# MCSE Consulting Bible

# MCSE Consulting Bible

Harry Brelsford

IDG Books Worldwide, Inc.
An International Data Group Company

Foster City, CA ✦ Chicago, IL ✦ Indianapolis, IN ✦ New York, NY

**MCSE Consulting Bible**

Published by

**IDG Books Worldwide, Inc.**

An International Data Group Company

919 E. Hillsdale Blvd., Suite 400

Foster City, CA 94404

www.idgbooks.com (IDG Books Worldwide Web site)

Copyright © 2001 IDG Books Worldwide, Inc. All rights reserved. No part of this book, including interior design, cover design, and icons, may be reproduced or transmitted in any form, by any means (electronic, photocopying, recording, or otherwise) without the prior written permission of the publisher.

ISBN: 0-7645-4774-7

Printed in the United States of America

10 9 8 7 6 5 4 3 2 1

1B/RX/QR/QR/FC

Distributed in the United States by IDG Books Worldwide, Inc.

Distributed by CDG Books Canada Inc. for Canada; by Transworld Publishers Limited in the United Kingdom; by IDG Norge Books for Norway; by IDG Sweden Books for Sweden; by IDG Books Australia Publishing Corporation Pty. Ltd. for Australia and New Zealand; by TransQuest Publishers Pte Ltd. for Singapore, Malaysia, Thailand, Indonesia, and Hong Kong; by Gotop Information Inc. for Taiwan; by ICG Muse, Inc. for Japan; by Intersoft for South Africa; by Eyrolles for France; by International Thomson Publishing for Germany, Austria, and Switzerland; by Distribuidora Cuspide for Argentina; by LR International for Brazil; by Galileo Libros for Chile; by Ediciones ZETA S.C.R. Ltda. for Peru; by WS Computer Publishing Corporation, Inc., for the Philippines; by Contemporanea de Ediciones for Venezuela; by Express Computer Distributors for the Caribbean and West Indies; by Micronesia Media Distributor, Inc. for Micronesia; by Chips Computadoras S.A. de C.V. for Mexico; by Editorial Norma de Panama S.A. for Panama; by American Bookshops for Finland.

For general information on IDG Books Worldwide's books in the U.S., please call our Consumer Customer Service department at 800-762-2974. For reseller information, including discounts and premium sales, please call our Reseller Customer Service department at 800-434-3422.

For information on where to purchase IDG Books Worldwide's books outside the U.S., please contact our International Sales department at 317-572-3993 or fax 317-572-4002.

For consumer information on foreign language translations, please contact our Customer Service department at 800-434-3422, fax 317-572-4002, or e-mail rights@idgbooks.com.

For information on licensing foreign or domestic rights, please phone +1-650-653-7098.

For sales inquiries and special prices for bulk quantities, please contact our Order Services department at 800-434-3422 or write to the address above.

For information on using IDG Books Worldwide's books in the classroom or for ordering examination copies, please contact our Educational Sales department at 800-434-2086 or fax 317-572-4005.

For press review copies, author interviews, or other publicity information, please contact our Public Relations department at 650-653-7000 or fax 650-653-7500.

For authorization to photocopy items for corporate, personal, or educational use, please contact Copyright Clearance Center, 222 Rosewood Drive, Danvers, MA 01923, or fax 978-750-4470.

**Library of Congress Cataloging-in-Publication Data**

Brelsford, Harry M., 1961-

    MCSE consulting bible / Harry Brelsford.

      p.   cm.

    ISBN 0-7645-4774-7 (alk. paper)

    1. Electronic data processing personnel--Certification. 2. Microsoft software--Examinations. 3. Electronic data processing consultants. I. Title.

QA76.3 .B74   2001

005.4'4769–dc21

                                         00-053993

 is a registered trademark or trademark under exclusive license to IDG Books Worldwide, Inc. from International Data Group, Inc. in the United States and/or other countries.

# ABOUT IDG BOOKS WORLDWIDE

Welcome to the world of IDG Books Worldwide.

IDG Books Worldwide, Inc., is a subsidiary of International Data Group, the world's largest publisher of computer-related information and the leading global provider of information services on information technology. IDG was founded more than 30 years ago by Patrick J. McGovern and now employs more than 9,000 people worldwide. IDG publishes more than 290 computer publications in over 75 countries. More than 90 million people read one or more IDG publications each month.

Launched in 1990, IDG Books Worldwide is today the #1 publisher of best-selling computer books in the United States. We are proud to have received eight awards from the Computer Press Association in recognition of editorial excellence and three from Computer Currents' First Annual Readers' Choice Awards. Our best-selling ...For Dummies® series has more than 50 million copies in print with translations in 31 languages. IDG Books Worldwide, through a joint venture with IDG's Hi-Tech Beijing, became the first U.S. publisher to publish a computer book in the People's Republic of China. In record time, IDG Books Worldwide has become the first choice for millions of readers around the world who want to learn how to better manage their businesses.

Our mission is simple: Every one of our books is designed to bring extra value and skill-building instructions to the reader. Our books are written by experts who understand and care about our readers. The knowledge base of our editorial staff comes from years of experience in publishing, education, and journalism — experience we use to produce books to carry us into the new millennium. In short, we care about books, so we attract the best people. We devote special attention to details such as audience, interior design, use of icons, and illustrations. And because we use an efficient process of authoring, editing, and desktop publishing our books electronically, we can spend more time ensuring superior content and less time on the technicalities of making books.

You can count on our commitment to deliver high-quality books at competitive prices on topics you want to read about. At IDG Books Worldwide, we continue in the IDG tradition of delivering quality for more than 30 years. You'll find no better book on a subject than one from IDG Books Worldwide.

John Kilcullen
Chairman and CEO
IDG Books Worldwide, Inc.

**Eighth Annual Computer Press Awards ≥1992**

**Ninth Annual Computer Press Awards ≥1993**

**Tenth Annual Computer Press Awards ≥1994**

**Eleventh Annual Computer Press Awards ≥1995**

IDG is the world's leading IT media, research and exposition company. Founded in 1964, IDG had 1997 revenues of $2.05 billion and has more than 9,000 employees worldwide. IDG offers the widest range of media options that reach IT buyers in 75 countries representing 95% of worldwide IT spending. IDG's diverse product and services portfolio spans six key areas including print publishing, online publishing, expositions and conferences, market research, education and training, and global marketing services. More than 90 million people read one or more of IDG's 290 magazines and newspapers, including IDG's leading global brands — Computerworld, PC World, Network World, Macworld and the Channel World family of publications. IDG Books Worldwide is one of the fastest-growing computer book publishers in the world, with more than 700 titles in 36 languages. The "...For Dummies®" series alone has more than 50 million copies in print. IDG offers online users the largest network of technology-specific Web sites around the world through IDG.net (http://www.idg.net), which comprises more than 225 targeted Web sites in 55 countries worldwide. International Data Corporation (IDC) is the world's largest provider of information technology data, analysis and consulting, with research centers in over 41 countries and more than 400 research analysts worldwide. IDG World Expo is a leading producer of more than 168 globally branded conferences and expositions in 35 countries including E3 (Electronic Entertainment Expo), Macworld Expo, ComNet, Windows World Expo, ICE (Internet Commerce Expo), Agenda, DEMO, and Spotlight. IDG's training subsidiary, ExecuTrain, is the world's largest computer training company, with more than 230 locations worldwide and 785 training courses. IDG Marketing Services helps industry-leading IT companies build international brand recognition by developing global integrated marketing programs via IDG's print, online and exposition products worldwide. Further information about the company can be found at www.idg.com. 1/26/00

# Credits

**Acquisitions Editor**
Nancy Maragioglio

**Project Editor**
Marcia Brochin

**Technical Editor**
James R. Kiniry, Jr.

**Copy Editor**
Kevin Kent

**Project Coordinators**
Joe Shines
Danette Nurse

**Book Designer**
Drew R. Moore

**Quality Control Technician**
Dina F Quan

**Graphics and Production Specialists**
Robert Bihlmayer
Rolly Delrosario
Jude Levinson
Michael Lewis
Victor Pérez-Varela
Ramses Ramirez

**Illustrators**
Gabriele McCann
Ronald Terry
John Greenough

**Proofreading and Indexing**
York Production Services
Robert Campbell

**Cover Image**
Anthony Bunyan

# About the Author

Seasoned MCSE consultant and Bainbridge Island, Washington, author Harry Brelsford is the founder and CEO of NetHealthMon.com, a Seattle-based firm providing fee-based remote network monitoring for BackOffice 2000 and Small Business Server 2000. The author of eight technology books including *Active Directory Planning and Design* and *Windows 2000 Server Secrets,* both published by IDG Books Worldwide, Inc., Harry is a longtime faculty member at Seattle Pacific University (www.spu.edu) where he teaches online MCSE certification courses. Harry holds several network certifications including MCSE and MCT, and he also holds an MBA (University of Denver). A contributing editor and regular columnist for *Microsoft Certified Professional Magazine* (www.mcpmag.com) from early in its existence, Harry also writes the monthly column "Nothing But Networks" for *Computer Source Magazine* (www.sourcemagazine.com). Harry can be reached at harryb@nethealthmon.com or www.nethealthmon.com. Harry and his family enjoy cross-country skiing and sailing in the Pacific Northwest.

*To my wife, Kristen, sons, Geoffrey and Harry,*

*and the good citizens of Bainbridge Island!*

# Foreword

**A**long with its loads of information on writing business plans, assessing your skills, getting started with your own business, finding clients, and marketing yourself, the *MCSE Consulting Bible* offers something that may be just as valuable: your invitation into a community of other MCSEs worldwide who are working as or aspire to be IT consultants.

When I was a technical writing consultant for a number of years, one of the biggest challenges I faced wasn't finding clients, balancing the books, staying motivated, or growing my business. It was simply this: dealing with the isolation of working largely alone, without feedback or coworkers to bounce things off or to offer advice, support, or reality checks. Suddenly, I was CEO, accounting department, secretary, and everything in between, all in an office of one. Who could I consult with when I had a new idea? Who could I ask about handling a difficult client? Who could I turn to when I needed to partner on a project? Who could I compare notes with on hourly billing rates, technical questions, growing the business, and operational logistics? The answer was no one.

As an MCSE interested in pursuing a consulting business or already pursuing one, you're facing that same challenge. Yet, because you're an MCSE, you're already part of an exclusive club of fellow technical experts — those who have studied for and passed a challenging set of networking administration exams. Because Harry has been part of that club for years, he breaks through the isolation and offers advice specifically targeted to MCSEs. With Harry's insights, advice, hands-on experiences, and the advice he includes from others, you're no longer alone. Instead, you have a ready guide to all of the ins and outs of the consulting life, written by someone who has been there.

As the editor of *MCP Magazine*, I often receive letters from readers asking about careers in consulting. You ask about deciding when to make the leap from employed to self-employed. You wonder what sorts of technical skills you'll need. Should you earn more certification titles first, or is an MCSE enough? How do you decide what to charge? How much can you expect to earn? Where does your first client come from? What about marketing? Should you plan for eventual employees or subcontractors? Taxes? Health insurance?

In nearly all of your questions, there's a common thread: the need for help with some good solid business planning — with a technology spin on all of it. Consulting suggestions are readily available from many sources; finding information specifically for MCSEs attempting to start or building on a career in consulting is tougher.

Fortunately, Harry's book delves into that very subject from Chapter 1, and he knows what he's talking about, since he has advised thousands of *MCP Magazine* readers through his "Professionally Speaking" column and has spoken at our conferences on both technology and career topics. In short, Harry walks the talk. He's been out there doing all of it for years as an MCSE consultant — and making a good living.

When I was consulting, I could have used a book like Harry's. His warm and encouraging tone, tempered with plenty of realism, would have been a big asset in allaying that inevitable sense of isolation. You can take advantage of someone else's experience, war stories, and advice to help you become that highly envied individual, a successful MCSE consultant. With Harry at your side, I wish you the best of luck!

Linda Briggs
Editor-in-Chief, *Microsoft Certified Professional Magazine*

# Preface

**W**elcome to the *MCSE Consulting Bible*, a book that addresses an overwhelming need in the MCSE community: how to use your MCSE-based technical skill set to make good money and have fun as a successful consultant. That is the focus of this book: being a successful MCSE consultant with a focus on best business practices. For some, being a successful MCSE consultant means making a lot of money. Others are seeking professional fulfillment, client service opportunities, and perhaps self-employment. Some want it all. This book is for all parties.

## What This Book Is About

This book focuses on the business side of being an MCSE consultant and running a professional services practice. I use the popular finder (sales), minder (management), and grinder (work) model, shown in Figure P-1, of professional services to present my MCSE consulting wisdom. My words to you are based on my real-world experiences as a longtime MCSE consultant. And as you'll see when you turn the pages, I invite other real-world professionals to share their stories by delivering Guest Sermons in many of my chapters.

More importantly, this book calls it like it is. I speak towards the good, which is making six-figure incomes without a boss and setting your own work schedule (within reason), but I don't shy away from the bad, such as forcing you to honestly assess your fitness as an MCSE consultant and your ability to weather long hours and client tirades. The big dollars and big fun don't come cheaply. I hope you'll find my honesty refreshing, and I hope it lends credibility to the words in this tome. While this book won't always make you feel good about the world of MCSE consulting, it will help protect you in your professional career. Perhaps you'll break the *MCP Magazine* Salary Survey numbers for MCSEs. On the other hand, you may find this book leads you to a different decision — to keep your existing salaried staff job and not to endeavor to excel as an MCSE consultant. I'd like everyone that buys the book to become a successful MCSE consultant, but if that goal can't be reached, I'd like this book to prevent people from becoming an unsuccessful MCSE consultant.

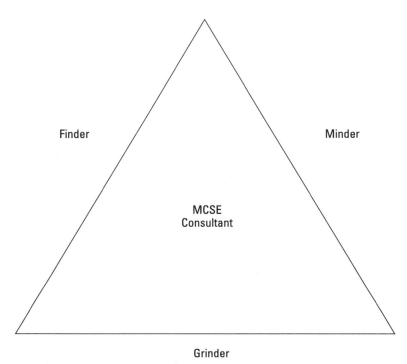

Finder

Minder

MCSE
Consultant

Grinder

**Figure P-1:** The finder, minder, and grinder professional services model is the basis for this book.

I never leave the practical and pragmatic world of MCSE consulting for comfort of the academic ivory towers. That would be inappropriate. But I've brought over one practice from my service in the education realm, the propensity to create a new theory or law. In most chapters of this book, you will find a Rule of Ten. By consistently applying an easily understood framework to complex, real-world MCSE consulting matters, you can see how the advice applies to you, the MCSE consultant seeking to do a better job without feeling like you're being told to do what I say and do myself. A Rule of Ten is a way for me to show you that every major and critical success factor in the MCSE consulting community is divisible by the number ten. I hope you'll find my insights to be both enlightening and enjoyable. I also throw in case studies and reader mail from my *MCP Magazine* column to provide even more real-world perspective.

I also sprinkle in tidbits of technical information where appropriate. This book certainly isn't a rewrite of the online help system or product resource manuals, a common reader complaint posted with online book resellers for technical books. Nor does the limited technical discussion in any way replace technical texts. Rather, I attempt to present billable opportunities to you. For example, Small Business Server installations are a tremendous MCSE consulting opportunity, and supporting Microsoft Exchange Server 2000 provides many billable hours for MCSEs. Plus, I've personally billed many good hours planning for, implementing, and supporting front office applications such as Office 2000 and Project 2000. If you're like me, you probably like billing a lot of hours, too. So it is in that spirit that I present targeted technical discussion.

Another interesting aspect to my take on this subject is my use of third-party applications. My belief is that this book should mirror the real world of MCSE consulting as closely as possible. In order to accomplish that, I break away from the strict Microsoft mindset of using only Microsoft solutions. Instead, I look at how I run my MCSE consulting practice and with what software tools. I find that I use software solutions from a wide range of independent software vendors (ISVs). That's why you'll find me singing the praises of QuickBooks and Timeslips. On the other hand, I think you'll find between these covers a book with an appropriate Microsoft focus that honors the MCSE community and its Microsoft-centric world.

MCSE consultants work in a competitive business environment. In many parts of this book I put on my MBA hat and present competent competitive analysis. Not only does my competitive analysis cover your direct consulting competition (a good thing to know), but I also profile what software solutions compete with Microsoft offerings. One of the best chapters detailing such competition is Chapter 21 in which I discuss Oracle as a competing database product for Microsoft SQL Server. Not only do I feel strongly that a superior MCSE consultant should be well versed in the competition, but also and more importantly, as an MCSE consultant acting in an advisory role, you will often encounter situations where you'll recommend non-Microsoft solutions. I've done it myself on several occasions and gladly billed my clients consulting hours to do so.

# Who Should Read This Book

This book serves several masters, much as an MCSE consultant does. I sincerely believe the following people can all benefit from reading this book:

+ **Those considering an MCSE consulting career** — If you are a potential MCSE consultant, you are clearly the largest audience for this book. Hopefully, you'll read this book with interest from cover to cover as you make the professional decision to become an MCSE consultant. This book has been written as a one-stop resource for your occupational research undertaking.

+ **Existing MCSE consultants seeking higher professional performance levels** — As a longtime columnist for *Microsoft Certified Professional Magazine* and an equally longtime Microsoft Certified Trainer teaching MCSEs, I have heard time and time again that while the MCSE consulting field is great in general individual performances can be improved. If you are an existing MCSE who strives to deliver better customer service, to pick better clients, and to select better technology solutions, you will benefit from this book.

✦ **Consulting managers** — Perhaps you've traded the TechNet CD-ROM technical library for life behind the desk as an MCSE consulting firm manager or owner. This book can improve your effectiveness in this role by not only speaking directly to you from time-to-time, but also by educating you on what your consulting staff does. When I incorporated this thinking into my text, I drew on my time as an MCSE consultant working for a regional accounting firm. If only I had had a book like this at the time to hand to the CPAs and say, "Read this. This is what I do," my life would have been much more pleasant.

✦ **MCSE candidates** — Perhaps you're an MCSE candidate, taking classes and studying hard to earn the coveted certification designation. Perhaps you've stumbled across this book in your quest to know what awaits you at the end of the rainbow. This book will not only help you in your search for a rainbow, to quote from the song "Searching for a rainbow" from The New Riders Of The Purple Sage, a late 1970s country and western rockabilly band, but will also help you cross to the other end of it.

✦ **Project managers** — One critical member of the consulting team on large engagements is the project manager. I've worked side by side with several project managers on technology projects who could benefit from an education on the inner workings of MCSE consulting.

✦ **Salespeople** — The members of the sales force are important people in many consulting organizations. They get the work for MCSE consultants. This book can make the lives of those in the professional services business development field much easier. By knowing more about what they're selling (your MCSE consulting services), the salespeople can be more successful. And that can only make you more successful. Take my friendly advice and buy an extra copy of this book to give to the salespeople at your consulting firm.

✦ **Spouses, partners, parents, and siblings** — I certainly plan to give copies of this book to my wife, folks, brothers, sister, kids, and in-laws. It is my highest hope that by reading this they'll know what I do for a living. Hopefully, the book can save me a lot of time having to explain both why I work long hours and how I got my new late-model Volvo. Perhaps they'll finally stop asking me what I do for a living.

# How This Book Is Organized

Simply stated, this book is organized into sections that honor the finder, minder, and grinder consulting practice business model.

1. Foundation

2. Finder

3. Minder

4. Grinder

5. Appendixes

## Part I: Foundation

Before getting into the details, I spend some time providing foundational knowledge about running a business, writing a business plan, and defining professional services consulting.

## Part II: Finder

Clearly, you have to get the business in the door to stay in business, so accordingly, the finder role is explored over several chapters. By the end of this part, you'll have a newfound appreciation for business development.

## Part III: Minder

You'll find early on in your career that managing the business is as important as getting the work and doing the work. I speak to management issues in this part. And if management isn't your gig, I also speak towards outsourcing some business functions, such as accounting, so you can focus on your strengths and not dwell on your weaknesses.

## Part IV: Grinder

"Ah, the good stuff," as many MCSE consultants have remarked to me. In this part of the book, the largest, I speak towards providing appropriate solutions for your beloved clients. I cover a wide range of solutions, ranging from general technology advising to narrow and lucrative consulting niches in security and Small Business Server.

## Appendixes

In the back part of this book, you'll find many goodies, including MCSE consulting working papers, resources, and information about the almighty *MCP Magazine* MCSE Salary Survey.

# Conventions Used in This Book

Icons appear in the left margin. The following icons are used to call your attention to additional information or points that are particularly important or insightful:

When something stands apart from the general discussion, I give it a Note to draw your attention to it.

Occasionally, I offer a bit of advice that needs special treatment. That's what the Tip icon is all about.

While many of you will read this book from cover to cover, hopefully all of you will consider the *MCSE Consulting Bible* to be your business buddy. I extensively cross-reference other chapters where I can for a given topic, allowing you improved access to and application of the content of this work.

I use the Caution icon to denote things in the MCSE consulting industry that you should be careful of.

# Acknowledgments

Even though I live on an island, it took a lot of people living on the mainland to make this book happen. All books are an exercise in synergy, with the sum of everyone's contributions exceeding what any one person could accomplish alone.

First and foremost, I want to acknowledge my clients and fellow MCSE consultants who have taught me more about business and technology than I can find words to express.

The team at IDG Books Worldwide, Inc., has been more than fair in their accommodating my harried submissions, often a few days late because I put the needs of my clients first. This group includes Nancy Maragioglio, Marcia Brochin, Kevin Kent, and Judy Brief.

Additionally, the good people at Compaq-Redmond who loaned me test servers need a serious round of applause from me. Here it is.

Finally, I acknowledge my modern influences in the MCSE community who've gotten me where I am today, including Linda Briggs and Dian Schaffhauser at *Microsoft Certified Professional Magazine* and John Martinez at *Computer Source Magazine*.

# Contents at a Glance

# Contents

# Foundation

This part explores some of the reasons for choosing to become an MCSE consultant. It walks you through developing a viable business plan and details the MCSE consulting fundamentals you'll need to know to get started in the business.

# Making the Break

**S**o you want to be a consultant? And not just any consultant, but an MCSE consultant. Congratulations. This is the start of your journey to becoming an MCSE consultant! Savor the moment, because the pace for the balance of your MCSE consulting career will increase rapidly, starting with the next paragraph. Many people want to become MCSE consultants, but few of these people truly accomplish that goal. For most, the MCSE consultant plans never progress beyond idle chatter with neighbors while standing over the barbecue. But by all appearances, you've taken your desire to become an MCSE consultant further than that, just by reading one paragraph at a time.

The goal of this book is to help you lead a better life, both financially and in terms of professional satisfaction. MCSE consulting, when done correctly, can be profitable and pleasurable. Done poorly, MCSE consulting is a nightmare, as the guest sermon in this chapter will demonstrate. This chapter sets the foundation for making the best decision for you as you consider a career in MCSE consulting. Now, I want to move on to the next section to discuss the reasons why you should become an MCSE consultant.

## Why Be an MCSE Consultant?

You and I probably have both common and dissimilar reasons for becoming MCSE consultants. That is, our motivations may be the same or not. That's okay, as it is in keeping with my theme of managing your expectations at each and every turn. In this section, I explore the most frequent motivations for becoming an MCSE consultant.

## Working for yourself

It has been my observation as an MCSE consultant, a trainer, and an author that the number one reason people make the break and become MCSE consultants is to work for themselves. Working for yourself has different meanings to different people. For me, it means having flex time and not riding the ferry into Seattle from Bainbridge Island with the nine-to-five crowd each day. For you, it might be that you are seeking self-employment as a way to follow the family tradition or as a way to rebel against authority. I've witnessed very successful MCSE consultants who weren't good employees when they were beholden to a boss. These people didn't like taking directions and orders from higher-ups. But once they blossomed into a self-employed MCSE consultant and their rebelliousness had been addressed, they thrived as MCSE consultants.

**Note**   Becoming an MCSE consultant doesn't necessarily mean self-employment. Many MCSE consultants work for consulting firms ranging from Big Five accounting firms to local contract houses and temporary agencies. While it's true that you can work your magic and practice your trade as a salaried (or W-2) MCSE consultant for a firm, you'll find that many of the same MCSE consulting dynamics — such as billing for your time and the high degree of freedom that MCSE consultants love — exist no matter where or how you work.

I end on a theme common to those who work for themselves that holds true for MCSE consultants. This theme is the notion that by becoming an MCSE consultant you are escaping some form of day-to-day drudgery, whether it be a difficult boss or the rote and routine of being a LAN administrator. Hey — escapism works for me.

## Making money

Close behind the working-for-yourself motivation is the MCSE consultant's desire to earn a fair, if not more than fair, financial return for his or her work efforts. MCSE consulting promises exactly that, albeit you earn each and every one of those dollars (to which the next several hundred pages of this book will attest). There are no windfalls here, fellow MCSE consultants. That said, MCSE consultants are routinely improving their financial situation over salaried day jobs and meeting or exceeding the oft-quoted *Microsoft Certified Professional Magazine's* Salary Survey (see Appendix E for the 2000 Salary Survey).

A cautionary few words of wisdom. If your primary motivation is money as an MCSE consultant, you're probably not going to last for the long term. Money is great, but if you're ill-equipped in other departments, such as managing or enjoying the actual work, your wanderlust will overcome desire for dough. Trust me on that, as I've seen it many times before.

Also, people don't simply write you checks once you become an MCSE consultant. Not only do you have to get, manage, and perform the work, but also you must keep your perspective appropriately fixed on making a profit. I've witnessed many MCSE consultants who have a huge top line (revenue), but a negative bottom line. In short, they spend everything that they earn, so they're really not making any money. The next few hundred pages will show you not only how to get and do the work but also how to still have at a little money left after you've paid yourself a salary and settled your tax obligation.

## Helping others

A few MCSE consultants enjoy working with people and make the break from other jobs so they can do more of exactly that. As you know, many "regular" MCSE jobs, such as system engineer positions, offer limited opportunities to interact with people (but lots of opportunities to interact with servers in air-conditioned rooms). It has been my observation that extrovert MCSE consultants are in business as much to work with people as to make money, and there are plenty of people who might be classified as introverted who also enjoy working with other people.

I've witnessed a few MCSE consultants who forego the big bucks to focus on the people dimension. These are MCSE consultants who work with not-for-profit organizations, who are hobbyists (having made their millions at Microsoft or the neighborhood dot-com startup), or who are true trainers. In short, some members of the MCSE community truly like helping people.

## Variety in applying technology solutions

Speaking only for myself, but many years ago, I learned that my grade school teachers were absolutely correct in their assessment of my hyperactivity. Not only do I need variety, but also the variety must be engaging. Routine administration, which can often be mindless, isn't my specialty. My life as an MCSE consultant has been a true lifesaver given my need for engaging variety. MCSE consulting has provided the both the variety and technical challenges I crave.

I'm not alone in this need for variety in applying technical solutions. More MCSEs than I can recall have commented on how bored they are once their salaried day-to-day LAN administration or system engineering job has become dull or routine. Becoming an MCSE consultant allows you to do what many of you love best, apply technical solutions. In the "A Day in the Life of an MCSE Consultant" section later in this chapter, I provide a glimpse of the variety of technical solutions an MCSE consultant can be expected to apply in any given day.

## Cost recovery

Many MCSEs become consultants out of a sense of duty or guilt over the sheer amount of dollars and time they spent getting certified. To be honest, basing future decisions on past outlays is typically a poor strategy, but MCSEs are only human and sometimes human nature takes over.

# A Day in the Life of an MCSE Consultant

So perhaps you're more convinced than ever that you want to become an MCSE consultant. Fair enough. Now let me take another approach at managing your expectations — by outlining the day-to-day life of an MCSE consultant.

Contrary to popular belief, the MCSE consultant's day doesn't commence with dawn, but rather with the darkness of the night before. I'll pick it up from there in Table 1-1.

| Table 1-1 MCSE Consultant's Typical Day | |
|---|---|
| *Time* | *Task* |
| 1:00 a.m. | You've just turned off your laptop, having answered all your e-mails, having submitted a BackOffice work proposal to a prospective client, and having run a few billing invoices to your mailbox. Time for a quick bowl of ice cream and bed. |
| 7:00 a.m. | You're awakened by your pager. Your clients, who don't stay up till 1:00 a.m. and pride themselves on being both titans of business and early risers, page you with a STOP error message from a legacy Windows NT Server 4.0 installation. You work through it over the telephone for the next 45 minutes. |
| 9:00 a.m. | In route to your first engagement, you receive three telephone calls from clients on your cellular phone. |
| 11:30 a.m. | You've successfully applied a couple of BackOffice service packs and downloaded the latest virus definition files at your first client site. Time for lunch. |
| 1:00 p.m. | Lunch was successful. The prospective client wants to receive a BackOffice work proposal from you by tomorrow morning. You know you can write and e-mail this proposal tonight after the family goes to bed. |
| 2:45 p.m. | After you leave a client site after fixing a SQL Server 2000 report, you return several calls from the car. |
| 4:00 p.m. | You emerge from a disappointing interview for a prospective employee who will work under you. Your thoughts are to remain a small consulting practice and not to grow your head count. You proceed to your final consulting visit of the day. |
| 7:00 p.m. | You're back in your car after a few hours of BackOffice needs analysis and systems planning. Fortunately, dinner was brought into the meeting as you've missed dinner at home. |
| 1:00 a.m. | You've answered all your e-mails, have studied for an hour for your forthcoming Windows 2000 MCSE exam, and have written the sale proposal you promised your prospect earlier in the day. You'll get up early to review it one more time before sending. |

# Business Planning

Woven into this book is something that's frequently overlooked in the real world of MCSE consulting and completely absent in the traditional MCSE certification exams in the Windows NT era: business planning. Business planning applies to the MCSE consultant on two fronts.

First, there is the business of running a business. An MCSE consultant must possess sound business skills. You can't make it on technical skills alone. Second, MCSE consultants are increasingly participating in a client's business decisions and interacting more and more with business people. One reason this is occurring is that new tools such as Active Directory require that MCSEs work side-by-side with MBAs to implement technology solutions that are in alignment with the greater business organization. And in fairness to Microsoft, the Windows 2000 MCSE certification exams that focus on designing, listed as follows, place significant emphasis on business needs analysis.

✦ 70-219: Designing a Microsoft Windows 2000 Directory Services Infrastructure

✦ 70-220: Designing Security for a Microsoft Windows 2000 Network

✦ 70-221: Designing a Microsoft Windows 2000 Network Infrastructure

# MCSE Consulting Success Factors

With the popularity of the MCSE certification has come sufficient information as to what the general qualities of a successful MCSE consultant are. Many of these observations are my firsthand experiences, confirmed time and time again in the MCSE consulting trenches.

✦ **Communicator**—Hardly a day goes by where I'm not made aware of an MCSE who worked magic and solved a complex technical problem revolving around Microsoft technologies but didn't tell anyone. For example, an MCSE at a local college fixes the online campus servers name resolution problem and doesn't tell the college staff and faculty for several hours. This time lapse prevents numerous students from accessing their course work, communicating, and taking exams. MCSEs, often armed with abundant technical aptitude, need to constantly check themselves when it comes to communicating (more on this in future chapters).

✦ **Technical skills**—While it's assumed an MCSE has the technical skills to solve technical problems (the old "merchant of the trade" assumption in the Uniform Commercial Code legal treatise), such is not always the case. Many smart people have used test-taking aids to pass MCSE exams while still being technically unqualified. Clients pay for technical solutions when they retain an MCSE. You're really there to solve a technical problem or reach some desired technology outcome. I've seen clients become frustrated at paper MCSEs who are great communicators but can't make BackOffice budge. Bottom line, while all the other MCSE consulting success factors are important, you still have to produce.

✦ **Business acumen** — Do you know how to work? Can you schedule and budget your time? Do you show up on time or even at all for your appointments? I have witnessed brilliant MCSEs who have been very poor business people. And by poor, I mean both incompetent and unprofitable.

✦ **Business development** — You're doing everything right technically and people think you're a great guru, but you have little or no business activity. Something many MCSE consultants remark about after one or two years is how much selling they must do. A successful MCSE consultant is always developing business.

✦ **Ability to deal with madness and confusion** — MCSE consultants are subject to rapidly shifting technology solutions from Microsoft as well as rapidly shifting client priorities. Many of the best MCSE consultants thrive in this volatile professional environment. Each day is typically different from the last.

✦ **Successful track record** — A key indicator of having a successful MCSE consulting career is to look at your past. Many star performers who hold in-house positions as network administrators make great MCSE consultants. Past performance is usually the best predictor of the future when it comes to achievement in professional services.

✦ **Countless other variables** — If any of us knew the true predictors of what makes a successful MCSE consultant, we'd bottle the formula, and Bill Gates would be shining our shoes. The point is that your unique gifts may make you a successful MCSE consultant where others have tried and failed. Because you're providing professional services, there is a huge human element here.

# Who Shouldn't Be an MCSE Consultant

Some people simply shouldn't be MCSE consultants. Hopefully they'll arrive at that decision before hurting themselves, a client, a computer system, or the MCSE profession as a whole. Here's a short list of those who might not thrive in an MCSE consulting environment:

✦ **Process-oriented types** — It has been my experience that MCSEs who like to come to the same job, office, desk, and chair each and every day make poor consultants. These folks are typically happiest with established routines.

✦ **Those who dislike change** — Individuals who admittedly don't like change or are frustrated by the constant learning curve confronting the MCSE consultant should consider keeping that in-house network administration position.

✦ **Undercommunicators** — A true MCSE consultant should have the ability to shift between his or her introverted side to the extroverted side when speaking with clients, because the clients will have an expectation of constant and consistent communication.

✦ **Mistake-prone individuals**—Some people have the special touch when it comes to computers and others never will. It was the same way, so I'm told, in the 1950s when the tech heads of that day analyzed and repaired cars. Some car mechanics could tell the problems just by listening to the car's engine. Others created more problems than solutions. If you're mistake prone with computers and software, consider a career as a software tester instead. Why? Because software testers are paid to break things and make mistakes. It's a job requirement!

✦ **Angry individuals**—You've likely seen them, and I certainly have: the macho MCSEs who have crossed the line and become angry. If you lose your temper or your patience often or easily, you're not going to be a successful MCSE consultant no matter what your technical skill set.

✦ **Goofy individuals**—Perhaps you're the class clown who never grew up completely. Fair enough, but your challenge in making it as an MCSE consultant might be your ability to inspire trust in your clients and, when appropriate, lend an air of corporate presence.

✦ **Those otherwise unemployable**—The old joke in consulting is that you're really a job seeker in disguise. Plying your trade as an MCSE consultant because you can't make it in business or technology any other way isn't the firmest foundation from which to work.

## Guest Sermon — A Cautionary Tale

I asked Steve Bloom, an Internet commerce expert at a regional online legal database Web portal called Versuslaw.com to speak about his brief tenure as a technology consultant (work he performed while earning his MCSE). Steve leaves no stone unturned in his Guest Sermon about his life as an MCSE consultant.

*I sat across the table at lunch with our client. Two of his underlings were there, and things seemed to be going well enough. I had invited them to lunch courtesy of our company. It was, for my part, a bit of a celebration. The installation was about to shift into a different phase after having installed and configured a new workstation for every employee. We were essentially on schedule and there had been a minimum amount of work interruption. I was feeling good. Still, this fellow seemed a little grumpy.*

*"Why doesn't my screen saver work," the client wanted to know.*

*Here was a client who by himself was worth millions of dollars, and our project would cost him around $200,000 when all the costs were put together. We were at budget, communicating clearly and often, yet he at that moment would characterize the entire project as deeply unsatisfying. Because his screen saver wasn't working. This situation embodies several of the biggest problems with technology consulting. They include resistance to change, technophobia, and having to be responsible for things you can't control.*

*Clients don't sit up and say, "I'm resistant to change" in the planning meetings or while responding to your proposal. They might snap at you or blame you when something isn't working as it should or as they think that it should. Change is inherently threatening, and failing to help manage it sufficiently could come back to bite you.*

*Continued*

*Continued*

*Technophobia is similar to resistance to change, but is more of a fear of the technology itself rather than a resistance or an inability to adapt to it. It's funny to think of someone as scared of Microsoft Outlook, but to the first timer it can be very intimidating. For people who use technology just to get their work done, a steep learning curve can be intimidating.*

*Technophobes and Resisters need to be shown one or two things that they can do right away. With Microsoft Outlook, walking a client through the implementation of the preview pane was enough to really impress a few clients. For another, a personal distribution list was a fine introduction. Something that runs them through the on-line help screens and makes their life better immediately is just the ticket. Try and leave them with a sense of trust towards you, and then leave them alone.*

*You'll get blamed for things that you can't control. The screen saver wasn't working properly on the client's workstation mentioned above, and we had no clue as to whether it was hardware, software, or barometric pressure.*

*Frankly, these kinds of issues lead me to feel glad that I'm no longer in the consulting business. Resistance to change, technophobia, and having to own circumstances that are not of my own choosing can make for a very unpleasant workweek.*

*Of course, the answer is to have great foresight; great communication skills, together with the ability to use them; and considerable technical skill. If you have these things then you're worth the big bucks and you should rake them in.*

Want to comment and share you thoughts with Steve? E-mail him at sbloom@versuslaw. com or visit `www.versuslaw.com`. He'll welcome your comments as Steve is a call-it-like-he-sees-it kind of guy!

## Summary

This is only the first chapter of a long book dedicated to making you a successful MCSE consultant. As such, it has cast a broad vision of the MCSE consulting profession with the details to follow in the chapters to come. Please read on before marching up to your boss' office and tendering your resignation.

This chapter introduced the world of MCSE consulting from a realistic perspective. Why realistic? Because while great riches and happiness await you as a successful MCSE consultant, so does a lot of hard work, worry and heartache. I also didn't pull any punches when it came to managing your expectations about what life as an MCSE consultant is all about. Let's face it. You'll be managing the expectations of your clients each and every day, so in the similar view, I'll manage your expectations in each and every chapter. The process started here by presenting reasons for MCSE consulting failure, including the guest sermon which showed why one person went back to the in-house cubicle as a salaried employee. Don't get me wrong. The world needs great MCSE consultants, but like any professional services field, we don't need misfits, malcontents and incompetent professionals. Wouldn't you agree?

But at the end of the day, the gains clearly outweigh the pain if MCSE consulting is indeed your calling. Bottom line? The chapter set the stage for making the best career decision for you when it comes to considering a career as an MCSE consultant. While not for everyone, those who are competent MCSE consultants do very well.

The major points discussed in this chapter included: reasons for being an MCSE consultant, factors that contribute to both success and failure, and the "good side" — as well as the "bad and ugly" side — of MCSE consulting.

✦     ✦     ✦

# MCSE Consulting Business Plan

◆     ◆     ◆     ◆

### In This Chapter

Defining a
business plan

Organizing your
consulting practice

Understanding your
consulting space and
the markets you serve

Honoring paperwork
requirements

Surrounding yourself
with business advisors

Making the final
decision to become
an MCSE consultant

◆     ◆     ◆     ◆

**D**on't ever underestimate the power of a business plan. Certainly one of my great career regrets is having dismissed business plans I've both seen and written as both impractical and/or unnecessary for future use. How could I have known that the original business plan shown to me that rainy morning in a Seattle coffee shop for Wizards of the Coast would grow into one of the largest game companies in the world? The point is this — not only do you need to create a business plan, but also you need to take it seriously. A business plan isn't just a static document sometimes bordering on boring to write. It's a dynamic road map for the MCSE consultant to follow and update frequently as conditions change. And it takes a good map to find the treasure.

This chapter defines and presents the mechanics of a business plan. You will literally use the remainder of this book to fill in the blanks. At every turn, I'll reference the business plan with respect to the topics being presented. For example, the marketing discussion in the Part II of the book will provide you the tools and information necessary to complete the marketing section of your MCSE consulting business plan. For example, in Chapter 6, I provide several practical business development strategies that will fit right into your MCSE consulting business plan. By the end of this book, if you've followed along, you should have successfully completed your MCSE consulting business plan.

## Writing a Business Plan

For many, writing a business plan is about as fun as completing a tax return. On the surface, it doesn't rank high on the list of preferred activities. However, in this book, the business plan is *your* business plan, and it's used as much to convince yourself you're making the right business decisions as it is to convince your stakeholders (bankers, landlord, or spouse) that this is the right direction for you to head. A business plan provides an opportunity to validate your business model sooner rather than later.

A business plan is a document ranging anywhere from 10 pages to over 100 pages, depending on the depth of the subject presented. But don't let formalities such as plan length get in the way of creating a business plan. It doesn't even have to be generated on a computer, as many success stories abound concerning business plans sketched out on napkins over lunch. If you have a business plan at all, you're miles (or kilometers) ahead of your competition. There are many good resources to help you complete your business plan listed at the end of this chapter.

It is important to note that a business plan isn't an end in the business planning process, but rather the start of a lifelong business planning process. An ongoing business plan encompasses surrounding yourself with advisors, completing the required paperwork for being in business, and constantly assessing if it is in your best interests to be in MCSE consulting.

Let me expand on that last thought. Much like in real estate where you attempt to put land to its highest and best use, your life as an MCSE consultant should represent your highest and best use of professional time. If for some reason being an MCSE consultant is your highest and best use of time, the business planning process often helps you discover that important fact. Your business plan and the business planning process will help you decide on a course of action to do just that, make the best use of your professional time. In Figure 2-1, the business planning process is presented graphically.

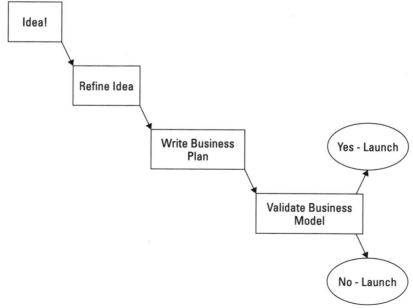

**Figure 2-1:** The business planning process

# Exploring the elements of the business plan food chain

Many people don't really know what a business plan is or isn't. This section will demystify that matter. A business plan is typically constructed from a top-down perspective, starting with the "Why are we here?" questions and ending with specific implementation tasks. As an MCSE consultant, you should have some guiding principle that gets you up each morning to go serve your clients. It should also be what motivates you to stay up late at night solving technical BackOffice problems, completing your invoices, and paying your bills. It all begins with the mission statement.

## Mission statement

Ironically, even though a mission statement traditionally appears first in the business plan, it is often one of the last parts of the business plan to be completed. I know that sounds like a contradiction to the last paragraph, but let me explain. It's easy to sit down and create a slogan such as "Quality is Job #1," call it a mission statement, and move on. However, the slogan or phrase you initially select in haste is unlikely to be the mission statement with which you end up. As you go through the business planning process, learn about yourself, your services, your market, your competition, and so on, you're likely to find your original mission statement is out of alignment with where you find yourself as an MCSE consultant. And your mission statement definitely needs to be in alignment with your MCSE consulting practice. Otherwise, you'll not only suffer from an identity crisis, but you'll also spend an inordinate amount of valuable time sitting around asking and trying to answer the following questions well after the business plan has been created and well beyond when you should be working (and earning money) as an MCSE consultant. The following list of questions represents the appropriate framework for selecting a mission statement that works for you, the MCSE consultant, as you launch your professional services practice:

✦ Why are we here?

✦ Who are we?

✦ What line of work are we in?

✦ What do we want to be known for?

**Note**

It is important to understand that arriving at answers to these questions is an important step in creating an appropriate mission statement for your MCSE consulting practice. After a reasonable amount of iterations, your mission statement should be acceptable and you should move on. If you find yourself asking these questions three months, six months, or nine months down the line, it suggests your mission statement is irrelevant and your business plan may be less than useful. In other words, sitting around day after day as an MCSE consultant asking, "Who are we?" is a serious organizational warning sign that things aren't going well. And that kind of bench time for an MCSE consultant isn't billable.

Here are a half dozen sample mission statements you might consider for now, subject to refinement as you develop your own MCSE consulting business plan.

✦ To make a difference with the technology solutions I implement

✦ To create wealth for my clients and myself via technology solutions

✦ To treat my clients with respect and to enjoy the trust of my clients

✦ To provide world-class technical solutions in our BackOffice niche while maintaining superior client relations

✦ To build a well-respected MCSE consulting practice

✦ To take pride in my MCSE consulting efforts at the end of the day, knowing I made the best decisions possible at the time, given the information available

Chapter 3 will help you prepare your mission statement with its overview of the world of consulting.

## Goals

From the mission statement, goals are derived. Goals are more detailed than is a mission statement. Goals might include statements relating to growth by referrals, to increasing profitability each year, to shedding day-to-day management responsibilities by recruiting a management team, or to acquiring a competitor.

## Objectives

Objectives follow goals and are even more pronounced. Objectives typically have details that separate them from goals. For example, an objective might be to start your firm by September 15 of this year, or to enjoy an after-tax return on your equity of at least 10 percent. Objectives are often what you're measured by in a traditional job, working for an employer from 8 a.m. to 5 p.m. five days per week, and are a useful way to measure your success as an MCSE consultant, assuming you'll be working for yourself. The point is that you need to be accountable to someone, even if that someone is yourself. In other words, we all have bosses. Objectives offer this form of accountability and comprise a common business management approach called Management By Objectives (MBO).

## Tactics

Tactics are how you get there. Once you are armed with objectives, you have to make choices about how to attain those objectives. Those choices are tactics. In day-to-day MCSE life, your tactics may well be your entries in your Outlook 2000 Tasks List.

# Explaining Your Services

Every business plan has a section defining products and services, and your MCSE consulting business plan is no exception. It is here that you will list the specific services (and perhaps products) you intend to offer. As you write this section, ask yourself, "Exactly what do I do?" This is the question you're attempting to answer in a fairly succinct manner. If you can't answer that question for yourself, you risk your practice being aimless.

Chapter 5 will help you select the types of services you want to provide in broad terms (that is, whether you want to generalize or specialize). Part IV is dedicated to helping you select specific work areas. For example, Chapter 16 addresses enterprise-level consulting. Chapter 24 addresses small business consulting using Microsoft Small Business Server 2000. For e-mail consulting, Chapter 20 looks at Microsoft Exchange 2000 Server. Chapter 21 explores the world of database administration-related consulting.

## Organizing your consulting practice

There are two critical issues to discuss in your MCSE business plan when it comes to organizing your consulting practice. These are substance and form.

### Substance

Each and every day, how do you as an MCSE consultant operate? Do you personally answer your telephone calls via a cellular telephone while at clients' sites? Do you recruit and manage staff so that you can better leverage your time as a consultant? Do you have a physical office location or a home office? What is the reality of making your MCSE consulting practice function like a business (billing, collections, paying bills, and so on)? The substance of organizing your MCSE consulting practice is making your dreams happen daily. It's implementing a business and management infrastructure to deal with the hundreds of little details that crop up in a given month. At worst, you want your business planning process and the resulting business plan to produce a functional organizational structure. At best, the outcome of writing a clear, substantive organizational section to your consulting practice's business plan could result in a practice that other MCSE consultants would envy. In a traditional business plan, the operations section outlines the organizational structure you desire.

### Form

In your MCSE business plan, you will want to spend a few minutes discussing the form of your MCSE consulting practice. Is it a sole proprietorship with you and only you at the helm? Have you retained a tax attorney or certified public accountant to help you organize your practice as a legal entity, such as a Professional Limited Liability Company (PLLC)?

When completing this section of your MCSE consulting business plan, you'll find guidance about organizational structure in this book in Part III. For example, in Chapter 11, I advise you about different staffing options.

# Financial considerations

One of the key reasons for becoming an MCSE consultant is to make money. Not only is it your right to do so, but also times are good for MCSE consultants. You should go forward with gusto, seeking to achieve your financial goals. For some people, that goal is to make a good living without a boss. For others, that goal involves really long hours to make loads of money. The choice is yours. The financial section of your MCSE business plan is critical. We're talking money here.

## What to charge

As a consultant, one of the key questions is what to charge. Few other financial variables will have a greater impact on your financial position as an MCSE consultant. Bill rates are a function of locality, expertise, specialty, luck, and ability to negotiate. Your MCSE business plan must include discussion and analysis of the revenues you intend to generate.

## Your costs

The second most important financial variable after determining your MCSE consulting bill rates is your costs. I've witnessed many technically competent MCSE consultants with more business than they could handle actually report losses from a pure financial point of view because they couldn't control costs. Leasing a flashy minivan with a company logo on it before your financial resources can justify such an expenditure is risky business. Your MCSE business plan must include discussion and analysis of the costs you will incur.

## Pro forma financial information

In a business plan, the financial analysis section typically results in pro forma financial information. A couple of thoughts for you to consider are the following:

✦ **Zero-based cost budgeting** — Believe it or not, as a budding MCSE consultant, you can more easily estimate your costs than your revenues. With some legwork and elbow grease, you can surf the Internet or call around and get cost estimates for nearly all the costs you'll incur. For example, suppose you're considering leasing a small office for your MCSE consulting practice. By calling a few real estate leasing agents, you could easily determine how much per square foot per month you will be paying. Other costs such as equipment outlays and fees for services can be estimated in a similar manner.

✦ **Break-even analysis** — If you are just starting your MCSE consulting practice without a track record, it has been my experience that the only type of valid pro forma budget is one based on break-even analysis. Here you are looking at how much business you have to bring in to make it. This should include the salary you will pay yourself. The only exceptions for using other budgeting techniques such as percentage of growth are when you have signed long-term consulting contracts as part of your MCSE consulting practice launch and when, months and years later, you have a business track record.

**Cross-Reference** See Chapter 12 for more information to help you complete the financial section of your MCSE consulting business plan.

# Your market

Up to this point in your business plan, you've determined why you're here (mission statement) and set goals and objectives to attain those goals. You know what services you intend to provide and how your MCSE consulting practice will be organized. You've even cast your eye towards profitability in the financial analysis section.

Now it's time to see if the marketplace agrees with your planning. You will define what your markets are, based on segments and geographic location.

## Segmentation

Your MCSE consulting business plan should include carefully considered analysis about the market you serve based on segment. A market segment is an identifiable group or niche. You could also think of it as a discrete territory. For some, this will amount to serving only law firms or some other specific industry. This is common in professional services. You might take a slightly broader view as an MCSE consultant and say that you intend to serve only service firms because they best suit your background and personality. Indeed, you might use this section of your MCSE business plan to list types of businesses with which you won't do business.

Another tack on segmentation is to consider business size. Perhaps you prefer to ply your craft as an MCSE consultant at the enterprise level because small businesses are of no interest to you. There are many MCSE consultants who feel just the opposite. The important point I'm making here is that you need to know your market(s) and communicate such understanding in your MCSE business plan.

## Local

For many MCSE consultants, all engagements are local. This is especially true when you work with small and medium-sized businesses. Your clients are the same people that you see at the checkout lines of the local grocery store. Local markets are often best suited for those MCSE consultants who want to minimize travel. I tend to define local as a 60-mile radius.

## Regional

If you envision a wider scope for your business, you may be well suited to being an MCSE consultant on a regional basis. Regional is a funny word, meaning different things to different people. In my world of the Pacific Northwest, I consider regional to be the four-state region of Washington, Idaho, Oregon, and Alaska. Not surprisingly, many firms that operate in the Pacific Northwest have a main office with branch offices dispersed across these four states. If my business plan targets regional clients, I'm well positioned when it comes to soliciting clients that fit the profile of close by regional operations. It's just a matter of knowing your market(s), which is a smart business practice for anyone.

### National

So you're one of those MCSEs who wants the recognition and all the other accolades that accrue when you're a nationally respected consultant. You may or may not be able to develop a national MCSE consulting practice as an individual, but perhaps you'll join a national consulting firm. Several of the Big Five accounting firms have formed alliances with Microsoft to deliver technology consulting services. In any event, your MCSE business plan should at least make mention of national markets and your willingness or unwillingness to serve those markets.

### International

Increasingly, MCSE consultants are beginning to cross borders to serve clients. This may occur because of wanderlust or a labor shortage in another country, or your level of expertise may have you in demand internationally. I've also witnessed bilingual MCSEs find interesting opportunities by combining their language skills with MCSE consulting capabilities.

 **Cross-Reference**    The MCSE consulting marketplace is further discussed in Chapter 5 and Chapter 13.

## Promotion/marketing/advertising

Now that you've identified your market, you've got to go out and get the business. Any worthwhile business plan demands a bona fide marketing section that details how you plan to get the business. Here you can put on your lender's hat and be critical of your own efforts. Remember that an excellent mission statement doesn't mean much if you have no sales. You need a marketing plan that not only is effective, but also isn't so costly that you end up unprofitable. That last point is important. Many eager MCSEs print good-looking color brochures and buy expensive telephone book advertising before they've earned one dollar.

 **Cross-Reference**    See Chapter 6 for a bevy of marketing tips ranging from free marketing opportunities (such as existing client referrals) to paid marketing avenues such as advertising.

## Competition

Next in your MCSE business plan is the competition section. I know what some of you are saying, "I don't have competition!" That simply isn't so. It's a fatal mistake to say you don't have competition. Not only are you fooling yourself, but also you won't be taken seriously if your business plan is being used to impress other stakeholders, such as a lender or landlord. Competition is typically discussed in a business plan as primary and secondary competition.

### Primary

The primary competition includes the other entities against which you are most likely to bid. This might be other individuals providing similar MCSE consulting services. Many times these individuals may be people you know. It is the primary competition that should receive your greatest attention both in your MCSE business plan and your day-to-day operations.

**Tip** Be sure to bookmark your primary competitors' Web sites. Revisit these sites frequently to monitor what services your primary competitors are offering, what marketing message they are communicating, and what rates are being charged.

### Secondary

This is a broader category of competitors that can potentially include everything ranging from high school students who work in technology at a fraction of your bill rate to big consulting firms who charge significantly more than you do. Be sure to include a list of secondary competitors in your MCSE business plan just so you're thinking about other forms of competitors.

### Repositioning to counter your competition

Once you've zeroed in on your competition, you need to think about how you will reposition to counter these competitive threats. As an astute MCSE consultant, you need to think about how you can reposition your practice to outfox the competition. For example, you may find that your competitors don't have after-hours services. Perhaps you should keep your cellular telephone on at all times, making you reachable 24 hours per day, 7 days per week. Repositioning your practice means refining your service offerings to fill a hole in the marketplace. For example, perhaps your primary competitors support Microsoft Outlook. Perhaps you could reposition your practice to provide Microsoft Outlook customization.

**Cross-Reference** See Chapter 5 for help in completing the competition section of your MCSE business plan.

## Presenting your skills/resume/management team

Simply stated, this section is your resume with a narrative profile that presents your MCSE skills in the most positive light possible. You should also include the resumes of co-workers and job descriptions of positions you intend to fill.

**Cross-Reference** More management-related discussion is found in Part III. For example, see Chapter 10 for information on how to better understand your client's personalities and work approaches.

## Risks

Your MCSE business plan should discuss business risks to which you are susceptible, including the following:

✦ **Economy** — Times have been very good for MCSEs. What will you do if there is a recession (local, regional, or national) that affects your ability to make a living as an MCSE consultant?

✦ **Key person** — What happens if something happens to you? For example, what if your health fails? Do you have enough cash in the bank to survive downtime?

✦ **Obsolescence** — What happens if you don't stay current with your skill set? Worse, what happens if you stay current but Microsoft stops producing BackOffice as part of its antitrust settlement? The skills you've worked so hard to build and refine might be in far less demand.

## Ask the Guru — Reinventing Oneself

This is the first installment of "Ask the Guru!", a rotating column that shares this space with the Guest Sermons and the case studies. In this column, I answer e-mail from a real reader seeking MCSE career advice. This particular e-mail relates well to strategic planning.

*Hi, Harry,*

*I was going through some old MCP Magazines, and I read your article in the December 1999 issue about reinventing oneself. I work for a solution provider in the central Florida area. We were a big Microsoft and Bay Networks shop when I first came aboard three years ago. I got my MCSE about a year and a half ago. I've basically worked a lot of PC support type of contracts with the occasional server rebuild or new deployment. I had hopes of becoming a Network Administrator with our company, but never had enough experience every time a review came around.*

*Then our company took a turn in direction. We became a big reseller of Cisco products. In fact, out of our 50 or so employees over half have some sort of Cisco certification. We have two CCIEs and will have three more shortly. We achieved Silver status with Cisco. All this is well and great, but unless you're a Network Engineer in our company, you're not going to get very far. So I decided to go for it and to try to make the Networking team. I got my CCNA a couple of months ago and have been begging to shadow on other contracts just so I can get some experience. I've gone back and redone my CCNA labs in our lab at the office just to get more hands on experience.*

*Well, as it turns out, I'm not getting a whole lot of experience. My review is due shortly, and I just know I'm going to get passed up again. We're selling a lot of hardware, but not that much in service. Otherwise, we would have more work than our engineers could handle. Anyway, I say all that to say that I've become very disenchanted. I've jumped through all the hoops put in front of me, to no avail. I'm still a PC tech. I read your article and said to myself, "I need to reinvent myself somehow." I don't know if I should forget about Network Engineering and go back to Network Admin. Maybe I should recertify in Windows 2K? Anyway, I've been in the field only three and a half years and wonder if I made a wrong turn. What do you think?*

*Sam R, MCSE, CCNA.*

*C T, Inc.*

Hi, Sam,

Thanks for the e-mail. Your story strikes at the heart of how fast businesses must adjust core mission statements and strategy in today's fast-paced world. It sounds as if the owners of your consulting firm decided to go in a different direction rather quickly. And Cisco isn't a bad horse to bet on.

Often, when a company changes strategic direction, the original purpose for your hire is no longer valid. That leaves two choices, as you've identified: either change your skill set to be in strategic alignment with your employer or find a new employer. Just as your company has done, I think you need to strongly consider reinventing yourself, but not necessarily jumping over to Cisco. Rather, I think another firm that is in mission alignment with your goals to be an MCSE consulting in the network engineering area is the best choice. It's perfectly valid to seek employment elsewhere under these conditions so that you can progress professionally and benefit from the commitment you made to learning and earning the MCSE. And the CCNA won't hurt you either.

The only part of the story I don't yet know is whether or not your region has prospective employers to your liking. Perhaps you could relocate to a larger market. And I have one final comment. I'm reading between the lines, but I sense that with their annual review process your existing employer is voting on how much they value your contribution. Being passed over for a promotion repeatedly suggests it's time to provide your skills elsewhere. Keep me posted.

Cheers,

harryb

# Business Plan Resources

Not only can the Small Business Administration (SBA), located at www.sba.gov, provide significant business planning resources, but you also might consider retaining a private management-consulting firm to help you get your great ideas in writing.

 **Cross-Reference** I discuss the SBA in greater detail in Appendix B.

A professional business plan can cost as much as $10,000, so be careful about this option. You can find the names of business plan writing firms from local accountants and business attorneys.

Better yet, approach the business department of your local business college and inquire about having a Master of Business Administration (MBA) student or upper-level student at the undergraduate level work for you on an internship basis. In my community, the University of Washington (www.washington.edu) provides such assistance to small businesses looking for a leg up in developing a business plan.

You can also use the Internet to find low cost or free business planning resources. For example, at www.planware.org, you can download Exl-Plan Super 2.1, a shareware business-planning template designed to work with Microsoft Excel and Word.

# Helping Others to Write Business Plans

Interestingly, you might well decide that writing business plans is your true calling, in addition to MCSE consulting. I've seen it done before. A student intern that I once hired came from the business community with a keen interest in Microsoft technologies. She ultimately returned to the business community as a small business banker after taking several MCSE certification classes. And guess what? She was the wiser for it when it came to both writing and reviewing technology-based business plans. When you write a business plan, you are really operating more as a management consultant than you are as an MCSE consultant, but the money is good (something you should consider). In fact, assuming you can position such a practice, you can earn as much writing business plans as you can serving as an MCSE consultant.

# Required Paperwork

Closely related to creating the MCSE business plan is identifying and obtaining the proper business licenses, permits, and certificates necessary to conduct business in your particular area. I can't hope to identify what those requirements are, given the thousands of distinct and separate municipalities that exist in the United States alone. However, I can cast some general thoughts your way that will guide you in this area.

At the federal level, you typically need to acquire a tax identification number, which can be an Employer Identification Number (EIN) or a Social Security number. Otherwise, few federal permits, licenses, or certificates are required to operate as an MCSE consultant. One fact of life in the United States is that you will need to file a federal tax return. In my case, with my MCSE consulting activities, this has historically taken the form of a Schedule C filing that is attached to my 1040 federal tax return. However, everyone's tax situation is different.

 **Note**     It is up to you to research what is required in the way of licenses, permits and certificates. These requirements change based on location and over time. A certified public accountant is usually a good source for helping you complete the required paperwork to start as an MCSE consultant.

Many states have business licenses and tax assessments. This clearly varies by state, but in Washington state, you need a business license and a registered business name, and you must file a business and occupation tax return.

At the local level, you may need another business license. Some municipalities also impose occupancy taxes on businesses. One other consideration at the local level is special assessment districts. These are often legally binding organizations of merchants and business people who have banded together and taxed themselves to accomplish some feat. Often, retailers will form a special business improvement district to hire private security details to improve the general atmosphere of the neighborhood (such as by driving drug dealers out).

**Cross-Reference** See Appendix B for more information on the topics discussed in this section.

# Business Advisors

Something I learned later rather than sooner in my career as an MCSE consultant is that successful business people are successes in large part because of the people with whom they surround themselves. Here common sense rules over ego. Egocentric business people will operate under the assumption that they don't need outside advice or help. The more pragmatic business people understand it isn't how hard you work but how smart you work. These people surround themselves with a whole host of business advisors. I learned this once I took a closer look at how my successful business clients operated. You might consider retaining the following business advisors as your needs and financial resources warrant (some on this list may well offer you free advice):

✦ **Bookkeeper**—Early on, you'll want to use a bookkeeper on an occasional basis to assist in your billings, collections, and general financial statement preparation. Trust me! These are dollars wisely spent.

✦ **CPA/accountant**—Not only should you enlist qualified accounting help to assist in your tax preparation, but before you know it, you may seek tax planning advice. It's nice to have such problems as an MCSE consultant, because when you need tax planning help, you're making money!

✦ **Lawyer**—As your MCSE consulting practice becomes more sophisticated, you may be seeking legal review of business contracts. Two thoughts here: First, don't try to be your own lawyer. Second, hire a good lawyer who specializes in the needs you have. A general practitioner lawyer probably doesn't even know what an MCSE consultant is.

✦ **Business consultant**—Perhaps you're a true tech head with limited business wisdom. And while you're financially successful, you could be missing out on some tremendous available business opportunities. I've always been impressed by technical types who accept their business limitations and hire a business consultant to guide them. In fact, you might find it your best use of time and money to hire a business consultant to complete your MCSE consulting business plan.

✦ **Other MCSE consultants**—There's nothing quite like running ideas by a valued peer group. Fellow MCSE consultants that you know and trust might be a tremendous source of business advice for you.

✦ **Banker**—Bankers review many proposals and business plans in the course of their work. So if you really want to get a thorough and revealing check on the validity of your MCSE consulting business plan, have it reviewed by a banker.

Why is this? Because a banker will point out weaknesses you might not otherwise have seen. However, be aware; it can be a critical review.

✦ **Spouse and other family members.** Your toughest critics will be those closest to you, including your spouse and family members. This group of business advisors can most likely be counted on for offering frank and brutally honest feedback.

In Appendix D, I list numerous business-planning resources for you, including agencies such as the Small Business Administration.

## Decision Point

At the time you complete your MCSE consulting business plan, which should also be about the time you finish reading this book, you'll face a decision point. It boils down to one of two alternatives: "Yes, I'll go for it!" or "Nope, I'll keep my day job!"

It should be strongly noted that you could go through this entire book, write an MCSE consulting practice business plan, and decide that you don't want to be an MCSE consultant. Is your time wasted by engaging in this process only to discover you aren't going to do it? Did you waste your money on the price of this book? The answer in both cases is *no*. Too often the business planning cycle is presented in the context that you have to go forward with your business plan. However, using your business plan to decide you don't want to invest in an endeavor is a perfectly acceptable and legitimate outcome.

## Ongoing Business Planning

So you've made the decision to become an MCSE consultant. The business planning process doesn't stop here. On an annual basis, you should be getting away from your practice for a few days to reflect on the past year and to engage in some strategic planning. A framework you can use for strategic planning is SWOT analysis, which stands for Strengths, Weaknesses, Opportunities, and Threats. Strengths and weaknesses are internal variables used to look at the pluses and minuses of your MCSE consulting practice. Opportunities and threats are external variables used to examine the competitive and economic landscape affecting your MCSE consulting practice.

## Summary

This chapter has covered the basic outline for your MCSE consulting business plan. You'll spend the rest of the book drawing out the answers needed for you to write your own MCSE business plan.

✦     ✦     ✦

# MCSE Consulting Fundamentals

**A**ll successful MCSE consulting practices are built on solid foundations. These foundations are typically bedrock values that define the consultant. This chapter presents a number of MCSE consulting fundamental tenets for your consideration. It's my belief that this discussion should occur earlier in the book rather than later, allowing you to build your own foundation before entering the wonderful and profitable world of MCSE consulting.

## Gaining Trust

When you get right down to it, all we sell as MCSE consultants is trust. Feature sets come and go, sometimes in the course of months. Because we live in the fast forward world of technology, aptly called Internet time, you can't hope to master more than a small fraction of the actual technology being introduced and used.

Because you're only one product release away from obsolescence, and because there's no sure way to know what features will be included in technology products one or two releases down the road, I recommend you stake your MCSE consulting claim on trust, not technology.

If your efforts are in part directed towards gaining and retaining the trust of your clients, you'll have the political capital necessary to survive technical mistakes you're bound to make or incur with new product introductions. In a strong trusting client relationship, I've even found that I can bill for much of my research time with clients as I learn how to deploy new product releases.

**Note**

I should mention that I've worked for years to build many of these relationships where trust is the cornerstone of the client relationship. So don't be too hard on yourself when working toward achieving this goal of client trust. Much like the self-actualization peak in Abraham Maslow's hierarchy of needs, it takes a while to get there.

Now, consider a relationship where trust is absent. Here you are truly only one reboot away from being fired by the client. If the client doesn't inherently trust you, your every move is questioned. And when you use that beta Agfa scanner driver on a new Windows 2000 Professional machine and the external Jaz drive is no longer visible in Windows Explorer, you're out the door. MCSE consulting relationships that lack trust tend to have a high consultant turnover, as measured by the parade of consultants that have come and departed such a client site.

The bottom line on trust is this: you won't make it if you can't get it, and you can't help but be successful if you've got it. If you're unable to inspire trust in your clients, you should question if you're going to make it as an MCSE consultant. Remember that trust is an ambiguous term and that it can be gained in a variety of ways. While it's hard to explicitly define (although I'll try in just a moment), you know it when you see it and you feel it when it's there. Many MCSE consultants garner client trust because of safe, conservative technology and sound business decision-making that keeps the client site up and running with a minimum of downtime. Other MCSE consultants earn trust as know-it-alls, a risky strategy that assumes you can keep current with and master a wide array of constantly changing technologies. I've even witnessed MCSE consultants gain great amounts of client trust by being on time to appointments, returning telephone calls, billing in a timely manner, and so on. These MCSE consultants are using better business practices to inspire client trust, and good communication skills and straightforwardness should never be underestimated.

You've made it as an MCSE consultant in the "trust" department when the client would rather sell his or her firstborn child before getting rid of you.

## Practicing Expectation Management

Not far behind the trust issue is expectation management. Rookie and other inexperienced MCSE consultants often fall into the trap of trying to please everybody. This can take several forms, including the following:

- ✦ **Overpromising** — Have you ever found yourself saying, "Oh yeah, Windows 2000 Server can do that," when you've never successfully implemented that particular feature?

- ✦ **The client is always right syndrome** — Have you ever been bullied by a client into committing to a technology solution that isn't feasible?

- ✦ **Next release syndrome** — Have you ever tried to duck and dodge a technical problem by promising it will be fixed in the next release (whether you know this to be true or not)?

✦ **Staff capabilities** — Have you ever said, "We've got someone who can do that," when you don't?

✦ **It'll only cost this much** — Have you ever knowingly or unknowingly under-quoted the true costs of an engagement?

All of these examples make one point: the importance of expectation management. Taken alone or as a whole, any of these instances can falsely raise a client's expectations so high that there's no chance to be successful. The point is that many technically adept, well-meaning MCSE consultants engage in self-defeating behavior with clients by not managing the client's expectations well.

This issue strikes at the heart of what an MCSE consultant is. A consultant, in my eyes, differs from a straight technician (tech head) because of the professional relationship dimension. A professional relationship requires relationship management, and to manage a relationship, you have to manage expectations. You probably don't have to look too far for an example of how best to manage expectations; just think about your marriage or a long-term relationship. Having been married for many years, I can tell you that I've learned all about expectation management. I'm very careful not to promise something I have no hope of delivering.

**Note**

Something you can do immediately to engage in client expectation management is avoid client surprises. I've found one easy area of expectation management improvement lies in billings. Not only should you carefully delineate what charges are within the project scope and what charges are outside of the scope, but you should perhaps call or e-mail clients to let them know about the bill they'll be receiving in the mail in a few days. Avoiding billing surprises is one of the best expectation management tricks around!

# Overcommunicating

Communicating is easy to do, and clients are begging for it. I've gained many good clients who were frustrated with past consultants who just didn't communicate. Undercommunication can occur in several forms:

✦ **Shyness** — Many MCSEs are introverted, a fact of life if you look at the field as a whole. That's not surprising, given the MCSE's natural affinity for technology. This introversion can often take the form of shyness in social interactions where communicating with other human beings (including clients) is key. Being a consultant is as much about communication as technical competency; thus, the importance of the communication discussion on these pages. The chronically shy are likely to be severely challenged to make it big as a MCSE consultant because their communications skills can hold them back. Likewise, these same individuals can be very successful as developers where communications isn't as large a success factor. This isn't intended to be a negative put-down but more a value-add in this consulting bible. I'll try to call it like it is so you, the reader, don't make a poor career decision.

✦ **Arrogance** — Almost 180 degrees opposite of the chronically shy is the arrogant MCSE consultant. A consultant who acts like he knows everything by sharing nothing will not only anger the client, but will completely leave the client out of the loop. So don't be the type that typically comes in, does the technical work, and leaves without uttering hardly a word to anyone. Ouch!

✦ **English as a second language (ESL)** — This isn't anyone's fault, but it is a fact of life. Many clients are alarmed and frustrated by the communication problems that can result from working with MCSEs who are unable to speak the English language well. In all fairness, I suspect those of us who speak English as a primary language would face the same communication challenge if we were to work overseas in a country where English was a secondary language.

✦ **Incompetence** — Some MCSE consultants either don't know better, don't care, or are incompetent. Whatever the reason, there is a simple lack of communication between the MCSE consultant and client.

Here are a few pointers about communicating with your clients.

1. Tell the clients what you're going to do. Take a moment to sit down and explain what your plan is. This typically only takes a few minutes. You might use e-mail to do this if a face-to-face communication isn't possible.

2. Do what you said you would do. If for some reason your plan changes along the way, it is critical you communicate this immediately to the client. Often, my plan as an MCSE consultant is to drop by a client site to install a new hardware device on a Windows 2000 network. On occasion, I've been surprised that no Windows 2000 driver exists for the device (such as an Agfa scanner). Caught by surprise, I endeavor to communicate this information to the client immediately and seek advice. In this example, the options might include using a Windows NT 4.0 driver, stopping the work and waiting for a Windows 2000 driver to be released, or advising the client to send the scanner back.

3. Tell the client what you did. This can be accomplished by a quick face-to-face meeting, but often that isn't practical for a few reasons: Maybe the client is unavailable (in a meeting, on the telephone, or you name it), or perhaps your work has occurred after hours (very common for an MCSE consultant) and the client is not on-site. My approach here has been to leave a site report on e-mail or voice mail telling the client exactly what I accomplished.

**Note**    When in doubt, overcommunicate. Until you read different, take the risk and be an overcommunicator with your clients. Believe me, they'll give you visual cues when you start to babble incessantly.

And don't forget to aggressively acknowledge the client's communication as a form of overcommunication. I look at it like sailboat racing, where the crew always repeats the skipper's command as a form of acknowledgement. That way, both parties know they've had a complete form of communication and understanding. You might try this by simply replying to clients' e-mail messages, saying, "I received your message. Thanks."

# Wearing Many Hats

MCSE consultants aren't just BackOffice heavyweights. At a client's request, MCSE consultants often have to make the coffee, lift over 40 pounds, run to the computer shop for a part, and so on. To some extent, these tasks are all part of the job and all part of serving the client.

Being an MCSE consultant isn't just bits and bytes. It's often about putting on an analytical hat and helping plan the strategic direction of the client's information infrastructure. Wearing many hats as a professional has often gone by another phrase: "doing whatever it takes."

## Case Study — Code of Ethics

Part of being a professional is to conduct yourself in an aboveboard and ethical manner. If you belong to a technology trade association, look closely at its Web site and you're likely to find a code of conduct. In the accompanying figure, I show the Etiquette page from the Network Professionals of Puget Sound (www.npps.org) as a plain-spoken example of best behavior guidelines. This group is also deeply committed to ethical standards that members adhere to.

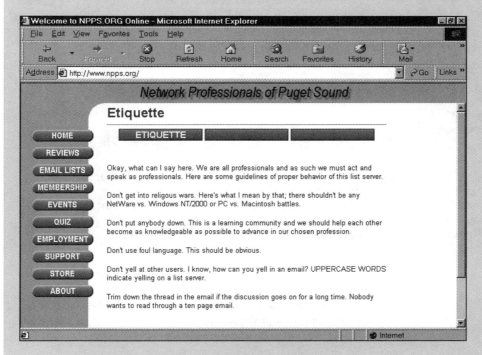

*Continued*

*Continued*

Another organization with a code of ethics is the Association of Microsoft Solution Providers (www.amsp.org). As you can see in the accompanying figure, this is a more formal code of ethics than the etiquette code from the NPPS. In all fairness, I'm comparing apples and oranges here, as the NPPS has an ethical code too. But what I'm attempting to accomplish in this case study is to educate you on the code of ethics area, with my goal being to make you a better MCSE consultant.

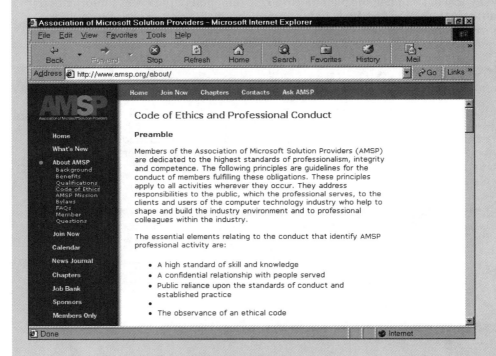

So here's your task as part of this case study. Search the Web and find other trade groups that publish a code of ethics for its membership. Take a moment to review these documents and consider whether or not the code of ethics from other organizations is in alignment with how your conduct yourself as an MCSE consultant. Call it a reflective moment, but I think it's a good use of your time.

**Note**      Start your search for the Network Professional Association at www.npa.org, a national trade group for network professionals.

# Becoming a Business Advisor

Microsoft got it, and as an MCSE consultant, it is critical you get it, too. The upper-level Windows 2000 MCSE exams now place a premium on business issues, in addition to underlying technologies such as Active Directory. For example, on the "70-221: Designing a Microsoft Windows 2000 Network Infrastructure" exam, you'll be responsible for analyzing existing and planned business models. The exam questions have taken the form of business story problems instead of strict technical definitions.

Life as an MCSE consultant closely mirrors the business paradigm shift on the Windows 2000 MCSE exams. Many of you already know this, but it's certainly worth discussing. As an MCSE consultant, you're increasingly being called upon to understand business needs and to implement technology solutions in the context of those needs. No longer is it sufficient just to know the cool feature sets of BackOffice 2000, unless you're shooting for a lower-paying, less value-added job as a technician.

The MCSE consultant adds value to the client relationship by serving as a business advisor. In fact, some of the most successful MCSE consultants I've met have mastered both BackOffice and the boardroom.

So why the concern about business models? What ever happened to good old-fashioned computing? The prevailing trend towards integrating business with technology can be attributed to several factors:

✦ **Maturity of operating systems and applications** — Basic technical needs are now being satisfied with the latest generations of operating systems and applications. An example of this is the front office product, Microsoft Office. This suite of business applications does just about everything now. People are literally starting to say they can't imagine what else they'd need technically in some areas of computing.

✦ **Profit pressures** — Businesses are looking for a higher return on investment (ROI) on technology expenditures. The financial types are looking closely at your bill rate, which isn't going down the way hardware and software prices are. If your bill rate remains stable or increases in a period of declining hardware and software prices, you have to do one of two things. You have to boost your productivity by accomplishing more amazing technical feats per billable hour. Or you have to add more value to the consulting engagement. A value-added feature is to participate as a business advisor, marrying technology to the client's business.

✦ **Better business practices** — Many clients view technology implementations as a fresh start. That is, they look at BackOffice 2000 and the like as an opportunity to change their procedures with tools such as the instant messaging capabilities of Exchange 2000 Server or the public folder–based group calendars in Outlook 2000. The savvy MCSE consultant will be able to see business opportunities for the technology being implemented. In effect, you might find yourself acting as a management consultant.

✦ **Competitive advantage** — The real hard-core business types, the MBAs, are looking to squeak out every competitive advantage they can in this new, what management guru Tom Peter's called " whacked out and crazy" Web-based world of business. In fact, you might want to try your hand at e-commerce consulting as an MCSE consultant, as I discuss later in Chapter 23. And you thought the Site Builder designation from the Windows NT 4.0 MCSE days wasn't going to do anything for you. Think again!

Some MCSE consultants naturally have a brain for business and others don't. Fair enough. If business issues escape you at first glance, consider attending a few business courses at your community college, or better yet, save a few bucks and take a free Web course. Barnes and Noble, as of this writing, is offering a free Web-based course you can download and complete (see www.bn.com). I'm sure other Web portals are doing the same.

# Focusing on a Long-term View

Imitation is the sincerest form of flattery, or so the saying goes. As an MCSE consultant, I've often looked at how my successful clients conduct business, hoping for some of that good luck to rub off on me. That is, by emulating successful behaviors, I hope to enjoy the same success as the people I'm emulating. As an aside, that's how I enjoyed success as a collegiate cross-country ski racer — by imitating the best practices of the faster ski racers. That same positive thinking applies to being in business as an MCSE consultant.

One of my most successful clients, a real estate advisory firm, considers its long-term relationships to be a foundation of success. This is a firm with decades of service to the local business community, working successfully in an industry that depends on and counts professional reputation as a critical success factor.

So what can you learn from this anecdote? Developing and maintaining long-term client relationships is critical to your success as an MCSE consultant. There simply aren't enough hours in the day to keep losing and acquiring clients. Such turnover is not only unprofitable financially, but also taxes your limited energy unnecessarily.

**Note**

A client today should be a client tomorrow, regardless of the operating system release. With the fast pace of technology product upgrades, it would be unprofitable for you to retain a client for only one product version release. Why? Just as you were getting to know a client and that client's information infrastructure, it would be time for you to hit the road.

# Act as a Client Advocate

As a professional service provider, the MCSE consultant represents the client as much as a lawyer or CPA does. In effect, on technology matters such as BackOffice technologies, you speak for the client. This relationship creates a fiduciary obligation for you to act in the best interest of the client. Ways that you can act as a client advocate include the following:

✦ **Represent the client, not the vendor** — When ordering hardware, software, and services for the client, remember that you are speaking on behalf of the client, not the wallet in your hip pocket or purse. You might find yourself farming out specialized tasks to your personal financial detriment because it is your fiduciary obligation in the context of your client relationship to do so.

✦ **Disclose conflicts of interest** — If you have a direct financial interest in a product being recommended to the client, it's your obligation to disclose such conflicts of interest. As an author, I'm often put in a tight spot where I'm recommending my own book to a client who has asked me for "some good Windows 2000 books." While I'm all too happy to recommend my own text, I usually make the point, via an appropriate dose of humor, that I'll pocket a buck and quarter in royalties from their book purchase. The point is typically well taken, appreciated, and accepted in the spirit in which it was delivered.

✦ **Practice tough love** — Part of the advocacy role will likely include a tough love dimension. An MCSE consultant, acting as the client's advocate, is honor bound to "call it like it is". Perhaps you have to tactfully tell your client something they don't want to hear. If the client has junk machines, you have to let them know. I remember all too well an example of telling a client in no uncertain terms that I couldn't support that company's decision to save money by not purchasing a new server to run the Great Plains Dynamics accounting system. This client sought to load Great Plains Dynamics accounting package on an overtaxed server already running several BackOffice applications as part of the Microsoft Small Business Server suite. Because I delivered the message based on fact and sincerity, I prevailed, and the client gladly purchased a member server for its network.

# Mentoring Your Clients

It's long been said in the consulting community that a great consultant is one that works their way out of a job. That is, if you're doing your job correctly as an MCSE consultant, the client shouldn't need you around. It's a lofty goal, and one that keeps you focused on provided exceptional customer service. The reality is different from the theory. Clients that like you tend to find more work for you, dishing additional work your way. So who's complaining?

I've taken a slightly modified view of working your way out of a job. I've found that many of my MCSE consulting hours come from helping a power user on the client's staff learn how to run the network. Perhaps you've seen this before. A business staff member is really a computer hobbyist at night and on the weekends. These people gravitate to you when you're working on-site so they can learn more. Over many months, you slowly allow these people to start performing maintenance tasks. Before you know it, they've added some technology management responsibilities to their job role. I've found this makes for great client relations to take someone under your mentoring wing. And these people are often enthusiastic referral sources for helping you obtain additional work.

# Providing Pro Bono Services

When I scan the horizon of business and commerce, looking for what makes an MCSE consulting firm successful in the long-term, there is one component that is common in many entities: volunteering services. Providing pro bono services means you provide some of your professional services without charge. It's a common practice for doctors and lawyers. Many professionals view this as a good way to give back to the community that's given to them. MCSE consultants should think no differently.

So what type of pro bono services can you provide as an MCSE consultant? I've seen the following services provided without charge:

✦ Wiring the local school for networking

✦ Teaching an introduction to computers at the senior citizen's center

✦ Donating computer equipment to the local library

In many communities, you can associate yourself with a not-for-profit organization that coordinates technology volunteers to help other not-for-profits. In the Pacific Northwest, one such group is NPower (www.npower.org), seen in Figure 3-1.

So why give away the milk and the cow when providing pro bono services? First, good things happen to good people. Those with a big heart tend to have a big paycheck as well (for reasons I can't fully explain). Note that I do believe you need to be selective in the giving of your services. Private firms that can pay for your services should do so. Remember that Bill Gates, Chairman of Microsoft Corporation, once stated that he puts as much time into giving away his money as he does making it!

# First, Do No Harm

Lastly, it should go without saying that above all, a key MCSE consulting foundation is to leave a system in the same or better shape than you found it.

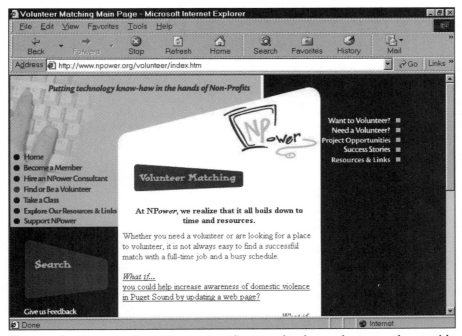

**Figure 3-1:** Groups such as NPower coordinate technology volunteers who provide pro bono services.

# Introducing Brelsford's Rules of Ten

This chapter is the foundation layer of your MCSE consulting career. But it's not the last you will hear about foundation-level issues in this book. At several points, I'll present pragmatic and practical MCSE rules — Rules of Ten — that sit right on top of the foundation you've built in this chapter. For example, in Chapter 6, I share with you two Rules of Ten for getting more business. And if you didn't notice, I presented ten MCSE consulting fundamentals in this chapter, which you should consider as your first Rule of Ten.

# Summary

This chapter brings to a close the introductory part of this book. Having completed your business plan in Chapter 2 and discovered the fundamentals of MCSE consulting in this chapter, the door has been opened to the next section, where you'll learn to go out and get the business.

✦          ✦          ✦

# Finder

**Y**our first task as an MCSE consultant after launching your practice is to go out and find business. This part will help you with business development focused on landing suitable clients and will help you avoid soliciting and engaging clients that are not right for you.

# Growing the Business

**W**hile there are many avenues to becoming an MCSE consultant, one of the most popular is to break out on your own. Here you are accountable only to yourself and the free marketplace. If you're the type of person who is self-reliant, this is tremendously exciting. On the other hand, if you harbor deep fears and lack confidence, breaking out on your own can be intimidating. For many of us, there is a fine line between excitement and intimidation.

This chapter is about growing your business by going out and getting the business. It starts with the first day of your life as an MCSE consultant and ends with some sage advice about client selection.

## Day One – You're in Business

If you're like me, you've spent the night before your new endeavor pondering the wisdom of your decision to become an MCSE consultant. Here are two thoughts to prepare you for your first day as an MCSE consultant. First, it may actually be difficult to identify your first day. Using some of the approaches outlined in this chapter and throughout the book, you might just find yourself acting as an MCSE consultant, with no big deal being made about the proverbial first day of business.

Second, the first day that you are officially open for business as an MCSE consultant may be anticlimactic. In most cases, it's unlikely you're booked full of engagements, and tasks such as getting your business cards and stationary designed and printed seem to take up an inordinate amount of time. I remember my first day as an MCSE consultant and the few days that followed as anything but MCSE-like. I felt I was in administration mode, opening a business bank account and purchasing a cellular telephone. These administrative tasks seemed to take hours. I felt very unproductive, but I knew that the work contributed towards my greater goal of being an MCSE consultant. That said, I had launched and was officially an MCSE consultant.

# Business Development Life Cycle

Rookie MCSE consultants often remark how surprised they are by the lead time necessary to procure business, to bill, and to receive cold hard cash in their bank accounts. The business development cycle alone is in the neighborhood of six months on average. Tack on another month to do the work and another month for the billing cycle, and it's possible that you can expect eight months between making the initial contact and actually getting cash in your hand.

Why does the business development cycle take six months? Don't calls come in from clients desperately asking you to start working immediately? Sure. In the market for technology consulting services, there are always spot buyers. However, not only are these clients the exception, but also their panicked call rife with immediacy and urgency may be a leading indicator of how they operate. I've also found these clients to have less loyalty to their consultant than the blue-chip or high-grade clients you should be cultivating. Many times, the spot buyer of your services has terminated another consultant, and you're just the next victim in line for an unsuccessful engagement.

**Note**   When you receive a panicked call from a client urgently seeking your services, be sure to ask if there was a previous consultant and, if so, what happened to that consultant. Remember that the same can happen to you. For example, if the client speaks poorly of the former consultant, they could certainly speak so of you. Ask yourself both if this is the type of client you want and if this is the type of client that will allow you to earn a profit in the long term.

The six-month business development cycle is an average. For every client that retains you inside the six-month window, take a moment to count how many clients took years to win over. Then don't forget to factor in those prospects you pursue for months and years that never become clients. Once you calculate these additional efforts into the business development cycle equation, the six-month average is a reasonable sales planning horizon. You'll be interested to know that I've confirmed this six-month business development cycle in other businesses. In fields such as commercial real estate leasing, it's not at all uncommon to spend half a year working on a transaction.

Table 4-1 reflects the business development dance that tends to occur between MCSE consultant and client.

The six-month business development cycle for MCSE consultants is just for business development. The actual work may begin the next day or a couple of months later. Needless to say, the business development cycle for MCSE consultants is surprisingly long and shouldn't be underestimated.

| | Table 4-1 |
|---|---|
| | **Business Development Cycle** |

| Month | Activity |
|---|---|
| One | Initial contact between MCSE consultant and prospective client initiated. Follow-up e-mail between parties. |
| Two | Follow-up meeting where MCSE consultant learns more about network. |
| Three | Prospective client gets busy at work. Doesn't return your call or answer your e-mail. |
| Four | Prospective client, cleaning out e-mail Inbox, replies to you and suggests another meeting. You're busy on a project followed by vacation for a week. You will have to meet next month. |
| Five | Another meeting at prospective client site. You submit proposal. Prospective client reads proposal and exchanges e-mail with you to clarify points and lower overall costs. |
| Six | Prospective client approves work and becomes a client. However, the signed consulting contract contains several stipulations, including one noting that the work can't start for 60 days because a new release of a narrow vertical market software application won't be available until that time. |

The sooner you accept the six-month business development cycle as a fact of life, the better. Not only will you start to manage your MCSE consulting practice from a visionary point of view where you're thinking six months out, you may also become a higher quality MCSE consultant. Here is what I mean. Like a fine wine, quality clients improve with age. You don't land the blue-chip clients in a short business development cycle. In fact, it may take years to land that icon of commerce and business in your market that every MCSE consultant is seeking. Perhaps you'll need to golf, sail, and ski for years with the business owner until you get a crack at the account, and you are allowed to bid then only because the existing consultant finally lost interest and didn't serve the client.

# 12-Month's Cash

Before you and I go one step further, it is important to understand that you need sufficient cash on hand to launch as an MCSE consultant. This is not unlike others you may know who've broken out as an independent business person, professional service provider or commission-based sales agent. All of these professionals, yourself included as an MCSE consultant, need starting capital.

Think about this. Maybe you've witnessed the following scenarios. Perhaps a friend or family member is in some type of commission-based professional capacity and started with a year of cash to initially cover living expenses. This area is so important that I'll restate it again. One fact about starting out that rings true with commission-based salespeople, small business owners, and MCSE consultants alike is that, when you break out on your own, you need a reserve of cash on which to survive until your business efforts yield a sustainable cash flow. In real estate sales seminars, you're advised to have a year of cash for living expenses. This is advice that applies equally well to the MCSE consultant just starting out.

Why should you have one-year's cash on hand to launch as an MCSE consultant? The billing cycle follows the initial contract, and accounting for write-downs. (Write-downs are charges against your billings when a client will not pay your consulting invoice. Accounting rules dictate that you write down doubtful accounts receivable balances after a reasonable period of time.) You're likely just a few months short of one calendar year before you see your first cash inflows from your consulting activities; hence the suggestion you have twelve months of cash on hand prior to launching as an MCSE consultant.

To some extent, the cycle I just presented affects even established practices. From the first sales call to the first satisfied invoice — which is cash to you, the MCSE consultant — it's not uncommon for nine to twelve months to have passed. So if you're just starting out as an MCSE consultant, these stark facts about timing and cash flow are even stronger. That is, the proper context for the discussion about setting aside 12-month's cash before making the break as an MCSE consultant is really to view your operation as a startup. Because startups are riskier and slower out of the gate than you expect, the extra few months' cash will be well appreciated.

# Interim Measures

So rich Uncle Richard didn't grease your bank account with a wad of cash. But you're not going to let this lack of one year's living expenses stop you from becoming an MCSE consultant. You need to look at other financial alternatives. I have seen two strategies used to overcome the cash nest egg problem. They are (in order of decreasing desirability): working a night job and borrowing money.

## Finding a night job

Some of the great fortunes in the small business community have come from those hard-working souls who toiled at a night job while cultivating their entrepreneurial endeavor. For the businessperson, this story is typically one of tending bar or delivering pizzas. These jobs are great and are the fodder for many American success stories. However, while I have nothing against budding MCSE consultants delivering pizzas on the way up, there are night shift alternatives that complement what you're trying to accomplish in the long term. For example, you could be an adjunct computer instructor at night at a local vocational-technical or community college. In many cases, these educational institutions will start an instructor with little or no formal teaching experience (including yours truly a dozen years ago). Not only does the old adage about teaching, "If you really want to learn a subject, teach it," apply in my case, but I've also found night teaching to be a good referral source for MCSE consulting engagements.

Another swing shift possibility is software product support. Many firms, primarily software companies, need to staff their help desks around the clock. This work often allows the MCSE consultant to increase his or her technical skill set while making a few dollars. I am aware of swing shift technical support opportunities in the following types of firms:

✦ **Software development firms** — Computers don't care what time it is, and many technology projects occur after hours when users have gone home. Both of these dynamics mean night work for you and others!

✦ **ISPs and telcos** — Internet service providers and the telecommunications firms that provide communication links experience some of the heaviest activity after hours. Any respectable ISP and telco will provide sufficient, bona fide 24-hour technical support.

✦ **Fortune 500 and other global firms** — Don't be lulled into thinking your community doesn't offer real technology-based night shift work. With the time zones that span the United States, morning on the east coast is just past the "witching hour" in Alaska. More to the point, firms with global operations, a common occurrence today, have business operations that are literally non-stop. Take a look around your town and see what firms have remote locations. They probably need to staff a technology crew on the night shift. Don't be afraid to dig deep in your search; it might be a law firm with ten offices worldwide that'll hire you for after-hours work.

✦ **Traditional night businesses** — Hotels have long hired night auditors to reconcile their accounting books while things are quiet in the lobby. These same firms should receive your resume seeking a swing shift, technology-based opportunity.

## Borrowing money

If you can get a dot-com entrepreneur to speak with you about how he or she started out, there is typically a maxed out credit card somewhere in his or her past. No matter what you choose to do for extra money, to launch yourself as an MCSE consultant, there comes a point where you'll probably have to borrow during your formative years. In itself, borrowing isn't a bad thing. Borrowing can be used to provide the working capital you need on that newly landed, enormous consulting contract. I did it myself, borrowing on a credit card to purchase a Dell laptop that was needed for my first contract as an MCSE consultant. It was a lucrative contract that paid on time 30 days later, but I needed the laptop in advance. You get the point.

There are various forms of borrowing, ranging from a commercial line of credit from a bank to pawn shops and loan sharks. But seriously, here are the most common forms of borrowing I've seen used by fledgling MCSE consultants:

✦ **Credit cards** — Few can resist the enticing preapproval offers of this high cost form of debt. Easy to acquire, credit cards are used at some point by almost every MCSE consultant.

✦ **Home equity loan** — This debt is reasonable both in its costs and in your ability to obtain it. You should obtain your funds via this avenue prior to leaving your day job and becoming a full-fledged MCSE consultant. It's much easier to get a home equity loan while gainfully employed. The nice thing about a home equity loan is that it allows you to feel that you're investing in your MCSE consulting business, given that you used some of the equity in your house to do it.

✦ **Friends, family, and in-laws** — While common, this form of debt carries the high cost of tension and hurt feelings when things don't go exactly as expected.

# Getting Your First Client

It's now time to get your first client. As with most anything, the first one is typically the hardest. This section speaks towards several strategies you might consider in gaining the first client.

## Capitalizing on an existing employer

A tried-and-true method of landing your first client is turning your existing employer into a client. This can take several forms, including the following:

✦ **Changing your status from W-2 to 1099** — This example, of course, applies to the United States, but here you can work for your existing employer as a contractor. This not only changes the treatment of your income, but also typically absolves you of the employer/employee relationship. As a contractor, you typically have fewer restrictions on additional, outside work, allowing you to build your MCSE consulting practice.

✦ **Change in hours** — Many people contract back to their existing employers so that they can work fewer hours. You might consider that same strategy when you make the break as an MCSE consultant. Instead of working 40+ hours (okay, closer to 60 hours) per week as a salaried or exempt MCSE, you might elect to work 20 hours per week as a contractor, freeing up the time you need to start your MCSE consulting practice.

The results of parlaying your existing employer into becoming your first client can be very positive.

Perhaps you've seen people return to their existing employers at a higher bill rate than their previous wage. There are several reasons why this occurs, including the contractor's absorbing overhead expenses such as medical insurance and self-employment taxes. Employers often have to pay a slightly higher wage for the flexible staffing option that contractors provide. Employers who are dissatisfied with contractors can typically terminate the relationship immediately with little fear of wrongful discharge litigation. Employers typically don't have to give layoff notices to contractors either (known as WARN notices).

## Volunteering

One way to establish yourself as a legitimate consultant and gain a reference letter and referral along the way is to volunteer. There are typically more volunteer opportunities than volunteers, so finding an unpaid opportunity to strut your stuff as an MCSE consultant shouldn't be that hard. Two volunteer organizations that I've seen MCSE consultants successfully use are not-for-profit organizations and political campaigns.

### Not-for-profit organizations

Not-for-profit organizations are chronically short on funds, yet have the same technology needs, both hardware and software, as private sector firms have. Pick a cause, and somewhere there is a not-for-profit organization behind it. Give them a call and see how you can help. Better yet, in major cities there are not-for-profit organizations that provide low-cost and no-cost technology consulting services for fellow not-for-profit organizations. In the Pacific Northwest part of the United States, there is one such group called NPower (www.npower.org).

### Political campaigns

Regardless of your political beliefs, there is a campaign out there that needs your MCSE consulting services. They just can't pay you. Find a candidate you support and volunteer to run the computer system. Not only is this approach a door opener for meeting the rich, famous, and politically connected, but your candidate just might get elected.

## Working for half price

If you properly propose it in such a way that you don't cheapen yourself, you can acquire your initial clients by offering to work at a reduced rate, recognizing your limitations (perhaps technical, perhaps management-related) as a new MCSE consultant. There is no shortage of clients willing to accept a lower price for your services. It's a fair deal. You get a client, and the client gets work performed at bargain rates.

These clients are seldom long-term fits for your MCSE consulting practice. A client that is susceptible to bargain pricing will likely trade you in for the next cut-rate deal that crosses his or her desk rather than pay your full consulting rate at a future date.

## Auctioning yourself

I didn't think of this one myself but observed other professional service providers in action on the auction catwalk.

### Charity auctions

The following is a true story that was widely reported in the Seattle-area newspapers. A medical doctor donated a vasectomy operation to a local school fundraising auction, spurring the question: Why can't an MCSE consultant donate a day of services for auction to the highest bidder? If you look closely, there are charity auctions literally every week in medium and large cities. What a wonderful way to market yourself!

### Online auction sites

Crafty technology professionals made headlines when they auctioned themselves through eBay. Today, the practice is more commonplace, but what have you got to lose? Put your MCSE consulting services up for sale at an online auction site.

### Ask the Guru — Just Say No!

This reader mail was received from someone interested in working with me. However, as you read closely, this individual was interested in something other than MCSE consulting opportunities. The point in sharing this with you is that, as you grow your business, you need to cast a critical eye towards business proposals that cross your e-mail inbox or desk. My view of business development and growing the business is qualifying opportunities and saying no at least as often as you say yes. Why? Because developing business isn't about engaging every opportunity that presents itself. It's about making key decisions that allow you to manage your time to maximize your potential as an MCSE consultant. Read on.

*"Dear Harry –*

*My name is Jeff Geiser. I read your recent article in* Computer Source *magazine. I am writing to you to explore the possibility of connecting on some research. I am an investor, stock analyst, and licensed broker. My company is The Pillar Financial Group, in Redmond Washington. If you have an interest in sharing research, read on... I believe it is appropriate to convey what it is I am trying to accomplish.*

*I am looking for someone who has an interest in technology, substantial expertise, and a willingness to share ideas and research. I have found that feedback from informed high tech folks has been extremely valuable in the past. One of the greatest investors of this century, Warren Buffet, has drastically underperformed the market recently, because as he says, "I don't buy what I don't understand". Meaning he doesn't buy technology stocks. I am aware of my limitations and don't want to fall into the same trap that Mr. Buffet has.*

*During recent years, I have struggled somewhat in evaluating technologies and technology companies. I am adept, however, at technical and fundamental analysis of companies and their stocks. I can read income statements, balance sheets, evaluate a company's valuations etc. In fact my stock picks have performed very well in recent years. This is all very useful; however, if I cannot understand a company's technology or its potential applications, then it is useless with respect to high tech companies.*

*For example, last summer a friend of mine asked me to look at F5 Networks (Symbol FFIV- It was $18/share). I looked at it and said, "I don't understand the technology." We talked about scheduling a visit to the company. Before we did anything, the stock was over $100/share (As high as $160 in November and has since settled down into the $90's). After snowboarding with an employee of FFIV two weeks ago, who explained a lot to me, I was finally able to be comfortable with the idea of owning the stock, which I recently purchased at $96 1/2. So, what does this have to do with you?*

*I have held some tech stocks during the last few years and done well with them. I believe, however, that I could likely enhance the performance. I currently have one research partner, an Aerospace engineer who has been investing for 20+ years. He is more well-versed on technology than I am. He knows a pretty fair amount about software etc., but neither us has our "finger on the pulse" of the high tech industries like someone who earns their livelihood in it would.*

*I am proposing the sharing of ideas and research. In that vein, I can tell you that I currently own Pervasive Software (Symbol -PVSW), which I have made money on but whose potential I am struggling to understand. I know they are big into embedded databases and that they work with Linux. They are a perfect example of the concept I am describing. From a technical and fundamental analysis standpoint, they looked excellent to me 3 weeks ago when I picked them up at $11.50/share. They are currently at about $15. As silly as it sounds, I am not comfortable with what they do and need help from someone to understand it more thoroughly. Evaluation of their technologies and potential would be extremely useful, for example, in deciding to sell soon at $16 1/2 with a 43% profit or holding for much longer term. (Could the stock return to its 1999 highs, in the $37 range? Only an understanding of their products, services, vision, and management will decide that!)*

*I am 35 years old and have been buying stocks for 20 years, 10 of those as a professional. I am not looking for a quick hit or get rich quick scheme, but rather, an informal partnership with someone willing to invest a little time and effort, ongoing, with the goal of identifying some promising stocks companies or technologies. I am really just wanting to find out if you, (or perhaps someone you could refer) is interested in just such a cooperative effort. Please e-mail me back if you are and we can discuss how we might move forward. Thanks. Sincerely,*

*Jeff G.*

*Investment Professional"*

You will be pleased to know that I graciously replied to Jeff's e-mail and politely declined his opportunity. I truthfully cited my busy and full schedule as an MCSE consultant, not allowing me the time to assist him in selecting technology stocks.

# Transition Plans

Any major life change requires a plan if you want to do it right. Becoming an MCSE consultant is a significant lifestyle change for many, so a transition plan is in order. This might include transitioning in stages. First, you might be a part-time MCSE consultant with other revenue-generating work in your life (such as that night job discussed earlier in the chapter). As your MCSE consulting practice becomes larger than your other activities, you can rightfully transition into becoming a full-time MCSE consultant. Here are a couple of ways to begin that transition. More importantly, these examples place you in a useful environment, working as a technology consultant for a client.

## Temp agencies

If I think back far enough, I benefited from the temporary agency path on the way up. By working as a technology temporary employee, I was exposed to a wide range of client sites, including a summer job at Microsoft testing Microsoft Excel 3.0 macros. (Now that was a long time ago!)

**Note**    Not only are temporary agencies a great place to gain legitimate consulting experience, but you can also often acquire your own clients this way. The temporary agency contract with the client typically won't let you take the client for your own billings. However, such contracts are often silent with respect to third-party referrals you receive. In other words, you work as a temp at a company. You demonstrate superior skills, and an employee at this company gives your name to his or her spouse who works for another company. The spouse calls you and retains your services as an MCSE consultant.

## Contract houses

The story is much the same working for contract houses. Here you are likely to be placed on longer term and more analytically demanding assignments than the temporary agency offered you. But you'll still gain important technology consulting experience and the possibility of referrals that are outside the scope of the contract house employment and client services agreement.

## Online employment agencies

Employment agencies have changed with the times and are now both bricks and clicks. The "clicks" are online employment agencies such as Monster.com (seen in Figure 4-1). By registering with a site such as Monster.com, you can easily advertise your skills to a much larger audience than your local hometown audience. This is an especially good way to jump start your MCSE consulting practice if you are willing to travel to distant lands to ply your craft.

**Figure 4-1:** Consider registering with online employment services to develop your MCSE consulting practice.

## Working for another consulting firm initially

If you look at other professions, you'll see the following trend. An attorney who starts a law firm first worked for another law firm and gained experience. This person then broke away and started his or her own practice. I've seen the same thing in certified public accounting and medicine. To start your own MCSE consulting practice, it often makes sense first to work in the industry as an MCSE consultant with an established consulting firm.

### Experience

One the key reasons to work for another consulting firm before making the break is to gain experience. It's one thing to read a book on MCSE consulting, but an entirely different thing to actually do it. By working for another consulting firm as an MCSE, you essentially learn on their payroll.

### Instant client base

Working for another consulting firm typically provides you with the instant client base you can take with you when you leave. This is seen in the legal and accounting fields all the time. Clients have a relationship with you and follow you when you make your move.

### Noncompete agreements

Typically when you are employed by a consulting firm, you'll sign a noncompete agreement on your date of hire. This will spell out how the firm must be compensated if you take existing clients to start your own consulting practice.

Read the terms and conditions of any noncompete agreement carefully. These are often written to protect the firm from being unduly raided. The agreement may spell out restrictive terms such as a distance radius (not within 50 miles), a duration (not within six months) or a financial penalty (all future client billings for one year paid to previous employer) under which you will have to operate when you leave the firm. You should consult an attorney on these agreements. The courts have a track record for frowning upon agreements that stifle competition and business growth.

# Firing Clients

Part of growing your business is about making the right engagement decisions along the way. A bad engagement, and you'll undoubtedly have a few of those, brings down your profit level, energy level, and kills your good attitude.

## Identifying bad fits

You can typically identify a bad fit without many words of wisdom from me. Things aren't going well when you're at the client site. The situation is constantly tense. Worse yet, the client isn't paying your invoice in a timely manner. And you certainly aren't going to get referrals from this client.

A point I'll make in Chapter 10 is that your goal is to have each of your clients be referenceable and referable. Clients that are neither are bad fits and should be fired.

## Terminating a relationship

Each situation is different, but often the easiest way to terminate the relationship is to explain to the client that you're taking the practice in a "new direction" and you'll be happy to help them line up another consultant. You will often need to dedicate a few hours, usually not billable, to the old client in helping transition the account to this new consultant. Why isn't this work, in reality, billable? A client that's been fired isn't pleased about paying you for additional work.

Be sure to time the termination of your client so that you have minimal outstanding accounts receivable or monies owed from this entity. You don't want to terminate an account and be out some serious money.

# Good Client Selection

The best way to avoid having to fire a client, or worse being fired by a client, is to do a better job of up front selection. A few thoughtful moments during the business development process can save untold hours of grief during the engagement.

## Making the decision is always critical

No matter how experienced and successful you are as an MCSE consultant, you're never far from making a bad client selection decision. You may be susceptible to the friendly demeanor of a client or a moving tale of woe. The bottom line is that a bad client is a bad client. It is incumbent upon you to remain as objective as possible at all times when considering a consulting engagement with a prospective client. This is a task that never goes away.

## Surviving early growth stages of business

As you build your MCSE consulting practice, it is especially important that you make the best client selection decisions possible. At this stage of your consulting practice, you literally can't afford a bad fit. If you were to land a big consulting gig where the client takes an excessive amount of your time and doesn't pay your bills, it could cause your young practice to falter and fail.

## Listening to your clients

Something that certainly took me a while to understand was the importance of hearing what your client is saying. If you make it a habit to do less talking and more listening when selecting clients, you'll find that many clients will either qualify or disqualify themselves from contention. Here is what I mean. Most clients are just interested in the report shown on the left-side of Figure 4-2. That is the output from all of the technology the client has implemented. Better reporting is a common reason for improving an information system and engaging an MCSE consultant to help out.

Working to the left, it likely takes a database, such as Microsoft SQL Server, to generate the wanted reports. And for a database to run properly, you need a network with a network operating system such as Windows 2000 Server. Digging deeper, the client likely wants e-mail and Internet connectivity, shown in the upper-right of the chart. Of course, Internet connectivity means a firewall tool such as Internet Security and Acceleration (ISA) Server 2000 must be considered. You get the point. The client communicates a business need without much knowledge of the technology. You, the MCSE consultant hear the business need and translate it into a technology solution. But if the client can't articulate a bona fide business need, they may in effect be disqualifying themselves from your consideration.

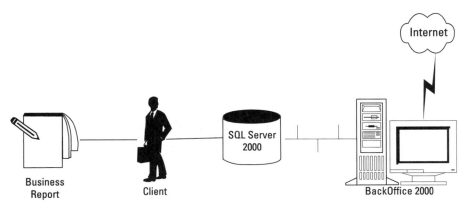

**Figure 4-2:** Viewing clients from a business focus

# Rule of Ten – Client Rejection Ratio

"In the long run, you should reject five out of ten clients."

My first MCSE consulting rule of ten came when I discovered I needed a guideline to help me stay focused on selecting good clients. If I operated under no such guide-line, client selection decisions tended to be emotional and political, if not made in occasional desperation. After looking over my business development working papers, I determined that I was rejecting about half the potential clients that asked for my services. A few explanations about this rule are in order:

✦ **The long run** — When you first open your doors for business as an MCSE con-sultant, it's probably not practical to say "no" to nearly anyone that wants to hire you. Sometimes you just have to take what you can get. Perhaps you'll reject only the most offensive prospects. To be honest, it took me years to get my practice to where I could comfortably turn away half the business.

✦ **Natural laws** — To some extent, the marketplace is already performing this rationing for you. If you count how many sales calls never go past discussing your rate or how many client meetings you've attended where you both (your-self and your client) discover that you provide a service different than the one required by the client, then you're probably close to a 50 percent client rejec-tion ratio without even knowing it.

✦ **Comfort zone** — If you have the confidence that leads will flow to you and being selective is critical to your success, you'll also have the confidence to say "no" when it doesn't feel right between you and a prospective client.

# Summary

This chapter was about how to initially build your business as an MCSE consultant. People I've observed who make it to this stage and beyond often comment that they didn't realize being an MCSE consultant would be such hard work and that so much selling and business development were involved. However, don't lose sight of the rewards of being an MCSE consultant. While it is difficult to build your business, the rewards are out there and will be discussed later.

✦　　✦　　✦

# Finding Opportunities

**S**o far in this book, you been planning, planning, planning. And while there is some planning discussion in this chapter, its focus is really on picking your area of consulting.

For the vast majority, making the right decisions and finding opportunities are a combination of timing, smart thinking, luck, and possession of a skill set that is in demand. For some, finding opportunities occurs by a process of elimination and by avoiding mistakes. However you find them, if the opportunities exist, the money is there for you.

## Selection of Consulting Service

The biggest decision you will make as an MCSE consultant is what type of consulting services you will offer and to whom you will offer them. No other decision will have a greater impact on your financial position. In reality, it's the same for nearly everyone in the working world. Choice of occupation has the largest impact on your financial net worth.

What happened to the old "do what you love and the money will follow" mantra? First, people that are doing what they love usually aren't in it for the money. Second, in many professions, money is both the inducement to work and the reward for unpleasantness. The higher you move in income tax brackets, the more work-related stress there typically is. Of course, this isn't always true, but it has been my observation that people who have high incomes have high stress levels. Those big dollars are earned, every single one of them.

**Note**

It is possible to love what you do and make a substantial amount of money along the way. I think MCSE consulting is potentially one of these rare professions. Most MCSE consultants that I know enjoy their jobs, as well as the financial rewards. It can be done.

# Areas of economic demand

The economic demand discussion occurs at five levels: general, specific, macro, micro and countercyclical. Remember that demand, as viewed by economists, concerns the wants and needs of rational purchasers.

## General

Perhaps your path to earning the MCSE designation is similar to that of many of my MCSE students. Many of my MCSE students were laid off from or otherwise exited declining industries such as timber logging, salmon fishing, and mineral mining. While these specific examples apply to the Pacific Northwest, perhaps you can think of similar examples in your area. If so, you've effectively exited a shrinking economic sector (manufacturing) for an expanding economic sector (technology). Welcome to the MCSE club.

So, if I were to advise a group of wide-eyed high school seniors as part of a graduation commencement address, I would tell them to avoid economic sectors that are in fundamental decline and pursue career opportunities in economic sectors that are expanding.

The point is that no one individual can swim against the current of economic decline. However, when you go with the flow and participate in an expanding economic sector, such as the MCSE community, you benefit from the economic boom and can secure against future decline.

## Specific

So you've made the rational economic decision to become an MCSE consultant. You now need to hone in on areas of demand that will potentially provide you the greatest return for the same or lesser amount of work compared to your competitors. In economics, this is called being efficient. For MCSE consultants, there are numerous opportunities on which to capitalize. Anything and everything having to do with Windows 2000 Active Directory is being rewarded right now (early twenty-first century) in the MCSE consulting field. A close second is the implementation of Group Policy.

**Cross-Reference**

In fact, I spend the better part of Part IV detailing specific MCSE consulting opportunities by Microsoft product lines. For example, in Chapter 20, I go to great lengths to promote Microsoft Exchange Server and e-mail consulting as a lucrative MCSE consulting field. In Chapter 22, I offer tips on how MCSEs can use Visual Studio to develop solutions for clients.

Demand for specific MCSE skills is often a function of how the Microsoft software is being used. For example, just about every business uses e-mail, and among e-mail users, Microsoft Exchange has established a dominant position. This translates into tremendous demand for Microsoft Exchange skills. However, I'd temper your enthusiasm with a small dose of reality. Many people know of the demand for Microsoft

Exchange skills, so there is potentially a greater supply of service providers with whom you will have to compete (however, demand still outweighs supply and will for the foreseeable future).

## Macro

Each and every day you've likely seen the macro economy at work right in front of your eyes. You've seen newly monied technology professionals, many with MCSEs, driving late-model foreign cars. That's a picture that has been painted as the MCSE lifestyle in the late 1990s. A large part of why this pleasant existence has been allowed to go on for so long has to do with the macro economic factors that support it. You may not think much about it, but the new money MCSEs in America have found that their standard of living has benefited greatly from such things as Federal Reserve Board economic policies, which have successfully created a growing economy with low inflation and low interest rates. These policies have had as much to do with MCSE money flows as the demand for Windows 2000 has. How is that the case? Because the favorable business environment that I just described has not only allowed many MCSEs to purchase a nice home with a reasonable monthly payment, but has also resulted in healthy technology budgets in companies. Those technology budgets are what pay MCSE consultants.

How does the Federal Reserve Board Chairperson affect your next lucrative MCSE consulting engagement? First, if he or she and the Federal Reserve Board raise the general level of interest rates, the cost of funds to businesses go up. Perhaps the business you call a client will notice it on the next draw of their commercial line of credit. That draw is used to satisfy your MCSE consulting invoice. While a quarter point increase in interest rates isn't the end of the world, such market maneuvers serve as a signal to business owners that tightening credit conditions are here, and businesses should scale back on their borrowings, capital expenditures (such as massive technology outlays), and luxuries. MCSE consultants are considered a luxury by many business owners. You could be the first to go when the macro economic conditions dictate. In Figure 5-1, I show the Web site for the Federal Reserve, where you can go for more information on U.S. macro economic trends and facts.

The Federal Reserve Board can also affect your livelihood as an MCSE consultant by passively allowing inflation growth. Inflation is the enemy of the stock markets. The threat and actual occurrence of inflation in the economy can send the stock markets into a downward spiral. If you have a portfolio of dot-com clients, the inability to attract necessary investment capital via the stock markets is a death sentence (as was seen in the general stock market correction of April-June 2000). Not only did many dot-coms close down, but also many healthy dot-coms had staff layoffs and a declining demand for outside services. In that kind of economic climate, MCSE consultants again become an unaffordable luxury. And keep in mind, those laid off dot-com staff members may become MCSE consultants too, potentially increasing the supply of similar service providers.

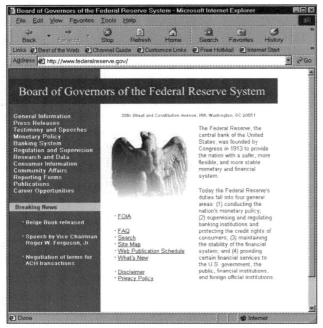

**Figure 5-1:** The U.S. Federal Reserve Web site at www.federalreserve.gov

Viewing the economy from a macro perspective is akin to looking at a challenging child. That is, when he or she is bad, he or she is very, very bad. When he or she is good, he or she is charming. This metaphor brings us back to the economy that most MCSEs know. Since before the MCSE title was created, the United States has enjoyed an amazing economic run. Low interest rates, low inflation, and low unemployment through the 1990s has created unprecedented wealth for both MCSEs and nonMCSEs alike.

The macro economic picture can be good and bad, and though there is not a lot you can do about it, a heightened awareness of events that affect your livelihood as an MCSE consultant makes you a better business person nonetheless.

The history of small business is filled with success stories about those intrepid entrepreneurs who, through time and circumstance, started businesses during economic down times. Once economic times improved, these people saw many others join their ranks, providing similar services. However, history shows that, in general, those who started their small business in down times have survived and outperformed those who started a business during the good times. It's much easier to start a business during good times, and many of those who do won't survive their first downturn. People who start businesses when economic conditions are tight really learn things such as how to control cost and how to get by with less. These lessons transfer to MCSE consultants directly and should serve as words of encouragement for you not to let an economic downturn deter you from your goal of becoming an MCSE consultant.

## Micro

Just as there are local politics, there are local economies. So while hypothetically the national economy might be in the doldrums, business locally might never have been better for you as an MCSE consultant. How can this be after the sobering macro economic discussion above? Micro economic influences (like a massive oil field's being discovered just up the road from you and spurring development activity surrounding it) shouldn't be underestimated. There's nothing like being an MCSE in a boomtown. It's both fun and rewarding.

Micro economic effects can also hamper your ability to make money as an MCSE consultant. For example, during the late 1990s, the general economic boom in the United States wasn't evenly distributed. While many regions did well, some did not. Cities that experienced plant closings during that time had people wondering aloud, "What boom?"

As you may know, economics is a dismal science. True to that reputation, it is important to keep in mind that being in business for yourself as an MCSE consultant brings no financial guarantee. For while I'm a big proponent of your becoming an MCSE consultant and earning a large income, I want to balance that idealistic view with the stark realities of being in business for yourself. Once you're a successful MCSE consultant, having avoided the numerous pitfalls that await you, you will truly take pride in both your professional and financial accomplishments.

## Countercyclical

This is the old zigzag routine. When everyone else is zigging one direction, you zag the other. This is especially prudent advice for the MCSE consultant during bad economic times. During a downturn, many MCSE consultants provide services to their tried-and-true client base. These MCSE consultants likely experience a downturn in business as well. However, by being an MCSE consultant who ascribes to a countercyclical economic strategy, decide to provide your services to entities that do well in bad times, including the following:

- ✦ **Bankruptcy courts**—More bankruptcies mean more activity at the courthouse.

- ✦ **Pawnshops**—These active places are where the financially challenged hock prized possessions.

- ✦ **Moving companies**—Rather than fight, many stricken with bad economic times flee to better business environments.

- ✦ **Educational institutions**—During economic downturns, many people use student loans and return to school to get retrained. These schools need MCSE consultants to implement new technologies such as MCSE labs. These schools often need adjunct technology instructors as well, so it's common for an MCSE consultant to become an MCSE trainer when working for an educational institution.

## Areas to avoid

MCSE consultants can be successful, in many cases, just by avoiding mistakes. In the case of technology, that would include avoiding technology solutions that have lost the hearts and minds of the IT community. The list is long and includes IBM's OS/2 operating system, certain releases of Novell NetWare, the really old C/PM operating system (now I'm really dating myself), and so on.

# Types of Work

Another factor that will affect the opportunities you are presented with is the type of work that you are seeking. In the world of MCSE consulting, this amounts to looking for project-related work, ongoing maintenance work, or both.

## Project work

Many MCSE consultants view consulting from a project orientation. That is because consulting is traditionally pitched as an engagement to engagement endeavor. This is a wonderful type of work with endless variety; the ability to see a beginning, middle, and end to your tasks; and enough mobility to prevent you for getting roped into internal politics at the client site.

It is project work that attracted me to MCSE consulting because, by moving from job site to job site, I see more in a year than many in-house network administrators see in several years. The variety breeds exposure to a wealth of technology problems and solutions.

What are the drawbacks to project work? First, it can result in erratic cash flow. Months with much project activity are very lucrative. Months in between projects are lean, sometimes forcing you to dip into retained earnings or savings. Second, the constant shifting of assignments doesn't sit well with all personality types. Some prefer a long-term relationship to project work.

## Ongoing maintenance work

There's nothing like the comfort of having a book of clients with whom you have long-term relationships of providing technology support services. You develop site-specific expertise that helps you retain the account (versus a new consultant who would have to relearn the computer system). Much of the work, at least in terms of managing the client, becomes routine. In consulting, a routine process is often a profitable process.

## Both

Your MCSE consulting practice will probably have both project and ongoing maintenance work. I encourage this as I do it by design myself. I enjoy the variety of projects, but I like the familiarity of my steady book of clients. More importantly, the dips in project work tend to be offset by my ongoing maintenance work. That's called diversification, which is something you should consider as an MCSE consultant.

# Generalization versus Specialization

As an MCSE consultant, you will need to confront just who you are at a very core level. Are you an advisor who works best as a generalist? Or are you a specialist who works best with the nuts and bolts of the technology? Choosing between being a generalist or a specialist will have a tremendous impact on the type of work you do, the way that you run your MCSE consultant business, and how much money you make.

### Guest Sermon — Go Get It for Yourself

I asked my fellow MCSE consultant Ron Hardesty to write about his life as a technology professional. Ron brings many years of experience to back up the words in his guest column, and his work experience is supplemented by his role as Marketing Director for the BackOffice Professional Association and his work at Microsoft in Redmond, Washington, as a contractor for a large consulting house. Here's Ron:

*When Harry asked me to write this column for his book, I wondered what I could add that Harry couldn't write about. I did start doing computer work in 1970, which seems like a long time ago (I don't think that Harry was even born then). The hardware, software, words, and acronyms we work with have certainly changed during that time. Even the way we find our next position, project, engagement, job, client, or employer to work has changed. But I don't know that the basic task has changed all that much. I would like to go over a few ideas that I believe are integral to a consultant's work life.*

*First, I believe that being a member of a professional organization is a critical. Being an active member is a must. I am a board member of the BackOffice Professionals Association (BOPA). Being a member of an organization like this allows you to get information before the general public gets it, and sometimes, allows you access to inside information that is possibly never made public. This helps sets you apart from other consultants. Another subtle benefit of being an active member is the networking that happens. You come to know people that have a need of your skills, they already know you, and the interview process is a nonissue. In some cases, you will have spent no time marketing yourself.*

*Continued*

*Continued*

*Second, certification is critical. Certification in your area of expertise is a must. I have a Certified Data Professional (CDP) certification given by the Institute for Certification of Computer Professionals. This was gained during the years that I worked primarily on mainframes and minicomputers. Upon making the transition to PCs, I immediately started studying to get a Microsoft Certified Professional (MCP) certification from Microsoft. At that time, it required a Microsoft Operating System and an elective. I passed Microsoft NT 4.0 Server and, as my elective, Microsoft SQL 6.5.*

*Being a member of a professional organization and having certification in the tools I use have made my consulting life considerably easier.*

*However, while professional organizations and certifications certainly make life as a consultant easier and help consulting assignments land in your lap from time to time, you still have to get up and do things for yourself. As a consultant you have to market yourself. A number of methods can make this task easier. If you're connected to the Web; your own Web site, the Web sites of companies you would like to consult to, online newspapers, and online job Web sites are all good avenues for marketing yourself. If you're not connected to the Web, consulting organizations, newspapers, and networking with like-minded technicians and potential employers are ways to make yourself known. In all that I have mentioned, you have to do it yourself. You have to be diligent even when applying to a consulting organization whose job it is to find you work. Your resume can easily get lost on someone's desk.*

*Also, adapt your resume to the format needed. As a consultant you can work a lot of different assignments. I could have a ten-page resume, but then no one would ever take the time to read it. Create your resume on a word processor so that it's in pieces. Then combine the pieces that are necessary to present yourself in the best possible light for the assignment. Leave out the superfluous information. In my immediate area (Seattle), most businesses, when you display your activism in a professional organization and you hold certification, want only a one-page recap of experience.*

*When you lay the groundwork, finding your next assignment can be relatively easy. I have personally experienced finding the right and perfect assignment in 24 hours.*

*I wish you much success in your future as a consultant.*

## Generalization

Many people either don't have the skills or desire to master Microsoft technology solutions at a granular level. These people would prefer to act as business technology advisors, emphasizing their communication skills over hands-on skills. Generalists typically serve as project managers and contract out much of the specialized work. There are significant opportunities for these types as MCSE consultants—something that shouldn't be overlooked.

## Specialization

These are the surgeons of the MCSE community, specializing in one niche or another. As in the medical profession, both demand and financial rewards tend to follow specialists. On the downside, specializations, especially in technology, can dry up and disappear. That's a fear that generalists typically don't have to worry about.

**Note**    It has been my experience that many MCSE consultants start as generalists and migrate to a specialization after they gain more experience as consultants. The migration also occurs because of two other factors. First, you discover where your interests are over time, working with a variety of technologies as a generalist. Second, you develop the bona fide expertise needed by a specialist as you focus on one area. To call yourself a specialist, you need to *be* a specialist.

# Areas Not Being Served Well

Ask the neighborhood millionaire how they made it, and often you'll get a story about his or her ability to find areas that others weren't serving well. The story is the same for successful MCSE consultants, too. Open your eyes and look at technology areas that are being ignored by others. I employed this strategy a few years back when no one in the MCSE community would touch Microsoft Small Business Server (SBS). Sensing there might be a need for MCSE-level services in the small business community, I made SBS one of my niches. It was a great decision. Even though many more MCSEs now provide SBS consulting services, it has never hurt me to be an early player in the SBS game.

A few Microsoft technology areas that I think are being underserved currently and warrant your scrutiny include the following:

✦ **Advanced Microsoft Outlook customization** — Many people use Outlook, but only for its four major functions of e-mail, Calendar, Contacts, and Tasks. Fewer people use it for its note-taking capabilities. Few people know and many could benefit from some of the advanced features of Outlook that require customization such as adding fields to Contacts. I'm convinced an MCSE consultant could sit down, teach himself or herself everything there is to know about Outlook, and be a world-class Outlook guru with only a reasonable amount of energy expended.

✦ **Digital Dashboard** — In the old days, enterprise-level executives spent enormous sums on a program known as an Executive Information System (EIS). An EIS provides a simplified view of critical business factors for the executive to scan on the screen. This information is typically presented in a traffic light metaphor of red, yellow, and green lights. For example, an accounting ratio that is presented as a red light needs the executive's attention.

EISs were a popular wave to ride in the late 1980s and early 1990s. In fact, not many people know that in 1992 Microsoft released a special product called the Microsoft EIS Kit that installed on top of Microsoft Excel 4.0. Today's EIS-type offering from Microsoft is Digital Dashboard 2.0. This is an application that allows the MCSE consultant to create an executive-level view of business activity ranging from e-mail and Web pages to business applications such as accounting and finance. I've yet to meet a Digital Dashboard specialist, which indicates to me this field is wide open. Microsoft's Web site for Digital Dashboard is shown in Figure 5-2.

✦ **Microsoft Small Business Server** — Given the several million businesses in the United States that fit the SBS profile, there still exists, and will continue to exist for some time, opportunities for MCSE consultants. If you find your personality type is more oriented towards a small business rather than a large enterprise, a SBS focus is for you.

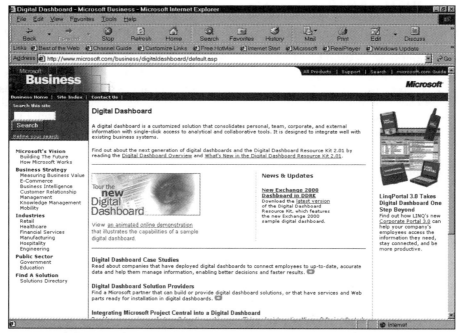

**Figure 5-2:** Digital Dashboard information is located at www.microsoft.com/digitaldashboard.

# Geographic Considerations

When looking for opportunities, geography can play a big role. It really comes down to size. Do you want to target a rural area? Or would you prefer being an MCSE in the big city? Here the choice is really yours as I've seen MCSE consultants who are successful at both. Working as an MCSE consultant in the big city is a well-documented path to success. But don't overlook rural or overseas opportunities. Two cases in point. First, in Alaska, I'm aware of a person who for a period of time was the only MCSE on the Kenai Peninsula, a rural area several hours from Anchorage (the largest city in Alaska). This individual served local governments, hospitals, and businesses. Being the only MCSE in this location for a while was very profitable, and even with a few more around, it's still profitable. Second, recognizing that over half of Microsoft's revenues now come from overseas should tell you something about where future opportunities lie. Perhaps you'd like to live the life of an American expatriate with a big house and servants in a banana republic. Some days of the week this sounds great to me.

# Summary

This chapter was a pragmatic and critical look at how you, the MCSE consultant, will fill your client list, meaning you must find opportunities to provide your services. This chapter demonstrated several ways to find the opportunities that best meet your needs.

✦　　✦　　✦

# Promotion, Marketing, Advertising

◆  ◆  ◆  ◆

**In This Chapter**

Marketing MCSE
services continuously

Considering
promotional
opportunities

Finding low cost
and free marketing
opportunities

Exploring advertising
approaches

◆  ◆  ◆  ◆

The reality of being an MCSE consultant is that you have to go out and find work. Before you build up your book of business and your referrals, you'll need to engage in the fine art of self-promotion. No matter who you are, you'll never fully get away from selling yourself as an MCSE consultant.

## Get the Word Out

You have to initially get the word out that you're an MCSE consultant open for business. Simply being an MCSE consultant doesn't generate business. You have to announce the availability of your services in some fashion.

Once established, it's in your best interest to keep your name visible so you can at least retain, if not gain, market share. Granted you'll have other, perhaps better ways of generating business (such as referrals), but as a self-employed MCSE consultant you should always be spreading the word about yourself and your services.

## Promote Yourself

There are several ways to promote yourself. In this section, I emphasize low cost ways to do just that. Promoting yourself with a large marketing budget isn't hard, as you can hire an advertising agency to get you market presence. Big budget advertising will be covered later in this chapter. The real trick is to promote yourself in a dignified way with few or no budgeted dollars. That's the situation you, as a new MCSE consultant, are more likely to find yourself in.

## Send press releases

One of the oldest tricks in the book is to use the sample template in Microsoft Word, write your own press release, and then e-mail, fax, or snail mail it to every paper in your area. This should include the dailies, weeklies, and monthlies. It has been my experience that the large daily papers might not print the press release or will print just a sentence in their business announcements column. These papers get many press releases and are selective.

You might have better luck with the smaller weekly business newspapers. These papers are often short on local content and may print your press release word for word. I've had good luck generating publicity with the regional weekly business papers over the years.

 **Tip**    Don't forget to include your photo with your press release. Many papers will print your photo along with your text-based announcement.

You might issue a press release when any of the following events occur:

✦ Opening for business

✦ Leasing new office space

✦ Hiring new employees

✦ Landing a new consulting contract

✦ Performing volunteer efforts (such as helping a school put in a network)

✦ Securing appointment to a board (such as a not-for-profit board or service organization board such as Rotary)

✦ Winning an award (Perhaps you've won an award for service. I was once named the service provider of the year for a not-for-profit organization. This generated both a press release and a photo opportunity.)

## Write an article

Consider writing an article. The weekly business papers seem to be more receptive than the daily papers for this type of activity. The monthly business magazines will also accept your submission. Writing an article allows you to enjoy the good publicity of having your name and maybe a photo in print along with your words of wisdom. Perhaps you want to write an article about how Windows 2000 is being implemented. Articles tend to lend an air of authority, so it's a great way to build up business.

You can use the articles again and again. Attach your articles to the back of your MCSE consulting proposals. Those articles can be confidence builders in the bidding process.

## Write a column

If you find you've got a knack for writing and your articles are thoughtfully received by the readership, consider leveraging your writing commitment into a regular column. This is a great way to establish yourself as an authority. More importantly, you enjoy the benefit of consistent publicity, appearing in print on a regular basis. This builds both recognition and a following.

## Write a book

Having a book on a technical topic, such as a Microsoft BackOffice component, will allow you to ascend to guru level status. Needless to say, writing a book is a great way to generate favorable publicity if you can justify the untold hours of writing (which likely take away from your hours of billing).

> **Note**  If you are interested in writing a book, one of the best ways to learn more about this avenue is to visit publishers' booths at technology trade shows. For example, *Microsoft Certified Professional Magazine*'s semiannual TechMentor trade show (www.techmentor.com) typically has several publishers present on the show floor. These booths are staffed with acquisitions editors who are on the constant hunt for the next Truman Capote. Perhaps that's you.

If you look at how the big-league consultants in both technology and business make it, you'll likely find that at some point these people have written a book. Moreover, writing a book is a time-tested promotional stunt. James Campy, for example, built his consulting practice around his books on downsizing and reengineering in the early 1990s. The other nice thing about a writing a book is that it also helps if you want to be an MCSE consultant in a larger firm. At interview time, whipping out your latest book can be an effective way to impress your future supervisors. Firms such as Big Five accounting firms (with their respective technology practices) appreciate this approach.

## Find speaking opportunities

Trade groups, social organizations, and the like are always looking for speakers for their monthly lunch meetings. In the past, I've found myself on the Rotary luncheon speaking circuit, telling the story about BackOffice.

### Seminars

A seminar is a tried-and-true way for an MCSE consultant to engage in a little educational marketing. In many cases, it's paid marketing where the attendees will pay for the privilege of your expertise. The key point with a seminar is that you need to appreciate from where the audience is coming. If it's a sales seminar about a new service or product, you probably can't charge the audience a fee to attend. If it's a technical seminar where you offer wisdom and insight, you can typically charge a fee, say $99 for a half day or $149 for a day (lunch included). You need to decide if you are going to put on a sales seminar, an educational seminar, or a combination of the two. If you are trying to close business that day (the closer approach), you are clearly delivering a sales seminar. If you are doing the old soft sale where you deliver more meaningful content, then you are taking the educational approach. It's up to you to decide what fits best for your personality style and the market you are trying to reach.

**Note** A classic though not always accurate view of a consultant is that of someone who works the speaking circuit. Still, many consultants are indeed in the business of giving seminars. These are the shuttle flyers who hop from one city to the next, day after day, to deliver an airport hotel seminar about guerilla marketing, success strategies, and so on, and I don't want to discourage you from pursuing this career path as a seminar specialist. Who knows? Maybe you'll fly around and deliver hit seminars on "Networking for Nontechnical People" as an MCSE consultant.

### Established seminars

Early on in the life of Small Business Server while I was developing my reputation as a niche specialist in this area, I gave a monthly educational seminar at Microsoft's Pacific West (PacWest) sales office in Bellevue, Washington. This was part of the monthly Solution Providers program whereby you could deliver a half-day seminar using Microsoft's lecture hall. The price was right as you only had to reimburse Microsoft for coffee and parking expenses. My topic, Networking Basics, typically brought in 30 to 60 people each month. From that crowd, I typically landed one engagement.

**Tip** Don't forget to consider joining the Microsoft Certified Solution Provider program as an MCSE consultant to help build your business and interact with other technology professionals in your area. More information on the Microsoft Certified Solutions Provider program can be obtained by calling Microsoft at (425) 882-8080 and asking for Microsoft Sales.

Today that program has been slightly revamped to include different types of seminars, including those produced by partners (that's you, the MCSE consultant), Direct Access, and TechNet. As an example, the Programs and Events home page for Microsoft's Pacific Northwest sales office is displayed in Figure 6-1. Here you can find out information on seminars or can list seminars you intend to give as part of your MCSE consulting promotion program.

If you're going to provide a seminar through Microsoft's sales office, be sure you are leveraging up. For example, if you specialize in SQL Server for not-for-profit organizations, your seminar should be on that topic. In that way, the people that attend will be interested in exactly what you have to say and do. Be careful, though; if you make your seminar topic too specific, you might scare away people who should attend but have disqualified themselves.

**Note** Using an established seminar channel is a great way to ride the coattails of others. Not only does Microsoft provide seminar opportunities for its partners but so do Novell, Cisco, Oracle, and most other major technology players. You should seriously consider taking advantage of these avenues.

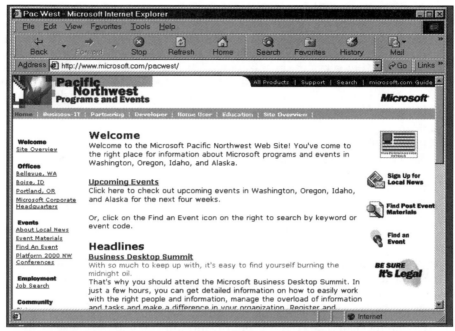

**Figure 6-1:** Seminar opportunities via local Microsoft sales offices

You might consider the following organizations when you're seeking out an established seminar channel through which to deliver your presentation (but take note that these organizations are biased toward nontechnology avenues because I firmly believe the MCSE consultant should be targeting different audiences than solely the technology crowd, audiences such as business people):

✦ **Chamber of commerce** — This might be the best one. Speaking in a credible manner as an MCSE consultant before a group of active business people is a great opportunity. You may need to join the chamber of commerce, but the $300 or so per year might be money well spent.

✦ **Regional economic development authorities** — These are typically quasi-government authorities charged with expanding the business base in a particular region. These organizations facilitate introductions in the business community in the form of conferences and pursue economic initiatives, such as having certain areas (such as a business park) declared duty-free zones for goods that are manufactured for export. Some regional economic development authorities have the power to issue bonds and debentures for financing public works projects, such as building parking garages. The way that an MCSE consultant can work with a regional economic development authority is to provide seminars at business conferences.

✦ **Service organizations** — These include Rotary, Masons, and Moose. You'll note I've listed these in the order you should consider these groups, with Rotary being the best selection because it, in my opinion, is populated with middle-aged business managers who have more purchasing authority than those in other services organizations. The Masons and Moose organizations among others tend to be more fraternal and social and don't claim to emphasize business and commerce (although many business people do belong to fraternal service organizations).

✦ **Professional associations** — There are two types of professional associations. First, there are the paralegals, legal secretaries, and office managers who meet each month for a formal luncheon. These groups are also seeking speakers, so you're likely to have success here. Don't underestimate this avenue. Remember that office managers and the like are key influencers when it comes to retaining the services you provide as an MCSE consultant. The second type of professional association includes groups who are organized for legal purposes. This includes accountants in the CPA Society, lawyers in the Bar Association, medical professionals, and so on. These groups need seminar speakers too.

✦ **Trade associations** — Industry-based trade associations represent a great seminar delivery avenue. Again, monthly luncheons or annual conventions are both possibilities.

✦ **Cause-based not-for-profit organizations** — Perhaps you support a medical research cause. The not-for-profit organization behind the cause of your choice may have a need for a seminar or speech.

✦ **Social organizations** — You might even get roped into giving an MCSE consulting speech to a social organization such as the Junior League.

✦ **Arts organizations** — Perhaps giving a speech or seminar during the dinner hour is more your style. Many arts organizations hold awards dinners and seek out speakers. The motivating factor in speaking before an arts organization is that you will find yourself before the barons and titans of industry in their off hours away from the office.

✦ **Clubs** — You can even successfully give a technical seminar before a club. I once gave a technical speech on how to use the Internet before the Dutch Club of Seattle, and several Microsoft employees were in attendance along with many successful Dutch-American business people.

### Create your own

You can also create your own seminars from scratch. The great thing about the homegrown seminar series is you control virtually everything: dates, content, promotion, and so on. One create-your-own seminar I put on with modest success was a series of executive workshops for Microsoft technologies (in this case, it was Windows 95). My feeling was that demand existed for business executives seeking to gain information on new Microsoft technologies. More importantly, these decision makers would be locked in a boardroom with me for a half day, a captive audience with budget authority. These seminars may not be instant moneymakers, but often pay off in the long term with new clients.

## Ask the Guru — I'm a Salesman

Here's a reader e-mail from the *Microsoft Certified Professional Magazine* column from someone who has been invited to work in technology sales and who is going to stop his designation at the MCP level and set his sights on working remotely from a home in the mountains. This e-mail offers a fresh perspective that might fit for some MCSEs who discover that selling technology services and products is more their calling than consulting is. For these people, selling MCSE consulting opportunities may be a career opportunity to explore.

*Harry,*

*I've enjoyed your articles during my brief tenure as a MCP. I have passed NT 4.0 Server, Networking Essentials, and Citrix Administrator. I had originally planned MCSE, but I am now working in sales with a friend who "rescued" me from "old war horse" stable. At 50, I was dumped from corporate America, and with no comparable jobs in sight, decided to move to IT (I had always loved computers). My real goal is to work from the mountains of North Carolina—from that little cabin with the view—so I'm looking to move in MCSD direction. I've always liked creating comprehensive spreadsheets and databases. You mentioned SQL as a possibility. I am thinking Visual Basic also. Do you have any suggestions on this choice? (Part of me is looking at Linux programming as well.)*

*Good luck, amigo!*

*John H.*

*Greensboro, NC*

John

I wish you the best. Thanks for the refreshing e-mail that provides a new perspective on certification tracks and employment opportunities.

Cheers,

harryb

The create-your-own seminar approach has been used for years by financial planners and stockbrokers, proving they do work. The key is to target your audience.

**Note**     Some technology consultants become so enamored with giving speeches that they effectively quit practicing as day-to-day consultants. These people are registered with speaker's bureaus, have agents, and so on. It's one way to have your time in the spotlight, but it's really not part of being an MCSE consultant.

## Conferences

Another promotional avenue, used more by established MCSE consultants than those new to the profession, is speaking at conferences. Not only do you have your time in front of an audience, but also you get your name and typically a short biography printed in the conference brochure. There are three types of conferences:

✦ **Local** — Your efforts may be best directed to local conferences if that is where your clients are (in your local community). Since I tend to focus on small and medium-sized firms for my MCSE consulting activities, local conferences make the most sense. In the Pacific Northwest, there is a local conference that travels from city to city called ITEC. Perhaps your community has a similar local technology conference.

✦ **Regional** — These conferences tend to be larger in scope and draw people from surrounding states. The caliber of attendees may be higher as well as the quality of the selected speakers. If your MCSE consulting business is regional in nature, speaking at a regional conference is a good use of time.

✦ **National** — Clearly this is where the heavyweights play. The type of MCSE consultant that can benefit from national exposure is someone working at the enterprise level. At these conferences, matching the clients' needs (enterprise, several locations) with an MCSE consultant who specializes in that market is the real promotional work.

**Note**    I can attest that those MCSE consultants focused on smaller companies should avoid putting a lot of effort into national conferences. To be blunt, your small clients won't be there (they'll be at the regional conferences).

# Free and Low-Fee Marketing Opportunities

You are probably surrounded by marketing opportunities each day, but you don't see them. Simply circulating at events is a tremendous marketing avenue. Here are some thoughts on that.

## Rule of Ten: Attend ten events per quarter

Make it your objective to attend ten events per quarter. That's almost one event per week, so be advised that you'll be busy. Just the act of circulating in public and meeting people is a legitimate form of marketing. Here are some suggestions:

✦ **Chamber of commerce events** — Yes, the chamber again. Instead of speaking at a chamber event (as discussed earlier in this chapter), attend a speech or seminar. Better yet, attend the monthly networking after-hours events where an emphasis is placed on meeting people.

✦ **Economic development authority events** — Likewise, you might start attending workshops hosted by the regional economic development authority. This is a chance to sit side by side with people who can potentially avail themselves of your MCSE consulting services.

✦ **Other business events**—By reading the business section of your local newspaper, you can learn about, register for, and attend other business events.

Initially, your goal will be to satisfy the ten events per quarter quota. Later, as you become savvier in your MCSE consulting operations, you'll likely learn how to pick the best events to attend.

It has been my experience that you should avoid hard-core technical events if your purpose is to market yourself to potential clients. Typically the type of client you're seeking with the authority and budget to hire you is attending a business event. Now if you want to attend a technical event to further your own knowledge, go for it.

## Rule of Ten: Give away ten business cards per quarter

Make it another MCSE consulting commandment to give away ten business cards per quarter. You can even place your business card on bulletin boards in coffee shops and grocery stores as you've no doubt seen service providers such as painters, carpenters, and handy people do.

With all the promotion and marketing ideas in this chapter, including activities such as giving away business cards, consider making it as easy as possible for people to reach you from their home, car phone, or even public telephone. I strongly encourage you to obtain a toll-free telephone number (if you have enough telephone traffic to justify it). Back when I was earning my MCSE designation, I worked for a contracting house/consulting firm that emphasized its telephone number. In fact, the name of the firm was the same as the telephone number (1-800-NETWORK). It was a brilliant move. All printed corporate communication had the easy-to-reach, toll-free telephone number for the firm. It resulted in a high volume of inbound telephone calls from prospective clients, which was appropriate for this particular firm. If you can justify the cost and use of a toll-free number, consider getting one.

## Case Study — Discover Ten Marketing Mistakes

In this chapter, I provide numerous ways for you to interact with the business community. For example, in the section on "Free and Low-Fee Marketing Opportunities" I suggest you attend local chamber of commerce events to meet perspective clients. For this case study, what I want you to do is this: When you interact with the business community, ask businesspeople what their top marketing mistakes have been. Mistakes made by others are lessons that you don't necessarily need to repeat. Compile this feedback into your own Rule of Ten list of the top ten marketing mistakes you wish to avoid.

## Rule of Ten: Collect ten business cards per quarter

Likewise, a marketing strategy for the MCSE consultant is to collect ten business cards per quarter. Not only does this greatly aid in the development of your book of contacts, but it is also a way to develop more meaningful business relationships. To collect business cards from people, you simply need to ask if you can have their business card. Further, the act of asking for a business card from someone usually results that person's asking for a business card from you, which may lead to a good opportunity.

# Advertising

If it makes sense for your business, by all means take a look at advertising. Advertising, which is considered an expensive marketing proposition, can be very effective. I've used two different types of advertising in my career: image and specific. With image advertising, I was trying to make an impression, not to sell a specific product or service. Image advertising contrasts with more specific advertising where the goal is to sell something (a product or service) at a specific price (and perhaps for a limited duration). This form of specific advertising for an MCSE consultant might be an offer like "First hour free between Thanksgiving and New Year's Day."

Advertising costs vary by medium, and many mediums exist, including print (magazine and newspaper), radio, TV, and even banner advertisements on Web pages of other companies (a local newspaper's Web site, for example). The effectiveness also varies depending on the type of ad, the market, and the product or service sold. Knowing how your ad will perform before it actually runs remains one of the great marketing mysteries. In Figure 6-2, I show a magazine (*Computer Source Magazine*) that not only has print display advertising available, but also has a Web site to post your ad a second time.

**Tip**

Another very interesting advertising possibility is the telephone directory. I have used this with the firms I've worked for as an MCSE consultant with varying degrees of success (mostly positive). In the case of the consulting firm that sold Great Plains business accounting software as well as consulting services (including those of yours truly), telephone directory advertising was successful. But when I worked for another firm that provided only services, the cost of the yellow pages ad (which exceeded $1,000 per month) was not considered to be the best use of the marketing budget. Results will vary, but consider this avenue a possibility.

One other point about telephone directory advertising — firms are typically listed alphabetically by business name. So if your firm is called "An MCSE Consulting Firm," you are listed ahead of a competing firm named "MCSE Consultants-R-Us." In telephone directory advertising, being listed earlier in the category listing is considered more desirable.

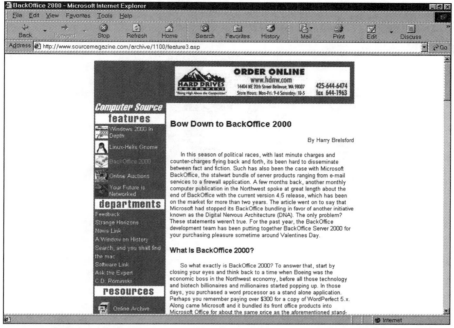

**Figure 6-2:** Magazines like *Computer Source Magazine* will work with you to develop tailored advertising campaigns.

# Public Relations Firms

Public relations firms, called PR firms in the business community, might very well have a role in your MCSE marketing plan. PR firms are retained for a number of reasons, including writing sales letters, writing and distributing press releases, and introducing you to media representatives, such as reporters and editors. My experience with PR firms has been positive. Typically, the senior professionals in these firms are well-established community icons of business and commerce. They are active in the community, sitting on boards of not-for-profit organizations and assisting in and contributing to political campaigns. If you retain the services of such a PR representative, you can typically expect them to call upon people in their extensive book of contacts to help you grow your MCSE consulting practice. In Figure 6-3, I show a PR firm on the East Coast of the United States that has a strong technology niche.

Note    Oftentimes, an advertising agency will have a PR subsidiary so they can provide full service to clients seeking marketing services.

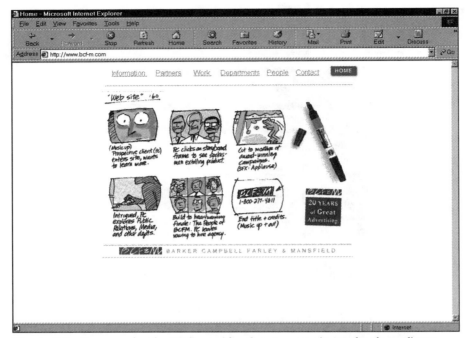

**Figure 6-3:** An example of a PR firm with a focus on serving technology clients

# Referrals

Don't overlook that fact that your existing client base can be part of your marketing program. A satisfied client who calls a business associate and recommends your services is one of your best and most cost-effective marketing avenues, as you don't have to write checks for display advertising and so on to obtain the new client. I've always likened my existing clients to being my virtual sales force.

 **Cross-Reference**    I discuss the importance and types of referrals in much greater detail in Chapter 8.

# The Web

Certainly one of the great marketing innovations in recent memory has been the Web. Whereas a few short years ago people were still discovering the Web for personal and business use, today it's primarily a line item on business marketing budgets. The Web has gone mainstream. Running the Microsoft FrontPage application to create and post your business Web page is fairly common and something you might consider doing as an MCSE. Microsoft FrontPage is include in the Professional version of Microsoft Office or can be purchased separately for under $150.00. Likewise, contracting with a Webmaster or Web programmer to develop your Web site using a variety advanced tools such as CGI scripts, the ColdFusion application, or the PERL programming language is another alternative to get your Web site up and looking professional.

But there is one alternative for creating and hosting your Web site that is relatively new. This is the business application service provider (ASP) approach behind Microsoft's bCentral (which stands for business central), which is shown in Figure 6-4 and can be reached on the Web at www.bcentral.com.

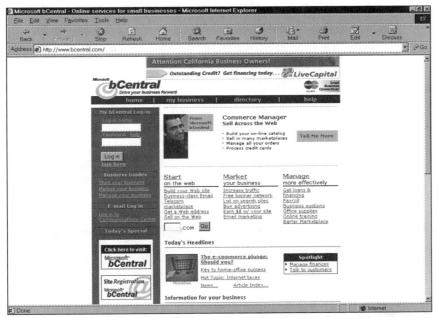

**Figure 6-4:** Microsoft's bCentral is a Web portal for building and hosting your Web site as part of your e-commerce strategy.

The idea behind bCentral is this — as a small businessperson (which is a common profile for MCSE consultants), you want a quick and cost-effective way to have a Web presence and Internet identity, and you will gladly pay Microsoft a monthly fee for this capability. The basics of bCentral, including terms and conditions, are discussed on the Overview page shown in Figure 6-5.

Next, assuming you plan to sign with bCentral as your Web portal, you obtain a Web address (which is a registered Internet domain name). As you know from being a practicing MCSE consultant, the Internet identity created by obtaining a Web address is very important. You need consider obtaining a Web address that is descriptive, relevant, and relatively easy to remember and spell. Most importantly, the Web address must be available for acquisition (that is, not already taken). Figure 6-6 shows information on obtaining a Web address.

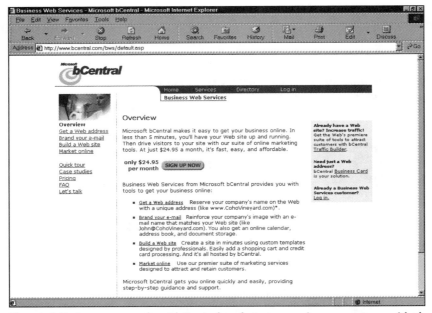

**Figure 6-5:** Learn more about bCentral and start your sign up process with the Overview page.

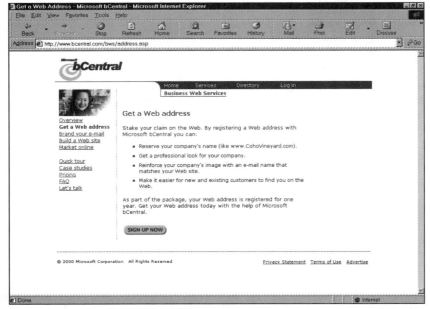

**Figure 6-6:** Obtaining a Web address via bCentral is the same as applying for a registered Internet domain name via other registration services.

The "Brand your e-mail" screen, shown in Figure 6-7, allows you to configure Post Office Protocol version 3 (POP3)–based Internet e-mail for your business. It is possible you will want to pursue this solution. The key point is to have e-mail tied to your Internet domain name for branding and identity purposes. You can clearly do this with bCentral and its POP3 approach, but it's been my experience that MCSE consultants tend to favor the Simple Mail Transfer Protocol (SMTP) capabilities of Microsoft Exchange Server.

**Cross-Reference**     Microsoft Exchange Server is discussed in Chapter 20.

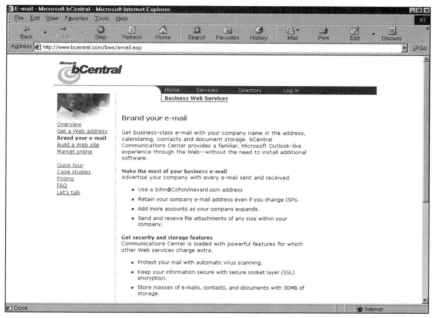

**Figure 6-7:** Microsoft bCentral offers an easy way to configure business e-mail.

The next step with bCentral is to start the process of building your Web site. In Figure 6-8, you can see the introductory discussion that raises several valid points about building a Web site with bCentral, such as not needing to purchase Web building applications like Microsoft FrontPage. Further, the Web site can have up to 200 pages or 40MB of storage space, an amazing amount of room.

The next step is one of my favorite parts of bCentral. In the past when I've worked with clients to introduce electronic commerce capabilities on their Web sites, the process was exceedingly complex. You had to program an actual payment mechanism on the Web page and then contract with and interact with third-party financial institutions that could accept and process credit card transactions quickly. That entire development process has become much easier with bCentral, as seen in Figure 6-9.

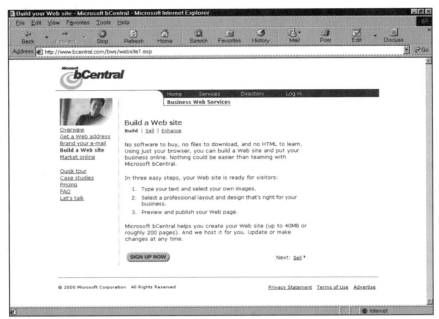

**Figure 6-8:** You can build a suitable business Web site directly interacting with bCentral.

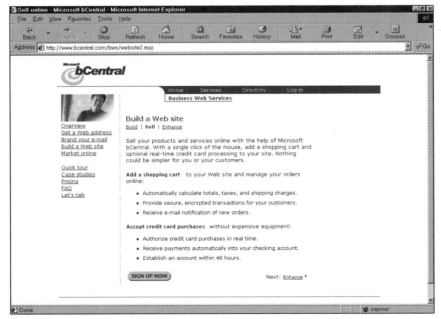

**Figure 6-9:** Microsoft bCentral's electronic commerce capabilities are very impressive and well worth the fees.

The next step on bCentral is the enhancement process to make your Web site more professional looking with the use of borders, backgrounds, frames, and animation. The Web site created by bCentral is sufficient for most small businesses, especially when you consider the low development costs. As you can see in Figure 6-10, examples of other Web sites created at bCentral are provided to help you think more creatively.

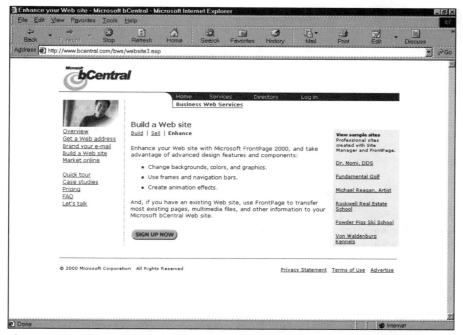

**Figure 6-10:** Microsoft bCentral's Web page enhancements allow you to create sophisticated and attractive Web pages.

Don't overlook the Market online page at bCentral for marketing tips. As you can see in Figure 6-11, the discussion is right on target about getting listed on Web search engines, using Web-based advertising, managing customer e-mail lists, and adding your business to the MSN Yellow Pages.

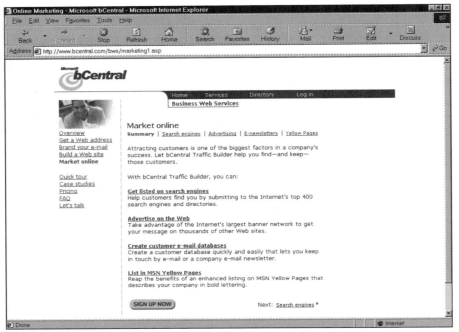

**Figure 6-11:** Microsoft bCentral's Market online page offers marketing tips that expand into more detailed discussion when you click the topical areas.

Banner Network is an online marketing and advertising agency that is partnered with Microsoft bCentral and can help to target your marketing. As you can see in Figure 6-12, by using the services provided by Banner Network, you can target thousands of prospective accounts that might have an interest in your services. However, to be honest, the consulting services provided by an MCSE consultant aren't necessarily sold to thousands of clients at a time, so closely scrutinize whether Banner Network provides a service you need.

After signing up and following the bCentral process just described to obtain an Internet domain name, to configure your Internet e-mail, and to create and promote a Web site, you're up and running as a Web-enabled small business. You should take the time to see if bCentral or other similar sites meet your need for Web-based promotion.

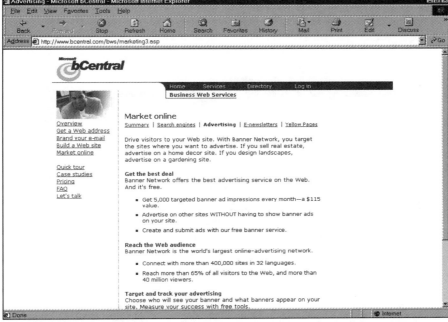

**Figure 6-12:** The services offered by Banner Network are likely a better fit for firms targeting large audiences.

# More Marketing Tips

I end this chapter with a variety of marketing tips for you to consider as an MCSE consultant. And though some of these tips are surprisingly simple, people often overlook them as being too obvious:

✦ **Search engines and online directories** — Many people use popular Web-based search engines and directories to find the products and services they need. Potential clients of your MCSE consulting services in your region may be searching for you online with keywords like MCSE or consulting. At a minimum you should register with the major search engines such as Yahoo!, GO.com, Google, Excite, and About (just to name a few). You should also verify that your MCSE consulting practice will appear when prospects search using the online directory supported by the telephone companies. In Figure 6-13, I show how such a search might occur on the Qwest directory page.

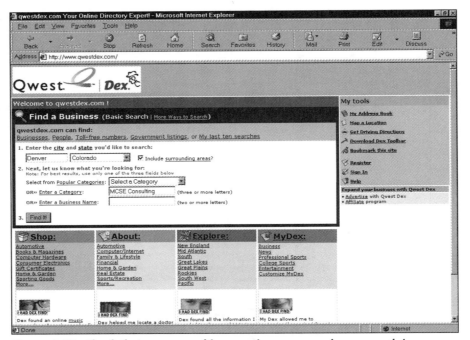

**Figure 6-13:** Check that your consulting practice appears when a search is conducted in online telephone company directories.

✦ **Document headers/footers**—A simple and effective trick is to place your MCSE consulting firm name and telephone number on either the header or footer of printed documents that leave your office. For example, if you write a proposal and send it to a client, make sure this key identification information is present on each page (name and telephone number in header or footer). That way, the client can call you by glancing at the page for your name and telephone number. More importantly, other staff members at the client site and friends of the client site who might be impressed by your proposal or other written matter will know how to reach you. Having my name and number in the footer of each page of my printed documents has generated calls for me.

✦ **E-mail signature**—Every piece of e-mail you send out is an opportunity to advertise and market yourself as an MCSE consultant. In the signature for your e-mail, provide basic contact information such as firm name, address, telephone number, Web page, and, of course, e-mail address. That way each of your e-mails is working for you. When e-mails are forwarded by your recipients, others see your e-mail signature. And don't forget to list your credentials, such as your MCSE designation, next to your name in your e-mail signature for an added touch of credibility.

✦ **Instant Messaging**—Consider being an active participant on an instant messaging system such as those offered by Microsoft's MSN or America Online's AOL. Instant messaging would allow a client to immediately ask you a question if you were online at the same time and accepting messaging. I discuss Microsoft's instant messaging in Chapter 20.

✦ **Voice mail**—One of my longtime career mentors who is very skilled at relationship marketing enlists his voice mail greeting in his marketing strategies. Each day in the early morning, he updates with a message giving the day's date and a general idea as to how promptly he can return calls. For example, the message may say, "Hello. It is July 18th, and you've reached Dick. I can't take your call right now, and I'll be in meetings until 3:00 p.m. I will attempt to return your call by the end of the day." I've found clients and others really appreciate this communication. It also sells more business because people have a good feeling about your ability to communicate and be responsive.

✦ **Guerrilla marketing**—Some true marketing stories in the professional services area involve strategies that won't be a perfect fit for everyone. For instance, a realtor in Dallas, Texas, is well known for attending Dallas Cowboys games and throwing a stack of business cards from the upper desks of the stadium when her team scores. The throw, accompanied by a loud cheer, is her own unique approach to marketing, and it has apparently proven effective for her. This type of creative marketing is known as guerrilla marketing (named after unconventional guerrilla warfare). You may take time to consider what creative marketing approaches will help to promote your MCSE consulting practice.

✦ **Vendor booths at trade shows and conferences**—Consider attending trade shows and conferences not as a speaker to market your business but as an attendee to learn more about a technology or industry. Further, you can use trade shows and conferences to engage in marketing intelligence. By visiting the booths of your competitors, you can learn what approaches they are using to serve customers and what rates they are charging. Such visits are an effective way to know who your competition is and what they are doing, and when I have visited vendor booths, I have left those booths knowing that I had to treat my MCSE consulting clients better or risk losing them to my competition.

# Summary

In this chapter, I focused on the important details of promoting, marketing, and advertising your MCSE consulting services. Promotion was presented through high-level approaches such as writing and speaking. Marketing encompassed more tactical approaches, such as attending business social events to both give away and receive business cards. Advertising addressed using all media forms available, using an advertising or public relations agency, and having an appropriate Web presence.

✦     ✦     ✦

# Scoping – Developing Winning MCSE Consulting Proposals

**S**ee if any or all of the following story meant to highlight technical writing skills applies to you. If you were the one in high school that took Honors English and wrote papers for others for hire, then bumped into Microsoft technologies and the MCSE certification program, and further decided you wanted to be a consultant, then this chapter is for you. This chapter will show you how to merge your writing skills and technology prowess to become a successful MCSE consultant.

Still, this chapter is for rest of you as well. If you don't feel that proposal writing is your strong suit, then this chapter can provide you with the elements you'll need to write a winning proposal. In short, over the next several pages, I will give advice that addresses what might be one of your weakest links as an MCSE consultant: writing proposals. Many technology professionals (including MCSEs) who easily know how to write great scripts via Windows Scripting Host (WSH) or stored procedures in SQL Server 2000 need a helping hand in writing winning technology proposals. And that is the purpose of this chapter.

# Writing a Technology Proposal

At some level, writing a technology proposal is as simple as taking a dictionary and just putting the words in order. While I share that thought with you tongue-in-cheek, perhaps that light-hearted view of proposal writing will help you exhale deeply and release some of your writer's anxieties.

Of course, writing a technology proposal is much more than just putting the words in order, which is a small part of the writing process. Many preparatory steps occur before you start striking the keyboard at all. This chapter walks through many of those steps, including boundary definition, scoping, and estimating.

 **Cross-Reference**   For an example of how to put the framework of an MCSE consulting proposal into practice, refer to Appendix C.

Before jumping into some of the details, I'll share a few observations about writing a technology proposal I have gleaned as a technology consultant:

✦ **Just do it** — You basically have to launch Microsoft Word 2000 and start with Document1 (an untitled blank page). Hopefully, if you're properly prepared, the writing is easy.

✦ **Just do it smarter** — You can visit Microsoft's document Template Gallery (`http://officeupdate.microsoft.com/TemplateGallery/`) for Office 2000 and download starter document templates to get started. Such templates help guide you, help fight off that writer's block you feel, and make you far more efficient than the old recreating-the-wheel approach that starts with blank Document1. In Figure 7-1, you can see numerous bid and proposal templates.

✦ **If you can't beat them, join them** — If you are soundly beaten time and time again at the proposal stage, a critical self-assessment may be necessary. If the factors contributing to your failures are not your skill set or the fees you are charging, then perhaps your written communication skills in the technology proposal need some help. In this case, don't hesitate to ask the lost client what they liked about the winning proposal.

✦ **Best of breed** — Similar to the preceding point, start and maintain a proposals file of competitors' proposals. You can then use these proposals as examples, selecting a format here, a well-worded paragraph there, and so on. Of course, I'm not suggesting that you break into you competitors' offices and photocopy their proposals, but rather that you ask for proposal copies from friendly competitors, mentors, and clients. This practice is used in many professional services environments, so you're not really breaking new ground here. But you are working smart.

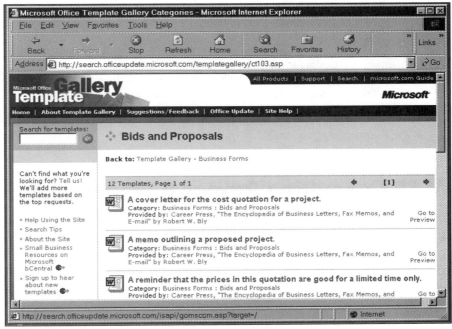

**Figure 7-1:** Microsoft Template Gallery is a rich collection of business forms.

✦ **Hire the best**—If you're the one that hired the Honors English student mentioned at the start of this chapter to write your school papers, then consider doing it again. If it worked in high school, it will work in the world of private sector consulting as an MCSE consultant, where you can hire gifted proposal writers to write your winning proposals, allowing you to focus on running an MCSE consulting practice. Many times, companies that provide typing services (typically located around college campuses) also provide excellent writing services.

✦ **Surf the net**—When in doubt, don't forget to surf the Internet. Later in this chapter, I'll give examples of the Internet-based Microsoft Direct Access Proposal Builder and another technology vendor site with proposal guidelines. You can also surf on your own using your favorite search engines such as GO.com, Google, Northern Light, Dogpile, and AltaVista to find technology proposals that have been advertently and inadvertently posted to the Web. Using Web-based search engines, you'll want to search on terms such as *proposal* and *technology*. The more narrow your query, the better so that you eliminate the millions of sites that contain the word *proposal*.

**Tip**

When searching the Web for technology proposal samples, it has been my experience that some of the best resources are government sites. Government entities are often subject to full disclosure laws such as the Freedom of Information Act in the United States. Government sites, therefore, publish massive quantities of information, including technology proposals from consulting firms seeking government work. I'm sure this occurs much to the chagrin of the submitting technology consulting firm, but the fact is these resources are widely available.

By thinking smart, you can be surprisingly successful and efficient in generating MCSE technology proposals.

## MCSE Consulting Proposal Framework

The MCSE consulting proposal framework is shown in Figure 7-2 and outlines the start-to-finish process for generating a winning MCSE consulting proposal.

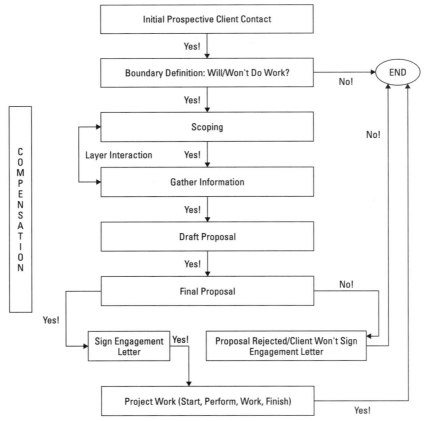

**Figure 7-2:** Consulting proposal framework

You start by knowing what you will and won't do. If you decide that the work fits within your purview of services offered, you'll proceed to scope (define) the project. Once you have an agreed upon scope with the client, you can gather information such as cost bids for hardware and software, for outside services, and even for your own services. That results in enough material to create the first draft of the technology proposal, which the smart MCSE consultant will endeavor to review with the potential client for feedback. An MCSE consultant acting in a communicative mode will proactively schedule an appointment with the potential client to see if he or she is on the right track. Use the feedback you receive to create the final draft of the technology proposal. This level of communication is critical consulting behavior that will allow you to separate yourself from your competition and to develop winning technology proposals every time.

For more information about communication as an MCSE consulting strategy, refer to Chapter 3.

## Getting paid to propose

Another component of the MCSE consulting proposal framework is to be compensated for your proposal generation efforts. Compensation for proposals is an ambiguous area encountered by consultants of all types. However, public accounting firms typically view such proposals as part of a bill-for-everything perspective (and that perspective is one of the key ways you make money as a consultant).

The idea behind that perspective is that an hour worked that produces bona fide value-added results for a client should be compensated. Putting together a technology proposal that is well scoped is often akin to writing a technology planning document (complete with needs analysis) that is of great value to the client. In the best-case scenario, such a technology proposal allows you to show how good you are at what you do, resulting in a winning proposal.

You may also use the compensation issue for proposal writing to assess whether or not a client is a good fit for you. Chances are a client that understands the value of a well-scoped proposal and is willing to pay for your proposal services is a good client to have.

In the worst-case scenario, unscrupulous clients may take your technology bids and go bid shopping. It has happened to me, and quite frankly, you can't do much about it beyond picking your prospective clients as carefully as you can. One legal step you can take is to insert language in the cover letter that accompanies your technology proposal that indicates that "this proposal is submitted in confidence." You might also have a footer on each page of the proposal that says "Confidential" and lists your name and date. That way the client will think twice about photocopying it for distribution. You should never submit an electronic version of your technology proposal to the client because an electronic version of your proposal would allow the client to copy and paste your work into a Request for Proposal (RFP) that could be bid shopped all around town.

**Tip**

In a bid-shopping scenario where your technology proposal is bid against by other technology consultants, it's entirely likely you would lose the job because the other bidders, using your proposal information, can minimize the time spent bidding on the project and may be able to undercut your price. The other bidders may also point to the tasks you have listed and claim, "We can do that for a lot less." Many clients are receptive to this message. Maybe it's in your best interest to let these clients go.

On a more positive note, you can institutionalize the bid-shopping process and get paid at the same time. If the client recognizes that there is value for him or her in receiving a well-written technology proposal from you, the MCSE consultant, then such a proposal can become a for-hire work element. You scope the work and prepare a technology proposal for the client, for which you are a paid a reasonable amount of money, perhaps by the hour or for a flat fee of $1,000 (a fee I've pulled out of thin air as an example). The technology proposal then serves as the RFP on which you and other consultants submit bids. At that point, it becomes "May the best technology consultant win." However, note that you'll have several distinct advantages over the competition at this point:

✦ **Relationship continuation** — You have assessed the client while preparing the technology proposal, and you can decide if you want to continue the consulting relationship. This is akin to job hunting as a temporary employee. You go in, look around, prepare a technology proposal for which you are compensated, and then decide if you want to go any further with this client. Sometimes the answer is no, and you don't want to work with this client anymore. One way to get out of this working relationship is to bid the actual work at a high rate so you effectively lose by choice. This allows everyone, including yourself, to save face in a situation that just isn't working out right.

✦ **Working relationship** — By working side by side with the client while preparing the work-for-hire technology proposal, you develop a working relationship that shouldn't be undervalued. In these scenarios where you divide the project up and are paid to develop the technology proposal, the client tends to develop a very trusting relationship with you. More often than not you'll be asked to evaluate the competing proposals because the client trusts you to work at arm's length and to represent the client's best interests by picking the best technology proposal for the client. Hopefully the best technology proposal for the client is also the best technology proposal for you (that is, your proposal is justified and selected).

Why would the client let the fox guard the hen house? Clients do so not only because they trust you for having developed the initial technology proposal used for RFP bidding purposes, but because you have the technical expertise to assess the fitness of the competing proposals. Typically the client hasn't the time, interest, or expertise to read the technology proposals that are returned.

Part of your being paid to write the initial technology proposal that was turned into an RFP is to purchase your independence in helping the client select the consultant who will perform the work. The planning work that generated the RFP may turn out to be the end of your engagement. The work from that point on may be awarded to another consultant. The good news is that under this business model, you won't be doing the planning work for free.

Further, when you're paid for writing a proposal and find yourself helping the client solicit other bids, you are a better MCSE consultant for it. By observing other competing proposals you are, in effect, building that proposals file in your own mind. You can't help but become a better MCSE consultant by seeing how your competitors are soliciting work, what their costs are, how they format a proposal, and so on. As long as you are party to this information in the capacity of serving the client, no one can fault you for becoming a better MCSE consultant by what you hear and see.

✦ **Favorable perception of qualifications**—If you write the technology proposal that is used for the RFP, the client may have the perception that you know the project best. I liken this to an adjunct instructor's getting a tenure-track teaching job at a public university. Often, the adjunct instructor at a public university has the inside track on tenure-track positions offered at that university. That is, the tenure-track teaching position is his or hers to lose. The university must still run ads announcing the opening for a tenured professorship for equal employment purposes, but a favorite candidate for the job already exists, one who has already been working with the school and the department offering the job. Your role in preparing the technology proposal used for the RFP gives you the inside track for being selected as the incumbent technology consultant. The job is yours to lose.

Tip    Assuming you're awarded the work and acknowledged as the most qualified, don't overlook that the competing technology proposals can help you to deliver a better technology solution. Your competitors may well expose some weaknesses in your approach that can be corrected.

## Reputation is paramount

Your reputation in the technology community is important when you are paid by the client to write the technology proposal that is used as an RFP. If other consultants and vendors sense an insincere or less than competitive bidding situation, they won't bid because it isn't worth their time. This process must be aboveboard, or you'll only attract bids from consultants at the bottom of the MCSE consulting food chain. More importantly, your professional reputation in the MCSE consulting community will suffer.

Tip     Consider the reverse situation. You are asked to bid on a technology project not
only for which another technology consultant has prepared the RFC but also on
which that same consultant is bidding. At a minimum, when you are bidding on
technology engagements, ask the client who else is bidding and whether or not an
existing technology consultant is bidding for the work. This might help you avoid
committing a lot of bidding time to an engagement you are unlikely to win.

Project work may be accomplished in different stages by the same or different technology consultants. For example, you may complete the technology proposal for
hire, another consulting firm may do the implementation work, and yet another
consulting firm may be selected for the ongoing maintenance work.

It has also been my experience that much of the work available to MCSE consultants,
especially lone ranger MCSE consultants who are not part of a large organization, is
often on the small to medium-sized project. That is, MCSEs often work on projects
starting in the five-figure range (up to $10,000), moving into the six-figure range
($100,000 and up), and capping in the low seven-figure range (around $1 million). You
typically don't see MCSE consultants serving in important or lead roles in $50 million
technology projects (these projects often implement solutions beyond Microsoft's
capabilities with the BackOffice suite of projects). In the $50 million and above range,
getting paid for your bid work is a time-honored tradition. But in the typical MCSE
project, there often isn't enough fat for you to be paid for considerable up-front
planning and scoping before you submit your proposal (and certainly before you are
awarded the engagement). If you can develop client relationships where you get paid
for your proposal generation efforts, consider yourself ahead of the game.

# Boundary Definition

Part of business development (which certainly includes writing winning MCSE technology proposals) is to know what work to pursue and accept and what work to
avoid and from which to run. As an MCSE consultant seeking to build your business,
you will need to be part salesperson and part lawyer when it comes to the boundary
development area of business development. Boundary definition is about deciding
what work you will perform (profitably) and what work you will reject. Lawyers are
good at looking at business deals (such as technology consulting engagements) differently than commission salespeople often do. Many commission salespeople will
sell into any deal that walks through the door. On the other hand, attorneys tend to
scrutinize deals more closely and don't hesitate to recommend against those business arrangements that seem less than beneficial. You need to adopt both personas
to be an effective MCSE consultant in the business development area and boundary
definition in particular.

One way to face the challenge of deciding which technology engagements are acceptable is to know what and who you are and what and who you are not. That's called boundary definition. It strikes at the core of how you present yourself as an MCSE consultant, whether you're a specialist or a generalist and so on.

My point about boundary definition is simple. Don't be afraid to put on your lawyer–turned–business development professional hat to reject work that doesn't feel right. On the other hand, don't reject so much work that you go hungry.

Also understand that defining your boundaries is a dynamic process, not a static line in the sand. Your skill set may change, allowing you to consider more difficult, challenging, and perhaps rewarding technology assignments that you previously might not have considered. Perhaps you've grown into an MCSE consulting practice and added some fresh talent to your staff that allows you to bid for work you previously shied away from. Conversely, maybe you stretched on the last engagement, got your fingertips burned, and want to pull back on the types of engagements you'll consider. These are all acceptable outcomes as you understand the shifting nature of boundaries.

**Tip**    I cannot emphasize enough the importance of boundary definition to the MCSE consultant. Knowing your boundaries will make you more successful. That's the bottom line. You'll bid on and win technology engagements on which you can be successful. You'll avoid wasting time on bidding technology engagements on which you can't be successful.

# Scoping

*Scoping* is the job of a pre-sales engineer. Pre-sales engineers typically put together the scope of work that allows a technology proposal to be generated.

In different industries scoping is identified by different terms and is performed by estimators. For example, in project management, scoping might be called developing the work breakdown structure (WBS). The WBS is used to create the project schedule. In construction, scoping refers to creating the specifications that are used for construction. Specifications are used to create construction blueprints.

**Cross-Reference**    For further discussion on project scheduling, refer to Chapter 9.

Scoping is busy work performed by someone with sufficient technical knowledge to call around to get part numbers and pricing from hardware resellers and so on, to collect cost estimates from other services providers (Internet service providers and so on), and to estimate the hours necessary to successfully complete each work area. Scoping is hard to teach someone. One learns typically through baptism by fire.

An example of a scope of work for a technology proposal is provided in Appendix C for your reference.

# Gathering Information

While the scoping discussed in the last section tends to have a quantitative bent to it, the information gathering stage is typically more qualitative. This is more akin to high-level needs analysis, an art that has enjoyed a resurgence in popularity due in large part to Microsoft's emphasis on business technology planning in the new Windows 2000 MCSE track. In other words, questions like "Tell me what your organization does?" are being asked again.

Experienced technology consultants will concur that the best way to gather information in an organization is to interview management, staff, and possibly suppliers and vendors depending on the size of the technology project for which you're preparing a proposal.

When constructing a list of interview questions, work smart. Go to college libraries and thumb through books on systems analysis to gather questions to add to your list. These few hours committed to research can save many more hours by helping to avoid the Document1 blank screen syndrome where all your questions have to be created from scratch.

## The draft

All of the work so far leads up to the first draft of the technology proposal. The major sections should be filled in, and the draft should have an appearance similar to a complete proposal. However, the first draft is not intended to be a final version of your technology proposal. Not only may your proposal contain grammatical errors (which reflect poorly on you), but also mathematical errors may possibly have crept into the cost estimates. Making math errors in a technology proposal can cost you real money.

For more information on the structural appearance of a technology proposal, refer to Appendix C.

Nothing improves a technology proposal like getting feedback in time to revise the draft. Accordingly and as mentioned in passing earlier in this chapter, you will want to meet with your prospective client to review the draft proposal and solicit feedback. This is typically a session that allows you to express what you thought you heard from the prospective client and find out if your proposal reflects that understanding. Often you'll find small errors that need correction, and, hopefully, you'll have a satisfied prospective client who will be impressed with your work style.

If you have this option available, you should consider submitting your draft technology proposal to peer and superior review. Peer review is having a fellow employee look over your draft technology consulting proposal to make suggestions and corrections. Even a lone ranger MCSE consultant should have some type of peer review process, though this process can be as simple as e-mailing your draft proposal to a buddy.

Having a superior review your proposal is a more formal process seen in larger technology consulting organizations. Here your boss or your boss's boss looks over every proposal that goes out the door. This procedure is often seen in two types of consulting practices — consulting practices that have learned the hard way and made a mistake somewhere along the way (which is the basis for most rules and procedures in business) and consulting firms that work on enterprise-level projects in an environment that requires such review. For example, if your firm is bidding on government contracts or military work, senior review of proposals is just a necessary step in the process. Sometimes the legal department even gets involved and eyeballs proposals to make sure the firm isn't making commitments it can't even hope to honor.

## The final copy

The technology proposal draft and subsequent corrections lead to a final copy. This copy is submitted to the prospective client. A final technology proposal should be devoid of mistakes and professional in appearance. It should represent you in a competitive and competent way as you try to win the business of the client.

**Note**  In many cases, the technology proposal is the first meaningful extended communication you will have with the prospective client. I've won many wonderful and lucrative consulting engagements not necessarily because I had a cheaper or better solution than my competitors had, but because the client responded more warmly to my well-written technology proposal.

### Ask the Guru — Who Would Hire Me?

Here is a letter from a reader of my column in *Microsoft Certified Professional Magazine* who comes from the business community and is seeking work in the technology field with newly minted MCSE certificate in hand.

*Harry,*

*I had the opportunity to briefly read your article on the benefits of having both the MBA/MCSE+I. I too have my MBA, and I am currently in process of finishing up my MCSE+I. I certainly can relate to those long hours studying. I also have spent time trying to justify the expense of the schooling and the time away from the family.*

*Continued*

*Continued*

*I really appreciated your article. I have been in financial services for 15 years, and the plan is to transition into the IT side. The MCSE+I plays a big part in that transition. I have been a little concerned about how my experience, the MBA, and the MCSE will help me, what areas of the tech side to go into, and so on.*

*Again, thanks for your article.*

*Sincerely,*

*Rene F.*

Hi, Rene,

Thanks for writing! It seems to me your business background is a perfect fit with the business development and proposal writing areas of MCSE consulting. Your significant business experience (especially the financial part) plus your MBA degree make you uniquely qualified to tackle the toughest engagement proposals. More importantly, I think you would have the ability to keep your eye on the broader financial objectives in an MCSE consulting practice (to make a profit and accumulate wealth). Go ahead and give it a shot; look for something that capitalizes on both your MBA and your MCSE+I credential. Good luck.

harryb

# Creating the Proposal

You can create the MCSE consulting proposals that you provide to clients in hopes of being awarded business in a number of ways. You can create a unique and custom proposal for each bidding situation. Or you can create a form letter–style proposal in a word processing program like Microsoft Word so you can just open the proposal document file, insert the date, client's name, address, and limited customized information such as pricing, and print it out. However, both of these approaches have some drawbacks. First, the custom approach for each bidding situation might clearly take too much of your administration time to effectively implement. The second approach with a form letter might be too robotic and make the customer feel that you haven't paid attention to their unique needs. However, I have found a tool that strikes the balance between custom proposals and the form proposal approach—the Microsoft Direct Access Proposal Builder.

## Microsoft Direct Access Proposal Builder

A surprisingly strong tool that is easily accessed at the Microsoft Direct Access (MSDA) Web site is the MSDA proposal builder. I consider this to be one of Microsoft's early attempts at being an application service provider (ASP), where you essentially run an application over the Internet. As you will discover, by working through a series of screens, you can build a basic technology proposal that can kick-start your career as an MCSE consultant. You will first configure the Proposal Builder and then create an actual technology proposal.

# Configuring the MSDA Proposal Builder

1. Assuming you are at a computer with an Internet connection, launch a Web browser such as Internet Explorer and type the following address: www. microsoft.com/directaccess.

2. Click on the Channel Biz option on the Microsoft Direct Access Web page and select Proposal Builder.

3. Click the Start Proposal Builder link when the Proposal Builder Web page appears.

4. Click the Register Me! link to complete a sign up form that allows you to access the MSDA Proposal Builder.

5. Provide your e-mail address on the Register page and click Next.

6. Assuming you have registered with the MSDA Web site before, the Sign In page will appear. Complete the password and preferred language fields and click Next. If you haven't registered at the MSDA site before, you will be prompted for specific registration information that you must provide before continuing.

7. Confirm your choice of your preferred language, such as English, and click Next.

8. The Welcome to Proposal Builder page appears, as seen in Figure 7-3. Complete the Options questions relating to storage and click Start Using Proposal Builder.

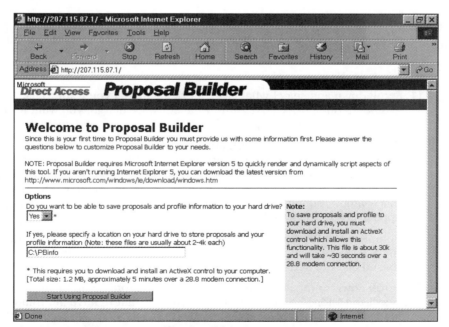

**Figure 7-3:** Welcome to Proposal Builder

9. Agree to the End User License Agreement by clicking I Accept.

10. Complete the Personalize Your Profile page with basic company and location information, as shown in Figure 7-4.

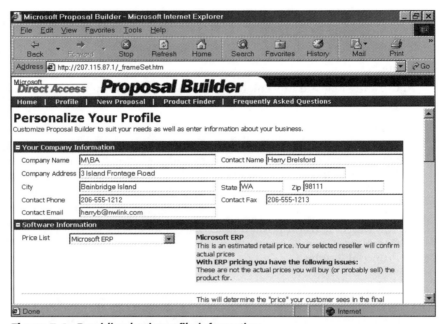

**Figure 7-4:** Providing basic profile information

11. Scroll down and select what type of pricing model you want to use, such as estimated retail price (ERP), and what software margin you want for pricing purposes, as shown in Figure 7-5. Scroll down to the next section.

12. Complete the Hardware Information section, including information on markup, type, and number of desktop units, servers, and printers. This is shown in Figure 7-6. You may customize, add, and delete any hardware peripherals. For example, to change the model number of the Dell desktop computer shown in this example, simply double-click the entry, and a modification dialog box will appear. Scroll down to the next section.

13. Complete the Proposal Builder Options shown in Figure 7-7. This will steer the MSDA Proposal Builder program to different screens for you to complete (based on your selections).

14. Scroll down to the Proposal Builder Downloadable Components section and select the Microsoft solutions for which you want to have information downloaded as part of your proposal process. This is shown in Figure 7-8. Click Download Selected Items. The information is downloaded as Microsoft documents that can be attached to your technology proposal.

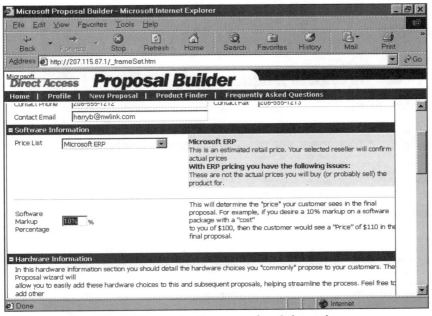

**Figure 7-5:** Providing pricing and software markup information

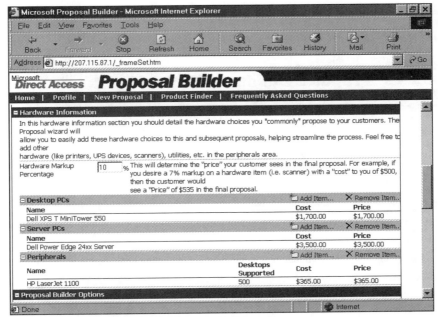

**Figure 7-6:** Providing hardware-related information

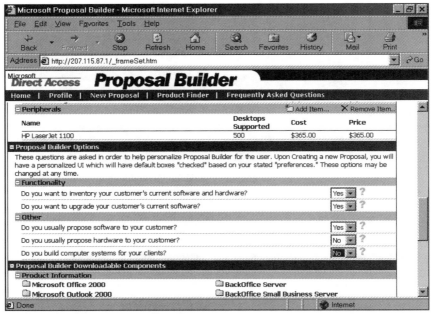

**Figure 7-7:** Answer the questions in the Proposal Builder Options section.

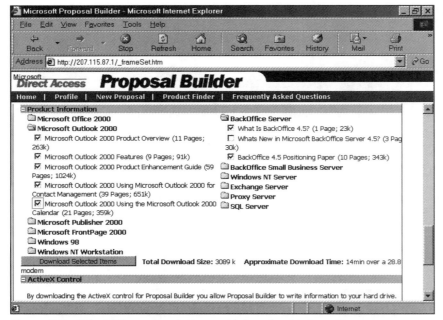

**Figure 7-8:** Select Microsoft solutions and download information.

15. Scroll down and answer the questions regarding storing the proposals locally on your hard disk and downloading an ActiveX control. Click the Submit all Information button.

You have now configured the MSDA Proposal Builder with generic information and can move on to creating a proposal.

## Creating a technology proposal

1. Select Create a New Proposal on the Proposal Builder page, shown in Figure 7-9.

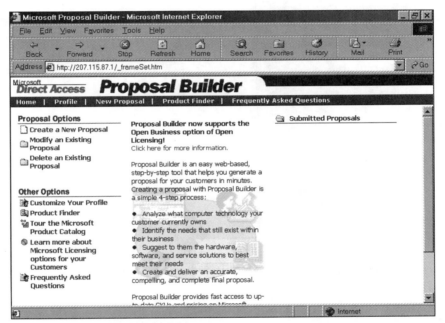

**Figure 7-9:** Proposal Builder home page

2. Complete the Proposal Information screen with project and client name and click Next.

3. Assuming you elected to inventory your client's existing hardware and software (a wise step, indeed), the Inventory page (also called the Current Technology Configuration page) will appear, and the Inventory Wizard will launch. After reading the basic welcome information, click Next.

4. The Inventory Wizard displays the Existing Microsoft Desktop Software page advising you that your client may qualify for upgrade pricing in certain scenarios. Click Next.

5. Complete the Existing Microsoft Desktop Software page that has appeared, allowing you to enter inventory quantities. This is shown in Figure 7-10. Click Next.

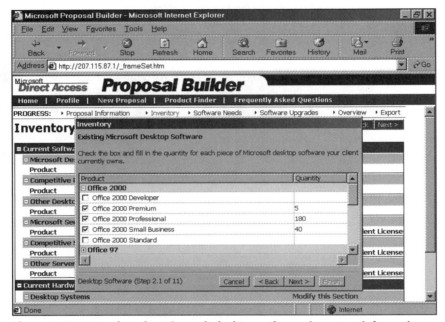

**Figure 7-10:** Complete the Microsoft desktop software inventory information.

6. Click Next after reading the Existing Competitive Desktop Software screen. This screen advises you about competing software that may be a qualifying upgrade to Microsoft desktop software products. The Existing Competitive Desktop Software screen changes to allow you to enter inventory information. Click Next after you complete that screen.

7. The Existing Other Desktop Software screen advises you that you may inventory other desktop software. Click Next, complete the appropriate inventory information, and click Next again.

8. The Existing Microsoft Server Software screen appears advising that you may inventory Microsoft server software. Click Next, complete the Existing Microsoft Server Software screen, shown in Figure 7-11, and click Next again.

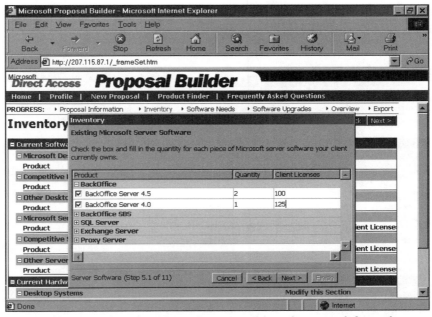

**Figure 7-11:** Complete the Microsoft server software inventory information.

9. Read and complete the next two screens relating to competitive server software. Click Next after each screen.

10. Read and complete the next two screens relating to other existing server software. Click Next after each screen.

11. Read and complete the next two screens relating to existing desktop systems. Click Next after each screen.

12. Complete the Existing Server Systems screen, shown in Figure 7-12. Click Next.

13. Read and complete the next two screens relating to existing peripherals. Click Next after each screen.

14. Click Finish to close the Inventory Wizard. The completed Inventory page will look similar to Figure 7-13. Click Next to move to the Software Needs section of the MSDA Proposal Builder.

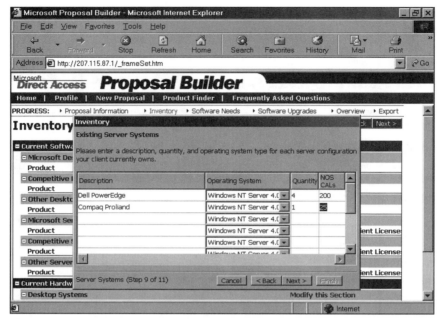

**Figure 7-12:** Provide existing server systems information.

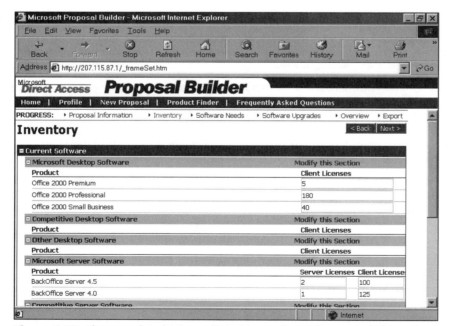

**Figure 7-13:** The completed Microsoft desktop software inventory information

15. Complete the Task List on the Software Needs page, shown in Figure 7-14, and click Next. Notice how the Software to Purchase section automatically updates when you make selections.

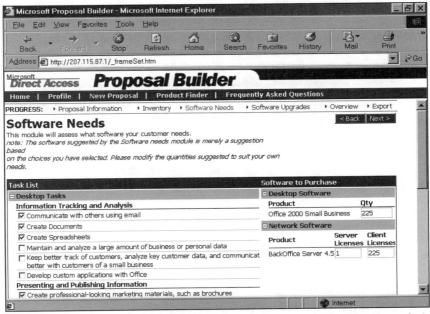

**Figure 7-14:** Answer the questions in the Task List as part of the needs analysis.

16. The Software Upgrade Wizard launches. Click Next after reading the Welcome notice.

17. Select which items you would like to upgrade on the next screen (which lists eligible items). Click Next.

18. On the next screen, select any existing Microsoft desktop software eligible for upgrading and click Next.

19. Complete the Upgrade Existing Competitive Desktop Software screen and click Next.

20. The Upgrade Existing Microsoft Server Software screen appears and allows you to clarify the quantity of Microsoft server products and licenses you want to upgrade. After answering the query, click Next.

21. If necessary, provide upgrade quantity information on the Upgrade Existing Competitive Server Software screen. Click Next.

22. Click Finish to close the Software Upgrade Wizard.

**23.** The Software to Upgrade page is updated to reflect information obtained from the Software Upgrade Wizard, as seen in Figure 7-15. Click Next.

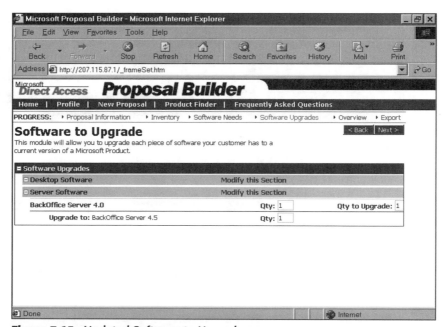

**Figure 7-15:** Updated Software to Upgrade page

> **Note**
>
> The MSDA Proposal Builder also allows you to create a Hardware Needs section similar to the Software Needs analysis steps immediately above. This allows the MCSE consultant to assess what hardware, such as workstations, should be included in the technology proposal, a useful feature area if you are a hardware reseller as well as an MCSE consultant.

**24.** The Proposal Overview, summarizing your analysis, appears as seen in Figure 7-16. You may click Back to change information and then return to this page. You may also print this page and consider it your draft proposal, subject to final adjustments.

**25.** Assuming you have made your final adjustments to your proposal, click Next to display the Export/Generate Proposal page. You may select what additional information you want included in your proposal, as shown in Figure 7-17. Click the Generate Proposal button at the bottom of the page.

> **Note**
>
> You must set your Web browser to a low security level in order for the Proposal Builder to write to your hard disk. With Microsoft's Internet Explorer 5.x, this is accomplished via the Tools menu by selecting the Internet Options menu item. Click the Security tab and change the security level to Low.

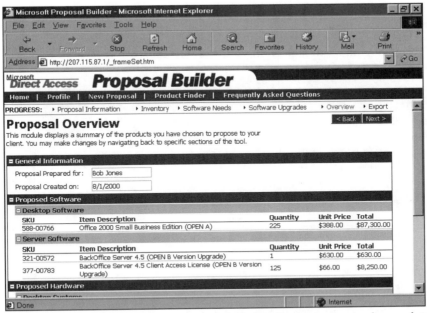

**Figure 7-16:** The Proposal Overview page summarizes your proposal, complete with Microsoft purchase information.

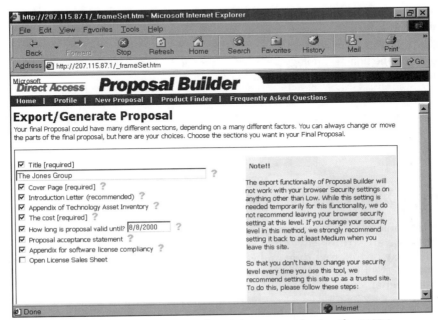

**Figure 7-17:** You have almost completed the proposal using the MSDA Proposal Builder.

After clicking the Generate Proposal button, your computer will whirl for several minutes as the actual proposal is built. The end result, shown in Figure 7-18, is a final technology proposal presented as a Microsoft Word document. You will need to mold this document to make it fit your exact needs.

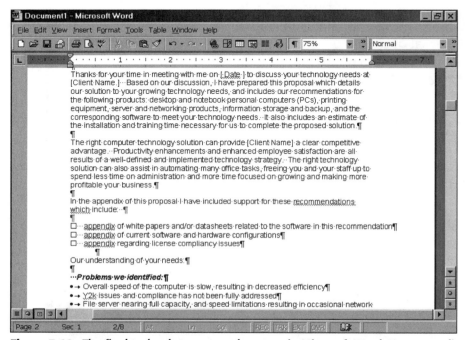

**Figure 7-18:** The final technology proposal as seen in Microsoft Word. You may edit and customize this technology proposal as needed.

> **Tip**
>
> Other vendors offer proposal builders for use by consultants. For example, if you are a Great Plains reseller, you are granted access to the secure partner site where you can use Great Plains–specific tools for generating proposals.

# Knowing Your Audience

As the technology proposal writer, it's ultimately up to you to know the audience for whom you are writing. If you're working with dairy farmers in Wisconsin, your approach may be different than one you would employ for a big city conglomerate. You'll have to be the judge in this area, but all proposals should be well thought out and professional.

# Rule of Ten: Scope a 10 Percent Fudge Factor

All of your proposals should include at least 10 percent padding or inflated cost estimates to account for unknowns and mistakes. In actuality, this 10 percent value is pretty lean, because it doesn't take much of a mistake to cut through 10 percent padding. In your niche area of MCSE consulting, you can probably get away with 10 percent padding. However, if you are bidding outside of your niche, consider estimating a 30 percent padding to cushion your lack of experience and to account for the unknowns and the unpredictable.

# Notes from the Field—Bad Proposals

Just as your proposal file should contain great proposals to model after, your proposal file should contain bad proposals to avoid. It's amazing what you see floating around the MCSE consulting community. There are some really bad proposals being written. My all-time favorite bad proposal was the Microsoft Small Business Server (SBS) 4.*x* proposal that scoped out the additional purchase of Windows NT Server 4.0 and Microsoft Proxy Server, apparently ignorant to the fact that SBS includes these two items as part of the bundled package, making the purchases of the additional software components unnecessary. I prevailed in that bidding situation simply because my proposal was factually correct.

As a practicing MCSE and budding MCSE consultant, you won't have to look far for similar bad proposal examples in your technology career. Hopefully, your days of committing such gaffes are behind you.

# Negotiating

The exhilaration you feel when being awarded a technology engagement is wonderful, albeit quickly tempered when you need to sit down with the client and sign an engagement letter. An engagement letter is typically the contract between MCSE consultant and client. It's one thing to win a bidding war with a superior technology consulting proposal, but it's an entirely different thing to get a signed engagement letter.

In commercial real estate leasing and other business transaction environments, there is a phenomenon called signature fright. In appearance, the client may have awarded you the technology engagement, but the deal isn't done until the engagement letter is signed, sealed, and delivered. Clients can back out of technology engagements at engagement letter signing time because their basic modus operandi (MO) is to avoid commitments or because they have a newly developed case of buyer's remorse. Other clients who might balk at signing are the "conditioners." These clients often change the rules of the consulting engagement, known as moving the yardsticks, and are hard to do business with.

Other points to consider while negotiating include the following:

✦ **Win-win situations** — Management texts abound espousing the need for win-win negotiations. In plain English, that means don't thump your clients so hard in the negotiation stages that they'll never do business with you again. Pursue long-term relationships, which require give and take.

✦ **No money, no problem** — Sometimes a potentially good client doesn't have the money. I've found that these clients are occasionally diamonds in the rough, so I work the deal to make it fit for everyone. For example, perhaps the client can pay for the majority of the work on the back end, so the engagement can be staged over a longer period to account for this.

✦ **Equity** — In today's dot-com business world, professional services providers, accountants, for example, are taking equity in the form of stock instead of cash payments. Perhaps this strategy works for you, too.

✦ **Trades** — I'll occasionally provide services to publications in order to receive free ads to promote my consulting practice. The publication saves money, and I take advantage of another marketing avenue.

# Summary

This was an important chapter in your journey as an MCSE consultant. Writing winning proposals is just as important as your technical, sales, and management capabilities. If you can't land the business at the technology proposal stage, not much else matters as an MCSE consultant. In this chapter I provided the important reasons for writing winning proposals and presented the use of the MSDA Proposal Builder tool.

✦      ✦      ✦

# Customer Service – Referrals and Additional Work

**T**his chapter is about conveying the importance of customer service in the MCSE consultant's life. I will spend time discussing customer service approaches that have worked from generation to generation, such as getting referrals from an existing customer as a reward for a job well done, but I'll also focus on specific customer services issues that affect the MCSE consultant, such as teaming with other professional service providers to the benefit of all involved.

## Tackling Customer Service

A few technical types often cringe at the term *customer service* for two reasons. First, that term is usually associated with a load of marketing hype, and second, a few technical types aren't especially good with social protocols. For those who take more than a day to return a phone call and let e-mails go unanswered, customer service can be a nightmare.

For those of us who are or are aspiring to become MCSE consultants, however, we must march to the beat of the customer service drummer because MCSE consultants depend on customers for their livelihood.

Customer service isn't about being the corporate cheerleader. Rather, customer service is about managing clients' expectations. It's about confronting customer problems head-on in a cheerful, nonoffensive way. Here's a short list of attributes that, if followed, will improve you customer service capabilities. (The expectation is that you'll make your own additions to it as you see fit):

✦ **Manage technology** — Manage the client's expectations about MCSE-related technologies, such as Microsoft BackOffice.

✦ **Meet the customers' needs in a timely manner** — Customers like to know you're dependable at some level and will come through.

✦ **Be honest** — Customer service is gaining the trust of your clients. They believe what you say.

✦ **Execute your duties** — Arrive at the client site, do your work, communicate what you did, and leave. Good customer service means using good judgment and not overstaying your welcome.

✦ **Be consistent** — Clients like consistent behavior. From that perspective, it's actually okay to be ten minutes early if you're consistently ten minutes early (though I wouldn't recommend it). More importantly, are your billings consistent with the time you've communicated you will bill for?

You really want to avoid this following definition of customer service, so kindly provided to me by a Microsoft Solution Provider consulting firm in deep decline. Tongue in cheek, one staff member shared with me that his firm no longer had any problems with customer service, his competition did. His point was that his firm was losing customers in droves to its competition. Not only did it not have any customer service, but it ultimately had no customers.

## The Ultimate Feedback Loop

Whether you like it or not, you will get customer feedback. With that said and accepted, your goal as an MCSE consultant is to listen to the feedback with an open, nondefensive attitude. You also want the feedback to be honest: false praise is easily unmasked.

Another point to remember is that the feedback you receive is largely based on the customer service you provide. This can be thought of as the ultimate feedback loop, which lets you know whether or not you're making it as an MCSE consultant. Sufficient, if not superior, customer service will lead to referrals, a key point of this chapter. If you're delivering great customer service to your clients, the referrals will take care of themselves.

## How am I doing?

One way to force the customer service feedback loop won't cost you any money. Simply walk into your client's office and ask, "How am I doing?" This proactive approach will leave a favorable impression. Catching the client slightly off balance can usually defuse any consulting/client tension that may exist. Often the client exhales a sigh of relief, and then proceeds to give you an earful (both good and bad).

## When to ask

The "How am I doing?" technique is of special benefit at the enterprise level if you're not endowed with keen enterprise-level political savvy and can't read the corporate tea leaves for how your performance is being judged. On more than one occasion, I have stepped into an enterprise client's office and solicited feedback. Granted, I usually begin by talking about project schedule milestones or some other technical detail as a way to initiate communications, but when the moment is right, I'll communicate (using a little humor) that, as a consultant, I have an important need to know how things are going.

# Client Surveys

A no-cost way to not only garner customer feedback but engage in good old-fashioned customer service is to periodically survey your clients. If you work for yourself, you might simply e-mail your clients with a few questions, making sure you don't tip them off to the fact that you're conducting an official and scientific poll.

If you're with a medium-sized or large consulting firm, you might institutionalize the survey process as part of your operations. For example, you might consider sending a five- or ten-question survey form to the client contact at predetermined points of the engagement — say, the 50 percent and 100 percent milestones. Surveying the client at mid-point affords you the opportunity to make course corrections while still making a difference on the project. Surveying the client at the end of the project allows you to see how you did and to determine if this client will be either a referral source or a reference for you in the future.

**Note** In my experience, it's often easier for another staff member to send out the client survey, tally the results, make a follow-up telephone call to the client to discuss, and so on. Why? First, you (the MCSE consultant) are too close to the project to be objective. Second, the client may be reluctant to be completely honest with you, even if it's warranted, because it's likely that both you and the client will have to work together again tomorrow, the day after that, and so on. In larger consulting firms, a front desk person can handle this chore.

The lone-ranger MCSE might need a spouse or family member to handle this function. Granted, the client realizes the MCSE consultant will ultimately receive and review the information, but having a third party perform the survey functions has proven to be an effective method for eliciting greater feedback from the client.

It is mission critical that the survey process not be a sham. Both you (the MCSE consultant) and your client need to find the survey process to be credible and lead to improvements as needed. In my career as an MCSE consultant, I have noticed two survey delivery problems that invalidated the results. First, the way in which the questions were worded pushed the client into selecting a negative response (called push polling in the world of government and politics). Second, the only clients surveyed were problem clients. Either of these survey mistakes are very sad to witness as a lot of time and effort is spent gather information that isn't valid. Strive to avoid politicizing or otherwise damaging the customer surveying process.

## Improving quality

Why the soapbox speech on client surveys? The bottom line is to improve quality. The cheapest route to financial success as an MCSE consultant is to have a quality practice that is not only on autopilot but also has referrals fed to it.

### Feedback Comes in Many Forms

As a teacher, I'm subject to the same feedback and customer surveys that you and other MCSE consultants receive. Twice each term, the wonderful MCSE students that I teach online for Seattle Pacific University complete teacher and course evaluation forms on a secure Web site that allows them to speak freely about how things are going (or in their opinion, not going). University network security has thwarted my most ardent attempts to discover who has commented on what topics. Kidding aside, you get used to the feedback — brutal as it may be. More importantly, with a consistent survey base of several years, you can see which ratings fall in and out of range. So is there any tidbit of feedback that modified my behavior? After receiving some feedback that I lectured to the chalkboard and had my back turned to the audience, I changed my lecture style to use a wireless microphone and walk around the audience more.

The second form of client survey I read with interest is from you, the reader. My books are listed at major online book retailers, such as Amazon (www.amazon.com), Barnes and Noble (www.bn.com), and Fat Brain (www.fatbrain.com). Readers can anonymously post reader reviews on my books. I've found these reviews to be fair, and I encourage you to post your feedback on this book. I look forward to it and will incorporate your suggestions into future releases of this title.

Part of improving quality is having thick skin. As mentioned earlier, feedback is often direct, and your first reaction may be a defensive one. However, feedback is, more often than not, sincere and on target. The good news is that it gets easier to accept client feedback over time. For one, some of the comments may become familiar to you (for example, "Harry accommodates our business work schedule by coming in after hours"). Also—knowingly or unknowingly—you develop a large data set of responses to which you can compare any new responses. It's your own form of filtering that allows you to determine if a particular piece of feedback is in or out of bounds, given the feedback you've received over the years. Having such a reference point is refreshing on those particularly dark days of MCSE consulting.

## Making every client referencable

A noble mission statement (discussed in Chapter 2) is to make every client referencable. This will not only reflect the quality of your work as an MCSE consultant, but your client selection capabilities. Not every potential client is going to be so enamored with your MCSE consulting skills that you'll be able to list him or her on your references list. In that case, you want to see that reality up front and not select these people as clients.

## Making every client referable

In addition to making every client referencable, strive to make every client a referral source. In other words, try to create a situation where your clients feed you referrals. Clients who feed you referrals are the most effective form of marketing in the land. In reality, the only way to achieve this lofty goal is to be really good at client selection. Once you've got your MCSE consulting practice to that stage, you've made it!

## Putting things in perspective

Now that I've pumped you up about delivering high-quality services as an MCSE consultant (and accepting the client accolades that await you), I'm going to present you with a more sobering fact: you can't make everyone happy. That's helpful to remember when you don't.

# Referrals

You can't afford to buy enough display ad space, yellow pages ads, or even skywriting airplane services to be a successful MCSE consultant. You can certainly purchase these high-priced advertising avenues, but the cost will far exceed what you could reasonably expect to earn as an MCSE consultant.

Your success, rather, will depend on the referrals you receive. It's an unmistakable key tenet to success that I've seen played out time and time again.

A referral from a client is a vote of confidence. It's the best form of feedback you can hope to receive. Most MCSE consultants on the way up don't get as many referrals as they would like, so referrals shouldn't be taken lightly. It has been my experience that referrals are earned over time, not necessarily early in your consulting career. That's fine, as long as you manage your expectation about the time it takes to get the referral food chain going and are committed to being an MCSE consultant over the long haul.

**Note**  Referrals from friends, family, and others (such as people you don't directly do business with) are fine and are all part of the referral mixture. While your customer service skills may not have directly resulted in these ancillary referrals, they didn't hurt either. Truth be told, many of my referrals come from secondary sources. These secondary sources apparently have confidence that I'll perform as expected.

# Rule of Ten — Eight Out of Ten New Clients Must Be Referrals

In the long run, eight out of ten new clients must be referrals or else you are facing an uphill battle to be truly profitable as an MCSE consultant. The *long run* means different things to different people. For a day trader, it means holding a stock overnight. For a real estate investor, it means holding a rental property for 30 years until it's paid for. And for the MCSE consultant, it lies somewhere between these two extremes. For me, the long run has proven to be a decade. I left the comfort of a corporate desk job in 1989. I made a few, quick dollars on the Exxon Valdez project in Valdez, AK and used that as my launch money into the computer consulting business. With the exception of one in-house job along the way (where I was a consultant to members of the association), I've been a billable-hour consultant in the same market for over a decade. It's just in the past couple of years that I've actually had referrals coming in on e-mail, voice mail, and through face-to-face conversations over lattes. You, too, will build your ability to gain referrals in your own time.

So how do you get eight out of ten of your clients to come from referrals? Being a competent technical professional with great customer service skills is the first step. Look around right now and see if there's just one tiny thing you could do better. Have you answered that client's e-mail sitting in your Inbox? No? Then put this book down, double-click on the e-mail, and hit Reply. I'm betting in less than ten minutes you can complete a customer service task that'll make your client feel good. Still sitting here? Go do it. The book will be here when you return.

**Tip**  If you really want to impress your clients, call them up and ask how things are going since your last visit. Tell your client you just wanted to check in and make sure the fix you implemented is working as planned. Since few people in the MCSE consulting industry do this any more, you'll stand out in a very positive way.

One way to boost the number of referrals you get is to look closely at the industries you are serving. Some industries and sectors of the economy lend themselves to being better referral sources than others. For example, excellent referrals are freely given in the not-for-profit sector, where the organizations keep in close contact with each other. You might be serving the wrong type of business if you're seeking to grow by referrals.

**Caution**   Remember that these same referral channels can turn against you if you disappoint any of them. Do a poor job at one not-for-profit organization and you can be blackballed from all the rest.

In general, small businesses aren't generous with referrals. Not that small business owners — those dawn-to-dusk, hard-working individuals — don't appreciate good customer service and quality work, but they simply don't have much time to mingle with others and share the good word about you. Many small business owners are married to their jobs. It's fine to serve small businesses (I have many as my clients), but understand that you'll be in a difficult environment to garner referrals.

Another way to get referrals is via vendor reseller programs. For example, from time to time Microsoft has tried to implement a bona fide referral program, where referrals are actively pushed to solution providers and other Microsoft friends and partners. Solution providers are a partner class in the Microsoft sale program where, with an appropriate number of certified professionals (MCSEs) on staff and an annual fee, you get a solution provider plaque, a software library, support incident vouchers, and training and marketing opportunities. All in all, it's a good deal — except for one observation. Microsoft hasn't been very successful at pushing referrals down to you and me. Although they implemented the Windows 95 specialist program in late 1995 that provided solution providers with call lists of hundreds of potential clients, generally speaking, small and lone MCSE consultants have fallen through the cracks in Microsoft's referral program.

Under the Microsoft referral program, a potential client needs to perform the following steps to access Microsoft's Web site and find an MCSE consultant (or MCP service provider):

1. Launch an Internet Web browser, such as Internet Explorer 5.*x*.

2. Type the following uniform resource locator (URL) in the Address field and then hit Enter: `www.microsoft.com`. You are taken to the main Microsoft home page.

3. Click the Support link in the upper right corner of Microsoft's home page.

4. Select Service Partner Referrals. The Technology Services page under Microsoft Business Advantage appears, as shown in Figure 8-1.

5. Click the "I want to hire an outside expert to plan and/or deploy a solution for my business" link. The Hire an Expert page appears.

6. Select your country and language, as shown in Figure 8-2. Click Continue.

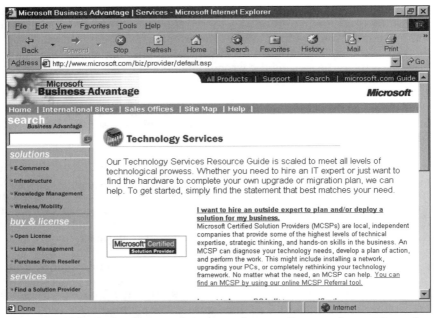

**Figure 8-1:** The Technology Services page allows a client to select a Microsoft Certified Solution Provider.

**Figure 8-2:** The Hire an Expert page allows the client to narrow the query.

**7.** Select a state, province, or region on the Find a Microsoft Certified Solution Provider in your area page, as shown in Figure 8-3. Click Continue.

**Figure 8-3:** Select the geographic area you want to have results returned for.

**8.** Complete the Hire an Expert that appears next. You will select at least one of the following: service, product, industry, area of business (horizontal market). Provide information on the number of PCs in the organization and select the city you live in. Your screen should look similar to the one shown in Figure 8-4. Click Submit.

You can use the screen shown in Figure 8-4 to select a Microsoft Certified Technical Education Center as well.

**9.** The results are returned for your query on the MCSP Search Results page, as shown in Figure 8-5.

In my experience, this referral tool from Microsoft is good for conducting broad services (for example, finding a firm that works with Windows 2000 Server in Seattle), but inadequate for narrow searches (for example, finding an expert in SQL Server for small law firms in Seattle). Such a narrow search returns a "no results error." The lesson learned here is that, when seeking a specialist, word of mouth is still best!

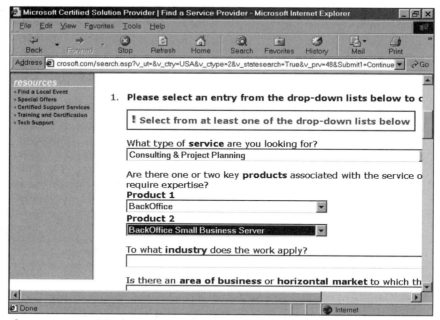

**Figure 8-4:** Provide details on products and services, as well as your city.

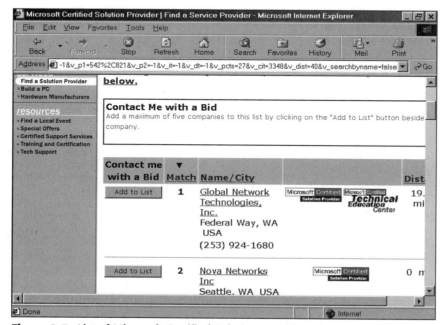

**Figure 8-5:** List of Microsoft Certified Solution Providers that meet your search criteria

Clicking on the name of your choice will provide a brief description page of that service provider. What you'll typically see is a service provider list of every product it's ever installed and every industry it's ever worked in, which again validates the observation that the Microsoft referral tool is sufficient for generalists, not specialists.

If you click on the Add to List, a bid list is built that allows up to five vendors to be contacted with a request for bid. This is shown in Figure 8-6. Building the bid list is the only official mechanism used by Microsoft to forward client information to its solution providers.

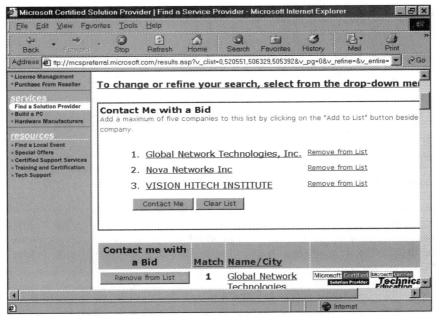

**Figure 8-6:** Creating a bid list in the Microsoft referral tool

Clicking the Contact Me button displays a screen where you (the potential client) place your contact information and a brief description of your needs. Be advised — this is a short form that is hardly qualified to be a full request for proposal, project specifications, or needs analysis. The bid list simply sends an e-mail to a sales contact at the consulting firm or reseller, who will then respond to your request by giving you a call.

So how do you get real referrals from Microsoft? It's been my experience that you have to cultivate and develop personal relationships at your regional Microsoft sales office. Business at Microsoft is still done, at some level, with those you know. I've enjoyed a lucrative relationship with the BackOffice marketing and development teams at Microsoft over the years because I live in the Seattle area and have niched on BackOffice solutions. Having contributed my expertise to the BackOffice team in the form of beta testing, I've been rewarded with referrals directly from those guys and gals in Redmond, Washington. By developing a rich relationship with your nearest Microsoft sales office and contributing specific expertise to the Microsoft cause, it's possible you'll benefit in a similar manner.

Other vendors have referral programs that, quite frankly, can be more helpful than the Microsoft referral page previewed above. For example, Great Plains has a partner program where consultants receive multiple leads from Great Plains on an occasional basis. I've seen this program in action and have always been just a little jealous that the Great Plains consultants got warm leads referred to them. To Great Plains' credit, it has a quality control program where clients complete a post-project survey. Scoring poorly on this customer satisfaction survey results in a low or no flow of future referrals. It's a good program and surfaces a valid issue for MCSE consultants to consider: whether or not you should take on a third-party software product as part of your offering. If you do, it's been my experience that you can still practice your MCSE craft. If you think about it, in this day and age, another software product is likely to run on top of a Microsoft infrastructure solution such as Windows 2000.

You are encouraged to consider this multi-vendor approach to building your MCSE consulting practice and building up your referrals. Many third-party application vendors work this way, so it's likely the product you're interested in has some form of consulting support program. I've even seen ISPs with partner programs where referrals are dished out.

So, how do you get the referral food chain going? Start asking your existing clients for a reference letter. This may get them thinking about how you're doing, but more importantly, it may get them thinking about helping you get business. In many cases, if you don't gently nudge your clients into a referral mindset, they'll forget about you and your business development needs. You can't blame them, as they've got their own business challenges to confront.

Another way to get the referral ball going in your MCSE consulting practice is to give a referral. It's the old "you've got to give a referral to get a referral" theory. On occasion, I've been known to give recommendations for "Bob," who works for the real estate services firm that I serve. It's not lost on Bob that I've been buttering his bread, so he occasionally remembers to butter mine.

## Guest Sermon—Making Money with Customer Service

The guest sermon for this chapter comes from Roy Riley, an MCSE with his own consulting practice. Roy now focuses on writing computer help systems and documentation with the belief that helping the technology consultant and user with software applications is in itself a form of customer service:

*We're all in business to make money. As an MCSE consultant, your money comes from your clients. The best means to getting those clients are referrals.*

*Now, the way I see it there are two types of referrals:*

1. *Passive referrals, where you did enough right on a job (or enough that wasn't wrong) that when a potential client needs your services someone, somewhere, remembers your name*

2. *Zealous referrals, where you have dazzled customers by solving their technology-based problems, and they actively send business your way*

*Which would you rather have? The answer, of course, is obvious. Word-of-mouth marketing is the most powerful business tool available today. It is priceless, but it cannot be purchased. The question arises, then, how do you get these zealous referrals? I will share a story with you that may help illustrate.*

*My friend Todd owns a roofing business. He has never taken out a yellow pages ad, bought a second of radio advertising, or blanketed a mall parking lot with flyers; he doesn't even post a yard sign when he's roofing a home. Yet, Todd is so busy that he's literally booked months in advance and has to turn business away. I tell you, an MCSE consultant, this story about my roofing buddy because it so perfectly illustrates the power of referral-based business.*

*Suppose you have started a consulting practice to small businesses and assume for a moment that you and all other consultants out there are pretty equal in skill and experience in your particular area. What makes you stand out? What makes you different? Why would a client choose you in the first place and then (more importantly) tell all their friends about you?*

*Well, what's different about my friend Todd? Well, for starters, he doesn't look, act, or sound like a roofer. You see, people have expectations set about the people with whom they do business. Roofers, for one, can be a bit unkempt and rough around the edges. My friend Todd, by contrast, is polite, articulate, personable, and clean-cut: as roofers go, atypical. But the differences don't end there. Todd shows up on time for appointments, explains specifically what he will and will not do for a price, and then does what he says.*

*On the job, he doesn't let his crews use profanity, and he insists they clean the area surrounding the house, even if it means cleaning some small messes they didn't make. Todd even makes a visual sweep through the grass and shrubs for shards, nails, or scraps. A couple weeks after the job is complete, Todd stops by or calls just to check on the customer even though he has no service contract opportunities and even though the customer has paid the bill.*

*Continued*

*Continued*

*Todd works at a level above expectations for his industry, and he has former customers that not only recommend him to their friends that need their roofs done, but also actually recommend to their friends that they should get their roofs done. Wouldn't you like to have that kind of MCSE consulting business?*

*Part of your success as a consultant is in how you treat your clients. Fortunately for you, much of treating clients well is largely common sense: don't lie, don't cut corners, keep your commitments, do excellent work, don't condescend to them, do the little things, listen to them, and so on.*

*But the real key to being an MCSE consultant to small businesses is this: understand what you are really selling.*

*You are not selling them computers, computer networks, or service contracts. You are not selling them e-mail servers, database servers, firewalls, or fax servers. Small businesses do not purchase technology. Do not sell hardware or software or even services; sell them solutions. Sell them solutions that help them run their businesses more efficiently and make more money. In fact, the components of those solutions—be they hardware, software, or services—should be transparent to them. If they have an e-mail and faxing problem, sell them an e-mail and faxing solution (though it may well include a new server computer running e-mail and faxing applications and perhaps even a monthly service contract). Sell them a solution.*

*I'll tell you what this does for you. People always talk about their problems, right? The person with a faxing problem will invariably complain about their problem. If you solve this problem for them, anytime they talk to someone with a similar problem, you stand a chance for a referral. (This isn't limited to faxing, of course, but to all the solutions you can provide as a consultant.)*

*As an MCSE consultant, if you can provide solutions to technology-based problems, if you will—like my friend Todd—be more than they expect and do more than they expect, then you will get their business, and you will get your zealous referrals.*

# Additional Work

Another customer service barometer is the area of additional work. If you're doing a great job as an MCSE consultant, you may find yourself overwhelmed with opportunities to do additional work for existing clients. Such a situation is advantageous because it lets you:

✦ **Sell yourself to existing clients**—It's a case of familiarity breeding comfort. It's always easier to sell yourself to existing clients. Not only that, but it's easier for you to be successful, given you already know the client site, the computer system, and so on.

✦ **Market yourself in the most effective way possible**—Hour for hour, obtaining additional work from your existing clients is the most effective marketing program you'll ever launch. Think about that the next time you're stuffing direct mail envelopes to promote your practice.

✦ **Market yourself in the cheapest way possible**—Having an existing client walk up and say, "Harry, could you spend a few hours looking at this?" is much cheaper than purchasing display advertising to attract new clients.

## Ask the Guru—Lessons Learned

Here is an e-mail from a reader of my *MCP Magazine* column who learned a lesson or two along the road of being an MCSE.

*Harry,*

*About two months ago, I was reading an article you wrote in* MCP Magazine *regarding MCSE free agents. Great article. I did not think two months from then I would be sending you this e-mail, but you never know. I had a job at Michigan Caterpillar making $86,000 base salary plus up to $10,000 per year in bonus checks, not to mention a company car. Then my boss and I got into an argument regarding expenses; to say the least, it got heated, and I resigned. I am now in the free agent market, and it is unfamiliar territory.*

*I am a MCSE + I, MSS, MCT, CNA, as well as Checkpoint Firewall certified. I am having a hard time finding the salary and bonus that I was making at Caterpillar. I am proficient at configuring Cisco routers, all aspects of Microsoft networks, business logic, firewalls, and so on, but it seems as if companies want only MCSEs for a specific function instead of utilizing all of my experience. This makes it difficult to negotiate salary.*

*I was wondering if you had any advice on how to make the low six-figure salaries. Attached is a copy of my resume if you have time to review it.*

*Thank you for your time,*

*Brady P.*

Hi, Brady,

That's an incredible story. As I was reading it, I couldn't help but think there is a real lesson learned here. While I applaud your good attitude about being an MCSE consultant (freelancer), I think the dispute you had with your boss points toward a real customer service issue. Undoubtedly, you will have billing disputes with clients in the future as an MCSE consultant. These disputes may involve simple matters such as expenses for computer parts (a discussion not unlike you had with your former boss about expenses). If you learn from your past and commit yourself to handling billing disputes better than you did at Caterpillar, I think you'll be all the better for it and a great MCSE consultant. But if you don't learn from your past, the Promised Land of six-figure earnings will seem very distant indeed. So start with customer service (you've clearly got the technical skill set based on your credentials), and the income you are seeking to earn will, in all likelihood, be a possibility. Good luck and keep me posted.

harryb

# New Work — Following the Last Consultant

New work is always welcome if there's time to do it. My favorite scenario is when — via word of mouth — I'm invited to help a client site following another consultant who was unsuccessful. After assessing that I can be more successful than the last consultant, which is always a legitimate concern, I arrive at the site and assess what the problem(s) is/are. If the last consultant was terminated, it was usually for cause.

In general, these follow-up situations are marked by clean-up activities that enable the client site to return to a functional state. More importantly, they allow you to be a customer service hero.

# Partnering

Another way to obtain referrals to grow your practice is to partner with other closely aligned professional services firms. In other words, it may be advantageous for you to partner with like-minded professionals where organizational synergy exists.

## Partnering with accountants

CPA firms long interested in technology for their clients (especially technology that runs accounting systems) have sometimes aligned themselves with MCSE consultants. It's a popular marriage, enabling accounting firms to provide a breadth of services to clients without having to build full-fledged technology consulting practices. More important, it's a practical marriage. The CPA firm protects its clients from other, larger CPA firms that have a full-fledged technology practice, and the MCSE consultant picks up client referrals. In fact, Microsoft touts the value-added provider (VAP)/accounting firm relationship as one of the smarter business decisions a VAP (like an MCSE consultant) can make. On Microsoft's Direct Access site (www.microsoft.com/directaccess) in the Value-Added Forum, there is a story of a VAP who, aligned with a CPA firm, doubled its revenue and cut its marketing expense 35 percent in one year.

 **Tip**

I've found, after working in the technology consulting division of a CPA firm and now partnering with CPA firms, that the purse strings prevail when it's time to sign an engagement letter. Accountants and clients tend to have really long-term relationships, often exceeding ten years in length and passing from one generation to another. The accountant becomes a trusted business advisor (when it comes to money, a fair amount of trust is necessary).

The accountant also interacts with the top decision-makers at the client site: the owners and the chief financial officer (CFO). Not only does the buck stop here, but the accountant knows how many bucks are being stopped. To put it briefly, there are fewer, stronger business relationships than between an accountant and a business owner. Understand that, and you'll do fine in the accountant/MCSE consultant partnership.

# Marketing to accountants

Just as the accountant is a trusted party in the MCSE consultant/accountant partnership, you need to become a trusted party yourself. An accountant is less impressed by stories of bleeding edge beta releases than by the fact that you strive to make every client referencable and referable. A provision that you'll call and provide the accountant with an update after each visit is solid marketing talk when you're dealing with an accountant.

As with any solid marketing effort, you should know your customer. Similarly, you should know what type of accountants there are.

There are different accounting designations. The Certified Public Accountant (CPA) designation is akin to the MCSE designation in technology consulting, with one minor difference: the CPA is required, whereas the MCSE is not. There are accountants without the CPA designation, working in-house in firms. These individuals have no public accounting responsibilities. There are other accounting designations, such as Certified Management Accountant (CMA), that won't be discussed here. Basically, MCSEs have their designations and accountants have theirs, and since professionals like working with professionals, MCSEs and CPAs can coexist just fine.

The services offered by accountants fall into a few distinct areas:

✦ **Accounting** — This includes financial statement preparation, setting up the chart of accounts in an accounting system all the way down to bookkeeping. Professionals who work in a true accounting function learn a great deal about the businesses they serve and may be your best resource for landing technology engagements as an MCSE consultant.

✦ **Auditing** — This is a true public accounting function and involves testing the validity of a firm's financial reports, transactions, and systems. Every CPA must spend a certain amount of time in auditing, but most accounting professionals move on to other accounting areas.

✦ **Taxes** — It has been said that from January through April, every accountant in a public accounting firm is involved in the tax area. To some extent this is true. But tax season aside, some specialized tax accountants help wealthy individuals year round with tax advice and so on.

✦ **Specialized niches** — Many accountants specialize after gaining general experience. Specialized niches that I've witnessed include estate planning, pre-IPO accounting services, divorce and litigation-related accounting, and so on.

✦ **Business advisory services** — Seasoned accountants with years of experience under their belts sometimes gravitate away from accounting and become general business advisors. These individuals provide business planning services and lead strategic planning seminars.

Another consideration when marketing to accountants is the size of the accounting firm you're partnering with. I've heard it said that large clients like large accounting firms and small clients like small accounting firms (and the lower bill rates). Because my primary MCSE consulting niche is Small Business Server (SBS), I have partnered with smaller accounting firms (with small business clients) who can benefit from what I have to offer, and vice versa.

One additional consideration when marketing the "partnership" idea to accountants is the calendar. There are at least two times per year you won't receive much attention from the accounting firm you've partnered with: the regular tax season and the mini-tax season in October, when firms file mid-year returns and fulfill outstanding extensions. If the accounting firm you've partnered with has a not-for-profit clientele, the month of June is busy when tax and accounting information is prepared for this area.

## Doing business with accountants

So you've got this great idea to partner with an accounting firm to fill your MCSE consulting book with referrals! Early on, you'll have to confront certain mechanical issues. For example, will you carry your business card — or theirs — to their clients?

### Fee splitting

There is the question about charges to the client. Will the client receive multiple bills, including your bill for MCSE consulting services? Most clients would probably agree that the fewer bills they have, the better. If the arrangement is to have the accounting firms you're partnered with handle the billing; you'll realistically need to do some fee splitting to compensate the accounting firm for its administration and collection activities.

This arrangement can be viewed from this perspective. As an MCSE consultant, you really have two bill rates. You have your retail rate (for example, $125 per hour). When you bill this rate, you've gone out and marketed, won over the client, performed the work, and handled the administration and collections. You also have your wholesale rate. Your wholesale rate charged to your accounting partner might be $80 per hour. The account firm then bills you out for $125 per hour. The difference is the amount contributed to the accounting firm's overhead and profit. I actually like the whole rate arrangement, as it allows me to let someone else handle the marketing, administration, and collections. When you step back and lucidly look at the difference between your retail and wholesale rate (and what the difference means practically), the bottom line is about the same, give or take a dollar or two per hour. Don't overlook the opportunity, under the right conditions, to bill at the wholesale rate.

Under any financial arrangement, bend over backward to honor the fact that the accountant owns the client if the client was delivered via your accounting firm partnership. Watch the accountant's backside at the client site (pass on gossip you might hear about the accountant in a professional way). Be technologically conservative. Few accountants that have partnered with you would appreciate an aggressive, bleeding edge MCSE consulting attitude.

## Regulations

Be advised that you as an MCSE consultant cannot and should not provide accounting advice. Likewise, you might ask your CPA buddies not to provide BackOffice advice.

## Type of services to provide

Depending on the type of MCSE consultant you are, you can provide different types of services. For example, if you're a network infrastructure type like me (Windows 2000, Microsoft Internet Security and Acceleration (ISA) Server, Microsoft Exchange 2000 Server, and Microsoft SQL Server 2000), you might deliver basic BackOffice services. That's ideal for situations where an accounting application is being installed or upgraded on top of Microsoft infrastructure. The last time I looked, there were plenty of these opportunities.

If you're more of a developer type, there are also wonderful opportunities in the MCSE consulting/accounting firm partnership. For example, the e-commerce module from Great Plains — part of the Great Plains Dynamics accounting solution — requires SQL Server and Site Server from Microsoft. These aren't out-of-the-box setup wizard installations; rather, they require SQL statements to implement this e-commerce solution, ideal for a developer niche. Other developer opportunities include report writing in SQL Server and using Crystal Report.

Many accounting packages also support common programming languages for customization purposes or have a programming language built-in. This customization and programming area is a consulting niche to consider if you think you might be successful at it. Figure 8-7 shows how Great Plains Dynamics supports customization work.

## The bottom line

Accountants are often bottom line professionals with a focus on profits, and because of the regulatory nature of accountants' job (auditing and taxation, for example), accountants tend to be more conservative than other types of business professionals. More importantly, however, accountants often have very high standards of professionalism, so if you can partner and get referrals from an accountant, you're doing a great job with customer service.

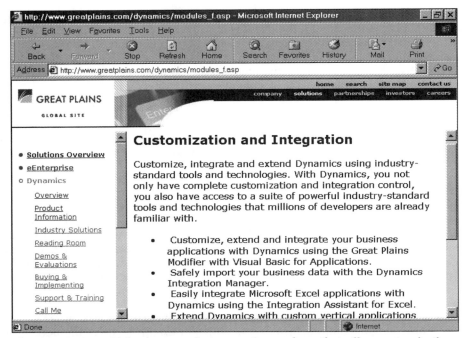

**Figure 8-7:** Great Plains is a popular accounting package that offers customization opportunities for the MCSE consultant.

# Summary

One of the main points of this chapter was to present the idea that receiving referrals and additional work from existing clients is an implicit reward for great customer service skills. Partnering with accounting firms was also presented as another way to go out and get referrals for your MCSE consulting practice. Think of clients as if they were sourdough starter in baking. You only need a little sourdough starter to make a lot of sourdough bread. The same concept applies when building your MCSE consulting practice on referrals. You need only one client to get the ball rolling, and if you're doing your job right in the customer service area, you'll get a referral (and a new client). The process will repeat itself until you've got more sourdough bread than you know what to do with. All analogies aside, though, great customer service boils down one thing: Your clients should be enthusiastic advocates for you and your services.

✦   ✦   ✦

# Minder

**A**fter you have gone out and obtained clients, the next step in running an MCSE consulting practice is to manage your client engagements and your own business. This is the minder role and is critical to the long-term viability of your MCSE consulting practice. This part navigates you through the many facets of MCSE consulting practice management.

# Managing the Engagement

**M**ore MCSE consulting engagements fail from misman-agement than for any other reason. That's why I have an entire part of the book dedicated to the minder function of professional services consulting. It is important that the management discussion begin with a chapter dedicated to managing the engagement.

## Good Old-fashioned Management Skills

Some would argue that in the field of MCSE consulting the management function has put the *M* back in the acronym *MCSE*. Others in the MCSE community would cringe at such suggestions, considering management something of a malady. Kindly allow me just a few pages to talk to you about the old school of management.

### Client file system

You need to have an updated client file system to manage each engagement. This file system can be a simple notebook for each client or a manila folder in a filing cabinet. Not only should the client file contain client engagement documentation, including the engagement letter, contracts, change orders, field notes, receipts, bills, and so on, it should also contain the network notebook and programming comments–related documentation, which I discuss next. Finally, be sure the client file also contains logon passwords, contact names, and so on. You would be amazed at how many MCSE consultants try to keep all that information in their heads. Without a file system in place, if something should happen to the MCSE consultant, there is no way someone else can easily step in and pick up the pieces, a clear example of bad engagement management.

## Documentation

Put yourself in the client's shoes. Part of the value they receive from the MCSE consulting relationship is the documentation of the work you do. If anyone follows in your footsteps, they will easily start work where you left off.

### Network notebook

At my sites, I maintain a network notebook with anything and everything related to infrastructure operations. This includes an as-built drawing created in Microsoft Visio (Microsoft Visio is introduced at the end of this chapter), site visit reports (you can see an example of a site visit report in Appendix D), user account information, vendor application information, and so on.

### Programming comments

One MCSE consulting engagement I remember in particular is the time I was hired by a lumberyard owner to verify the work of his database administrator. While I wasn't qualified to verify the development work in a database program called Clipper, I was qualified to look at how well the database was documented. What I found was a pleasant surprise. The database administrator had commented out his work, had printed out the comments, and had saved them both in a fireproof file cabinet and as comment files to the server (which meant a bona fide tape backup system with off-site storage was protecting the comments). The lumber owner slept much better at night knowing this.

# Status Meetings

Communication is critical to managing the client relationship. One way that communication occurs is the status meeting.

## Formal meetings

A status meeting can be a formal meeting that occurs on a regular schedule. This meeting is a good exercise in client service, as well as a good way to keep any outstanding projects on schedule, on budget, and at the level of quality you expect. A formal meeting should be limited to an hour in my opinion, because your clients probably don't have much time, and you should watch your charge hours here. All formal meetings should have an agenda to keep everyone on track and to keep the meetings efficient.

## Frequent telephone calls

A consulting firm president with a nontechnical background runs a very successful technology consulting practice. Part of his routine is overcommunication with clients. Not only does he have his MCSEs report on a regular basis what they've done and what they plan to do, but also the president takes this information and calls the client personally with an update. In cases where the work is continuing, the president updates the client daily. A frequent strategy of his is to say, "I'll call you in exactly 24 hours with another update." Indeed, he does call the next day at the same time, even if there is nothing new to report. His clients feel cared for. This approach is known as *massaging,* and it works.

## Status reports and invoices

Regular client status meetings are an important time for reviewing your regular status reports with the client. A status report may be nothing more than a site visit report that you complete each time you work at the client site, or the report may be a more formal document, such as a memorandum. I've also found the status meeting is an ideal time to present and review your regular billing invoices with the client.

# Contract Administration

You might want to farm out this management role to someone on your staff, even if it is to a part-time office manager you hire to help administer your successful MCSE consulting practice. Someone has to manage the letter of the law, as evidenced by the engagement letter, signed contract, and other contractual paperwork, such as approved change orders.

## Terms and conditions

The reason I mention contract administration is to protect you, the MCSE consultant. You've got to be familiar with the terms and conditions of the client relationship. There are some gray areas in the contract administration side of the business, but you need to have basic familiarity in terms of how you will be paid and how approval will be given for different types of work (such as work outside the scope of the project specifications). If you haven't done this in the past, put this book down now and don't return until you've thumbed through your client files. This review of your files will allow you to mentally revisit the terms and conditions of the working relationships you have with each of your clients as you proceed. I can also share a few insights with you about different consulting terms and conditions that I've written into contracts:

✦ **Project-based work** — This is a discrete relationship that has a limited scope and duration. The compensation paid to the consultant relates to the work performed on the project and nothing else.

✦ **Service contracts** — Perhaps you don't perform much project work and prefer to work with maintenance agreements (such as monthly printer maintenance). Service contracts are a wonderful way for MCSE consultants to even out their workloads and avoid much of the cyclical work pattern of project work. Note that the biggest challenge in service contracts is defining service levels and quality of work. For example, are return visits to fix the same problem billed separately from the main service contract?

✦ **Fixed-price arrangements** — It is possible that you want a fixed-price arrangement to be work project–based or ongoing.

✦ **Time and materials arrangements** — If the contractual relationship with the client is a time and materials arrangement, you bill by the hour and for materials with less regard for billing limits and budgets.

✦ **Per incident arrangements** — Perhaps you want an MCSE consulting practice where you charge per incident, for example, $150 flat fee per site visit.

## Reconciling planned against actual

If the contract calls for work items A, B, and C and you perform A, B, C, and D, you are at risk for not getting paid for D. I remember the painful scrutiny in staff meetings when I was with a Northwest technology-consulting firm. A co-worker was quick to point out statutory shortcomings pertaining to the MCSE consultants' performing work that wasn't explicitly specified in the client contracts. In fact, years later, it was discovered that she was advising the clients not to pay for work that fell into gray areas in the contract. The other MCSE consultants and I quickly learned about contract administration after that.

## Change orders

How will you evidence client work that is outside the scope of the contract? Will you accept change orders orally (such as via a telephone call) or in writing? Can the written form be an unsigned e-mail you receive or do you insist on a signed changed order that can be placed in the contract file? The choice is yours and, to be honest, may vary from situation to situation. The world of MCSE consulting is often filled with gray areas. Take my MCSE consulting practice. Whereas one client may be asked to submit written change orders, other clients whom I trust can call me on my cellular telephone and place a change order with me. The key point is to have some type of change-order mechanism in place for your MCSE consulting practice.

# Warranties

Part of contract administration is honoring the warranties associated with your work. This area for most MCSE consultants is left dangerously ambiguous with such phrases as "we'll make good on it" or "we adjust the bill for those things." If you live by ambiguity, I can assure you that you'll die an unambiguous death as an MCSE consultant: you won't get paid. Better to apply a little contract administration skill here; know what you are warranting and what you're not. I also advise you to cure what ails the client before they file a warranty claim against you.

# Single point of contact

In the professional services delivery business, which is what MCSE consulting is, you clearly want to have a formal contact for communication in the client organization. I've placed this discussion under contract administration, but it could fit under management skills, status meetings, or even project management. Having a formal communication conduit to a person with authority in the client organization is paramount to the success of the engagement. That's because you, the MCSE consultant, need to try to avoid serving several masters.

Taking direction from several client-side representatives is often confusing and can result in unexpected conflicts between the MCSE consultant and the client organization. How? The stories you hear from multiple client contacts are filtered and often don't represent the client organization's true position. One client-side employee might have a political agenda to miscommunicate about another client-side employee in order to gain some type of workplace victory. But more often, miscommunication is a case of the right hand not knowing what the left hand is doing. One department in the client organization may tell you, the MCSE consultant, to perform a task with a certain set of guidelines. Another client-side department representative may ask you to perform work that is at odds with the first instructions. It happens, and having a single point of contact with the client organization can avoid such miscommunication.

Another angle on the single point of contact issue is that your organization, the MCSE consulting firm, should offer a single point of contact for the client. A client wants good service, which includes clear and consistent communication. This type of communication can better occur if you or someone else in your MCSE consultant organization acts as a single point of contact for a given client.

# Role of subcontractors and vendors

Another contract administration issue in the MCSE consulting world is the use of subcontractors and vendors. In this section, I'll ask more questions than I have answers to because every situation with subcontractors and vendors is different. More importantly, you should visit with your business attorney when you plan to engage subcontractors and vendors on an MCSE consulting project. Are these subcontractors and vendors parties to your contract with the clients? Are the subcontractors and vendors allowed to communicate directly with the client? What liability issues exist with when you have a primary contract with client yet you use subcontractors and vendors to perform some or much of the work?

# Problem Solving

One of the things that separates consultants from technicians in the MCSE community is problem-solving capabilities. It's the added value of the consulting relationship versus the client's just calling a computer repair shop to fix a broken PC.

## What good MCSE consultants are great at

Not only are great MCSE consultants good at getting the business, managing the relationship, and doing the work, but they bring something extra to the table. This something varies by individual, but in the context of this section, it's problem solving. Great MCSE consultants don't necessarily need to know the answer; they just need to be able to solve the problems through research, grit, MCSE buddy calls, technical support, and so on. In essence, you fortify the trust you've already built with the client with the problem-solving capabilities I'm now suggesting you promote.

## Nonlinear thinking

One dimension of this problem solving discussion is nonlinear thinking. Nonlinear thinking is almost a day-to-day occurrence for the MCSE consultant. Here is an example from my own experience.

My longtime client had converted its Seattle-area offices from Integrated Services Digital Network (ISDN) to Digital Subscriber Line (DSL) and were using the virtual private network (VPN) capabilities of Windows NT Server 4.0 and the remote session capabilities of Terminal Services on Windows 2000 Server; this was a very nice setup for running this firm's corporate database between offices.

A few months later this firm acquired another company a couple hundred miles away in rural Washington, where the only high-speed connection possibilities were ISDN and dish-based wireless communications. The ISDN was cheaper and, given that I could recycle the now dormant ISDN router sitting in Seattle, I figured it seemed the way to go.

A local computer firm was retained to reprogram the Cisco ISDN router and to go out to this outback branch office and implement it. Not surprisingly, the small network then connected to the Internet just fine, and the users had access to point of presence (POP) e-mail and Web browsing. However, a VPN connection could not be established to the Windows NT Server back in Seattle. The local technician performed numerous other tests over four hours before determining that this older Cisco ISDN router, using an address translation scheme called Personal Address Translation (PAT) instead of the more conventional Network Address Translation (NAT), couldn't deal with Point-to-Point Tunneling Protocol (PPTP) traffic.

The technician hired in the rural community wanted to solve the problem in a linear fashion. She wanted to call Cisco, see if firmware could be downloaded to implement NAT functionality, upgrade the router, and so on.

Instead of doing that, I halted the work and met with the client. Taking a half step back allowed us to see the bigger picture. Given that DSL was coming to that rural community in three months and that the firm's database was being significantly upgraded in the same time frame, the better and nonlinear decision was to have the rural office stay with the ISDN access for POP e-mail and Web browsing for 90 days and to bring the rural office online with the VPN and Terminal Services solution after the database was upgraded. Everyone seemed pleased with this new approach. More importantly, the client gladly paid the consulting invoices associated with this exercise.

## Creative problem solving

I've always felt standardized tests like the SAT, LSAT, GMAT, and even the MCSE exams are good at measuring linear thinking and test-taking skills. But standardized exams as a whole do a poor job of measuring creative thinking. Perhaps Cisco in its demanding Certified Cisco Internetwork Expert (CCIE) program recognized this when it added a two-day practicum performed by visits to the Cisco labs (for example, the Cisco lab in San Jose, California). The labs are interactive. The first day you fix a broken wide area network (WAN) only to return a second day and find the WAN broken again. The idea is to test creative problem solving. Hats off to Cisco!

A true MCSE consultant will consider creative problem-solving activities to be part of the job. At a minimum, you need develop your creative problem solving and add it to your bag of MCSE consulting tricks.

# Rule of Ten: Client Treatment

As part of your engagement management approach, I suggest that you treat your clients ten times better than you would want to be treated. If you stick to that rule, which really allows you to put yourself in your client's shoes, you'll do fine.

## Guest Sermon — The Client Speaks

If you really want to learn about engagement management, what could be better than hearing from a client. For this chapter's Guest Sermon, I asked someone I know well from the business community. Dick Brandenburg is the Executive Director of the Port of Bremerton. He has had a career in real estate and has been involved primarily in high-rise office building development in Seattle for the past 30 years. He is presently developing activities for an industrial park, the 6,200-foot runway at Bremerton National Airport, and the expansion of the 400-slip Port Orchard Marina. He is a slave to the Ports Computer System, which is the "interpreter" of the daily business. Dick is a demanding but fair client to those that serve him. Here are some words from Dick that I believe you'll respect:

*The world of computer technology is the great equalizer in the business world, because the all-too-self-important chief of the company is brought to his or her knees and the company's activities stop when the plug is pulled (and once the plug was literally pulled) on a stack of gray and black boxes that are back in a corner of the office that was once used to store the janitor supplies.*

*I remember items of business that our best service techs have never even seen, such as carbon paper, a mimeograph machine, and an operable Selectromatic, and I have found by experience that those techs that show up that do remember these symbols of antiquity either are not competent or are so slow that we can't afford them. When our system is not working, we're just like that incompetent service tech, slow and unable to do our work. I have traveled to Russia on business and have had to use the services of an interpreter and have experienced the awkwardness of having the interpreter leave the room. Communication stops, and the two parties just sit there and wait until the interpreter returns. It's is the same with a broken system.*

*Our bookkeeping requirement is to keep track of our 400 marina tenants, our 150 hangar tenants, and our 600-acre industrial park with its 95 tenants. We also have the usual business requirements for a computer system that allows 12 desks in the office and 5 satellite stations to communicate to the stack of gray and black boxes in the corner. Whenever we can't do that our in-house tech head gets very grouchy and runs to check the plug. Once it is determined that the plug is in, we call the contracted service company and hope that the technician who spent several hours analyzing our system the last time is still with the company.*

*We have had more that the usual episodes in finding a consultant that will perform to our satisfaction for two elementary reasons: We are geographically isolated from the mainstream supply of experts, and we are on a tight budget and used to think that we couldn't afford the best on that budget. We were wrong. I will give you a sequence of consultant contacts that we have had over the past three years. This isn't a mystery novel, so I will tell you at the beginning that this story has a happy ending.*

*We knew that we needed a system such as Novell to bring us up to a higher level of performance. We called a local three-man shop, and one consultant showed up hours after the appointed time to discuss the mission. This guy spent weeks at our office with actually a day or two at each workstation trying to set our system up right.*

*One day I was looking over his shoulder watching him peck away, when it dawned on me that this guy remembered carbon paper and even the Selectromatic. We called local associates and were referred to a whiz that had his office about 45 miles away. We then called a highly regarded consultant in Bellevue who was interested in coming 75 miles to interview. The Bellevue consultant was the ultimate in business sophistication. He arrived on time, was well groomed, spoke fluently, and surveyed the scene efficiently. He sent us a bid to do all we needed, for $125 per hour. So we contracted with the local guy for $75 per hour. He was very likable, and since he was a one-man shop, we forgave him for not returning phone calls for a day at a time or for arriving hours late or for telling us that he would not be available for a week at a time. He was very hard working when he was with us, and we trusted him so much that we let him lock up when he would leave at 2 a.m. However, the one-man shop burned himself out, went to work for someone far away, and left us in limbo. And further, our $75 per hour guy, took 250 hours to do the job that the $125 per hour company man could have done in 125 hours. You figure it out. It is no consolation that this story has been repeated thousands of times in this new world without carbon paper. We now have service consultants that are knowledgeable, have backup, and are reliable. We like them because they are reliable in all aspects of our expectations, and we don't have to show them how to lock up at 2 a.m.*

# MCSE Project Management

A critical part of managing the consulting engagement is project management. All MCSE consulting engagements, whether ongoing or truly project-based, benefit from project management. This section of the book defines project management by looking at specifications, which drive the creation of the work breakdown structure, which drives the project schedule.

## Project management secrets

Being a good MCSE project manager, a bona fide role in the MCSE consulting community, is more than writing reports and creating charts. There are a few secrets to the project management craft that I'll share with you here.

### Balancing time, budget, and quality

A good project manager tries to achieve high marks in three categories: time (being on time), budget (being on budget), and quality (delivering what the client expects). The trick is to balance these three dimensions, which are often at odds with each other. In Figure 9-1, I show the project management triangle that depicts the legs of time, budget, and quality.

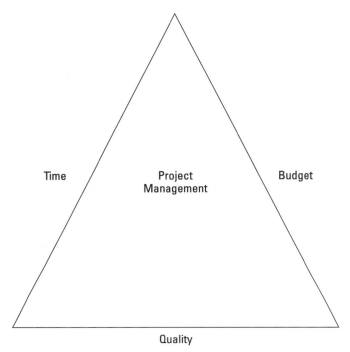

**Figure 9-1:** Time, budget, and quality legs form a triangle.

## Crashing

The bottom line with project management is to get the work done. Often you have to crash a project (apply extra resources or cut back on quality) to achieve this goal. In technology in particular, crashing a project to reach completion is not uncommon. Crashing a project is done in several different ways:

✦ **Budget busters** — If the critical deadline is time, a project management ploy is to throw money at the maligned project. That means hiring more laborers on a construction project or hiring more contractors (developers and so on) on a technology project. I've seen cases where the project manager doubled the size of the staff to get a project done on time.

✦ **Missed deadlines** — Another way to crash a project is to let the date slip, but to stay on budget and at the same level of quality. This option is much less common in the world of project management as the emphasis often is placed on meeting deadlines more than on meeting the requirements of any other category.

✦ **Cut feature sets** — A common project crashing approach in software development is not only to freeze the feature set, but also to cut features not critical to get the software shipped. You've unknowingly or unwittingly seen this in Microsoft solutions you've purchased. Cut features typically appear as a new features in the next software release. How does this relate to general product management in the MCSE consulting field? Often in the professional services area, the scope of the work is scaled back in order to crash to project. That is, the project is effectively made smaller by reducing the tasks that must be completed and the deliverables that are expected.

**Tip**     The law of crashing is this. You can trade off any leg of the project management triangle (time, budget, or quality) to crash the remaining two legs.

## Backward pass

My favorite trick in project management is the backward pass. All too often, when people sit down to create a project schedule, they work from left to right. That is, they start at time period zero and work toward the project deadline. This approach tends to create schedule creep as people add more time to tasks, a true luxury in project management.

A backward pass is project scheduling going from right to left. You start the project schedule with the final deadline and work your way left, determining what day you should start the project.

**Tip**     Be aware that a backward pass when used to determine the start date of the project usually results in a start date of yesterday.

## Showstoppers

The following is a short, but not inclusive, list of maladies that can negatively impact the success of your MCSE consulting engagement. Be aware of these showstoppers and be prepared to take corrective action as necessary:

✦ **Too many opinions** — This is the case of collaboration taking the form of too many cooks in the kitchen. Leadership is necessary to prevent a project or engagement from being bogged down in a quagmire of unfocused work efforts.

✦ **Inflexible baseline project schedule** — Being too focused on a static project schedule that doesn't allow for the ebbs and flows of real-world timing adjustments can bog down an engagement. Stay flexible as the last project schedule you print will look far different from the first project schedule (baseline) your create. It's natural for a project schedule to change during the course of a project, so be flexible.

✦ **Vendor and service provider delays**—You've done everything right on your end, but the telecommunications company is late getting the DSL service to your client site. Being dependent on third-party service providers is an uncontrollable area of project management that can truly be a showstopper.

✦ **Additional (and extracontractual) engagement work**—This is the "Oh by the way" method clients sometimes use to add work on to an engagement. Not only does the added work delay the project, but also it can result in billing disputes if you perform work outside the scope of your contractual engagement.

✦ **Phase skipping to save time and money**—If you eliminate a critical phase to save either time or money (or both) on an engagement, you haven't really accomplished the project as intended.

✦ **Technological incompatibilities**—Since MCSE consultants work primarily with technology, the likelihood that you'll discover technology on projects that has incompatible hardware and software is entirely plausible. You must exercise great care not to let software and hardware compatibilities be engagement showstoppers.

✦ **Pirated software**—It's not in your best interest to perform work on an MCSE consulting engagement where unlicensed software is being deployed and used. Why bother with the mess when there are plenty of honest consulting opportunities for you. And don't ever loan your software to clients with the understanding that clients will order their own copies. They won't.

## Specifications

Specifications are the document that defines the work at a granular level. In construction, specifications are the quantities ordered, the length of wood cut, and so on. With technology, the specifications are the scope of work. Scoping was discussed Chapter 7. An example of specifications might contain the following Statement of Work (SOW)—"Develop a relational database system to drive business process in the firm. Adequately train staff."

## Work breakdown structure

The work breakdown structure (WBS) is based on the information provided by the specifications. The WBS organizes work into manageable groups of tasks. The WBS is the way in which tasks are listed in a Gantt chart. A WBS, based on the sample specification mentioned in the previous section, looks like Table 9-1.

| | | Table 9-1<br>**Work Breakdown Structure** | |
|---|---|---|
| *Task* | *Subtask* | *Description* |
| 1.0 | | Start Database Development |
| | 1.10 | Needs Analysis |
| | 1.20 | Purchase Database |
| | 1.30 | Install Database Engine |
| | 1.4 | Start Database Development |
| | 1.4.1 | Review Needs Analysis Documentation |
| | 1.4.2 | Create Data Dictionary |
| | 1.4.3 | Create Active Directory Schema Modification Plan |
| | 1.5 | Install ISV Database Applications |
| 2.0 | | Database Training |
| | 2.1 | Assess Training Needs |
| | 2.2 | Develop and Publish Database Training RFP |
| | 2.3 | Contract with Database Training Firm |
| | 2.4 | Develop Database Training Program |
| 3.0 | | Testing |
| | 3.1 | Develop Test Plan |
| | 3.2 | Create Model Office |
| 4.0 | | Database Rollout to Control Group |

# Project schedule

The outcome most identifiable with the practice of project management is the project schedule. The two types of project schedules are Gantt charts and critical path method (CPM) charts. In this section, both the Gantt and CPM charts are shown for the database development example started in the previous specification section and detailed in the WBS in Table 9-1. As mentioned once before, the WBS drives the project schedule, which is exactly what I'm doing with the database development example in this discussion. The list of tasks in the WBS must be assigned durations and resources. Set this information on a chart, and you have a project schedule.

## Gantt

Gantt charts are basically horizontal bar charts that show activity against the y-axis of time. For example, a two-week task would be a horizontal bar that occupies two weeks of time. This is shown in Figure 9-2, which you will create in step-by-step fashion later in this chapter.

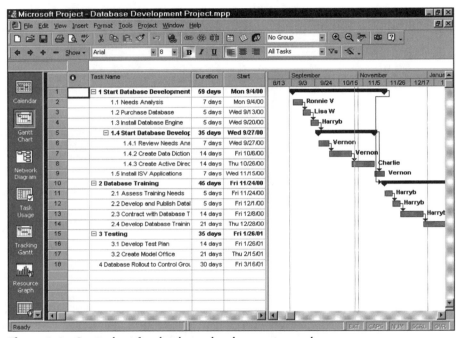

**Figure 9-2:** Gantt chart for database development sample

**Tip**　A Gantt chart is the easiest form of project schedule to understand, but it does not explicitly show relationships between tasks. That is, if Task 1.15 is a predecessor of Task 2.43 in a large project, that dependency would not be apparent in a Gantt chart.

## Critical path method

The project management diagram chart of connected boxes uses the critical path method (CPM). Task boxes are connected to each other by lines. The longest path through the project, measured by time, is the critical path. Tasks on the critical path have no slack time or room for slipping the schedule without affecting the entire project. The CPM chart (also called the network diagram view in Microsoft Project 2000) for the database development example is shown in Figure 9-3.

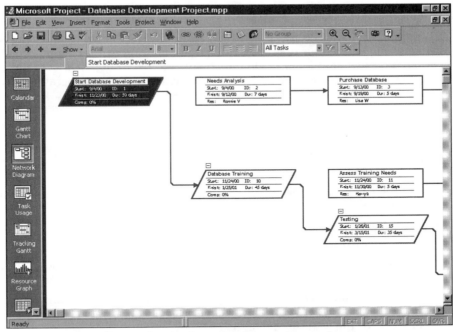

**Figure 9-3:** CPM diagram for database development example

**Tip**    The CPM project schedule is considered more sophisticated than the Gantt chart, but it doesn't show time durations very well. The length of line connecting the task boxes has no relationship to the duration of the task. Furthermore, a CPM project schedule has no time axis.

In the next section, you will develop a Gantt chart and a CPM diagram for the sample database project in this chapter.

# Using Microsoft Project

MCSE consultants working on medium and large technology implementations will want to purchase, install, and master the use of Microsoft Project (in this book, I profile Microsoft Project 2000, but the product is frequently updated). Microsoft Project is a big-league project management tool that can be used to manage everything from pipelines across Alaska and multimillion-dollar technology implementations down to relatively modest BackOffice implementations in the five-figure budget range. Microsoft Project is overkill for smaller technology projects such as Small Business Server. I speak towards managing small projects in the "Other Project Management Tools" section later in the chapter.

## Defining Microsoft Project

As a program, Microsoft Project is relatively mature, exceeding ten years in age and evolving through numerous upgrades during that time. Microsoft Project was originally released as version 1.0 in 1990. At its heart, Microsoft Project is a resource-based project management system running on Microsoft desktop operating systems such as Windows 2000. It has the following features:

✦ **Calendar** — You may view task information set against a traditional 30-day gyfcalendar.

✦ **Gantt Chart** — This is the default view in Microsoft Project and shows tasks set against time.

✦ **Network Diagram** — This shows the critical path method project schedule view. Task boxes are connected by lines.

✦ **Task Usage** — This is a spread view of tasks. Tasks are listed in a table format similar to a WBS.

✦ **Tracking Gantt** — This is a modified view of the Gantt Chart to show percentage of completion on the list of tasks.

✦ **Resource Graph** — This view shows resource allocations in a histogram view. This is the chart where you learn you've assigned someone to work 80 hours per week for the next three months.

✦ **Resource Sheet** — This is a table view of the resources you have available. Resources are listed by type, such as people (by different labor classifications), machines, conference rooms/facilities, and so on.

✦ **Resource Usage** — This is a table view of how you've committed your resources.

✦ **Custom views, reports** — Microsoft Project is very strong in the customization area, especially with views and reporting.

**Tip**    Microsoft Project was designed to be used in the following fashion. First, you enter your resources such as labor units (people) or machinery. You then enter tasks with durations and assign resources to the tasks. You proceed to manage the resources as much as the tasks themselves throughout the project so that no one resource becomes overburdened and the project can finish on time.

## Installing Microsoft Project 2000

After purchasing Microsoft Project 2000, you install it by running `Setup.exe` from the CD-ROM. The Setup Wizard behaves similarly to that of other Microsoft products, where you click Next and accept the typical installation defaults. You will need to run Microsoft Project setup a second time if you want to install Microsoft Project

Central, a project management collaboration tool (which allows the coordination of multiple projects by a single project manager). A good source for more information on Microsoft Project Central is the *Microsoft Project 2000 Bible* by Elaine Marmel, published by IDG Books Worldwide, Inc.

**Tip**     You can download a 60-day version of Microsoft Project 2000 from Microsoft's Web site (http://www.microsoft.com) or install it from the TechNet monthly CD-ROM. This is a great way to try before you buy or, better yet, manage a one-time project that is 60 days or less in duration.

## Step-by-step use

In this section, you will create a project schedule for the sample database project being used in this chapter. I assume you have installed either the full version of Microsoft Project or the 60-day trial version. As you will see in a few steps and in reference to Table 9-2, the task numbering that matches the WBS numbering is automatic. The task description is entered in the Task Name column. The Resources information is entered in the Resource Names column. The duration information is entered in the Duration column in the Gantt chart (this information is entered as days, but other time scales are possible, including hours and minutes).

| | | Table 9-2 | | |
| | | **Project Task List** | | |
| **Task** | **Subtask** | **Description** | **Resources** | **Duration** |
|---|---|---|---|---|
| 1.0 | | Start Database Development | Harryb | (Sum of subtasks) |
| | 1.1 | Needs Analysis | Ronnie V. | 7 |
| | 1.2 | Purchase Database | Lisa W. | 5 |
| | 1.3 | Install Database Engine | Harryb | 5 |
| | 1.4 | Start Database Development | Vernon | (Sum of subtasks) |
| | 1.4.1 | Review Needs Analysis Documentation | Vernon | 7 |
| | 1.4.2 | Create Data Dictionary | Vernon | 14 |
| | 1.4.3 | Create Active Directory Schema Modification Plan | Charlie | 14 |
| | 1.5 | Install ISV Database Applications | Vernon | 7 |

*Continued*

| Table 9-2 *(continued)* | | | | |
| --- | --- | --- | --- | --- |
| **Task** | **Subtask** | **Description** | **Resources** | **Duration** |
| 2.0 | | Database Training | Harryb | (Sum of subtasks) |
| | 2.1 | Assess Training Needs | Harryb | 5 |
| | 2.2 | Develop and Publish Database Training RFP | Harryb | 5 |
| | 2.3 | Contract with Database Training Firm | Harryb | 14 |
| | 2.4 | Develop Database Training Program | Joan | 21 |
| 3.0 | | Testing | Charlie | (Sum of subtasks) |
| | 3.1 | Develop Test Plan | Charlie | 14 |
| | 3.2 | Create Model Office | Charlie | 21 |
| 4.0 | | Database Rollout to Control Group | Charlie | 30 |

To create a project schedule in Microsoft Project 2000:

1. Click Start ➪ Programs ➪ Microsoft Project. Microsoft Project 2000 starts in the Gantt Chart view.

2. Save the project schedule as a file ("Database Development Project") by selecting Save from the File menu.

3. Enter the information in Table 9-2. The result should look like Figure 9-4.

4. In order to create the appropriate subtasks for the database development project, Microsoft Project makes use of outlining, which you may have used in Microsoft Word. Observe in Table 9-2 that subtasks 1.1 to 1.5 are beneath task 1.0. In Microsoft Project, highlight rows 2-5. Click the indent arrow icon on the toolbar (the right arrow on the left side of the formatting toolbar).

5. Based on the subtask information in Table 9-2, complete the remaining subtask relationships for the sample database project.

6. Click Tools ➪ Options. The Options dialog box appears. Click the View tab, and select the Show outline number check box. Click OK. This adds the WBS numbering to your Task Name column. Verify the WBS numbers are correct against the information in Table 9-2.

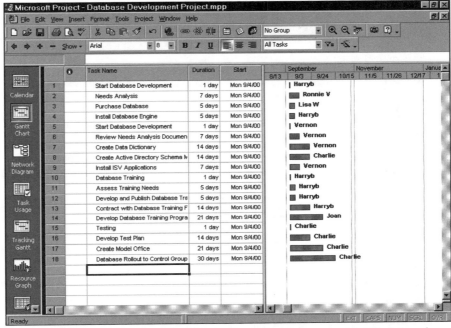

**Figure 9-4:** Base task information for database development project is entered.

7. Enter today's date (for example, 9/4/00) in the Start cell for the first task.

8. Highlight all tasks in the Task Name column. Click Edit ➪ Link Tasks to create a predecessor/successor task relationship. You have now created the Gantt chart view of the sample database development project. Your screen should look similar to Figure 9-5.

You may click on the other Microsoft Project views, such as the Network Diagram, to see the sample database development project schedule from different views. You might recall that Figure 9-3 shows the CPM or network diagram view of this project.

The intent of this step-by-step exercise was to show you how easy it is to manage your MCSE consulting engagements with Microsoft Project 2000. This is a very powerful project management tool. In the next section, I show you some timesavers in the form of the built-in sample templates that ship with Microsoft Project.

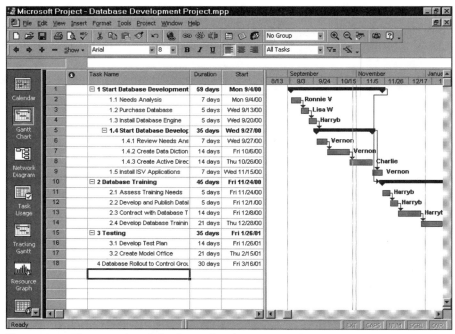

**Figure 9-5:** The completed database development project

## Sample templates

Give the Microsoft Project program managers credit. They have included sample templates as timesavers for the MCSE consultant. By creating sample projects that are already formatted, you don't suffer from the blank screen syndrome, where you rightfully ask, "What do I do now?" Follow these steps to use a preconfigured sample template in Microsoft Project 2000:

1. Assuming Microsoft Project 2000 is running, click File ➪ New.

2. Click the Project Template tab in the New dialog box.

3. The following sample templates, included with Microsoft Project, are displayed:

   - Commercial Construction
   - Engineering
   - Infrastructure Deployment
   - Microsoft Project 2000 Deployment
   - MSF Application Development

- New Business
- New Product
- Office 2000 Deployment
- Project Office
- Residential Construction
- Software Development
- Windows 2000 Deployment

4. For the purpose of this example, select the Windows 2000 Deployment project template. Click OK. The Windows Installer will install the Windows 2000 Deployment template, which appears with a preconfigured project schedule of common tasks, as shown in Figure 9-6.

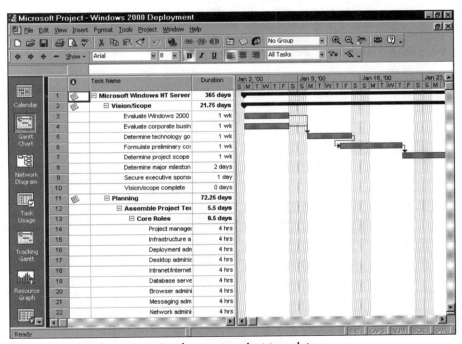

**Figure 9-6:** Windows 2000 Deployment project template

You can add, delete, and modify these templates' tasks to your own needs.

 **Tip**    To learn more about project management, see the excellent online help system in Microsoft Project 2000. It's a project management textbook.

# Other Project Management Tools

Microsoft Project is a huge program. In fact, some MCSE consultants have niched on Microsoft Project 2000 itself as trainers, project managers, and developers (who customize Microsoft Project 2000). However, not all projects require a General Patton–level tool. For the rest of us, working on small projects might suggest the use of a small project management tool.

## Microsoft Outlook 2000

In the keep–it–simple school of project management, I typically recommend using Microsoft Outlook 2000. Just enter your tasks as appointments, as seen in Figure 9-7.

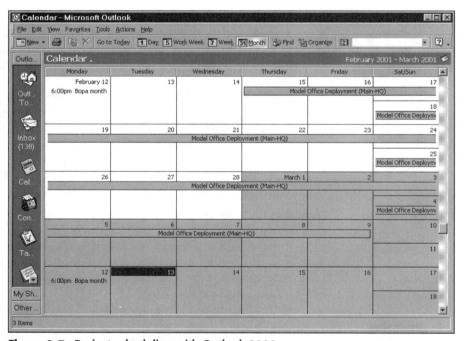

**Figure 9-7:** Project scheduling with Outlook 2000

**Cross-Reference**   Microsoft Outlook 2000 is discussed in greater detail as an MCSE consulting platform in Chapter 17.

Something you should consider implementing is Outlook Team Folders. Outlook Team Folders, which are essentially public folders that have been preprogrammed, can be downloaded from Microsoft at `www.microsoft.com/outlook`. After you download and run the self-extracting executable file for Outlook Team Folders, you implement Outlook Team Folders directly from Outlook 2000:

1. Start Outlook 2000.

2. Select File ⇨ New ⇨ Team Folder in Outlook 2000. The Outlook Team Folder Wizard runs. It will create a sophisticated public folder application under Public Folders in Outlook 2000.

3. Click Next after reading the Outlook Team Folder Wizard welcome notice.

4. Select from the following Team Folders that are available for your implementation in the Outlook Team Folder Wizard and click Next:

   • **Team Project**—This helps a project team work closely together by providing a shared calendar, contacts list, task list, a discussion forum, and a document library. I have used this Team Folder and found it to be very impressive.

   • **Discussion Forum**—This is a bulletin board where project team members can exchange ideas in threaded conversations.

   • **Document Library**—This is a place where project team members can share documents with each other.

   • **Team Calendar**—This is a place where project team members can post appointments, meetings, and events that pertain to the project team.

   • **Team Contacts**—This is a place where project team members can share important contacts.

   • **Team Tasks**—This is a shared task list that project team members can use to plan projects together.

5. Type a name for the Team Folder and then click Next.

6. Click Choose Folder and select a public folder where the Team Folder will reside.

7. Replace `<YourServerName>` with the NetBIOS name of your server in the Web Page destination field.

8. Click Next.

9. Select members for the team, set permission levels, and then click Next.

10. Click Yes when the Security Warning dialog box appears warning you that the Microsoft Outlook View Control (consisting of the files olTFACL.ocx and oltfacl.inf) will be installed over the Internet (you must have a live Internet connection to complete the Outlook Team Folders installation).

You are now ready to use Outlook Team Folders for assisting in the management of your MCSE consulting engagements.

## Visio

Another Microsoft product, Visio, has a project management template that is also useful. I rate this product as slightly more sophisticated than Outlook 2000 and less sophisticated than Microsoft Project 2000. In Figure 9-8, I display the project management template for Visio.

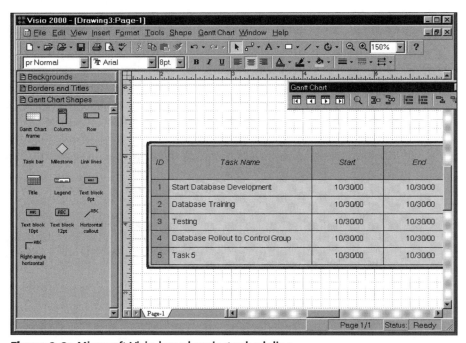

**Figure 9-8:** Microsoft Visio-based project scheduling

## eProject.com

One enterprising dot-com, eProject.com, offers online project management collaboration for project teams. This capability allows widely dispersed project teams to work together on a project by collaborating over the Internet with eProject.com. The basic idea is for you to log on and access your project area. You can communicate about the project and make additions to the project schedule. eProject.com is displayed in Figure 9-9.

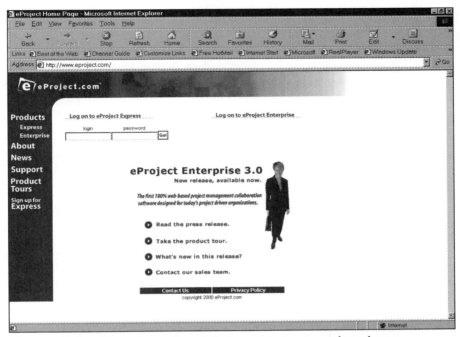

**Figure 9-9:** Consider using online project management portals such as eProject.com to assist you in managing your MCSE consulting engagements.

## Summary

This chapter focused on the critical MCSE consulting area of client engagement management. If you can't manage your engagements, you aren't fit for duty as an MCSE consultant in the long run. Sound management of your consulting engagements is an undeniable reality of running a profitable MCSE consulting practice. The good news is that every day, MCSE consultants are excelling in the client engagement management area using many of the techniques described herein. These MCSE consultants enjoy profitable operations. The first part of the chapter focused on soft skills such as communication. The second part of the chapter focused on hard skills such as project management.

✦     ✦     ✦

# Managing the Client Relationship

Т his chapter is, of course, the successor to Chapter 9 on engagement management. The topic at hand is managing the client relationship. That's relationship with a capital *R*, and this means managing communication, feelings, perceptions, and many other things not included on the MCSE certification exams.

## Revisiting Human Communications

In your freshman year of college you may have had to take a mandatory communications 101 course that emphasized sender/receiver (S/R) communications, such as the type presented in Figure 10-1.

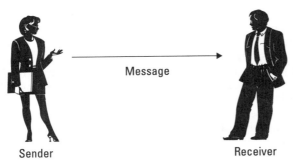

Message

Sender

Receiver

**Figure 10-1:** Sender/receiver communications model

The basic premise with the S/R model is that a sender "sends" a message that is "received" by the receiver. The model becomes more complex when the receiver hears something different than the sender intends. When you think about it, both human communications and modern networking are based on this basic S/R model. With human communications, typically one person speaks (sends a message) while the other person hears (receives a message). Now relate this to a computer network. A sending host sends a message (in the form of a packet) to a receiving host. The receiving host accepts the packet and typically replies with an acknowledgement packet. After processing the packet, it's common for the second host (the original receiving host) to send a packet of information back to the first host (which likely requested some information be returned as part of the communication sequence). And, just like when human communications experience interruptions, network communication models become more complex when packet collisions occur, packets are dropped, or noise interferes.

This procedure for communicating is very similar to how humans communicate between each other, how we take turns to talk. Don't believe me? Let me use token-ring networking as an example. Turn the clock back in time and look at how American Natives managed communications with a talking stick. When you held the talking stick, you talked, and the others listened. This is analogous to how hosts on a token-ring network communicate. The host holding the token is allowed to communicate on the network.

I've emphasized communication skills as much as technical skills for defining the prototypical successful MCSE consultant. I stand by that base argument now as before, because communication is the answer to my basic question as to why widely divergent salary ranges may exist for two comparable MCSEs standing side by side.

The first MCSE is making in excess of $100K per year as a consultant. The second MCSE is making $40K per year as a break-fix technician. Both passed all of their exams, are experienced in the field, and considered technically competent. It is likely that the first MCSE is a superior communicator compared to the second MCSE.

In this example, the first MCSE doesn't necessarily have a larger vocabulary or use more technical terminology than the second MCSE has or uses. Rather, the first MCSE communicates clearly (as in straightforward with no embellishment) and consistently. The first MCSE still communicates bad news, such as "You'll need a new server" or "I'll be one hour late." But because this form of communicating is direct, the client receives the same message the consultant intended to send. That's the definition of communication.

The second MCSE in my example is the one that walks in, performs the work, and leaves without telling anyone at the client site what work was accomplished, what the next steps in the process are, and so on.

# Rule of Ten: Communications

Communicate with your clients frequently on a clear and consistent basis. For clients with whom you have an ongoing relationship, communicate every ten business days. I selected this number as it fits with my style of checking in with my portfolio a couple of times per month. I've found that not adhering to the MCSE consulting Rule of Ten for communications results in the following outcomes:

✦ **Crises-based negative communications**—If you don't proactively communicate a couple of times per month with your active clients, the communication channel can take on a consistently negative tone. That is, the only time you communicate with your client is when there is a problem. Perhaps you've had such clients that call only when something is broken! This is not the firm foundation of communication you're seeking as an MCSE consultant.

✦ **Manufactured information**—I've also found that if I don't proactively initiate communications a couple of times per month with my clients that, with the passage of time, clients will start to manufacture information, resulting in an unintentional fabrication. If you don't provide a constant stream of communication, your clients will create information to fill this void and honor their perceptions of what the communications should be. In other words, a lack of clear and consistent communications from you will create a void in the client communication model that will be filled by your clients. That sounds risky to me. I'll never forget a time when I was breaking my own rule and not being communicative with my client. Having not heard from me and having misinterpreted my parting comment one visit about performing surgery on a server, the business owner called one day to find out if I was out of the hospital yet. He had confused my surgery comments in his own mind and, when he didn't hear from me again, assumed I'd gone into the hospital. We enjoyed a good chuckle when we found out that information had been manufactured, but it sure illustrated the power of imaginary information. You should strive to prevent this with constant communication because the outcome might not always be so humorous.

By saying that you should communicate with clients a couple of times per month, I don't mean to suggest you need to sit at a telephone and "power call" for several hours straight. Mix it up. Some weeks call a few clients. Other weeks e-mail a note to other clients. The communications can often just be a quick, "How is it going?" I've found clients appreciate the gesture, and such behavior has resulted in additional work for me.

# Defining Personality Types

At some level, all clients are different. Clients are human beings and come in all shapes, sizes, and personalities. You need to appreciate that and, more important, need to know what you're dealing with on a client-by-client basis. A rundown of different client types follows to increase your awareness (the first solid step toward better communication with your clients). You should modify your communication style accordingly to work with the various client personality types you're serving.

✦ **Passive** — Mellow people, who are passive in nature, tend to like to work with other mellow people. Hint: Tone down your aggressiveness when dealing with such clients.

✦ **Aggressive** — These hard chargers will roll right over you if you let them. Hint: Drink a triple espresso on the way to these client sites to reveal your aggressive attitude. More often than not, aggressive clients respect aggressiveness, but use your best judgment as each situation is unique.

✦ **Perceptive** — This client relies on their intuition and judgment about people. You're being watched and judged. Hint: It takes a while to earn the trust of perceptive people, but once you do, it's typically easy to keep.

✦ **Listener** — Perhaps you've worked with these analytical thinkers who take it all in, process what they've heard, and then make decisions. Hint: These people typically like a lot of information. You can pour it on here and arm these people with more than enough information for them to process.

✦ **Talker** — These quick decision makers don't desire or need all the information given to them. Hint: You're not going to shout down a talker. Let them talk and steer them toward decision making. How do you steer a talker? It's been my experience that talkers like to think that they created the proposed solution, so you might steer them by saying, "As you were just proposing …". In that way, you lead them into arriving at a decision.

# Personality Assessment Tools

There are numerous tools available for assessing different personality types, communication strengths and weaknesses, and so on. Many of these are in a testing format. You complete the survey or test and have it scored. One of the best that I've worked with is the Myers-Briggs Type Indicator. The guest sermon that follows goes into great detail about this tool.

**Note**    I've used and had used on me these personality tests as part of the recruitment process. When interviewing for a job, I've completed the Myers-Briggs Type Indicator. It allows you and your prospective employer to decide if there is a good fit between you. You might want to use such tools when you're recruiting for staff in your own MCSE consulting firm.

## Guest Sermon — Intellectual Capital Tool

It is with great pleasure I present the following discussion from someone I've admired for years — Bill Bergman, a business consultant and Change Agent Coach with Bergman & Associates, Inc., in Chico, California (billbergman@email.msn.com). Bill extends my discussion on client types by adding his wisdom:

*Thanks, Harry. This is a subject I love to share with others. Leadership, change, and empowerment affect individual and interpersonal effectiveness, personal and professional development of intellectual capital, and bottom-line satisfaction. Millions of people have experienced some level of the Myers-Briggs Type Indicator (MBTI) globally and in at least 17 different languages. This intellectual capital tool, developed by Isabel Myers and Katherine Briggs, is based on the writings and insights of C.G. Jung, the Swiss psychiatrist and spiritualist, who studied people's behaviors and invited them to honor each other's differences. Like any tool, its usefulness and accuracy depend greatly on the craftsman's creativity and innovation and his/her practical and common-sense application both personally and professionally.*

*The MBTI describes personality preference styles with four bipolar scales that occur in daily interpersonal and intrapersonal interactions both proactively and reactively.*

✦ *Extrovert and Introvert focus on our personal energy level.*

✦ *Sensate and Intuitive are perceptions of information.*

✦ *Thinking and Feeling/Valuing differentiate decision-making styles.*

✦ *Judging/Organized and Perceiving manage daily lifestyle.*

*One's personal preferences may vary as to strength and application. Preferring one more than the other is similar to people preferring to be either right-handed or left-handed. Most of us are not ambidextrous. We have both hands, and we use both hands. However, one is more effective, and the other is less efficient. One is natural and habitual; and the other takes more time and effort to accomplish similar tasks. The former is the leader, the later the supporter. How we manage all eight personality preferences, shown in the sidebar table, will both indicate our maturity and impact the global world.*

| Extroverts (E) | Introverts (I) |
| --- | --- |
| Talk things out | Think things internally |
| Actions and stories | Ideas and values |
| Energy = outside focus | Energy = inside focus |
| Speak to think and feel | Think and feel to speak |
| When speaking — not necessarily decided | When thinking — not necessarily shared |
| [Exaggerate and repeat] | [Withhold and contain] |

*Continued*

Continued

| Sensing (S) | Intuition (N) |
|---|---|
| Five senses, experience | "Sixth sense," options |
| Past and present | Future and present |
| Facts and details | Big picture and patterns |
| Practicality | Innovation |
| Live life and let live now | Change and rearrange life in the future |
| [Misses big picture] | [Misses details] |

| Thinking (T) | Feeling (F) |
|---|---|
| Objective — air | Subjective — supportive |
| Impersonal and brief | Personal and friendly |
| Analytical truth, principles, competency | Human values, needs, spirituality |
| Intellectual criticism | Loyalty and caring |
| Costs and benefits | Value-added |
| [Can be insensitive] | [Avoids conflict] |

| Judging (J) | Perceiving (P) |
|---|---|
| Focus on decisions | Focus on information |
| Thinking — feeling | Sensing — intuition |
| Closure with planning and systems | Possibilities with brainstorming |
| Finish tasks — closers | Begin tasks — starters |
| [Decide too soon] | [Inform too much] |
| [Right/Wrong] | [Procrastination] |

*Some people believe their own style is often the other's preferred style. We know in physics that opposites attract and the like repels. Knowing, understanding, and honoring one another's differences empower the individual, the work group, the corporation, the family, and the relationship. Such meaningful, internal, and external communication and awareness heighten productivity, creativity, innovation, research, teamwork, and profitability.*

*The MBTI has practical applications for leadership and management within corporations, education, personal and career development, cultural understanding, research, and spirituality. Further professional information about the MBTI may be obtained by contacting the Association for Psychological Type (APT) at* www.aptcentral.org *or calling (847) 375-4717.*

# Identifying Personality Strengths and Weaknesses

Your ability to be smart and assess both your and your client's personality strengths and weaknesses will directly affect your financial bottom line as an MCSE consultant. In other words, miscommunications will cost you money you could have otherwise earned from your clients.

There is no real trick here other than to devote seriously the energies necessary to attempt to assess personality strengths and weaknesses. Keeping a score card on a pad of paper listing the personality strengths and weaknesses of each of your clients is a useful idea, but obviously, such information is for your use only, is very sensitive, and should remain private.

# Building Successful Relationships

On the whole, you'll be judged as an MCSE consultant not for what you know but for the business relationships you build. Talk to management consultants who aren't necessarily practicing a technical craft, and you'll consistently hear the emphasis that's placed on strong consultant/client relationships.

The outcome of building successful relationships with your clients is trust. Trust between a consultant and client will survive operating system releases, application versions, and anything else in the fast-changing world of technology.

# Failed Engagements

My experience has shown that more client engagements will fail from poor relationships than bad technology. While blue screens happen, being terminated for a server crash is often not the real reason for a termination. Rather, the client relationship was most likely the trouble, whether you knew it or not. When a technical failure occurs, that's often used as the excuse for the termination of the MCSE consultant.

**Cross-Reference** You might recall Steve Bloom's guest sermon in Chapter 1 spoke towards blaming environments in the world of MCSE consulting.

# The Body Politic

Being a consultant instead of a technician working behind closed server room doors means you have to address politics. Human beings are political animals. Put two people together in the same room and, poof, you've got politics, as one person attempts to outmaneuver another and so on. In the context of the politics encountered by MCSE consultants, some people try to elevate their status via maneuvers such as telling someone one thing in private only to contradict that statement in a larger meeting.

The good news is that you don't have to be a master politician to be an MCSE consultant. Political skills are critical with top management at large corporations. However, you're likely to have your political skill set tested from time to time as you follow client instructions you may not agree with. For example, MCSE consultants are often brought in to situations where they assist in the termination of an existing network administrator and the recruitment of the replacement. You might be the one the business owner has hired to change the soon-to-be-terminated employee's account password and disable his or her e-mail. It's not a pleasant part of MCSE consulting, but it has been known to happen.

# Making Every Client Referencable and Referable

The outcome from effective relationship management is that every active client becomes "referencable" and referable. This lofty goal, in reality one that is rarely achieved, is the benchmark standard you should strive for as an MCSE consultant.

# Summary

This chapter discussed the critical nature of client relationship management. It started with a discussion of the sender/receiver communication model. Discussion about different types of client personalities followed. Bill Bergman delivered a guest sermon on using a tool to assess personality types. Political awareness as an MCSE consultant was emphasized. Finally, the chapter discussed the goal of having a client relationship be positive so that each client becomes referencable and referable.

✦    ✦    ✦

# Managing Staff

There are some MCSEs among us that are excited by human resource management. I don't necessarily count myself amongst these blessed souls, but I respect them nonetheless. This human resource management matter is one of the most challenging and difficult areas that will confront an MCSE consultant in growth mode, and it is the topic of this chapter.

## The Eye-opener

I remember being taken to school on a Saturday by the president of a regional consulting firm for which I worked. He asked that I meet him in his office over the weekend to address his longtime client's dissatisfaction with an MCSE consultant who reported to me. Not one to tell the company president no, I arrived at 10:00 a.m. on Saturday as promised. What transpired over the next two hours wasn't a talk about Microsoft Back Office technologies, but rather one about human resource management. Managing staff is one of the most puzzling and bewildering task areas an MCSE consultant will ever encounter. "You can do everything right and still lose," Todd H., the company president said. "You never really perfect staff management because you're dealing with people."

Put on your Zen hats. This chapter is about the journey, not the finish line. Staff management is an evolutionary process, not a discrete event. Figure 11-1 depicts the input variables for managing staff.

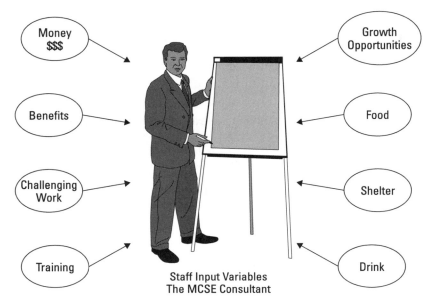

Figure 11-1: The complex creature known as the employee as shown by input variables

Assuming you are running an MCSE consulting firm, remember that your stock in trade isn't materials or finished goods. Rather, what you offer is professional services delivered by humans. Thus, your primary working assets are people. That's why staff management demands your attention. Call it asset management by any other name.

# One of the Biggest Challenges — Recruiting

First, you have to hire the staff. In this era of labor shortages, attracting competent and qualified MCSE consulting talent is exceedingly difficult. You are competing with other employers for a limited talent pool. There are many MCSE candidates and newly minted MCSEs with inadequate skills seeking the compensation promised land, but once you weed through the stack of resumes and conduct a handful of interviews, you will have invested significant time in the recruiting process.

## Avoiding the beer-and-buddy system

A time-tested lesson in business is to avoid hiring your friends. I present that point by taking a moment to discuss what MCSE consulting is not about in the recruiting area. It isn't an exercise in getting the fraternity brothers together and hanging a shingle outside announcing yourself as an MCSE consulting firm. The way you used beer and buddies to move from your apartment to your first house doesn't work here. In fact, MCSE consulting is such a high-caliber occupational endeavor that I've not seen much success where good friends are recruited to help out. Is that another way of saying you shouldn't do business with friend? You'll have to decide for yourself as you take the MCSE consulting journey.

## Attracting top talent

You have to sell yourself to potential employees. Top talent in the MCSE consulting field, hopefully yourself included, will typically receive multiple offers when job hunting. If you're the employer, how on earth do you attract the best employees?

Tip It's widely believed in the Silicon Forest of the Pacific Northwest that Microsoft's success is as much attributable to Bill Gate's early recruiting strengths as it is to anything else. Apparently, Bill Gates is mesmerizing in telling the Microsoft story and painting his picture of occupational opportunity. The tradition continues today.

I'm sad to say there's no snake oil solution you can buy for successful recruiting. The process is clearly trial and error. Offering competitive wages and an enthusiastic work environment is a great start.

Tip My advice would be for you to read regional and national business magazines that occasionally print "best companies to work for" articles. In Washington state, *Washington CEO* magazine prints an annual best companies survey that imparts secrets to recruiting and retaining top talent. Be advised that these lists have become somewhat cliché with featured firms allowing you to bring your dog to work, endorsing casual Fridays, and placing Foosball tables in the employee lounge.

# Hiring Strategies

Just do the best you can do when it comes to hiring MCSE consultants to work for you. This section presents some proven hiring strategies.

## Homegrown talent

A break-fix repair business in North Seattle that I have the utmost respect for is well known for being an MCSE consulting training ground. They believe in growing your own when it comes to recruiting. MCSEs are hired as break-fix technicians, often starting at the bottom cleaning printers. Slowly, the MCSEs are given more challenging assignments and ultimately are allowed to assist in the management of the client relationship.

This approach often means you train and lose a few good ones along the way. Sometimes you even train your competition, as the people you train may open up shop using many of the same consulting techniques you use. But that's life in the fast-paced world of MCSE consulting. More importantly, in the case of the respected break-fix shop, the MCSE consultants who came up through the ranks and stayed on were real gems.

# Outsourcing

You can outsource the human resources function in three ways. First, you can sub-contract out a lot of your work to other firms. In that case, your role as an MCSE consultant is more that of project manager.

 **Cross-Reference**   The roles of project management are discussed in Chapter 9.

You can outsource the human resources function by using headhunters to do your recruiting. A headhunter will work on a fee basis to find, screen, interview, and otherwise qualify (check references and work history) candidates for you. Headhunters typically charge a percentage of a candidate's first year salary (sometimes as high as 30 percent), payable after a 90-day warranty period. This warranty period, which starts on the date of hire, ensures the candidates are expected to fit in your organization before the headhunter is paid. Many headhunting firms can also provide you with temporary employees and contracts.

Finally, there are organizations in the business of serving as your human resources department on an outsourced basis. These firms assist not only in the hiring process, but also in developing, maintaining, and enforcing employee policies. Other services provided by outsourced human resources departments include conducting salary surveys, helping to set compensation levels, and performing terminations.

# Using temps and contractors

Past newspaper articles in the Seattle area, where Microsoft is located, have estimated Microsoft's workforce as consisting of up to 30 percent temporary employees and contractors. Microsoft and other companies pursue this workforce strategy for a number of reasons including the following:

✦ **Lower benefit costs** — Temporary employees and contractors typically don't receive benefits, and if they do, the benefits don't closely compare to those received by full-time employees. This translates into lower benefits costs.

✦ **Flexible staffing levels** — On a macro level, executives like the flexible staffing option as a human resource policy in order to be able to shift the focus of the company quickly. Imagine this. You're a large MCSE consulting firm. You decide to pursue consulting opportunities that are in alignment with Microsoft's dot-NET (.NET) direction. One day, Microsoft abandons the .NET initiative. If you have a staff augmented for .NET, you could be faced with the extremely unpleasant task of large-scale terminations. With a flexible staffing solution in place, you can call the temporary agency or contracting house and have them adjust your staff to eliminate the unneeded workers. A few days later, that same temporary agency or contracting house can send over a workforce that meets the needs of your new direction.

✦ **At-will terminations** — On a more individual basis, substantial legal maneuvering is avoided when you want to terminate an incompetent individual. I discuss termination of full-time employees at the end of this chapter, but suffice it to say, the standard that must be met to terminate a temporary employee or contractor is much lower. And the temporary agency or contract house can conveniently perform the termination for you.

✦ **Try before you buy** — Many firms use the temporary employee and contractor approach to test-drive employees before hire. There's nothing like seeing someone in action for several months before you extend a full-time offer. Many temporary agencies and contract houses have turned this "try before you buy" option into a service offering by including a break on the headhunter placement fee you ultimately pay.

One of the odd jobs I had on the way up in the technology community was as an account manager for a national temporary agency. It provided an interesting look inside the placement field. One thing I learned that has been invaluable is that temporary agencies and contract houses enjoy significant markups on the rate you are paid as the temp. A markup is the difference between the price paid by the customer and the cost paid for something. In the retail field, 100 percent markups are common on merchandise, a practice known as keystone pricing. In the temporary agency context, a markup is the difference between your labor rate per hour and the charge to the customer per hour. The high-volume national temporary agencies have lower markups and make it up on volume. The markups here can be in the 20 percent range. The middle-tier placement agencies that tend to be more specialized operate with markups in the 50 percent range. Very specialized placement agencies enjoy markups in excess of 100 percent.

**Caution**

If you work with temporary agencies and contract houses, understand that the placement field if full of unsavory characters. Be sure to ask what the person being placed at your site is making. Be sure to receive assurances that the person being placed knows what you are paying the temporary agency or contract house. If the agency or contract house isn't willing to participate in the full disclosure of this information, then you are advised to shop for another placement firm.

## Full-time employees

You might just want to hire a full-time employee as your next MCSE consultant and be done with it. It's what most of us do. It's what our parents and our grandparents did.

# Compensation Guidelines

There are many ways to pay your staff. I discuss a few approaches here, including the popular salary and per hour wage options.

## Salary

It's fun each year when the *Microsoft Certified Professional (MCP) Magazine* Salary Survey hits the streets. MCSEs across the WAN (and the land) become deeply concerned about how much money they are making. In some cases, they're deeply concerned about how much money they're not making. The *MCP Magazine* 2000 Salary Survey is found in Appendix E of this book.

Given that the national U.S. average for MCSEs tends to be in the high $60,000 salary range, what's a poor consulting firm owner to do? Read the *MCP Magazine* Salary Survey yourself. You will see that salary levels vary by region and by years of experience. Salaries also vary by gender, but even though that observation is brought out in the *MCP Magazine* Salary Survey (and other salary surveys), it is illegal for you to pay one gender more or less than the other.

The only MCSE salary level that ultimately matters is the salary that to which you and your employee agree. Salary negotiations are emotional, and often nonsalary factors enter the decision-making matrix. Do your homework, be prepared, and hope for the best outcome. Remember that you're running an MCSE consulting business, and your financial model has to justify the outcomes.

**Tip**    Ratios vary, but in general the MCSE consultant you hire needs to earn two to two and a half times his or her salary for the firm. If you hire someone for $60,000, then they need to pull in $120,000 to $150,000 for you. This pays the benefits, overhead, rent, and most of all, contribution to owner's equity.

## Per hour wages

It may make more sense for you to pay by the hour, especially if you're at the low end of the MCSE consulting market where you still perform break-fix work. Certain work environments are traditional wage environments, and it's not the intent of this book to address that issue.

Assuming you work in a per hour environment, think through your financial business model. If the MCSE consultant earns $30.00 per hour and that includes many hours of shop time (since not every hour is billable), then you've got to bill out at several times the hourly wage. A good MCSE consultant has a 50 percent utilization rate, an observation I've made several times in this book. If you pay someone $30.00 per hour for full-time employment (about 2,000 hours per year) and he or she bills only 1,000 hours per year, their effective wage rate matched against the billable hour is $60.00 per hour. In that scenario, you would need to bill out at $120.00 per hour (at least). Viewed a different way, the MCSE consultant employee might think he or she is earning only $30.00 per hour and being billed out at $120.00 per hour (and may feel he or she is being taken advantage of). You'll want to be sensitive to this issue and work through the math with your employees.

## Eat what you kill

Another type of compensation method, one that I personally like, is the "eat what you kill" method. Basically this involves an agreement or understanding with a consulting firm where you earn a percentage of what your make for the firm. To make my point, I cite an example of an MCSE consulting firm in the Pacific Northwest. The owner, I'll call him Wayne, recruited MCSEs to be consultants. His compensation system was easy. He paid you half of what you earned. So if you billed out at $120 per hour, you earned $60 per hour. More importantly, and here's the part I like, you were part of an organization with infrastructure and support that theoretically allowed you to earn more money more easily than being on your own allowed. Wayne's support structure was particularly effective in generating workflow. Wayne, free to market and manage, brought the business in and kept his consultants' plates full. Also, this form of compensation is a lot like a commission environment: you can earn what you want. So if you want to work enough to earn $60,000, Wayne's "eat what you kill" approach works. If you want to earn $80,000 per year, Wayne's world likely works for you, too.

## Partnerships, equity, and so on

You might consider partnership distributions as a form of compensation. Given the right situation, you might take on a partner in your MCSE consulting practice. The only caveat in this scenario is never to forget that owners are always the last to get paid. If you have ever run a business, you may recall that only after your suppliers, vendors, and employees are paid do you finally get paid.

Appendix B further discusses partnership as an organizational structure to consider when starting your MCSE consulting practice.

## Profit sharing and options

You can consider offering profit sharing to employees to sweeten the compensation pot. In this day of dot-coms, compensation forms like profit sharing bring a twinkle to the eyes of prospective MCSE consultants you're recruiting. If you are organized as a corporation and have hopes of going public, you might grant stock options to your employees to give them a sense of ownership.

## Sweat equity

My favorite compensation form is a deal that, unfortunately, never happened. I was looking at the manufacturing molds of the San Juan Sailboat Company and the company was communicating it needed a new network, but didn't have any money to pay for it. In fact, the company was in an early form of bankruptcy. No problem, I thought. I'll just take a San Juan sailboat in return for my services. I thought perhaps I could turn the job into a multiyear engagement and get a really big sailboat in return. As fate would have it, however, the sailboat company went deeper into bankruptcy, and I never got my sailboat. However, I'd sure entertain the same deal today, and I'd encourage you to do the same. Certain industries use this form of barter, including construction and construction materials. Think about that the next time you want to get a free hot tub installed on your patio deck in exchange for installing a Windows 2000 network.

# Benefits

Another part of the managing staff puzzle is the benefits area. This is a complex area. Some benefit consultants make a good living advising small business owners, such as you and I running MCSE consulting firms, on what benefit packages to provide. The good news is that, in addition to retaining a benefits consultant (who might be compensated on commission for the benefits they suggest to you), shopping among insurance companies is a great way to get free information.

## Health and life insurance

Without tackling the complexities of the health and life insurance policies, I can share the following observations. Health insurance is increasingly not offered to MCSE consultants working for consulting firms. If it's offered, it is typically a co-pay situation.

Life insurance is another one of the disappearing employee benefits. In general, employees and independent contractors are on their own when it comes to having any meaningful life insurance coverage. The Pacific Northwest regional consulting firm that I worked for as an MCSE consultant for a spell had a basic $10,000 life insurance policy for each employee. That policy would have about covered the funeral expenses. Having gone out and purchased my own life insurance, I can tell you that some ratios exist. At a minimum, you want three times your annual salary, roughly enough to pay off the house and provide several months cash for your family.

**Tip**   Bite the bullet and sit through a couple of insurance sales presentations. However, make sure you've fortified your constitution so that you don't get sucked into purchasing policies before you step back from the process and consider them as a rational buyer.

## Additional benefits to offer

Additional benefits are an area in which you can shine as an MCSE consulting firm trying to hire MCSE consultants without an enterprise-level benefits package. People appreciate creativity in the benefits department. Here are a few of things I've seen offered to recruits that fall under the creative benefits category:

✦ Work from home arrangements

✦ Elder care subsidies

- ✦ Child-care arrangements
- ✦ Tickets to sports team events
- ✦ Occasional use of the owner's ski condo

**Note** Many wonderful human resources sites are on the Web to guide you. For example, you can find sites that provide information on compensation. There is a small business Web portal with a bevy of human resources links and information. Go to bizbuilders.com (`www.bizbuilders.com`) and select the Human Resources link in the Small Business category.

## Guest Sermon—Recruiting, Another Tool of the Trade

This guest sermon is from a well-established headhunter in the Pacific Northwest named Michael Jones (majones@houser.com, `www.houser.com`), who shares some words that apply equally well to both hiring managers and job seekers. Here's Michael's contribution.

*Headhunter, flesh peddler, agent—whatever name you choose to use, recruiters can have a very significant impact on both your career and business. As an example, if most of us were going to build our dream home, we would have to seek out some advice and counsel. We would have a plan drawn up for the house, outlining how the house is going to sit on the property, how it is going to be built, and what we want to do with the property. If we are going to stay successful at our jobs, we are not going to have the time necessary to seek out and review all of the available listings, so we would need to find a real estate agent that could actively look for the right piece of property. We would contact an agent that we know personally or one who has been referred to us that we feel we can work with and trust, tell him or her all about our dream home and what we are looking for in a piece of property, and then leave it to him or her to search for the property and call us when he or she has found something that fits. We could then go about our daily lives and jobs, knowing a competent professional is watching out for our best interest.*

*Recruiting is much the same. Your career, whether you plan on working for yourself, starting a company, or working for a company, is much like that dream home. You need to have a plan, an objective, from which you can plan interim steps and against which you can measure all of your career decisions. But there is even more to building a career or company than just having a plan. What I recognize as an Executive Recruiter is that the best people, the people that companies are really looking for, are not out looking for the next big career move. In fact, they have their heads down and are working diligently at their jobs and refining their skills. Successful people just don't have time to go looking for a job, just as successful managers do not have time to spend reading through thousands of resumes and interviewing hundreds of people to find the real talent. Successful people have someone that knows what they are looking for and actively looks out for their best interests so that they can concentrate on being their best. In other words, do what you know best and let the recruiter do the rest.*

*Continued*

*Continued*

*A good rule of thumb when looking for a new job is that you will spend approximately one month looking for every $10,000 increment in salary starting at a base of zero. In other words, someone wishing to make $120,000 might spend 12 months finding the right position. That has been reduced substantially in this current market, but the point is still valid; there are a lot of jobs, but very few are just the right one for your next career move. That is why it is important to develop a good relationship with a recruiter that truly understands your objectives.*

*Likewise, when hiring new employees, the people you want to find are not the ones scouring the newspaper ads and Internet listings. The best of the best are the ones who are usually approached by people who already know them and know how good they really are,*

*just as you approach the best of the people that you have worked with in the past or I approach them for my clients. The problem is that as your business grows you will quickly run out of people that you already know. You will have to turn to other means of attracting highly talented people. A skilled recruiter has connections in many places and is constantly staying in touch with the movers and shakers and the people they know. His or her database of contacts in all relevant technologies is extensive, and he or she can pick up the phone and call any one of them for an update. In addition, a recruiter can help you stay tuned in on the marketplace and keep your compensation plans current. This will help you in retaining those good people you have. Too many times I have had a manager call asking that I replace an employee they have lost because they were not keeping up the pace in compensation.*

*I can offer one final advantage, especially from a business perspective. I am constantly asked who I know that could perform a contract project. I have referred a substantial amount of business to both client and candidates over the years. Having a relationship with a recruiter(s) will bring contract opportunities that you would not have otherwise had.*

*Partnering with the right recruiter(s) is another important tool that will help you be successful in your career, both as a hiring manager and a job seeker.*

# Training

As knowledge workers in the information sector, you have to stay current or become extinct. It's a fact of life. I discuss that reality in this section.

## All employees need training

You really shortchange yourself, your firm, and your employees if you neglect the training area. Believe me, I've seen it done time and time again, resulting in poor morale, high turnover, and poor delivery of services.

If you as a firm and an MCSE consultant don't stay valuable by keeping your skill set current, the demand for your services will decrease. And it can happen in a matter of months, not years.

I like to think of the ideal MCSE consulting firm as being a learning organization and the ideal MCSE consultant as being a learner. When I've supervised MCSE consultants in the past, I've tried to ingrain in them a learning culture. I raise such optimistic rhetoric early and often in the recruiting process so I lose the nonlearner and see the twinkle of excitement in the true learners. Once the right hiring decision has been made, I like to sit down with my consulting staff and come up with a learning plan. The intent is that staff will meet me more than halfway. These people should have already had a track record for continuing education, taking a class here or there at the community college at night. Therefore, the need for and commitment to training is a nonissue. Rather, the discussion focuses on questions such as "What classes you plan to take this quarter?" and "Is anyone planning to start their master's degree this fall?" Traditional business consulting firms and their business clients respond warmly to consultants who are pursuing or hold master's degrees. Some of the same dynamics exist in the world of MCSE consulting as well.

You should still be selective when it comes to choosing training. You have a training budget (which I discuss in the next section), and you want be prudent about how often people go to training and what courses are taken. Taking courses that focus on Borland software solutions might not make as much sense as taking courses that focus on Microsoft BackOffice technologies. As the old IBM slogan said, "Think Smart!"

## Training budgets

A wide variety of training options exists, ranging from the expensive private training center five-day MCSE certification courses to free seminars.

The training costs associated with an MCSE consultant tend to be dramatically higher than those for other business professionals are. For example, a seasoned CPA once expressed his frustration with MCSEs in his technology division compared to the CPAs in his auditing division. This accounting firm had enjoyed high profits from its accounting services, in part due to the minimal outlay for additional training after an accountant earns his or her CPA designation. Each year, approximately $1,500 was allocated for meeting continuing education requirements. Not only do MCSEs cost infinitely more to adequately train on an annual basis, in the neighborhood of $5,000 to $10,000, but also the knowledge imparted in the MCSE training process has a much shorter useful life. In other words, each year you spend all this money to train your MCSE staff on SQL Server 7.0, and months later SQL Server 2000 comes out and training must begin again. I haven't even mentioned recertification requirements that make MCSE training mandatory. Finally, consider the business model at play here. If a young CPA and a young MCSE bill at the same rate, for example, $125.00 per hour, and the training costs are as widely divergent as I've expressed in this section, guess where a CPA firm with a technology consulting division will place its emphasis. You can't really blame the firm from a strict dollars-and-cents management perspective.

**Tip**   I've seen and my research affirms that the average MCSE needs $5,000 to $10,000 of training per year.

Following are details on training alternatives at different costs. Note that the marketplace for MCSE-related training is considered efficient, meaning that, in general, you get what you pay for.

### Five-day courses at CTECs

The five-day Microsoft Official Curriculum (MOC) courses are wonderful and expensive. Not only are you drinking directly from the well of MCSE and Microsoft product knowledge, but I've also heard the courses compared to drinking from a fire hose. The five-day format has a very rapid pace. The people I've seen excel in this environment tend to be highly experienced and use the five-day course as something of a primer. That is, the experienced attendee brushes up on specific product area feature sets and functionality and prepares for the corresponding MCSE certification exam. This is the most expensive option and is delivered at Microsoft Certified Technical Education Centers (CTECs).

### Curriculum clones

Numerous third-party training organizations offer an array of MCSE training opportunities. Five-day funnel courses are similar to the CTEC approach, but use third-party or custom books at a reduced fee. These third-party organizations often offer one-week, two-week, and three-week boot camps. The bottom line on clone-based training options is this: You tend to get what you pay for. Let the buyer beware; shop wisely.

### Night school at AATPs

Perhaps you don't adhere to the rapid training approach enjoyed by some MCSE consultants. Long-term MCSE training approaches exist that mimic how college courses are delivered. In fact, these MOC-based courses are delivered at colleges as part of the Microsoft Authorized Academic Training Program (AATP). MOC courses offered at an AATP are, on average, delivered at a lower price than the ones offered at the CTECs, and they tend to last longer. At Seattle Pacific University (SPU), a Microsoft AATP where I teach MCSE courses, we've adopted the long-term delivery model more frequently seen in academic environments. The content of the traditional forty-hour MOC courses is spread over five weeks with training sessions two nights per week. This has proven popular as students have the time to digest the lectures, to repeat the labs, and even to prepare in advance of class by reading ahead.

### Online courses, anytime, anywhere

Further down the cost food chain are the online MCSE courses. Numerous training centers, including the three groups I have just discussed in the previous subheadings, are joining in the latest wave of education: online training. The idea is that with streaming media, a book in hand, and a couple of machines in your test lab you can learn on your own schedule at your own pace and have an educational outcome similar to that experienced in the classroom.

Online education is relatively new, and the area is still under development. Some things work better than others do in online education. For example, in the online world, the ideal student has five to ten years of experience. Seattle Pacific University found with its online MCSE offerings that inexperienced participants (career changers seeking to earn the MCSE) aren't wildly successful.

Online courses, at this point, are lower priced than in-class offerings. This is due in part to the fact that the marketplace isn't valuing online education at the same price as in-class instruction. In my opinion, this may be due to the fact the world of education is still in the process of learning to accept online education at the same value level as in-class instruction. That is, the education community still values bricks over clicks. In that sense, you should take advantage of the online education bargain. In the future, look for the price differential between online and in-class courses to narrow.

## Conferences

Perhaps your business snail mailbox is akin to mine. Hardly a week passes without my receiving an invitation to attend a professional conference that's being pitched to MCSEs. The topics presented run the gamut from A (Active Directory) to Z (Zero Administration). Currently, a glut of Windows 2000 workshops is being offered.

These professional conferences typically cost in the neighborhood of $300 to $400 per day. As an occasional conference attendee, I encourage you to ask the "what do I get" question up front rather than attend and be disappointed afterwards. It has also been my experience that attending one specific conference year after year tends to hold more value than does the shotgun approach of attending different conferences all of the time. If you focus on one conference, you can meet and get to know other attendees and develop valuable professional relationships. Once you have frequented a conference, you'll find you attend not only to engage in mind share and technology knowledge transfer, but also to conduct business.

There are two ways to reduce the financial pain of attending professional conferences while still enjoying some of the educational gain. The first method is to speak at a conference as a presenter. Professional conferences typically post a call for papers at least six months prior to the event. Take a chance and submit a speaking proposal. If accepted, not only do you get to attend the conference for free, but also typically you receive an expenses paid trip as well.

Another avenue is to attend a conference as a vendor. Perhaps the company you work for has a product or service that should be communicated to the technology community. Your employer might respond favorably to a proposal from you to set up and manage the booth at a conference (while attending a few technical sessions as well).

If you're creative, you can find a way to attend conferences yourself and send MCSE consultants on your staff without paying too much money.

A notable conference for MCSEs of all stripes that should be on your annual "must attend" list is the TechMentor conference hosted by *Microsoft Certified Professional Magazine*. Aside from its heavy technical content, this conference is emerging as an annual convention for MCPs. Contact www.techmentorevents.com, shown in Figure 11-2, for more details.

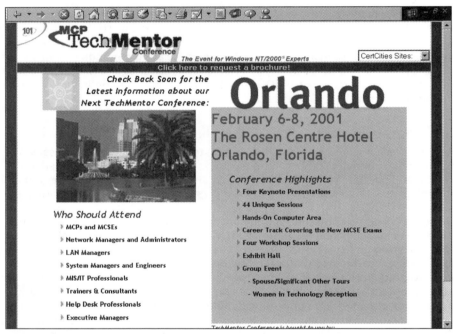

**Figure 11-2:** MCSE consultant managers and employees alike should strongly consider attending TechMentor each year.

## Seminars

Another old trick in continuing education for employees is to send them to vendor seminars. Many such seminars are available each month in urban areas, including those offered by local Microsoft and Cisco sales offices. The Microsoft TechNet and Direct Access seminars tend to be a good use of time and are typically presented without charge. If you visit www.microsoft.com/directaccess, not only can you view seminar offerings in your area, but also you can sign up for the periodic Direct Access e-mail newsletter seen in Figure 11-3. Be advised that the Microsoft seminars, selected wisely, are typically the same content presented at expensive professional conferences. However, the third-party applications seminars (such as for customer relationship management software), while technical in nature, tend to be more sales oriented.

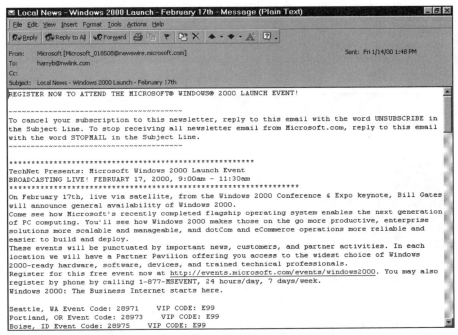

**Figure 11-3:** Microsoft's Direct Access e-mail newsletter

If you want decent router training for free, contact your local Cisco office to sign up for their highly acclaimed, very technical seminars. Check www.cisco.com for the telephone number of your local Cisco office. I have also attended free technical seminars from Novell, Oracle, Apple, and Sun.

## Workshops

Perhaps your MCSE consultant employees receive mailers for one-day, hands-on workshops held in hotel ballrooms near the local airport. This is the proverbial traveling road show, with instructors flying from one city to the next to deliver their workshops. These one-day workshops tend to offer topics outside the mainstream, such as document image management. In these seminars you typically have a PC at your desk, so it's a great educational opportunity for the active learner. These seminars do cost money, although many are presented in the $99 per day range.

One of the largest providers of these workshops is DataTech Institute via its TPG Technologies group. DataTech Institute, as part of TPG Technologies, offers credible workshops in most major cities, as shown in Figure 11-4.

**Figure 11-4:** TPG Technologies workshop offerings are typically held in all major cities at local hotels.

## Trade shows

Trade shows often offer little technical knowledge transfer. That doesn't mean you should not attend these. As a technology professional, attending trade shows goes with the territory. If you're shopping for hardware or software, there's nothing like stopping by a vendor's both and getting a free demo. I certainly feel this "try before you buy" approach is good use of an afternoon.

Many technology trade shows are held across the land, frequently at public facilities such as convention centers. A major technology trade show (with a seminar track included) is Information Technology Expositions and Conferences (ITEC). You can reach ITEC at www.itec.asmcorp.com, as seen in Figure 11-5.

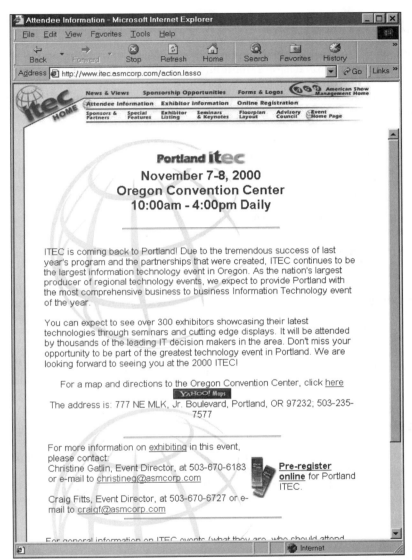

**Figure 11-5:** ITEC hosts some of the largest regional technology trade shows.

See Chapter 27 for more information on training topics.

# Retention Strategies

As you mature as a consultant manager and as your MCSE consulting practice matures, you'll place emphasis on retention. Seasoned human resources managers know that it's far cheaper to put a few dollars into retention rather than lose your talent. Staff turnover involves a very real cost. Here is a short list of retention considerations:

✦ **Paying for certifications**—You might pay for certifications. As an MCSE consulting manager, recognize it's in your best interest to sign a loan agreement with your employees whereby they pay you back for all or part of the certification courses if they leave within 12- or 18-months. This is common practice when a company pays for a graduate degree for an employee, too.

✦ **Paying for cost of courses**—As the previous point suggested, paying for an employee's course work is a valid retention strategy.

✦ **Paying for time away from the office**—You might grant paid hours away from the office both to attend class and to study for the MCSE certification exams. Employees appreciate it when their time isn't docked.

✦ **Increasing compensation for certifications earned**—A popular retention strategy is to pay your MCSE consultants more money as they earn more certifications. Perhaps you'll offer a $5,000 salary bump for these employees for each certification. In consulting, this retention strategy makes sense. An employee with more certifications should have a higher bill rate, and the whole arrangement should be both cost-effective and revenue generating.

# Mentoring Your Hires

Part of being an MCSE consulting manager is to be a coach and mentor to your staff. You'll likely mentor a few great MCSE consultants right out of your organization who will go on to do bigger and better things with their lives, but what goes around comes around. Sometimes those mentored MCSEs refer new candidates for hire to you.

# Rule of Ten: Annual Departures

No matter how wonderful your are, your firm is, and the salary is, you will lose MCSE consultants in your practice. It has been my experience that three out of ten employees will leave per year in high technology consulting. That's the complex paradox of managing human beings. Some are unhappy with their career choices.

Others are unhappy with you, but not their career choices. I've observed the following reasons for departures:

- ✦ Better offers
- ✦ Family matters (divorce and so on)
- ✦ Relocation
- ✦ Job not a good fit

# Terminations

Terminations happen. While I haven't been involved in many terminations, I cite the advice of a one-time speaker before my college class, the CEO of Egghead Software. He commented, and I believe correctly so, that most terminations occur too late. For the benefit of both employee and employer, issues surrounding termination of employment should be addressed earlier, not later. "No one ever got fired too early" were his exact words.

**Note**      Retain and seek the counsel of a labor lawyer in all matters involving employee terminations.

# Summary

This chapter addressed the complex and difficult area of managing staff. Numerous strategies for hiring, compensating, offering benefits, cultivating retention, and handling departures and terminations were presented.

✦      ✦      ✦

# Making Money – MCSE Style

**S**o now you and I finally get to one of the reasons we're really here as MCSE consultants: making money. You don't need to apologize for such less than puritan motives. Speaking only for myself, I've got kids to get through school, a house and car payment to make, and a retirement to fund. So making money is not only okay, but it's kind of cool.

## Determining What You Want To Make

The next step after deciding you want to make money is to determine how much money you want to make. You should assess your basic needs, what your other wants and desires are, and what foolish luxuries you would like. Somewhere between basic needs and foolish luxuries is the amount of money you need to make as an MCSE consultant. This amount will vary by individual.

Speaking more pragmatically, determining what you want to make is a function of many variables beyond your control. One of those input variables is what the marketplace will pay for your talents. The place to start this investigation is to look at salary surveys beyond this book and the words I share with you. Consider the following salary survey sources:

- ✦ *Computerworld* magazine
- ✦ IDC Web site at www.idc.com (IDC is a sister company to IDG Books Worldwide, Inc., the publisher of this book.)
- ✦ Robert Half International Inc. (www.rhii.com), which publishes an annual guide for the information technology field
- ✦ *MCP Magazine* 2000 Salary Survey, which can be accessed at www.mcpmag.com and which I discuss more in Appendix E

After discovering what the marketplace will pay for your services, the next step is to quantify your financial expectations, which is discussed in the budgeting section of this chapter.

# 50 Percent Utilization

I encourage you to consult with other MCSE consultants to confirm the observations that I present in this section. In plain English, you bill only half of your hours in a given year. Hang in there and I'll explain why.

## What is a utilization rate?

A utilization rate is the ratio of billable hours to available hours. It is a standard measure in professional services such as consulting, law, and accounting. In fact, the regional consulting practice I was with in the mid to late 1990s had a weekly charge hour report that displayed a column with the calculated utilization rate.

With MCSE consulting, your utilization rate is 50 percent. This is a truism observed year in and year out due to redundant tasks, incalls/outcalls, and recurring charge hours.

### Redundant tasks

Accounting has certain roles that are rote by nature, allowing efficiencies to be gained because of their predictability. For example, auditing and tax preparation tend to have more of a step-by-step workflow than many tasks performed by MCSE consultants. MCSE consultants tend to perform one task (for example, implement a service pack) and then move on to another client site and perform a completely different task (a data restoration, for instance). Different task sets eat into billable hours because the MCSE consultant has to shift his or her mindset.

### Incalls/outcalls

Accountants tend to work at their desks in their offices. The nature of the workflow is inbound from clients. That is, clients typically deliver paperwork to the accountant's office, a process often combined with a meeting in the conference room.

With MCSE consultants, the process tends to be exactly opposite. The work is performed at the client site instead of at the MCSE consultant's office. Performing outcalls instead of receiving incalls contributes to a lower utilization rate.

### Recurring charge hours

First, for comparison, I want to take a moment to look at how accounting firms bill for hours of work; then I'll transition to the MCSE consulting environment. It is a fact that the regulatory environment that businesses operate in dictates that certain accounting-related jobs, such as tax preparation and auditing, be performed once per year. Accountants are also retained to assist in the annual budgeting process and, perhaps, to update the business plan. To say that accounts are offered recurring billable hour opportunities in the context of their client relationships is an understatement. Basically in accounting, once you land an account, you can count on certain types of work each year from that account without additional marketing. And in many cases, state and federal law, tax rulings, and good old-fashioned government regulation mandate the work.

MCSE consultants in general perform more project-oriented work than other professional services, such as my oft-cited accounting field, perform. MCSE consultants start many client relationships with a project, such as implementing a Windows 2000 network or BackOffice components. Many times the greatest number of hours occurs early in the MCSE consulting relationship. In fact, it's not uncommon for MCSEs to comment that their better hours on a mature account are behind them. Long-term client relationships in the world of MCSE consulting are more than desirable, but you will rarely exceed the billable hours you'll enjoy at the beginning of a project.

**Note**     Some MCSE consultants, having wised up to the peaks and valleys of project-based consulting, sell maintenance contracts to their clients to increase recurring charge hour revenues and stabilize the organization's cash flow.

For these reasons and more, MCSE consulting is different from other professional services. Without naming the guilty party, I can't help but smile at the longtime career CPA who boldly stated he wanted to run a technology consulting practice just like his accounting practice. That is, he expected the same utilization rate from his technology consulting accounts as he did from his loyal accounting accounts. Given his lofty expectations, I regret to say his career could have ended only in disappointment. The point is this: MCSE consultant is different from other types of professional services-based consulting.

## Use of remaining hours

If you've accepted the premise that an MCSE consultant bills only half of the available hours in the long run, you may be curious as to what happens to all of those remaining hours. For some consulting managers, it's one of the greatest mysteries of running a consulting practice. Some skeptical businesspeople think consultants, under this scenario of a 50 percent utilization rate, are working only part time.

### Marketing

Certainly near the top of the list for time robbers is the marketing function. MCSE consultants are constantly marketing, placing follow-up telephone calls with leads, attending a chamber of commerce after-hours mixer, writing and delivering a proposal, and so on. MCSE consulting is as much a finder exercise as it is a minder and grinder exercise.

One interesting point about marketing and the MCSE consultant is this: Because much of the new work awarded to an MCSE is project-based, expending the same marketing effort to land a one-time MCSE consultant engagement that an accountant expends to land an account with recurring annual work and a very long life is not uncommon. In other words, the lunches, letters, and telephone calls that are requisite to consummate a professional services transaction (such as landing the client engagement) are often the same when comparing accountants and MCSE consultants. The difference is that the MCSE consultant may well be expending the same marketing effort for a one-time event that an accountant puts forth for a ten-year relationship and constant workflow. This drives the marketing time commitment and associated marketing expenses higher for MCSE consultants than for those in other professional services capacities.

## Administration

Assuming that you're a sole proprietor MCSE consultant or run a small MCSE consulting firm, you clearly perform much of your own administration (perhaps with the assistance of your long-suffering spouse or soul mate). It's shocking how much time the administrative function takes in the day-to-day world of MCSE consulting. Faxing a document or mailing a letter at the post office can take a significant amount of time. It's these administrative tasks that often result in your looking up at the clock at midday and not only feeling like you haven't accomplished a thing but also pondering where all the time went. E-mail may be the biggest culprit.

One administrative task of critical importance is the accounting function. The hours spent billing your time and recording your financial activity are more than well spent and necessary.

In larger consultant organizations, the administrative function is ever present as well. While you may have administrative minions to send your faxes and mail your letters, you have to contend with a whole different layer of paperwork, such as time and expense (T&E) reports. I've personally found big company paperwork and reporting requirements to be more frustrating than the mindless tasks of mailing my own letters as a lone ranger MCSE consultant.

## Full cost principle

Accounting recognizes an idea known as the full cost principle that basically says you must realize and recognize the full costs associated with your revenues. In MCSE, if you want a way of truly appreciating the hours you put in (both billable and nonbillable), you have to realize and recognize your learning hours. It's the only fair way of truly assessing how hard you're working for those MCSE consulting revenue dollars. Under this full cost model, you'll probably find you're working more than you thought.

## Learning activities

Do you recognize any of the following behaviors?

✦ You've followed many of the sage tips presented in this book and subscribed to the local business newspaper (typically a weekly business journal in your region). You read this newspaper for one hour per week.

✦ You read the business section of the local paper each day, looking for interesting stories that might spur some creative MCSE marketing ideas. You are also on the lookout for articles about troubled businesses so that you don't perform services for such entities and unwittingly become an unpaid creditor.

✦ You purchase third-party computer books on products such as Windows 2000 Server. You then proceed to spend hours reading the book at night and tinkering with step-by-step exercises in your home computer lab.

✦ You delve into the resource kit of a BackOffice application in the middle of the night to resolve a bedeviling conflict that has turned into a recurring nightmare.

Assuming you've displayed any of these symptoms before, you're suffering a lower utilization rate as an MCSE consultant than you know. If you spend 15 hours per week reading, these hours need to be thrown into the mix of total hours worked. This has the practical effect of lowering your utilization rate as an MCSE consultant because time dedicated to the MCSE consulting professional is time taken away from other endeavors. This time must be added to the utilization rate equation. It is added to the denominator value, which is the whole of the hours you've committed professionally to being an MCSE consultant on an annual basis. A larger denominator with the same size numerator in a fraction results in a smaller decimal value. In this case, the decimal value is the utilization rate of the MCSE consultant. Try the math yourself, but you will find that the result is a lower utilization rate.

# Time for formal training

Every technology professional faces the unrelenting challenge of staying current. One popular avenue for increasing your knowledge is to attend training courses and conferences.

### Courses

If you've attended those five-day MCSE certification courses at Microsoft Certified Technical Education Centers (CTECs), you already know that the time commitment away from your MCSE consulting practice is at least 40 hours. This is a huge chunk of time that you've got to throw into the unbillable hour bucket when calculating your utilization rate.

### Conferences

"Got to go to them," said the seasoned MCSE consultant to the novice. As a professional, you should attend at least one professional conference per year.

**Cross-Reference**    For more discussion on the importance of attending conferences, see Chapter 11.

The best conference I've found in terms of its relevancy for MCSE consultants is *Microsoft Certified Professional Magazine's* TechMentor conference (see www.mcpmag.com for details). This conference not only has a few technical tracks for increasing your knowledge about Microsoft-based solutions, but also has management and certification tracks, two other very important topics to MCSE consultants. The management track is consistent with the minder role in MCSE consulting. The certification track is relevant to retaining your MCSE designation (and it's hard to be an MCSE consultant if you don't have the MCSE certification).

**Tip**

Both courses and conferences can result in major hits against the utilization ratio because these are large chunks of hours dedicated to learning. While important, courses and conferences should be selected wisely so that you get the most for your hours and ultimately your money. You should also avoid getting conference syndrome, where you compulsively attend conferences to collect trade show trinkets, t-shirts, and backpacks. Attending too many conferences wreaks havoc on your MCSE consulting utilization rate.

### On-the-job training

Another use of nonbillable hours is on-the-job (OTJ) training. Perhaps you've made an agreement with a client to implement a solution, and you'll have to learn the product to implement it. You agree not to bill for these hours, or you bill and then write off these hours, which I discuss later in this chapter. All MCSE consultants do this at one time or another, and such a strategy contributes to the consumption of your time, resulting in a lower utilization rate.

### R and R

The biggest fear of all consulting managers is rest and relaxation (R and R). These activities include taking long lunches, attending doctor's appointments, hiding at the local beach with the pager turned off, and going on vacations. All of these R and R activities are nonbillable.

## In the long run

Armed with the understanding that a great MCSE consultant has a 50 percent utilization rate, you can appreciate that this rate translates into billing 1,000 to 1,200 hours per year, assuming a work year of 2,000 to 2,400 hours. If your assumption is 2,000 hours per year, you're likely working a 40-hour workweek. If your assumption is 2,400 hours per year, you're likely working closer to a 50-hour workweek (which is probably more realistic).

You may occasionally work 80-hour weeks; however, few do this for extended periods of time. For every 80-hour workweek in MCSE consulting, there is a shortened week of 10 work hours lurking. The law of consulting that for every peak there is a valley holds true for MCSE consultants.

The key point is that the hours tend to balance out to a 50 percent utilization rate. You should keep short-term long hour aberrations in proper perspective.

# Moneymaking Strategies

By digging deep into the MCSE consulting financial model, this section presents a few Rules of Ten that are part of the moneymaking framework.

## Rule of Ten: Assume a 10 percent profit margin

For the sake of argument, use a simple 10 percent profit margin rate in the world of MCSE consulting. This number is actually close to true, once you do the math for a large sample size of professional services firms. Consider that large law and accounting firms, after everyone is paid, are lucky to have a 10 percent profit margin. And this profit margin calculation accounts for the compensation paid to the lawyers of the law firm. It also accounts for the depreciation expense over three years to recover the costs of the state-of-the-art network that hardworking MCSE consultant implemented.

For MCSE consultants, understanding that profits are truly the bottom line is critical. After you have paid yourself a salary and have paid all of your taxes and expenses, you need to have about 10 percent of the gross revenue left (this is your 10 percent profit). Profit is the reward above and beyond just making a living as a consultant, the reward for taking a risk to start your own firm. It's also the money used to pay for capital additions and acquisitions.

 **Tip**    If you're not making a 10 percent profit margin in the long run, consider packing up your MCSE shingle and becoming someone else's employee. Why bother with the headache and frustration of running your own consulting practice when for the same approximate compensation you could work a set job. This is a strict financial argument that doesn't account for the freedom you have as an MCSE consultant, but you get the point.

## Rule of Ten: True costs can be ten times real costs

If you assume a 10 percent profit margin, you now need to understand how expensive your marginal costs are. That personal digital assistant (PDA) you've been eyeing to keep track of your tasks, address book, and calendar is more expensive in reality than it first appears to be. That additional certification above and beyond the MCSE, the Certified Cisco Internetwork Expert (CCIE), for example, is also surprisingly expensive.

Something like a PDA is useful to the MCSE consultant (I have one myself). A good PDA, for the sake of argument, costs $500. Assuming a 10 percent profit margin in MCSE consulting, it takes $5,000 in revenue to earn a $500 profit. That PDA you want to purchase for $500 will suck the profit out of $5,000 of billable time. If you didn't buy the PDA, your profit would be $500 higher. Addressing the $5,000 in billable time, if your bill rate is $100 per hour, you would need to bill at least 50 hours to generate the profit needed to pay for the PDA (actually slightly more hours when you account for write-offs, which are discussed in a later section).

Perhaps you're a certification addict. Many MCSEs are. You've mastered the Microsoft certification path, and now, looking around at other vendors, you've decided you want to conquer Cisco. Your hard costs for an advanced certification such as the CCIE may exceed $20,000. This is a staggering number when you consider that just ate all of the profit out of $200,000 in MCSE consulting revenue. That could possibly be all of your profit for two years worth of work. Don't forget your MCSE consulting utilization rate is going to take a hit for the hundreds of preparation hours you'll incur to pass the intensive CCIE exams (both written and hands-on lab). You really have to ask yourself whether or not such an expensive designation will truly pay off for you.

## Reducing costs

Now is a good time to discuss lowering costs, given the alarming true cost model I've just presented. With MCSE consulting, a dollar saved is truly a dollar earned. Perhaps low-end business cards costing $19.95 per 1,000 cards will meet your needs as well as fancy business cards costing $400 per 1,000 cards. Do you really need to order that expensive embossed stationary when you can use the laser printer to print out your own masthead?

The lowering costs discussion is often presented in the context of lowering overhead. By reading small business magazines and Web sites, you can easily find articles about how to lower your business expenses. One noteworthy and timely article link is presented here for you to consider. At the ZDNet Web site, Jacquelyn Lynn shares some cost reduction tips in the article "28 ways to save money in your home-based business." Visit `http://cgi.zdnet.com/slink?52250:4481172` for more information.

In this age of the Internet, you can lower your overhead by taking advantage of free goods and services. One such opportunity is the free faxing service at Onebox.com (`www.onebox.com`). By signing up for this service, I have a fax number that clients and others can use to send me faxes without the added expense of maintaining a second telephone line in my MCSE consultant office. Free services that help the MCSE consultant lower business overhead are detailed in Jesse Berst's ZDNet AnchorDesk column of April 7, 2000, which can be accessed at `www.zdnet.com/anchordesk/story/story_4648.html`. Berst speaks about the following free resources in his excellent article:

- ✦ Free retail storefronts on the Web
- ✦ Free Web site promotion
- ✦ Free file storage
- ✦ Free e-mail, voice mail, and fax

## Guest Sermon—Making Money

Tom Broetje, principal in CFO-2-Go, an accounting and business consulting firm in Bothell, Washington, provides the following words of wisdom on making money. Tom can be reached at tomb@cfo2go.com and welcomes your comments (as well as your business):

*Experience has taught me that successful business owners are those who run profitable businesses. Unprofitable businesses are not much fun. Everyone is stressed trying to reduce costs and having to pick up more of the load. Profitable businesses are much more fun. Profits allow businesses to expand, hire new employees, pay employees bonuses, or pay owners handsome dividends. All of this would not be possible without profits.*

*Recently many startup technology companies believed wealth could be created without generating profits. Unfortunately, venture capitalists believed them and gave them a seemingly endless supply of capital in exchange for shares of stock in the company. All of this was done in anticipation of the company's going public and selling shares in the stock market. The employees were given stock options that would be worth millions once the company went public.*

*As more and more unprofitable technology companies went public, investors finally figured out they were far from making a profit, and the stock prices of these companies fell. Unfortunately, once this happened, the venture capitalists' stock and the employee stock options became worthless.*

*Generating profits is not easy. Sadly, most businesses do not generate profits sufficient to make it through their first year. It takes discipline, tenacity, vision, creativity, intelligence, and patience, as well as many other attributes. However, the most important trait the entrepreneur commonly demonstrates is the willingness to take risks.*

*Many businesses are started because the owner is an inventor, a salesman, a craftsman, or an excellent manager of people. This owner starts out with a passion for what he or she does well and starts producing that product or offering that service. Managing the business is time consuming, but due to the business' small size it is controllable. However, as the business grows, the owner starts having problems managing all of the demands on his or her time.*

*This is the critical point. The owner has to let go and hire a quality management team to help run the business. This is extremely difficult. To grow the owner needs to hire quality management and empower them to run the business; otherwise the business will stagnate and stop growing. If the business isn't transitioned, timely competition chips away at its market share, and before long the owner is forced to sell or close the business.*

*I have seen many businesses struggle with this transition. Most entrepreneurs' personal identity is tied to their business. Their personal assets are generally encumbered by the business, as well as by countless hours of their time. Handing off the business to a management team is generally more difficult than sending their first born to college.*

*Continued*

*Continued*

*My company, CFO-2-Go, helps the entrepreneur transition from doing it all to utilizing a management team. We help the owner get refocused on what he does best by managing the financial aspects of the business. We bring in the right amount of expertise for the right amount of time. Outsourcing part-time help is a cost-effective way to get the experienced management on board earlier during the critical transition phase.*

*My company recently worked with a small service business. The business was started several years before and was owned by a few individuals who were also active in the business. After a few years of modest growth, the company started growing rapidly, and they decided it was time to hire a CEO. The owners had trouble turning over the reins, and we were brought in to help mediate and improve their financial management.*

*What we found was a very lucrative business whose owners were concerned that the CEO would squander the profits. They micromanaged the CEO and questioned all of his decisions, causing him to be ineffective and eventually causing employee morale to suffer.*

*In this situation CFO-2-Go was forced to push the board in the correct direction. We informed the owners that we would work for them only through an effective and empowered CEO. We would report only to the CEO and would take direction directly from him. Otherwise, we saw no point in continuing the engagement. This was a significant gamble on our part, but we were convinced the company would fail unless the transition was made.*

*Fortunately, the owners were able to make the change. The CEO was able to focus on building the management team, and the result was doubled sales, quadrupled profits, and a forecast for sales to double again the following year. Morale is up, management is effective and productive, and the owners are receiving dividends that far exceed their expectations.*

*My advice to future entrepreneurs is if you want to make money then make one of your goals to generate profits. To get to those profits, stick to what you do best and be sure to bring in qualified management when your business starts to grow.*

## Rule of Ten: Assume a 10 percent write-off rate

Another Rule of Ten in the world of MCSE consulting concerns write-off rates. All MCSE consultants do and should take write-offs. Believe it or not, it's good consulting practice management.

### Dissatisfied clients

At one time or another, you'll have one or more dissatisfied clients. You may not know it from their communication with you, which might be very pleasant. Rather, you'll know it by observing your accounts receivable balance. When a client's account ages 30, 60, or 90 days, they are typically showing with their pocketbooks how dissatisfied they are with your services.

Client dissatisfaction results for many reasons, such as technical competence and communications, explored in this book. The reason for the client dissatisfaction is not the point here; rather, the point is that unhappy clients will cause hits against your consulting revenues as an MCSE consultant.

### Learning curve analysis

You have picked a niche, have mastered client relations, and are making money. Do you really need to recognize this 10 percent write-off rate? Yes. For example, suppose you are an MCSE in the networking niche who started in the Windows NT 4.0 days. Over the years, you master Windows NT 4.0 and enjoy client respect. Then Windows 2000 is released, and you run head-on into Active Directory. Billing adjustments are made to account for time you spend learning Active Directory at the client site. This is time you can't reasonably expect the client to pay. So, you've got a legitimate write-off on your hands. Such write-offs are an acceptable part of being an MCSE consultant. You need to factor in learning curve analysis for product upgrades and new releases. It's all part of your budgeting model.

### Trying new niches

Professional services firms are often looking for new opportunities. One reason is that niches, while well defined and lucrative, can also mature and dry up. For example, suppose you're a Microsoft Small Business Server (SBS) consultant and Microsoft decides to release no future SBS upgrades. Over a couple of years, your SBS consulting niche can be expected to dry up.

Be thinking about and developing new niches. Such development is just good MCSE consulting management. The drawback is that in developing new niches you often have to take significant write-offs (which some MCSE consultants call write-downs) as you refine your consultant methodology and technical expertise. Many times such development comes through an implicit understanding with clients that you'll work for half-price on their job in order to break into that niche.

**Tip**

A good consulting manager knows to expect reasonable write-offs. In fact, if such write-offs are absent, the consultant manager knows that the MCSE consultants on staff are hiding mistakes, loafing on the job, or not expanding their professional and technical boundaries. A small number of mistakes go with the MCSE consulting territory, and if you are developing a new consulting niche, your propensity for making mistakes is higher while you are learning and mastering this new area.

# Budgeting Using Microsoft Excel

Time to convert the preceding guidance into a practical outcome: an MCSE consulting budget. So far you've thought about what you want to make (for example, $100,000 per year) and you've seen how the 50 percent utilization rate applies to you.

## Ask the Guru

I felt so strongly about the points raised in this reader e-mail that I've included it in the book to teach a lesson in negotiating. An MCSE consultant will negotiate financial matters on two fronts: client and staff. With clients, you will negotiate bill rates and the like. With staff that you supervise, you'll negotiate compensation matters such as salaries. The insights from a reader named Brian show in their own way that money isn't necessarily everything when negotiating in the business world.

*Dear Harry,*

*I just wanted to applaud you for your article on negotiations. This is a very important skill to have. I just switched jobs, and I had to do a lot of negotiating to get what I wanted. This meant at least three rounds of "back and forth." However, after the dust cleared, I think both the company and I were happy. Here's a brief outline of what we negotiated on:*

   - *Salary $X (about $5,000 below market average)*

   - *Laptop computer (top of the line)*

   - *Stock options roughly valued at $10,000 when the company goes IPO*

   - *Three weeks of vacation*

   - *Guaranteed performance review in six months*

*I feel quite happy with the deal we made. Maybe my salary is a bit lower; however, I have a 400 MHz Pentium II with a 15-inch screen, 3 weeks of vacation, and the possibility of getting more base salary money in six months.*

*Regards,*

*Brian Lee C.*

Brian,

Thanks for the e-mail and enlightening story. While financial rewards are important, it's sometimes more important to make good deals happen between good people. That can include your looking at nonfinancial rewards to make a job a great fit. It can also include MCSE consultants' working creatively with clients (perhaps taking an equity stake in the client company in lieu of cash compensation).

Best wishes,

harryb

## Supported bill rate

Part of the budgeting process is gathering information. You clearly need to know what markets you plan to operate within when it comes to bill rates. In general, urban markets tend to pay more than rural markets, reflecting increased cost of living. An MCSE consulting billing $125 per hour in Denver, Colorado, may only bill $40 per hour in Missoula, Montana. This example isn't far-fetched. Big cities offer a wonderful top line (the revenue picture), but sometimes the rural market offers the same bottom line with their lower cost of living. Two very different markets might offer the same financial compensation when all factors are taken into consideration.

Establishing your bill rate is critical because other key budget variables such as number of hours billed per year, profit margin, and the write-off rate have been established. In my simple examples in the next sections, I'll assume a bill rate of $100 per hour.

## Creating a budget

Microsoft Excel is the tool of choice when it comes to using a spreadsheet application to create a budget. Figure 12-1 shows the typical layout of a budget. The top section typically reflects revenues, both total gross revenues and the gross margin (which is net of write-downs). The middle section reflects expenses. The lower section speaks toward profitability.

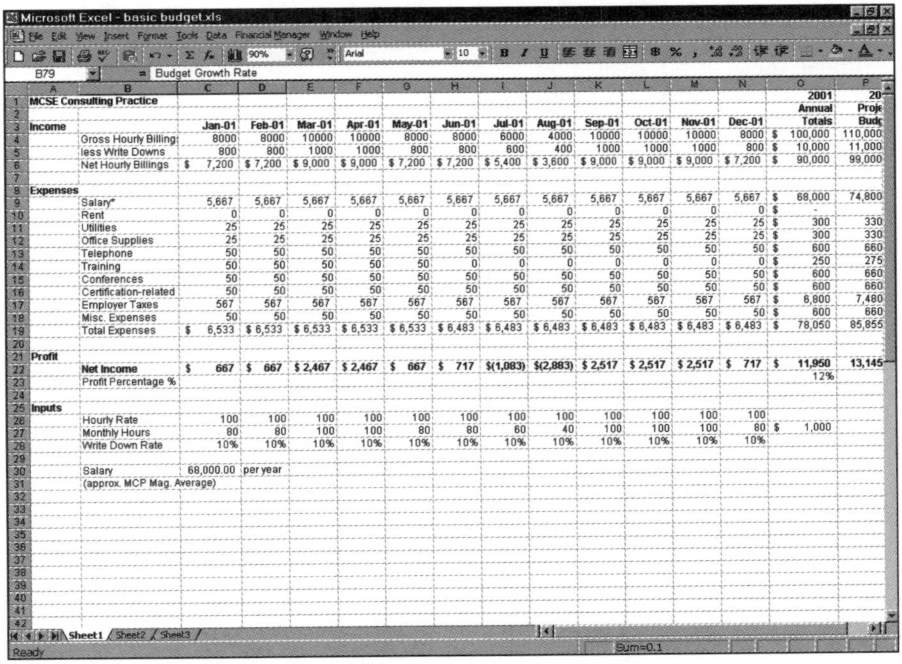


| | A | B | C | D | E | F | G | H | I | J | K | L | M | N | O | P |
|---|---|---|---|---|---|---|---|---|---|---|---|---|---|---|---|---|
| 1 | MCSE Consulting Practice | | | | | | | | | | | | | | 2001 | 20 |
| 2 | | | | | | | | | | | | | | | Annual | Proje |
| 3 | Income | | Jan-01 | Feb-01 | Mar-01 | Apr-01 | May-01 | Jun-01 | Jul-01 | Aug-01 | Sep-01 | Oct-01 | Nov-01 | Dec-01 | Totals | Budg |
| 4 | | Gross Hourly Billing: | 8000 | 8000 | 10000 | 10000 | 8000 | 8000 | 6000 | 4000 | 10000 | 10000 | 10000 | 8000 | $ 100,000 | 110,000 |
| 5 | | less Write Downs | 800 | 800 | 1000 | 1000 | 800 | 800 | 600 | 400 | 1000 | 1000 | 1000 | 800 | $ 10,000 | 11,000 |
| 6 | | Net Hourly Billings | $ 7,200 | $ 7,200 | $ 9,000 | $ 9,000 | $ 7,200 | $ 7,200 | $ 5,400 | $ 3,600 | $ 9,000 | $ 9,000 | $ 9,000 | $ 7,200 | $ 90,000 | 99,000 |
| 7 | | | | | | | | | | | | | | | | |
| 8 | Expenses | | | | | | | | | | | | | | | |
| 9 | | Salary* | 5,667 | 5,667 | 5,667 | 5,667 | 5,667 | 5,667 | 5,667 | 5,667 | 5,667 | 5,667 | 5,667 | 5,667 | $ 68,000 | 74,800 |
| 10 | | Rent | 0 | 0 | 0 | 0 | 0 | 0 | 0 | 0 | 0 | 0 | 0 | 0 | $ - | |
| 11 | | Utilities | 25 | 25 | 25 | 25 | 25 | 25 | 25 | 25 | 25 | 25 | 25 | 25 | $ 300 | 330 |
| 12 | | Office Supplies | 25 | 25 | 25 | 25 | 25 | 25 | 25 | 25 | 25 | 25 | 25 | 25 | $ 300 | 330 |
| 13 | | Telephone | 50 | 50 | 50 | 50 | 50 | 50 | 50 | 50 | 50 | 50 | 50 | 50 | $ 600 | 660 |
| 14 | | Training | 50 | 50 | 50 | 50 | 50 | 0 | 0 | 0 | 0 | 0 | 0 | 0 | $ 250 | 275 |
| 15 | | Conferences | 50 | 50 | 50 | 50 | 50 | 50 | 50 | 50 | 50 | 50 | 50 | 50 | $ 600 | 660 |
| 16 | | Certification-related | 50 | 50 | 50 | 50 | 50 | 50 | 50 | 50 | 50 | 50 | 50 | 50 | $ 600 | 660 |
| 17 | | Employer Taxes | 567 | 567 | 567 | 567 | 567 | 567 | 567 | 567 | 567 | 567 | 567 | 567 | $ 6,800 | 7,480 |
| 18 | | Misc. Expenses | 50 | 50 | 50 | 50 | 50 | 50 | 50 | 50 | 50 | 50 | 50 | 50 | $ 600 | 660 |
| 19 | | Total Expenses | $ 6,533 | $ 6,533 | $ 6,533 | $ 6,533 | $ 6,533 | $ 6,483 | $ 6,483 | $ 6,483 | $ 6,483 | $ 6,483 | $ 6,483 | $ 6,483 | $ 78,050 | 85,855 |
| 20 | | | | | | | | | | | | | | | | |
| 21 | Profit | | | | | | | | | | | | | | | |
| 22 | | **Net Income** | **$ 667** | **$ 667** | **$ 2,467** | **$ 2,467** | **$ 667** | **$ 717** | **$(1,083)** | **$(2,883)** | **$ 2,517** | **$ 2,517** | **$ 2,517** | **$ 717** | **$ 11,950** | **13,145** |
| 23 | | Profit Percentage % | | | | | | | | | | | | | 12% | |
| 24 | | | | | | | | | | | | | | | | |
| 25 | Inputs | | | | | | | | | | | | | | | |
| 26 | | Hourly Rate | 100 | 100 | 100 | 100 | 100 | 100 | 100 | 100 | 100 | 100 | 100 | 100 | | |
| 27 | | Monthly Hours | 80 | 80 | 100 | 100 | 80 | 80 | 60 | 40 | 100 | 100 | 100 | 80 | $ 1,000 | |
| 28 | | Write Down Rate | 10% | 10% | 10% | 10% | 10% | 10% | 10% | 10% | 10% | 10% | 10% | 10% | | |
| 29 | | | | | | | | | | | | | | | | |
| 30 | | Salary | 68,000.00 | per year | | | | | | | | | | | | |
| 31 | | (approx. MCP Mag. Average) | | | | | | | | | | | | | | |

**Figure 12-1:** Basic budget showing key formulas

Notice the dates across the side of the budget, going from left to right. These are typically displayed by month with an annual total after 12 months. The consultant referenced in Figure 12-1 earns an average MCSE salary of $68,000.

Notice that the employer contribution of taxes was expensed at 10 percent. This is the self-employment contribution tax. The profitability rate of 12 percent is slightly ahead of the profitability rate goal of 10 percent. The $68,000 salary paid the MCSE consultant is before standard employee wage withholding. This budget analysis didn't account for the MCSE consultant's insurance and benefits, which suggests the MCSE consultant, working for himself or herself, receives no benefits and insurance under this scenario or pays for these costs out of profit. In fact, this MCSE consultant would be advised to raise his or her bill rates to fund a retirement and benefits package next budget year.

# Extrapolation

A popular way to budget is to simply add a growth factor to the prior year's budget. Add 10 percent to last year's budget to account for inflation, new consulting activity, and so on. Figure 12-2 displays this practice where an additional annual column for the year 2002 has been added to reflect 10 percent growth in everything across the board.

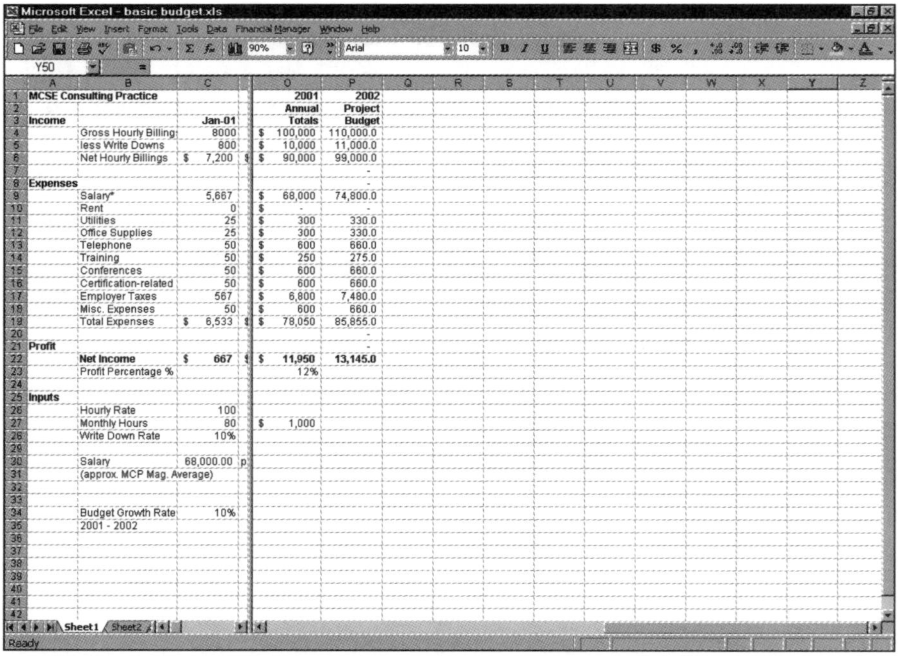


| | A | B | C | O | P |
|---|---|---|---|---|---|
| 1 | MCSE Consulting Practice | | | 2001 | 2002 |
| 2 | | | | Annual | Project |
| 3 | Income | | Jan-01 | Totals | Budget |
| 4 | | Gross Hourly Billing | 8000 | $ 100,000 | 110,000.0 |
| 5 | | less Write Downs | 800 | $ 10,000 | 11,000.0 |
| 6 | | Net Hourly Billings | $ 7,200 | $ 90,000 | 99,000.0 |
| 7 | | | | | - |
| 8 | Expenses | | | | - |
| 9 | | Salary* | 5,667 | $ 68,000 | 74,800.0 |
| 10 | | Rent | 0 | $ - | - |
| 11 | | Utilities | 25 | $ 300 | 330.0 |
| 12 | | Office Supplies | 25 | $ 300 | 330.0 |
| 13 | | Telephone | 50 | $ 600 | 660.0 |
| 14 | | Training | 50 | $ 250 | 275.0 |
| 15 | | Conferences | 50 | $ 600 | 660.0 |
| 16 | | Certification-related | 50 | $ 600 | 660.0 |
| 17 | | Employer Taxes | 567 | $ 6,800 | 7,480.0 |
| 18 | | Misc. Expenses | 50 | $ 600 | 660.0 |
| 19 | | Total Expenses | $ 6,533 | $ 78,050 | 85,855.0 |
| 20 | | | | | - |
| 21 | Profit | | | | - |
| 22 | | **Net Income** | **$ 667** | **$ 11,950** | **13,145.0** |
| 23 | | Profit Percentage % | | 12% | |
| 25 | Inputs | | | | |
| 26 | | Hourly Rate | 100 | | |
| 27 | | Monthly Hours | 80 | $ 1,000 | |
| 28 | | Write Down Rate | 10% | | |
| 30 | | Salary | 68,000.00 | | |
| 31 | | (approx. MCP Mag. Average) | | | |
| 34 | | Budget Growth Rate | 10% | | |
| 35 | | 2001 - 2002 | | | |

**Figure 12-2:** Extrapolated budget growth of 10 percent

This form of budget is a massive oversimplification of how the real world works. Nonetheless, it's a favorite among entrepreneurs and MCSE consultants alike who just want to get the general picture about how things look now and in the future.

**Tip**　The 10 percent growth in revenues can be accomplished one of two ways. The first method is to work 10 percent additional hours. This increases your total working hours for the year when you factor in the 50 percent utilization rate. The second method for increasing revenues is to increase your bill rate. It is common for professional services firms to announce rate increases to reflect inflation, increased efficiency, more value-added services, and so on.

## Zero-based budgeting

My favorite budgeting method is the zero-based budgeting. This method is from the land of MBAs; it is detail oriented but surprisingly accurate. With zero-based budgeting, you typically use linked spreadsheets that allow you to enter the details of a particular budgeting category, such as the telephone expenses seen in Figure 12-3, on a child spreadsheet. The detailed information is then summarized as a category in the master budget (which was shown previously in Figure 12-1).

| | | Jan-01 | Feb-01 | Mar-01 | Apr-01 | May-01 | Jun-01 | Jul-01 | Aug-01 | Sep-01 | Oct-01 | Nov-01 | Dec-01 |
|---|---|---|---|---|---|---|---|---|---|---|---|---|---|
| **Telephone Expense** | | | | | | | | | | | | | |
| **Regular Service (US West)** | | | | | | | | | | | | | |
| | Monthly Flat Fee | 10 | 10 | 10 | 10 | 10 | 10 | 10 | 10 | 10 | 10 | 10 | 10 |
| | Voice Mail | 2 | 2 | 2 | 2 | 2 | 2 | 2 | 2 | 2 | 2 | 2 | 2 |
| **Cellular Service (Verizon)** | | | | | | | | | | | | | |
| | Basic Plan | 18 | 18 | 18 | 18 | 18 | 18 | 18 | 18 | 18 | 18 | 18 | 18 |
| | Roaming | 2 | 2 | 2 | 2 | 2 | 2 | 2 | 2 | 2 | 2 | 2 | 2 |
| **Long-Distance (Sprint)** | | 18 | 18 | 18 | 18 | 18 | 18 | 18 | 18 | 18 | 18 | 18 | 18 |
| Total | | | | | | | | | | | | | |
| | Link To Row 13 | | | | | | | | | | | | |
| | Basic Budget | $ 50.00 | $ 50.00 | $ 50.00 | $ 50.00 | $ 50.00 | $ 50.00 | $ 50.00 | $ 50.00 | $ 50.00 | $ 50.00 | $ 50.00 | $ 50.00 |

**Figure 12-3:** Details for the telephone expenses in a linked spreadsheet

In a true zero-based budgeting scenario, you create a child spreadsheet for each budget category. These child spreadsheets are then linked to the master budget spreadsheet. You then call around to get costs (for example, estimated utility expenses) or look at actual bills (for example, from the telephone company). For the client billings, your spreadsheet may look similar to Figure 12-4 where the clients are listed by name and the monthly billings are inserted into the appropriate spreadsheet cells. To arrive at these billings, you would be advised to sit down with your clients and discuss their expected needs over the next year (monthly maintenance, upgrades, and so on).

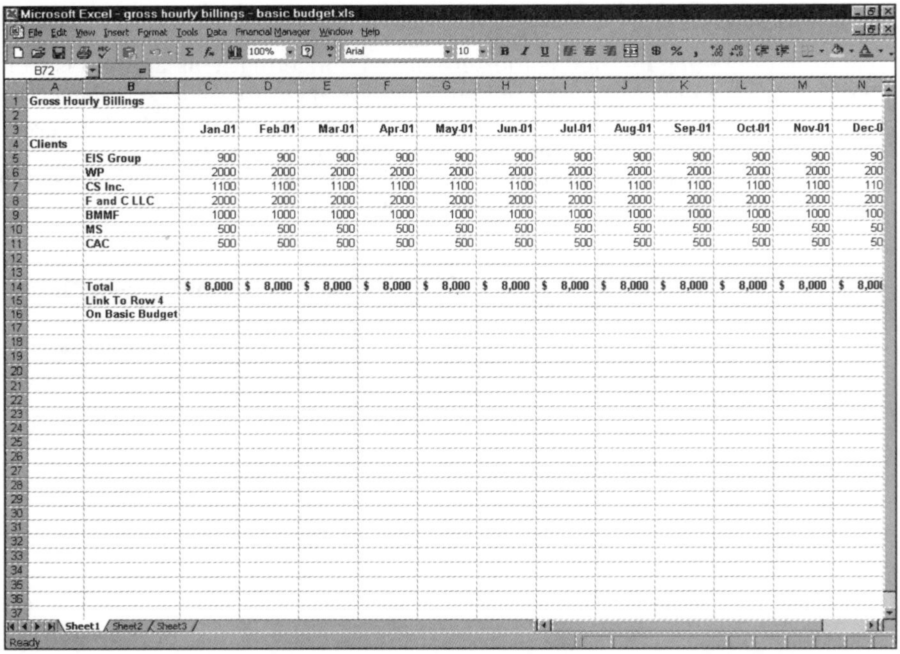

**Figure 12-4:** The framework for estimating your client billing on a monthly basis

## Break-even analysis

Budgeting has a very important role in the MCSE consultant's life. But a budget requires you to make assumptions. In budgeting, especially the extrapolation method, the inherent assumption is that you have an operating history on which to base your budget numbers.

What's an MCSE consultant to do if they have no operating history and just want to know if they'll make it or not? To answer that, I use the break-even analysis method in Microsoft Excel. I've changed the MCSE consulting scenario slightly so you can see the outcome in detailed numbers. As seen in Figure 12-5, the MCSE consultant wants to gross $125,000 per year billing at $105 per hour. The answer, via break-even analysis, is to bill 1,190 hours, which is a considerable amount of work.

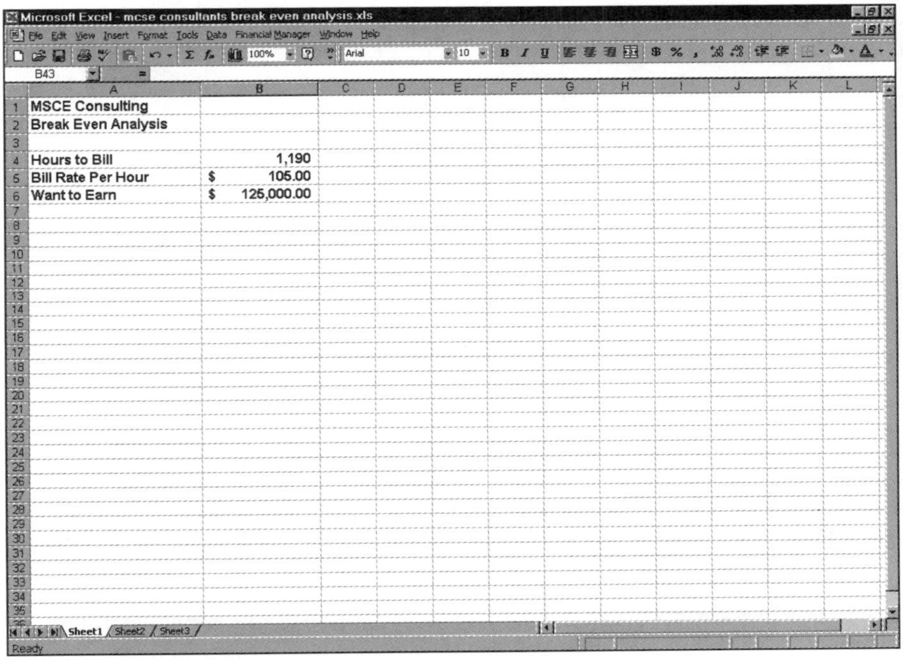

**Figure 12-5:** Break-even analysis using Microsoft Excel

In break-even analysis, you interpret the results by asking yourself if you believe you can bill that many hours at that rate in your marketplace. If you feel confident about it, you have your answer. Break-even analysis, in spreadsheet form, is wonderful for playing *what if* or what is more formally known as sensitivity analysis. In this form of analysis you change your variables to create different financial scenarios. For example, perhaps you think billing the nearly 1,200 hours mentioned in the previous example is too aggressive. What if you raised your bill rate to $125 per hour as part of testing a different scenario? As seen in Figure 12-6, in this new scenario you have to bill only 1,000 hours, which is a much more reasonable number with which to work.

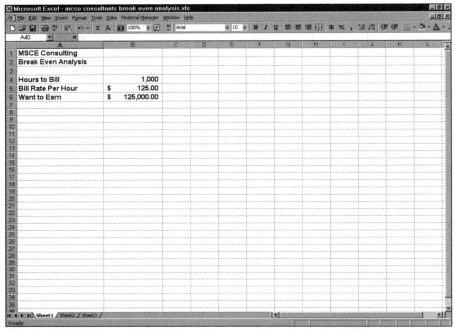

**Figure 12-6:** Testing a different scenario using break-even analysis for sensitivity analysis

The keystrokes for the break-even analysis spreadsheet are shown in Table 12-1.

## Table 12-1
## Creating A Break-even Analysis Spreadsheet

| Cell | Input |
| --- | --- |
| A1 | Type **MCSE Consulting** |
| A2 | Type **Break-even Analysis** |
| A4 | Type **Hours to Bill** |
| A5 | Type **Bill Rate Per Hour** |
| A6 | Type **Want to Earn** |
| B4 | Type **=B6/B5** |
| B5 | Type your hourly bill rate ($105) |
| B6 | Type the gross consulting income you want to earn ($125,000) on an annual basis |

Assuming you have completed the keystrokes in Table 12-1, you have now created a break-even analysis spreadsheet that allows you to play *what if* using sensitivity analysis. More importantly, you can answer your own questions about whether or not you can really make it or not as an MCSE consultant.

# Planning Your Accounting System

You have to have one. That's certainly the first response from any businessperson about accounting systems. MCSE consultants are no different. Whether you love, hate, or are indifferent to accounting system applications, they are necessary. In this section, I discuss QuickBooks and a Web-based accounting service.

## QuickBooks

QuickBooks is a popular small business accounting program from Intuit, the makers of the Quicken home accounting application. Some of the key features of QuickBooks include the following:

✦ **Ease of setup** — QuickBooks' Wizard-based installation is essentially bullet-proof if you simply click Next and accept the default setup conditions. Ease of setup also includes selecting from a sample chart of accounts to ease the company creation process.

✦ **Basic general accounting support** — This kind of support includes general ledger (G/L), accounts payable (A/P), and accounts receivable (A/R) functions.

✦ **Basic job costing, time tracking, and estimating** — These features are helpful in tracking budget versus actual performance on a per client or per job basis.

✦ **Multiuser support** — QuickBooks can run over a network using this support.

✦ **Reporting and graphing** — QuickBooks has a sufficient reporting function that allows the small business, such as the MCSE consulting firm, to understand where it's at financially.

✦ **Other features that may or may not suit your needs** — These features include payroll, inventory, and invoicing capabilities. Note that while invoicing is important, for that function you may want to use a more robust time and billing package such as Timeslips (which I discuss in Chapter 13).

**Note**  I've always felt QuickBooks does a great job of managing user expectations. The features are clearly identified on the retail packaging, and the product never claims to work for anything other than small businesses. Clearly, QuickBooks isn't designed for the medium or large MCSE consulting firm, so if you grow into a sizeable operation, you will need to select a more robust business accounting solution such as Great Plains Dynamics. Great Plains Dynamics is more modular, allowing you to purchase specific modules that you need while ignoring others. For example, if you were seeking sophisticated job costing, you would want to consider the job cost module for Great Plains Dynamics.

The following steps will walk you through installation of QuickBooks and setting up a consulting practice in QuickBooks.

To install QuickBooks:

1. Place the QuickBooks CD-ROM in your CD drive.

2. Click Install when the QuickBooks splash screen (with logo) appears. This is an autorun screen and will appear automatically when the CD drive reads the QuickBooks CD-ROM. If your computer doesn't have autorun capabilities, simply run the setup program (setup.exe) on the QuickBooks CD-ROM.

3. Click Next after reading the Welcome screen.

4. Click Yes on the Software Licenses Agreement screen.

5. Type your key code in the Key code field of the Enter Installation Key Code screen. Click Next.

6. Accept or change the program installation folder on the Choose Destination Location screen. Click Next.

7. Accept or change the program group name on the Select Program Folder screen and click Next.

8. Review the setup information on the Start Copying Files screen and click Next. The QuickBooks program will be installed, and a progress bar will be visible.

9. Agree or disagree when asked in the Question dialog box about placing a QuickBooks shortcut on your desktop.

10. Click Finish on the Setup Complete screen. You are now ready to use QuickBooks.

To set up a company in QuickBooks:

1. Click Start ➪ Programs ➪ QuickBooks Pro program group.

2. Select the QuickBooks Pro program item. QuickBooks Pro launches.

3. Click the "Setup a new data file for a company" button on the Welcome to QuickBooks Pro for Windows dialog box.

4. Click OK.

5. The EasyStep Interview Wizard launches. In Figure 12-7, you see the Welcome tab. Click Next.

6. Select whether or not you are upgrading from another Quicken or QuickBooks product on the screen that follows. In this example, the "No, I'm not upgrading" radio button was clicked. Click Next.

7. The next screen allows you to terminate the interview process by selecting the Skip Interview process. Ignore this button and click Next to continue with the QuickBooks setup interview.

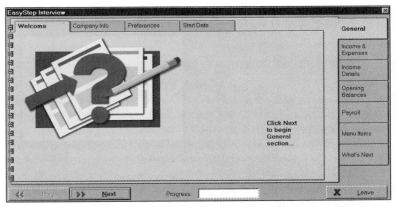

**Figure 12-7:** The first screen of the EasyStep Interview process

8. Click Next after reading the navigation screen.

9. Click Next after reading the information screen about EasyStep Interview sections and topics.

10. Click Next after reading about the ability to change selections during the EasyStep Interview process.

11. Click Next when the Welcome completed screen appears.

12. The general Company Info screen appears. Click Next.

13. Type your company name and legal name on the "Your company name" screen, as seen in Figure 12-8. Click Next.

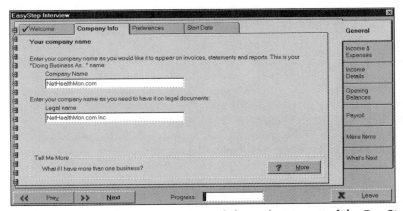

**Figure 12-8:** Providing company name information as part of the EasyStep Interview process

**14.** Provide company address information on the "Your company address" screen and click Next. This is shown in Figure 12-9.

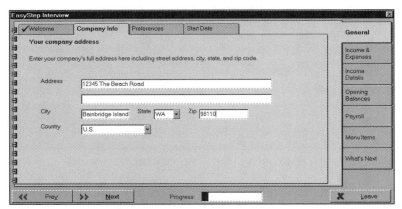

**Figure 12-9:** Providing company address information

**15.** Provide a federal tax ID number on the "Other company information" screen. Confirm the first month for the income tax and the fiscal year. This is shown in Figure 12-10. Click Next.

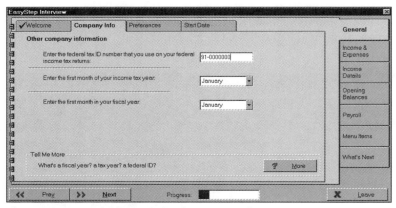

**Figure 12-10:** Providing a federal tax ID number

**16.** Select the income tax form your company uses on the "Your company income tax form" screen and click Next.

**17.** Select the type of business you are in the list under Industry on the "Select your type of business" screen. MCSE consultants would select Consulting (see Figure 12-11). Click Next.

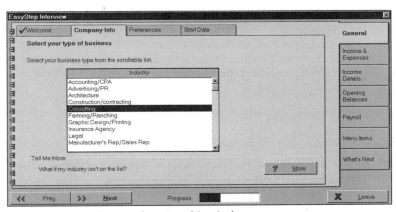

**Figure 12-11:** Selecting the consulting industry

18. Read the "Setup tips for business" screen and click Next.

19. Click Next when notified that QuickBooks is ready to create your company file.

20. Provide a file name in the Save As dialog box that appears and click Next.

21. This is a key setup step. Select the Yes radio button when allowed to use the suggested consulting-related chart of accounts, as seen in Figure 12-12. Click Next.

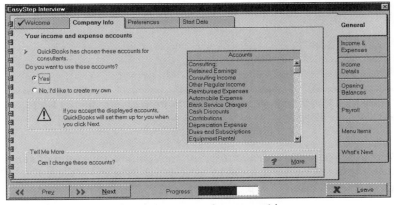

**Figure 12-12:** Accepting the suggested account titles

22. Complete the "Accessing your company" screen where you indicate how many people will have access to your QuickBooks data. Click Next.

23. Click Next when you see the "Company Info completed" screen.

You have now set up the QuickBooks accounting system for an MCSE consulting firm. The EasyStep Interview continues with the Preferences and Start Date sections. The Preferences section allows you to determine what QuickBooks features you want turned off or on. The Start Date section allows you to provide critical opening date information so that the historic balance sheet and income statement reporting are calculated and displayed correctly.

To complete the Preferences and Start Date sections:

1. Read the "What are preferences" screen and click Next.

2. Answer Yes or No on the Inventory screen regarding whether or not your company maintains inventory and click Next.

3. Answer Yes or No on the Sales tax screen regarding whether or not your company collects sales tax (your answer will vary based on government regulation). This is shown in Figure 12-13.

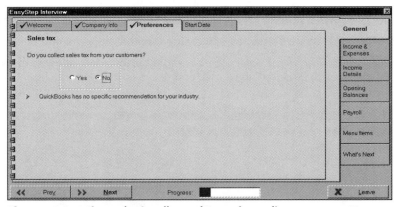

**Figure 12-13:** If you don't collect sales tax from clients, answer No to the Sales tax screen.

4. Select the appropriate invoice style on the "Your invoice format" screen. In my case, the Service invoice format was selected, as seen in Figure 12-14. Click Next.

5. Answer how many employees you have on payroll on the Employees screen and click Next.

6. Answer whether or not you prepare written or verbal client estimates on the Estimates screen, as shown in Figure 12-15. Click Next.

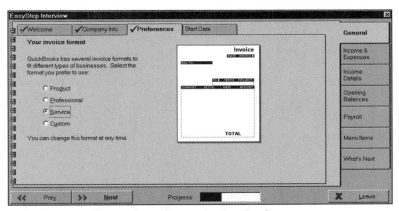

**Figure 12-14:** Observe how the Service invoice format appears.

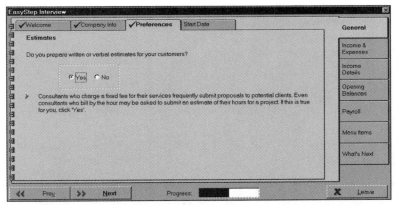

**Figure 12-15:** Tell QuickBooks whether or not you provide estimates to your clients.

7. On the Progress Invoicing screen indicate whether or not you bill for partial work completed, as seen in Figure 12-16. Click Next.

8. Answer Yes on the Time tracking screen if you want to track time (your time and employee time) by job and project. Click Next.

9. On the "Track segments of your business with 'classes'" screen, advise QuickBooks as to whether or not you have discrete business units or divisions by answering Yes or No. This is shown in Figure 12-17. Click Next.

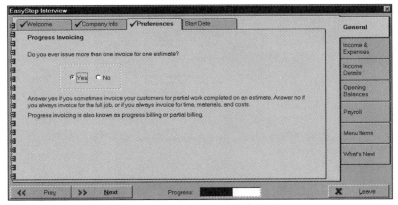

**Figure 12-16:** If you engage in partial billing, your answer on the Progress Invoicing screen is Yes.

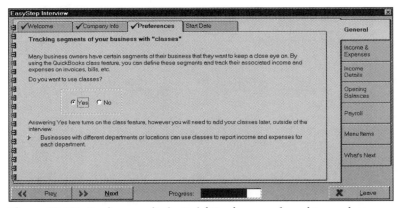

**Figure 12-17:** Business units in QuickBooks are referred to as classes

10. Advise QuickBooks on how your handle bills and payments on the "Two ways to handle bills and payments" screen, as seen in Figure 12-18. Click Next.

11. Answer when you would like to receive reminders on the Reminders list screen and click Next.

12. Define your business as cash-based or accrual accounting–based. Most small MCSE consulting practices tend to be cash-based. Click Next.

13. Click Next on the Preferences completed screen.

14. Read the information on the "Understanding your QuickBooks start date" screen and click Next.

15. On the "Information for your start date" screen, read the educational information about what start dates are and how they impact you and click Next.

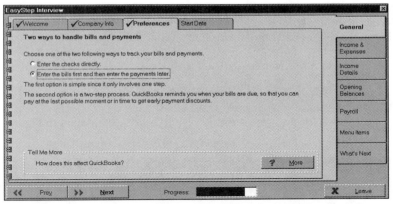

**Figure 12-18:** You may enter checks first or bills first depending on your answer.

16. Enter your start date on the "Choose your QuickBooks start date" screen and click Next. This is shown in Figure 12-19.

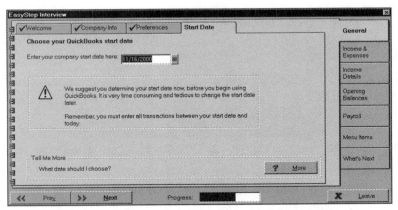

**Figure 12-19:** Your company start date is a critical value entered as part of the QuickBooks setup.

17. Click Next on the General section completed screen. Close the EasyStep Interview Wizard.

QuickBooks is now ready for basic use. There are more advanced configuration areas that may require the advice of an accountant, but at this stage, QuickBooks is functional. The advanced areas are on the right side of the EasyStep Interview dialog box. There you will notice tabs for Income and Expenses, Income Details, and Opening Balances. You complete this information to provide a complete financial profile for a snapshot in time. This time snapshot is typically based on the day you installed and set up QuickBooks, which in the world of finance is referred to as time period zero. Rarely does someone go back and input historic data.

You enter a transaction, such as writing a check, in QuickBooks with the following steps:

1. The QuickBooks Navigator appears when you start QuickBooks. It is the central interface for your accounting activity and is displayed in Figure 12-20.

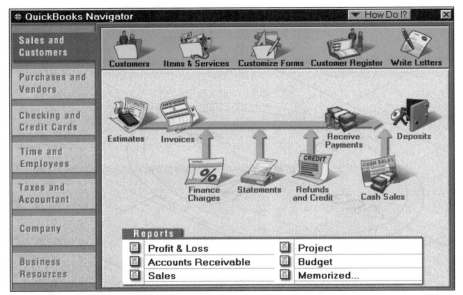

**Figure 12-20:** The user interface for QuickBooks is considered to be very friendly.

2. Select Purchases and Vendors.

3. Click Enter Bills. The Enter Bills screen appears.

4. Enter a vendor name on the Vendor line.

5. Select Quick Add when the Add Vendor dialog box appears. You are returned to the Enter Bills screen.

6. Complete the Amount Due and Memo fields on the Enter Bills screen similar to Figure 12-21.

7. Click on the Accounting column in the Expenses section of the Enter Bills screen and assign an expense account to this transaction.

8. Click OK. You have now entered a transaction in QuickBooks.

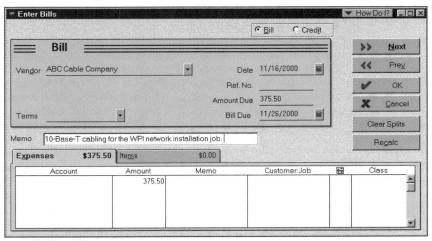

**Figure 12-21:** Complete a bill to be paid transaction in QuickBooks.

After you enter in your income and expense transactions for your MCSE consulting practice, you can generate accounting reports, including balance sheets, income statements, cash flow positions, project accounting reports, and a number of custom reports. A basic report with limited financial information entered in the QuickBooks system is displayed in Figure 12-22.

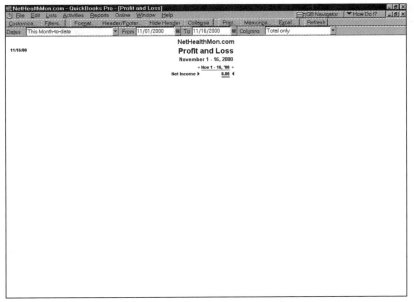

**Figure 12-22:** A sample Profit and Loss statement for a sample MCSE consulting practice with limited information entered in the system

## Web-based accounting

Another consideration for your MCSE consulting accounting needs is Web-based application service providers. One benefit to using a Web-based accounting system is that you can access it from nearly any location you work (even client sites) as long as you're connected to the Internet with a compatible browser. Two such providers are ready to serve the MCSE consultant who doesn't want to have a local accounting system — NetLedger (www.netledger.com) and ePeachtree (www.epeachtree.com). NetLedger, seen in Figure 12-23, charges approximately $4.95 per month for basic accounting services. More robust services, such as allowing customers to log on with limited rights to look at their account balances, run $19.95 per month.

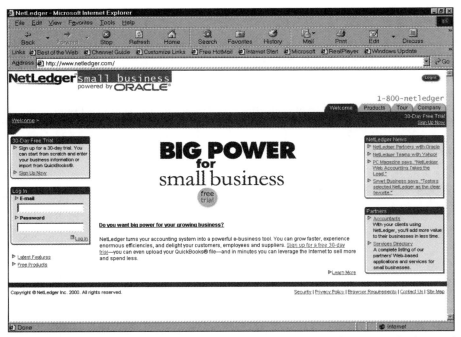

**Figure 12-23:** NetLedger offers online accounting services with basic and advanced capabilities.

Peachtree is a well respected small business accounting application that has sold very well for years. The Web-based accounting service of Peachtree, called ePeachtree, is shown in Figure 12-24. This system offers features comparable to NetLedger, and prices start at $9.99 per month.

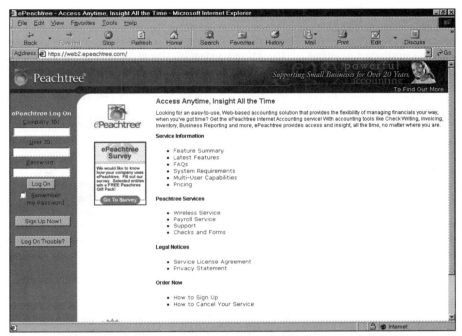

**Figure 12-24:** Web-based accounting services from ePeachtree

# Boosting Your MCSE Return on Investment

Once you've looked at making money from an MCSE consulting point of view and considered how to account for this money, it is important to visit the mathematics of certification return on investment (ROI). That is, how has the MCSE certification made money for you and how can you boost your return on the certification component? My thoughts here speak toward MCSEs in general, including MCSE consultants and in-house IS employees on salary.

## ROI mathematics

An ROI equation has three variables:

✦ **Costs** — These are your certification costs, which include course fees, exam fees, book purchases, lost wages at work while studying, and so on. In this example, I'll assume $10,000 in costs to get certified.

✦ **Inflows** — Inflows are the extra cash you will make because you are certified. For this example, assume that you will enjoy an extra $5,000 per year once you're certified.

✦ **Duration**—How long is the ROI relationship valid? Does your certification have a useful life associated with it? You bet it does. Assume the useful life for the MCSE is about four years because within four years it's likely you'll need to pursue yet another certification to stay on the cutting edge of your field as a technology professional.

The ROI formula is as follows: ((Inflows × Duration) – Costs) / Costs. In English, you invest $10,000 and receive an extra $5,000 a year for four years because of your certification investment. Here the ROI is 100 percent. Obtaining the MCSE certification is a good investment in this case.

However, should you somehow account for the many hours you toiled to earn your MCSE? That's bound to reduce your ROI. Ongoing certification costs, while not overwhelming, also reduce ROI values (remember that you'll probably need to take a certification exam each year to maintain your MCSE designation). Further, in the world of corporate finance, a thing called *time value of money* penalizes inflows in the future by some rate to account for risk, inflation, and the fact that said dollars aren't in your hand today, ready to be invested by you.

## Lowering your costs

There are several ways to boost your MCSE ROI. An often overlooked way is simply to lower your certification costs. Instead of attending fancy MCSE classes and running up that $10,000 certification bill, perhaps you could get certified for $1,000 using videos, software-based practice assessment exams, and free advice from your MCSE buddies. If you're able to do that (lower your MCSE certification costs to just $1,000), your ROI (based on the same assumptions from the previous example) increases dramatically to 1,900 percent. That's the power of controlling your costs.

This example isn't far-fetched. Many of you are forming study groups to save money, using a variety of software-based practice assessment exams, attending online training courses, and so on. The lesson learned is that it's not always how much you make but how little you spend (see the book *The Millionaire Mind* by Thomas J. Stanley, published by Andrews McMeel Publishing).

The best way to lower your costs is to get your boss (if you work for an MCSE consulting firm) to pay for your certification. At that point, your ROI is off the charts because you have no explicit costs in your ROI model. But beware, because now it's your boss who's looking for a significant ROI.

## Raising your bill rates

I've saved the best advice for last. One of the most obvious ways to boost your ROI, based on the mathematical equation, is to raise your effective bill rate. You can raise your bill rate effectively in several ways.

## Inflation

The old saying that "all politics is local" can be changed to "all inflation is local" when MCSEs look at reasons to raise their bill rates. Here is what I mean. You can track the broad inflationary measures such as the Consumer Price Index (CPI) and consider how that relates to you, but you're far better off looking at how costs around you are rising. I recently raised my bill rates $5 per hour to account for an increase in my health insurance costs. In the past, for my family, I was paying $400 per month for full health insurance coverage. When it came time to renew, the costs for the same policy had increased to $650 per month. It was necessary for me to increase my MCSE consulting bill rate slightly to pay for this inflationary effect of increasing costs for my health insurance.

## Increased skill set

Suppose you've added another certification from Microsoft. This effort to gain another certification represents an increase in your basic skill set. Perhaps a bill rate increase of $10 or more per hour can now be justified.

## New title and responsibilities

If your role has fundamentally changed and you have risen in rank from MCSE consultant at the hands-on level to MCSE consulting manager, a higher bill rate is justified. In this latter role, you are likely providing management expertise and project management services. These skills tend to be valued higher than technician skills when such skills as management and project management are warranted on a consulting engagement.

## Billable hour minimum

Another way to raise your ROI via your effective bill rate is to impose a one- or two-hour minimum per client call. If you tell your clients that you have a two-hour billable hour minimum, the clients will think twice about calling you out for small tasks they can solve on their own. And these are typically tasks that you have little interest in solving. Imposing such a minimum is also a legitimate way to bill up. If you make five client visits in an eight-hour day with a two-hour minimum (assuming all parties are in agreement with this provision), you will have mathematically billed ten hours in an eight-hour day, which raises your effective bill rate by approximately 20 percent.

## Travel time

Another overlooked billing category that will contribute to your profitability is billing for travel time. Think for a moment about what you sell in any workday: time. At some level, you are indifferent as to whether that time is billed sitting in a car commuting to an engagement or working at a client site. When I was with a large consulting firm, we billed for travel time. This act had a way of contributing positively to the bottom line of the financial statements.

**Tip**

I recently mentored a new MCSE consultant along the path to profitability. When I met James, he was billing at a rate nearly 40 percent below market. He was booked so solid on his consulting schedule that he was to the point of being fatigued and not giving his best effort to any one client. In the final analysis, both James and his clients suffered from less than stellar outcomes. Later, when James raised his rate to market, he lost a couple of clients but ended up making more money because of the higher bill rate. His schedule wasn't booked solid, he had time for technical training to increase his skill set, and he enjoyed a few afternoons of long-deserved rest. He thanked me for teaching him how to work smarter and more profitably.

## Rule of Ten: Survey Ten Competitors for Bill Rates

Now that you've read about ways to make money as an MCSE consultant, you need to perform a reality check and make sure the market will bear the bill rates you have in mind. Contact ten competitors in your consulting space (ones that you consider to be viable competitors) and ask what their bill rates are. Much of this research can be performed over the Web, as many consulting firms are proud to publish what they charge clients. Assess the results of your research to either affirm or further question the bill rate you intend to set for charging clients.

**Tip**

One client explained bill rates to me this way. Bill rates are all relative. He commented that I could charge $300 per hour if I wanted and that he would gladly pay this fee if it quickly solved a huge problem. He was alluding to the fact that I could potentially solve a $10,000 problem for him in just a few billable hours. But, he cautioned, on the other hand, I could charge $100 per hour, and if it took tens of hours longer to solve the problem (or worse yet, I never solved his problem), he would dispute my bill to him. He might ultimately pay part of it, but he would be dissatisfied. The point is that good clients will gladly pay more than a fair bill rate to an MCSE consultant who produces results.

## Summary

This chapter covered a very important area for all MCSE consultants: making and accounting for your money. It is essential that you manage your MCSE consulting practice to be profitable in the long run. Specific discussion areas included determining the income you want to earn from consulting, understanding the 50 percent utilization rate of MCSE consulting, and reviewing MCSE moneymaking strategies. This chapter also presented budgeting and accounting methods in great detail, as well an advanced financial discussion on return of investment (ROI) concepts.

✦    ✦    ✦

# Running the Business — Workload, Paperwork, and Administration

◆   ◆   ◆   ◆

**In This Chapter**

Appreciating the day-to-day focus of running an MCSE consulting practice

Working within the constraints of the organizational structure you have selected

Understanding inherent limitations in client size and scope

Understanding how to manage and bill for your time

◆   ◆   ◆   ◆

**I**t is possible the one activity that will take as much, if not more, time than any other work you do as an MCSE consultant will be to run the business. The act of running the business you've created is distinctly different from other activities, such as managing client relationships, installing BackOffice, and so on. This chapter is Business Management 101.

## Managing Land, Labor, and Capital

As a businessperson, you wear many hats. The three big ones in this book are the finder, minder, and grinder hats. In the minder role, which is also the title of the part of the book we're in, there are additional hats. I've found management by its very definition to be a variety of hats worn by one person performing lots of general tasks. It's the economist's vision of managing land, labor, and capital.

## Organizational structure

If you haven't already done so, you need to look at how your business is organized. Many MCSE consulting practices start with just one person calling himself or herself an MCSE consultant and billing clients for services rendered. It's easy to let too much time pass without revisiting whether or not your organizational structure is appropriate.

### Sole proprietorship

Combine an MCSE, a business license, and business cards, and you're a sole proprietor MCSE consultant. It's possible you're doing business under your own name, so clients write checks directly to you. Perhaps you use your own personal checking account. In fact, your checkbook may well be your accounting system. Again, this is how most MCSE consultants begin operations. This system may meet your needs only for a short while, or it may suffice over the long term.

### Partnership

Now envision two or more MCSEs, a partnership agreement, a business license, and business cards, and you have a partnership. There are many different types of partnerships, but basically you're looking at MCSE consultants who've grown beyond the sole proprietorship stage. It is common to see MCSEs form a partnership together after they've been working side-by-side on common projects and the clients are tired of receiving two separate bills from two separate sole proprietor MCSE consultants.

Note    Understand that all of my discussion about organizational structures needs to be followed up with a visit to the business attorney of your choice. A business attorney is best qualified to advise you on what organizational structure is the best fit for your situation.

### Corporation

Another viable business organization, which comes in different shapes and sizes, is the corporation. Here you have MCSEs working together but seeking the corporate shield of limited liability to protect their assets. Running a corporation is more complex than running other organizational forms. It involves reporting requirements, especially if you are a public corporation (which means you will need to file numerous reports with securities regulators). It also involves more administrative tasks — such as the issuance of corporate stock certificates and the procurement of a corporate seal — as well as increased communication requirements, since certain forms of information must be provided to shareholders and the public (if it is a public corporation).

Cross-Reference    I include a general discussion about organizational structures in Appendix B.

## Management tips

In this world, there is no shortage of business people willing to give you free advice. Typically such advice is worth exactly what you paid for it: nothing. Part of your maturation process as an MCSE consulting practice manager will be your ability to separate the good advice from the bad advice. Better yet, you'll want to develop your own management "do's and don'ts" based on your own experiences. It's something that managers do. Following are some management tips I've learned along the way as an MCSE consultant.

## Managing growth

First and foremost, I advise you not to fall into the trap of growing too quickly. It's an easy trap to fall into, given an MCSE consultant's natural enthusiasm to do more, take on more work, and so on. In your MCSE practice, assuming you are competent and do good work that is appreciated by your clients, you're far more likely to fail from growing too quickly than from not growing fast enough.

Perhaps you've seen this with other consulting practices in your area. A couple of technology practitioners get hot in the marketplace soon after launching their practice. Late nights and a flurry of activity follow, with maybe even a few hurried hires along the way. This upward slope of activity continues unimpeded for a while. Then an implosion occurs. The consultants miss deadlines because they took on too much work. Client dissatisfaction grows. New business dries up and existing contracts mature, strangling cash flow.

In the next few sections, I provide growth management tips based on marketplace size.

## Small marketplace

The small business market known as the small organization (SORG) marketplace is illustrated in Figure 13-1.

**Figure 13-1:** Welcome to the small business marketplace.

This is the easiest market to break into because of its large number of potential clients and high turnover. Small business technology consultants, many of whom are MCSEs, come and go. Some burn out and seek jobs on salary (say as in-house LAN administrators). Others use the small business marketplace as a launching pad into MCSE consulting and move on to the medium- and enterprise-sized marketplaces.

### Rule of Ten: Ten clients

You need only 10 clients that average 100 billable hours per year in the SORG consulting space. I've learned this the hard way and ascribe to this rule religiously.

Once, while short staffed at the Pacific Northwest regional consulting firm I worked for, I had my own area of consulting responsibility grow to 20 clients. This went on for a couple of months, and fairly quickly, the fallout arrived. I found my response time for accommodating existing clients slipping. It took me over a week to get to a landscaping company site to fix a relatively easy Microsoft Exchange e-mail problem. This particular client found another consulting firm to take care of them shortly thereafter, correctly assessing that they needed a faster response time.

What good did I do having a portfolio of 20 small businesses? Not only did I lose clients, but also my other clients sensed my stress. More importantly, I didn't have time to replace the clients I was losing, as there certainly wasn't sufficient time to go out and market my wonderful services (which during those couple of months weren't exactly a model of MCSE consulting service).

If you're going to practice everything I'm preaching in this consulting bible, first and foremost, you need to restrict the number of clients you take on. Otherwise, there's time for little else but fighting fires.

### Medium-sized marketplace

The middle markets, defined by medium organizations (MORG), are more ambiguous than the smaller markets when it comes to determining client limits. It may be that two or three well-selected, medium-sized clients will more than meet your needs as an MCSE consultant. It may be that you'll have ten medium-sized clients that have internal IS staffs who call you occasionally for advice. You may be brought in on a project-by-project basis with your medium-sized clients. In this scenario, you would potentially have one client at a time. The medium-sized marketplace is depicted in Figure 13-2.

### Enterprise marketplace

Just like the small business market, I believe the enterprise market is easy to define. It has been my experience that MCSE consultants have one enterprise client at a time. The engagements can last from months to years. I think back to the enterprise environments I've both participated in and witnessed. In these environments the consultants (often called contractors) are given desks or offices and are placed on a long-term and lucrative assignment. In effect, enterprise MCSE consultants sometimes act as outside subject matter experts brought in for a long-term engagement. I have vivid memories of the Oracle developer (whose name I unfortunately can't remember) from a reputable Pacific Northwest consulting firm named Aris Corporation who camped out at an enterprise site month after month. The enterprise market level is displayed in Figure 13-3.

Medium Markets

**Figure 13-2:** The medium-sized marketplace

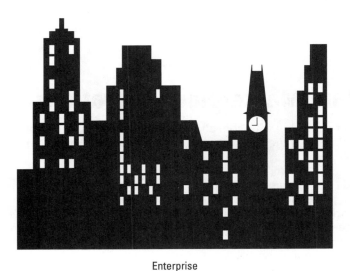

Enterprise

**Figure 13-3:** The coveted enterprise consulting space

Don't be lulled into a false sense of complacency about having one enterprise-level client. It's easy to become comfortable at the enterprise-level, where the living is easy, the work appears to be ongoing, and you start to cultivate meaningful business and personal relationships. In effect, you may start to act like an employee, becoming laid-back about your external marketing efforts (efforts which allow you to always keep an eye open for future clients). You may develop bad work habits; you may not communicate as strongly as an outside consultant to not only keep the client appraised of the work efforts underway, but also to remain of value to the enterprise (remember that I've stressed the importance of abundant, clear, and consistent communications as an MCSE consultant).

Still unconvinced? Consider the following. I realize many of the Rules of Ten and other tips and tricks in this book center on MCSE consultants with multiple clients. However, you as the enterprise-level MCSE consultant likely have the common sense enough to know that enterprise clients need constant communication. These clients also need a certain amount of sales effort because the enterprise-level MCSE consultant must not only play politics, but also often must hunt for the next consulting engagement inside the enterprise account. I can speak about this matter from experience. I recently served the BackOffice development team at Microsoft in a consulting role. When BackOffice Server 2000 and Small Business Server 2000 were released as products to the public, there was little need for my consulting services. However, I still made a point to cultivate relationships in other parts of the enterprise. I also attempted to communicate my forthcoming availability to the other departments I was meeting and greeting. The result was that I was made aware of six other consulting engagements inside Microsoft, and I ended up accepting one in the wireless division.

# MCSE Consultant Marketplace Migrations

While I'm talking about managing your consulting practice based on different sizes of consulting marketplaces, I want to take a moment to discuss the evolution of MCSE consulting practices.

I had it first explained (and perhaps best explained) to me by an old hand in the technology consulting profession. He spoke about how his firm started years ago in the small business marketplace to get business in the door, to get experience as a consulting firm, and to get letters of reference. Once these three goals had been achieved, he took his practice to the next level, the medium-sized market. Here the projects were larger, and the money was better. Finally, he broke into the enterprise market, where he found big budgets and big assignments.

I asked him, "Why did you migrate from small to large? Aren't the politics less than pleasant at the enterprise level?" He explained that the market effort to get a small job compared to a large job isn't that different. You still take months to land an account in the both the small and large markets. However, since the large markets have larger projects and larger budgets, this translates into a better use of time. Small clients also tend to be fussier about "I can't print" problems than enterprises are and require more time fixing little problems that often aren't billable. I summarize this view using the small marketplace as a launching pad toward eventual enterprise-level work in Figure 13-4.

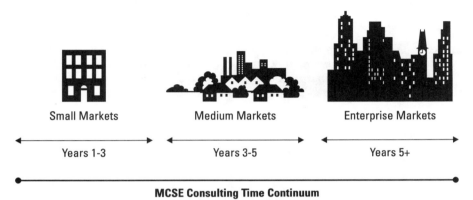

**MCSE Consulting Time Continuum**

**Figure 13-4:** A common evolution in MCSE consulting practices

What's interesting about this evolution is that your skills as an MCSE consultant or MCSE consulting manager will really be tested over time. The skills you developed that made you successful in the small organization space aren't the same skills that will make you successful in the large organization. For example, in the small organization space, politics don't play as critical a role in success. In the large organization space, politics are often your primary job as an MCSE consultant. In the small organization space, your technical skills may be broad to accommodate a wide range of computer problems you might encounter. In the large organization space, your skills might be very specific. You get the point. If you're going to migrate between markets as an MCSE consultant, you might need to modify your skill set.

## Ask the Guru

No discussion on running the MCSE consulting business would be complete without a look inward at yourself and your own management style. This reader of my monthly column in *Microsoft Certified Professional Magazine* really brought home the need to undertake the look in the mirror with these pointed words:

*Hi Harry!*

*I read your article in the Jan 99* MS Certified Professional *and enjoyed it. As a recent graduate into the ranks of middle management (at 52, after 27 years as a techie—believe it or not), I was pleased to see that I was actually aware of, and attempting to avoid, most of your "10 Mistakes."*

*Continued*

*Continued*

*However, one thing you said really bothered me. "I know that my employees must tire of my late-night phone calls to their homes, but that's often the only time I have a chance to return their calls and/or when my best ideas hit me. Such late-night calls are made in the spirit of overcommunication."*

*C'mon, Harry, give them a break. Your employees are your most important asset. MAKE the time to return their calls during the day. If you can't contain your need to talk shop in the middle of the night, send them an e-mail; don't phone them. People, quite appropriately, have other lives outside of work. As managers, we need to respect that.*

*Fred H., Systems Analyst*

*Hendersonville, NC*

*My response was:*

*Dear Fred,*

*Thanks for the feedback. I think you're on target with your assertion, and even we MCSE consulting managers (and writers) need to be reeled in occasionally. Your e-mail has served such a purpose for me. Upon further review, while I might be a night owl, it's more than understandable that my co-workers and subordinates may have well-defined limits between their personal and professional roles. So from this day forward, I'll use e-mail when I have a midnight flash of insight that can't wait to be communicated. No more telephone calls after 10pm! You have my word on it, this being a case of the guru needing to follow his own rules. Thanks again....harryb*

# Rule of Ten: Daily Limits

Realistically speaking, we all have daily limits that we can productively work in our professional roles. Here's an example to map my point. Leave it to the airlines and some pilot overtime–related flight delays I've suffered to provide this example. Perhaps you've been on the type of flights I've had in the early twenty-first century. The United Airlines pilots were refusing to work overtime. Once their allotted flight time of 12 hours per day was up, they refused to work any more. The plane sat on the ground while another crew was brought in.

I formulated an MCSE consulting Rule of Ten suggesting the MCSE consultant should work no longer than ten hours a day. In reviewing my Outlook calendar and my own work habits, I detected a dark and disturbing trend.

No one is truly capable of putting in more than ten hours of work per day and staying functional. MCSE consulting work that exceeds ten hours per day suffers. It's like slow water torture. Slowly but surely fatigue sets in, and fatigue leads to burnout and bad decisions.

If you can't self-regulate your work hours and you work too many hours in too short of a time, the result is burnout which can, in turn, lead to your missing out on future consulting opportunities.

If you don't burn out, you might make bad decisions in situations where you exceed your daily limit of ten working hours. Looking back, I can trace several bad decisions to my being fatigued late at night. For example, more than once I've gotten tunnel vision at 1:00 a.m. where I narrowed in on a simple stupid problem and didn't think of the obvious solution (which appeared to me as a vision the next day when I was rested).

# Time Management

One of the great pleasures in writing a third-party independent book such as this compared to a user manual for a particular product is that I can share with you the way things work in the real world. When it comes to MCSE consulting, the solutions you deploy may well be Microsoft-centric. This might include Microsoft BackOffice Server 2000 or individual Microsoft Server applications such as Systems Management Server. However, when it comes to actually running your MCSE consulting practice, the solutions offered by Microsoft might not always be the best fit. This is truly a case of MCSEs indulging in heresy! In this section on time management, I'm pushing Timeslips For Windows, an application from Sage (visit www.timeslips.com). I feel very strongly that it's the best timekeeping software on the market, and managing your billable time is paramount to your success as an MCSE consultant. In many cases, billable time is all that the MCSE consultant sells.

Timeslips has been around for a number of years and is popular in professional service environments such as the legal community. Not only does Timeslips provide the functionality you need to keep track of your billable time and bill clients, but it also interfaces with popular accounting programs such as QuickBooks. Another appreciated feature is the Timeslips personal digital assistant (PDA) interface. You can load Timeslips on your Windows CE-based PDA and keep your time while at the client site. Once you return to the office and synchronize your PDA with your personal computer, the billing information is uploaded to your full version of Timeslips.

**Note** Timeslips is also available in application service provider (ASP) mode. Sage has introduced Timeslips eCenter where you can log on over the Internet to enter your time and billing information. Go to www.timeslips.com for more information on this. Ideally, you and the other MCSE consultants you work with would enter your time and billing information from a Web browser at a client site while the information is still fresh in your minds.

I want to spend a few pages with you on how to use Timeslips, given it may well be your choice of timekeeping software applications. It wouldn't surprise me if you elect to go with Timeslips, a category leader in timekeeping software for professional services firms.

To install Timeslips:

1. Close open applications on your Windows-based personal computer.

2. Place the Master Configuration Disk in your floppy disk drive (drive A)

3. Insert the Timeslips Disc in your CD-ROM drive.

4. Assuming your system is AutoPlay enabled, the setup program will automatically launch. Otherwise, you will need to run Setup directly from the Timeslips Disc.

5. Click Install Timeslips when the Welcome to Timeslips dialog box appears.

6. Click Next when the Welcome page appears in the Setup Wizard.

7. Click Yes to approve the software license agreement.

8. The Select Setup Type page appears. Select the type of setup you intend to perform (single machine, network, or configure the product). In my case, the correct choice was Single. Click Next.

9. The Server Installation Type view page appears. You may select a typical, complete, custom, or work from network installation. Typical is the selection that should meet your needs (the only two components not installed will be a Procedure Editor and a Navigator Editor).

10. Click Next to confirm the installation location on the Choose Destination Location screen.

11. Assuming you selected the Single choice in Step #8, you will click Next when the Connecting to your Network page appears. Leave the network location field blank.

12. When the Upgrading from Prior Version page appears, click Next (assuming you are not upgrading from a prior version of Timeslips).

13. On the User Information screen, provide your name, company name, and serial number. Your serial number is printed on your Master Configuration Disk (which should be in drive A).

14. The Master Configuration Disk page appears, confirming its location is drive A. Click Next. The Master Configuration Disk is read by the Timeslips setup program.

15. The Enter Additional Configuration Disk page appears, as seen in Figure 13-5. Confirm the configuration information, and click Next.

16. Click Next on the Installing page to start file copying.

17. Click Next when the Select Program Folder page appears to accept the default program group name of Timeslips.

18. Elect whether you need to install Adobe Acrobat 4.0 when the Install Adobe Acrobat Reader v.4 page appears. Click Next.

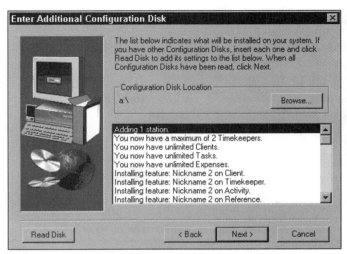

**Figure 13-5:** The Master Configuration Disk provides critical setup information.

**19.** Click Next when the Review ReadMe screen opens. It is not mandatory to review the readme file.

**20.** The Web Sites Update page appears. Select if you want to update Timeslips with any patches from the Sage Web site. Click Next.

**21.** When the Setup Complete page appears, click Finish.

**22.** Click Exit on the Welcome to Timeslips dialog box (which remained open in the background).

You have completed the setup of Timeslips. Following are the steps for creating a Timeslips database:

**1.** Click Start ➪ Programs ➪ Timeslips, and select the Timeslips program item.

**2.** Select Make a New Database when the No Database Selected dialog box appears.

**3.** Select Templates by Profession when the Create a New Database dialog box appears. Click Next.

**4.** If necessary, insert your Timeslips Disc and confirm the CD-ROM drive. This step is necessary for Timeslips to read the professional templates. Click Next.

**5.** Select the Computer Consultant choice, as seen in Figure 13-6, and click Next.

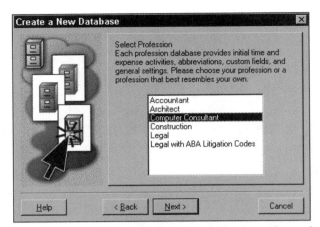

**Figure 13-6:** Computer Consultant choice is made on the Select Profession page.

6. Provide a location to store the new Timeslips database, and click Next.

7. Select a currency format, as seen in Figure 13-7, and click Next.

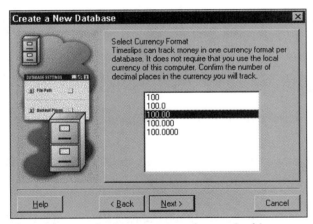

**Figure 13-7:** Selecting a currency format; in this case, the format is displayed to two significant digits.

8. Click Next on the Create New Database page. The Timeslips database will be created.

9. Click Finish.

10. Complete the General Settings dialog box that appears. You will provide basic information about your MCSE consulting firm, as seen in Figure 13-8. Click OK when complete.

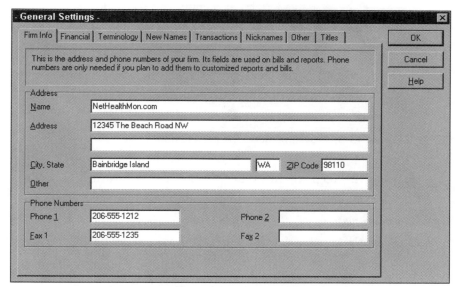

**Figure 13-8:** You provide basic firm information via the General Settings dialog box that will appear on printed matter such as bills and invoices.

11. Select Yes when asked about exchanging information with accounting programs on the Use Timeslips Accounting Link dialog box.

12. Click Next when the Getting Started Wizard appears.

13. Provide your full name and initials on the next screen, and click Next.

14. Provide your nickname, and click Next. This is shown in Figure 13-9. The nickname is a concept in Timeslips used to quickly query the database and return settings and information specific to you. You may enter any name you like, since many of us do not have true nicknames (such as "The Reverend" or "Billy Boy" or "The Man" or other irreverent silly names used between good friends to identify each other). If you do not have a nickname you are comfortable with, might I suggest you simply use the first name of your given or Christian name.

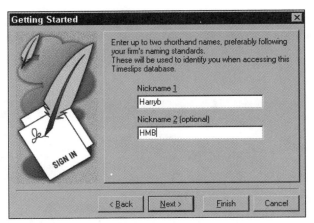

**Figure 13-9:** Providing nickname information

15. Select the Keep current settings option and click Next.

16. Select No when asked about a personal abbreviations file, and click Next.

17. Click Finish.

18. Select the starting date for your billing system on the Bill and Aging Date page, as seen in Figure 13-10. Click OK.

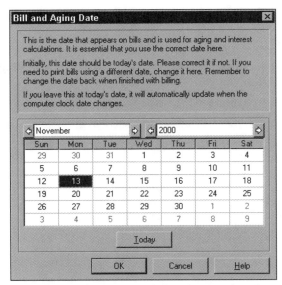

**Figure 13-10:** Selecting a bill and aging date for the system

At this point, Timeslips is functional. Steps for entering and billing your MCSE consulting client follow:

1. Start at the Basic Navigator as seen in Figure 13-11. This dialog automatically appeared after the last step above was completed.

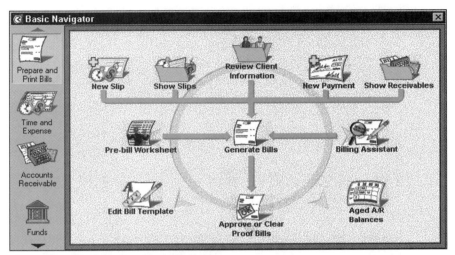

**Figure 13-11:** Timeslips Basic Navigator

2. Click New Slip.

3. The Slip Entry screen appears. You can select the Consultant name (that's you) from the drop-down menu. You will need to create a new client by right-clicking on the client field and selecting New from the secondary menu.

4. The Client Information screen appears. Click the Apply Defaults button to display all client fields. Complete the page similar to Figure 13-12, and click the Save and Return button on the far right vertical toolbar.

5. Complete the Slip Entry screen similar to Figure 13-13, and click the Save icon on the far right vertical toolbar.

6. Close the Slip Entry screen and you are returned to the Basic Navigator screen. You've now billed your first MCSE consulting client using Timeslips.

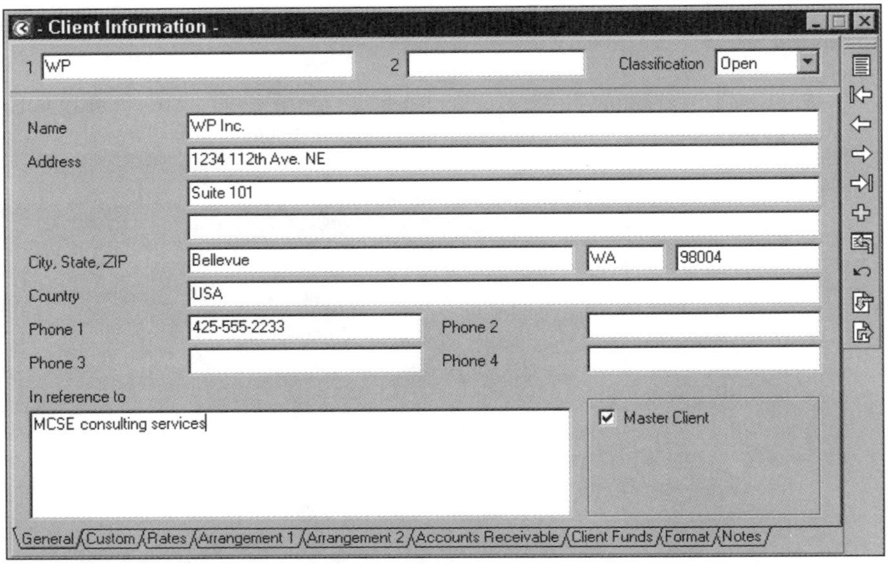

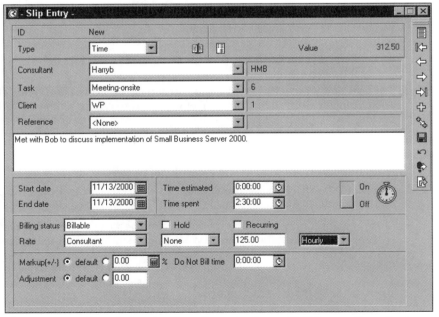

**Figure 13-12:** Client setup information

**Figure 13-13:** Completing the Timeslips entry for an MCSE consulting client

At this point, you will process the time billed and invoice the client. Follow these steps.

1. Select Show Slips on the Basic Navigator screen to observe the Timeslips you have entered. The Time and Expense Slip List appears similar to Figure 13-14. This is your first opportunity to see, in aggregate, the slips you've entered. More importantly, this is a chance to see if you've forgotten to enter a billable time into the system using the steps in the immediate section above.

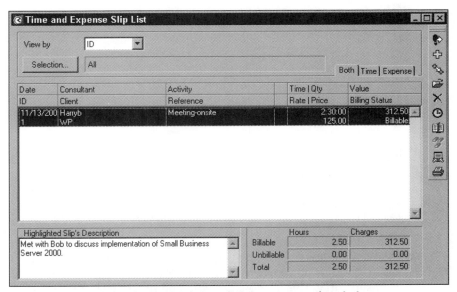

**Figure 13-14:** Review the entered Timeslips for errors and omissions

2. Click the upper-right Close icon (shaped like an X) to close the Time and Expense Slip List. You are returned to the Basic Navigator screen.

3. Select Pre-bill Worksheet and click Print when the Set Up Report dialog box appears. This will print billing information to the computer display by default, as seen in Figure 13-15.

4. Click More to see the remainder of the Pre-bill Worksheet. You may also click Print to print the Pre-bill Worksheet (which I personally prefer to do).

5. Click Done to close the Pre-bill Worksheet.

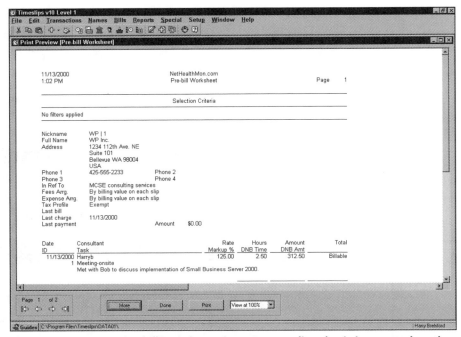

**Figure 13-15:** Extensive billing information on a per-client basis is reported on the Pre-bill Worksheet. This allows you to verify the correctness of the billings.

6. Close the Set Up Report dialog box. If you need to correct a billing, you would select the Show Slips icon on the Basic Navigator and correct a specific Timeslip entry. This is actually a common practice as entry mistakes occasionally occur.

7. Assuming the Pre-bill Worksheet reported the billing information correctly or you have corrected any errant Timeslip entries, click Generate Bills on the Basic Navigator screen.

8. The Setup Report dialog box appears. Click Print to print the billing information to the computer display.

9. The print preview screen for Generate Billings will appear and show you what the client invoice will look like (see Figure 13-16).

10. Click Print. This will initiate a process to finalize the billing. A warning message confirming the process is shown in Figure 13-17. Click Yes to include the Approval step.

11. Click OK when the Print dialog box appears.

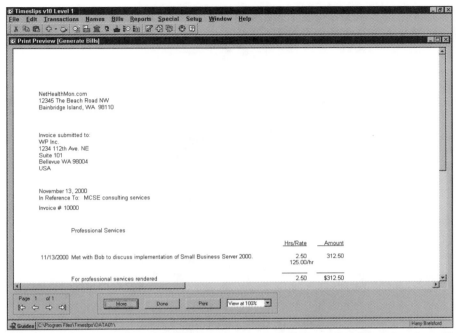

**Figure 13-16:** Generate Bills displays a realistic view of how the client's invoice will appear.

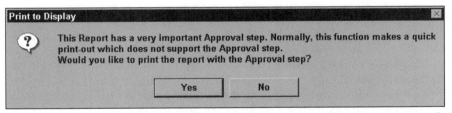

**Figure 13-17:** The Print message provides an important reminder about approvals.

12. Read and make a decision about how you will treat the bills on the Generation of Bills Completed screen, as seen in Figure 13-18. I recommend you select Put Bills in the Proof Stage while reviewing them and click OK.

13. Done. Close the Set Up Print dialog box (that remained open in the background).

14. One of the final steps, now that you have looked at and possibly edited the bills, is to approve the billings. In a MCSE consulting firm, it might be the consulting manager who reviews and approves the final bills. To do this, click Approve or Clear Proof Bills on the Basic Navigator screen.

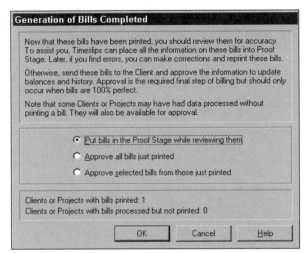

**Figure 13-18:** This is an important screen that allows you to approve the bills immediately or wait to give approval.

15. The Bill Stages dialog box appears. Select the bills you want to approve on the Proof tab, as seen in Figure 13-19, and click Approve. You may select only some bills for approval, you may view the billing again or even clear the billing. If you select Approve, you will need to confirm the Approve Bills warning box with Yes.

16. After making your selections, click Done.

You would now take the printed billing invoice and place it in an envelope for mailing to your client (don't forget to address the envelope and add postage). Timeslips allows you to track when clients pay, when the accounts age over 30-, 60- and 90-days and even apply late fees to your aged accounts. Needless to say, Timeslips is a very sophisticated program that you should plan on spending between 10 to 20 hours learning over your first month of operations. I believe that it is time well spent. In fact, there are certified Timeslips consultants in many areas that offer training classes and setup help. A list of these consultants may be obtained from Sage U.S. Holdings (the developer of Timeslips) at www.timeslips.com.

# Rule of Ten: Bill to the Tenth of an Hour

Whether it is a telephone call, research on the Web, or a dose of additional work at a client site, I bill to the tenth of an hour. It's a fair division of time that I don't believe is as usurious as lawyers' billing to the quarter hour. The six minutes represented by the tenth-of-hour billing concept is representative of what it takes me to shift my attention to a quick telephone call and then shift back to other MCSE consulting matters. I've had success with this approach to billing, best measured by the lack of grumbling when I bill for telephone calls and so on.

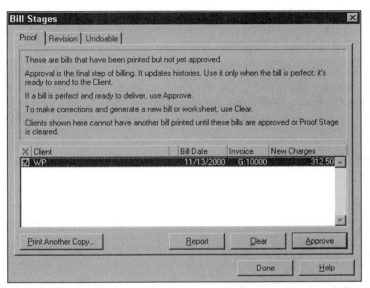

**Figure 13-19:** A consulting manager would approve or clear billings on the Bill Stages dialog box. This is the final billing step in Timeslips.

# Additional Management Tips

There are a few other management tips for you to consider in making your way through the MCSE consulting maze. Again, I'd emphasize these are just a few of my own observations as a practicing MCSE consultant. It would be a healthy exercise for you to take a few minutes to add your own tips that you've learned along the way.

## Outsourcing administrative functions

I've worked closely with an accounting firm, CFO-2-Go , in the Seattle area to assist in performing some of my administrative functions, primarily in the accounting area.

There are outsourcing firms in the following fields that you might want to avail yourself of, so you can focus on the things you do best.

✦ Accounting and bookkeeping

✦ Payroll

✦ Human resources (discussed in Chapter 11)

✦ Marketing

✦ Public relations

✦ Legal

**Tip** Another management consultant I speak with occasionally spoke about a CEO he was advising. This CEO had retained a consultant as a success coach. A success coach is someone who for a fee makes executives more successful. In this case, the success coach worked with the CEO to let go of his weaknesses and outsource those weak areas to service providers that could perform the work in question much better than the CEO could. This CEO was especially strong in selling but weak in administration, so he let go of the business administration functions. This is an application of the old "you're only as strong as your *weakest* link" theory of running a company. In other words, by propping up your weaknesses, which in this example was the act of seeking help in the administrative area, your greater overall work effort is stronger and more effective.

## Bartering

Great opportunities exist for savvy MCSEs to swap services with other professional service providers so both sides get what they want. I've swapped out network consulting services with the accounting firm CFO-2-Go to the satisfaction of all parties. I get accounting assistance when needed, and they have a Microsoft Small Business Server network that keeps on ticking.

## Working smarter — geographic issues

You need to have your client located in close proximity to your operations to maximize your MCSE consulting profitability. Let me make the point with a story about my dear friend, Vern. Vern is a lifelong consultant who aggressively serves almost any client that walks through his door. Because it's not Vern's practice to discriminate among his potential clientele, he has built a portfolio that is geographically diverse. And because they are in a small business consulting space, Vern and his staff are running 60 miles north to fix a database problem and then 60 miles south to upgrade a software module. It's hard to make money when you're on the road so much, even if you charge for travel.

Pick your clients wisely. Vern would be better off both financially and physically if he limited his clients to within a 20-mile radius of his consulting firm. This suggestion is illustrated in Figure 13-20.

## Working smarter — cool tools

Lastly, there are a few cool tools that I recently bumped into that I think are of value in performing administrative functions better than I did before. These include the following four small business tools provided by Microsoft as part of the Microsoft Office 2000 Small Business Tools. The idea is that, in addition to using Microsoft Office 2000 to run your business, you can benefit and save time by using the Microsoft Office 2000 Small Business Tools. While many of the forms are obvious, it's the time you save in not having to conceptualize and create these forms by using Microsoft Office 2000 Small Business Tools that makes the cut for being "cool tools."

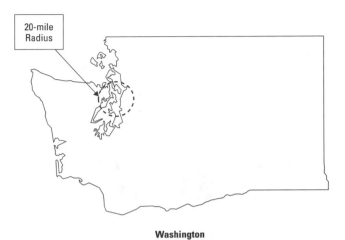

**Washington**

**Figure 13-20:** Limiting your geographic scope to a 20-mile radius

## Microsoft Business Planner

You may recall that the need for an initial business plan was discussed early in the book, before you gave up your day job and leaped into the exciting and profitable world of MCSE consulting. But creating a business plan is not a one-time event. Rather, you should endeavor to update your business plan annually to account for a new area of focus, the hiring or termination of key staff and whatever events have impacted your business. The Microsoft Business Planner starts with a personal interview, as seen in Figure 13-21.

**Figure 13-21:** Starting the personal interview with the Microsoft Business Planner

## Microsoft Direct Mail Manager

It is entirely possible that you've selected direct mailing as one of your marketing avenues for your MCSE consulting practice. Direct mail is one of those marketing approaches, in my opinion, that either works very well or doesn't work at all. There doesn't seem to be any middle ground with direct mailings, as the customer feedback tends to be skewed one way or the other (successful or not successful). Assuming you'd like to try a direct mail campaign, the Microsoft Direct Mail Manager is a tool to help you with the process. This is shown in Figure 13-22.

**Figure 13-22:** Consider using the Microsoft Direct Mail Manager to help manage your campaign.

## Microsoft Small Business Customer Manager

The idea behind the Microsoft Small Business Customer Manager is to provide a mini-customer relationship management (CRM) application for you. As you know, the CRM area is wildly popular in business technology circles as a way for enterprises, MORGs, and SORGs to listen to its customers and respond faster and better to any customer want or need than a competitor could. CRM applications are typically expensive applications programs, starting in the thousands of dollars and skyrocketing upward from there. Microsoft Small Business Customer Manager provides a way to integrate customer information from disparate applications such as accounting programs and Outlook contacts in one location. This information can then be managed in a more meaningful, effective, and efficient way. The Microsoft Small Business Customer Manager is shown in Figure 13-23.

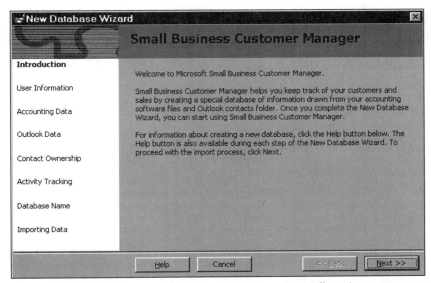

**Figure 13-23:** Whether you knew it or not, Microsoft Small Business Customer Manager can be your own low-cost CRM program.

## Microsoft Small Business Financial Manager

A favorite area of computing of mine has been executive information system (EIS) applications. Microsoft offers EIS-like solutions on a couple of fronts, including the Microsoft Small Business Financial Manager discussed in this section and its Digital Dashboard solution (which you can see at www.microsoft.com/digitaldashboard). Basically, Microsoft Small Business Financial Manager, seen in Figure 13-24, allows you to integrate financial information from several sources, such as spreadsheets and business accounting systems, into a single report or view.

I don't know about you, but my list of cool tools is always growing. When I'm at numerous client sites as an MCSE consultant, it's amazing the good administrative work habits you can pick up by looking at how your clients perform their work. For example, it was a law firm client that introduced me to Timeslips for managing my billable hours.

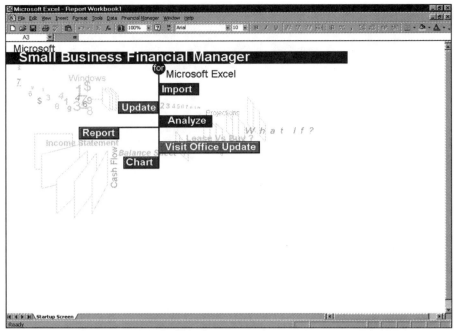

**Figure 13-24:** Gathering and integrating financial information from different sources is the key idea behind Microsoft Small Business Financial Manager.

## Summary

This chapter was about running your MCSE consulting practice as a business. Several important management topics were discussed, including the need to understand how the organizational structure you select will affect how you run your business. You must also decide whether it's in your best interests to serve small, medium, or large markets. Perhaps one of the most important administrative tasks an MCSE consultant must perform is keeping track of billable time. Timeslips was demonstrated extensively as a tool to help you do exactly that. Also, a few sage management tips were provided from the real world of MCSE consulting to supplement the administrative discussion.

✦    ✦    ✦

# Leaving – Retirement and Exit Strategies

So the day arrives when you ride off into the MCSE consulting sunset, either by choice or by cause. The idea of retiring is an interesting consideration, given that MCSE consultants as a whole tend to be a younger segment of the workforce focused on just staying current with rapidly changing technologies from day to day. In other words, it's really not part of the MCSE consulting mindset to dwell on the golden years.

As a result, I am spending only several pages to survey MCSE consulting retirement and exit strategy issues with you. In the same spirit, I'd be remiss if I presented a consulting guide that didn't heighten your awareness about planning for the future. Okay, I can hear the groans! You think a long discussion of mutual funds, retirement planning, and the need for a personal financial planner awaits you. Such is not the case, as I use the next several pages to focus on retirement and exit strategy topics specific to MCSE consultants. And since I'm not a licensed securities broker/dealer, I won't try to close you on any tremendous investment opportunities.

First, let me paint a picture of MCSE consulting career paths. Early in your MCSE consulting career, you're really just an MCSE candidate. Then you're MCSE acquired. After decades of toil, you're MCSE retired. This is shown in Figure 14-1.

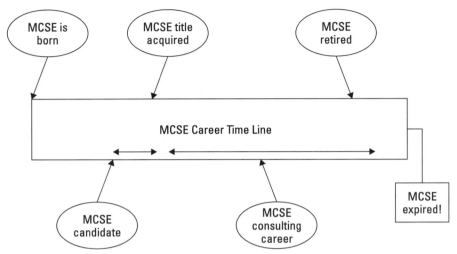

**Figure 14-1:** The MCSE consultant's life cycle

# Taking Care of Yourself

The MCSE designation is relatively new (less than ten years old), and it's hard to say if it will be here in ten years. Consider how vendor certifications come and go. For a while, IBM's OS/2 Certified LAN Server Engineer (CLSE) title showed promise, but it has since faded from the scene. Likewise, Novell's Certified Novell Engineer (CNE) title was as dominant several years ago as the MCSE is today, but it, too, has faded. The point I'm trying to make is that in your lifetime you will likely have several careers. This is a fact noted in several popular human resources–related studies. I'm sure you've heard of the phenomenon before. There are two ways to relate to this observation: by choice and not by choice.

## By choice

It's entirely possible that one day you may wake up and find yourself sick and tired of computers. A Denver real estate developer building urban condos, when pressed, admitted to me that he was a burned-out computer guy and wanted as far away from computers as he could get (land development is a good start). I discuss burnout later in this chapter.

You may find your intellectual curiosity takes you away from being an MCSE consultant. Perhaps you'll want to code programs in the C programming language, which isn't really the stuff of MCSEs.

A third possibility is that, while you're not burned out as an MCSE consultant, you may find that your priorities have changed and you must leave to go take care of yourself and others.

## Not by choice

The old saying that "things work out for the best" often comes true. Perhaps you've tried MCSE consulting, and someone (a boss), in no uncertain terms, lets you know that this line of work isn't for you. While you may not see it at the time, this individual is really helping you take care of yourself, assisting in steering you into a career where your gifts are best deployed.

# Reasons for Leaving

There are as many reasons for leaving the MCSE consulting field for other careers or retirement as there are MCSEs. In this section, I focus on a few reasons that I've either observed or experienced personally.

## Burnout

MCSE consulting is hard work. The long hours, incessant pager, and relentless cellular telephone calls can take their toll. I've experienced MCSE consulting burnout and used escape hatches such as teaching and book writing to renew myself. Burnout is a leading cause for exiting from the MCSE consulting business.

**Note**    At one time or another, all MCSE consultants will suffer burnout. This is inevitable with the long hours of work and everything that goes along with them. The key is to cope with burnout. There are many wonderful personal wellness books on coping with occupational burnout, stress, and so on at the same bookstore you purchased this book from. Read them before it's too late.

## Stress

Stress, in its severe states, is psychologically and physically debilitating. Ever wonder why your body truly aches at the joints after many months of nonstop hard work? Ever wonder why you can't concentrate or focus on what's in front of you?

The answer, of course, is that you are suffering from stress. Stress can be combated with exercise, diet, and everything else your doctor says is good for you. Stress is a common reason cited by many ex-MCSE consultants for leaving the business.

## Cashing out

What? Cashing out? That statement reminds me of the time I called a Microsoft product manager and got voice mail. The recorded message said that as of a few days prior to my call, this individual had retired from Microsoft (a true story I might add). If we all could have such problems . . .

I haven't seen the huge run up in personal net worth in the MCSE consulting community that early Microsoft employees enjoyed. However, I have worked with MCSE consultants who are making more money than they ever imagined possible. In fact, some of these individuals viewed the money as coming at a steep price: workaholism. In one case, feeling financially rewarded as an MCSE consultant and seeking a simpler life, a friend left the world of MCSEs to pursue a peaceful existence on an island. Cool.

## Retirement age

When you work for yourself as an MCSE consultant, there is no mandatory retirement age. If you work for a consulting firm, especially a national consulting firm, retirement age may be defined by policy. So, whether you or someone else determines what retirement age is, the fact is that getting too old to keep up with the younger MCSE consultants is a legitimate reason of sorts to exit the consulting business.

# Retirement Planning

Speaking of retirement leads the discussion to retirement planning, a timely topic for any MCSE consultant. Several retirement issues directly confront MCSE consultants, the least of which is the war story I share with you now.

A tried-and-true MCSE consulting strategy is to serve as a contractor to large corporations. The pay for contractors is higher than that given to salaried employees to account for both risk pay and the fact that the employer typically doesn't have to pay out benefits (retirement contributions, health insurance, vacation pay, and so on). The benefits of being a contractor (freedom, higher pay, and so on) were spelled out in great detail earlier in Part II of this book.

I was working side by side with a *blue card* at Microsoft. A blue card is a permanent employee. She had been a contractor for five years before going blue. I asked her why she hired on as a permanent employee. She responded that she needed to start saving for retirement, and as a contractor, she wasn't able to reasonably do that. Taking a full-time job at Microsoft was her form of retirement planning, but in the same breath she lamented how much she missed her freedom as a contractor.

That is the paradox of MCSE consulting: how to have it all. Having it all includes the following:

✦ Freedom

✦ Varied and challenging engagements

✦ A full plate of work

✦ Staying current with technology and certifications

✦ Health insurance coverage

✦ A fully funded retirement

As any retirement planner will tell you, aside from contributing the right amount towards your retirement, the other objectives of a sound retirement investment plan are avoiding taxation and beating inflation. I'll weave these ideas into my retirement discussion over the next several pages.

## Rule of Ten: Contribute 10 percent to retirement

Thou shalt contribute at least 10 percent of your *gross* consulting revenues toward a bona fide retirement system. That would suggest that if you make $125,000 per year as an MCSE consultant, you should be placing $12,500 into a retirement investment vehicle of some kind.

This retirement Rule of Ten speaks of retirement contributions you would privately make above and beyond the self-employment Social Security contribution you already make (which I discuss next).

This Rule of Ten doesn't necessarily mean you need to be making a huge cash outlay to fulfill the letter of the law. A 10 percent retirement contribution can come in many forms, ranging from retirement fund contributions to real estate.

## Social Security contributions

You can't avoid death, taxes, and recertification requirements. When I broke out on my own as an MCSE consultant, I was truly surprised at how big a chunk the Internal Revenue Service took in the form of a self-employment assessment. It gave me greater respect for my past employers, who were shouldering this tax burden in the form of the employers' payroll tax contribution.

Roughly 10 percent self-employment tax is imposed against your taxable income. This is an unavoidable fact, so you need to factor this into your bill rates and income projections as an MCSE consultant. Don't get caught by surprise like I did in year one as an MCSE consultant when it came time to calculate my taxes. And in year two, I had no guilt whatsoever charging the bill rates I did (truly knowing the full cost of doing business).

There are ways to reduce the effect of this tax burden. This tax is assessed against taxable income, which is typically calculated as a net of deductions and credits against gross income. So if you have more deductions or credits, you lower your taxable income and lessen the bite of your self-employment tax contributions.

I don't factor this item, Social Security contributions, into my Rule of Ten on retirement contributions because of concerns about the Social Security pot of retirement gold that awaits us all at the end of our careers. Social Security is a serious political hot potato that changes directions with the political winds of Congress and the White House. It's prudent as an MCSE consultant to plan for your own retirement and not count on the politicians to do it for you.

# 401K

Popular with salaried employees working for companies is the much ballyhooed 401K plan. These plans come in many shapes and sizes with accompanying tomes of policies, procedures, rules, and regulations. The three points I want to make about 401K plans are to trumpet the viability of this retirement vehicle, to speak towards its ability to keep pace with inflation, and to acknowledge the 401K plan approach as a way to lessen your income tax burden.

## Cool retirement plan

401K plans, done right, can be an inducement to join one employer over another when you are job hunting. There is a wide range of 401K type plans, and some of them are good. If you're an MCSE consultant that intends to join a consulting firm as an employee, read the fine print on these plans so you aren't surprised when you turn 65.

 **Note**    When you participate in a 401K plan as an employee, you typically benefit from matching contributions, up to a point, from the employer. This is easy money and significantly boosts the amount contributed to your retirement fund.

## Keep up with inflation

By and large, 401K plans have you place your precious retirement contributions in the hands of professional planners. In general, 401K plans outperform the Consumer Price Index (CPI) and other forms of inflation measures.

## Pretax contributions

The dollars you contribute into your 401K plan are typically tax deferred (again, plans vary). These pretax dollars have the effect of reducing your taxable income today. Tomorrow, when you're 65 years of age or older and cash out, these dollars are taxed. The tax strategy here is based on two assumptions. First, you had those dollars working for you for many years in a tax-free scenario. Second, when you are finally taxed against plan dollars as you withdraw them from the plan for living purposes in your golden years, in all likelihood you have a much lower marginal income tax rate. This assumption is typically valid because you are well past your peak earning years at that point.

# Life insurance–based retirement plans

Life insurance-based retirement plans are a bona fide way to build a nest egg for your golden years. The first step is to contact a life insurance company and ask for a sales presentation. Armed with charts, handouts, and forms to sign, these people will legitimately recommend you purchase life insurance that is several times your annual salary and also present a plan whereby your life insurance is also a retirement fund. I don't have enough pages available to go into the details of such propositions here, but be careful and do your homework. I'd recommend you ask for referrals and speak with people who pursued one of these strategies. How did it work out for them?

There is a prevailing paradigm in the financial community that I bumped into when researching insurance-based retirement plans: that life insurance should be used for insurance purposes, that retirement plans should be used for retirement, and that the two should never meet. That is just a thought to keep in mind as you navigate through the complex world of personal financial planning.

## Other retirement investments

Many financially successful MCSE consultants like to tinker with investments as part of their retirement planning. At a minimum, investing is a fun hobby. At a maximum, investing is a serious endeavor that consumes many of the free hours an MCSE consultant has off of the job. Following are a few of the investment avenues being used.

### Stocks

Ever since the MCSE program has been in existence since the early/mid 1990s, the stock market has produced astounding annuals returns. The facts bear out that, year to year, the stock market on an aggregate basis has beat inflation. However, I'll pass on some advice from a wealthy client that I serve as an MCSE consultant. This gentleman, with over $30 million invested in individual stocks, told me that if I ever got excited about the stock market, I should just put my money in a well-regarded mutual fund and forget about it for 20 or 30 years.

Stocks typically have very high liquidity. If you have a bad few months of MCSE consulting, you can sell some of your stock portfolio to survive. That's comforting for many MCSE consultants.

### Real estate

Real estate holds the favorite son status as an investment vehicle for retirement plans for several reasons, in my humble opinion.

✦ **Beats inflation**—As a real asset, real estate consistently beats the rate of inflation. That is because it's a law of economics that real assets increase in value in an inflationary environment while financial assets decline. This is a complex area of study, but it has to do with both scarcity and too many dollars chasing too few goods (the classic definition of inflation). When you look closely at inflation numbers, you find the real estate component (such as housing) is a large component of inflation. This is called being on the right side of inflation.

✦ **Leverage**—Where else will you contractually control assets of significant value with a relatively small amount of cash? It's common to see real estate transactions where $30,000 cash can control real estate worth $300,000. That really isn't feasible with other retirement investment vehicles.

✦ **Maturity matching**—Real estate mortgages 30 years in duration nearly match the remaining working years of many MCSEs. Assuming you pay down your loan on schedule, in 30 years you'll own the property outright. Maturity matching is a significant component of being a successful investor.

As an aside, maturity matching is also important when running the business side of the MCSE consulting practice. You don't want to be in a situation of going broke while being highly profitable. An example of this is your accounts receivables balance (the billings you've sent to clients) growing to sky-high levels while your on-hand cash dwindles. I discuss business practices more in Chapter 12.

✦ **Tax benefits**—You need to minimize your tax liability. Real estate provides this capability like few other investments with the deductibility of interest expenses. In the case of real estate rentals, you can also deduct legitimate business expenses and enjoy the benefits of depreciation deductions.

✦ **Contractual return**—The real estate loan that you pay off month by month is a contract. The interest rate effectively represents a rate of return you're making on your money (in the context of opportunity cost). For example, take an 11 percent loan and $1,000 in hand. You could invest the $1,000 in the stock market and make an unknown return (possibly very high), or you could pay down the loan so at least a small part of the principal balance doesn't accrue interest charges at the 11 percent rate in this example.

✦ **Rentals at retirement**—Assuming you've focused on real estate as your retirement plan, built up a portfolio of rentals, and paid off the mortgages, here's what you're facing. You'll have a high net worth and monthly rental income flowing in for you to live on.

✦ **Own your home outright**—Similar to the point above, if you own a home and have paid it off, at least you have a roof over your head.

✦ **Other people's money**—Earlier in this chapter I presented the Rule of Ten that you should fund your retirement with at least ten percent of your gross income. I also alluded to the fact that this can be done without your necessarily making a cash outlay each month to reach this goal. Here's the way it can be done. Suppose you buy your first house, live in it ten years, turn it into a rental property, and move to a bigger and better home. That's a good plan. After ten years, the mortgage on the now rental property is amortizing more quickly, so the monthly rental being paid by the tenant is in effect going into your retirement fund.

## Commodities, options, and day traders

While this isn't an area for me and my investments personally, there is certainly more than one high-flying MCSE playing with day trading. This can be fun if you have mad money to burn, but I wouldn't tie up my long-term retirement fund in something that has such excessive volatility.

## Case Study—Net Worth Exercise

Visit one of the many life insurance Web sites and calculate your net worth, how much life insurance you need, and how much money you would have available at retirement. I'll warn you that this can be a sobering exercise. I know when I first undertook such an exercise several years ago, I quickly determined that I needed to make more money and that I needed to contribute more to my retirement program.

One site that has such a net work calculator is Northwestern Mutual at `www.northwestern mutual.com`. I told the net worth calculator the following:

- ✦ I was 39 years old

- ✦ Earned $150,000 per year as an MCSE consultant

- ✦ I expected to retire at 65 years old

- ✦ My income would grow five percent per year

- ✦ My investments and savings earn, on average, a seven percent return per year

The Northwestern Mutual net work calculator returned the following results:

- ✦ I will earn over $7.7 million in income over the remaining 26 years I plan to work

- ✦ If I needed to replace that income, I need to have $3.1 million in savings today earning a seven percent annual return

And since I don't have $3.1 million in insurance, I need to purchase a lot of life insurance from Northwestern Mutual. Fair enough. The exercise is both entertaining and educational. I'd highly recommend you complete such an exercise now.

**Note**     If you're interested in learning more about retirement planning and investments, consider reading other books dedicated to that subject, including a couple of the *...For Dummies* financial planning books from IDG Books Worldwide, Inc. Also, don't hesitate to engage the services of a financial planning professional, such as an accountant.

# Exit Strategies

This part of the chapter is dedicated to various exit strategies you can use to exit the MCSE consulting business.

## Becoming "of counsel"

Suppose you make a name for yourself as a hotshot MCSE consultant and you're ready to cut back your workload. But you've heard over the years that full retirement isn't healthy, because after years of toil, it's too traumatic to downshift to idle. You want to work, but part-time instead of full-time.

In this case, an appropriate exit strategy is to work as an "of counsel" to a large consulting firm. This is seen all the time in the legal profession where marquee players with rainmaking skills (sales abilities) lend their name to the law firm to practice part time and generate business leads. This is not bad work if you can find it.

 **Tip**    One way to become "of counsel" to a large consulting firm is to speak at conferences and publish books. I know from personal experience that this is a time-tested avenue for becoming a player in the consulting community.

## Adding partners

You might aggressively seek to dilute your MCSE consulting practice so you can spread the workload (and work less yourself), select a successor, and keep your practice alive as a business entity long after you are gone. An appropriate vehicle to do this is to take on more partners, which is a time-tested exit strategy. Adding partners is also considered a value-added process where the contributions of the individual partners add more value than is extracted. This is how long-term wealth can be created in a professional services firm. So, not only can you find a way to possibly work less, but you can become richer along the way. This sounds like the best of all worlds to me.

## Merging

A plan that often works very well and allows you to extract maximum financial value from your exit efforts is to merge with another firm. Not only can you receive a payout from being acquired if you are the acquired, but you can also use a few years to blend the two MCSE consulting practices together and create true synergy.

## Selling

Perhaps you just want to sell everything and cash out. You'll want to obtain the assistance of a business broker to value and dispose of your business. The more time you have to accomplish this the better, as a distress sale of an MCSE consulting practice typically yields less than market value.

## Family matters

Perhaps you've raised a son or daughter who wants to take over the family business. Perhaps your son or daughter married an MCSE consultant who will be your successor.

### Family succession planning

Family succession in professional services is rare, but not unheard of. That's because clients are hiring the individual professional as much as the firm itself. It's hard to sell a son, daughter, son-in-law, or daughter-in-law into these consulting engagements, but not impossible.

### Marrying into it

It's not uncommon for a family member to marry someone from the family's line of work. This occurs because many social opportunities revolve around business. MCSEs tend to hang out with MCSEs. Don't be surprised if your son or daughter brings home an MCSE bride or groom who'll some day fit your succession plans.

# How To Value Your Business

Last and certainly not least is the topic of business valuations. In preparing this chapter, I interviewed people who had recently sold business practices in the professional services area.

As a general rule, professional services firms sell for twice annual gross revenues. Other observations on business valuations include the following:

✦ **Selling for less, but attaching debt** — You might sell for less than this 2:1 ratio because the buyer will assume a debt attached to your business.

✦ **Establishing purchase requirements** — To purchase an MCSE consulting firm, you really need to be an MCSE consultant, a credential that requires time and money to obtain. Having a requirement as a condition of sale limits your liquidity.

Tip

My best advice with respect to business valuations is to hire a business valuation firm. Period.

# Summary

This chapter focused on a topic that, while germane, is probably considered mundane by MCSE consultants: retirement and exit strategies. There are numerous approaches to funding your retirement, but the biggest step is to have at least some type of retirement plan. Anything is better than nothing. Numerous exit strategies, such as merging or selling the MCSE consulting practice, were also presented in this chapter.

✦    ✦    ✦

# Grinder

This part highlights, in great detail, many potential MCSE consulting opportunities, including small, medium, and large organizations; general and specific niche consulting; operating systems; bundled solutions such as Microsoft BackOffice and Small Business Server; specific applications such as Microsoft Exchange Server and SQL Server; and even developer opportunities with Visual Studio. Additional certifications such as MCDBA, MCSD, and MOUS are also presented.

# Doing the Work – Methodologies

**M**ethodologies are a way of standardizing business practices. Appreciating the role of methodologies and, more importantly, using a methodology in your MCSE consulting practice are highly desirable goals because methodologies bring order and structure to, in this case, technology-based implementations. In the absence of a defined methodology, work habits become random, circular (redundant), and many times confused. If you're going to be a successful MCSE consultant who can grind out the work with the best, you will need to have a clear methodology.

## Maturing as an MCSE consultant

You know you've matured as an MCSE consultant when you start talking about methodologies. This is an advanced consulting topic and reflects a mature MCSE consultant who has the following qualities:

- ✦ **Awareness** — To even have the term "methodologies" uttered by an MCSE is music to a consulting manager's ears. If you're not aware of consulting methodologies, it is highly unlikely you're actually using one.

- ✦ **Reflection** — A reflective soul is contemplative and has the ability to reason and think things through.

- ✦ **Seasoning** — In all fairness, we don't arrive at the end of our MCSE journeys thinking and breathing consulting methodologies. Part of what introduces the methodology mindset into an MCSE's behavior is experience. Over time, you learn which consulting approaches work and which don't work. This seasoning alone allows you to develop a casual, living MCSE methodology.

✦ **Professionalism**—When you are working with executive-level clients, being able to articulate your MCSE consulting services in the context of a methodology gains the client's confidence. More importantly, having a consulting methodology puts the word "professional" back into professional services as it helps you coordinate, organize, and apply your work habits successfully.

✦ **Structure**—Formal methodologies bring necessary structure to your MCSE consulting practice. As you mature as an MCSE, ad hoc approaches will serve you less and less effectively.

# Avoiding Defeats

My take on consulting methodologies is pragmatic: avoid defeats. You can be successful by simply not making mistakes. If you consistently deliver what you promised, making money and enjoying your jobs won't be problems. Consulting methodologies bring the consistency element and effectively allow you to avoid defeats.

Depending on your consulting philosophy, you may be playing to win or playing not to lose. The playing to win approach includes such things as introducing bleeding edge solutions. You're trying to hit the home run. Many times you do, but other times you strike out. The playing not to lose approach is more akin to the public accounting approach to consulting: conservative. Here an emphasis is placed on risk adversity, management of the engagement, and avoidance of surprises. Both approaches can be profitable, but the playing not to lose approach is clearly a more consistent delivery mechanism and in alignment with consulting methodology thinking.

# Value of Repetition

Another view of MCSE consulting methodologies is to appreciate the value of repetition. Repetition breeds familiarity and allows you to debug your process. It's much easier to bid work when you've done it several times before. One entire school of consulting believes that sound consulting practice management involves performing the same work over and over again. I've seen this firsthand with accounting application installers who install the same package week after week at different client sites.

**Note**

Too much repetition can be boring with a capital *B* and may not present much personal enjoyment or fulfillment. If your main concern is making money, my advice is deal with the repetition and find satisfaction where you can.

# Turning Your Consulting Practice into a Franchise

What if something happened to you and you could no longer perform professionally up to the levels you desire? This could include an extended illness (either physical or mental) or a tragedy such as your passing away. I don't want to cast the dark cloud of doom over this discussion, but believe it or not, I'm trying to make a point about consulting methodologies.

In a professional services practice, such as an MCSE consulting firm, you're typically a key person. Your competencies are essential for the practice to be successful. That's because you are selling and delivering professional services, which when all rhetoric is set aside are personal services. You can purchase key person insurance at a price to mitigate the loss of your services and allow the MCSE consulting firm to continue its existence, but without the qualities you brought to the table the business cannot function in the same way.

Good MCSE consulting practice management dictates that you attempt to turn your consulting practice into a franchise. I'm not talking about hamburger stands that look and feel the same at any location. I'm talking about the application of a consulting methodology that would allow someone (another competent MCSE) to wear your shoes in your absence and successfully run your practice. Another way to view the franchise approach in a much less sinister light than the how I started this section is in terms of growth. Could it be that if you apply a sound consulting methodology to your MCSE consulting practice that you could open additional offices? Yes. That's exactly how consulting firms grow into multioffice operations. They have a consulting methodology that allows them to be consistent in the delivery of their professional services.

# Don't Reinvent Consulting Methodologies

It's important to think efficiently when looking into the development and application of your own MCSE consulting methodology. Keep in mind that the process of creating and improving your consulting methodologies shouldn't overcome your practice of delivering services.

Caution

It has been my experience as a businessperson, an MCSE consultant, and a manager that a business warning sign is too much time spent on process and too little time performing real work. Perhaps you've worked for the type of company I'll cite here. Consultants and employees spend more time talking about what the firm should be instead of going out, doing the work, and building the practice. More to the point, I've observed that it's often the malcontents who are lagging in billable hours that seek to push the organization into a focus on process instead of production. Perhaps because these underperformers don't have much billable work to do, they have time to sit around and proffer opinions about what the firm should be.

Efficiently select the appropriate consulting methodology for you and then go out and practice what you preach, go out and apply your consulting methodology by billing hours and making money as an MCSE consultant.

**Tip**    As you'll see in a moment, my method for having you implement a consulting methodology is based on a best-of-breed approach. Look around at what other successful firms are doing, select specific traits that appeal to you, and efficiently devise your own consulting methodology.

## Guest Sermon – Advice from the Trenches

My good friend and one of the first MCSE title holders Kevin Wagner is a technology professional in Chicago, Illinois, specializing in high volume systems design and performance tuning. Speaking from many years of experience, Kevin gives us the following guest sermon touching on the issue of methodologies:

*As a consultant and longtime MCSE working with Microsoft's SQL Server product, I have run into many different variations of the same theme. Get to know Microsoft's solutions framework, and you will have at least 85 percent success out of the box with a new gig. Most of the methodology I see in practice ranges from having no methodology at all to applying an archaic and antiquated methodology that is a realization of outdated best practices (probably from version 1.0 of the product being used) that are gained over the years by a central IT and are usually obsolete before implementation. These obsolete practices are discarded in favor of "shooting from the hip," which usually leads to some sort of unpredictable system failure down the road. The way the industry changes and the rate at which that change occurs means that the THERE often has changed before you leave the HERE. I cannot stress enough the value of knowing Microsoft's solutions framework. This collection of methodologies can see you through any project if you apply those parts that fit your current situation.*

*Two scenarios from real life that illustrate my point come from my work at Weyerhaeuser and at Western Wireless.*

### Life at Weyerhaeuser — antiquated methodology

*One of the qualities of this company is the extensive use of methodology and best practices. They designed and published their own methods and practices that they learned from over 100 years of continued business. Since their main product, trees, had a life cycle of 50 to 75 or more years, the methods they used to run their business reflected the long life cycle approach. Developing the scope of an NT deployment took many meetings and more than six months. During this time, NT had jumped versions and was about to go to version 4.0. The scope had not been hammered out before the change in technology, and the project timeline slipped. While NT development marched on, the project was locked into deploying an outdated version. Needless to say, they had to put another project together to upgrade all the outdated installations of NT around the world. What should have taken place was a change in methodology and an accelerated change management cycle implementation embracing the rapid change of computers into their business process. What should have been en easy deployment of NT turned into a never ending project to install and upgrade equipment.*

**Change at Western Wireless**

*This second example demonstrates starting with no methodology and going to a full-blown implementation of Microsoft's solutions framework. Western Wireless was a small wireless communications outfit located in the Northwest. They had no formal methodology in place when I started a two-year (or more) engagement. In the beginning they had system failures due to mismanagement of patch implementations and system software upgrades. Users could not be guaranteed of system availability during any particular time frame as the IT department was adding patches to take care of some software bugs. Further, they were supposed to be a "24 hours a day, 7 days a week, 365 days a year" operation as the information provided by the system was used by telephone operations to manage the cellular network. Fixing their problems required a change in thinking at the top level of IT. They hired a new Director of IT that understood the problem and was able to bring in some order. What we ended up with was a change management methodology implementation that required signatures of the user community before any critical system was brought down for any maintenance. This single change took a system availability rating of 70 percent planned uptime and raised it to nearly 99.999 percent planned uptime. The only real change was the addition of effective communication between the user community and IT. After the successful implementation of the change management, the company started looking into the other areas of IT and R&D. In the end Western Wireless was able to provide over 99.999 percent planned uptime to all critical systems by implementing a reliable and fluid methodology based on Microsoft's solutions framework.*

*As with anything in life, change is inevitable. If you embrace change as a friend instead of a mortal enemy, you will go far in consulting. Part of the responsibility that goes with consulting is to bring to the table your unique life- and job-related experiences and meld them into the current situation for the betterment of your client. Your clients are looking for those experiences to help them get ahead in their market, and you are the one chosen to bring it to them. Don't be self-righteous and unwilling to learn new ideas. Those new ideas and methodologies will make you a better consultant and more valuable to your future clients.*

# Existing Consulting Methodologies

In reality, none of us have enough time available to devise the ultimate workable consulting methodology. Add to that fact that we constantly tinker with our consulting methodologies once we have one, and you'll quickly see a methodology is a living, not static, framework. Because you'll pick and play with your MCSE consulting methodology, I have a few suggestions for minimizing the time you spend selecting the consulting methodology that works best for you. It's another Rule of Ten and suggests you take a best-of-breed approach, picking the germane points you like best and discarding the others.

# Rule of Ten: Best of Breed

The most efficient way to devise your MCSE consulting methodology is to refine existing proven methodologies. Look at ten Web sites for other consulting firms, study each consulting methodology, and select ten attributes as the baseline for your own MCSE consulting methodology. Figure 15-1 shows the Top 50 consulting firms listed by Kennedy Information research group (www.kennedyinfo.com).

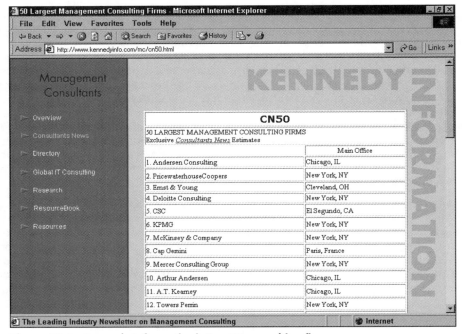

**Figure 15-1:** Kennedy Information's Top 50 consulting firms

**Tip**    I found this list of top consulting firms by searching on the keywords "consulting firms" using the Google search engine (www.google.com). You are encouraged to perform a similar search using the search engine of your choice.

It is interesting to note that Figure 15-1 presents primarily management consulting firms. However, each of these management consulting firms is involved in technology consulting. Also, it is legitimate to look into the consulting methodologies from the management consulting realm, as the same methods used to deliver management consulting can often be applied to MCSE consulting.

In the next several sections, I will present ten different consulting methodologies taken from the Kennedy Information's Top 50 consulting firms list and tailored for my own use. While you are welcome to use my work in developing your own MCSE consulting methodology, I encourage you to substitute some of your own competitive resources, such as local technology consulting firms in your region, to make the sampling more relevant to your particular situation. In fact, later in this chapter I'll show you two regional firms that aren't on Kennedy Information's Top 50 consulting firms list just to provide that kind of research balance.

Note that I start by taking selected consulting firms from the Kennedy Information's Top 50 consulting firms list and reclassifying them as either Big Five accounting firm–related consulting firms, management consulting firms, or technology consulting firms. For all ten samples, I display their respective Web pages that discuss consulting methodologies.

# Big Five accounting firms

Each of the largest accounting firms has, or recently had, technology consulting practices as of this writing. From time to time a Big Five firm will sell its consulting practice in order to focus on its core competencies such as accounting. Andersen Consulting is one such example that I'll discuss in a moment. Such realignments are to be expected in the consulting field. Following is a list of the Big Five accounting firms:

+ **Arthur Andersen** — Consulting is conducted via Andersen Consulting, but Andersen Consulting plans to become its own firm on January 1, 2001.

+ **PricewaterhouseCoopers** — The parent firm was created by the merger of Price Waterhouse and Cooper & Lybrand (which is why the largest accounting firms are now called the Big Five and not the Big Six anymore).

+ **Ernst & Young** — This firm sold its technology consulting practice to Cap Gemini.

+ **Deloitte & Touche** — Consulting is conducted via Deloitte Consulting.

+ **KPMG** — The consulting work is performed by KPMG Consulting.

A closer look at the consulting practice of each of these five firms follows.

## Andersen Consulting

Andersen Consulting (`www.ac.com`) is the consulting arm of Arthur Andersen that is in the process of being spun off as a separate company. Its most current consulting methodology is articulated through its eInfrastructure service offering, shown in Figure 15-2.

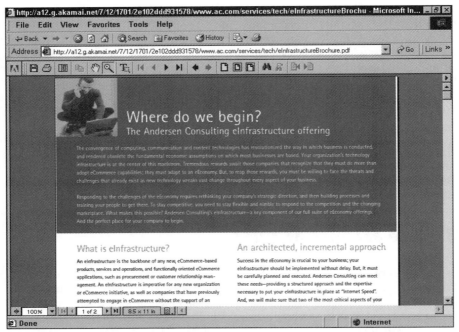

**Figure 15-2:** Andersen Consulting's eInfrastructure consulting methodology

Some key points about Andersen Consulting's eInfrastructure consulting methodology are as follows:

✦ Diagnose and assess your strategic direction. Then, evaluate your existing infrastructure and identify areas for improvement and future infrastructure needs.

✦ Determine the impact new applications may have on your infrastructure components and vice versa.

✦ Select infrastructure components that support new e-commerce strategies, products, services, or operational techniques.

✦ Develop and deploy a robust infrastructure, integrated with legacy systems and positioned to support future applications.

✦ Operate, manage, and evolve the new infrastructure.

## PricewaterhouseCoopers

PricewaterhouseCoopers (www.pwcglobal.com) displays general, not specific, consulting methodologies at its Web site, seen in Figure 15-3. Perhaps the reason for this is to prevent competitors from borrowing its methodologies right from its Web site.

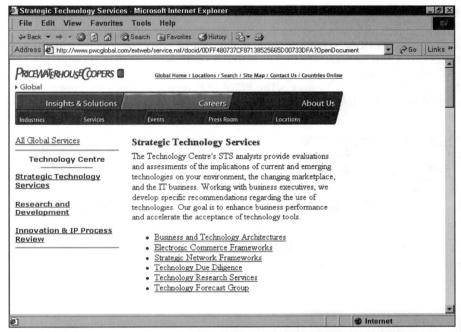

**Figure 15-3:** Strategic technology consulting services provided by Pricewaterhouse Coopers

However, if you dig just a little deeper, by selecting the Innovation and IP Process Review link, you get into more specifics. The typical service approach here involves the following:

✦ Competitive benchmarking

✦ Conducting cross-functional company interviews and facilities inspections

✦ Analysis and assessment

These three approaches result in the following deliverables:

✦ Situation analysis

✦ Leading practical comparison

✦ Business improvement recommendations

## Ernst & Young

Taking a back-to-basics approach, Ernst & Young recently returned to traditional accounting services, spinning off its management and technology consulting practice to Cap Gemini, a huge consulting firm headquartered in Paris, France, with offices around the world (`www.capgemini.com`). The example I'll use here for consulting methodologies is the PERFORM Applications Management consulting methodology, shown in Figure 15-4.

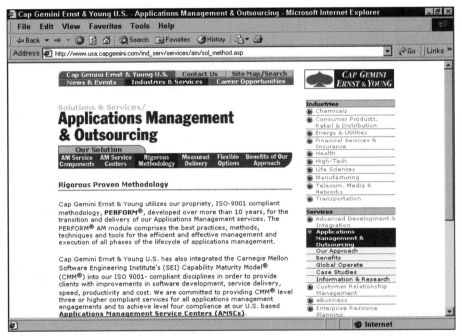

**Figure 15-4:** PERFORM Applications Management consulting methodology

Some key aspects of PERFORM are the following:

✦ ISO-9001 compliance

✦ A defined set of best practices, methods, techniques, and tools:

- A **Statement of Work (SOW)** that defines the what of service delivery

- **Service Level Agreements (SLAs)** that define the what, how much, and how well of the engagement

- **Operating Level Agreements (OLAs)** that define the how well and how much among multiple service providers

- A **Service Quality Plan** that defines the roles and responsibilities between all parties involved

- An **On Time and Above Customer Expectations (OTACE)** method that measures customer satisfaction

## Deloitte Consulting

Another worldwide consulting firm with accounting origins, Deloitte Consulting (www.dc.com) has a methodology called FastTrack for its SAP R/3 database implementations. I'm sure Deloitte Consulting has many additional consulting methodologies, but this one seemed closest to home when discussing MCSE consulting. On Deloitte Consulting's Web site, you'll find FastTrack presented as success stories, as examples of how successful implementations of their FastTrack methodology have been. In Figure 15-5, I show the Microsoft engagement success story.

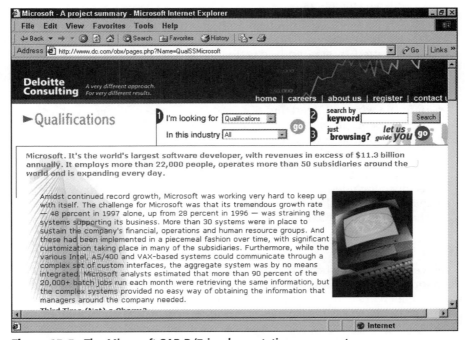

**Figure 15-5:** The Microsoft SAP R/3 implementation success story

**Note**   It shouldn't surprise you that Deloitte Consulting would profile Microsoft. Deloitte Consulting has a long history of success with Microsoft. It's literally fact that half of Microsoft's finance department came from Deloitte & Touche, the accounting firm that launched Deloitte Consulting.

The key attributes of Deloitte Consulting's methodology, as presented in the context of the Microsoft project and found in the Microsoft engagement success story on the Deloitte Consulting Web site, are as follows:

✦ **Stressing the importance of a main business objective** — Streamlining and making uniform Microsoft's global business practices was the objective in this case.

✦ **Setting project goals** — In the Microsoft example, successful R/3 implementation to support all business processes was the goal.

✦ **Designing clear criteria for solutions providers** — In addition to knowledge of the business and industry, the vendors needed experience in R/3 implementation and configuration represented at different physical sites.

✦ **Selecting the makeup of the team** — Creating the project team is an important (and sometimes large) task; in the case of the Microsoft engagement, the team exceeded 65 members.

✦ **Choosing a method of implementation** — This is the key point. The Fast Track methodology provided the foundation upon which the team planned, implemented, integrated, and tested the R/3 project.

✦ **Devising a training plan** — The Deloitte Consulting Training for Results methodology was used to account for user training as part of the implementation.

✦ **Defining what will lead and did lead to success** — Success in the case of the Microsoft project came about because of top-level executive support that grew out of well-defined business goals, conscientious project management, and clear communication of knowledge and expertise.

✦ **Recognizing the benefits gained** — A few of the benefits that Microsoft received included quick implementation, monthly books that were closed much more quickly, access to real-time information for financial managers, and significant annual savings.

## KPMG Consulting

If you've been around the business community a decade or two, you might remember a former Big Six accounting firm called Peat, Marwick, and Mitchell. Along the way, with mergers and consolidations, this firm became KPMG (www.kpmg.com). Not surprisingly, this firm also has a consulting arm, KPMG Consulting (www.kpmgconsulting.com).

The consulting methodology I'm presenting from KPMG Consulting is its Strategic Enterprise Management (SEM) approach, as seen in Figure 15-6.

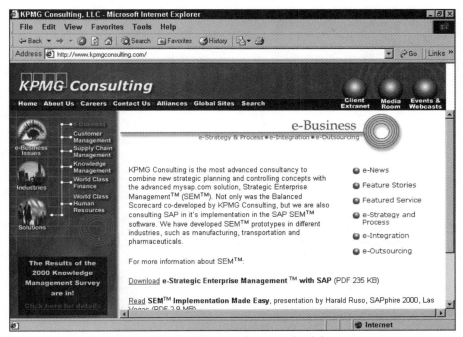

**Figure 15-6:** KPMG Consulting's SEM consulting methodology

The key point to SEM is its implementation model, listed here and shown in Figure 15-7.

✦ Strategy Definition

✦ Process Analysis

✦ Enterprise Data Model

✦ Design of User Interface

✦ System Implementation

I also thought KPMG's marketing message of achieving a Balanced Scorecard, shown in Figure 15-8, was especially compelling for its management consulting views of financial, customer, organizational development, and process perspectives. The idea behind the Balanced Scorecard is easy to understand. A firm's strategic vision is keenest when its core strategic components are in balance and harmony. This is akin to what psychologists and others profess makes a "whole person": a person who has balance between their personal and professional lives (including elements of spirituality, fitness, relaxation, and so on).

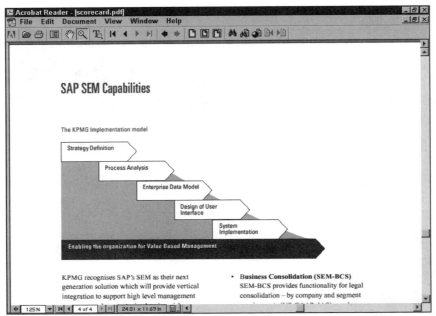

**Figure 15-7:** SEM implementation approach

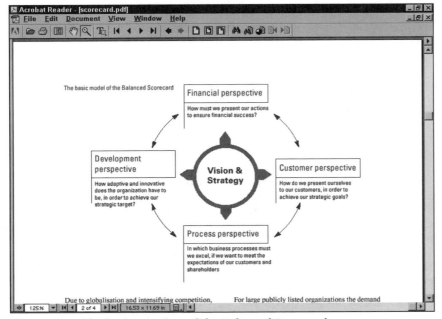

**Figure 15-8:** The basic overview of the Balanced Scorecard

This concludes the discussion on the Big Five consulting methodologies. I find the exercise of visiting the Web pages of the Big Five on an occasional basis to be a good use of time because many smart consultants and managers at these firms are putting a lot of thought (and time) into developing and presenting their consulting methodologies. It's time and brainpower I don't have, so by perusing what the Big Five present as effective consulting methodologies, I can benefit from their wisdom without the significant time investment they made in developing these insights.

**Tip**    The Big Five tend to be big employers of MCSE consultants. That's something to strongly consider if you're looking for a break into the big-time MCSE consulting arena.

## Management consulting firms

Next in the implementation of the best-of-breed Rule of Ten consulting methodology exercise are management consulting firms. These firms provide consulting services in the lucrative technology niche as you might expect. Here I focus on three such firms, which are well known to the Masters of Business Administration (MBA) crowd but less well known to MCSE consultants:

✦ McKinsey & Company

✦ Booz-Allen and Hamilton

✦ The Boston Consulting Group

As I will discuss, in general these consulting methodologies tend to be higher level, meaning more focused on the kind of planning and strategic thinking that may encompass writing white papers and conducting studies. However, high-level consulting activities do not include installing Microsoft solutions at the keyboard level (where you actually insert the CD-ROM into the server).

### McKinsey & Company

McKinsey & Company (www.mckinsey.com) is an old East Coast (U.S.) consulting firm that has historically provided management consulting services such as strategic planning and business plan writing. Today, it claims over 30 percent of its consulting activity is related to electronic commerce.

It was difficult to find its consulting methodology on its Web site, but I did under the recruiting section. Its approach is shown in Figure 15-9 as part of a case study.

**Note**    The consulting methodology example is shown in the context of being completed in six weeks. The model could certainly apply to longer term or shorter term projects.

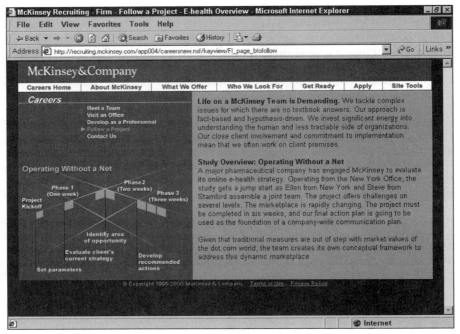

**Figure 15-9:** McKinsey & Company consulting methodology example

The key points displayed in Figure 15-9 are as follows:

- ✦ **Project kickoff**—The work begins and the engagement is entered into.
- ✦ **Phase 1: Evaluate client's current strategy**—Consulting work parameters are set.
- ✦ **Phase 2: Identify opportunity areas**—A framework for the e-marketplace is developed.
- ✦ **Phase 3: Develop recommendations**—The basic question of "What actions would most benefit the client?" is answered.

## Booz-Allen & Hamilton

Another old management consulting firm with technology niches is Booz-Allen & Hamilton (www.bah.com, www.boozallen.com). Booz-Allen & Hamilton has an especially strong niche in computer security consulting. In Figure 15-10, you can see its consulting methodology for end-to-end solutions presented as quick and easy to read bullet points.

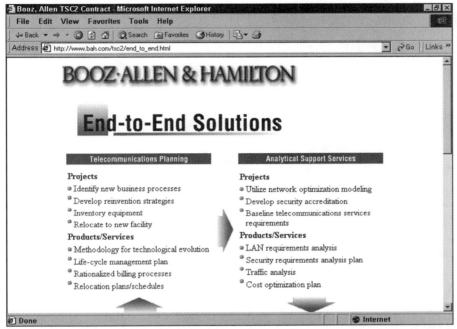

**Figure 15-10:** Booz-Allen & Hamilton's end-to-end technology consulting methodologies

## The Boston Consulting Group

Here's a quiz (an easy one if you're an MBA). What firm invented cows, dogs, and stars? The answer is The Boston Consulting Group (www.bcg.com). The basic model used by The Boston Consulting Group and shown in Figure 15-11 groups business firms into four categories:

✦ **Stars**—These are fast rising firms that are in growth mode. They may or may not be profitable but are considered a key to the future.

✦ **Dogs**—These are laggards. They should be retired to the apple farm to live out their golden years.

✦ **Cows**—This is a positive connotation that addresses cash cows. These are mature firms that spin off considerable cash.

✦ **Question Marks (?)**—This is the ambiguous, unknown position in which many firms find themselves. Will they be a star, cow, or dog in the future?

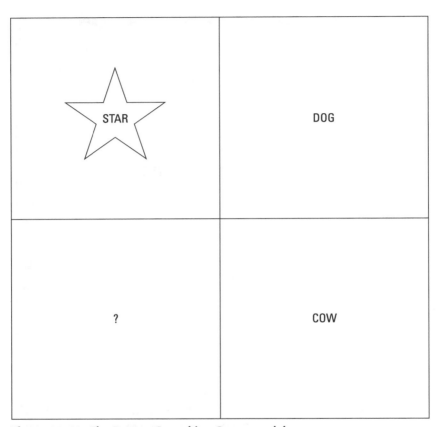

**Figure 15-11:** The Boston Consulting Group model

More to the point in the world of e-commerce and technology, The Boston Consulting Group has a refreshing approach to technology consulting methodologies, stating that their approach varies on a case-by-case basis. This is mentioned at the bottom of Figure 15-12. I suspect The Boston Consulting Group has avoided posting much information on specific consulting methodologies to avoid enabling their competitors to access their methods too easily.

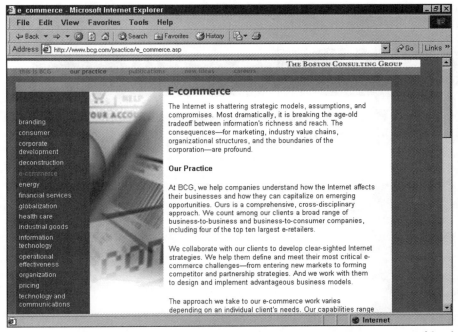

**Figure 15-12:** The Boston Consulting Group's approach to e-commerce consulting is more ad hoc than formal methodology.

## Technology consulting firms

To round out the investigation of ten different consulting methodologies as a vehicle to develop your own MCSE consulting methodology, I will look at two large technology consulting firms found on Kennedy Information's Top 50 list:

✦ IBM Global Services Consulting

✦ Cambridge Technology Partners

### IBM Global Services Consulting

Found at www.ibm.com, this one ton elephant of the technology world has countless consulting methodologies. I've focused on its e-business strategy and design consulting practice as referenced in Figure 15-13, where the consulting methodology is based on best practices.

**Figure 15-13:** IBM's e-commerce consulting service

Highlights of IBM's e-commerce consulting methodology include the following:

✦ Develop a competitive e-business strategy.

✦ Identify, develop, and act on e-business opportunities.

✦ Establish, improve, and sustain your competitive advantage.

✦ Accelerate the growth of your business with strategic and complementary initiatives.

✦ Maximize the return on your Web technology investment.

✦ Implement the processes, organization, and IT for your total transformation strategy.

## Cambridge Technology Partners

This fast-growing firm, which has grown largely by acquisitions, is based in Boston, Massachusetts (www.ctp.com). The regional accounting firm I used to ply my MCSE consulting craft with was the accounting firm for a consulting organization that was acquired by Cambridge Technology Partners (CTP), so I've had first-hand experience with this aggressive firm. Its consulting services are depicted in Figure 15-14. If I were to summarize my observations of this firm's approach, it would be as doers not planners. The point is intended as a compliment. This firm is interested in doing the work, not just proposing it.

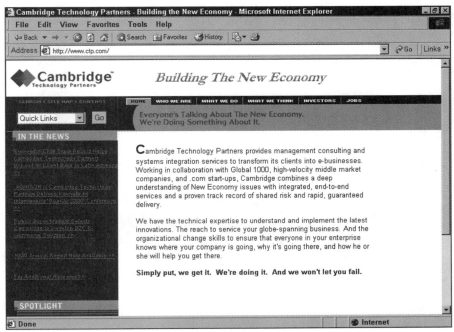

**Figure 15-14:** Cambridge Technology Partner's consulting services

The CTP consulting methodology listed here relates to technology value chain leadership, which emphasizes adding value each step of the way in a consulting engagement (value can be measured as increased accumulation of wealth or increased profitability):

1. Create new business models and specialized value chains to increase customer-perceived value.

2. Form collaborative alliances to strengthen and extend the value chain.

3. Use electronic commerce to integrate the value chain with your customers and collaborating partners. CTP displays this in Figure 15-15.

4. Build business relationships built on openness and trust.

5. Focus on quality, speed, and cost for competitive advantage across the extended enterprise.

6. Share risk and benefits with your value chain partners, based on key metrics.

7. Align your business processes, structure, and reward systems with value chain strategies.

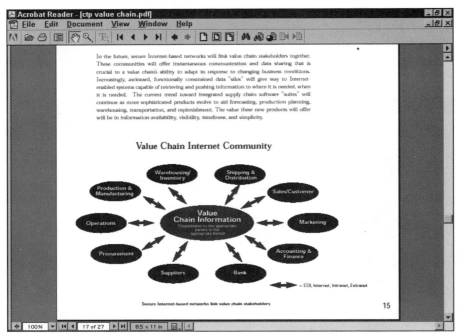

**Figure 15-15:** Graphically displaying the CTP value chain Internet community

This concludes the formal look at ten differing consulting methodologies as part of the best-of-breed Rule of Ten. In this section, I reviewed a number of different consulting firm's methodologies, including those from Big Five accounting firms and national technology consulting practices. I looked at some traditional management consulting firms as well. It is now time for you, the MCSE consultant, to consider what points in this section stood out the most and made the most sense for you to incorporate into your own consulting methodology.

# Regional and Local Firms

As I mentioned earlier in this chapter, you in all likelihood will want to look at the Web sites for local consulting firms in your region. It is possible that regional cultural norms come into play with respect to how MCSE consulting services are delivered. I have selected two firms, Aris and Best Consulting, as examples of this.

## Aris

Aris (www.aris.com) is based in the Seattle area of Washington and primarily focuses on e-business consulting. I've highlighted its 4D consulting model that emphasizes discovery, design, development, and deployment. This is shown in Figure 15-16.

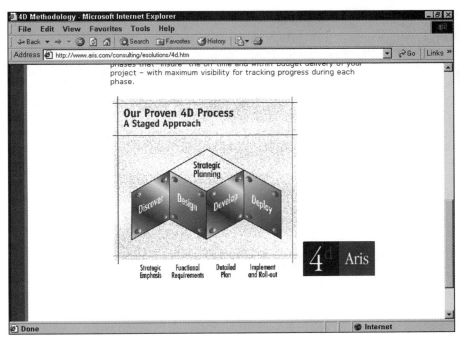

**Figure 15-16:** Aris' 4D e-commerce consulting model

## BEST Consulting

This firm has offices in several major cities, including a large office in Bellevue, Washington. BEST Consulting (www.bestnet.com) is both a consulting firm with full-time employees and a contracting house that provides temporary employees. BEST Consulting's consulting methodologies are to manage engagements within the structure of the Project Management Institute's compliant project management methodology and systems life cycle development methodology, so no new ground is being broken here. BEST Consulting is using proven industry methodologies.

Tip

By the way, the practice of observing the above firms' consulting methodologies was also part of the process of competitive analysis. Assuming you've read the past few sections, you could now speak at length about the competitive climate of technology consulting to a potential client. That type of knowledge is always impressive during the business development phase.

# Microsoft Solutions Framework

Microsoft has a technology implementation methodology it will gladly teach you as part of the Microsoft Official Curriculum (MOC). In Figure 15-17, I display one of the methodology courses you can attend.

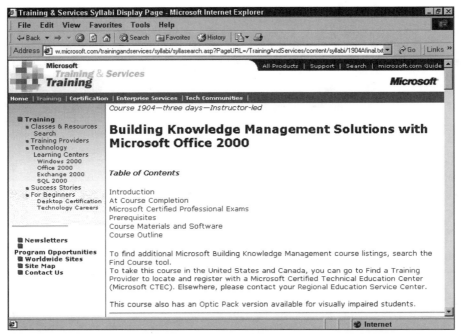

**Figure 15-17:** Course 1904: Building Knowledge Management Solutions with Microsoft Office 2000.

Other MOC courses to consider include the following:

✦ **1917:** Deploying and Managing Windows DNA applications in the Corporate Environment

✦ **1910:** Designing and Implementing Distributed Applications on Windows 2000

✦ **1608:** Designing Business Solutions

✦ **1609:** Designing Data Services and Data Models

✦ **1585:** Gathering and Analyzing Business Requirements (MDAD 2)

✦ **1298:** Mastering Distributed Applications Design Using Microsoft Visual Studio (Classroom View)

✦ **1044:** Microsoft Windows Architecture for Developers Training Kit

✦ **1934:** Principles of Modeling Windows DNA-based Applications with Rational Rose

# Microsoft Consulting

Who better to learn about MCSE consulting from than the founders themselves? You may not have known that Microsoft Consulting Services, shown in Figure 15-18, is a major player in the MCSE consulting market. Accordingly, they hire a large number of MCSE consultants.

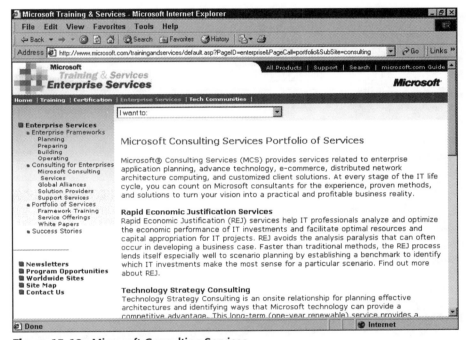

**Figure 15-18:** Microsoft Consulting Services

One consulting methodology used by Microsoft Consulting is the Rapid Economic Justification (REJ) approach. The key steps to REJ are as follows:

1. Understand the business.

2. Understand the solution.

3. Understand the cost/benefit equation.

4. Understand the financial metrics.

5. Understand the risks.

# Visio 2000 and Software Development

Other hidden jewels available to you for consulting methodologies development are the methodology templates included in Visio 2000, the design program from Microsoft. While these are oriented toward software development, you can pick and choose the best components that fit your MCSE consulting engagements. Figure 15-19 shows the Yourdon and Coad template.

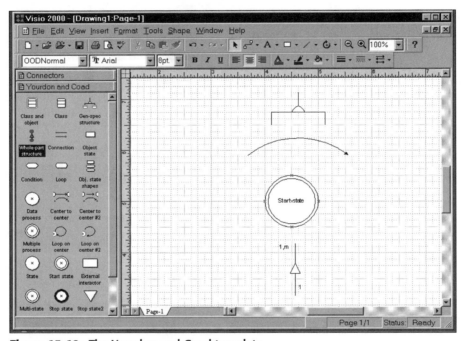

**Figure 15-19:** The Yourdon and Coad template

Other methodology templates in Visio 2000 include the following:

- ✦ Booch OOD
- ✦ COM and OLE
- ✦ Gane-Sarson
- ✦ Jackson
- ✦ Jacobson Use Cases
- ✦ Nassi-Schneiderman
- ✦ ROOM
- ✦ Rumbaugh OMT

✦ Shlaer-Mellor

✦ Ssadm

✦ UML

# The MCSE Consulting Framework

The MCSE consulting proposal framework, shown in Figure 15-20, is one more important consideration when developing a consulting methodology.

 **Cross-Reference** More information on the MCSE consulting proposal framework can be found in Chapter 7.

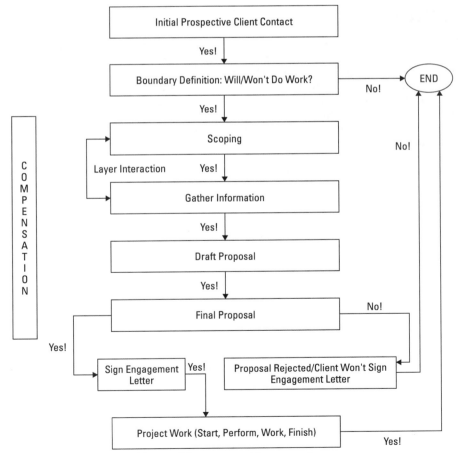

**Figure 15-20:** The MCSE consulting proposal framework

I offer this framework to serve as the launch pad for you to go forward and to quickly develop your own unique MCSE consulting methodology. An emphasis in the MCSE consulting proposal framework is placed on boundary definition and information gathering.

**Tip**    Another way to jumpstart your MCSE consulting methodology is to use the Windows 2000 MCSE exam objectives for the business and technical needs analysis sections of the 70-219, 70-220, and 70-221 MCSE certification exams. If you look closely at the exam objectives, you'll see that these can easily be recast as a consulting methodology. This will save you countless hours at this stage.

I consider this activity of developing an MCSE consulting methodology to be a key to your long-term MCSE consulting success.

## Summary

This chapter was presented as a primer on technology consulting methodologies. By observing existing consulting methodologies, you can develop your own MCSE consulting methodologies, which will speak volumes to your clients and peers about how you do business. Topics covered included defining the term *methodology,* recognizing the maturity it takes to implement a consulting methodology, observing the consulting methodologies in use with leading consulting firms, and recognizing the tools such as the Visio 2000 templates that can help you map out your consulting methodology.

✦        ✦        ✦

# Enterprise-level Consulting

**W**ith Microsoft's emphasis on the enterprise in the Windows 2000 MCSE certification, it's not surprising that many MCSE consultants have an enterprise mindset. Microsoft has set its eyes on being successful at the enterprise level, which is the one market it hasn't conquered and in which it faces stiff competition from the UNIX and mainframe vendors.

This is confirmed by the conference offerings at *Microsoft Certified Professional Magazine*'s TechMentor conference (see www.mpcmag.com) held twice per year. The conference content is aimed squarely at MCSEs serving the enterprise, with topics ranging from complex security topics to clustering. That said, the enterprise market represents a huge opportunity for MCSE consultants.

In fact, Microsoft is not only trying to be more successful in the enterprise space with its products, but also trying to respond to enterprise complaints about failures to provide reliable around-the-clock enterprise-level support. Through the course of this chapter, you'll see how much Microsoft is pushing its MCSEs and partners, such as certified solution providers, to migrate to the enterprise.

## Welcome to the Enterprise

The enterprise is different from the small organization (SORG) and medium-sized organization (MORG) markets. It has been my experience that MCSE consultants who are comfortable at the enterprise level aren't the same MCSE consultants who serve the SORG and MORG space. This section will explore the enterprise space and compare and contrast it to the SORG and MORG space.

## Politics as usual

Speaking only from my own limited enterprise-level experience and the experiences shared by readers and fellow MCSE consultants, the enterprise space is more political than other environments. This is to be expected and accepted.

Rather than fight the enterprise political environment, one of your earliest clues that you're fit for enterprise-level MCSE consulting duties will be your ability to adapt to that world. Are you a consensus builder? Are you a team player effective in working with groups of people? If you can answer in the affirmative, the enterprise space might just be for you, assuming you have a technical skill set that is valued.

If your political skill set lags far behind your technical skill set, the enterprise might not be for you. Some warning signs you should be aware of are as follows:

✦ Does it bother you when people say one thing and do another?

✦ Does it bother you to attend meetings all day?

✦ Does it bother you to contribute to and participate in fundraising causes such as the United Way?

Many subtle success factors at the enterprise level are not spoken but implied. If you have a good sense for these political issues, welcome to the enterprise!

## Risk adverse

What business isn't risk adverse? As comedian Pat Cashman has deadpanned, "Big companies love surprises." He was only kidding, of course. Perhaps more than those in any other environment, managers of all stripes in the enterprise level are taught to be risk adverse.

In general, the enterprise level won't present the best opportunity for you, the MCSE consultant, to work with cutting-edge technology. That's because the political and structural constraints demand conservatism. For example, in the era of Windows 2000 Professional, Boeing (a large aerospace manufacturer in Seattle, Washington) was just wrapping up its Windows 9x installations at the desktop level. This clearly shows that enterprises can lag behind the technology curve.

**Tip**    I don't want to leave you hanging if you're an MCSE consultant that thrives on risk. There are opportunities for you as well. It has been my experience that two types of firms embrace the most recent technology. The first are technology companies themselves, which include software firms such as Microsoft, hardware firms such as Compaq, and dot-coms such as HomeGrocer.com. When you have companies run by technical people, it's a given that these people will go for the latest and greatest technology solutions. The other environment I've observed that lets you play with the latest toys is a test lab affiliated with either hardware and software manufacturers or traditional companies. For example, at Motorola in Chicago, Illinois, there is a test lab dedicated to testing the latest hardware and software before it's distributed to employees.

## Getting along with difficult people

For some reason, enterprises can be a safe harbor for "difficult people." Perhaps that's because the enterprise has the capacity to carry dead weight, something that's typically not possible for the lean and mean MORG or SORG. This leads to a Rule of Ten for dealing with difficult people.

## Rule of Ten — Ten difficult people profiles

Thanks to Dr. Rick Brinkman and Dr. Rick Kirschner, authors of the excellent book *Dealing With People You Can't Stand,* published by McGraw-Hill, I present the ten difficult people types and how to deal with them MCSE consulting style.

1. **The Tank** — is confrontational, acerbic, and angry and may display aggressive and pushy behavior.

2. **The Sniper** — has a sense of humor that's dry as a martini, and a repertoire of rude comments and sarcasm that are well placed to make you look like a fool, not an MCSE consultant.

3. **The Grenade** — lulls you into complacency by being calm, and then explodes into a ranting and raving session.

4. **The Know-It-All** — is supremely self-confident, with a low tolerance for corrections and contradictions.

5. **The Think-They-Know-It-All** — Brinkman and Kirschner said it best, "[This person] can't fool all of the people all of the time but can fool some of the people enough of the time, and enough of the people all of the time — all for the sake of getting some attention." So what does this mean for the MCSE consultant? In larger organizations, you're likely to confront people that talk big but in the long run prove to be vulnerable.

6. **The Yes Person** — basically says yes without thinking things through. Yes people are abundant at the enterprise level.

7. **The Maybe Person** — procrastinates as a stalling tactic, hoping a better choice will come along.

8. **The Nothing Person** — gives no verbal or emotional feedback.

9. **The No Person** — surrounds himself with negativity; fights a never-ceasing battle of futility, hopelessness, and despair.

10. **The Whiner** — feels overwhelmed and helpless.

What is the magical solution for dealing with these ten types of difficult people? Essentially, you can change your attitude about these difficult people or you can change your behavior. Both are difficult choices, but it's up to you.

## Ask the Guru — Difficult People

Working closely with difficult people isn't limited to any one organization type or country even, as this reader's e-mail reminds each of us.

*Dear Harry,*

*It was wonderful reading your war experiences and the advice you have given. I too face a lot of such instances myself here in college. It would do me a great deal of good if you could send me some information and or URLs that deal with getting along with difficult people. I am an MCSE and MCP+I and am pursuing my Masters of Computer Application in India. I am also interested in psychology.*

*Thank You,*

*Best Regards,*

*Arjun T.*

Arjun,

Thanks for your e-mail. I know that there are several good books dedicated to this topic. One such books that takes the high road and offers words of encouragement is *Coaching & Mentoring For Dummies* by Marty Brounstein, published by IDG Books Worldwide, Inc. More importantly, I think experience is the key here. Learning to get along with difficult people is often something you learn by doing, regardless of how many articles and books you read on the subject. I am very impressed with the background you have, including your interest in psychology. Perhaps you could open a niche counseling practice where you cater to helping MCSE consultants. Best of luck to you.

harryb

## Other cultural considerations

I want to close the enterprise welcome section with a few observations about the enterprise that you should take to heart.

✦ **Rah-rah is in** — By and large, the people you'll answer to at the enterprise level have been successful in this environment. These are typically company people who are enthusiastic about the firm. People who move up in the enterprise environment and have the budget authority to hire you are typically not malcontents.

✦ **Serious attitudes** — The small business sense of humor you might have typically doesn't play well before the enterprise crowd. I learned this lesson the hard way — not as an MCSE consultant, but as a Microsoft Certified Trainer (MCT). I had the good fortune (or misfortune) one term to teach an MCSE course in the classroom before twenty Boeing employees. My humor fell flat and I was banned to the online MCSE classroom.

✦ **Slow decision-making**—Something that shouldn't surprise you is the slow speed at which enterprises make decisions. If you've worked for small businesses and had the owner make on-the-fly decisions, the enterprise will be a change for you.

✦ **Wear a tie**—As an MCSE consultant at the enterprise level, you may actually have to dress for success. Are you willing to wear a tie or dress stylishly to make it at the enterprise level? I've seen highly qualified MCSE consultants shun the enterprise level because the Fortune 500 look wasn't for them.

# The Enterprise Architect

Need more fodder to feast on about Microsoft's enterprise-centric view for the MCSE community? Stop by your local Microsoft sales office or attend any number of Windows 2000 half-day seminars. Doing so will indoctrinate you into Microsoft's enterprise message, including the popular PowerPoint slide show (also called a slide deck) that defines the enterprise architect. Here are a few highlights from Microsoft's view of what an enterprise architect should be.

## What is an enterprise architect?

Enterprise architects perform tasks that are more planning- and design-oriented than MCSEs at the keyboard level. In the broadest sense, an enterprise architect wants to know the what and why instead of the how.

**Note**  An enterprise architect has the requisite technical skills to make planning and design decisions. Often, an enterprise architect has been promoted from the ranks of the hands-on MCSE crowd.

This difference means that while the enterprise architect is concerned about lowering the costs of wide area network (WAN) telecommunications by increasing the latency in Active Directory replication, the hands-on MCSE actually makes Active Directory site replication settings in a dialog box on the Active Directory Sites and Services snap-in. The questions an enterprise architect might ponder include:

✦ What is the cost and risk of implementing this solution or technology?

✦ What are the alternatives?

✦ What are the performance implications?

✦ What is the deployment and management strategy?

Figure 16-1 compares the job tasks that an enterprise architect performs with those of an end user, an administrator, and a support professional. In general, the chart demonstrates that the analytical tasks an enterprise architect performs are more complex and global in scope than those tasks performed by a support professional, network administrator, or day-to-day end user. Note that I designate the roles of the senior support professional and the enterprise architect as falling within the MCSE consultant realm. This means the MCSE consultant who is well positioned to bill at high hourly rates and seek out professional challenges at the enterprise level will find their engagement activities skewed to the right side of the chart.

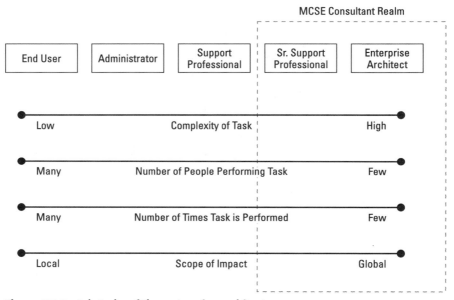

**Figure 16-1:** Job tasks of the enterprise architect

Another look at the enterprise architect and the MCSE consultant comes from Figure 16-2, where the enterprise architect profile is shown as a triangle and mapped to the certifications as well as to the MCSE consulting role.

## Requirements

What personal qualities should you have before you reprint your business cards, pitching yourself as an MCSE consultant with an enterprise architecture niche? Ask yourself these questions:

✦ Do you understand enterprise business models?

✦ Are you open to change, such as the change you'll introduce to the enterprise?

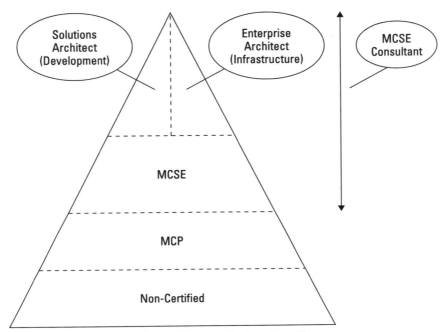

**Figure 16-2:** The enterprise architect professional profile

✦ Do you have the ability to walk a kilometer in another person's shoes? Can you see where other people are coming from?

✦ Are you willing to think outside the staid enterprise technology box?

✦ Do you have sufficient technical expertise? Remember that the enterprise architect doesn't have to be the most technical person in the enterprise.

## Challenges

Microsoft suggests that the enterprise architect will encounter the following challenges:

✦ Remaining customer-focused

✦ Staying passionate about the business

✦ Staying sincere about his or her work

✦ Taking the time to grow continually

# Adopt the Digital Nervous System

If you want to ride the Microsoft horse as an MCSE consultant acting as an enterprise architect, you've got to master the Digital Nervous System (DNS), as shown in Figure 16-3.

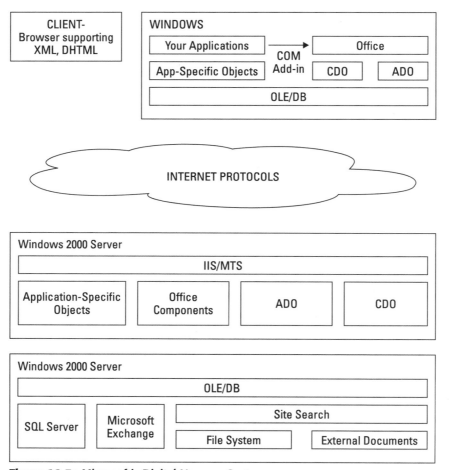

**Figure 16-3:** Microsoft's Digital Nervous System

The Digital Nervous System is a metaphor for the human nervous system; in the context of business computing, the Digital Nervous System is meant to be a Microsoft technology implementation based on Microsoft solutions such as Windows 2000, Active Directory, and BackOffice that will motivate knowledge workers, allow you to manage your business process (such as ERP), and allow you to remain competitive and stay ahead. Microsoft is marketing the Digital Nervous System paradigm as the best way to position your business for the new e-commerce world.

**Tip**     Worrying about being fired is another sign of enterprise thinking!

# Nontechnical Considerations

The MCSE consultant should consider certain nontechnical issues — such as slow decision-making, longer payment cycles, and need for personal enrichment — concerning the enterprise space.

## Longer decision-making time frame

I mentioned earlier in the chapter that enterprises take longer to make decisions than small firms (often because the decisions are weightier). Of course, this can impact the tie between enterprise engagements. Specific to the MCSE consultant, the following pro-enterprise argument presents a contrary view of the decision-making process.

Many large consulting firms avoid small business environments for one simple reason. The salespeople at these consulting firms have found it takes as much effort (but not always as much time) to sell into a small firm as a large firm. They prefer to market to larger firms, such as those found in the enterprise space, given the larger contracts that are awarded.

I'm not sure the preceding statements always hold true, but it is the perception among large consulting firms — at any rate, this time argument should be of interest to the fledging MCSE consultant.

## Longer payment cycles to consultant

Something you will notice in the enterprise environment is the turnaround time on invoices. My smaller customers often write me a check the same day they receive my consulting invoice. However, enterprises with a longer payment cycle will introduce you, the MCSE consultant, to terms such as *line of credit* and *factoring*. Here's what I mean.

When your enterprise consulting invoices age past 45 days and you call a client's accounts payable department, you'll likely hear phrases such as, "We're converting from PeopleSoft to SAP." Six months later, you'll hear the opposite: "We're converting from SAP to PeopleSoft." Meanwhile, you've still got payroll to meet, so if you're going to work at the enterprise level, be sure to get a commercial line of credit at the bank of your choice. When your invoice ages, you can draw down on the line of credit to meet your financial obligations. When your enterprise ship comes in, you can pay back the line of credit. Factoring works in a similar manner, since you get cash before you're paid. Here, you sell your account receivable (A/R) to a factoring firm at a deep discount. Thus, factoring companies can be thought of as the pawnshops of corporate finance.

## You are a small part of the solution

As an MCSE consultant at the enterprise level, you'll often find yourself acting as a small fish in a large pond. Many MCSE consultants find this comforting, as no one person can cause extreme harm to the enterprise network (at least in theory). Others find that the enterprise does not allow significant professional and personal growth. Why? Large organizations often value team process more than individual creativity. It is possible that you'll be assigned duties that are performed in conjunction with other enterprise employees, and your individual contribution might be just a small part of the overall picture. More importantly, your creative insights might not mesh well with enterprise thinking where decisions are often made by committee. And if you are truly a creative thinker with an overabundance of new ideas, you might get frustrated by this type of environment.

# Competitive Analysis

There are many consulting firms competing for enterprise business. These firms might be traditional management consulting firms dabbling in technology, accounting firms with a technology division, and so on. Table 16-1 displays the full list of the top 50 consulting firms, as compiled by Kennedy Information (`www.kennedyinfo.com/mc/cn50.html`). It's very possible that you'll bid against these firms as you solicit enterprise-level work. Better to know who your competitors are than not.

## Table 16-1
### Kennedy Information's Largest 50 Management Consultant Firms

| Ranking | Firm | Headquarters |
|---|---|---|
| 1 | Andersen Consulting | Chicago, IL |
| 2 | PricewaterhouseCoopers | New York, NY |
| 3 | Ernst & Young | Cleveland, OH |
| 4 | Deloitte Consulting | New York, NY |
| 5 | CSC | El Segundo, CA |

| Ranking | Firm | Headquarters |
| --- | --- | --- |
| 6 | KPMG | New York, NY |
| 7 | McKinsey & Company | New York, NY |
| 8 | Cap Gemini | Paris, France |
| 9 | Mercer Consulting Group | New York, NY |
| 10 | Arthur Andersen | Chicago, IL |
| 11 | A.T. Kearney | Chicago, IL |
| 12 | Towers Perrin | New York, NY |
| 13 | Booz-Allen & Hamilton | McLean, VA |
| 14 | IBM Consulting | Somers, NY |
| 15 | American Management Systems | Fairfax, VA |
| 16 | Keane | Boston, MA |
| 17 | Hewitt Associates | Lincolnshire, IL |
| 18 | Sema Group | Paris, France |
| 19 | Logica London | United Kingdom |
| 20 | The Boston Consulting Group | Boston, MA |
| 21 | Watson Wyatt Worldwide | Bethesda, MD |
| 22 | DMR Consulting Group | Montreal, PQ, Canada |
| 23 | CMG | London, England |
| 24 | Aon Consulting | Chicago, IL |
| 25 | Cambridge Technology Partners | Cambridge, MA |
| 26 | Arthur D. Little | Cambridge, MA |
| 27 | Bain & Company | Boston, MA |
| 28 | debis Systemhaus | Fasanenweg, Germany |
| 29 | PA Consulting Group | London, England |
| 30 | Woodrow Milliman | Seattle, WA |
| 31 | Origin | Eindhoven, The Netherlands |
| 32 | Telcordia Technologies (formerly Bellcore) | Morristown, NJ |
| 33 | Buck Consultants | Secaucus, NJ |
| 34 | Metzler Group | Chicago, IL |

*Continued*

| | Table 16-1 *(continued)* | |
|---|---|---|
| *Ranking* | *Firm* | *Headquarters* |
| 35 | Roland Berger & Partner | Munich, Germany |
| 36 | Technology Solutions Company | Chicago, IL |
| 37 | Whittman-Hart | Chicago, IL |
| 38 | CTG | Buffalo, NY |
| 39 | CBSI | Farmington Hills, MI |
| 40 | Renaissance Worldwide | Newton, MA |
| 41 | Hay Group | Philadelphia, PA |
| 42 | Mitchell Madison Group | New York, NY |
| 43 | Perot Systems | Dallas, TX |
| 44 | INS | Sunnyvale, CA |
| 45 | McGladrey & Pullen | Schaumburg, IL |
| 46 | CIBER | Englewood, CO |
| 47 | Monitor Company | Cambridge, MA |
| 48 | First Consulting Group | Long Beach, CA |
| 49 | Horwath International | New York, NY |
| 50 | Hagler Bailly | Arlington, VA |

## Guest Sermon — Life Is Good

Chicago-based Kevin Kocis is a former self-employed MCSE consultant who has worked in the information technology field for over ten years and who has served enterprise accounts. He now works for a large electronic manufacturer (one with over 130,000 employees worldwide). Kevin is also a skilled author and presenter of technology topics, with a book to his credit, several articles and reviews published in *Microsoft Certified Professional Magazine,* and presentations delivered at TechMentor conferences in Atlanta and San Francisco. He has unique insights to share on the enterprise consulting space with the following guest sermon:

*Ah, the life of an enterprise consultant.*

*My experience with consulting has been predominantly in the enterprise arena. Sure, I've worked with some smaller firms, and the scope is definitely different. What oftentimes is viewed as a defined specialty (say a strong MCSE skill set) can be viewed differently in the enterprise.*

*What do I mean by that? Well, when I began consulting, my area of competency was in the Macintosh arena. I focused solely on supporting companies that were predominantly Macintosh-based. While this focus seemed excellent at the time, we all know where it would get one of us today.*

*Fortunately, the heterogeneous enterprise offers the opportunity to learn a variety of platforms and architectures. During my Macintosh days (yes, I still have several at home on my W2K network), I was exposed to flavors of UNIX and Windows. As a result, I inherited a wealth of information from colleagues regarding these operating systems and began pursuing my MCSE. I also had the opportunity to slap an older Sun Sparcstation (UNIX) on my desk.*

*Before I go further, let me establish a point. I don't believe there is anything wrong with focusing on an area of expertise. Consultants are often categorized and hired for a specialty, and possessing a major strength is definitely not a mistake. However, I encourage you to also pursue diversity, which I'll examine next.*

*As a direct result of my exposure to the various platforms, not only did I become more marketable for various consulting firms (and myself), but also I could better leverage my rates and employment opportunities (if I were interested in a permanent opportunity). Knowledge will always translate to power, and the IT professional sometimes pushes this power over the edge.*

*In many of my consulting roles, interoperability was a key concern. I watched as NT consultants bucked heads with UNIX on Web hosting and DNS issues. Collaboration was a constant struggle and usually management intervention prevailed (which usually meant managers decided based on what they found to be the focus). With diversification, you are better qualified to lead efforts in situations such as this.*

*If you are considering the opportunity for a lead or management role, having a heterogeneous background puts you in a better position politically. Since many IT groups in the enterprise are aligned by specialty (UNIX, NT, networking, and so on), if your experience has transcended these stereotypes, you are better qualified to make sound objective decisions.*

*The opportunities that were presented to me while consulting were 100 percent based on my exposure to heterogeneous environments. While consulting, I was offered the opportunity to lead the group that had trained me (which was quite an honorable offer). I accepted this position and eventually landed an IT management position with another group at this Fortune 100 company.*

*Currently, I manage UNIX, NT, networking, software development, and Oracle teams. The benefit I have is that when I was consulting, I maintained an open and eager perspective on technology. I learned the nuances, the pros and cons, to each platform and operating system. I challenge you to go into your situation with this approach. If you are an MCSE on NT4, learn more about UNIX and networking (and I don't mean studying network essentials). Learn more about Macintosh. I'm sure you won't be too surprised to learn that Windows really is an inherited hybrid of these two technologies marketed very effectively. In doing this, you will have a more rounded approach, and may find the opportunity you've been after.*

# Rule of Ten — Enterprise Case Studies

In this section, I'll present ten case studies for you to analyze, discuss with other MCSE consultants, and consider solutions for. MCSE Consultants-R-Us will be the sample consulting firm in our case studies. At the end of the chapter, I'll present a suggested solution set.

## Case study #1 — National Stock Exchange

This is a case study about one of the major stock markets and how it addressed the challenge to modernize.

### Just the facts

Building relationships with its listed companies through the timely and efficient delivery of information is very important for National Stock Exchange (NSE), the largest electronic stock market in Africa. As the speed of business increased, however, NSE found that existing information products, delivered in a mix of hard copy and electronic formats, weren't keeping pace with its clients' needs. NSE was quick to identify the valuable role the Internet could play in reinventing the way it delivers market, financial, and analytical information.

### MCSE Consultants-R-Us arrives

Never before had NSE addressed such a comprehensive array of information needs, so NSE turned to MCSE Consultants-R-Us. Using Rad-Rad, a customer-oriented, rapid application development process for delivering electronic commerce solutions, MCSE Consultants-R-Us rapidly deployed a timely and content-rich interactive market information delivery system. See the "Case Study Results" section later in the chapter for the solution.

## Case study #2 — A medical health maintenance organization

This case study is about a health maintenance organization addressing legacy database issues.

### Just the facts

Blue Heart of Alaska's legacy human resources management system (HRMS) was built in the late 1960s. When it came time to upgrade, Blue Heart originally planned to develop a new HRMS in-house. However, with the Year 2000 looming ahead, the company realized that developing an in-house system would take much too long.

### MCSE Consultants-R-Us arrives

The insurer hired MCSE Consultants-R-Us to help it become Y2K-compliant and to automate its benefits operations, which were still being manually administered via the mainframe system. Blue Heart was attracted to MCSE Consultants-R-Us because of its track record of successful and rapid PeopleSoft (the insurer's chosen application) implementations.

## Case study #3 — European telecommunications operations

This case study focuses on both an international company and the telecommunications industry.

### Just the facts

Stung more than once by their American counterparts, European telecommunications companies pursuing world leadership in rapidly deregulating markets know that merely satisfying customers is no longer enough to keep the shareholders happy. As with any industry, the companies that create and cultivate customer loyalty have a distinct competitive edge.

### MCSE Consultants-R-Us arrives

Five European telecommunications companies chose MCSE Consultants-R-Us based on its extensive experience, services, and the right approach to build end-to-end customer service solutions that met the clients' unique needs.

## Case study #4 — A large life insurance company

This case study addresses the client/server needs of a large life insurance company.

### Just the facts

Canada's largest provider of individual life insurance needed to enhance its new sales compensation package.

### MCSE Consultants-R-Us arrives

This was the company's first large-scale client/server implementation, so management looked for a systems integrator that would develop the system and empower members of its IT staff along the way. MCSE Consultants-R-Us satisfied these selection criteria.

# Case study #5 — A government tourism promotion department

This is a case study about a not-for-profit tourism agency.

## Just the facts

The tourism industry is extremely competitive and Alaska competes with other destinations for tourists. The prospective audience and the tourism department's sales and marketing efforts are global and spread throughout specialty markets, from travel wholesalers to outfitters to marinas. Reaching this varied audience requires a carefully coordinated sales effort.

## MCSE Consultants-R-Us arrives

The Alaska tourism department realized that using technology to enhance the flow, exchange, and use of information from its sales and marketing efforts was critical to continued success. The organization turned to MCSE Consultants-R-Us to help it build a knowledge management solution that would give Alaska a competitive edge with tourists.

# Case study #6 — A large pizza chain

This is a case study about a pizza delivery chain.

## Just the facts

Dino's Pizza Distribution supports the operations and growth of over 7,800 stores worldwide by providing exceptional service and quality products at the best available price. Through a network of ten distribution centers, Dino's supplies stores with a variety of products, ranging from basic food items to pizza boxes, ovens, and cleaning supplies. To enhance its distribution centers' service to stores, Dino's recognized the need for operational and financial technology solutions that would ensure Y2K-compliance of existing financial systems. They also wanted to streamline their supply chain and eliminate the burden of inventory management for the franchises, allowing them to focus on sales and customer service.

## MCSE Consultants-R-Us arrives

A long-standing PeopleSoft HRMS customer, Dino's licensed PeopleSoft Manufacturing, Distribution, and Financials applications to provide a complete enterprise solution to its corporate, distributorship, and internal productions. Dino's chose MCSE Consultants-R-Us as their implementation partner for its successful experience with over 100 PeopleSoft implementations, its proven methodology that ensures on-time and on-budget solutions, and its ability to reengineer processes around the PeopleSoft functionality.

# Case study #7 — A state university

This is a case study from the academic community. Don't forget that the enterprise space includes colleges as well as private sector firms.

## Just the facts

The second largest university in Florida has a student population of 21,000. In order to meet their growing information needs and provide functionality that will meet their long-term goals, the University needs to replace its dated payroll and student administration systems, consisting of several stand-alone packages. These systems, which are redundant, are also too costly to maintain. They lack the flexibility to keep pace with changing requirements and new technology, and are not Y2K compliant. To meet each of these requirements, the University selected PeopleSoft's HRMS and SA systems.

## MCSE Consultants-R-Us arrives

The University selected MCSE Consultants-R-Us as its implementation partner because of its strong Mo-Mo methodology, which would give their project team the drive and direction it needed for such a large project, as well as ensure that the project is completed on time and on budget. Another major factor for the University was the breadth of MCSE Consultants-R-Us' education experience and the quality and quantity of consultants with extensive student administration and PeopleSoft experience.

# Case study #8 — A foreign airline

This case study is about a European airline. The MCSE consultants on this one earned frequent flyer miles.

## Just the facts

Air-Air Airlines (AAA) is constantly looking for ways to improve its service and thereby increase customer loyalty and retention. To that end, the airline decided to extend its customer service leadership position by building a Web site that would provide a comprehensive travel planning experience.

## MCSE Consultants-R-Us arrives

The success of this site depended on more than just great technical tools. It also required sophisticated design techniques to ensure that the site would be easy for people to use and navigate, as well as business process expertise to fully integrate the site with the airline's operations. AAA found, in MCSE Consultants-R-Us, a consulting firm that could combine all of these skills.

## Case study #9 — A large aerospace concern

This is a case study about a large American aerospace company, known as LAC.

### Just the facts

Faced with increased competition in the post–cold war world, LAC needed to improve procurement processes for its five divisions. The company's existing system required employees to manually fill out "requests to buy" and route them to the approving manager. In addition, inventory purchasing and price histories resided in two stand-alone systems, adding to an already lengthy process.

### MCSE Consultants-R-Us arrives

To save time, reduce costs, and achieve results, LAC partnered with MCSE Consultants-R-Us to develop a streamlined procurement system. LAC chose MCSE Consultants-R-Us based on its object-oriented technology expertise, willingness to transfer knowledge to its team, and ability to build the system in rapid timeframes.

## Case study #10 — An independent software vendor

This case study is about a large software development firm based in India.

### Just the facts

With global competitive pressures, customer expectations, and more complex support problems on the rise, software giant MiaMia wanted to implement a customer service system that would enable it, and other leading high-tech companies, to communicate customer service issues among partners, vendors, and key customers. As a result, they would provide customers with the seamless support they deserve.

### MCSE Consultants-R-Us arrives

Delivering the industry's first open, standards-based, multivendor support center would be a challenge. MiaMia hired MCSE Consultants-R-Us to provide program management, design business processes, and help implement the new system.

# Ways to Serve the Enterprise

An MCSE consultant can serve the enterprise in numerous ways, which I discuss in the subsections that follow. I include the employee category so that you can compare and contrast the wide range of roles available for MCSEs looking to make some money.

# Consultant

You can serve the enterprise space as an MCSE consultant where you operate as a sole practitioner. That is the primary focus of this book. However, you might consider joining a consulting firm. Here is a recent job opening for a consultant in a large consulting firm, seeking someone to join one of its European offices.

## Description — Business analyst

The MCSE consultant, serving as a business analyst, would work as part of a multi-disciplined team under the guidance of experienced consultants to provide a variety of consulting activities, to contribute to the development and delivery of business consulting project solutions, and to enhance the capacity of the Project team to meet client needs.

## Qualifications

✦ Able to contribute to business model discussions both internally and with clients.

✦ Able to conduct activity and process modeling, including current and future processes.

✦ Able to lead best practice discussion around future business processes.

✦ Able to facilitate discussion around organization structure and roles and responsibilities around future processes.

✦ Able to lead discussions on business concepts.

✦ Able to undertake interviews of clients. This requires the ability to be both an active interviewer and listener in client settings. The candidate must be articulate and able to comprehend client responses, as well as generate follow-up questions.

✦ Able to display an understanding of the key elements of a complete business system design.

✦ Able to run round table meetings, single-handedly, with up to 10 client participants.

✦ Able to plan and run a workshop successfully.

✦ Able to confirm business assumptions and drive assigned issues to closure.

✦ Complete tasks within budget.

✦ Able to estimate accurately the time necessary to complete an assigned task and take proper account of all activities that must be undertaken, such as scenario development.

✦ Keep the Project Manager informed accurately and promptly of the status of tasks and other issues.

✦ Able to build a business case.

✦ Able to build measurement architecture.

✦ Has vertical or industry experience.

## Latest starting date
Within 4–6 weeks.

## Travel requirements
Travel may be expected depending on the location of the project, although many of our projects are conducted within the consulting firm's offices.

## Salary, benefits, and stock
Salary depends on experience (DOE) but starts in the mid-$70,000 range. Standard health care package. Stock grants dependent on seniority.

## Culture
The consulting firm is a goal-oriented, dynamic, and informal culture. The environment is relatively unstructured and focused on empowerment and responsibility for all staff. The consulting firm is primarily involved in software development projects using advanced technologies. A project will typically last between three months and one year and is delivered by a team of between 7 and 20 people. Each team member is expected to take ownership of the part of the project on which they are working.

# Contractor

Another popular avenue for MCSE consultants within the enterprise is as a contractor. Contractors enjoy flexible assignments without the headaches of running a competitive consulting practice. The compensation is typically lower than that of consultants. Here is a sample contracting assignment for a contract house. The position was located in California.

## Description — Advanced network engineer
Responsibilities include network configuration and design, proposal development and presentation, application and industry support, project management, and technical assurance. The advanced network engineer will perform technical assurance on customized integrated network services ensuring customer's equipment and software capabilities are incorporated into the design process. He or she will analyze the customer's technical operating environment and design network solutions as appropriate. He or she will engineer all digital access arrangements, including line coding and format specifications, synchronization design, and disaster recovery,

and ensure design integrity throughout the implementation process. The engineer will design routing arrangements and features to create the customer application and perform complex engineering studies to determine optimal network configuration, address design changes, and resolve subsequent implementation problems.

### Qualifications

Five years of relevant work experience in network design techniques and standards including access LAN/WAN, circuit/trunk sizing, terminating equipment, routing design, contingency, and recovery planning is required. Knowledge of various network service architectures, transport technologies, and access/egress arrangements is also required. Candidates should be familiar with facilities engineering, procurement and diagnostic techniques, project coordination, and project management.

### Duration and pay rate

This advanced network engineer position is by contract for a duration of 120 days or more. The pay rate is to be determined.

## Temp

I've never looked down on the temp avenue for getting work as an MCSE. First of all, it's a great way to get experience at the enterprise level. Second, you can try the firm out before you accept an offer for full-time employment. It might well be that you won't care to work for the firm you're interviewing with after seeing it in action. The job description below is a temporary assignment at an enterprise in the Boston area that was recently posted by a large international temp agency.

### Description — Windows NT network engineer

The responsibilities for this position are as follows: the setup and configuration of Windows NT Servers; maintenance of user accounts, hosts, and domains; possible administration of DNS, e-mail, HTTP, remote access, and backups; integration with MacOS, NetWare, or UNIX; and possible responsibility for administering and troubleshooting SQL, Exchange, or SMS servers.

### Qualifications

Three to five years of technical support/administration experience is required. Familiarity with Windows 95, Windows NT, Network Administration, Windows 3.*x,* and E-mail Administrator is also required. Excellent customer service skills, project management, and strong knowledge of TCP/IP certifications (MCSE, A+, CNE) are a plus.

### Pay rate

This temporary technical position begins immediately and will pay $25–$30 per hour.

# Employee

You may decide to just become an employee for an enterprise. Many enterprise organizations hire qualified MCSEs, as the job description that follows shows.

## Description — Senior network analyst (LAN/WAN)

The senior network analyst will provide third-level technical support to Network Services Group architectures, in particular to local and wide area networks, including Cisco and Bay Networks equipment and software. Other tasks will include performing project management, completing analysis of operations and user needs. The incumbent will also be responsible for designing, engineering, and implementing mission critical data network systems.

## Primary job functions

✦ Prepare and maintain complex router configurations and microcode.

✦ Design network topology using various protocols and transport architectures such as Layer 2 and 3 switching, Token Ring, Ethernet, Frame Relay, ATM, and SNA.

✦ Coordinate with vendors for equipment readiness (includes new installations, troubleshooting current installations, and upgrades).

✦ Redesign the physical network to allow for new additions or upgrade service to existing locations, while planning for future network needs and growth.

✦ Accept responsibility for LAN/WAN design, administration, and troubleshooting at all levels of complexity.

✦ Utilize intelligent network management tools to isolate problems or improve network performance (HP Openview, Cisco Works, Network General Distributed Sniffer, NetScout).

✦ Create and maintain well-documented project plans related to system analysis and implementation. Effectively communicate project plans and updates to other team members as well as other groups.

✦ Create and maintain technical drawings and documentation for all LAN/WAN topologies.

✦ Provide third-level technical support for network-related problems and escalations.

## Required qualifications

✦ Five or more years of experience in LAN/WAN design and components used (Cisco routers/switches, Bay Networks hubs, VLANs, CSU/DSU, and so on).

✦ MCSE certification holder for Windows 2000.

✦ Fluent in LAN/WAN network components, protocols, and connectivity issues.

✦ Experienced in data network troubleshooting methods and network protocol analysis tools (Network General sniffers, HP Openview, Cisco Works, and Net Scout).

✦ Able to learn independently and apply learned concepts quickly in order to design and manage enterprise systems efficiently.

✦ Able to successfully manage multiple projects and responsibilities at the same time. Able to deal with changing priorities.

✦ Demonstrated use of a systematic approach in solving problems through analysis of problem and evaluation of alternate solutions.

✦ Able to start and persist with specific courses of action while exhibiting high motivation and a sense of urgency. Able to work flexible hours when needed.

✦ Able to work with people in such a manner as to build high morale and group commitments to goals and objectives.

✦ Excellent customer and communication skills.

### Desired qualifications

✦ Three or more years designing, implementing, and supporting Extranets/Virtual Private Networks. Advanced understanding of Extranet architectures.

✦ Two or more years implementing and maintaining traffic prioritization schemes in data networks.

### Pay rate

Depends on experience (DOE) plus full benefits.

## Outsourcing

Don't overlook the opportunity to serve the enterprise consulting space by providing outsourcing services. Many enterprises subscribe to the management philosophy that they should focus on core competencies and not distractions. Accordingly, many enterprises view technology functions such as infrastructure administration as not central to their key business goals and objectives. These enterprises are prime candidates from which to solicit outsourcing engagements.

For example, perhaps in your region a large manufacturing concern wants to focus on manufacturing and marketing its product. Perhaps they consider their Web site to be a necessary evil to have for the purposes of having an Internet identity in the twenty-first century, but they still do business the old-fashioned way with telephone calls and face-to-face sales meetings with customers. Such an enterprise would probably be interested in outsourcing its Web site, including the development and maintenance of its Web pages and content, to an MCSE-type consulting practice that focuses on outsourced Web site management. It's likely that such an MCSE consulting firm would be more nimble and update the Web content faster than the manufacturer would, given the manufacturers preference to focus on its core competencies. This is but one example of the outsourcing opportunities that exist for MCSE consultants at the enterprise level.

There are many great resources for learning more about outsourcing, two of which are the following:

✦ **IBM** — IBM provides outsourcing services for large customers and has posted a significant outsourcing discussion at `www.ibm.com/services` (select "Focus on core competencies/Consider Outsourcing" on the "Option 1: Custom service list" drop-down field).

✦ **Deloitte Consulting** — At `www.dc.com`, you should type the word *outsourcing* into the Search by Keyword field. You will be presented with numerous outsourcing resources including the hyperlink to the Services — Outsourcing page on the Deloitte Consulting Web site. In particular, I found the Services — Outsourcing page to offer excellent advice on why an enterprise should outsource some of its business and technology functions.

# Serving Microsoft

Microsoft has been a great consulting account for me personally, where I've served as a vendor on an occasional basis. Microsoft pays a fair consulting rate in a timely manner. More importantly, Microsoft is vendor-friendly. Many MCSE consultants serve Microsoft exclusively and make a great living doing it.

There are three classes of workers at Microsoft.

## Blue cards

The permanent employees are known as *blue cards* and enjoy something of a mythical status. Not only do they get full benefits, but they are also awarded stock options.

## A-

The A- status is for temps and contractors who work at Microsoft via temp agencies and contract houses. These individuals typically earn 50 percent to 70 percent of what the temp agency or contract house is billing them out for. An A- worker cannot work more than 12 consecutive months at Microsoft without taking a three-month break from work. These employees have the lowest status at Microsoft, so it's not surprising that they have formed a voluntary union, called the Washington Alliance of Technology (WashTech for short), to help improve their working conditions. The WashTech Web site is shown in Figure 16-4. As an MCSE consultant, you should visit this site if you plan to work for Microsoft as a temporary employee.

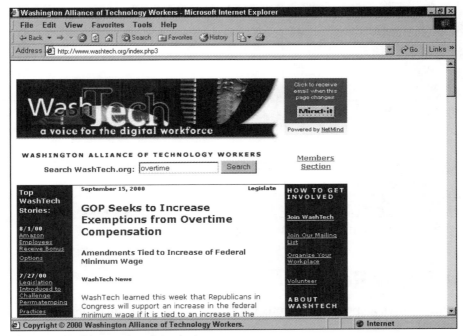

**Figure 16-4:** The WashTech Web site

## V-

The V- status is for vendors. Microsoft vendors enjoy several benefits, such as the ability to quickly bid on and be awarded Microsoft work. You must be sponsored by a Microsoft manager to become a vendor, and after completing vendor application paperwork, you'll receive notice that you have a vendor account. Once you have a vendor account, you can bill against outstanding Microsoft purchase orders using the online invoice program shown in Figure 16-5.

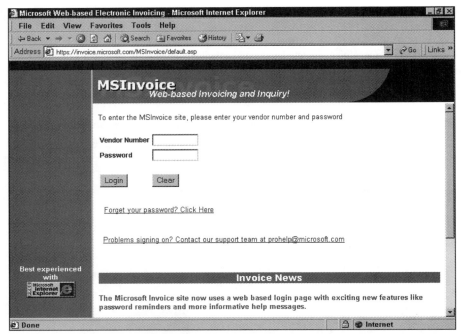

**Figure 16-5:** Electronic billing system using Microsoft Invoice

# Case Study Results

In this section, I'll present the outcome for each case study involving MCSE Consultants-R-Us.

## Case study #1 — National Stock Exchange

Here is the outcome of the stock exchange case study.

### The solution

The MCSE Consultants-R-Us team balanced all of the elements — business, technical, creative, and cognitive — needed to develop and deliver a system that not only fits with NSE's business but is technically sound, graphically compelling, and rich in timely and accurate information. NSE Online provides executives of NSE-listed companies with an up-to-the-minute picture of what's happening in the market and with their company's stock. It further enables them to make strategic decisions and increase their reach to investors.

## Results

NSE Online is a high-value information resource that shows listed companies that NSE understands their needs. It distinguishes NSE from other exchanges, helps build customer loyalty, and provides yet another incentive to list on the NSE stock market.

# Case study #2 — A medical health maintenance organization

Here is the outcome of the health maintenance organization case study.

## The solution

With the help of MCSE Consultants-R-Us' functional and technical consultants, who developed mainframe interfaces, complex reports, and necessary customizations, the PeopleSoft system was up and running in less than eight months. The MCSE Consultants-R-Us team also transferred its technical knowledge throughout the project and helped Blue Heart make important improvements to its business processes to leverage the best practices built into PeopleSoft.

## Results

With new business processes and automated benefits procedures, Blue Heart has reduced the number of inquiries made to HR staff and has transferred ownership of data to the appropriate users. The company is Y2K-compliant and empowered to manage system upgrades on its own.

# Case study #3 — European telecommunications operations

Here is the outcome of the European telecommunications case study.

## The solutions

✦ **Switzerland** — In just eight months, MCSE Consultants-R-Us built a solid customer service foundation that enabled one Swiss telecommunications start-up to provide superior service. The system provides customers with a single point of contact for service, pricing, order processing, and problem resolution.

✦ **The Netherlands** — For a firm in the Dutch mobile telecommunications market, MCSE Consultants-R-Us defined and implemented the supporting workflows to drive superior service. Then MCSE Consultants-R-Us wrote much of the required technology functionality from scratch. With the new system, the company now closes 85 percent to 95 percent of calls on the first try.

✦ **Germany** — MCSE Consultants-R-Us worked closely with individuals at all levels of one of Germany's top telecommunication companies (telcos) to define optimal service processes and create new job roles and descriptions. Then MCSE Consultants-R-Us developed the system that has improved customer service quality, enhanced employee morale, and built the internal customer loyalty that's so critical to success.

✦ **England** — When a British telco giant began forming partnerships with telephone service providers in more than a dozen countries across Europe and Asia, it asked MCSE Consultants-R-Us to develop a central, easily accessed repository of customer and product information and problem resolutions. The system enables the telecommunications company and all of its partners to share best practices, collaborate more effectively, and elevate the quality of customer service.

✦ **Sweden** — From the very start of the project, MCSE Consultants-R-Us worked closely with users from across the Swedish company's many departments. This ensured that they felt a sense of ownership in both articulating the business challenges and crafting the customer handling application that would help the company achieve its goals, cultivate customer loyalty, and support the workforce's needs.

### Results

Now that they've become customer-focused, these companies are ideally positioned to manage customer relationships and build the long-term loyalty that is critical to winning the race to the top of the telecommunications field.

## Case study #4 — A large life insurance company

Here is the outcome of the large life insurance company case study.

### The solution

In just ten months, MCSE Consultants-R-Us partnered with the life insurance company to design and deploy an object-oriented application to handle general and district agent compensation. MCSE Consultants-R-Us transferred technical and project management expertise to the life insurance company's IT staff every step of the way.

### Results

The large life insurance company has a more streamlined approach to compensation processing. With the knowledge employees gained during the project, they can maintain and enhance the application themselves, and apply MCSE Consultants-R-Us' methodology to future internal development projects.

## Case study #5 — A government tourism promotion department

Here is the outcome of the tourism department case study.

### The solution

Following an initial scoping effort, MCSE Consultants-R-Us recommended a Lotus Notes solution and worked closely with the tourism department to implement Notes across the enterprise. Four key databases — marketing, special events, activities and sales goals, and lead tracking — serve as the heart of the tourism department's sales and marketing efforts. The Notes system gives everyone access to the same information, allowing for new levels of global communication and collaboration.

### Results

The new knowledge management infrastructure enables the tourism department to benefit from the shared information, strategies, and experience of all personnel. Plus, field personnel can work at home, in the office, on the road, or at client sites, dialing up their office for immediate access to up-to-date information on events, accounts, sales plans, and more.

## Case study #6 — A large pizza chain

Here is the outcome of the pizza chain case study.

### The solution

MCSE Consultants-R-Us worked with Dino's to reengineer production, planning, and distribution processes across their nineteen distribution centers to prepare the organization for the new technology. Working with the Dino's team, MCSE Consultants-R-Us implemented ten new Distribution and Financial PeopleSoft 7.5 modules to be rolled out to each distribution center. Development and initial implementations were completed in approximately one year. MCSE Consultants-R-Us also developed and conducted a comprehensive training program, ensuring that new processes and technologies were fully understood and utilized by Dino's staff. This program included a customized system and process training as well as enterprise-wide communications initiatives.

### Results

With new Y2K-compliant systems in place, Dino's has a streamlined supply chain system that automatically ensures that franchises receive the right supplies at the right time, fueling their success and paving the way for future growth. Dino's has greatly enhanced production, planning, and distribution processes that maximize the effectiveness of the PeopleSoft solutions. They now have a staff that understands why the new processes and systems are important and how to fully leverage each element of the solution.

# Case study #7 — A state university

Here is the outcome of the state university case study.

## The solutions

The engagement began with a four-week scope to identify the University's requirements. Next, the MCSE Consultants-R-Us team ran simultaneous Business Process Prototype (BPP) phases for the HRMS and SA products that kick-started the package development efforts by defining detailed application functionality and developing alternatives to existing issues. During the prototype, the team learned that certain components of SA functionality, originally slated for release 7.0, would not be available until release 7.5 (due out several months later). Despite the software setbacks, the team kept the project on target. Multiprogram tracks were developed to bring a crucial element of the SA module live, to continue the development and testing activities for both HRMS and SA, and to upgrade the software to the latest release, once available. The team was successful in choreographing the rollout and upgrade maneuvers in sync with the University's processing time schedules.

## Results

The University realized a quick return on their investment. Employees now have the ability to gain immediate access to campus-wide, centralized data, alleviating the difficulties that university faculty and advisors experienced when trying to access student records. The ERP implementation has also eliminated "shadow" systems and redundant data entry, as information can be entered into the system just once, then automatically integrated into each department's system. Moving forward, the University anticipates many additional business benefits, such as student and employee self-service via the Web, which will provide easier, more immediate access to the University's programs and policies.

# Case study #8 — A foreign airline

Here is the outcome of the airline case study.

## The solution

MCSE Consultants-R-Us kicked things off by defining the required functionality for AAAirlines.com. Next, a team of business, technical, and cognitive experts worked alongside the designers to bring the site to life. Later, MCSE Consultants-R-Us linked the Web site to the rest of AAA's reservations systems to make sure reservations were booked and paid for accurately and securely.

## Results

AAAirlines.com reflects AAA's ongoing commitment to its customers. By placing the emphasis on customer service and giving fliers a more convenient channel for doing business, AAA will be able to increase customer loyalty, broaden its global customer base, and increase its online revenue streams.

## Case study #9 — A large aerospace concern

Here is the outcome of the large aerospace company (LAC) case study.

### The solution

LAC's IT staff worked with MCSE Consultants-R-Us to deliver the Procurement Management Information System (PMIS). By using an object-oriented development approach, Consultants-R-Us designed a leading-edge system while helping LAC build expertise in object-oriented technologies.

### Results

With PMIS, the aerospace company cut procurement cycle time by 40 percent and reduced overhead costs by $8.75 million in just over one year. In addition, the system streamlined procurement process has enhanced the productivity of more than 1,400 users, thereby improving both employee and customer satisfaction.

## Case study #10 — An independent software vendor

Here is the outcome of the ISV case study.

### The solution

Working closely with MiaMia and one of its hardware partners, MCSE Consultants-R-Us developed a common vision for the support center and a joint implementation plan. MCSE Consultants-R-Us worked with IT and business process experts from both companies to resolve critical issues around collaboration and redesign processes to support the new environment. Consultants-R-Us was closely involved in taking the support application from the alpha phase through testing and piloting.

### Results

Once the project completes rollout, MiaMia will be able to collaborate with other hardware and software companies that comprise the customer's computing environment as well as exchange information with strategic partners. Customers will be able to use one support center, regardless of the support issue.

# Rule of Ten — View Ten Online Seminars

I end this chapter on enterprise-level MCSE consulting by directing your attention to a free training resource that has several online seminars. This resource is the Seminar Online page at Microsoft's Web site. You can access this page at `www.microsoft.com/seminar`, as shown in Figure 16-6.

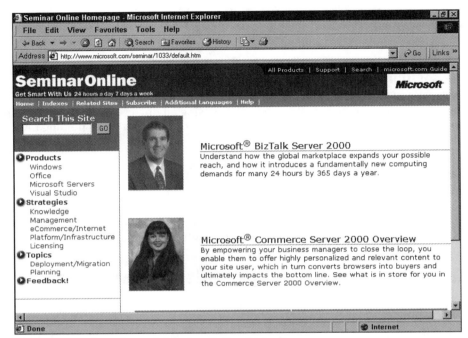

**Figure 16-6:** The Microsoft SeminarOnline Web site

**Tip**    The Microsoft SeminarOnline Web site is one of the best free resources to learn about enterprise-level MCSE consulting that I can think of. But there is another Web-based resource you should consider that is a portal for everything enterprise: `www.microsoft.com/trainingandservices/default.asp?PageID=enterprise`. At this site dedicated to enterprise services you will find extensive information on the Microsoft Enterprise Framework (planning, preparing, building, and operating), as well as training information, white papers, and success stories.

You should view ten enterprise-related online seminars as an MCSE consultant seeking to break into the enterprise space. Searching on the term *enterprise* at this site resulted in the following seminars of interest (over 80 seminars were found, but I list the top ten in my opinion):

1. Virtual Events — Development for the Enterprise Infrastructure

2. Extending the Enterprise with Microsoft and Baan E-Enterprise

3. Delivering Enterprise Intelligence with SQL Server and Sagent

4. How to use Windows 2000 Professional Deployment Tools in the Enterprise

5. The Mobile Knowledge Worker: High-Tech Tools in the Enterprise

6. Business Internet — Microsoft's Enterprise Technology Strategy

7. Building the Enterprise Directory

8. Microsoft Enterprise Agreement

9. Microsoft Software Licensing

10. Prevent Data Loss

# Summary

In this chapter, I focused on the enterprise consulting space that is favored by many MCSE consultants. The topics discussed included introducing the enterprise consulting space, defining the enterprise architect, and considering the technical and nontechnical roles present in large organizations (include politics). In addition, I presented several enterprise-level job descriptions, as well as offered tips on providing your services to Microsoft as vendor, temporary employee, or full-time employee. And finally, I offered numerous case studies for you to solve and went over case study answers at the end of the chapter.

✦    ✦    ✦

# Front Office Consulting

**A**t one time or another, all MCSE consultants serve in the front office. This includes helping users with desktop operating systems and applications, providing help with desktop support, and fixing hardware. It's unavoidable, and it's also a very good consulting opportunity.

No one is above helping fellow human beings, such as end users, in distress, and pleasing end users at client sites is a surefire way to continue a profitable consulting relationship.

This chapter explores the desktop operating systems, several front office applications, and a few suggested consulting opportunities with those applications. I'll discuss specific front office services that are available to you regardless of whether the end users are running Microsoft desktop applications or not. I'll conclude with an in-depth look at the Microsoft Office User Specialist (MOUS) certification.

## What Is the Front Office?

The term *front office* is a convenient metaphor to help you visualize the desktop and end user. This term is convenient because even people without a technical background know to what it refers.

As an MCSE consultant, I'll often use the term *front office* to contrast to the *back office*. The front office is end user desktop stuff, and the back office is the server stuff. This is an exercise in the minder role of consulting engagement boundary setting and expectation management. At my MCSE consulting bill rate and expertise level, I certainly prefer the back office role and often help my clients recruit a front office consultant at a lower bill rate to help out on "the floor."

When using the true BackOffice Server (BOS) product from Microsoft, the term *front office* often means Office 2000 and its desktop applications.

# Desktop Operating Systems

In this section, I define, compare, and contrast the desktop operating systems you'll most likely see in the front office.

## Microsoft

Interestingly, the blending of the look and feel of the Microsoft desktop operating system is well underway, if not nearly complete. A complete code base merger and the death of DOS are expected in 2004 or 2005 with the widespread adaptation of Microsoft's operating system that is code named Blackcomb.

## Windows 2000 Professional

I've really fallen in love with Windows 2000 Professional as a desktop operating system and upgrade my client's legacy desktops to it when possible. In my eyes, Windows 2000 Professional overcame the reboot and device management shortcomings of its predecessor (Windows NT Workstation 4). More importantly, at a desktop where a bona fide MCSE consulting-level need exists to restrict how users operate the computer, Windows 2000 Professional simply can't be beat.

I lock down the Windows 2000 Professional machine one of two ways. The first way is to let NTFS security simply do its thing. A user logs on locally and either has permissions to certain folders, files, and printers or does not. The second approach is to use Group Policy in Windows 2000. Here, the back office works with the front office. The Windows 2000 Server performs logon authentication and applies Group Policy based on the logon name or computer name. Group Policy, shown in Figure 17-1, is infinitely configurable and represents one of the truly great consulting opportunities for MCSE consultants because with Group Policy, which requires an all Windows 2000 network, you can truly solve your clients' desktop access, control, and configuration problems.

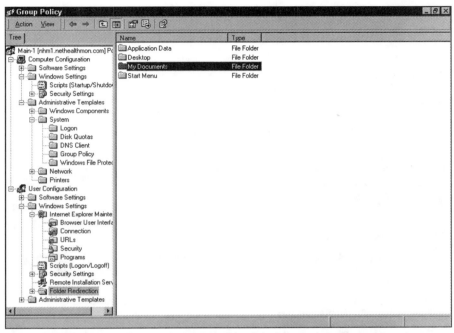

**Figure 17-1:** Group Policy on the server side showing workstation settings

# Rule of Ten — Windows 2000 Professional

Direct from Microsoft and its longtime public relations firm, Waggoner Edstrom, I present to you the top ten reasons to upgrade to Windows 2000 Professional. You can use this list to help your clients decide if Windows 2000 Professional is the right operating system for them to use in their business.

1. Value

2. Reliability

3. Mobility

4. Manageability

5. Performance

6. Security

7. Internet

8. Usability

9. Data access

10. Hardware

This list, shown in Figure 17-2, can be accessed at www.microsoft.com/
windows2000/guide/professional/solutions, where additional links
to studies and white papers support each of the ten reasons provided.

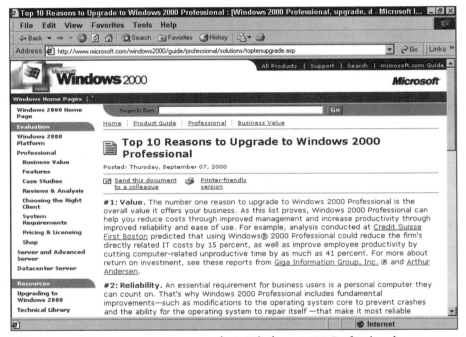

**Figure 17-2:** Top ten reasons to upgrade to Windows 2000 Professional

## Windows Me

Windows Me, the latest reincarnation of Microsoft's desktop operating system code
base, still honors legacy software and drivers. End users are happy with it and independent software vendors (ISVs) are writing software applications to take advantage of its new capabilities. Windows Me's Web page is shown in Figure 17-3.

**Figure 17-3:** Windows Me at www.microsoft.com/windowsme

## Rule of Ten — Windows Me

Microsoft has released the following top ten reasons to upgrade to Windows Me. As you can see, the list is distinctly different from the earlier list for upgrading to Windows 2000 Professional. The differences in the lists reflect the consumer and end user market into which Windows Me is trying to sell.

1. Import and edit your home movies.
2. Move your photo collection from a shoebox to the Web.
3. Archive and index your favorite music.
4. Protect your critical files.
5. Revert your computer back to normal.
6. Find the answers you need.
7. Use your computer to set your VCR and thermostat.
8. Link your household computers.
9. Contact friends and co-workers more efficiently than ever.
10. Take gaming to the next level.

To be honest, when confronted with the upgrade choice for my clients, I select Windows 2000 Professional over Windows Me. However, when my clients purchase a desktop machine on their own with Windows Me, I haven't had any problems placing Windows Me on the network. As an MCSE consultant, you make the decision at this juncture regarding what operating system to install.

**Tip**     For more detailed information on Windows Me, read the book *Microsoft Windows Me Millennium Edition Secrets,* written by Brian Livingston and Davis Straub and published by IDG Books Worldwide, Inc.

### Windows 9x

I still work with client machines (including a couple in my consulting office) that run Windows 9x. Some things never go away. Windows 9x basically did the job it was asked to perform, the least of which was it got users out of the clunky Windows 3.x/Windows for Workgroups era. I have a place in my heart for Windows 9x as an MCSE consultant and continue to support it with pride.

### Terminal Services — application mode

I've billed wonderful hours as an MCSE consultant implementing Terminal Services session-based solutions. I've done this three ways. The most common way is to install the Terminal Services client on the desktop computer. Here, you run a window-within-window and enjoy a Windows 2000 desktop environment.

Another way is to install the Terminal Services on a workstation at home for an end user. The end user connects over the Internet via a modem session or virtual private network (VPN) connection and launches a Terminal Services session. It's the mobile worker using true remote computing.

The third way that I've implemented a Terminal Services solution is via thin clients. Also known as WinTerminals, these desktop devices (a keyboard, screen, and mouse) look much like a dumb terminal from the mainframe generation years ago. I implemented this solution at a regional theater company with over 50 users and it worked very well. The profiles were stored on the robust server, so when users connected, they were presented with their specific desktop environment. More importantly, if users trashed their desktop, it was as easy to recreate as a new profile. If one of the WinTerminals ever failed, all the network administrator had to do was take a spare off the shelf in the server room and deploy it at the desktop. The user was up and running in just a few minutes without the need to install applications and so on.

## Competing desktop operating systems

Other desktop operating systems exist, and it's likely you'll see them. Two such desktop operating systems are Macintosh and Linux.

## Macintosh

This venerable operating system from Apple Computer is very popular in specific narrow vertical markets such as the advertising and printing industries. I've supported many clients whose network contacted Macintoshes. In fact, I can trace my early roots in technology consulting to my temp days when I served MacTemps, Inc., with great pleasure. The Macintosh operating system is shown on the Apple Web page in Figure 17-4.

**Figure 17-4:** Mac OS X's look and feel

**Tip**

You might consider a consulting niche supporting Macintoshes on Windows 2000 networks. You'll learn a few tricks along the way, and Macintosh environments are accustomed to spending more for computer equipment, software, and even support than the personal computer crowd (where clone makers have driven down prices significantly more than a comparable Macintosh when measuring computing power). In other words, because the Macintosh crowd is accustomed to paying more for high quality goods and services, this can be a very lucrative consulting niche for an MCSE consultant.

## Linux

The biggest desktop operating system threat to Microsoft, Linux, should not be dismissed by the MCSE consulting crowd. The grass roots origins of this operating system means it comes in more than one variety. Figure 17-5 profiles Best Linux.

**Figure 17-5:** Best Linux is one of several Linux distributors.

There are several Linux distributors including, but not limited to, the following list:

- ✦ Best Linux
- ✦ Yellow Dog
- ✦ MkLinux
- ✦ Libranet
- ✦ Elfstone Linux
- ✦ Red Hat
- ✦ ASPLinux
- ✦ Corel Linux
- ✦ Stampede
- ✦ Debian
- ✦ Linux-Mandrake
- ✦ SuSE

- ✦ Phat
- ✦ LuteLinux
- ✦ Slackware
- ✦ KSI
- ✦ OpenLinux
- ✦ Storm
- ✦ LinuxPPC
- ✦ TurboLinux
- ✦ UltraPenguin

Part of the reason to show you this long list of Linux distributions is to expose a way that Microsoft desktop operating systems can be repositioned to the Linux threat in the following way: standards enforced by one vendor. Whether you like it or not, Microsoft desktop operating systems are from a single source. On a more positive note, if you'd like more information on Linux (perhaps to develop an MCSE/Linux niche), visit the Open Source Development Network (OSDN) at www.linux.com, as seen in Figure 17-6.

**Figure 17-6:** OSDN's Web page

# Office 2000

Office 2000 comes in several flavors including the highly prized Premium version that contains everything under the sun. The Office 2000 components, by Office 2000 suite version, are shown in Table 17-1.

| Table 17-1 Office 2000 Suite | | | | |
| --- | --- | --- | --- | --- |
| *Component* | *Standard* | *Small Business* | *Professional* | *Premium* |
| Word | X | X | X | X |
| Excel | X | X | X | X |
| Outlook | X | X | X | X |
| PowerPoint | X | | X | X |
| Publisher | | X | X | X |
| Small Business Tools | | X | X | X |
| Access | | | X | X |
| FrontPage | | | | X |
| PhotoDraw | | | | X |

**Note**    Office 2000 Developer includes everything in Office 2000 Premium plus some nifty developer tools.

As Office 2000 relates to MCSE consulting, I've identified the following three areas of interest: the Office 2000 Resource Kit, using transforms to install Office 2000 in Terminal Services environments, and deploying Office 2000 with Group Policy.

## Office 2000 Resource Kit

Microsoft posts its Office 2000 Resource Kit on the Web, as seen in Figure 17-7.

To access the Office 2000 Resource Kit, point your Web browser to www.microsoft. com/office/resource.htm and click the Office Resource Kit link. Whether you use the online version of the Office 2000 Resource Kit or order the print version from Microsoft Press, this tool is a must for your MCSE bookshelf for those times when you're involved with the front office. If you know a thing or two about advanced Office 2000 deployments, garnered from your research in the Office 2000 Resource Kit, you have discovered another way to make money as an MCSE consultant and truly help your clients.

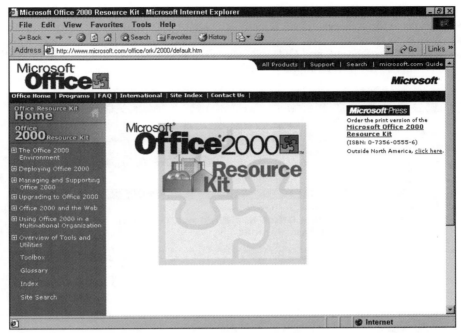

**Figure 17-7:** The Web-based Office 2000 Resource Kit

A few topics in the Office 2000 Resource Kit that I've researched and implemented while billing time as an MCSE consultant include the following:

✦ The Office 2000 Toolbox that contains utilities

✦ Custom installations, such as having people use the same set of corporate document templates

✦ The administrative installation of Office 2000 to a network share

✦ Over the network installations of Office 2000 both manually and using Windows 2000 Group Policy

✦ Use of transforms

## Transforms

The Office 2000 Resource Kit contains explicit instructions for installing Office 2000 in a Terminal Services environment using transforms. *Transforms* are essentially configuration scripts that are used as an installation tool. The transform approach allows you to modify the typical setup wizard approach. Transforms are used in a variety of installation scenarios and must be used when installing Office 2000 to a Terminal Services session.

You will find yourself needing to install Office 2000 while running under a Terminal Services session for one simple reason, the use of Terminal Services for remote workers who connect to the corporate network via a VPN connection and want to work using Word, Excel, and Outlook 2000. Figure 17-8 shows the page in the Office 2000 Resource Kit that explains this type of deployment scenario.

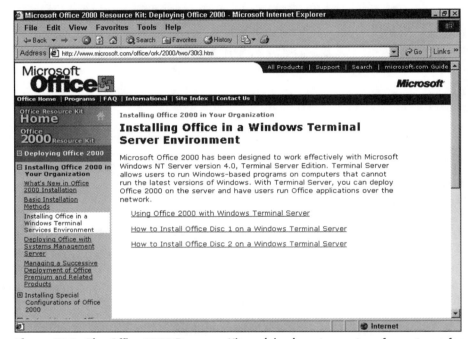

**Figure 17-8:** The Office 2000 Resource Kit explains how to use transforms to perform installations in a Terminal Service environment.

## Deploying Office 2000 with Group Policy

Another front office MCSE consulting area is the software deployment capability of Group Policy to implement Office 2000 in an organization. You will likely be brought in on this type of work. You should read up on how to create Microsoft Windows Installer package (*.msi) in order to use Group Policy software deployment. As you can see in Figure 17-9, Group Policy is asking for an *.msi file to proceed in creating a software deployment job.

Note    Overall, I give the Office 2000 Resource Kit a positive review. I have used this Web-based resource kit to solve some client problems and was very impressed with its depth and breadth of front office technology coverage.

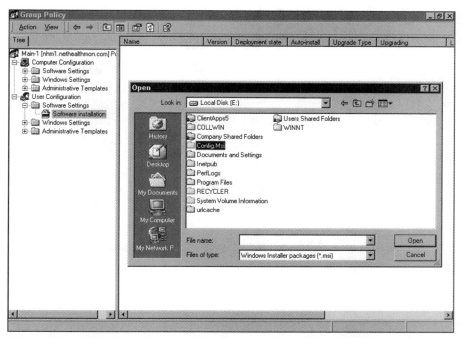

**Figure 17-9:** Using the software installation capability of Group Policy requires you to create a Windows Installer package.

# Outlook 2000

Few end users are left who don't know how to use Outlook. Many started with some of the early versions of Outlook, and their ranks have grown with the latest release, Outlook 2000. Clearly, the vast majority of Outlook users are content to use this tool for basic e-mail, scheduling, and contact management functions. Others use Outlook for managing tasks. However, this product does much more. Advanced information on Outlook 2000 may be found at the Microsoft Developer Network (MSDN) Office Developer Center, shown in Figure 17-10, at `http://msdn.microsoft.com/office`.

On the MCSE consultant billable hour clock, I've worked Outlook to benefit my clients in the following ways (and perhaps you can to): customization, Team Folders, and PDA synchronization.

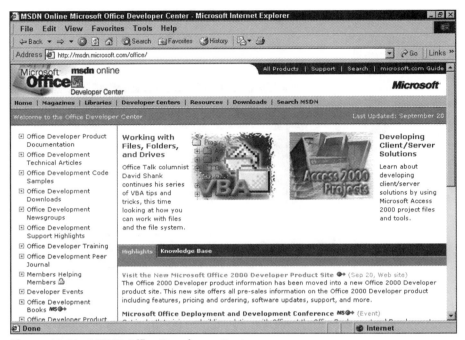

**Figure 17-10:** MSDN Office Developer Center

## Customization

I've had clients who "get it" when it comes to Outlook. Not only are they Outlook power users, but also they want to customize Outlook to extend it to perform sophisticated queries, such as sorting their Christmas list by zip code and printing only certain zip codes (something Outlook can't do right out of the box). Other clients want Outlook to behave like GoldMine, a robust third-party personal information manager application that is highly regarded. This is a tremendous consulting opportunity for the savvy MCSE consultant.

## Team Folders

A relatively new feature in Outlook is the Team Folders capability. This capability is designed to extend the collaboration capabilities of Outlook and reflects Microsoft's search for the Lotus Notes killer application. Team Folders can be a tight but profitable consulting niche for an MCSE consultant seeking such an opportunity. You can download the Team Folders kit from www.microsoft.com/outlook and take advantage of several pre-configured Team Folders, including one for project management. Once you work with Team Folders, you'll undoubtedly think of ways that your clients can take advantage of this tool.

## Outlook Web Access

Another MCSE consultant billing opportunity involves Outlook Web Access (OWA). Why? Because many of my business clients want a way to access their Microsoft Exchange–based company e-mail at any time from the Internet. I've seen traveling business people use OWA to access their e-mail from hotel rooms, ski condos, hotel lobbies, and even Internet cafes while on vacation! This is a service in Microsoft Exchange Server that allows you to configure the e-mail system so that it is accessible from the Internet using a current Web browser (such as Internet Explorer 5.*x* or higher or Netscape 5.*x* or higher). OWA is installed as a component from the Microsoft Exchange Server setup wizard. You then need to verify that your firewall (e.g., ISA Server) allows OWA-type Web traffic (typically, ISA Server is set up to allow this by default). Next, at the client machine (say a home computer connected to the Internet and running an acceptable Web browser), type the IP address of the Exchange Server running OWA back at the office (which I assume is connected to the Internet as well) and then /exchange. Your URL address should look similar to: http://10.0.0.9/exchange (understanding that your IP address will be different).

At this point, you will need to be authenticated on the network by providing your logon name and password in the Windows logon dialog box. Next, the OWA client runs and displays the Inbox. The look and feel of the OWA is very similar to the regular Outlook e-mail client. More information on Outlook Web Access can be obtained from the following Web site: www.microsoft.com/exchange.

## PDA synchronization

I've billed more than a few hours as an MCSE consultant helping executives synchronize their personal digital assistants (PDAs) running either Palm OS or Windows CE with Outlook. Even though this is easy to do, clients sometimes prefer to pay an MCSE consultant to do this work.

**Tip**  Outlook is a huge area of study, well beyond the scope of this book. Not surprisingly, there are some huge third-party books on the market that discuss advanced uses and customization of Outlook. These may be found by searching on the term *Outlook* at your favorite online bookstore.

# Other Front Office Applications

I'll quickly highlight a couple of other front office applications where opportunities lurk for the MCSE consultant.

## Microsoft Project 2000

Microsoft Project 2000 is a popular project management application that I profiled in Part III of this book as a tool to help you manage your MCSE consulting gigs. Assuming you've done exactly that and you now have a Project 2000 skill set, you can provide such services to your clients. I was at a medium-sized manufacturer installing a Windows NT Server–based network a few years back, and my client pulled me aside and asked if I could help him create the Gantt chart I had prepared in Microsoft Project for my records for some of his other work. It was billable work.

Another time I had an engagement with McCaw Cellular (before it was acquired by AT&T) to prepare the project schedule for the digital services rollout with the input of the Marketing department and others. It was a great six-week job. It paid well, and I grew as an MCSE consultant because of it.

**Tip** For more detailed information on Project 2000, see the *Project 2000 Bible* by Elaine Marmel, published by IDG Books Worldwide, Inc.

## Internet Explorer 5.*x*

Did you know that there is a sophisticated administrative tool kit known as the Internet Explorer Administration Kit (IEAK) that allows you to create advanced Internet Explorer (IE) implementations? One client had me use this to implement IE in his organization with a fixed list of Favorites. Favorites are the collection of favorite Web sites a user can specify to appear as a list in the Favorites drop-down menu in IE.

The IEAK can be downloaded from Microsoft at www.microsoft.com/downloads. Be advised this is a large download, and it is a sophisticated solution. You are encouraged to also download Course 1400: Deploying and Customizing Microsoft Internet Explorer 5 Using Microsoft Internet Explorer Administration Kit at the same download site. The self-study course is well worth your time.

**Note** Back in the old Windows NT 4 days in the MCSE community, the IEAK class and corresponding IEAK exam actually counted toward your MCSE credential. The exam was also part of the +Internet designation.

## Digital Dashboard

Many wonderful billable hours await you as an MCSE consultant suggesting and implementing Microsoft Digital Dashboard for your client. Digital Dashboard is an application that displays critical business information such as news, notices, reminders, and financial information on an easy to read "dashboard" on the user's computer display. The best analogy for Digital Dashboard is that it is the "reincarnation" of the Executive Information System (EIS). EISs were popular in the late 1980s and early 1990s with large companies. An EIS presented an attractive screen for, you guessed it, top executives seeking to view critical business data at a glance. EISs were known for presenting financial information such as the DuPont Ratio Model (a set of important financial ratios used by business people) and the use of traffic light metaphors. For example, a "green light" meant that the financial ratio did not need attention. Contrast that with a "red light" that identified a financial variable needing immediate attention. You can find more information on Digital Dashboard at www.microsoft.com/digitaldashboard.

# Competitive Analysis

You may recall that earlier in this chapter I discussed the desktop operating system competitors of Microsoft. Microsoft's front office products also have some competition. I've listed those competitors grouped by category.

Some competitors of Office 2000 are as follows:

✦ Individual applications such as Lotus 1-2-3

✦ Lotus SmartSuite

✦ WordPerfect Office 2000, shown in Figure 17-11

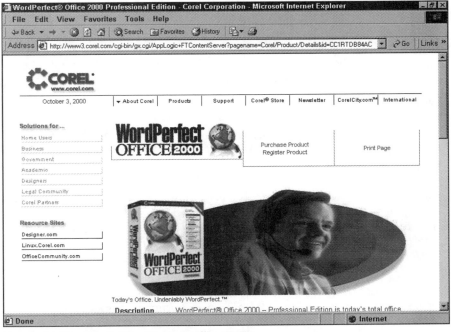

**Figure 17-11:** Corel's WordPerfect Office 2000

Competitors of Outlook 2000 include the following:

✦ Lotus Notes and Domino

✦ GoldMine

Some competitors of Project 2000 are as follows:

✦ PermaVera

✦ SuperProject

Competitors of Internet Explorer include the following:

✦ Netscape

✦ AOL's user application

## Guest Sermon — MOUS Basics for MCSEs

My longtime buddy from the publishing world Shelley Doyle is the editor of OfficeCert.com, an online magazine site dedicated to the Microsoft Office User Specialist certification discussed later in the chapter. She's a freelance Web site producer, Windows 9x peer-to-peer network manager, and general computer fix-it person who programs in C++ when given the opportunity. She provides a primer for MCSEs on this front office certification title as the guest sermon for this chapter. Take it away, Shelley.

### What's a MOUS?

The Microsoft Office User Specialist (MOUS) program is a Microsoft certification program administered by Nivo International. MOUS exams measure knowledge of and skill in using Microsoft Office applications and Microsoft Project. The exams run in a live application environment (you prove your expertise on a running version of the program) and are available worldwide.

For Office 2000, you can take Core level exams for Word, Excel, PowerPoint, Outlook, Access, and Project, as well as Expert (read "tougher") exams for Word, Excel, and Project. You obtain the MOUS Office 2000 Master certification on passing five exams: Word and Excel Expert and Access, Outlook, and PowerPoint Core.(The Project exam isn't required for Master status.)

The latest addition is the MOUS Authorized Instructor (MOUS AI) program, launched in February 2000. The requirements for AI certification include a minimum of two Expert-level MOUS certification exams, documentation of instructional skills (such as an MCT), a course outline for each Office application you'll be teaching, and (of course) a signed Program Agreement and $50 application fee. Unique to the Authorized Instructor program is a logo that MOUS AIs can use on business cards. (There's no logo as yet for MOUSs.)

You can learn more at these MOUS-related Web sites:

✦ www.mous.net: Nivo's "official" MOUS Web site, with MOUS and MOUS Authorized Instructor program details, exam objectives, test center locator, MOUS online store, etc.

✦ www.officecert.com: *An independent Web site for the MOUS community, sponsored by the same folks who publish Microsoft Certified Professional Magazine. OfficeCert.com has MOUS program news and information, MOUS exam reviews, book reviews, how-to articles, forums, chats, etc.*

**Why should an MCSE also be a MOUS?**

*To begin with, you use at least a couple of these programs regularly. Why not validate your skills with them? It's another way to make sure you're working as efficiently as possible, since you'll no doubt learn new tricks in your test preparation.*

*If you use MS Project, why not get the Expert level certification? It can't hurt to show the world you've really mastered it — and it could help you get that project lead position on the next major deployment your IT team tackles.*

*If you're a certified trainer, along with MCSE, adding the Office programs to your repertoire can make you only that much more attractive to prospective employers. A simple way to show you're qualified to teach those courses is to add the MOUS AI logo on your business card or resume.*

*Do you do Excel or Outlook customization for your clients? Having the MOUS certification in that application demonstrates to your client that you fully understand its built-in capabilities.*

*Finally, you know perfectly well that most folks out there in business-land don't know the difference between an operating system and a desktop application. You're lucky if they understand the difference between a programmer and a network administrator. It's all "computer stuff" to them and you're the expert — you're supposed to have all the answers. You don't want to find yourself in a situation where you're trying to answer one of those Outlook or Word how-to questions and the administrative assistant helpfully walks over to show you how to do it! Not good for your image as "the all-wise computer guru." If you've taken the MOUS exams, you'll probably know the answers — that's less annoying than when you have to figure things out on the fly. Plus, you'll be back to your real work sooner. (And then, when you do finally hire someone else to be the Office users' help desk, hire a MOUS and you'll be sure they can do the job.)*

# Outsourcing

Smart MCSE consultants are making a great living providing outsourced services to small and medium-sized companies in need of such front office support. Here I address the outsourcing issue from a front office and desktop support viewpoint.

## Support methods

Hardly a week passes when a very good client doesn't call with a desktop or front office question or problem. This is the gray area of MCSE consulting. The reality is that in many cases it's not possible for me to tell a longtime client that I can't help them. So instead I use some of the following tools that allow me to support my clients efficiently, effectively, and profitably.

## NetMeeting

One tool I've used to provide front office support is NetMeeting, Microsoft's remote control application that can be downloaded for free from `www.microsoft.com/downloads`. As you can see in Figure 17-12, you can use NetMeeting to chat with your client, they can see you on video, and you can take remote control of their desktop to solve a problem. NetMeeting works very well over the Internet, even at modem connection speeds.

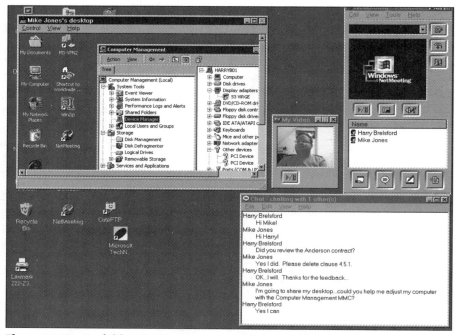

**Figure 17-12:** Exploiting NetMeeting to provide front office support

**Tip**    You can download the NetMeeting Resource Kit from `http://www.microsoft.com/downloads`. This is a valuable resource and even includes a tool for custom deployments of NetMeeting to the client desktop.

## Terminal Services

Terminal Services is technically more of a back office support tool than a front office support tool. However, sometimes you solve a front office problem in the back office by making an adjustment on the server that affects end users. This occurs countless times over the course of a year in your work as an MCSE consultant. When I'm solving a front office or back office problem from a remote location that involves a server, my preference is to use a Terminal Services session similar to that seen in Figure 17-13.

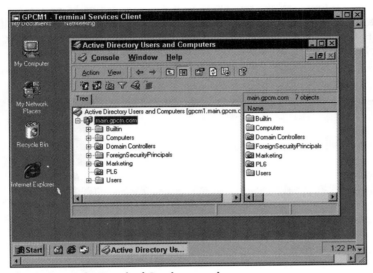

**Figure 17-13:** A Terminal Services session

# Help desk

While I'm not proposing you take your MCSE credentials and skill sets to return to the low-paying cubicle of customer service, I am suggesting you consider adding customer service as part of the product mix in your MCSE consulting firm. Perhaps you'll oversee those with only an MCP title as you provide outsourced help desk services to clients. It is an increasingly popular business model through which you can make good money.

## Common applications

You might want to offer a call center–like service where you provide support for common desktop applications such as Office 2000 to clients you have under contract. If this business appeals to you, a client is probably out there waiting to retain your services.

## Custom applications

I've previously been involved in a consulting firm that provided help desk services to clients that purchased a support contract. This particular scenario involved Great Plains accounting software, and the support agreement was a very profitable component of the consulting practice. I'd offer this type of service again if presented the right opportunity.

# Microsoft Office User Specialist

If you are eager to add as many vendor certifications to your list of credentials as you can, the Microsoft Office User Specialist (MOUS—pronounced "mouse") program might just be for you. Not only are the basic Office 2000 applications certification eligible, you can also become certified in other Microsoft front office products such as Project 2000. Basic information on the MOUS program can be found at www.microsoft.com/train_cert, as seen in Figure 17-14.

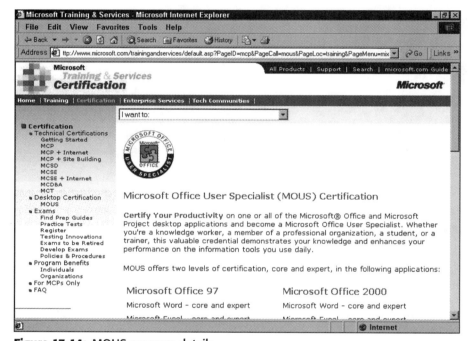

**Figure 17-14:** MOUS program details

The basic framework of the MOUS program is easy to understand. Each supported front office application has at least a core certification. Word, Excel, and Project have an expert certification.

The key to fully understanding the MOUS program and how to prepare for the exams is to monitor the OfficeCert site hosted by 101 Communications, shown in Figure 17-15.

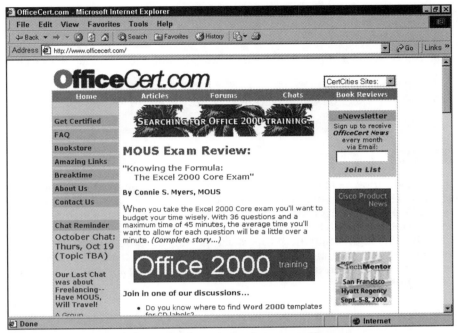

**Figure 17-15:** MOUS information is presented at www.officecert.com.

# Rule of Ten — Front Office Support

On a lighter note, I've come up with the top ten reasons for lending your MCSE consulting gifts to the front office. Some of my reasons are silly, and I ask that you read them in the spirit in which they were written. However, some of my reasons such as Group Policy are very serious.

1. You get to apply Group Policy.

2. You get to keep your job as an MCSE consultant, keeping end users happy.

3. You can earn another certification title (MOUS).

4. You will have the chance to master front office applications such as Word and Excel in ways you might not otherwise have the opportunity to do so.

5. You get to work with real human beings, not just network infrastructure components.

6. You will have the chance to learn about other areas of your client site, such as bookkeeping, executive management, and marketing.

7. You will be introduced professionally to a new technology area, different service providers and vendors, and even different specialized trade shows than you are used to.

8. You've been looking for a problem for NetMeeting and Terminal Services to solve.

9. You always wondered exactly what IEAK stood for.

10. You get to see the whole picture, a healthy exercise for any MCSE consultant.

## Summary

This chapter took a different view of MCSE consulting: the front office. If you look closely at the time you bill as an MCSE consultant, you will see that front office consulting likely represents a significant portion of your consulting income. Recognizing this fact, the chapter addressed how to be an effective MCSE consultant in the front office by addressing these topics: supporting desktop operating systems and desktop applications, understanding what non-Microsoft front office applications exist, considering front office outsourcing as a consulting service, and the MOUS certification.

✦     ✦     ✦

# BackOffice Consulting

**B**ackOffice Server (BOS) represents a tremendous consulting opportunity for MCSE consultants, as I will seek to point out in this chapter.

BOS is the bundled suite of Microsoft Servers applications sitting on top of Windows 2000 Server. Throw in a management console to ease administration and a real-time reporting tool, and you have an all-in-one solution for medium-sized organizations (MORGs).

I'll never forget three defining moments in my MCSE career when I developed my consciousness of BOS. First, there was the stark realization when BOS was released that Microsoft was extending the bundling concept from the front office product of Word, Excel, and PowerPoint. Youmightrecall that Microsoft's Office bundle was a true category killer, effectively sending the WordPerfect word processing program, Lotus 1-2-3 spreadsheet program, and Compel presentation programs to their graves. Second, BOS was placed firmly on my radar screen when I was interviewing a candidate at lunch one day to teach in the MCSE program at Seattle Pacific University (SPU). The candidate worked for a regional consulting firm, and his business card reported his title as *BackOffice Consultant*. That was a defining moment as it struck how right on target that job title was. BOS is a big product, providing many distinct consulting opportunities, which I discuss throughout this chapter. A third BOS milestone in my career came with the founding of the BackOffice Professionals Association (BOPA). BOPA is a user group for BOS enthusiasts to meet monthly and increase their BOS-specific technical skills. BOPA is also a great way to get a job, as joining BOPA often equals getting a job.

# BackOffice Opportunities

If, as an MCSE consultant, you promote yourself as a BOS specialist, you can truly position yourself as everything to everyone. It's the ultimate political tool in the world of MCSE consulting. Because BOS contains nearly every Microsoft Servers product, you have a chance to dabble here and there with it (be a generalist). You can also home in on one or two components (be a specialist). The opportunities as to how you can provide BOS consulting services are limitless.

**Caution**    I'd be remiss if I didn't honor one school of consulting that exists that I don't particularly ascribe to: the *anything consultant*. An anything consultant will do anything for a billable hour. I once worked for one of these guys, and this type of consulting is brutal. Your life as a consultant involves accepting any work that comes through the door with the phrase, "We can do that." You find yourself often staying one chapter in the user manual ahead of the client. You effectively learn on the job. Because of BOS's breadth, it tends to attract anything consultants seeking to do it all, but in the wrong hands, BOS can be a platform of hype where customers are sold the farm and delivered the T-shirt. Exercise your better judgment as a BOS consultant.

# BackOffice Features

So just what is BOS? Before jumping into the details, I want to share a couple ideas behind the development of the BackOffice Server, shown in Figure 18-1.

## Synergy

Clearly one of Microsoft's development goals was to make "the sum of the parts greater than the whole." The synergy obtained in BOS is amazing. For example, Microsoft Exchange 2000 Server is now primarily administered via Active Directory Users and Computers.

## Cheaper by the dozen

BOS is priced as a bundle. If you purchase Windows 2000 Server and just one BackOffice component, then you will have paid approximately the same price as you would for the BOS bundle.

**Figure 18-1:** BackOffice Server

## Rule of Ten: Top ten features

The Rule of Ten relating to BOS is as follows: As an MCSE consultant, it is paramount that you have an understanding of the top ten BOS features committed to memory, as you are an advisor for all matters technical and otherwise. In its current release, BOS 2000 contains the following components, my top ten list:

1. **Windows 2000 Server**—This underlying network operating system includes the Microsoft Management Console 2.1, Terminal Services, Active Directory, Group Policy, IIS, and many other features.

2. **Microsoft Exchange Server 2000 and Microsoft Outlook 2000**—These are the messaging and collaboration solutions.

3. **Microsoft SQL Server 2000**—This is the database solution.

4. **Systems Management Server (SMS) 2.0**—This enterprise tool is used for managing desktops, software distribution, inventory management, and remote diagnostics and troubleshooting.

5. **Internet Security and Acceleration Server 2000 (ISA)** — This component represents firewall and Web caching solutions.

6. **Host Integration Server (HIS)** — This host system gateway component facilitates mainframe and midrange connectivity.

7. **Shared Modem, Shared Fax** — These tools are communications solutions.

8. **Health Monitor 2.1** — This powerful real-time server monitor tool allows in-house IT professionals and consultants to constantly monitor network performance.

9. **Server Status Reports and Server Status View** — These tools allow in-house IT professionals and consultants to receive logs via e-mail. For example, a technology consultant could receive a tape backup log each morning.

10. **Wizards** — Numerous configuration wizards, above and beyond those found in Windows 2000 Server alone, are used in BOS to facilitate ease of implementation and administration.

The top ten features of BOS are displayed graphically in Figure 18-2.

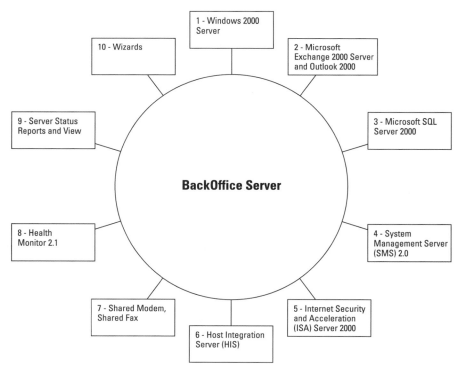

**Figure 18-2:** BOS viewed as an integrated suite

## What BOS isn't

BOS is positioned to serve the MORG, not the full-fledged enterprise. Microsoft's reasoning for this positioning is based on its experience that its largest clients have server farms and purchase Microsoft Servers components as needed. For example, an enterprise-level client might purchase one edition of SMS but five editions of Microsoft Exchange 2000 Server. BOS assumes a linear purchasing scheme, which isn't always the most cost-effective way to buy.

**Note**  BOS has a server limit, currently at four servers, which restricts its usefulness in large firms. This is done to define the market space that BOS will serve and is akin to the single Small Business Server (SBS) root-of-forest server restriction. In reality, both are marketing schemes that help to fit customers into different purchasing classes.

# Medium-Sized Organizations and Branch Offices

Part of BOS's appeal is its positioning for medium-sized organizations (MORGs) and branch offices. I'll address these two markets separately.

## MORGs

Microsoft has found, and I can confirm first hand as a practicing MCSE consultant, that MORGs have many characteristics similar to small organizations (SORGs). Medium-sized organizations might have an IT person on staff, but often *only* one IT person. This IT administrator is likely a jack-of-all-trades but a master of none. During any given day, this person will help a desktop "I can't print" problem as well as solve a firewall port opening problem. The MORG IT staff, small as it is, likely relies heavily on outside experts to perform precision surgery on the computer system as necessary.

**Tip**  The MORG's reliance on outside subject matter experts presents wonderful consulting opportunities for the MCSE consultant who has needed skills, is available to work, and is priced competitively.

Outside help aside, BOS uses Small Business Server–style management consoles and wizards to ease the administrative burden on the MORG IT staff.

## Branch offices

While considering the branch office concept, Microsoft BOS planners found that small businesses, which use Small Business Server (SBS), behave very much like branch offices in the following ways:

✦ Both have a power user on-site performing limited administration.

✦ Both have limited on-site IT expertise.

✦ Both have limited IT resources.

✦ Both rely on home office IT expertise or outside consultants.

Once these behavioral considerations were identified and analyzed, it was correctly believed that BOS could benefit from some of the groundbreaking features in SBS, such as administrative consoles, wizards, and server status reporting. In fact, Microsoft felt so strongly about this revelation that the BOS and SBS development teams were combined for the BOS 2000 and SBS 2000 release cycle.

This ease of use and these monitoring and reporting features in BOS make it ideal for branch office implementations.

## Other uses

I suppose Microsoft didn't want to lock itself into two market categories with BOS, so it has positioned BOS for other uses as well.

### Line-of-business application server

BOS provides all of the key components needed to deploy line-of-business (LOB) applications and connect to existing databases and transaction-based systems.

### Web application server

BOS can also be positioned as a Web server, given the Internet-related components included such as IIS, ISA Server, and so on. In fact, BOS contains an Intranet Starter Site with sample applications.

# Competitive Analysis

With BOS, Microsoft application developers and operating system developers truly are in bed together, and as such, they enjoy the ability to offer a product on the market that no other single vendor can match exactly. However, some noble attempts to compete have been made by vendors from different walks of life getting together to offer "bundles" to compete against BOS. I have found my clients love BackOffice because it comes from one vendor and they believe, and rightly so, that the software components work very well together.

In this section, I profile two BOS competitors: Novell and Oracle. Depending on how you define server suites, other competitors exist, ranging from IBM to UNIX vendors to Apple Computer. Other than a quick mention of IBM, I'll leave you to your own analysis of those other competitors.

# Novell

Perhaps more than any other competitor of Microsoft in the MORG space, Novell has most of the BOS-like components under one roof. These components include the following:

- ✦ **Novell NetWare 5.1** — This network operating system competes with Windows 2000 Server in BOS.

- ✦ **HostPublisher** — This gateway solution is used to connect to mainframe and midrange hosts and competes directly with BOS's Host Integration Server.

- ✦ **ZENworks and ManageWise 2.7** — These management applications assist in the deployment, administration, and maintenance of the network. They compete directly with BOS's implementation of SMS 2.*x*.

- ✦ **BorderManager Enterprise Edition 3.5** — This Internet firewall solution competes directly with ISA Server in BOS.

- ✦ **Novell Internet Caching Services** — This component's capabilities to cache Web pages and Internet content to improve Internet access performance competes directly with ISA Server in BOS.

- ✦ **Novell GroupWise** — Novell's e-mail and collaboration solution competes directly with Microsoft Exchange 2000 Server.

- ✦ **Novell NDS eDirectory and NDS Corporate Edition** — This is Novell's well-respected directory services implementation that competes very successfully against Active Directory in Windows 2000 Server.

The Novell offerings are listed on its Web site, displayed in Figure 18-3 and found at www.novell.com.

It should be noted that Novell doesn't have a bundle of these products for the MORG space. Each of the products must be purchased separately. Novell does have a small business bundle called Small Business Suite that competes strongly with Microsoft's SBS.

I discuss small business bundles more extensively in Chapter 24.

So what's Novell missing from its bundle as it competes against BOS? The most critical omission is the lack of a true enterprise-wide relational database. Novell has two database solutions. First, Novell promotes its NDS directory services as a viable database solution depending on your needs. If the need is to manage objects on the network, NDS directory services is a viable solution. If your need is to run an accounting system, the solution fails. Second, Novell's venerable Btrieve database engine is still alive and kicking, thanks in part to Novell partner Pervasive. In the past, Btrieve was a popular database engine for server applications to use. One such application was the Btrieve edition of Great Plains Dynamics, an accounting package. However, like so many applications that supported Btrieve in the past, Great Plains no longer supports Btrieve and currently uses Microsoft SQL Server.

**Cross-Reference**    I discuss Microsoft SQL Server more thoroughly in Chapter 21.

**Figure 18-3:** The Novell family of products that compete with BOS

# Oracle

Oracle is a second BOS competitor that has a killer database but no sincere infrastructure offerings. Oracle offers three application server bundles that compete indirectly with BOS.

## Oracle Internet Application Server 8*i*

This product is a suite of Web-enabled business solutions running on top of Apache Server. The services include the following:

- ✦ **Web/HTTP support** for high-end e-commerce applications
- ✦ **Java applets** and support for Java Virtual Machines (JVMs)
- ✦ **Caching server** to improve Web performance
- ✦ **File management capabilities** with Oracle Internet File System

✦ **Oracle Form service**, an optimized environment for instantly deploying Oracle Forms Developer applications on the Internet

✦ **Business intelligence functions** such as ad hoc reporting

✦ **Oracle Enterprise Manager**, a management framework that allows you to centrally manage data, applications, and access.

The Oracle Internet Application Server 8*i* is shown in Figure 18-4.

**Figure 18-4:** iAS from Oracle

## Integration Server

Another Oracle solution, Integration Server, is interesting in that it allows you to switch out the underlying operating system, as shown in Figure 18-5. The bundled solution provides the following:

✦ **Application messaging services** via the scalable and open Java Messaging Services

✦ **Business process coordination services** delivered via Oracle Workflow

✦ **Queuing services** providing support for asynchronous application communications

✦ **Data transformation services** providing support for XML formats

✦ **Application adapter services** for Customer Relationship Management (CRM) and Enterprise Resource Planning (ERP)

✦ **Directory services** with Oracle Internet Directory

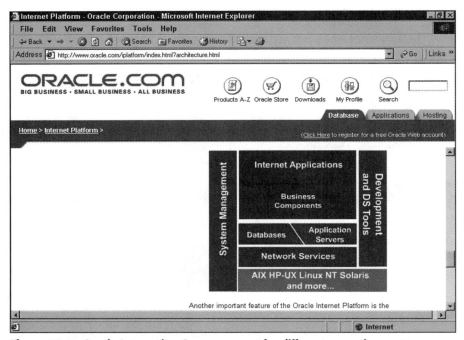

**Figure 18-5:** Oracle Integration Server support for different operating systems

## E-Business Suite

Oracle offers the following e-business applications either separately or as a suite. These Oracle applications expose a Microsoft product weakness in that Oracle has developed narrow vertical market solutions that have been overlooked by Microsoft.

✦ Oracle Exchange (which offers supply chain management capabilities)

✦ Oracle Financials (a well-respected financial reporting module)

✦ Human Resources

✦ International Procurement

✦ Manufacturing

✦ Marketing

- ✦ Payroll
- ✦ Projects
- ✦ Sales
- ✦ Service
- ✦ Strategic Enterprise Management
- ✦ Treasury

An example of an e-business suite component is shown in Figure 18-6.

So what's missing in Oracle's offering? For starters, true operating system integration is noticeably absent. In response to observations of its lack of integration, Oracle claims that business applications can now be uncoupled from the operating system. The choice is yours with respect to how strongly you support that reasoning and how important you find the system integration that is absent from Oracle. Second, Oracle isn't offering a true e-mail solution. Oracle can be reached at `www.oracle.com`.

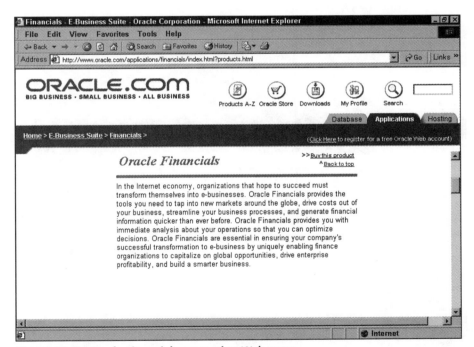

**Figure 18-6:** Oracle Financials promotion Web page

# IBM

In my eyes, the firm to monitor in the business applications suite game, the one firm that could put together a bona fide threat to BOS, is IBM. IBM is the granddaddy of them all when it comes to integrated solutions. IBM can even trump Microsoft with hardware offerings. IBM has the potential to offer a midrange solution that supplies hardware, operating systems, and applications to willing businesses. The applications could consist of technologies it acquired from the Lotus acquisitions (Domino, Notes, and so on), and the database component could be IBM's versatile DB2 product. The IBM Web page is displayed in Figure 18-7.

IBM has the following software products that should be considered competitors of BOS (see `www.ibm.com` for greater details).

✦ WebSphere Commerce Suite

✦ NetCommerce

✦ IBM Business Integration Suite for Windows NT

✦ IBM Suite for Windows NT

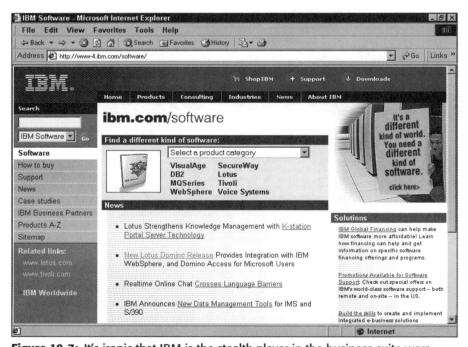

**Figure 18-7:** It's ironic that IBM is the stealth player in the business suite wars.

# Repositioning Microsoft and BOS

After digesting the preceding competitive analysis, you'll need to reposition BOS when asked by clients how it compares to these alternatives. At least in my mind, a few strengths stand out:

✦ **Operating system/application integration** — This is the single vendor argument that worked so well for IBM at its peak. Who better than Microsoft can provide a comprehensive solution?

✦ **Category killer applications** — Even on a stand-alone basis, many of the BOS applications are category killers. For example, Microsoft Exchange 2000 Server is widely hailed as superior to GroupWise from Novell.

✦ **Cost** — Certainly no one is going to undercut Microsoft in the integration suite wars. The other vendors' solutions have a hard time being price competitively when comparing the product you get for your buck.

**Tip**

It's in your best interest to monitor the Microsoft antitrust case, pending as of this publication, closely. If Microsoft is ultimately ordered split into two companies, an operating systems company and an applications development company, BOS is where you will see the fallout. BOS has just the type of operating system/application integration targeted by such a breakup decree. Be careful of placing all of your eggs in one BOS basket in light of the antitrust litigation.

## Guest Sermon — Protect Yourself

Roberta Bragg, an MCSE consultant who has niched on security matters (including ISA Server in BackOffice 2000), shares her observations on security and protecting yourself.

*"Protect Yourself" was a song when my boys were we're just approaching manhood. They got the message.*

*It's also my mantra when I talk to IT in my travels. And I'm not sure they do.*

*Oh, the product is different, and certainly the installation instructions are more complex, but the concept is the same. It's a nasty, evil world out there, and if you're going to live the good life, you'd better take action, or you're going to pay the price.*

*I'm talking about info systems security. I'm rapping about understanding what you have to lose and how you can prevent it. I'm exposing inadequacies and the tools that you use to correct them. I'm feverishly slamming and jamming and I'm beginning to feel like that street corner preacher, wrapped in rags and preaching doom and gloom — I'm being ignored.*

*For every "Roberta, I read your columns every month," and for every book that gets bought, firewall configured, hot fix applied, security policy implemented, I see and hear and find dozens of deaf ears. Or ears that just don't seem to understand.*

*Continued*

*Continued*

*Have I said something wrong? Done something untoward? Lost my skill at explaining the obtuse to the recluse?*

*I've written books, configured firewalls, locked down systems, and led many down the right path. What I can't figure out is what's wrong with those of you who bring up systems and fail to harden them. Your philosophy is "make-it-work-who-cares-about-reading-the-documentation." Then when your ill-configured, un-protected, under-resourced system crashes or is hacked, you blame the operating system.*

*If you run systems, do what's necessary to lock them down and protect them. If you tell other people how to run their systems, add security to every analysis, every proposal.*

*Read books. Subscribe to security lists. Go to classes and conferences. Visit the Web sites for the products you promote and those you don't. Build your own test networks and practice, practice, practice.*

Roberta Bragg is a Security Evangelist for Have Computer Will Travel, Inc. and happily preaches the benefits of security around the world when she's not locked in the attic writing books, teaching an online class for Seattle Pacific University (`www.spu.edu/prolearn`), writing her monthly column "Security Advisor" for *Microsoft Certified Professional Magazine* (`www.mcpmag.com`), or weaving blankets.

# BackOffice Technical Considerations

Can one individual truly master BOS? I'll wager the answer is no. BOS is too big for any one MCSE consultant to master at much more than a shallow level. I'll speak more about generalizing versus specializing in the next section, but suffice it to say, the BOS consulting opportunity is really a team opportunity. It has the characteristics of an enterprise deployment rather than an SBS deployment.

## Planning

A diverse group of parties are involved in the planning phase of a BOS implementation. You have messaging people, security representatives, end users, applications people (such as the accounting software consultant), and so on. This planning group or team reflects the multidimensional view of what BOS is. It's not just an operating system. It's not just an e-mail applications tool. It's not just a database.

## Installation

The installation of BOS itself has been simplified to the point of being anticlimactic. The step-by-step, wizard-based startup can likely be performed by a low-level technology employee, assuming the MCSE consultant has addressed all of the planning issues sufficiently.

## Maintenance

BOS is designed to be maintenance friendly with its use of Terminal Services in remote administration mode and its use of the different management consoles. The idea is that a power user or less experienced technology professional can perform much of the routine maintenance and administration once BOS has been implemented. Because of this maintenance friendliness, BOS is also a great platform to train up-and-coming MCSE consultants on increasingly sophisticated computing environments without giving them too much to handle too quickly.

## Reporting

BOS really excels when it comes to keeping an eye on operations. The aforementioned Health Monitor 2.1, shown in Figure 18-8, is truly an outstanding tool and competes favorably with the network monitoring tools from NetIQ and other vendors. The big difference is that Health Monitor 2.1 is free in BOS. Conversely, NetIQ software must be purchased separately.

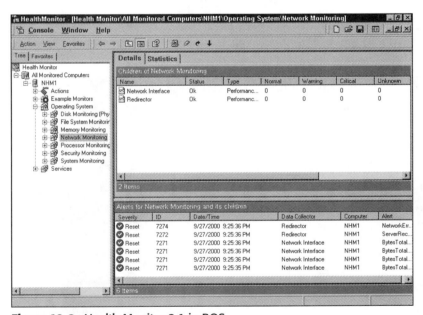

**Figure 18-8:** Health Monitor 2.1 in BOS

NetIQ is profiled in Figure 18-9.

Don't forget the server status reporting tools included in BOS. These tools send static reports, such as tape backup and virus detection logs, to the IT manager or technology consultant on a regular basis. The Server Status Report Configuration dialog box is shown in Figure 18-10.

**Figure 18-9:** NetIQ's monitoring tools compete with BOS's Health Monitor 2.1.

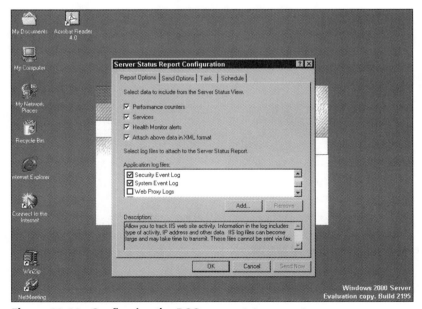

**Figure 18-10:** Configuring the BOS server status reports

# More information

In my view, the real secret to understanding and mastering BOS to the best of your abilities is to subscribe to Microsoft TechNet, the monthly CD-ROM library subscription service. TechNet is akin to legal information services such as WestLaw through which subscribed law firms receive a monthly set of CD-ROMs with the latest judicial rulings. In the case of TechNet, you receive a monthly package of updated CD-ROMs containing the latest technical library information. As a professional MCSE consultant, you need to make reading and researching in your TechNet electronic library a required activity.

But more specific to the BOS discussion, with TechNet you also receive the entire set of resource kits that apply to all BOS components. If you had to purchase these resource kits individually, your cash outlay would greatly exceed the subscription fee to TechNet. Figure 18-11 shows a sampling of a resource kit contained on TechNet.

You can subscribe to Microsoft TechNet in one of two ways:

✦ A regular subscription

✦ TechNet Plus, a premium subscription that includes beta software releases

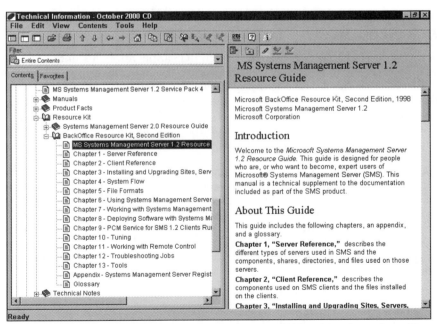

**Figure 18-11:** All BOS-related resource kits are available with Microsoft TechNet.

# Starting with BackOffice

All MCSEs should take BOS seriously as a consulting platform for a number of reasons. Not only does it offer you a great MCSE consultant training ground on your way up to the enterprise market, but also you get to see and learn so much about the Microsoft Servers family working with BOS. I find that to be very exciting and professionally rewarding. In this section, I present the general case for working with BOS, present the specific case for working with BOS, and highlight a BOS application.

## General

I'm supportive of MCSE consultants who want to use BOS to be general practitioners. While I prefer to specialize, some consultants enjoy having variety each and every day. Needless to say, BOS will give you that.

BOS addresses what I call the college major syndrome of MCSE consulting. With so many majors from which to choose, a freshman philosophy major may end their senior year of college with a finance major. The same analogy applies to MCSE consultants. You might very well enter this business dabbling and sampling each of the BOS components, changing your focus several times.

## Specialization

After you've looked at and worked with each BOS application, it's not unusual to select an area to niche on because the learning curve for mastering each BOS application is typically steep. Steep learning curves are often unprofitable because they translate into write-downs and inefficiencies. Write-downs are charges against current income to recognize uncollectables. For example, if you're spending too much time learning new features and functions on the job, clients may balk at paying for your on-the-job training time, resulting in write-downs.

One popular niche that MCSE consultants select is ISA Server in the security area. One MCSE consultant who I hold in high esteem is my fellow Seattle Pacific University online MCSE instructor Roberta Bragg. Roberta, who pens the monthly Security Advisor column for *Microsoft Certified Professional Magazine* (www.mcpmag.com), has taken her somewhat diverse career ranging from mainframes to motorcycles and niched in the security area. It's been a good choice as she now enjoys being able to pick and choose her engagements. More importantly for Roberta, her dance card is always full.

# Example – ISA Server

ISA Server is the firewall and caching solution in BOS. I've found it to be one of those deal closers when working with clients on the decision to implement BOS. When you note to clients that BOS comes with an effective firewall solution called ISA Server, that one statement often tips the scales for the MORG that was considering a separate pricey firewall solution.

ISA Server, shown in Figure 18-12, is a complex product, and I selected it for my BOS specialization example because the security area represents one of the most significant specializations an MCSE consultant can offer. Part of my reasoning is the importance of firewall security. It's one thing to have the e-mail system down and unavailable. It's an entirely different thing to have the fundamental security of your network compromised.

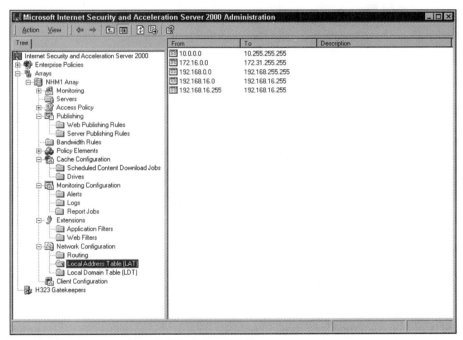

**Figure 18-12:** ISA Server Administration tool

# BOS Education and Exams

Microsoft has a suggested education track for immersing yourself in the world of BOS. Note this track will be updated for BOS 2000. Aside from any individual course you might take in specific BOS applications such as Microsoft Exchange 2000 Server or SQL Server 2000, you should consider the courses shown in Figure 18-13.

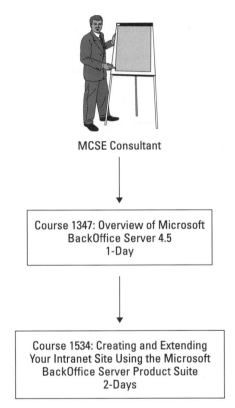

**Figure 18-13:** BOS education track

MCSE Consultant

Course 1347: Overview of Microsoft
BackOffice Server 4.5
1-Day

Course 1534: Creating and Extending
Your Intranet Site Using the Microsoft
BackOffice Server Product Suite
2-Days

The BackOffice training track consists of two courses as of this writing: —Course 1534: Creating and Extending Your Intranet Site Using the Microsoft BackOffice Server 4.5 Product Suite, and Course 1535: Analyzing and Tuning Microsoft Windows 2000 and Microsoft BackOffice 4.5 Performance. It is anticipated that additional training courses will be offered for future versions of BackOffice, and you should monitor training sites such as www.microsoft.com/backoffice and www.mcpmag.com periodically.

**Note**     Exams and their requirements frequently change. Be sure to check often for the latest exams and requirements.

There are no MCSE certification exams specifically oriented toward BOS. Rather, you pass the individual certification exams for each individual BOS component. Be aware that passing each individual exam is a tall order, so you might consider specializing in one or two BOS components and passing the associated certification exams for your specialization.

# BackOffice Professionals Association

The BackOffice Professional Association (BOPA) is first and foremost a user group focused on Microsoft solutions. BOPA is a community of fellow Microsoft Certified Professionals (MCPs) who meet monthly to hear a qualified guest speaker discuss a Microsoft Servers–related topic. Typically the guest speaker is an employee of Microsoft who for a couple of hours speaks about new products in the pipeline.

My take on BOPA is pragmatic. Instead of flying to expensive conferences around the country, I can hear from the same speakers who are using the same PowerPoint slide deck for the cost of my annual dues. I consider BOPA to be quite a bargain. As of this writing, BOPA is considering streaming video solutions that would allow members at a distance to participate in real time. I suggest you monitor the BOPA Web site (`www.bopa.org`), shown in Figure 18-14, for more information.

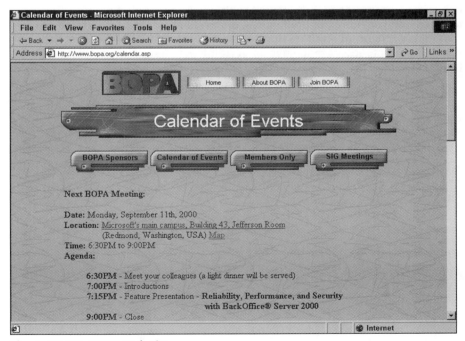

**Figure 18-14:** BOPA Web site

# The Future of BackOffice

Microsoft has actually dropped the term *BackOffice* in reference to its family of server products. The server products are now referred to as Microsoft Servers. The term *BackOffice* is now relegated to a single stock keeping unit (SKU), the BackOffice 2000 product. Even Small Business Server dropped the term *BackOffice* from its official title.

Personally I'm sorry to see the term *BackOffice* de-emphasized by Microsoft, as it allows for an easy contrast with the front office Office 2000 suite.

In the future and for financial reasons, Microsoft may well disband the BackOffice product and focus on the sale of individual components. It is more profitable selling the individual components separately at retail, and since most Microsoft server products are indeed sold individually, the extra expense to create an integrated server suite isn't justified. Personally I think they'll keep BackOffice around for some time to come, as it fits a market segment so well.

# Summary

This chapter was a complete MCSE consulting reference for BackOffice Server, known in the trade as BOS. Specific topics covered included defining BackOffice features and consulting opportunities, understanding the organization types (medium-sized, branch office) that can benefit most from BackOffice, listing BackOffice competitors, and suggested training courses and certification exams for BackOffice.

✦    ✦    ✦

# Windows 2000 Consulting

**A** straightforward consulting opportunity that focuses on the operating system is Windows 2000 consulting. This consulting area is consistent with Microsoft's new MCSE track under Windows 2000. As you likely know from other chapters and your own real-world experience, the MCSE track is operating system–centric with no less than seven exams focused on Windows 2000.

In this chapter I will focus on Windows 2000 Server as a network operating system. I will profile specific Windows 2000 Server features such as Active Directory and Group Policy as consultant opportunity areas. I will present daily, weekly, monthly, and annual tasks as administration-related consulting areas. I will mention Windows 2000 Professional as a desktop operating system in passing, but I will not emphasize it.

## Defining Windows 2000 Server

As a Windows 2000 MCSE (or MCSE candidate), you're likely quite familiar with Windows 2000 Server already. However, if for some reason, you're still learning about Windows 2000 Server, I present the following features list to make sure everyone is on the same page before continuing with the Windows 2000 Server consulting chapter:

✦ **Network operating system** — Windows 2000 Server is a true network operating system (NOS) that can handle multiple requests from multiple client machines simultaneously. In conjunction with the Microsoft Client for Networks installed on client machines, Windows 2000 Server executes server-related tasks and commands initiated by users. Local commands are redirected to the local client machine for execution.

✦ **Security** — Windows 2000 Server invokes security in several ways. There is Kerberos-based logon authentication. There are the tried-and-true share-level and NTFS-based security implementations. Windows 2000 Server makes advanced network security solutions available such as PPTP, L2TP, and IPSec depending on your security needs. For more information on Windows 2000–related security, see Microsoft's security Web site at `www.microsoft.com/security`.

✦ **Storage** — Part of the job of a network operating system is to act as a reliable and secure data repository for the company. Windows 2000 Server acts as a file server in this capacity.

✦ **Printing** — Any good NOS acts as a print server. In that respect, Windows 2000 Server doesn't disappointment.

✦ **Directory services** — One of the major improvements in Windows 2000 Server over its predecessors is the inclusion of Active Directory. Active Directory is a directory services solution discussed in detail in the second half of this chapter.

✦ **Remote control** — Windows 2000 Server provides an integrated remote control solution with Terminal Services. Terminal Services may be run in two modes: remote administration and application. In remote administration mode, MCSE consultants can manage the server from remote locations. Application mode allows you to design a Windows 2000 network with thin clients or remote clients who can log on to Terminal Services sessions and run applications that are resident on the Windows 2000 Server. Terminal Services is discussed later in this chapter.

✦ **Centralized management and administration** — Windows 2000 Server provides a framework for more effective technology management. This effectiveness is accomplished primarily through Group Policy, which allows you to infinitely configure user and computer configurations. The more powerful scripting capabilities, based on Windows Scripting Host (WSH), also contribute to this centralized management and administration paradigm.

✦ **Networking standards** — Windows 2000 Server is the final step in making Microsoft networking solutions industry standards–based. Not only is Transmission Control Protocol/Internet Protocol (TCP/IP) the default (and required) networking protocol, but also the Domain Name System (DNS) is the required name resolution system. Both TCP/IP and DNS are the most popular solutions in their respective worlds of network protocols and name resolution.

✦ **Other valuable features** — The list is long. It seems like each time you right-click on an object or click Next in a wizard, you make a new feature set and functionality discovery in Windows 2000 Server. Those discoveries include the following:

• Wizards for ease of configuration

• Plug and Play (PnP) hardware detection to assist in hardware management

- Multimedia support for sound and video

- Device Manager from Windows 9*x* (finally!)

- Microsoft Management Console (MMC) for a consistent interface for managing Windows 2000 Server

- Web-enabled tools such as Internet Explorer 5.*x* and Internet Information Server (IIS) 5.0 to make Windows 2000 Server a more than sufficient Web citizen

- Disk quotas

- High-end capabilities such as clustering

- Very large memory configurations (in the Advanced Server and Datacenter Server releases that I discuss later in this chapter)

For more information, consult Microsoft's Windows 2000 Web site at `www.microsoft.com/windows2000`.

# LAN of Opportunity

Windows 2000 Server consulting opportunities run the full range from small firms to the largest enterprises. That one solution can span such a diverse audience is somewhat unusual in the world of computing. Windows 2000 Server can serve so many different firms because the product itself is so scalable, a design goal that has allowed Windows 2000 Server to win over the hearts and minds of technology professionals (and MCSE consultants) from its earliest days after release.

## Low-end market

The low end of the Windows 2000 Server market consists of smaller firms. My observation has been that this market is defined by two factors: upgrades and desires for Microsoft solutions. I'll also discuss different types of Windows 2000 solutions for the low-end market in this section.

### Upgrades

As you know, few businesses today are computerless, so the decision to implement Windows 2000 Server is typically an upgrade scenario from Windows NT Server 4.0 or earlier. The upgrade decision is typically based on the desire for increased stability in this smaller market segment. Windows 2000 Server has certainly delivered when it comes to fewer blue screens and fewer reboots.

I haven't observed the low-end market feeling the same pressure as the medium and high-end market to upgrade to stay current with application revisions. Low-end accounting systems such as QuickBooks have been relatively operating system agnostic and not the primary reason to upgrade to Windows 2000. Application-driven Windows 2000 Server upgrades will be discussed shortly.

### Desire for Microsoft-based solutions

Many small companies have been waiting for Microsoft to deliver a mature networking solution. Those low-end holdouts have met their match with Windows 2000 Server. In particular I'm thinking about firms in the architectural, advertising, and public relations fields that have embraced Macintosh networks. Windows 2000 has caught up in the eyes of these firms with increased support for multimedia devices, peripheral hardware such as plotters, and most importantly, Plug and Play device detection.

### Windows 2000 Server

As a stand-alone solution, Windows 2000 is easily implemented and maintained at the low end of the market. Firms are making this decision when economics are a concern. For under a thousand dollars, a low-end firm can purchase a world-class network operating system and get ready to put it to work. It's a compelling argument for firms on a budget.

**Caution**    It is both interesting and important to note that the deployment of Windows 2000 Server presented in the preceding text did not account for other applications such as e-mail. Ironically, the small firm that purchases Windows 2000 Server alone at a bargain price often returns to purchase an e-mail application such as Microsoft Exchange and a firewall system. Before you know it, the small firm has spent more on ad hoc application purchases than they would have if they had purchased a bundled solution such as Microsoft Small Business Server.

### Small Business Server 2000

Windows 2000 Server is also present at the low-end market space as the underlying network operating system in Small Business Server 2000. In addition to the Windows 2000 Server network operating system, Small Business Server 2000 contains several BackOffice applications, as shown in Table 19-1.

**Cross-Reference**    Small Business Server 2000 is discussed at length as an MCSE consulting opportunity in Chapter 24.

## Table 19-1
## Small Business Server Components

| Component | Description |
|---|---|
| Windows 2000 Server | Network operating system with Active Directory, Group Policy, Terminal Services, Kerberos security, and disk quotas. See the discussion earlier in this chapter for detailed Windows 2000 Server information. |
| Microsoft Exchange 2000 Server | Messaging and collaboration platform. See Chapter 20 for more details. |
| Microsoft SQL Server 2000 | Powerful relational database. See Chapter 21 for more details. |
| Microsoft Internet Security and Acceleration (ISA) Server | Firewall and Web caching solution. See Chapter 18 for more details on ISA. |
| Shared fax and modem pool | Allows network users to share fax devices and modem pools. |
| Performance monitoring | Provided by Health Monitor 2.1. Allows MCSE consultants to be e-mailed or paged based on alert conditions. |
| Small Business Server consoles | The Administrator and Personal consoles facilitate ease of use in performing Small Business Server management functions. |

**Note**  Microsoft has priced Small Business Server 2000 at a price point that makes a compelling argument for purchasing it outright over just purchasing Windows 2000 Server. Purchasing Small Business Server up front is typically cost-effective in the long run when small firms seek to add functionality such as e-mail and firewall protection to their computer network. This is clearly a chance for the MCSE consultant to offer sage advice to the client.

## Peer-to-peer networks

Believe it or not, the small firms in the low-end space are using peer-to-peer networks. Windows 2000 Professional facilitates this solution. The MCSE consultant should discourage peer-to-peer networking, as the management of data is more difficult. Networking performance tends to suffer, as each client machine is acting as both a workstation and a server.

## Medium market

Windows 2000 sells very well in the medium-sized marketplace. This market space has long accepted Windows NT Server and is aggressively upgrading to Windows 2000 Server.

### Windows 2000 Server

Upgrades to Windows 2000 Server are the largest segment of the middle market. Upgrades occur to take advantage of the stability and reliability improvements in Windows 2000 Server, though application-driven upgrades occur as well. Application vendors in the middle market are releasing upgrades that are Active Directory–integrated. You'll see this in particular in the database and business applications areas.

Middle markets offer the opportunity to exercise your MCSE consulting muscles and be challenged with many responsibilities. Unlike when consulting at the enterprise level, you'll feel less like a cog in the wheel and more like one of the wheels.

### BackOffice 2000

It is imperative as an MCSE consulting in the middle market consulting space that you are well versed in BackOffice 2000 and can decide whether or not the BackOffice bundle (with its licensing limitations) meets your client's needs.

**Cross-Reference**    The specifics on BackOffice 2000 are discussed in Chapter 18.

Believe it or not, at the middle and high-end levels, purchasing Windows 2000 Server individually sometimes makes more sense than investing in BackOffice 2000. It just depends on the client's needs (which should underscore the importance of needs analysis).

**Note**    BackOffice 2000 contains the same components as Small Business Server with a few additions. BackOffice 2000 contains Systems Management Server 2.0 (for wide-scale server and client machine management) and Host Integration Server (the successor to SNA Server for mainframe host connectivity). BackOffice 2000 also has multiserver support, positioning it for branch office implementations.

## High-end market

As an MCT who trains aspiring MCSEs, I'm often surprised by the enthusiasm my students have for the enterprise space. They, as well as many working MCSEs in the technology sector, believe that real computing begins at the enterprise level. However, while you will work with some of the fastest and most impressive technology solutions when you work in the high-end market, temper that observation with the realization that you are part of a team effort, so you may work with only one specific component of a technology area (not the entire solution). In fact, at the enterprise level, rarely does any one person grasp the entire technology solution being implemented. Rather, each team member has a specific and defined area of responsibility.

Enterprise-level consulting is discussed in further detail in Chapter 16.

Microsoft has admittedly made great strides in the enterprise marketplace, an area that has typically been an IBM hotbed. With Windows 2000 Server, enterprise technology managers are taking a second look at Microsoft networking solutions.

## Windows 2000 Server

The product stock keeping unit (SKU) that is called Windows 2000 Server actually peaks at the lower end of the enterprise market. You're likely to find Windows 2000 Server acting as a department application server or as a member in a server farm. However, Windows 2000 Server has some bigger siblings aimed squarely at the enterprise level.

## Windows 2000 Advanced Server

A real enterprise workhorse, Windows 2000 Advanced Server addresses the more demanding needs of the enterprise including the following:

✦ **Eight-way symmetric multiprocessing support**—This version scales up to eight SMP processor configurations for much more robust processing power. This is an improvement over the four-way SMP support found in regular Windows 2000 Server.

✦ **8GB memory support**—This version can take advantage of very large amounts of memory. This is an improvement over regular Windows 2000 Server, which supports 4GB memory.

✦ **Advanced hardware configurations**—Windows 2000 Advanced Server supports Intel's Physical Address Extension (PAE).

✦ **Network load balancing**—Windows 2000 Advanced Server has the capability to distribute processing load over a server farm.

✦ **Cluster service**—Windows 2000 Advanced Server has a ten-node cluster service that supports fail-over when applications or hardware fails on a cluster partner. Basically the other cluster partners pick up the workload. The setup is considered a big improvement over Microsoft's other attempts at clustering. You may also manage clusters from a remote or central location.

✦ **Rolling upgrade support**—A combination of clustering and network load balancing allows you to take down a Windows 2000 Advanced Server machine, perform an upgrade, and then bring it back online. This first node to be upgraded can then be migrated to the other cluster partners.

An information sheet from Microsoft's Web site is shown in Figure 19-1.

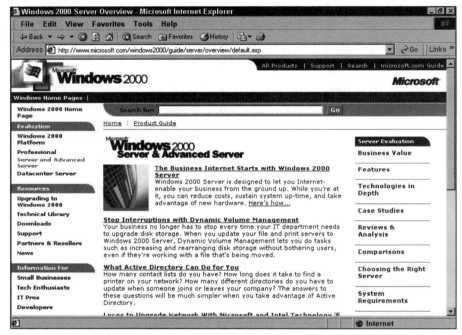

**Figure 19-1:** Windows 2000 Server and Advanced Server features

## Windows 2000 Datacenter Server

*Computerworld,* a widely read and respected weekly trade journal, called Windows 2000 Datacenter Server "Windows 2000 in Mainframe Land." I couldn't agree more. Datacenter Server picks up where Advanced Server left off. The two biggest incremental features it has over Advanced Server are as follow:

✦ Support for 32-way SMP

✦ Support for 64GB memory

If you're intent on becoming the next Amazon.com, these features are exciting. An information sheet on Datacenter Server is shown in Figure 19-2.

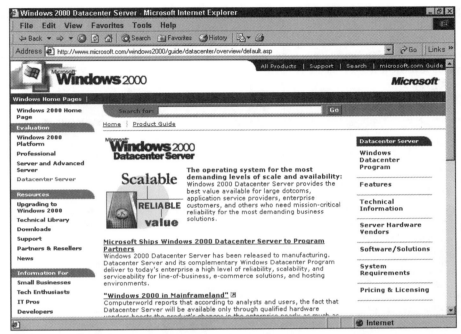

**Figure 19-2:** Windows 2000 Datacenter Server features

# Competitive Analysis

Windows 2000 Server has competitors, a statement you should be comfortable hearing. As an MCSE consultant who is most likely a proponent of Windows 2000 Server, your job is to reposition against the competition. The first step for doing this is to know the competition. This section explores two popular competing operating systems and mentions a few other competitors in passing.

## NetWare

NetWare by Novell arguably has a larger installed base of network nodes worldwide than Windows 2000 Server and Windows NT Server combined, a statistic that reflects Novell's early 1990s dominance. In reality, the hearts and minds of many in the technology community have shifted to Microsoft networking solutions, based on Windows 2000 and Active Directory.

NetWare 5.1 is a robust network operating system and, ounce for ounce, is competitive with Windows 2000 Server on many fronts. Ardent NetWare proponents are
often loaded with facts that pit NetWare against Windows 2000. A favorite tactic is
to emphasize NetWare Directory Services (NDS), which is the mature directory services solution from Novell. NetWare 5.1 is profiled on the Novell Web page shown
in Figure 19-3.

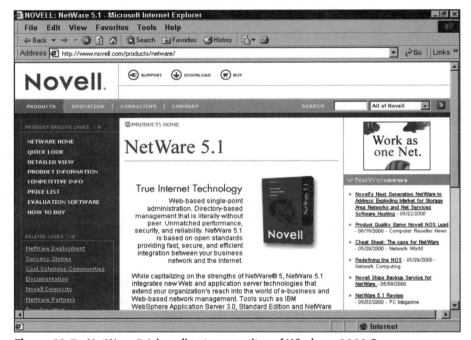

**Figure 19-3:** NetWare 5.1 is a direct competitor of Windows 2000 Server.

The primary advantage that Windows 2000 Server holds is application support.
Many NetWare applications have been ported over or completely redesigned for
Windows 2000 Server. In many cases, the independent software vendors (ISVs) have
stopped developing for the NetWare platform. Ask your clients where they want to
place the emphasis when selecting a network operating system, including considerations of support for business applications.

## UNIX

UNIX is a mature network operating system that in many cases matches Windows
2000 Server stride for stride. Comparisons can be made in the areas of application
availability, clustering support, performance, and reliability.

However, Microsoft, as the sole provider of Windows 2000 Server, can set standards for the operating system to which application vendors and hardware manufacturers will adhere. In contrast, there are many flavors of UNIX, including the popular Linux shown in Figure 19-4.

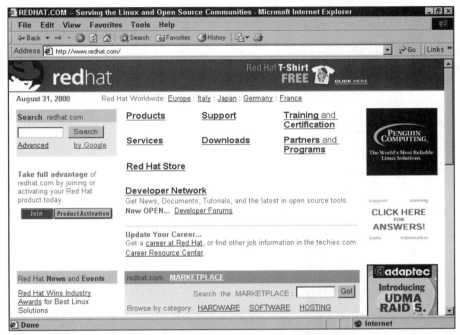

**Figure 19-4:** Red Hat Linux is a bona fide competitor of Windows 2000 Server

Usability is a standard argument used by MCSE consultants to select Windows 2000 Server over UNIX. The effort put into the Windows 2000 user interface is commendable, but if you or your client inherently like command-line scripting, then UNIX is for you.

## Others

Windows 2000 Server has other competitors, depending on the market size. Table 19-2 summarizes those competitors, as well as NetWare and UNIX, arranged by market size.

| | Table 19-2 | | |
|---|---|---|---|
| | **Windows 2000 Server Competitors** | | |
| **Product** | **Small Market** | **Middle Market** | **Large Market** |
| NetWare | X | X | |
| UNIX | X | X | X |
| IBM (AS400, mainframes) | | X | X |
| Data General | | | X |
| Other mainframes | | | X |
| Apple Macintosh | X | | |

# Windows 2000 Setup and Implementation

The Windows 2000 Server setup and implementation process is deceptively easy. Four setup floppy disks, one setup CD-ROM, and an hour later Windows 2000 Server is up and running in a basic configuration. Setting up Windows 2000 Professional on a client machine takes even less time.

## Server-side setup

The server-side setup and implementation is uneventful after you've performed the activity several times. Before you install Windows 2000 Server on a production machine, do it on a test network first. Still, the setup process is the easiest work you will do on Windows 2000 Server. The devil is in the details, as the latter part of this chapter will explore with the Active Directory, Group Policy, and Terminal Services discussion. After the Windows 2000 Server setup is complete, many hours of configuration await you.

## Windows 2000 Professional

The smoothest running Windows 2000 network will have Windows 2000 Professional clients to complement the Windows 2000 Server machines. One reason this network configuration runs so smoothly is that it allows you to fully exploit the functionality of Windows 2000 by using such capabilities as Group Policy.

I have personally found Windows 2000 Professional to be a very stable desktop program that supports the applications I need to run. Of course, the majority of my applications are Microsoft-based such as Office 2000; still, it is nice to say good-bye to unresponsive application errors and the like. To date, Windows 2000 Professional has done a good job with hardware driver support, including support for multimedia devices. With Microsoft's commitment to Windows 2000 Professional, look for the drivers library for new hardware devices to stay current.

## Ask the Guru — Getting Experience

The following e-mail is from a reader looking to leverage his MCSE into a better paying and more exciting position. I offer a few words of advice about picking a specialty within the networking area, specifically Windows 2000.

*Hi, Harry,*

*I know you're a busy guy, so I'll get right to the point. I went to a technical training school (Strategy Computers) in Bellevue last year to obtain my A+ and MCSE certifications. The school was great, I learned a lot, and now I am certified. I live in Wenatchee and got a job here right away in June 1999 without a whole lot of effort. The company is all right, but I don't see my IT career going far here.*

*I've looked around (Seattle, Portland, and Northern California) and most of the Network Admin jobs I come across are now asking for at least three years experience. I don't have a BS in CS so that eliminates me as a candidate on many jobs as well. (I do have two years of college at Portland State, however.) I wouldn't mind doing consulting work, but that also usually requires more experience than I currently have.*

*I am a Junior Net Admin and Exchange Administrator at my current job and would like to move up and not into a help desk/tech support position. I guess what I'm trying to say is this: "Am I stuck where I'm at or do you think I might be able to grab a similar or better position elsewhere?"*

*I really respect your opinion so if you could send me a quick note I'd appreciate it. I appreciate you taking time out of your schedule to read this.*

*Ed A., MCSE, A+*

Hi, Ed,

Thanks for the e-mail. I've thought a long time about what you said. You are seeking interesting opportunities and, I suspect, sufficient pay. But you're realistic about the limited work experience you have. Here is what I suggest. Consider MCSE consulting to quickly gain the experience you are seeking. A year of MCSE consulting is worth a couple years as an in-house administrator because MCSE consultants see so many different networks in a given month that their experience level quickly increases. More importantly, by serving as an MCSE consultant, you will see different types of companies and how they operate. You might well find one that you'd like to join as a full-time, in-house employee. I've seen that occur many times. My final point is that you should consider picking a specialty within the Windows 2000 community, such as Group Policy. Learn an area like Group Policy from start to finish and you'll be very valuable despite your limited years of work experience. Best of luck and keep me posted.

harryb

# Types of Windows 2000 Server Consulting

Concentrating your consulting on Windows 2000 Server provides you with many significant opportunities, particularly in the planning area, which includes both annual tasks and day-to-day support for existing Windows 2000 networks.

## Planning

If your strength is planning and you want to participate in a technical capacity as an MCSE consultant, Windows 2000 Server may just be your calling. Windows 2000 implementation requires more planning than the implementation of previous releases have required. First, the push into the enterprise with Windows 2000 immediately places MCSE consultants in more of a planning role. This planning paradigm is clearly reflected in the Windows 2000 MCSE track. Second, certain features such as Active Directory lend themselves to planning. At Microsoft's Windows 2000 Web site (`www.microsoft.com/windows2000`), in the Technical Library area, you will find significant planning and deployment resources just waiting for your perusal. This Web page is shown in Figure 19-5.

**Figure 19-5:** You can find tremendous planning and deployment guides for MCSE consultants in the Microsoft Windows 2000 Technical Library.

MCSE consultants who focus on planning issues are typically acting as designers and architects. In fact, it's not uncommon for MCSE consultants to be listed as Active Directory architects as a job title. MCSE consultants in a planning role may well be brought in to participate in a number of annual exercises, as displayed in Table 19-3.

### Table 19-3
### Annual Windows 2000 Network Planning Tasks

| Task | Description |
| --- | --- |
| Budgeting | The IT budget is the lifeblood of technology professionals everywhere. It's an annual exercise you should give top priority. |
| Fire drill | You need to undertake this painful and necessary disaster recovery exercise annually to test the fitness of your backup procedures and IT staff. Can you truly recover in a reasonable amount of time from a natural or man-made disaster? |
| Security audit | Typically a security specialization firm is retained to conduct a third-party security audit of the network. |
| Application upgrades planning | You will want to work months in advance with your ISVs for any software upgrades. Plenty of planning opportunities exist here, to say the least. |
| Application upgrades implementation | The actual implementation of application upgrades falls into the annual category. At least once per year, a busy MCSE consultant in the Windows 2000 consulting space will be involved in upgrading business and other applications at client sites. |
| IT staff training/certifications | An MCSE consultant can advise management on the need for IT staff training, certification tracks, and so on. The goal is to provide training opportunities for staff so that the network infrastructure operates more efficiently and existing staff is retained. |
| Annual planning retreat | This retreat is where the real fun begins. Typically the management team, the top IT staff, and selected consultants (including you) and vendors huddle away from the company site to engage in some forward thinking. This group of heathens is typically known as the technology committee, a topic discussed further in Chapter 25. |

*Continued*

| Table 19-3 *(continued)* | |
|---|---|
| **Task** | **Description** |
| Corrupt servers rebuilds | Machines, and Windows 2000-based computers are no exception, get trashed sometimes. Once a year, you — the MCSE consultant — are likely to find yourself rebuilding badly behaved machines. |
| As-built full network diagram | A fun planning engagement is the as-built network diagramming exercise. Each year, you should diagram your network so that you have a current blueprint of your network infrastructure. |
| Corporate networking policies updates | Times change, and corporate network use policies need to stay current. A couple years back the issue was junk e-mail, but today the concern is more likely to be Internet stock trading on company time. |

# Administration

MCSE consultant is a blanket job description that can refer to a high-end designer or a temporary employee at the low end of the pay scale looking for experience and that breakthrough job. Perhaps you're the high-end designer I alluded to in the previous section on planning. Perhaps you're really a glorified temporary employee at the low end of the pay scale, just looking for a break to gain valuable experience and to make a few bucks along the way. This section on administration speaks more toward the low end of the marketplace than it does to the high end. Contractors and permanent temps are often assigned to medium and large companies to work as network administrators.

Administration of a Windows 2000 network is a downstream function that has a day-to-day focus. An MCSE consultant can anticipate performing the Windows 2000 network administrative tasks summarized in Table 19-4 (call it my baker's dozen activities list) on a regular basis. Not all of these tasks will be performed each day, and some may only be performed weekly or monthly. Still, these tasks are important regularly occurring concerns.

### Table 19-4
### Day-to-Day Administrative Tasks

| Task | Description |
|------|-------------|
| Tape backup | The most important Windows 2000 Server task each day is a backup. This can be confirmed by reading the tape backup logs and performing a quick test restore of a text file. On a monthly basis, a full restore to a spare hard disk should be performed. |
| Virus detection | A close second in importance to backups is the issue of virus detection. There are at least three tasks related to virus detection: read the virus detection logs, implement the latest virus detection signature files (most commonly referred to as DAT files), and monitor virus vendor Web sites (like Network Associates at `www.nai.com`) and even popular news organization Web sites (like the Microsoft/NBC News joint venture (JV) at `www.msnbc.com`) for mentions of new predatory viruses. |
| Firewall logs | Closely monitoring firewall activity is a daily event. |
| Event logs | System, security, application, directory service, DNS server, and file replication service logs can be viewed in Event Viewer. |
| Connectivity testing | It's never a bad idea to run connectivity tests before your users attempt to log on. You can use tools such as PingPlotter (a widely available shareware program) to run ping tests. |
| Group Policy updates | In a homogenous Windows 2000 network, you will find yourself frequently modifying Group Policy to satisfy organizational needs. Group Policy has many configurations that can be modified. |
| Application support, troubleshooting, and installations | Being an MCSE consultant is not as Microsoft- or BackOffice-centric as you might have thought. I often myself assisting in the administration of third-party find business applications (even if all I do is call a business software specialist for advice). Though your consulting job may be Microsoft-centric if you're supporting Microsoft front-office applications such as Office 2000. (I discuss front-office consulting in more detail in Chapter 17.) |

*Continued*

## Table 19-4 *(continued)*

| Task | Description |
|---|---|
| End user support | Many MCSE consultants want to avoid end user interaction as much as possible. However, if you work in the Windows 2000 Server network infrastructure field, you can't avoid interacting with end users. Don't forget end user support also includes adding and deleting users and computers in Active Directory. |
| Performance monitoring | Using some of the Windows 2000 built-in tools such as System Monitor and Network Monitor to analyze and boost network performance is a common task. There are common object:counters (measurements by System Monitor) used to track critical operational areas such as disk, memory, and processor performance. Many third-party software developers also provide object:counters that monitor the performance of the specific applications (for example, accounting applications). |
| | You might consider providing a consulting service to your clients where you periodically log critical performance object:counters and report back to the client on the condition their network. I've charged for this type of work by coming in each calendar quarter, logging the data in System Monitor, and advising my client. Over time (several quarters, for example) the data becomes more meaningful and valuable because you can observe progressive changes. |
| Server reboots | Reboots are fewer in Windows 2000 than they were in Windows NT Server, but you can't completely avoid them. A badly behaved service will still cause memory leaks that are best flushed away with a server reboot. |
| Permissions management | Requests to modify a user or group permission to allow or restrict network access are frequent. |
| Service packs and fixes implementation | Such implementation is a big part of the administrative burden for MCSE consultants because not only are you expected to track and test Microsoft service packs and fixes, but you also need to do the same for third-party applications. |
| Network notebook updates | Because you need to be an effective communicator, in this case through written communications, you should religiously update network notebook with reports. |

**Tip**

If I may be so bold as to recommend another of my published works, I spend hundreds of pages discussing Windows 2000 Server administration in *Windows 2000 Server Secrets,* published by IDG Books Worldwide, Inc. You might enjoy that book as a follow up to the Windows 2000 Server discussion contained in this chapter. In particular, the performance analysis section of the preceding book advises you on critical performance counters you can log and interpret in System Monitor for your client's benefit.

## Specialization

A very strong argument can be made for considering a specialization as an MCSE consultant. In the context of Windows 2000, it might be Active Directory, Group Policy, or Terminals Services. I discuss these three specializations in the last part of this chapter.

Another consideration is to specialize by industry. This is more common in the world of applications, such as business accounting software (where a consultant may specialize in construction firms), but the same ploy can be played as an MCSE consultant. The idea is to have specific industry knowledge so that you are more than competitive as an MCSE consultant. That way, when you solicit new consulting engagements, you can truly claim that you know the client's industry. This type of insight can often tip the scale your way in a competitive bidding scenario.

### Case Study — Rule of Ten: Purchasing Windows 2000 Server

This case study asks you to develop your own list of top ten reasons for purchasing and deploying Windows 2000 Server. By completing this exercise, you will be well prepared to face a client when you are trying to persuade them to purchase Windows 2000 Server. I realize this may require you to research Windows 2000 Server to complete the assignment, which is exactly my point. You can find significant amounts of Windows 2000 Server information at Microsoft's Windows 2000 Web site at www.microsoft.com/windows2000. Consider reviewing the list of Windows 2000 features earlier in this chapter as a starting point for completing your top ten list.

# Windows 2000 Server Consulting Specializations

This final section of the chapter details three Windows 2000 Server specializations you might consider as an MCSE consultant: Active Directory, Group Policy, and Terminal Services.

## Active Directory

Active Directory is the directory services implementation in Windows 2000 Server. There are two ways to consult in the Active Directory niche, both of which can be performed by the same MCSE consultant. The Active Directory design and planning area is the first method of consulting in the Active Directory niche. Active Directory is often thought of as both a technical and an organizational implementation. Not only do you confront technical requirements, but also you must typically address business requirements of the organization to implement an Active Directory infrastructure that is both technically and politically sound. A few Active Directory planning issues that come to mind include the following:

✦ Using organizational units (OUs) to reflect the organization chart

✦ Considering application support for Active Directory

✦ Considering the placement of domain controllers (DCs) on the network

✦ Collapsing Windows NT Server resource domains into Windows 2000 OUs

✦ Delegating administrative authority to power users

✦ Laying Active Directory over other directory services to create a metadirectory

The other Active Directory consulting consideration is the administration area. Active Directory administration is largely performed by three tools: Active Directory Users and Computers, Active Directory Domains and Trusts, and Active Directory Sites and Services. Each of these tools is found in the Administrative Tools program group from the Start menu. These tools, known technically as snap-ins, are based on the Microsoft Management Console (MMC) framework.

### Active Directory Users and Computers

Shown in Figure 19-6, the Active Directory Users and Computers tool is used to manage users, computers, distribution and security groups, and other objects in the Active Directory. This is the tool used to apply Group Policy at the OU level.

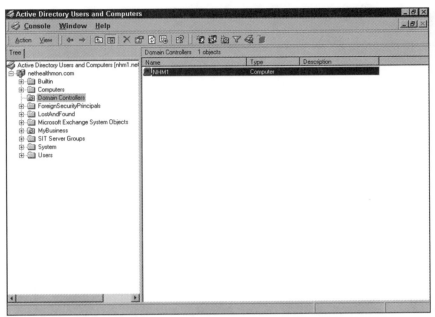

**Figure 19-6:** Introducing the Active Directory Users and Computers tool

**Tip**     A user may be a member of only one OU. This is a known MCSE exam stumper.

### Active Directory Domains and Trusts

Active Directory Domains and Trusts allows you to manage the trust relationships between domains as well as apply Group Policy at the domain level. Windows 2000 sets explicit two-way trusts between domains automatically, but this may be over-ridden using Active Directory Domains and Trusts. This tool is shown in Figure 19-7.

### Active Directory Sites and Services

An interesting and often overlooked area of Active Directory is the management of sites. Active Directory objects such as domains and OUs typically map to the logical view of the organization, but sites map to the physical view of the network infrastructure. More specifically, sites map to IP subnets. Active Directory Sites and Services is where you manage replication traffic and replication schedules. Active Directory Sites and Services is shown in Figure 19-8.

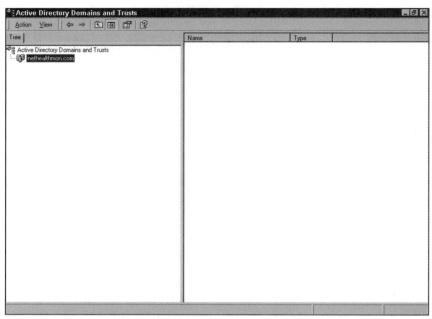

**Figure 19-7:** Active Directory Domains and Trusts

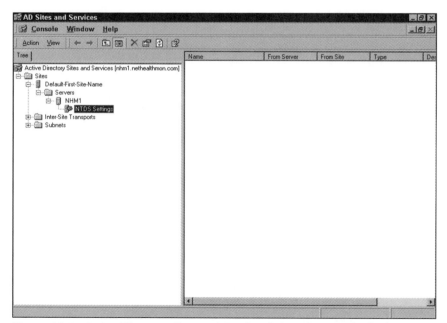

**Figure 19-8:** Active Directory Sites and Services is an often overlooked management tool.

Tip
To quickly become a Windows 2000 and Active Directory specialist, visit www.reskit.com and complete the online deployment exercises. You will create the deployment plan for a large Windows 2000 network with an Internet connection.

## Group Policy

A hidden jewel in Windows 2000 networking that hasn't received near the press coverage of Active Directory is Group Policy. There are more settings than you can imagine in Group Policy that may be configured for the user, computer, or both. Group Policy is applied to sites, domains, and organizational units (this statement is a known MCSE Windows 2000 examination area). The following example, where Task Manager will be disabled when users who are members of the OU log on to the network, demonstrates a Group Policy implementation.

The steps to implement Group Policy are as follows:

1. At the Windows 2000 Server machine, click Start ⇨ Programs ⇨ Administrative Tools ⇨ Active Directory Users and Computers.

2. In the console tree (the left pane), right-click on an OU (for example, MyBusiness) to which you want to apply Group Policy.

3. Select Properties from the secondary menu. The property sheet for the OU will appear.

4. Select the Group Policy tab. Your screen should look similar to Figure 19-9.

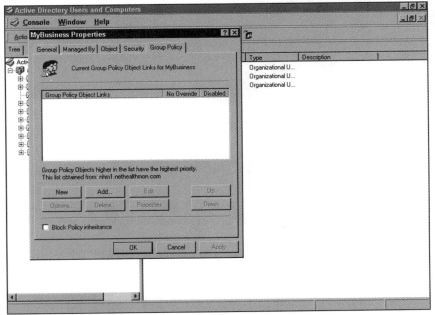

**Figure 19-9:** The Group Policy tab on an OU's property sheet

5. Click New to create a new Group Policy object (GPO) that will be applied to this OU.

6. Name the GPO (for example, Main-1).

7. Click Edit. The Group Policy MMC for the GPO you just created appears.

8. Expand the Administrative Templates folder under User Configuration in the console tree.

9. Expand the System folder in the console tree.

10. Expand the Logon/Logoff folder in the console tree. Observe the numerous policies in the detail pane (the right side of the MMC).

11. Double-click on the Disable Task Manager policy. The Disable Task Manager Properties dialog box appears.

12. Select Enabled. The Disable Task Manager Properties dialog box should look similar to Figure 19-10.

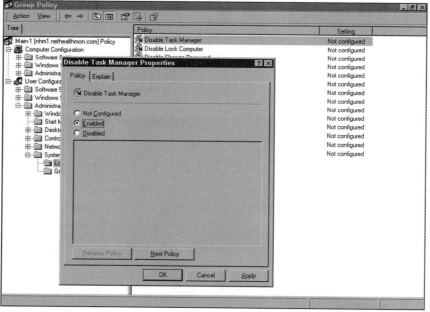

**Figure 19-10:** Enabling the Disable Task Manager policy will effectively restrict Task Manager from running when OU user accounts log on to the Windows 2000 network.

**13.** Click OK. The Group Policy MMC should look similar to Figure 19-11.

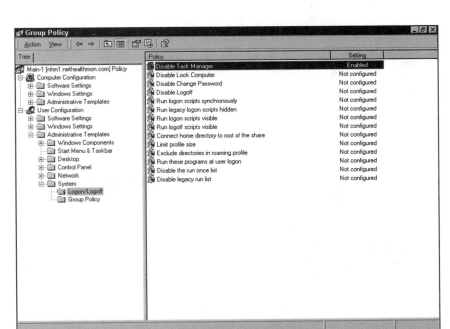

**Figure 19-11:** The Group Policy MMC reflects the Task Manager policy that has been set.

**14.** Close the Group Policy MMC.

**15.** At the property sheet for the OU, determine whether you want to block inheritance (which prevents higher-level GPOs from overwriting this GPO). Click Close.

When a user who is a member of the MyBusiness OU performs a Windows 2000 network logon on a Windows 2000 machine, Task Manager will be disabled. This was just one example to demonstrate how to configure Group Policy. There are over 600 policy settings out of the box with Windows 2000 Server of which I'm aware. Further, you can even create your own.

## Terminal Services

Another area of excitement among Windows 2000 MCSE consultants is the use of Terminal Services. Not only are MCSE consultants using Terminal Services to remotely manage client sites, but also Terminal Services is being implemented as an application server solution. With Terminal Services, remote workstations (such as executives working from home) and thin clients (such as low cost point-of-sale terminals that provide limited local functionality) can connect to the Windows 2000 Server machine and enjoy a full Windows 2000–based computing session. More information on Terminal Services may be obtained from `http://www.microsoft.com/windows2000/guide/server/features/terminalsvcs.asp`, as seen in Figure 19-12.

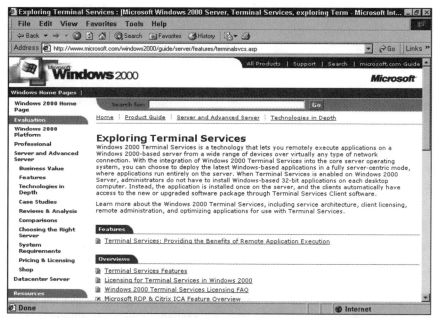

**Figure 19-12:** The Exploring Terminal Services Web page at the Microsoft Web site is a great place to learn more about Terminal Services.

# Summary

In this chapter, I presented Windows 2000 Server opportunities for the MCSE consultant to consider. I discussed compelling reasons for becoming a Windows 2000 MCSE consultant, different releases of Windows 2000 and its competitors including NetWare, and the different areas of consulting specialization available in Windows 2000.

✦     ✦     ✦

# Microsoft Exchange Server Consulting

**E**-mail is everywhere. A recent poster advertisement in the Denver International Airport where the underground train shuttles people from terminal to terminal said it best: "You've received eight e-mails while waiting for the train." Not only was the message on target, but the audience, intense business travelers, heeded these words of wisdom like gospel. Remember that in many cases networking and communication technologies were sold as elixirs of efficiency, as solutions that would make our lives easier and free up our time. In reality, e-mail has improved communications, but I'm not sure it has freed up time for people. People now spend a lot of time answering e-mails.

Exchange Server has emerged as a category killer in much the same way as Microsoft Word eclipsed WordPerfect some years ago in the word processing market. In the electronic mail category, it's Microsoft Exchange taking the lead over Lotus Notes/Domino, with Novell's GroupWise a downtrodden and distant third. And that's just the server side of the e-mail equation. It's hard to find anyone that isn't using Outlook or Outlook Express on the client side.

Turn the Exchange Server stone over and you find an MCSE consulting opportunity. Because everyone uses e-mail and because Exchange has the major share of the market, Exchange Server has become a valuable consulting niche.

## Core Organizational Application

Is it not true that e-mail is perhaps the most important application in an organization today?

## E-mail Has Come a Long Way

Certainly you couldn't say that e-mail was a core business application back when Microsoft Mail 3.x ruled the land. Microsoft Mail 3.x had limited capabilities and a hard disk–based folder system for storage that made it unsecure and often unreliable. More importantly, the connectors for Internet mail with Microsoft Mail 3.x never really worked well, relegating Microsoft Mail to an internal, not Internet, e-mail solution.

By the way, did you know that Microsoft Mail was one of the original MCSE elective exams? It's true, and I took it to complete my MCSE (it was my last MCSE exam). So why did I select the Microsoft Mail exam as my last elective exam when I originally became MCSE certified? There were two reasons. First, the exam was easier than the other electives offered. This exam had questions like how many subdirectories are there beneath the MSMAIL directory. Second, the firm I worked for as a LAN administrator used Microsoft Mail, and I worked with the product. During that time, e-mail was just emerging as a core organization application.

Think about how you might spend today as an MCSE consultant. What application would you spend most of your time with as measured by minutes and hours? E-mail is almost certainly number one. It certainly is for my consulting clients on any given day. I have watched them work while I'm on-site and have noticed they will pop in to Word to write a letter and into Excel to update a spreadsheet. But for most computer users, such activities don't consume their day. But when it comes to e-mail, I have observed clients that spend hours responding to e-mails.

Need more empirical evidence that e-mail is central to all things related to technology in the firm? Look over your billing records to your consulting clients. Assuming you provide e-mail support as part of your consulting services, a common offering for consulting in the infrastructure space, you might be surprised how significant your e-mail–related billings are in your practice. Second, close your eyes and think back to the panic-stricken calls you receive on your cellular telephone from clients. Is it not fair to say that many of these calls include shrieks about e-mail not working? The point is that a crashed e-mail system is a sure source of stress and billable hours for the MCSE consultant.

# Niching on Microsoft Exchange

Many MCSE consultants have found a niche in Microsoft Exchange and discovered the space to be fertile ground for billable hours. Many consultants find working with messaging applications to be an enjoyable expedition.

## Small, medium, large

An MCSE consulting buddy named Peter who has focused his skill set on Exchange offers the following observation about the Exchange consulting space.

According to Peter, Exchange is one of those products that scale very well. It works for the smallest firms as part of Small Business Server (SBS). At the other end, it drives the messaging function in the largest enterprises.

What Peter points out is that once you learn Exchange thoroughly you can support it in organizations of all sizes. Many MCSE consultants start with SBS to get their professional feet wet. These SBS MCSE consultants can then take some of the BackOffice skills learned in SBS, such as Exchange, to the next level and target medium-sized and large firms. Peter further shares that in his professional opinion SBS exposes the MCSE consultant to approximately 80 percent of the features and functionality in Exchange. If the MCSE consultant in the SBS space wants to move to the next level of organization size, the learning curve for scaling Exchange is relatively tame.

Once you learn Exchange, taking your skill set to a larger organization is a matter of learning a tad more here and there in the core products. Two Exchange elements that you wouldn't see in a smaller firm but would need to become proficient in with a larger organization are Exchange sites and organizations. These concepts are further explored on Microsoft's Exchange Web site at `www.microsoft.com/exchange`, where you can look at product specifications and download white papers. This Web site is displayed in Figure 20-2.

## X-Large

While I can't speak from direct experience about Exchange in the largest enterprises, I can share a few facts that turned up during my research for this book.

Many Internet service providers (ISPs) are using Exchange as the core messaging solution for customers. This is a trend that started to emerge in the Exchange 5.*x* era, when Exchange was taken much more seriously by the technology community. The trend has only accelerated with Exchange 2000 Server. While ISPs have relatively small staffs (regional ISPs typically have fewer than 100 employees), the number of mailboxes they serve is 10,000 or more, placing them squarely in the enterprise environment.

In addition to providing core messaging services with Exchange, ISPs are using Outlook Web Access (discussed later in this chapter) to provide Web-based access to users. This is significant in that it signals that ISPs are using some of the more advanced (and resource-intensive) features of Microsoft Exchange.

# Introducing Exchange 2000

I can't hope to make this chapter an A-to-Z reference on Microsoft Exchange 2000 Server. That's not my intent, as I first and foremost want to present MCSE consultant guidance with a sprinkling of technical goodies here and there. In fact, searching the online bookstore at IDG Books Worldwide, Inc., (www.idgbooks.com), the publishers of this book, reveals numerous books on Exchange. And several of those are thicker than this entire tome, a testament to how rich the study of Exchange is.

Exchange 2000 is the latest upgrade of Microsoft's successful messaging system application. Many of the improvements you would expect in this release are present:

✦ More speed

✦ New features

✦ More functionality

✦ Bug fixes

But those generic improvements aside, a couple of things stand out with the particular upgrade, including its integration with Active Directory. Much of the Exchange-related administration that previously occurred in Exchange-specific administration tools now occurs at the operating-system level. In this case, the Exchange-related management occurs within Active Directory Users and Computers (see Figure 20-1). You can expect this integration between Exchange and the underlying operating system to continue to grow over the years.

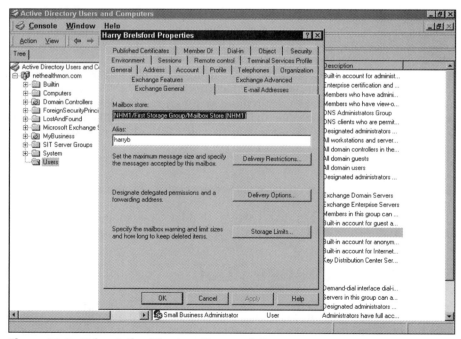

**Figure 20-1:** Using Active Directory Users and Computers to manage Exchange 2000 Server

Later in this chapter I will profile a few additional Exchange 2000 Server features that represent billing opportunities for MCSE consultants. The Exchange 2000 Server Web page at Microsoft (`www.microsoft.com/exchange`) is shown in Figure 20-2.

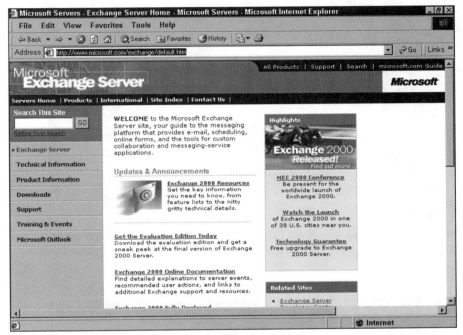

**Figure 20-2:** Microsoft Web page for Exchange

# Competitive Analysis

There are two significant competitors to Exchange. The greatest competitor is the Notes and Domino combination from the Lotus division of IBM. The other competitor, on the strength of its parent operating system (NetWare), is GroupWise from Novell.

## Notes/Domino

The messaging application offerings from IBM via its Lotus division should not be discounted. IBM is the one company with enough resources to make good things happen in the new Internet era. While Microsoft is just starting to define its .NET strategy (.NET is Microsoft's Internet strategy) and operate as an application service provider (ASP), IBM has decades of experience on this playing field. Lotus Notes is shown in Figure 20-3.

IBM's Lotus Domino is shown in Figure 20-4.

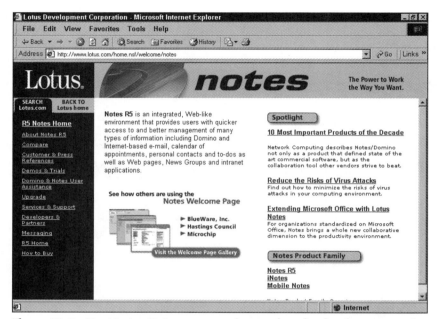

**Figure 20-3:** Meet Lotus Notes, a messaging product that has been around as long as Exchange.

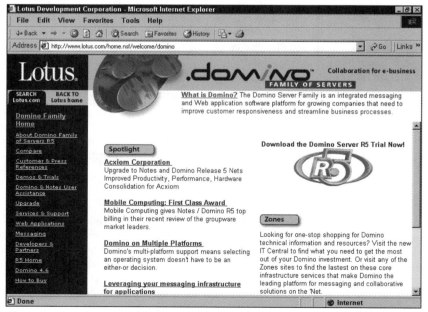

**Figure 20-4:** Lotus Domino is a sophisticated messaging and collaboration application.

## GroupWise

GroupWise is here, and it's likely to be here for years to come. I don't have its sales figures, but I suspect it has carved out all the market share that it's going to manage. Novell continues to develop GroupWise and to release upgrades. GroupWise is shown in Figure 20-5.

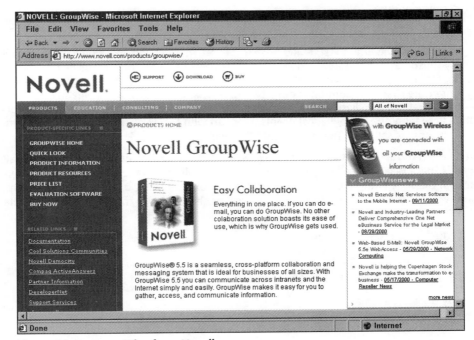

**Figure 20-5:** GroupWise from Novell

## Ask the Guru — Remote Consulting Possibilities

In this Ask the Guru installment, I share reader mail from someone who read a column of mine in *Microsoft Certified Professional Magazine* and wrote the following query to me:

*Harry,*

*My name is Darrick and I am interested in getting your opinion on how to break into the field of consulting. I read an article written by you some time ago where you explained that you were now consulting remotely for several clients, and I've been dreaming of working for myself ever since as a goal of my own.*

*Continued*

*Continued*

*I wanted to solicit your advice on how to go about finding clients that could use the services of a consultant who's not on site all the time. If you could point me in the direction of where to start that would be greatly appreciated.*
*Darrick T.*

*Tampa Bay, Florida*

Dear Darrick,

Thanks for taking the time to write and pose this excellent question. In a single word, e-mail will be your solution for remotely supporting clients. Sure, you can plan on using other tools such as Terminal Services and NetMeeting, but on a day-to-day basis, by far my strongest tool for remote client site support is e-mail. Here is what I mean. On any given day, I receive a few e-mails from my clients with computer-related questions. I've pasted one such interchange here with one of my largest clients. I replied with the answer to solve the problem, and the user was satisfied. That's good MCSE consulting.

Here is my remote support example using e-mail. What's significant in reading the e-mail thread is that I was able to suggest a solution to a problem that the user was able to perform and that this entire communication scenario took less than 30 minutes (far less time than it would have taken me to drive to the client site). Look at the time stamps on the e-mail thread to confirm for yourself.

-----Original Message-----

From: Ellen P

Sent: Thursday, November 16, 2000 2:41 PM

To: Harry Brelsford (E-mail)

Subject: More "stuff"

Hi, Harry,

I have had two "Attune Intelligrams" pop up on my computer as I have used programs. One is alerting me of a security problem in Excel 2000 that there is a security update for; the other has the same message regarding Internet Explorer 5.01. I have kept these messages minimized on the bottom toolbar of my computer. Would you advise me if I should download these updates, if I should disregard/delete these messages, or if you want to look at the messages when you are at our office on November 21?

Thanks!

Ellen P

-----Reply Message-----

From: Harry Brelsford

Sent: Thursday, November 16, 2000 2:58 PM

To: Ellen P

Subject: RE: More "stuff"

Thanks for the e-mail.

First, please try to upgrade the affected applications as the message directs you. Second, I can look at it on Tuesday

Thanks,

harryb

-----Reply Message-----

From: Ellen P

Sent: Thursday, November 16, 2000 3:06 PM

To: Harry Brelsford (E-mail)

Subject: RE: More "stuff"

I was able to download the updates successfully, at least as far as I can tell.

Thanks!

Ellen

# Hands-on Exchange Consulting Opportunities

I've identified at least five Exchange 2000 Server work areas that represent consulting opportunities for the MCSE consultant. These suggested opportunities would be in addition to the general technology consulting services such as the following:

✦ **Planning** — Because e-mail is a core application and Microsoft Exchange Server is a complex product, it behooves you and your client to engage in sufficient planning to make sure the proposed solution meets the e-mail–based communication needs of the organization.

✦ **Design** — The next process after planning, once the e-mail–based communication needs have been identified, is the design of the e-mail system. The design process is traditionally more technical than the planning discussion and might involve determining where to place multiple Microsoft Exchange Servers in the organization.

✦ **Implementation** — After the necessary planning and design work for the Microsoft Exchange project has occurred, you as the MCSE consultant would likely be selected to implement the solution.

✦ **Administration** — You may well have a role in providing administration services, such as applying Microsoft Exchange Server service packs and fixes for your client site.

✦ **Troubleshooting** — Because e-mail is a core organizational application, you will have an important role in troubleshooting Microsoft Exchange Server when it is not functioning optimally.

✦ **Training** — I have found that client sites get very excited about e-mail as a bona fide business tool. Many times the users want to know more about Microsoft Exchange Server and other components that can be added to it. This level of interest from users represents a training opportunity for the MCSE consultant.

See Chapters 15, 16, and 25 for more discussion on general technology planning, design, implementation, administration, and troubleshooting types of service offerings. Training is discussed in Chapter 26.

The following hands-on opportunities are related to components that Microsoft has built into Microsoft Exchange Server or ones that can be purchased from Microsoft:

✦ **Outlook Web Access** — There are good billable hours waiting for you if go into an organization, implement Outlook Web Access (OWA), and train users on its proper usage. I've racked up ten hours to implement and train on OWA, which isn't a bad day of work for an MCSE consultant.

✦ **Public folders** — Another popular request is to have a common calendar and contact list for the organization to use. This can be accomplished with public folders in Exchange. You can count on more than a few billable hours here.

✦ **Recipient policies** — A new feature in Exchange 2000 Server that you'll want to learn more about is the recipient policies. The idea here is that Exchange can support multiple organizations easily with one server. For example, if you consult to a business known as *executive suites* that houses several businesses under one roof, all with different Internet identities, you'll want to learn about recipient policies.

✦ **Instant messaging** — Instant messaging is very popular around Microsoft and among America Online (AOL) users. Instead of doing the old linear back-and-forth of traditional e-mail, you can have real-time mini-chats with users anywhere in the world. This is akin to the chat application in Windows for Workgroups in the early 1990s that disappeared from Windows 9*x*. It's back as instant messaging, and your clients will allow you to bill a few hours to implement it. Note that Microsoft Exchange Server uses Microsoft-based instant messaging, which is separate from AOL's form of instant messaging. In fact, the instant messaging platform as a whole is still being developed so that disparate instant messaging systems can trade messages. For a quick look at how instant messaging can work (as part of your proof of concept), visit MSN at `www.msn.com`.

✦ **Exchange Conferencing Server**—Exchange Conferencing Server facilitates multicast video conferencing. This is how you turn NetMeeting from a unicast video conferencing solution to multicast mode. The Web page for Exchange Conferencing Server is shown in Figure 20-6.

**Figure 20-6:** Exchange Conferencing Server

Other hands-on consulting opportunities (based on third-party add-ons to Microsoft Exchange Server) exist, but I don't explore those third-party add-ons here. These include integrating voice mail functions with Microsoft Exchange Server–based e-mail so that you can see voice mails in your Inbox; you then double-click the sound icon to hear your message over your computer. One vendor that produces a voice mail solution that is integrated with Microsoft Exchange Server is Active Voice (`www.activevoice.com`), which recently became a wholly owned subsidiary of Cisco.

# Exchange Server Courses and Exams

There are numerous Microsoft Official Curriculum (MOC) and certification exams you can take relating to Exchange. A sampling of such courses is shown in Figure 20-7.

**Note**    Both the MOC and certification exams are frequently updated to reflect new Exchange releases.

**Figure 20-7:** Exchange training courses available for you to take

# Exchange Resources

There are two great ways to position yourself in the Microsoft Exchange Server niche as an MCSE consultant focused on communication solutions. The first is an industry newsletter, and the second is a conference. The *Exchange Administrator* newsletter is a highly respected avenue for the transfer of Exchange knowledge. Found at www.exchangeadmin.com and shown in Figure 20-8, this newsletter not only presents technical discussion on the finer points of Microsoft Exchange Server but also has an interesting column called reader-to-reader where you can contribute your own war stories to benefit others in the Microsoft Exchange Server community.

The Microsoft Exchange and Collaboration Solutions Conference (MEC), shown in Figure 20-9, is a must for the MCSE consultant who wants to be a player in the Exchange community. This conference is the largest conference dedicated to serving the Microsoft Exchange community, and as such, deserves your consideration if you plan to make this your consulting niche. It is a technical conference with limited management and planning topics.

**Figure 20-8:** *Exchange Administrator* newsletter

**Figure 20-9:** MEC—the premier Exchange conference

# The Future of Exchange

Clearly, Microsoft Exchange Server is here to stay. It is a category-leading e-mail application and is central to Microsoft's messaging strategy. But I suspect you can look for further improvements as the product upgrades. One improvement may well be integration with SQL Server.

You probably know that Exchange Server uses its own proprietary messaging database. It doesn't use the Active Directory database explicitly for that purpose, nor does it use SQL Server. It seems to me that with SQL Server as a part of the BackOffice family integrating SQL Server with Exchange would be a natural marriage. Plus, that integration would allow corporate IT departments to extend the messaging database and would allow independent software vendors (ISVs) to add Exchange functionality not envisioned by Microsoft more easily. It wouldn't hurt the sales of SQL Server either (just a hint to the marketing group at Microsoft).

# Summary

Numerous MCSE consulting opportunities exist with Microsoft Exchange, the premium messaging system from Microsoft. This chapter focused on recognizing e-mail as a core business application and provided information about Microsoft Exchange Server, its competitors, and general and specific Microsoft Exchange Server consulting opportunities.

✦    ✦    ✦

# DBA – Microsoft SQL Server Consulting

◆   ◆   ◆   ◆

**In This Chapter**

The importance
of data to any
organization

Consulting
opportunities in
the Microsoft SQL
Server arena

Software applications
that compete with
Microsoft SQL Server

The Microsoft
Certified Database
Administrator
(MCDBA)
certification title

◆   ◆   ◆   ◆

**M**icrosoft SQL Server is a hidden jewel in the MCSE consulting community. Long overlooked by MCSEs with an infrastructure focus, SQL Server is the powerful relational database that Microsoft offers as its answer to Oracle and other competing database products. SQL Server as a product is well respected in the business community for its speed, capabilities, reliability, and competitive cost.

In this chapter, I'll make the case for MCSEs to add SQL Server to their service offerings as a consulting area.

## Data Reigns Supreme

If not for the data, none of us would be here. Infrastructure such as Windows 2000 networks can be thrown out if you take your eye off the data. The data is the ultimate reason we're here. It's the reason clients hire MCSE consultants. Are you hired for the chance to improve WAN logon speed, or are you really hired to improve access to information stored on the computer network, such as accounting reports? The endgame for most clients is access to information (typically business-related information).

I next direct your attention to a lower-level argument about data and SQL Server. It's my contention that as the infrastructure side of the MCSE consulting business matures, the data side will receive attention. Many networking bandwidth issues have been resolved as far as basic productivity is concerned. The big infrastructure speed issues, such as working remotely from home by attaching to the corporate network, have been solved with widely available broadband connection options.

However, when it comes to the data, I still have clients that can't find information on their networks. As an MCSE consultant, it's common for me to overhear clients lament that they can't find a file, can't remember what reports contained specific information, and so on. Again, for the typical end user, it's the ability to access and interpret information that allows tasks to be completed and work to be performed.

A database design that hinders the retrieval of information and its effective use will slow down a technology infrastructure implementation more than enough to undo all the good you can accomplish as an MCSE consultant implementing a routed, switched, 100 Mbps network. The nanoseconds you save the organization with your know-how is dramatically overshadowed by an organization that doesn't manage its data well. This is the appeal of SQL Server as a database management application. Imagine the professional pride you can take in a job well done if you help an organization more efficiently manage its data because of a SQL Server–based solution you implement. Specifically, perhaps you have an insight into how the data can be indexed in such a way as to result in much faster sorts when a query is executed. A practical achievement like that can literally save an organization hundreds of hours of time over the course of the database's life. Many MCSE consultants will understand this and go from the LAN of infrastructure opportunity to the land of database opportunity.

# General SQL Server Consulting Opportunities

As you've gathered, I'm particularly excited about why the database area, with SQL Server, represents one of the great hidden consulting opportunities for MCSE consultants. One reason is that the assignments in the database field tend to be of longer duration and, thus, in some ways more profitable.

## One long-term client

Here's what I mean from a firsthand perspective. As an MCSE consultant with an active portfolio of clients, it's not uncommon for me to visit ten different client sites in a month. Some visits are as short as my two-hour minimum billing. Other client visits can last as long as several days for special projects. Occasionally, I'll have a work assignment that lasts several weeks. However, it struck me one day at a client site as I watched a database consultant at work that the database assignments tend to be much longer, often at the same bill rate. At the same client site, I observed and got to know the Oracle consultant acting as a database administrator (DBA). He was, for lack of a better phrase, camped out at this client site. He had been there for nine months and had at least another year to go on a huge database development and implementation project. He was working at least eight-hour days and billing for all of his time. While his rate was actually $25 per hour less than mine was, he clearly made up that differential by working at one site for a long duration.

That experience taught me a very valuable lesson in MCSE consulting — there are different consulting models, depending on your skill set. My discussion in Chapter 12 about a 50 percent utilization rate assumed infrastructure consulting with a port-folio of clients. As you can see in the preceding example, the business model for the database developer was a single client with a long-term assignment. During the pro-ject, his utilization rate was likely approaching 100 percent, save a few hours written down here and there for personal leave, sick days, and technical mistakes. (Of course, his overall utilization rate likely dropped from those lofty levels once you factor in the down time, also known as bench time, between assignments.)

**Note**    The consulting model I've presented for database developers of one client and a long-term assignment also applies to programmers. I don't go deep into program-ming consulting opportunities in this book, as that work area fits the Microsoft Certified Solution Developer (MCSD) more than the MCSE. However, I do speak toward the MCSD title in Chapter 22. Let the record reflect, however, that pro-grammers do very well financially adhering to the same consulting model to which many database developers ascribe.

## Breadth of opportunities

The database community presents a wide range of consulting opportunities from high-level business analysis down to programming. You can even be a data entry clerk, but I'm not recommending that as a lucrative MCSE consulting opportunity. The point is that there are general opportunities if you have limited technical acu-men but are stronger in business. Thinking about general consulting opportunities with SQL Server is a primary focus of this chapter.

**Tip**    If you're a hard-core infrastructure-oriented MCSE who would like to learn more about SQL Server by dabbling in database consulting, consider the following. It's in your best interest to start in a general role such as a business analyst consulting position while you develop your SQL Server–specific technical skill set. In the gen-eral roles, your infrastructure know-how will be appreciated and called upon.

## Specific opportunities

Here is an example of a general SQL Server–related consulting opportunity in the form of a job listing by a Seattle-based firm called Aris seeking a Senior Consultant. Note the high-level emphasis:

"The firm is seeking Senior Consultants with a desire to maximize operational effi-ciency to improve bottom line results. Applicants must demonstrate a solid under-standing of business process, organization design, and information technology. Responsibilities include conducting substantive analysis, identifying key issues, generating recommendations, developing financial justification that support a com-pelling rationale for change contributions, and owning production of final reports. Qualified candidates must have obtained a minimum of two to four years of consult-ing or project-based work. SQL Server, E-business, technology delivery, organization design, and/or business process improvement experiences are beneficial. An MBA is a plus. An MCSE is desired but not required."

# Competitive Analysis

Assuming you're considering consulting opportunities in the database space with SQL Server, you need to know who the product competitors are. The primary competitor is Oracle, but since there are other database products that compete with SQL Server beyond Oracle, I'll profile Sybase for comparison purposes as well.

## Oracle

As of this writing, Oracle's flagship database product is called Oracle8*i*, shown in Figure 21-1. Since all independent software vendors (ISVs) upgrade their respective software releases periodically and it's entirely possible the product has been or will be upgraded and improved, I'll restrict my comments on Oracle to a more general vein.

**Figure 21-1:** Oracle8*i* — Enterprise Edition

The database family from Oracle is more entrenched and well established than Microsoft's SQL Server. This is, in part, because Oracle has been in the database business longer than Microsoft has. It has also been more focused on database applications as its core competency.

Oracle8*i* comes in five varieties:

- ✦ **Oracle8*i* Enterprise Edition**—This edition includes advanced security, parallel server architecture, spatial database support, a diagnostic management pack, a tuning management pack, and a change management pack.

- ✦ **Oracle8*i* Standard Edition**—This version includes easy management tools and Oracle interMedia to manage rich content including text, documents, images, audio, video, and geographic location. The Oracle Internet File System (iFS) allows users to find any Microsoft Office files, e-mail, XML files, and Web pages better than the simple Find command in Windows 2000 Server.

- ✦ **Oracle8*i* Personal Edition**—This desktop database system is designed for Windows 2000, Windows NT, Windows Me, and Windows 9*x*.

- ✦ **Oracle8*i* Lite**—This small Java-based database application is designed for PDA devices.

- ✦ **Oracle8*i* Appliance**—This hardware-based solution is used to rapidly deploy Oracle8*i* in the organization.

For more information, visit Oracle's Web site at `www.oracle.com`.

**Tip** You need to institutionalize upgrade thinking as an MCSE consultant. Just when you think you've seen it all, vendors such as Microsoft will upgrade the products with which you're keenly familiar. You'll have to educate yourself on the product's new features so you can advise your consulting clients. You need to read a considerable amount in this industry, Web sites, trade journals, and books, just to stay current with the products offered in your consulting space.

## Sybase

Sybase, a longtime player in the database field, is a worthy competitor of Microsoft SQL Server. As you can infer from Figure 12-2, Sybase has many different products, including its traditional relational database family.

The Sybase database family includes the following:

- ✦ **Adaptive Server Enterprise**—This product is designed for mission critical, high-availability scenarios.

- ✦ **SQL Anywhere Studio**—This Sybase offering is used to develop corporate database solutions at the workgroup level. Also supports mobile and distributed database scenarios.

- ✦ **Adaptive Server IQ**—Sybase designed this product for Web-based data warehousing, with the emphasis on fast retrieval times, easy maintenance, data compression, and data scalability.

For more information, visit the Sybase Web site at `www.sybase.com`.

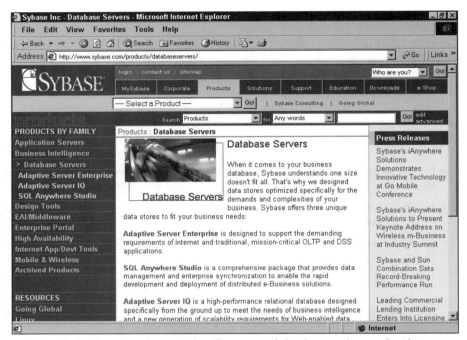

**Figure 21-2:** Sybase is a large and well-respected database software developer.

# Repositioning Microsoft SQL Server

Microsoft has mastered certain areas such as the Office suite and is still playing catch-up in other areas. One such area is in database applications, where Oracle occupies the dominant position. As an MCSE consultant in the database space, you can reposition SQL Server against Oracle and other database competitors using the following two arguments.

## Microsoft integration

To me the best argument for selecting SQL Server is integration. Microsoft enjoys some distinct competencies when it comes to running its business applications such as SQL Server on top of its Windows 2000 Server operating system. I have observed that Microsoft products just run better as an integrated whole than many third-party applications under the same scenario. This integration argument is very effective when advising and persuading businesspeople on technology directions.

## Database applications run on SQL Server

The best repositioning Microsoft can do for its SQL Server product comes directly from the ISV community. If the ISV's product needs SQL Server or will run on SQL

Server, the selection decision is typically an easy one. If your client's accounting system needs SQL Server and will run only on SQL Server, the decision is automatic.

The current release of SQL Server is SQL Server 2000, and its informational Web page is displayed in Figure 21-3.

**Figure 21-3:** Microsoft SQL Server 2000

# Hands-on SQL Server Consulting Opportunities

In this section, I'll profile several hands-on consulting opportunities for MCSE consultants seeking to work in the database space. This list is not meant to be inclusive of all consulting opportunities in this space, as such opportunities are limited only by your imagination. Rather, it represents a sampling of common SQL Server–related opportunities.

## Guest Sermon—The Good Life as a DBA

This guest sermon on DBA consulting comes from Bob Watkins, a database professional and MCSE who lives in the Pacific Northwest. Bob is a computer professional with 25 years of experience in programming, systems analysis, consulting, and training. He is vendor certified by Microsoft (Microsoft Certified Systems Engineer), Oracle (Oracle Certified Professional) and Hewlett-Packard (HP-UX Technical Consultant and NetServer Technical Consultant). He is currently a senior instructor (Oracle) at SQLSoft+ in Bellevue, Washington (www. sqlsoft.com). He can be reached via e-mail at either bob.watkins@sqlsoft.com or bwatkins@bwatkins.com. Here is Bob's contribution to the discussion:

*Many companies are finding that managing their corporate databases is a significant, but less than full-time job. Enter the consulting database administrator or DBA. I've been taking care of other people's databases for about five years now, and in that time I've learned that the technology is only about 15 percent of the job. The other 85 percent of the job is dealing with people. The next paragraphs include some of the things I've learned, some that are specific to the DBA role and others that apply to consultants in general:*

✦ ***Share the power***—*With smaller clients I can be both DBA and system administrator. But in larger firms these two roles are separate. As a DBA, I find my work often requires system privileges, but the system administrator may be reluctant to give me the keys to his or her kingdom (the Administrator password). I've learned to relax and go with the flow in these cases. I ask politely for what I need and follow up as often as necessary so that my timetable doesn't slip. Being upset or demanding typically doesn't work.*

✦ ***Protect the data***—*All consultants try to safeguard their clients' systems and not break more than they fix. For a consulting DBA, however, the integrity of the database is the primary job. Database administrators have a reputation for being anal retentive, but I prefer the term detail oriented. Shortcuts kill: dot the I's and cross the T's.*

✦ ***Stay centered***—*Both DBAs and sysadmins are on call when something breaks. People are unable to get their work done, and senior managers are apt to call every half hour to see if the problem is fixed yet. I've learned that it's important to resist the temptation to take risky shortcuts, particularly where the integrity of the database is concerned. For example, I back up a broken database before trying to fix it even though that takes precious time. My first try at a solution might be incorrect, and I'll need the files in their original state to try something else. It is possible to make a bad situation worse if you panic. Also, my remaining calm tends to calm the client as well.*

✦ ***Focus on the customer***—*It's easy to fixate on the technology and forget that the reason I'm there is to make it easier for people to do their jobs. I try to get out from behind my keyboard and talk to as many different people in the client company as I can. I ask for their wish lists; even though I can't always implement their ideas, it gives me vital information about their needs and priorities.*

✦ **Blend into the culture** — As a consultant, I might visit several companies during a week, each with a different way of doing things. I tend to dress fairly conservatively on site, but one client wrote into my actual contract that I was not allowed to wear a tie while working there. I need more of those in my client list.

✦ **Prepare for resistance** — Change is not always welcome, and people resist in various ways. I know some people who argue openly but eventually go along with the plan; others who are closed-mouthed and don't volunteer information that may be helpful; and still others who work behind my back to sabotage my efforts. When I have gone into a client situation with the attitude that such resistance is always a possibility, it's easier to stay calm when I encounter it. Instead of fighting back, I work on removing the underlying fears that are causing people to behave that way.

✦ **Learn multiple technologies** — It's difficult enough to master one vendor's technologies, much less several, but most companies have a mixture of systems. My focus is database administration, but I need to know how to implement those databases on both Microsoft and UNIX platforms. Taking the time to become certified on Microsoft Windows NT and UNIX has enabled me to adapt to whatever the client needs and makes me a more valuable resource to them.

## SQL coding

SQL Server is a strange product in that it clearly has several dimensions. One of the largest opportunities available is to write SQL code. SQL coding gives you the opportunities to create applications, write stored procedures, and so on. I've listed a typical application development opportunity for SQL coding (this one was posted by Cambridge Technology Partners):

"There is an *immediate* opportunity. The needs of this project require us to look for five client server programmers with at least three years' development experience with Oracle and SQL Server. Each candidate will have experience with Web-enabled technologies and have excellent communications skills and be able to work as part of a team."

## DBA stuff

Another role an MCSE consultant can fill is the database administrator (DBA) role. Perhaps a client site can't afford or doesn't have the need for a full-time SQL Server DBA. As a consultant, this might be a service you can provide on a cost-effective basis for the client. The following two subsections present a sample DBA job description posted by SEI Information Technology that could easily be converted into a statement of capabilities for an MCSE consultant to market.

### Database administrator

The focus of this position will be to prepare and "clean" data from several sources. This data will come from databases (SQL SVR, Access) or spreadsheets (Excel). It will need to be combined and split multiple times so that it can be submitted to Trillium (data cleansing and standardizing software). After being cleansed the data will be sent to outside vendors for call downs to verify profile information from customers. The data will then come back, need a final grooming, and be submitted to Siebel for MORG mining. The consultant will need to keep track of how the data was combined and from what resources.

### Requirements

✦ Good organizational skills

✦ Multitasking is important because different sets of data will need to go through the processes simultaneously, but will be on different schedules

✦ SQL

✦ Ability to do moderately complex joins (merges) and selects

✦ Access

✦ Excel

## Install applications on top of SQL Server

One of the largest SQL Server–related consulting opportunities for MCSE consultants is the planning, installation, and support of applications that run on top of SQL Server. A prime example of this is for the popular high-end business accounting package Great Plains Dynamics. The following subsection contains a job description posted by Great Plains, Inc., for an MCSE consultant who would provide such services.

### Career title: Great Plains SQL Consultant

Want to be part of a growing company with vision, integrity, great employees, and a successful future? The consulting firm is a software consulting company specializing in implementing Great Plains Dynamics and eEnterprise. We offer an excellent work environment, learning opportunities, and personal and professional growth potential. We need someone with a set of strong work ethics, a commitment to learning, and personal values that align with our company's shared values. This position requires a highly professional individual to install, train, and support accounting software. Must have a strong accounting knowledge, the desire to work with people, and solve problems. Work with variety of clients and the latest technologies. Knowledge of Microsoft SQL and Great Plains' products a plus. Help us grow our company!

✦ **Employer type:** Great Plains Partner

✦ **Employment type:** Full Time

✦ **Career category:** Consulting

✦ **Location of career:** Seattle/Washington/USA

✦ **Travel:** Less Than 25 Percent

✦ **Education and experience:** Bachelor's Degree

✦ **Majors:** Accounting

✦ **Skills and knowledge:** Accounting, Consulting, Crystal Reports, Customer Service, FRx, Great Plains Dynamics, Great Plains Dynamics C/S+, Microsoft SQL Server, Microsoft Windows 95, Microsoft Windows NT, Novell, Project Management, Training

✦ **Certifications:** Certified Public Accountant, Dynamics C/S+ — SQL Certified Installation Specialist (CIS-SQL), Dynamics C/S+ Certified Installation Specialist (CIS-C/S+), Dynamics Certified Accounting Applications Specialist (CAAS), Dynamics Certified Installation Specialist (CIS-DYN). MCSE highly desirable.

✦ **Years of experience required:** 1–2

## E-commerce

One of the most appealing areas for SQL Server professionals is the e-commerce area. Depending on which way the venture capital winds are blowing, e-commerce is also one of the fastest growing SQL Server–related opportunities. Below I've listed the type of opportunity you might expect to find as an e-commerce specialist in the SQL Server community (from Aris in Seattle).

"The consulting firm has an immediate opening for the Web Application Architect to join our development staff in our growing downtown Seattle Solution Center. We help organizations maximize their competitive advantage through the planning and development of customized, high-end, interactive Web sites, applications, and eBusiness solutions. You will be asked to provide a high degree of development expertise throughout our projects, as well as technical oversight and design reviews development of complex Web applications for clients in accordance with their specifications and eBusiness visions. Coding tool-set skills should include senior level expertise in the majority of the following: SQL Server, Visual Basic, VBScript, Java, JavaScript, ASP, Windows NT, IIS, and OLE components to support technical design."

# Next Steps: MCDBA

If you jump into the world of SQL Server, you might soon discover that your MCSE, while strong in the infrastructure realm, doesn't prepare you for a full-blown SQL Server consulting career. The good news is that Microsoft understands that shortcoming and offers the Microsoft Certified Database Administrator (MCDBA) certification.

## Defining the MCDBA certification

This certification is geared toward technology professionals seeking to implement and administer Microsoft SQL Server and associated databases. Upon completion, Microsoft expects the MCDBA certificate holder to be able to do the following:

✦ Derive physical database designs

✦ Develop logical models

✦ Create physical databases

✦ Create data services using Transact-SQL

✦ Manage and maintain databases

✦ Configure and manage security

✦ Monitor and optimize databases

✦ Install and configure Microsoft SQL Server

While this certification is being promoted toward consultants, the MCDBA is also appropriate for database administrators, database architects, and database developers. It is Microsoft's stated desire that candidates have one year of SQL Server experience before starting the MCDBA track.

## Certification steps

Like the aspiring MCSE, an MCDBA candidate has to pass certification exams to achieve the title. You are required to pass three core exams and one optional exam. The exams, both core and elective, are shown in Table 21-1.

Note    Exam versions and requirements frequently change. Be sure to check the latest MCDBA certification requirements at www.microsoft.com.

### Table 21-1
### MCDBA Exams

| Exam | Title | Required/Optional |
|------|-------|-------------------|
| 70-215 | Installing, Configuring, and Administering Microsoft Windows 2000 Server | Core = Required |
| or | | |
| 70-240 | Microsoft Windows 2000 Accelerated Exam for MCPs Certified on Microsoft Windows NT 4.0 (if you qualify) | |
| 70-028 | Administering Microsoft SQL Server 7.0 | Core = Required |
| or | | |
| 70-228 | Installing, Configuring, and Administering Microsoft SQL Server 2000 Enterprise Edition | |
| 70-029 | Designing and Implementing Databases with Microsoft SQL Server 7.0 | Core = Required |
| or | | |
| 70-229 | Designing and Implementing Databases with Microsoft SQL Server 2000 Enterprise Edition | |
| 70-216 | Implementing and Administering a Microsoft Windows 2000 Network Infrastructure | Elective |
| 70-015 | Designing and Implementing Distributed Applications with Microsoft Visual C++ 6.0 | Elective |
| 70-019 | Designing and Implementing Data Warehouses with Microsoft SQL Server 7.0 | Elective |
| 70-155 | Designing and Implementing Distributed Applications with Microsoft Visual FoxPro 6.0 | Elective |
| 70-175 | Designing and Implementing Distributed Applications with Microsoft Visual Basic 6.0 | Elective |

## Courses

Consider taking the following Microsoft Official Curriculum (MOC) courses to both become an MCDBA and become proficient in SQL Server.

✦ **Course 1140:** Microsoft SQL Server 7.0 Overview

✦ **Course 832:** System Administration for Microsoft SQL Server 7.0

✦ **Course 833:** Implementing a Database in Microsoft SQL Server 7.0

✦ **Course 1131:** Upgrading to Microsoft SQL Server 7.0

✦ **Course 1502:** Designing and Implementing a Data Warehouse Using Microsoft SQL Server 7.0

## Summary

In this chapter, I presented database consulting opportunities for the MCSE consultant to consider. The specific focus was on Microsoft SQL Server. I discussed the importance of data to an organization, Microsoft SQL Server and its direct competitors, specific MCSE consulting opportunities related to SQL Server, and the MCDBA certification title.

✦    ✦    ✦

# Developer –
# Microsoft
# Visual Studio
# Consulting

**F**or many MCSE consultants, offering services in the developer community can be both professionally rewarding and profitable. I have known many MCSE consultants who have programming skills and have embraced the opportunity to serve clients as a developer in addition to being an engineer. Microsoft has a bundled product called Visual Studio that, for one price, provides you with Microsoft's leading developer tools. That is the purpose of this chapter, to define and appreciate what Visual Studio can do for you as an MCSE consultant. Note that I discuss Visual Studio with a focus on the Visual Studio.NET release in this chapter.

## The Value of Visual Studio

Historically, Visual Studio was and remains the most valuable gift selection when offered as a gratuity for MCSE consultants who participate in software product usability testing at Microsoft. Let me make a comment about Microsoft usability testing, which will help you better understand the gratuity process and the value of Visual Studio. Microsoft is always soliciting MCSE consultants to participate in usability testing for future product releases. I've done this several times at Microsoft's Redmond, Washington campus. Microsoft conducts similar testing at its other major facilities in North Carolina and the Dallas, Texas area.

**Tip**  If you would like to participate in Microsoft usability testing, attend Microsoft Direct Access and TechNet events, where usability testing forms are distributed. You can also contact your regional Microsoft sales office directly and ask about participating in usability tests.

Upon completion of one usability testing session, I selected Visual Studio as my gratuity from the gratuity list because Visual Studio was by far the most valuable software (it has a retail price in excess of $1,000). It's an old trick MCSE consultants play when participating in Microsoft usability tests. Score the most valuable software.

# Wearing the Developer Hat

Before jumping into the details on Visual Studio.NET, which is a suite of developer tools, I want to explain the scope of the developer consulting opportunity. I'll focus on your developer mindset, long-term opportunities, and full billing schedules in the context of the developer community. And no discussion of Visual Studio.NET is complete without a look at the Visual Studio development methodology.

## Are you wired that way?

Either you are or you aren't wired to be a developer. After flunking out of C programming, I concluded that developers are born that way, not created afterward. No matter how hard I tried to learn programming, I just didn't get it. Instead, I took up Novell networks as an infrastructure specialist. Be true to yourself when assessing your gifts. Perhaps you're one that can do both developer work and infrastructure work.

## In the long run

Much like database developers, programmers enjoy nice long-term assignments. It's clearly a different consulting model than the one under which most MCSE consultants operate. MCSE consultants typically visit multiple sites in any given week, billing discrete chunks of hours here and there. However, developers often focus on one project at a time and typically spend the entire week at one client site.

## No bench time

While infrastructure consulting for the MCSE consultant can be expected to have its peaks and valleys, I've noticed that the developer community doesn't typically suffer from bench time (also known as downtime). It seems developers, often working through contract houses, have projects lined up in a row. Clearly the combination of long-term engagements with no downtime means a very high utilization rate.

## Ask the Guru

This e-mail was one that I received from a foreign reader from India who was considering doing both networking and programming. He is referring to one of my columns in Microsoft Certified Professional Magazine. It is a fitting discussion for this chapter on the developer community and the discussion on Visual Studio.

*Dear Sir,*

*I am a graduate in Electronics and Communications and recently got my MCSE certification. Your article on salary negotiation, "You Can Get Whatever You Want," was very informative and helpful to the unemployed. Thus, I thought you would be the right person to help me take the right steps toward a bright career. I would be very thankful if you could do this. Sir, I have developed an interest in both the networking and programming fields. Now I find myself on a path which is split in two. One leads to the networking and the other to the programming world. Both the networking technologies and hardware, and the creativity in programming, equally fascinate me. Which is best for an unemployed graduate like me? Which field has the brighter future and which would be more lucrative? Which field offers more scope for developing a career? Hoping to get a career-guiding response from you.*

*Regards,*

*Kusha D.*

*India*

Dear Kusha,

Thank you for your e-mail and your great story. It sounds like you've worked hard to get where you're at as a technology professional. Regarding your central question about which career path (programming or networking) is better, I can't offer a simple answer. You will need to be the one that makes that decision. However, I can suggest that you're not worse off if you consider both paths (even though I agree there is a fork in the road between the two disciplines after a certain level of competency). I have believed for some time that there is a role for someone to be both an MCSE in networking and an MCSD (the solution developer certification from Microsoft) with a focus on programming (perhaps with Microsoft's Visual Studio bundle). It may be that this dual skill set of yours, which is very rare indeed, could land you a position in management, allowing you to participate in both realms and oversee staff members (if that appeals to you).

Regarding pay rates and so on, it just depends on the opportunities you have in your region. For example, in the Pacific Northwest (United States) where I live, I have seen the following situations. Standout experienced MCSE consultants with a focus on networking and infrastructure can earn in the upper five figures to low six figures (for a mean or average compensation of around $100,000 per year). MCSE consultants with less developed skills earn less (of course). Programmers and developers can typically match those compensation levels as consultants, so that part of the equation is a draw. However, take an

*Continued*

## Visual Studio.NET development life cycle

While you and I are wearing our developer hats, kindly allow me to present the Microsoft .NET development methodology, as shown in Figure 22-1, which includes Visual Studio.NET. It's presented in the classic life cycle perspective.

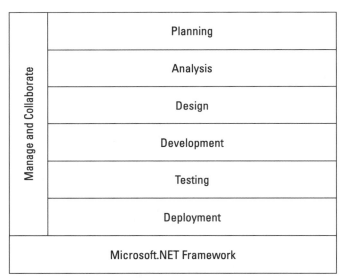

**Figure 22-1:** Microsoft .NET development life cycle, which includes Visual Studio.NET

# Defining Microsoft Visual Studio.NET

Simply stated, Visual Studio.NET is the BackOffice bundle for developers. True, Visual Studio.NET doesn't have any actual BackOffice applications, but it's akin to the way business applications are bundled with BackOffice. Instead, Visual Studio.NET bundles developer tools and toys.

Whether Microsoft designed it to be this way or not, I've promoted the Visual Studio.NET bundle in the following context: It provides all the tools you need to be the next Amazon.com. With the components listed below, a powerful personal computer, lots of know-how, and even more gumption, there's really nothing holding you back from being the next dot-com success story! Someday you'll see someone say they owe all of their success to Visual Studio.NET. Visual Studio.NET is seen in Figure 22-2.

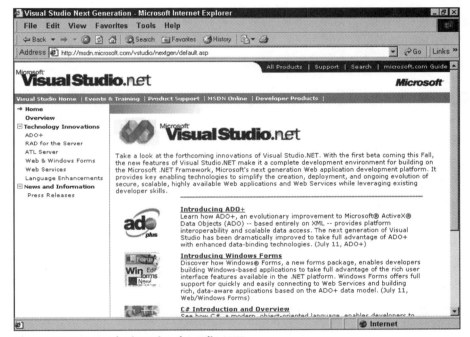

**Figure 22-2:** Introducing Visual Studio.NET

## Specifics

As of this writing, the final feature set for Visual Studio.NET is in the process of being frozen, but in Table 22-1, I list the Professional and Enterprise Edition features for Visual Studio 6.0.

| Table 22-1 Visual Studio 6.0 Components | | |
| --- | --- | --- |
| **Component** | **Professional Edition** | **Enterprise Edition** |
| Visual Basic 6.0 | X | X |
| Visual C++ 6.0 | X | X |
| Visual FoxPro 6.0 | X | X |
| Visual InterDev 6.0 | X | X |
| Visual J++ 6.0 | X | X |
| MSDN Library | X | X |
| Windows NT 4.0 Option Pack | X | X |
| Professional Visual Database Tools | X | X |
| Windows 2000 Developer's Readiness Kit | X | X |
| Microsoft Data Engine (MSDE) for Visual Studio | X | X |
| Visual Studio Installer | X | X |
| Complete debugging support | X | X |
| Rapid application development (RAD) Web development | X | X |
| Visual SourceSafe 6.0 | | X |
| Microsoft BackOffice Server 4.5 Developer Edition | | X |
| Enterprise Visual Database Tools | | X |
| Visual Modeler | | X |
| Visual Studio Analyzer | | X |
| Visual Component Manager | | X |
| Lifecycle Support | | X |

In Table 22-2, I list the features that are announced for Visual Studio.NET.

### Table 22-2
### New Components in Visual Studio.NET

| Component | Description |
| --- | --- |
| ADO+ | An improved version of Microsoft ActiveX Data Objects. |
| Windows Forms | A new forms package that allows developers to reuse forms in building Windows-based applications. |
| C# | This next-generation C programming language brings rapid Web development to the C programming language. |
| RAD improvements | Server-side RAD improvements. |

## Architecture

Visual Studio.NET is being promoted by Microsoft as a rich set of tips, tricks, and tools to rapidly develop enterprise-scale applications for the Web. The Visual Studio.NET architecture is displayed in Figure 22-3.

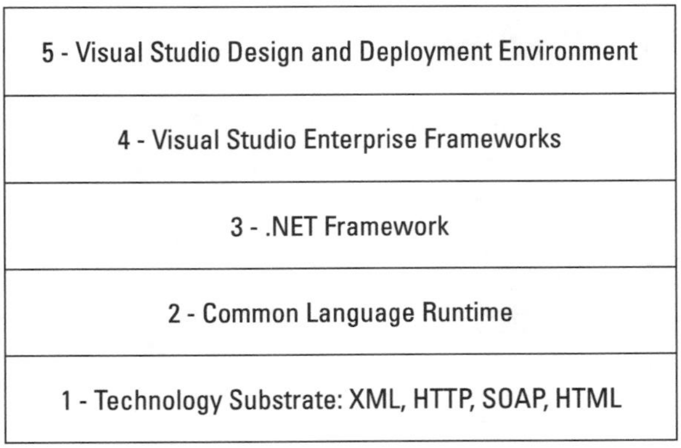

```
┌─────────────────────────────────────────────────────┐
│ 5 - Visual Studio Design and Deployment Environment   │
├─────────────────────────────────────────────────────┤
│        4 - Visual Studio Enterprise Frameworks        │
├─────────────────────────────────────────────────────┤
│                 3 - .NET Framework                    │
├─────────────────────────────────────────────────────┤
│              2 - Common Language Runtime              │
├─────────────────────────────────────────────────────┤
│    1 - Technology Substrate: XML, HTTP, SOAP, HTML    │
└─────────────────────────────────────────────────────┘
```

**Figure 22-3:** The modular architecture of Visual Studio.NET

Layer one of the architecture reflects Microsoft's use of open Internet standards. Layer two is a common infrastructure for loosely coupled objects. Layer three is a class framework (which Microsoft claims is "simplified") that serves as the building blocks for forms and data. Layer four is architectural templates and design patterns with policy enforcement. Layer five is the visual designer's drag-and-drop environment.

# Competitive Analysis

Proving the Justice Department right again in its antitrust litigation against Microsoft is the fact that there are few competitors for Visual Studio.NET. In conducting my research for this chapter, I found that Borland (www.borland.com) with its JBuilder 4 visual development suite, seen in Figure 22-4, is the closest competitor to Visual Studio.NET.

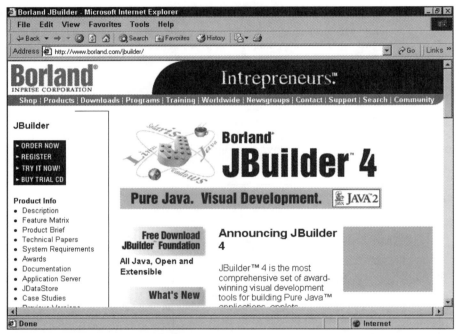

**Figure 22-4:** Borland's JBuilder 4

JBuilder 4 contains the following selected features, arrayed in Table 22-3 by version (Foundation, Professional, and Enterprise). If you visit Borland's Web site, you can see the latest features for the JBuilder product.

| Table 22-3 JBuilder 4 Feature Set | | | |
|---|---|---|---|
| *Feature* | *Foundation* | *Professional* | *Enterprise* |
| **Developer Productivity** | | | |
| 100% Pure Java applications, applets, and JavaBeans with no proprietary code or markers | X | X | X |
| Visual Java 2 two-way designers and wizards for drag-and-drop JFC/Swing application development | X | X | X |
| 100% pure Java IDE hosted on Java 2 SDK 1.3 | X | X | X |
| XML-based project manager with new JPX project file format | X | X | X |
| Advanced syntax highlighting for XML, WML, IDL, JSP, and XSL, CSS style sheets | | X | X |
| **Debugging** | | | |
| Debugging of any JDK with Java 2 JPDA debug API support | X | X | X |
| ToolTip Expression Insight with detailed structure view of member instances | | X | X |
| Multiplatform and Remote debugging for debugging complex distributed applications on a variety of platforms | | | X |
| Thread deadlock, stalls, and race conditions detection on precise error location | | | X |
| Native JSP debugging with full breakpoint, watches, evaluation, and context information support | | | X |

*Continued*

| Table 22-3 (continued) | | | |
| --- | --- | --- | --- |
| *Feature* | *Foundation* | *Professional* | *Enterprise* |
| ***Integrated Team Development*** | | | |
| Revision browser for displaying history information of source versions | X | X | X |
| Visual source-level display of differences between source revisions | | X | X |
| Conflict resolution for reconciling source versions between workspace and repository | | | X |
| Integrated Version Control System with support for update, merge, add, and check-out | | | X |
| ***Rapid Internet Development*** | | | |
| Full support for Servlet 2.2/JSP 1.1 standard | | X | X |
| Executes JSP and Servlet in the built-in Web server | | X | X |
| InternetBeans Express presentation components for rapidly creating Web-driven Internet applications based on DataExpress database components | | X | X |
| CodeInsight, ErrorInsight, ToolTip Evaluation for JavaServer Pages (JSP) embedded Java | | | X |
| Remote execution and debugging of Servlet | | | X |
| ***Open Database Support*** | | | |
| DataExpress data access components with JDBC database connectivity, including support for Master-Detail relationships, Picklists, Lookups, Multiple Table Joins, and Transactions | | X | X |

| Feature | Foundation | Professional | Enterprise |
|---|---|---|---|
| **Open Database Support** | | | |
| Pure Java JDataStore 4 Development License for high performance data caching and compact persistence of data, objects, and arbitrary files | | X | X |
| DataExpress Source Code for control and flexibility in building your Pure Java database applications | | | X |
| **Rapid J2EE compliant development and deployment** | | | |
| Visual creation of Enterprise JavaBeans (EJBs), 100% compliant to the latest J2EE standard | | | X |
| Two-way editing of deployment descriptor for home and remote interface, container transactions, security roles, and data sources | | | X |
| Entity Bean Modeler to create Container Managed Persistence (CMP) and Bean Managed Persistence (BMP) entity beans including home and remote interfaces as well as primary key classes | | | X |
| Dynamic Hot-deploy, to deploy/ undeploy/redeploy EJBs to container without shutting down or restarting | | | X |
| Inprise Application Server 4.1 Development License, a complete EJB 1.1 implementation | | | X |
| Integrated WebLogic Server 5.1 development support | | | X |

# Case Study — Decoding the Code

Are you a coder and you just don't know it yet? Perhaps the developer track is your calling as an MCSE consultant. Here is a quick test of your code aptitude. Look at the sample code below and determine if you can understand what is going on. If you can, consider adding a developer angle to your MCSE consulting practice. If not, perhaps you're better off focusing on networking and infrastructure matters. Here is the code sample:

```
#include <windows.h>
#include <shellapi.h>
#include <shlobj.h>
#include "CabView.h"
#include "Cabinet.h"
#include "Resource.h"

LPSTR lpExtractPath = NULL;

//
//   BrowseCallbackProc - Callback function for
SHBrowseForFolder
//
INT CALLBACK BrowseCallbackProc (HWND hWnd, UINT uMsg, LPARAM
lParam, LPARAM lpData)
{
    switch (uMsg)
    {
        case BFFM_INITIALIZED:
            SendMessage (hWnd, BFFM_SETSELECTION, TRUE,
lpData);
            break;
    }
    return 0;
}


//
//   CabView_GetDestinationPath - Prompts user to select a
destination
//                                folder for extracted files.
Uses
//                                SHBrowseForFolder.
//
VOID WINAPI CabView_GetDestinationPath (HWND hWnd, LPSTR
lpDestination)
{
    CHAR szDisplayName[MAX_PATH] = "";
    BROWSEINFO bi = {0};
    LPITEMIDLIST pidl = NULL;
```

```
    bi.hwndOwner = hWnd;
    bi.pidlRoot = NULL;
    bi.pszDisplayName = szDisplayName;
    bi.lpszTitle = "Select the destination folder for extracted
files.";
    bi.ulFlags = BIF_RETURNONLYFSDIRS;
    bi.lpfn = BrowseCallbackProc;
    bi.lParam = (LPARAM) lpDestination;

    pidl = SHBrowseForFolder (&bi);
    if (pidl != NULL)
    {
        SHGetPathFromIDList (pidl, lpDestination);

        LPMALLOC pMalloc = NULL;
        SHGetMalloc (&pMalloc);
        pMalloc->Free ((LPVOID) pMalloc);
        pMalloc->Release ();
    }
}


//
//  CabView_IsFileInFileList - Called to determine if the
current file being
//                           examined in the FDICopy function
is in the list
//                           of files to be extracted.
//
BOOL CDECL CabView_IsFileInFileList (LPSTR lpFilename, LPSTR
*lpFileList)
{
    UINT nIndex = 0;

    while (lpFileList[nIndex] != NULL)
    {
        if (lstrcmpi (lpFilename, lpFileList[nIndex]) == 0)
            return TRUE;
        nIndex++;
    }
    return FALSE;
}


//
//  CabView_ExtractNotifyCallback - Called by FDICopy to notify
the
//                           of file operations on a CAB
file
```

```
//                                    or to provide information
about
//                                    the CAB file.
//
//                                    Used here to extract a list
of
//                                    files from a CAB file
//
INT CDECL CabView_ExtractNotifyCallback (FDINOTIFICATIONTYPE
fdint, PFDINOTIFICATION pfdin)
{
    LPCABINET_EXTRACT_INFO pcei = (LPCABINET_EXTRACT_INFO)
pfdin->pv;
    LPSTR *lpFileList = pcei->lpFileList;
    CHAR szFileToCreate[MAX_PATH] = "";

    switch (fdint)
    {
        case fdintCOPY_FILE:
            if (CabView_IsFileInFileList (pfdin->psz1,
lpFileList) == FALSE)
                return 0;

            // Create the file to extract to.
            wsprintf (szFileToCreate, "%s\\%s", pcei-
>lpDestinationDir, pfdin->psz1);
            return Cabinet_CreateFile (szFileToCreate, O_CREAT
| O_RDWR | O_BINARY, S_IWRITE);

        case fdintCLOSE_FILE_INFO:
            if (Cabinet_CloseFile (pfdin->hf) == 0)
                return 1;
            return 0;
            break;
    }
    return 1;
}
```

# A Visual Studio.NET Example

To fully explore Visual Studio.NET is a book in itself. Being solidly from the infrastructure side of the MCSE community, I'm not qualified to speak in great depth about many Visual Studio.NET features. However, I can speak as an authority on one component, Visual SourceSafe, shown in Figure 22-5.

I use Visual SourceSafe every day as a writer to maintain version control of my documents. My documents are my lifeblood in the same way code is to a coder. I simply can't afford a version control mistake. When I'm working on a document, it needs to be the most current version. Visual SourceSafe provides this capability and more, such as the ability to roll back to older document editions.

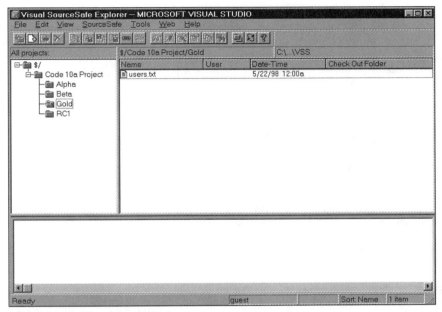

**Figure 22-5:** Visual SourceSafe

Visual SourceSafe is a sophisticated library and document management program. It allows a team working on a development project to check in their source code to the "safe" (hence the product name SourceSafe) for safekeeping. Later, the developers may check out their source code to work on again knowing that SourceSafe has managed version control issues. As part of the version control management capabilities, SourceSafe keeps track of who checked code (or documents) in or out of the "safe" (which is a storage folder on a server machine). If for some reason you need to get back to a prior version of code or a document (before a mistake was made, for example), Visual SourceSafe supports this capability. More importantly, it's a way for program managers to control and manage the coding and document assets. Developers and writers who use Visual SourceSafe appreciate the order it brings to the saving and revising process. Plus, properly implemented, it means that the coders and writers don't have to worry about their work being properly backed up. If it's in Visual SourceSafe, the most current version and all prior versions are backed up.

If I were to sum up Visual SourceSafe in two words, the words would be *version control.* As a writer, you no longer need to have some funky naming convention like Chapter1.rev2.doc to maintain version control. Visual SourceSafe keeps the original document name (for example, Chapter1.doc) and manages all of the version control issues, even among teammates working on the same documents. The same capabilities apply to coding.

**Tip**    Even if you have little need for Visual Studio.NET in your professional life, you should strongly consider implementing the Visual SourceSafe component. I can think of numerous areas where an MCSE consultant benefits from Visual SourceSafe, including managing the versions of consulting proposals that go out the door. If you have ever sent out the wrong proposal version to a client, Visual SourceSafe is for you.

# Visual Studio Integration Program

One early step you should take if you plan to add the Visual Studio.NET arrow to your MCSE consulting quiver is the Visual Studio Integration Program. This is a like-minded community of developers in the Visual Studio space who enjoy a special relationship with Microsoft, including additional support such as free Software Development Kits (SDKs), business development opportunities, and enhanced developer support. The Visual Studio Integration Program is shown in Figure 22-6 and can be accessed at www.msdn.microsoft.com/vstudio/vsip.

**Figure 22-6:** Microsoft maintains a Web page with information on the Visual Studio Integration Program

The following firms have pledged support for the Visual Studio Integration Program in word, deed, dollars, services, and products. That's good news for the MCSE consultant with a keen interest in Visual Studio.NET.

✦ ActiveState

✦ AppForge

✦ ASNA

✦ Cast

✦ Compaq

✦ ComputerBoards, Inc.

✦ Compuware

✦ Continuus

✦ Elsinore Technologies

✦ Icras

✦ InstallShield

✦ Intel

✦ Liant

✦ MERANT

✦ MKS

✦ Mutek

✦ National Instruments

✦ POET Software

✦ Rational Software Corporation

✦ Seagate Software

✦ Starbase

✦ Stingray

✦ SuperNova

✦ TowerJ

✦ WebPutty

# MCSD Designation

As you know, many MCSE consultants don't stop with the MCSE designation but start collecting vendor certifications like fine wine, present company included. Some MCSEs move on to obtain the Cisco certification or Novell certifications. Others are content to add more Microsoft certifications.

Assuming you have an interest in both Visual Studio.NET and earning additional certifications, the Microsoft Certified Solution Developer (MCSD), affectionately known in certain social circles as "The Big D," is for you. This is the Microsoft certification that is in alignment with Visual Studio.NET.

## Specifics

The MCSD is the certification for technology professionals who design and develop business solutions with Microsoft programming tools such as Visual Studio.NET. The typical certification candidates, according to Microsoft, include the following:

- ✦ Software engineers
- ✦ Software application engineers
- ✦ Software developers
- ✦ Technical consultants (that's you, the MCSE consultant)

Aside from the title, the benefits include a one-year subscription to the Microsoft Developer Network (MSDN), special offers, a wallet card, logon pin, and peer recognition.

**Tip**    Speaking of the MSDN subscription, you can elevate your MCSD benefit to receive a $500 discount on MSDN Universal. I'd recommend you take this option instead of the basic MSDN for free. MSDN gives you free copies of the Microsoft family of software products in the business, servers, and developer areas. You also get comprehensive technical support without charge.

## Exams

You must pass six certification exams to be MCSD certified. The exams, three of which are required core exams, are presented as follows. For starters, you will need to pass the following three core exams:

- ✦ **Exam 70-016:** Designing and Implementing Desktop Applications with Microsoft Visual C++ 6.0
- ✦ **Exam 70-156:** Designing and Implementing Desktop Applications with Microsoft Visual FoxPro 6.0
- ✦ **Exam 70-176:** Designing and Implementing Desktop Applications with Microsoft Visual Basic 6.0

You must then pass one distributed applications development exam from this list of three:

✦ **Exam 70-015:** Designing and Implementing Distributed Applications with Microsoft Visual C++ 6.0

✦ **Exam 70-155:** Designing and Implementing Distributed Applications with Microsoft Visual FoxPro 6.0

✦ **Exam 70-175:** Designing and Implementing Distributed Applications with Microsoft Visual Basic 6.0

You must then pass the solution architecture exam titled: Exam 70-100: Analyzing Requirements and Defining Solution Architectures

Finally, you will need to select and pass one exam from this list of electives:

✦ **Exam 70-015:** Designing and Implementing Distributed Applications with Microsoft Visual C++ 6.0

✦ **Exam 70-016:** Designing and Implementing Desktop Applications with Microsoft Visual C++ 6.0

✦ **Exam 70-019:** Designing and Implementing Data Warehouses with Microsoft SQL Server 7.0

✦ **Exam 70-029:** Designing and Implementing Databases with Microsoft SQL Server 7.0

✦ **Exam 70-229:** Designing and Implementing Databases with Microsoft SQL Server 2000 Enterprise Edition

✦ **Exam 70-055:** Designing and Implementing Web Sites with Microsoft FrontPage 98

✦ **Exam 70-057:** Designing and Implementing Commerce Solutions with Microsoft Site Server 3.0, Commerce Edition

✦ **Exam 70-091:** Designing and Implementing Solutions with Microsoft Office 2000 and Microsoft Visual Basic for Applications

✦ **Exam 70-105:** Designing and Implementing Collaborative Solutions with Microsoft Outlook 2000 and Microsoft Exchange Server 5.5

✦ **Exam 70-152:** Designing and Implementing Web Solutions with Microsoft Visual InterDev 6.0

✦ **Exam 70-155:** Designing and Implementing Distributed Applications with Microsoft Visual FoxPro 6.0

✦ **Exam 70-156:** Designing and Implementing Desktop Applications with Microsoft Visual FoxPro 6.0

✦ **Exam 70-175:** Designing and Implementing Distributed Applications with Microsoft Visual Basic 6.0

✦ **Exam 70-176:** Designing and Implementing Desktop Applications with Microsoft Visual Basic 6.0

## Courses

There are numerous courses you can take to prepare for the MCSD exams. However, I want to list a couple of Microsoft Official Curriculum (MOC) courses that are Visual Studio–compliant. The other MCSD courses are detailed at `www.microsoft.com/train_cert`.

✦ **1013:** Mastering Microsoft Visual Basic 6 Development

✦ **1633:** Building Data-Centric Business Applications with Microsoft Visual Basic 6

✦ **1582:** Building Web Applications Using Microsoft Visual InterDev 6

✦ **1011:** Mastering MFC Fundamentals Using Microsoft Visual C++

✦ **1298:** Mastering Distributed Applications Design Using Microsoft Visual Studio

✦ **1303:** Mastering Microsoft Visual Basic 6 Fundamentals

✦ **1016:** Mastering Enterprise Development Using Microsoft Visual Basic 6

✦ **1015:** Mastering MFC Development Using Microsoft Visual C++ 6

✦ **1608:** Designing Business Solutions

✦ **1629:** Building Applications for Microsoft Windows CE with Visual Basic 6

✦ **1587:** Introduction to Programming with Microsoft Visual Basic 6

**Tip**

Just look at the byline for many of the writers for *Microsoft Certified Professional Magazine* (`www.mcpmag.com`) and you will see that many of them have added the MCSD title to their MCSE designation. It's something you should strongly consider doing if it makes sense.

## Summary

This chapter tackled the Big D—the developer side of the Microsoft community. A surprisingly large number of MCSEs also attain the MCSD certification and work with Visual Studio.NET. Because of that fact, offering Visual Studio.NET consulting services is a legitimate category to consider for your MCSE consulting practice. This chapter covered several topics defining the developer community and the MCSD program, defining Visual Studio and its .NET release, and how the SourceSafe application works inside of Visual Studio. This chapter also looked at a competitor of Visual Studio, the JBuilder product line from Borland, and discussed the Visual Studio Integration Program.

✦     ✦     ✦

# Dot-com Consulting

I f you thrive on challenge, risk, and volatility, then dot-com consulting is for you. Though it seems like most businesses have expanded to the Internet in this day and age, according to Prodigy Communications, only 40 percent of small and medium-sized businesses (the SORG and MORG markets I refer to in numerous other chapters in the book) have Web sites. The dot-com consulting field is ripe for the picking.

The Prodigy Communications study continues with analysis of the 60 percent of SORG and MORG businesses without Web sites. Nearly 70 percent of companies without Web sites would use such a site for promoting products and services to customers. Just over 55 percent of the same group would sell products or services over the Web. Finally, just under half (48 percent) would use a Web site to promote better customer service.

MCSEs are at the epicenter of opportunity when it comes to dot-com consulting. You will see in this chapter that you're in alignment with Microsoft's new twenty-first century thinking — the dot-NET strategy (.NET).

## Microsoft .NET Strategy

If you listened to Ty Carlson, Microsoft's program manager for .NET at the Fall 2000 TechMentor conference (sponsored by *Microsoft Certified Professional Magazine*), you would have gotten an earful on Microsoft's organizational paradigm shift to .NET. You would have also been in good company if you didn't quite grasp what Microsoft was really trying to do (Ty admitted he didn't get it for the longest time either).

The paradigm shift is away from PC-centric computing to Internet-centric computing. Today, that thinking is meaningful to developers who are working with new tools such as eXtensible Markup Language (XML), the Simple Object Access Protocol (SOAP), and a new version of the C programming language called C Sharp (which is written as C#). Today, the focus is on middleware applications that facilitate Internet-based computing such as application service providers (ASP).

Where will MCSE consultants see the .NET strategy in action? First, there is the rebranding of Microsoft Servers from the BackOffice moniker to .NET Enterprise servers. Microsoft defines it as being built from the ground up for third generation Internet support. This includes ASPs who will rent or lease applications and services to clients over the Internet. Microsoft believes that software will be delivered as a service. The .NET Enterprise Server family includes some familiar faces:

✦ **Microsoft Application Center 2000** — This tool facilitates the deployment and management of high-availability Windows 2000–based Web applications.

✦ **Microsoft BizTalk Server 2000** — This tool set coordinates business processes and Web services inside and between organizations.

✦ **Microsoft Commerce Server 2000** — This solution is used to rapidly deploy online businesses.

✦ **Microsoft Exchange 2000** — This is the good old e-mail and collaboration solution you've come to love.

✦ **Microsoft Host Integration Server 2000** — This is used for host system connectivity.

✦ **Microsoft Internet Security and Acceleration Server 2000** — This is the firewall and Web-caching solution from Microsoft.

✦ **Microsoft Mobile Information 2001 Server** — A tool for extending the .NET paradigm to wireless devices.

✦ **Microsoft SQL Server 2000** — The enterprise-level and Web-enabled relational database product.

Microsoft .NET Servers are displayed in Figure 23-1.

MCSEs will also see .NET in action with Blackcomb, which likely will follow Whistler (the code name for Microsoft's next generation of operating system) in late 2002/early 2003. The word on the inside is that Blackcomb, code named after a popular Canadian ski resort, will be named Windows.NET and will be a major rework of Windows 2000.

My take on the .NET initiative is that it's another MCSE continuing employment opportunity. After you've satisfied your clients with the current offering of

Microsoft solutions, you'll get to come back in a couple of years and do it all again. That's clearly the good news. The bad news is that you'll need to satisfy a whole new round of MCSE recertification requirements. For more information on .NET, see the following Microsoft Web site: `www.microsoft.com/servers/net`. At that Web site, you'll find countless valuable white papers on Web business applications and so on.

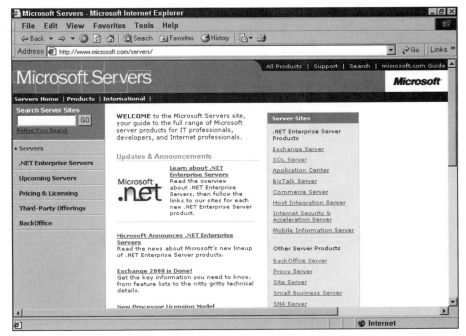

**Figure 23-1:** Microsoft .NET Enterprise Servers

# Dot-com Methodologies

If you share the same vision of the future as Microsoft with its .NET strategy and you've turned your MCSE consulting practice on a dime, everything from this point forward is Internet.

Will the tried-and-true methodologies you've developed as an MCSE consultant work for you in this new consulting role? Perhaps. However, just in case the lateral transfer of MCSE consulting methodologies doesn't go as smoothly as you'd like, I'll share two dot-com consulting methodologies that might help.

## Leading Way Knowledge Systems

I met with James Li, Ph.D. — the CEO and founder of Leading Way Knowledge Systems — at the Online Learning 2000 conference in Denver, Colorado. His story was compelling and had a practical application for MCSE consultants seeking to go dot-com. Dr. Li had positioned his firm not only to serve clients in a consulting capacity, but also to license his Knowledge Management methodology to other consulting firms. In effect, one of his services is to consult to consulting firms seeking to become dot-com consultants. Here is Dr. Li's Knowledge Management methodology, which he freely shared with me during our interview for the purposes of presenting it in this book. The methodology is first presented in Figure 23-2, and the details follow.

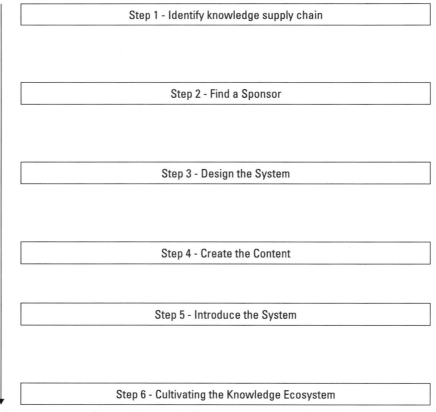

**Leading Way's Knowledge Management
Dot-Com Consulting Methodology**

Step 1 - Identify knowledge supply chain

Step 2 - Find a Sponsor

Step 3 - Design the System

Step 4 - Create the Content

Step 5 - Introduce the System

Step 6 - Cultivating the Knowledge Ecosystem

**Figure 23-2:** Leading Way's Knowledge Management methodology

## Step 1 — Identify knowledge supply chains

✦ Audit knowledge assets and delivery channels.

✦ Identify the current knowledge production process.

✦ Document costs of the current process.

✦ Measure the time-to-market of the current process.

✦ Map the knowledge capture process.

✦ **Solution** — One integrated Knowledge Management and eLearning system.

## Step 2 — Find a sponsor

✦ Identify sponsors who can ensure your success.

✦ Seek to understand the psychology of your sponsor.

✦ Consider the Technology Adoption Life Cycle. (This is Dr Li's way of presenting his vision of the life cycle for technology adoption.)

✦ Develop psychographic profiles of your sponsors.

✦ Identify the innovators, early adopters, and early majority in your organization.

## Step 3 — Design the system

✦ Ask, "Who are the users?" (Here Dr. Li asks you to investigate who the users of the system are.)

✦ Ask, "What are the critical components?" (Here Dr. Li asks you to identify what the critical components of the system are.)

✦ Draw up a feature checklist for inclusion in the design spec.

## Step 4 — Create the content

✦ Manufacture or craft knowledge. (Dr. Li's methodology calls for what he terms knowledge manufacturing or crafting.)

✦ Ask, "What is the Knowledge Factory?" (Dr. Li has applied the analogy of a factory to knowledge management by creating the term *Knowledge Factory*.)

✦ Create knowledge objects. (According to Dr. Li's methodology, the process of knowledge manufacturing creates knowledge objects. In this context, knowledge objects are identifiable information items.)

✦ Examine the principles of content creation. (Dr. Li's methodology is driven by principles, in this case the principles of content creation.)

✦ Coordinate content creation process and team. (Essential to Dr. Li's methodology is the creative process and the team that work together.)

### Step 5 — Introduce the system

✦ Assess your organization's readiness for change. (Dr. Li recognizes that his methodology, when applied, will cause change in the organization. Some of the changes are unknown in quantity and scope. Thus, Dr. Li challenges you to ask if your organization is ready for change.)

✦ Assess your organization and yourself.

✦ Design system introduction and adoption programs.

### Step 6 — Cultivating the knowledge ecosystem

✦ Perform maintenance.

✦ Appreciate the role of knowledge manager. (Dr Li believes a new professional role is created as a central part of the knowledge management philosophy, the position of the knowledge manager.)

✦ Evaluate. Improve. Grow.

**Note**   I have recast Dr. Li's Knowledge Management methodology to be more descriptive and conversational in the context of this chapter. The actual methodology is addressed in great detail in Dr. Li's workshops.

Dr. Li has a one-day seminar well worth attending that presents the methodology displayed above in much greater detail. At the end of your day, you'll have a dot-com consulting methodology ready to be implemented.

Leading Way, shown in Figure 23-3, can be reached at `www.leadingway.com`.

## www.workz.com

A ferryboat ride away from my home, in downtown Seattle, resides workz.com. This firm, whom I've had the great pleasure to meet first hand, confirms all that I thought was good about the Web. Workz.com, reached at `www.workz.com`, is shown in Figure 23-4.

This company has positioned itself to be a one-stop portal for small businesses seeking to become an online business quickly. The site offers free information and premium content for a modest subscription fee. Specifically, workz.com provides small businesses with a one-stop resource for marketing and managing a Web site, maximizing online e-commerce opportunities. The site includes how-to checklists, utilities, resources, and references needed to build, manage, promote, and maintain a profitable online business. A sample of its wares is shown in Figure 23-5.

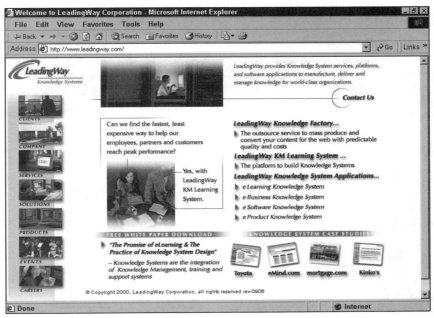

**Figure 23-3:** Leading Way's Web site

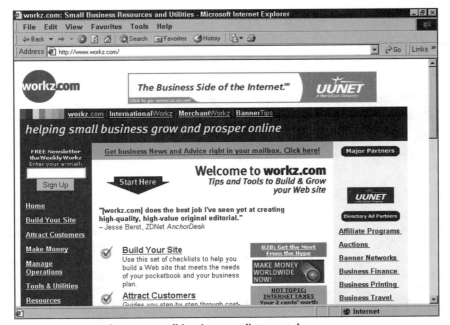

**Figure 23-4:** Workz.com small business online portal

**Figure 23-5:** Workz.com generously shares its Web implementation methodology at its Web site.

Visiting a site such as workz.com can save you hours in defining and developing your dot-com methodologies and MCSE consulting practice.

## Guest Sermon — YnotLearn

I asked Betsy Harrison at the Online Learning 2000 conference to write up a description of a dot-com system consultancy she represents in her role as public affairs consultant. I wanted to find out what the business model of a successful firm in the online world is and what lessons can be learned. She offers the following insights by both introducing YnotLearn and sharing a case study.

*Thanks, Harry! This is about e-learning, a large and growing segment in the dot-com commerce world. My client, based in Virginia Beach, Virginia, YnotLearn.Com, LLC, is a new provider of online learning solutions for organizations. The company supports developing and implementing training solutions in its client organizations through easy-to-access and easy-to-use tools for eLearning content development, maintenance, assessment, and management. YnotLearn provides eLearning infrastructure, tools, and services and is the only eLearning firm today providing a single integrated system that is completely browser based. Its goal is to supply centralized training management for organizations of all sizes on a one-stop-shop basis or customized by specific components.*

## Products

*My client's products include the following:*

✦ **YnotAssess**—*to identify knowledge weaknesses and assess attitudes and opinions.*

✦ **YnotPublish**—*to create courseware to address those knowledge weaknesses.*

✦ **YnotEdit**—*to update that courseware as business changes demand.*

✦ **YnotManage**—*to manage the learning environment, control access, and monitor student progress.*

✦ **YnotServices**—*to assist the client during implementation of the YnotLearn solution and to ensure full utilization of the learning system and its features. Via its services group, YnotLearn can host the administration, hardware and software maintenance, and logistics of enterprise training. In addition, YnotLearn can create specific curricula and courseware and develop interfaces for the efficient flow of training data to and from corporate human resource information systems (HRIS) and/or enterprise resource planning (ERP) systems.*

## Outsourcing

*For those customers who wish to outsource all or a portion of their eLearning program, YnotLearn is prepared to offer a turnkey solution including any or all of the following services:*

✦ *Web site and application hosting with full system maintenance and support*

✦ *Integration between YNL and third-party courseware*

✦ *Electronic interface to existing human resource management and ERP systems*

✦ *Custom courseware development from scratch*

✦ *Courseware conversion from classroom, video, CBT, CD-ROM*

✦ *Software installation and configuration on customer servers*

✦ *International language courseware and software conversions/translations*

✦ *Job task analyses and automated employee profiling*

## Case Study

*The ABC Corporation has a comprehensive line of products that are represented by 500 geographically based sales representatives, domestic and international. The company has identified the need to improve product knowledge among its sales force. The ABC Corporation takes advantage of their new Learning Management System (LMS) purchased from and implemented by YnotLearn with YnotServices. Using YnotLearn's YnotManage and YnotPublish toolsets, ABC's training department, along with YnotServices, develops the specific product knowledge curricula encompassing the mission and goals of the ABC Corporation. The curriculum is interactive and feature rich, yielding a dynamic training process delivered via the Web.*

*Continued*

*Continued*

With YnotManage in place, ABC determines a specific timeline and level of expertise that all sales representatives need to obtain. ABC utilizes YnotAssess to develop a product knowledge assessment to administer to all field sales representatives via the Web. YnotManage is utilized to administer and track the responses from all salespeople. From the assessment, each individual's knowledge gap is determined by the YnotManage LMS, and each individual is automatically enrolled into the specific curriculum needed to reach the necessary level of expertise concerning all products.

Since the training is Web-based and self-paced, each representative has the flexibility to access the product training on his or her own schedule. As the reps complete sections of their training, YnotManage automatically administers the necessary testing to confirm the proper level of expertise has been met. During the entire process, YnotManage tracks the progress of all reps, giving ABC full reporting capability. Through the communication components offered with YnotLearn's solution, each rep has the ability to communicate with training personnel as well as participate in information forums with peers.

Upon completion of this particular training, data is now available to determine the impact on sales and customer satisfaction and to define the next focus for product training. As new products are introduced and existing product features change, ABC utilizes YnotEdit to keep product courseware current.

As an added bonus, trained and educated sales representatives are now on the job calling on prospective clients. When a client poses a question a rep can't answer immediately, the rep hops on the Internet, connects to the company virtual learning center supported by YnotLearn, queries the system, and provides an answer to that customer's specific question.

## Consultancy

YnotLearn's goal is to enable our clients to tap expertise across their entire organization in a structured way. With this in mind, YnotLearn's consultant group will focus on the development of organizational training objectives to help the client understand better not only what training should be delivered, but also which technology platform would provide the most effective and efficient training vehicle.

The YnotLearn approach is built upon a partnership in which the YnotLearn team becomes a natural extension of the client's own internal team. Both work together to ensure that the training applications developed meet or exceed the client need. For more information, visit www.ynotlearn.com.

# Microsoft Dot-com Certification Exams

Microsoft is revamping its certification program for Windows 2000 and the .NET revolution emerging out of Redmond, Washington. Until that happens, you might consider taking the following Microsoft certification exams that will position you to be a "+I" or "plus Internet" in the MCSE community. Note that in this discussion, I'll assume you have earned the MCSE designation (thus, I won't repeat the basic MCSE certification requirements here).

 **Note**    The MCP+I designation was retired by Microsoft on December 31, 2000. You must now have the MCSE designation in order to add the +Internet certification.

In order to add the "+Internet" designation to your MCSE, you must select three of the following four exams as of this writing. This exam list will be updated as the new .NET exams are released.

- ✦ **Exam 70-05:** Internetworking Microsoft TCP/IP on Microsoft Windows NT 4.0
- ✦ **Exam 70-067:** Implementing and Supporting Microsoft Windows NT Server 4.0
- ✦ **Exam 70-077:** Implementing and Supporting Internet Information Server 3.0 and Microsoft Index Server 1.1
- ✦ **Exam 70-087:** Implementing and Supporting Microsoft Internet Information Server 4.0

 **Note**    Microsoft freely admits these exams are subject to retirement. I've presented them here for the purposes of discussion. You will want to check the latest list of certification exams at www.microsoft.com.

# Microsoft Office User Specialist

Another less well known angle for proving your dot-com skill set to potential clients is the Microsoft Office User Specialist certification (MOUS, pronounced "mouse"). I suggest you give consideration to the MOUS program, shown in Figure 23-6, which is specific to dot-com consulting.

The MOUS certification program is oriented toward Office 2000. Don't forget that tools contained in Office 2000 are often used for the development of Web sites including Word 2000, PowerPoint 2000, Access 2000, and perhaps even Microsoft Project 2000 (which isn't part of Office 2000, but is part of MOUS).

I would encourage you to continue monitoring the MOUS program for more exams, such as a certification on FrontPage 2000. The best site to monitor on the Web for MOUS news is the Officecert site at www.officecert.com, shown in Figure 23-7.

**Figure 23-6:** How to become a MOUS

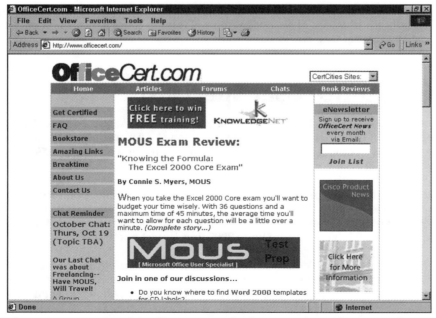

**Figure 23-7:** Monitor the Officecert.com site for news about changes to the MOUS program.

# Dot-com Certifications

There are other professional certifications in the Web world where you can prove your dot-com competence. The most popular dot-com certifications are from CompTIA, an industry training and certification group. Officially called the Computing Technology Industry Association, CompTIA is a 17-year-old association that represents over 7,500 computer hardware and software manufacturers. The i-Net+ Internet Technician Certification from CompTIA is designed to test a candidate's knowledge of various technologies and tasks related to Internet technology. It is proudly vendor-neutral. The exam covers basic networking, HTML authoring, multimedia, security, client/server administration, e-commerce practices, and legal issues. For those who want to enter the Internet job market, this certification is quickly becoming a baseline requirement by many employers. IBM and Novell have already announced that they will include i-Net+ certification as part of their Internet certification tracks.

The I-Net+ certification test measures the following areas:

✦ Net Basics (10 percent of the exam)

✦ Net Clients (20 percent of the exam)

✦ Development (20 percent of the exam)

✦ Networking (25 percent of the exam)

✦ I-Net Security (15 percent of the exam)

✦ Business Concepts (10 percent of the exam)

For more information, visit CompTIA at `www.comptia.com`, as shown in Figure 23-8.

# Jobs

You may want to be an MCSE consultant in the dot-com space but not want to go it alone. What opportunities with existing consulting firms await you, then? Can you break into the e-commerce area? To assist your journey, I present below two recent job postings from a national consulting firm for Web-related openings. The first listing is for a senior position. The second is for a junior position. The point is to show you the high and low ends of the dot-com consulting market.

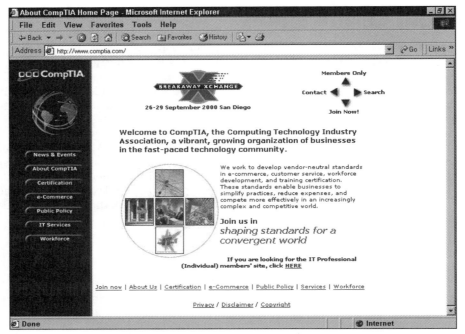

**Figure 23-8:** CompTIA's Web site

## High-end dot-com opportunity

"The consulting firm has an immediate opening for a Web Application Architect to join our development staff in our growing Denver office. Coding tool-set skills should include senior-level expertise in JAVA and experience on full life cycle Web development projects. We help organizations maximize their competitive advantage through the planning and development of customized, high-end, interactive Web sites, applications, and eBusiness solutions. You will be asked to provide a high degree of development expertise throughout our projects, as well as technical oversight. You will participate in design reviews and the development of complex Web applications for clients in accordance with project specifications and eBusiness visions."

This consulting opportunity paid in excess of $100,000 per year.

## Low-end dot-com opportunity

"Hot Shot Web Designer—We are looking for a real Hot Shot! If you can design for print and Web, you may be perfect for us! We need an Artist who has been designing for print and Web for at least three years. Show us your samples with concept and designs, with style and functionality. An ideal candidate will specialize in good design, animation, and content. Your technical skills will include Photoshop, DreamWeaver, Go-Live, ImageReady, and HTML, Quark, and Illustrator. Additional skills will be a plus."

This consulting opportunity paid $25 per hour.

# Getting Business

Dot-com skill set in hand, you're now an MCSE consultant who must go out and mingle with the online crowd. Start by making the rounds with the Internet crowd after hours in your region. In Seattle, SeattleNetwork — a group that is more social than technical — serves as the focal point for dot-com gatherings. Here, movers and shakers mix it up with venture capitalists. In Figure 23-9, I show you a recent invitation to a SeattleNetwork event. Again, check around in your community for a similar quasi-social/quasi-technical dot-com association.

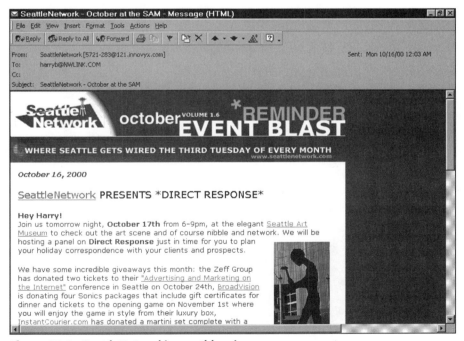

**Figure 23-9:** SeattleNetwork's monthly mixer announcement

Tip    Keep your chin high during excessive turbulence and volatility in the dot-com sector. For all of the ups and downs of the stock market as it relates to dot-coms, you
might be surprised what the actual facts reveal. A recent reporting period, after the
famous dot-com market correction of early 2000, revealed that 93 percent of venture capital funds (over $16 billion) went into technology investments (according to
PricewaterhouseCoopers). That figure is eight times the amount directed to technology companies in 1998 and four times the amount similarly directed in 1999.

## Summary

This chapter focused on positioning the MCSE consultant for dot-com consulting
opportunities. This included reviewing the dot-com opportunities that exist, understanding Microsoft's .NET strategy, learning about various Internet certifications,
and looking at specific dot-com job opportunities.

✦    ✦    ✦

# Small Business Server Consulting

O ne of the truly special consulting opportunities for MCSEs is Small Business Server. I boldly state this for several reasons, which I'll explore in detail after defining Small Business Server. I will then focus on the technical side of Small Business Server in the second part of the chapter.

## Defining Small Business Server

For something so straightforward and simple, defining Small Business Server can be a trying experience. Depending on how you interact with Small Business Server, you and I could have profoundly different definitions and viewpoints. Allow me a few pages to work through that discussion.

### A large and largely underserved market

Long ignored by Microsoft and other major software vendors, the small business market now enjoys newfound popularity. Microsoft has certainly mastered marketing to middle-sized organizations and is quickly making major inroads into the enterprise market. That begs the question in the halls of Microsoft's Redmond, Washington, campus: "What's left?" In answer to this question, someone noticed the huge, under-served small business market, and Small Business Server was born.

There are over 30 million small businesses in America alone. That number increases exponentially when you consider the world economy. That number dwarfs the Fortune 500 (limited, of course, to 500 entities) or any enterprise-level measurement you like. More interestingly, study after study has shown that the greatest job growth occurs in the small business sector, while the largest companies routinely report declines in employee head count as retrenchments and reorganizations play out.

One more interesting small business market fact the MCSE consultant should be aware of is volatility. The facts show that more small businesses fail than succeed in the long run. However, more business start-ups commence in the small business sector than in any other part of the economy. Nearly all of these small businesses need computers that are networked and connected to the Internet. You as an MCSE consultant might implement ten Small Business Server networks in a year, and perhaps one or two of the businesses that you networked will fail. Not to worry, there's another small business waiting to launch in need of your MCSE consulting skills.

## All-in-one solution

I personally can't think of anything else that Small Business Server needs. I'm pleased with its performance as is, so I hope it won't be overloaded in future releases at the cost of degraded performance. The following subsections discuss the capabilities of Small Business Server 2000, the current release.

### Windows 2000 Server

As an MCSE, you certainly know what Windows 2000 Server is capable of. What's significant is that Small Business Server 2000 is built on Windows 2000 Server and enjoys all the capabilities that the regular Windows 2000 Server provides (subject to a couple of limitations).

Windows 2000 Server is a robust 32-bit network operating system that supports the following functionality (available in Small Business Server 2000).

✦ **Active Directory** — This is Microsoft's directory services solution. Small Business Server uses it, but not nearly to the extent that Active Directory is deployed at the enterprise level. Small Business Server simply installs and configures Active Directory and creates a single organizational unit (OU). I actually view this as positive for MCSEs who are new to Windows 2000 and Active Directory. Here's a chance to learn more about Active Directory in a relatively safe environment, the small business.

✦ **Terminal Services** — The remote control nature of Terminal Services allows MCSE consultants to service their Small Business Server clients from remote locations, such as the consultant's office.

Note    Terminal Services in Small Business Server 2000 is configured to operate in remote administration mode. That's because Small Business Server is so busy running the suite of BackOffice applications on one server machine that it can't support Terminal Services in application mode.

Microsoft has communicated this up front and directly, so my expectations are suitably managed. Having Terminal Services in remote administration mode has made my life infinitely easier as an MCSE consultant because I can remotely connect to client sites and perform surprisingly sophisticated administration. For Small Business Server sites demanding more intensive Terminal Services interaction (to run tax preparation programs on the company network while working from home, for example), the solution is to add another Windows 2000 Server to the Small Business Server network and configure this machine to run Terminal Services in application mode.

✦ **Group Policy** — Assuming you're equipped with an all Windows 2000 network (including client machines), you can take advantage of one of the strongest capabilities of Windows 2000: Group Policy. Group Policy allows you to configure, down to a very granular level, what users and machines can accomplish on the network. For example, you can empower users to customize their desktops, modify application settings (such as store Favorites in Internet Explorer), and so on. On the other hand, Group Policy can be viewed as centralized management run amuck. Not only can you restrict what actions users may perform, but also you can assign or restrict mandatory software deployments. In other words, in the wrong hands Group Policy is a very dangerous thing on homogeneous Windows 2000 networks.

✦ **Disk quotas** — Another goodie needed by small businesses and enterprises alike is disk quotas. Even though gigabytes of storage are cheap, the fact of the matter is that, just as with Internet connection bandwidth, you never have enough disk space. Disk quotas are a popular implementation with my Small Business Server clients because rogue users with a passion for hard disk sector consuming audio video (.avi) files can be denied.

✦ **Miscellaneous qualities** — While your list probably will be different than mine, I find the fewer reboots, the greater stability, the built-in disk defragmentation, the encryption file system (EFS), and the use of the Microsoft Management Console (MMC) for consistency when working with native Windows 2000 tools all to be key features of Windows 2000 Server functionality. Additionally, Windows 2000 functionality provides more security than my Small Business Server clients will ever need.

 I discuss Windows 2000 in much greater detail in Chapter 19.

## Internet Information Server (IIS) 5.0

"New and improved" is an understatement for this Small Business Server component that provides Web functionality. In the early MCSE certification days, the IIS exam was the easiest exam of all. That has changed, and it has become one of the more difficult exams. The development of the IIS product parallels that increase in the exam's difficulty.

### Microsoft Exchange 2000 Server

Microsoft's intent with Microsoft Exchange 2000 Server in Small Business Server is both to shore up the suite offering with the latest product releases and to provide additional functionality and robustness. The additional functionality includes the addition of instant messaging. The robustness includes the integration of Microsoft Exchange with Active Directory so that you can now manage the e-mail accounts directly from the Active Directory Users and Computers MMC.

A few tried-and-true Exchange Server features such as Outlook Web Access (allowing you to remotely check your e-mail) have been upgraded as well.

 I discuss Microsoft Exchange 2000 Server in much greater detail in Chapter 20.

### Microsoft Internet Security and Acceleration (ISA) Server 2000

Even small businesses need an effective firewall, right? Small Business Server delivers with ISA Server and the use of configuration wizards to remove the great mysteries of firewall tuning. For example, using the Internet Connection Wizard in Small Business Server allows you to easily configure the NAT and dynamic port filtering capabilities.

 ISA is discussed in more technical detail and as a viable consulting platform in Chapter 18.

### Microsoft SQL Server 2000

Many MCSEs overlook the power of SQL Server in part because they don't understand it. The SQL database administration and programming areas are difficult to grasp. While I am SQL Server certified, I'm ashamed to say I took the SQL Server Administration test five times.

But trading SQL Server war stories isn't the intent of this snippet. My intent is to have you view the SQL Server component in Small Business Server from a business perspective. SQL Server is a robust relational database application. Popular business applications, such as complex accounting packages, run on top of SQL Server. Businesspeople, especially those who work with accounting systems, make technology purchase decisions. These purchase decisions include the need for MCSE consultants.

### Shared Fax and Modem Services

Microsoft has reworked both the Shared Fax Service and the Shared Modem Service in Small Business Server 2000. Both of these components now really work. I'm an especially big fan of inbound faxes being distributed over the e-mail system. The Shared Modem Service isn't exactly a hot item in today's world of Internet connectivity and virtual private networks (VPN). The only uses I've seen in the early twenty-first century for true modem pooling (which is what we're talking about here) are to dial banks, payroll firms, and drug testing labs. These are information service providers who in many cases still prefer a modem connection to an Internet connection.

## Management Console

Ease of use and consistency of experience are a couple of the design goals behind the improved Small Business Server Management Consoles. Later in this chapter I'll describe the consoles in greater depth, but suffice it to say, this management tool has been improved. There are now two Small Business Server consoles: Personal and Administrator. The Personal Console is for power users entrusted to perform low-level duties. The Administrator Console for the MCSE consultant to manage the Small Business Server network is shown in Figure 24-1.

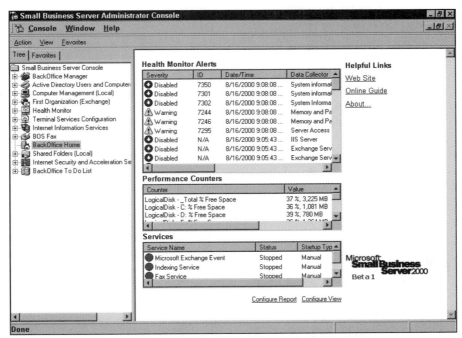

**Figure 24-1:** Many people think of the Small Business Server Administrator Console as the most representative view of Small Business Server 2000.

## Health Monitor

One of the truly exciting developments in Small Business Server 2000 is the advent of Health Monitor, which allows you to monitor critical network management measures, such as free disk space. This monitoring can occur from distant locations, as the alerts can be e-mailed to you. The monitoring is also continuous, 24 hours a day, 7 days a week. This tool presents significant consulting opportunities for the MCSE, as you may now proactively present solutions without falling into the trap of always receiving a call when something is broken.

## Limitations

So far I've painted a rosy picture of Small Business Server. I now need to temper your enthusiasm with a few facts that limit how and when you can place Small Business Server in an organization:

✦ **Fifty computer limit** — Only fifty computers may be attached to the Small Business Server network.

✦ **Root of the Active Directory tree** — This is another way of saying that you may have only one Small Business Server machine on a network.

✦ **Terminal Services in remote administration mode by default** — There is a two-user logon limit for Terminal Services sessions. You can change the Terminal Services service to application sharing mode, a last minute modification in Small Business Server 2000 made by the Microsoft development team. As of this writing, however, Microsoft product support will not provide technical support for application sharing mode. You should also be aware that application sharing mode will greatly tax your machine's resources such as RAM memory.

✦ **Overhead footprint limits** — Applications have been optimized in order to "fit" on to one box. This is evident because many of these applications, such as Microsoft Exchange 2000 Server, often require their own machines at the enterprise level.

## Resources

For more information on Small Business Server 2000 features and capabilities, start by visiting Microsoft's Small Business Server Web site at www.microsoft.com/smallbusinessserver, shown in Figure 24-2.

Another important Small Business Server 2000 information resource is Grey Lancaster's Small Business Server Web site located at www.smallbizserver.com. This is shown in Figure 24-3.

**Figure 24-2:** Microsoft's Small Business Server Web site is the central portal for information on Small Business Server.

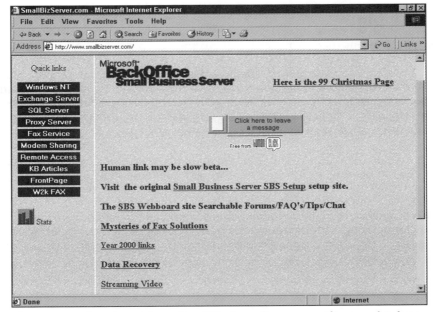

**Figure 24-3:** Grey Lancaster, a Small Business Server consultant, maintains a Web site widely regarded as the best third-party Small Business Server source of Web-based information.

## Small Business Server Zen

Some MCSE consultants view Small Business Server as something larger than a bundled application, server machine, and network. For them, Small Business Server is a community that they want to "live in." In other words, Small Business Server is a consulting space that has definition (as a small business technology solution), boundaries (the 50 machine limits), and the need for technology consultants (small firms typically don't have in-house technology expertise).

There are MCSE consultants that have niched their consulting practices on Small Business Server. To SBSers, the Small Business Server consulting space is more than a job; it's a lifestyle.

## Cheaper stock keeping unit

One thing you can count on as an MCSE consultant in the Small Business Server consulting space is that your small business clients, as a general rule, really watch their expenditures. Small businesses don't have the large technology budgets found at the enterprise level. Small Business Server, in the spirit of Microsoft's bundling practices, is significantly cheaper than purchasing the same components individually. As a comparison, if you were to purchase Windows 2000 Server and one other application (such as Microsoft Exchange), you will have basically paid the same as Small Business Server costs by itself.

## Looking big

I've heard numerous times from my small business clients that they need to look big. This concept was especially important to one of my Small Business Server clients, a real estate services firm. The president of this firm stated that the biggest problem the firm faced was the perception that they weren't big enough to handle large assignments. Small Business Server delivered an infrastructure for this firm that not only allows them to look like a bigger firm but also gives them the capability to handle the biggest assignments thrown their way.

Another take on the bigger is better argument is that with Small Business Server clients can run big-league applications, such as manufacturing applications. If you know anything about installing narrow vertical-market applications, the actual cost of the software and hardware tends to be a small component of the total cost of operations. Indeed, the labor component measured in fees paid to consultants typically far outweighs other technology costs. For the MCSE consultant, Small Business Server is often the good way to a long-term and mutually beneficial consulting relationship.

## Trust

You and I are riding an elevator. I'm the MCSE consultant, and you are the small business owner. I have 60 seconds to "close" you on implementing Small Business Server. I use half of my time to define it as Baby BackOffice with Windows 2000, e-mail, and an effective firewall. But with my remaining 30 seconds, I tell you that Small Business Server can be trusted because it comes from a reliable vendor (Microsoft) who supports it today and will support it tomorrow. With Windows 2000 Server as the underlying operating system, it's the most reliable Small Business Server release ever. And as an MCSE consultant, having your trust and providing a solution you can trust is of the utmost importance to me.

# Consulting Opportunities

What does Small Business Server do for the MCSE consultant? In this section I offer several perspectives on being an MCSE consultant in the Small Business Server space.

## MCSE Consulting training grounds

Small Business Server is a great consulting avenue for both newly minted MCSEs seeking technology experience and experienced MCSEs seeking to learn the consulting business.

### Seeking technology experience

One of the best tips for new MCSEs seeking Microsoft technology experience is to start with Small Business Server. That's because Small Business Server exposes you to nearly all of the BackOffice family and runs on a single machine. It's also a low-cost learning environment. If you make a mistake, you realistically impact only a handful of users, not the thousands of users you might affect at the enterprise level.

### Seeking consulting experience

Small Business Server is a great path to follow for getting significant technology consulting experience. You are exposed to a range of business applications from Microsoft and are allowed to sample each one. Later, when you're comfortable working as a consultant and running a fledgling consulting practice, you'll likely find one Small Business Server component in which you would like to specialize. For example, you may discover you have a passion for electronic mail and want to become an Exchange guru. Small Business Server is a fine place to start the journey.

## I'll have it fixed by morning

Personally speaking, the thing I like so much about being an MCSE consultant in the Small Business Server space is that I always (with no exceptions at this point) get the company back up and running by morning. Sure, I've made mistakes, especially during the first release of Small Business Server. However, by sunrise I always had those problematic client sites up and running. I look at Small Business Server as a way to mitigate consulting risk (risk of failure and so on). Even a superstar MCSE consultant can dig a hole so deep at the enterprise level that it might take weeks to recover.

## Rule of Ten

It has been my experience that a network with ten users can be repaired or rebuilt and up and running within ten hours. How did I learn this? Many Small Business Server networks have around ten users, and I've been able to do an overnight rebuild on more than one occasion to cure cataclysmic ills.

## Nonenterprise personalities

Not all of us were raised to wear suits and ties, and despite Microsoft's greatest desires, not all MCSEs work at the enterprise level. Some MCSEs are happy to work in the often more casual small business space with Small Business Server.

## Wearing many hats

Working with Small Business Server and small businesses affords the opportunity to perform many different sorts of tasks. Contrast this with some enterprise-level engagements where you are narrowly typecast into very specific technical roles. If you like variety as an MCSE consultant, Small Business Server may just be for you.

## Business advising

Because you're front and center as the MCSE consultant implementing Small Business Server, you'll often consult on business issues as well. Small business owners, once turned on to the power of Small Business Server, often ask for your feedback on broader business issues, such as should a new line of online services be offered by the small business?

## Serving bigger clients sooner

Many small businesses start with Small Business Server knowing full well that the business will upgrade to BackOffice as the firm grows and has more funds available.

So in a sense, small businesses are often following the same strategy you might be using as an MCSE consultant.

It is common for a professional services provider to start with small clients and grow with these same clients over the years. That's a relationship component of MCSE consulting I'm fond of emphasizing. By picking small businesses with growth potential and peddling Small Business Server consulting services, you may find yourself growing beyond your expectations without much additional effort required on your behalf.

**Note**  Small Business Server also provides another way to look at the bigger client proposition in that the product modestly understates the size of organization it can serve. Small Business Server's licensing model allows a maximum of 50 client machines to be physically connected to the network. However, a company with 50 client machines attached to a Small Business Server network may indeed have over 100 employees. Not all employees in a company use personal computers. I've witnessed this firsthand in companies with trade-related practices. For example, a small administrative office of 20 client machines on a Small Business Server network was all that was needed to support the technology requirements of an Issaquah, Washington, landscaping firm with over 300 employees. In general, Small Business Server tends to serve larger-sized organizations than the strict licensing count would suggest.

# Competitive Analysis

What alternatives to Small Business Server from Microsoft exist for small businesses? Two major alternatives stand out: Novell's Small Business Suite 5.1 and Windows 2000 Server (standalone). I'll also discuss BackOffice 2000, the Microsoft server solution for larger firms, as well as the unbundlers.

As an MCSE consultant in alignment with Microsoft's product offerings, it's important that you know who your competition is and how to reposition to compete with them.

**Note**  Some of the best consultants I've ever seen operate are armed with extensive information about competing products. Not only does this knowledge allow them to better understand the client's needs and determine whether their consultant skills are a match for the client and engagement, but it helps when selling the client a solution. You want to be an educated consultant who knows the pluses and minuses of both your favorite solution and competing solutions.

# Novell Small Business Suite 5.1

Novell Small Business Suite 5.1 (NSBS) is Novell's response to Small Business Server. Much of the market positioning for this product sells its ease of use and the way it allows the technology consultant to assist the small business, a marketing position that is directly comparable to the Small Business Server product message. Specific features and how they compare to Small Business Server are described in the following sections.

## Operating system

NSBS is based on NetWare 5.1 operating system and the NDS eDirectory directory services solution. There are many technologists who enthusiastically approve of NetWare 5.1 and the mature NDS directory services solution, so you would be unwise to marginalize NSBS in this area. While I prefer Windows 2000 Server over NetWare (and I've worked with them both as a practicing MCSE and CNE), I'm willing to acknowledge that competing camps feel strongly about both NetWare and Windows 2000 Server. Both camps have technical white papers to back up their claims, as you might expect.

There are two ways that I reposition Small Business Server against NSBS in the operating system area: vendor support and application support.

✦ **Vendor support** — For a few years in the mid-1990s, Novell seemed asleep at the wheel and couldn't decide if it wanted to be in business. Novell and its NetWare product lost the support of a large part of the business and technology community. So today, when faced with a significant technology decision, small business owners tend to favor Microsoft, knowing it will support the business and technology community through shifting markets and the like.

**Note**  CNE consultants may well counter here that the uncertainty of judicial actions against Microsoft in the antitrust area make the selection of Microsoft products a risk choice at the time of this writing. You need to be aware of that valid point.

✦ **Application Support** — The real trump card for the MCSE consultant in the NSBS and Small Business Server matchup lies in ISV application support for NetWare. The list is long, so you don't have to look far for a vendor that has stopped developing NetWare-specific versions of its products and now only supports the Windows NT/Windows 2000 platform. My favorite business software example, the Great Plains Dynamics accounting system, is a case in point. Some years back, Great Plains stopped supporting the NetWare platform. This occurred about the time Small Business Server 4.0 was released in late 1997. Needless to say, my clients running NetWare were easy to convert over to Small Business Server: they had to join the Microsoft camp if they wanted to continue using Great Plains Dynamics in the future.

In many industries, the popular narrow vertical-market software applications that were previously supported on NetWare are now supported only on Microsoft Server–based solutions such as Small Business Server. This is powerful ammunition for the MCSE consultant to use in the business development cycle.

One other point that may or may not be helpful to you in comparing the two products is that Microsoft has embraced the TCP/IP networking protocol longer than NetWare has. Previously, NetWare used its IPX/SPX networking protocol.

## Firewall

NSBS ships with BorderManager Enterprise Edition 3.5 Firewall, a credible firewall product. This is comparable to ISA Server in Small Business Server 2000. Call it a draw here. In general, the security delivered by both NSBS and Small Business Server is effective for the small business.

Like ISA Server in Small Business Server, BorderManager can be configured to cache frequently accessed Web pages for faster access by network users.

## E-mail

GroupWise 5.5 is the e-mail solution in NSBS. Like Microsoft Exchange 2000 Server, GroupWise also has calendaring and scheduling features. Nevertheless, Small Business Server with its Exchange-based e-mail repositions very strongly against GroupWise. Exchange is much more widely accepted and enjoys significant vendor support with ISV add-ons. It has also been my experience that Exchange is more reliable and able to handle larger e-mail stores than GroupWise, but take that statement as an opinion, not necessarily fact.

I once bid on installing a network for a small business and lost the bid. Months later I learned the NetWare network solution that was implemented ultimately included a Microsoft Server solution using Exchange as its e-mail application. So instead of having an all-in-one Small Business Server network, this client ended up with a hybrid network of NetWare and (in this case) Windows NT Server. This meant managing two different server environments (which often required calling in two different consultants), and troubleshooting was more difficult as it wasn't always clear which networking environment was causing a problem.

## Web

NSBS supports Web and e-activity with two components: IBM WebSphere and NetWare Enterprise Web Server.

### IBM WebSphere

This is the Web server integrated into the NetWare 5.1 operating system that provides secure Web services.

### NetWare Enterprise Web Server

This is a second component of NSBS's Web solution. NetWare Enterprise Web Server is an open-standards, enterprise-strength Web server that provides built-in Web publishing functionality, full indexing, and search tools.

### Repositioning

The difference here between Novell's Small Business Suite and Small Business Server is clear. Whereas Novell uses two separate components from two separate vendors to provide the Web solution in NSBS, Small Business Server offers the single vendor, single component solution, IIS 5.0. When it comes to the Web, I'm all for the functionality that comes from Microsoft's having its operating system (Windows 2000 Server) developers and application (IIS 5.0) developers collaborate early and often.

## Faxing

With Tobit FaxWare 6 in NSBS, you can send and receive faxes on your computer, just as you can with Small Business Server. Call it a tie in this department between Small Business Server and NSBS.

## Database

This is nothing short of the classic Oracle versus Microsoft SQL Server debate. NSBS collaborated with Oracle for a database solution, and I certainly can't settle the Oracle versus Microsoft SQL Server debate on these pages. In truth, choosing a database really depends on the client's needs. If Oracle is the manufacturing software choice for a small business client, then NSBS might deserve the client's nod, all other things being equal, such as the need for e-mail communications, Internet connectivity, firewall protection, and so on.

Note

The classic way for consultants to assist clients in selecting a technology solution was to first assess the business needs of the client irrespective of the operating system or application. The consultant would then find the appropriate solution for the client. This is great advice when it comes to databases.

In terms of development environments, such as grow-your-own databases, the two environments are comparable. Both have strengths and weaknesses as development platforms. I suggest you consult other books specifically dedicated to Microsoft SQL Server 2000 and Oracle to address the development environment issue.

## Management

Many MCSEs take a full frontal assault approach in their peer groups about Microsoft's purchasing technology, not developing it. In other words, Microsoft copies from others. In the case of Small Business Server and the management area, such is not the case, as Novell has adopted some of the user interface and tools that have worked so well in Small Business Server. It is easy to confirm this fact by looking at the old character-based NetWare family of operating systems and comparing that to Novell's new consoles.

✦ **Consoles**—NSBS uses the ConsoleOne and ZENworks to perform console-based management functions. Small Business Server uses consoles based on the Microsoft Management Console (MMC). Microsoft's solution has more maturity in this area, but ZENworks is also an effective tool.

✦ **Wizards**—Wizard-based management for setup and maintenance occurs via the Novell Easy Administration Tasks tool (NEAT). Still, Microsoft has more experience in wizard-based scripting.

✦ **Remote management**—NSBS provides the NetWare 5.1 Management Portal that enables you to perform server management tasks from any Web browser on the network. Small Business Server 2000 uses Terminal Services in remote administration mode for a full, remote control session. Clearly the advantage here goes to Small Business Server with Terminal Services (which is integrated at the operating system kernel level). Terminal Services can also be accessed with a Web browser (either on the LAN or over the Internet).

## Additional features

There are a few other points of comparison between NSBS and SBS, including the following:

✦ **Virus detection**—NSBS has virus detection in the form of Network Associates VirusScan and NetShield for a six-month free trail. This is a nice touch that is missing in Small Business Server. To come close to this functionality, you could download the same products in the form a 30-day free trail from Network Associates (www.nai.com).

✦ **Licensing**—NSBS allows you to add users one at a time. Small Business Server sells its license bump packs (also called add packs by some vendors) in quantities of five.

✦ **Upgrade path**—NSBS facilitates upgrades for growing small businesses to full NetWare 5.1 networks. Small Business Server has an upgrade path to BackOffice 2000.

✦ **Pricing**—The pricing is comparable between NSBS and Small Business Server 2000.

✦ **Modem pooling**—NSBS doesn't have explicit modem pooling support, but Small Business Server does.

✦ **Health monitoring**—NSBS doesn't have powerful health monitor tools for use by the technology consultant. Small Business Server 2000 ships with the powerful Health Monitor 2.1.

To me it is significant that Small Business Server is an integrated business networking solution from a single vendor. NSBS relies on the contributions of multiple vendors. You're welcome to draw your own conclusions armed with these facts. My portfolio of clients seeks several things from their small business computer network, one of which is reliability. It has been my experience as an MCSE consultant that an integrated solution from a single vendor tends to work better in the reliability department than a technology solution built on a patchwork quilt of different vendors and different solutions. When given the choice, I prefer a single vendor solution such as Small Business Server to other business suites that incorporate solutions from multiple vendors. For more information on NSBS, contact Novell at 1-800-NETWARE or visit Novell's Web site, shown in Figure 24-4, at `www.novell.com/products/smallbiz`.

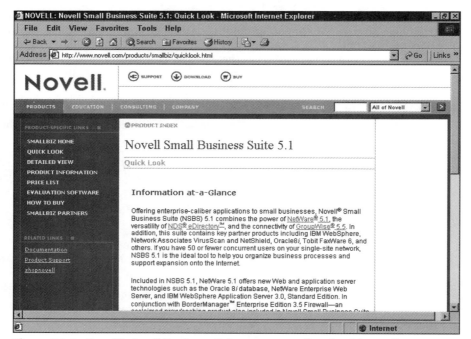

**Figure 24-4:** Novell's Small Business Suite competes directly with Small Business Server.

## IBM Small Business Suite for Linux

IBM has aggressively entered the small business space with a Linux-based bundle call Small Business Suite for Linux. Much as with the other small business bundles from Microsoft and Novell, IBM claims that inside a single box, the small business has everything it needs to become a fully networked business with electronic commerce capabilities. Small Business Suite for Linux focuses on three areas that IBM considers essential to small business computing: databases, e-mail, and Web serving. Specific components in Small Business Suite for Linux include:

✦ IBM Suites Installer

✦ Lotus Domino Application Server for Linux V5.0.4

✦ Lotus Notes for Windows V5.0.4

✦ IBM DB2 Universal Database Workgroup Edition for Linux V7.1

✦ IBM WebSphere Application Server for Linux V3.0.2

✦ IBM HTTP Server for Linux V1.3.12

✦ Lotus SmartSuite for Windows

✦ IBM WebSphere Studio Entry Edition V3.0.2

✦ Lotus Domino Designer for Windows V.5.0.4

✦ IBM WebSphere Homepage Builder for Linux V4.0

This small business offering from IBM should be taken seriously by MCSE consultants in the SBS niche. It's a single vendor solution, a tactic IBM has been well-known and well-respected for. The entry-level price for five users is approximately a third of the cost of the comparable Microsoft Small Business Server product. There is no question that there are certain small businesses that are cost-conscious and will be customers of IBM's Small Business Suite for Linux. Contact IBM at www.ibm.com for more information.

## Windows 2000 Server (stand-alone)

In many cases the stand-alone version of Windows 2000 Server steals sales from Small Business Server. This occurs for two reasons.

First, the small business computer advertisements from popular hardware providers such as Compaq and Dell typically list only Windows 2000 Server as a purchase or pre-installation option. This is done so that the vendor can have the lowest priced hardware/software bundled solution in print. If customers ask about alternatives, a smart order taker may tout the benefits of Small Business Server. In most cases, however, a small business owner reads the advertisement and places the order from what's listed (in this case, Windows 2000 Server).

Second, the small business owner, working without the guidance of a technology consultant, may know only about Windows 2000 Server, so that's what will be purchased and installed. Once educated, the small business owner may regret his decision and, if the election is made to migrate to Small Business Server, the price of networking goes up significantly because the cost of purchasing Windows 2000 Server followed by the cost of purchasing Small Business Server is considerable.

## BackOffice 2000

Small business people who go out and purchase BackOffice 2000 (designed for larger companies) are often unknowingly overbuying. BackOffice 2000 is significantly more expensive than Small Business Server and includes unnecessary components such as Integration Host Server for mainframe connectivity. When I've seen a small business opt for this mispurchase, the choice was often made because Small Business Server was perceived to be inadequate, to have poor performance, and so on. Such is not the case with the current release of Small Business Server. In these situations, it's paramount that the MCSE educate the client on the features of Small Business Server and at some level invoke trust in the product.

## Unbundlers

Closely related to the discussion on purchasing Windows 2000 Server in an unbundled manner is the issue of unbundlers. Unbundlers are people who purchase Windows 2000 Server and then purchase Microsoft Exchange 2000 Server separately. When they add a firewall to the mix, they've exceeded the bundled price for Small Business Server. As an MCSE consultant, if you can catch these clients soon enough, you can easily explain the money-saving alternative Small Business Server can offer.

# Bottom Line: You Are the Entire Solution

Let me drive one major point home by borrowing from Tim Catura-Houser, the founder of Tcatu.net, a certification training organization focusing on CompTIA certifications. Tim's slogan is "You're IT in I.T." Loosely translated, this means you are "it" when it comes to information technology. The MCSE consultant who works in the Small Business Server consulting space is the "solution." That's both exciting and scary. It's exciting because you run the show for the technology implementation for the small business client. It's scary because it's typically just you and you alone taking full responsibility. It's never boring as an MCSE consultant working with Small Business Server.

# Getting Technical

I've identified six phases to Small Business Server consulting.

1. **Design and planning** — Many of the engagement management techniques, such as proposal and engagement letter writing, client expectation management, and the upfront scoping and technical design process, are performed at this phase.

2. **Server setup** — Small Business Server is installed on the server machine. I provide the steps for this later in the chapter.

3. **Workstation setup**—After the server running Small Business Server is up and stable, the setup disk is created and used to configure workstations on the network. I provide the steps to configure workstations later in the chapter.

4. **Components configuration**—Here's where the consulting relationship finds traction. Over several weeks, you'll return for periodic visits to introduce new features, such as Internet e-mail and faxing. I've found that cataclysmic change such as the introduction of new networking infrastructure can be overwhelming for small business employees. Consider extending the rollout of all the Small Business Server tools over several weeks.

5. **Celebration**—The Small Business Server network is up and running. This discrete event brings closure to the Small Business Server implementation project, so you can now shift your billings to categories (such as maintenance) outside the initial project budget.

6. **Ongoing maintenance**—This is the phase that will truly test your client relationship management skills. Small Business Server clients are good clients in general, and the work is ongoing. You'll have add-on work such as adding new Web pages, using NetMeeting for video conferencing, implementing upgrades, installing new business applications, and so on. But with some Small Business Server clients you're never more than a bad "I can't print day" from failure.

## Guest Sermon – A Day in the Life of an SBSer

There is no one better than Grey Lancaster, big time SBSer, host of www.smallbizserver. com (an educational Web site for SBS), and SBS listserv coordinator (see www.egroups/ group/sbs2k for more information) to preach on the merits of Small Business Server.

*I was flattered when Harry asked me to write this little piece, "A day in the life of an SBS consultant." Obviously it would be no problem for me, as SBS is what I have done 12 hours a day, seven days a week, for the past three years. Now that the deadline is here and I start to type, I have no idea where to begin. Harry suggested . . . 4 a.m. beeper goes off . . . then go from there. First of all, I have one phone number to my office. After three rings it goes to my cell phone. Lately I have come to realize that I can only talk on two phones at the same time while typing replies to e-mails. Second, seems like this past week was full of those silly little nitpicking things that should take 20 minutes and end up taking three hours. Have you ever tried to reinstall Windows 95 after IE 4 has been installed?*

*An SBS consultant? Before I go any farther and forget, NT certification does not make a good SBS guru. May actually do more harm than good at first. You first look at your customers. Well, mine anyway. The idea/goal is you are their IMS manager. SBS gives small business the same powerful tools that the Fortune 500 companies have. This means not only NT as the backbone (Win 2k as you read this), but the excellent Exchange server, the practical Proxy Server (now ISA), and a fair Fax Server. SQL is also included, but to be honest, not one of my clients is using it. But then my niche is the legal market.*

*Continued*

*Continued*

*So what did I just say? When you leave your customer, he will have file and printer sharing. All users will have their own e-mail addresses and be able to send and receive e-mail across the hall or across the world. Everyone will have Internet access either through one phone line or a dedicated connection. Users can print to fax to one recipient and get an e-mail notification of the results of their fax. Different from a "patched" solution, SBS provides a secure robust solution. E-mails, files, calendars, contacts, etc., are stored and backed up in a central location.*

*Who are our/my customers? These people have no clue as to what a DNS server is. What is an MX record? Backup? Mirror? They don't know how to share a printer or do other stuff we take for granted. I have answered thousands of posts in the SBS newsgroup and SBS Listserv over the years, and my two favorite comments are as follows:*

✦ "I am the network guru in my office because I can clear the paper jams in the copier."

✦ An MSCE writes, "This is my first SBS install, actually my first NT install as well."

*So the SBS consultant is going to be the IMS Manager for this firm. How? I attended an SBS VAP Roundtable in Redmond this summer. One of the comments that stuck with me was that 8,000 engineers participated/provided code for this product. So the key here is that it will be very hard for anyone to "know it all." The SBS guru must know where the resources are. There are two Microsoft teams whose duties are to support SBS. One is in Texas, and the other is in North Carolina. They may monitor the calls you place to pay support. On their screen they have a form of instant messaging that they all log into to help each other. When I get the Exchange 2000 version figured out, I will probably do the same for the SBS community. The key here is to go ahead and familiarize yourself with your support options. One option would be critical need support. Then there are the Direct Access News groups at* http://www.microsoft.com/directaccess/. *Public newsgroups, such as* msnews. microsoft.com, *are also a good resource. My favorite, of course, would be the listserv I moderate. Details can be found at* www.smallbizserver.com.

*I do not mean to skip over some of the "value added" things I do such as VPN, OWA, VAP reporting tool, and Remote Control, but these are all addressed in SBS 2k. I think other than anti-virus products, such as The Trend Suite for SBS, the thing you need a firm grip on is an ISP that can work with you providing connectivity and e-mail.*

*Just because you are an "SBS guru" does not mean folks are not going to call you every time they get a GPF in Kernel32.dll or that a hard drive is never going to fail again. You still have to figure out PPPOE with DSL, roaming users, NDRs, and the POP3 connector. If you have configured SBS to receive and send e-mail for two people, or for those two to surf, you can do the same for 200 or 2,000. When you know how to back up and restore a nine gig hard drive including Exchange Server, you can do it for a 40 gig just as well. Microsoft offered a six-user NFR of SBS with no time bombs. I assume they will have a similar offering for SBS 2000. I encourage each of you to use it to grow into this lucrative market.*

*If you have any questions or comments, please holler.*

*Grey*

*MS MVP SBS*

*grey@smallbizserver.com*

*PS: I should say thanks for their support to Paul Fitzgerald (MS), SBS Development Redmond, and to my fellow MVPs, Michel Bordeleau, Jeff Middleton, Chris Hanna, and Mal Osborne. There are too many great folks on the listserv to mention them all, but I will mention Greg Martin and Gary Peterson, who have been loyal forever.*

# Installing Small Business Server 2000

You have to install Small Business Server 2000 to use it. This section is dedicated to installation of Small Business Server on the server machine. You start by making the four installation setup floppy disks and ultimately end with a final reboot.

To create the Small Business Server installation setup disks:

1. Insert Disc 1 into the CD-ROM drive.
2. On the Start menu, point to Programs ⇨ Accessories and then click Command Prompt.
3. In Command Prompt, change the drive to your CD-ROM drive letter. For example, if your CD-ROM drive is E, type **E:** and press the Enter key.
4. Type **cd bootdisk**.
5. Type **makeboot** and follow the onscreen instructions.

You will now use the four installation setup disks and the four Small Business Server CD-ROM discs to install Small Business Server 2000 on the server machine. It all starts with Step 1 in the next sequence.

To install Small Business Server 2000 on the server machine:

1. Insert the Windows 2000 Setup Boot Disk in floppy drive A. Power on the server machine.
2. When requested, insert Windows 2000 Setup Disk #2 and press the Enter key.
3. When requested, insert Windows 2000 Server Setup Disk #3 and press the Enter key.
4. When requested, insert Windows 2000 Server Setup Disk #4 and press the Enter key.

5. A Windows 2000 Server Setup screen appears after several minutes. Press Enter.

6. When requested, insert the Small Business Server CD-ROM Disc 1. Press Enter.

7. The Windows 2000 Licensing Agreement screen appears. Press F8 to agree to the license and continue. If you don't agree to the license, the setup process will terminate.

8. Assuming you have a new hard disk, you will need to create a partition for Windows 2000 Server and Small Business Server to install on. After a partition has been created, select it and press Enter to continue the installation.

9. You will be asked to format the partition. It is essential that you select the NTFS formatting option even though Small Business Server installs on either a FAT or NTFS partition. Press Enter after selecting NTFS. Setup now formats the hard disk partition you have just created. This formatting process takes several minutes. After the formatting is complete, the computer's hard disks will be inspected for hard disk errors.

10. Remove Small Business Server Setup Disk #4 from your floppy drive A. After several minutes of file copying from Small Business Server CD-ROM Disc 1, the computer automatically reboots itself.

11. An auto logon occurs, and the GUI-based Windows 2000 Server phase commences. The Windows 2000 Server Setup Wizard appears and automatically starts installing devices.

12. You are presented with the Regional Settings screen, where you may select the system locale and keyboard layout. After accepting or changing the defaults (via the Customize button), click Next.

13. You are next presented with the Personalize Your Software screen. This allows you to enter the appropriate name and organization. After entering this information, click Next.

14. The Computer Name and Administrator Password screen appears. Provide the computer name and the Administrator password and click Next.

15. Select what components you want to install on the Windows 2000 Components screen and click Next.

16. Select your date, time, and time zone when presented with the Date and Time Settings screen. Click Next.

17. Additional computer files to install the Windows 2000 networking components are copied and installed. You will then select either typical or custom settings on the Networking Settings screen and click Next. Additional Windows 2000 files are copied.

18. The Performing Final Tasks screen appears from which you can perform four tasks (install Start menu items on the computer, install registry components, save configuration settings, and delete any temporary files created during the setup routine). Click Finish when the Completing the Windows 2000 Setup Wizard appears. The Small Business Server computer reboots, and Windows 2000 Server starts.

**19.** After you log on, you are greeted by the initial Small Business Server Setup screen, as seen in Figure 24-5.

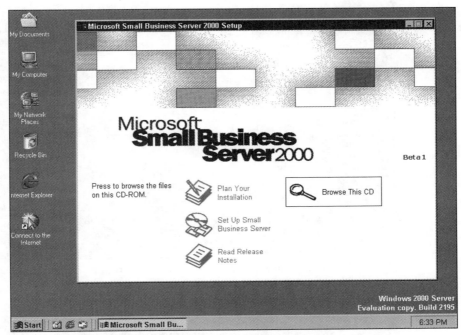

**Figure 24-5:** The Small Business Server Setup screen

**20.** Click Set Up Small Business Server. You will receive a notice to please wait while setup initializes. The Welcome to the Microsoft Small Business Server 2000 Setup Wizard appears. Click Next.

**21.** You are presented with the License Agreement screen. If you select the I Agree button, the setup routine continues. If you select the I Disagree button, the setup routine terminates. Read the software license agreement, select I Agree, and click Next.

**22.** The Product Identification screen now appears, as seen in Figure 24-6. You are shown the Name and Organization fields. This is your last chance to change the Name and Organization fields. You also need to enter the 25-digit CD key that is found on the yellow sticker on the back of your Small Business Server CD case. You will enter the 25-digit CD key for Microsoft Outlook as well.

**23.** Provide the Administrator account password on the Automatic Logon Screen. Click Next.

**24.** Complete the Company Information screen that appears, as seen in Figure 24-7. Click Next.

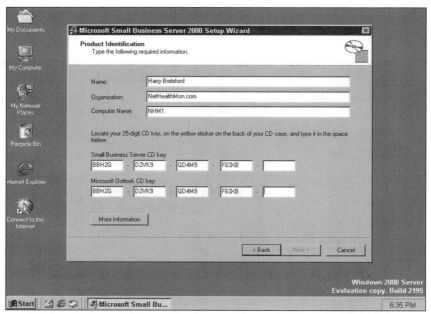

**Figure 24-6:** Complete the Small Business Server Product Identification screen with legitimate license numbers.

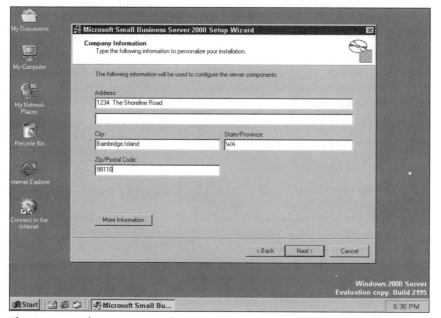

**Figure 24-7:** The Company Information screen captures information that is used again in the setup and the operation of Small Business Server.

25. Complete the Telephony information screen with a business telephone number, fax number, and dialing properties. Click Next.

26. Select which network adapter card is attached to the local area network (LAN) on the Local Network Card Information screen and click Next.

27. Complete the Server Network Card Configuration screen, shown in Figure 24-8. You may enter the IP address, Subnet Mask, and Default Gateway values of your choice, including real Internet public network IP addresses. You may accept the Class C private network address of 192.168.16.2, which is suggested (but not required) by default. Click Next.

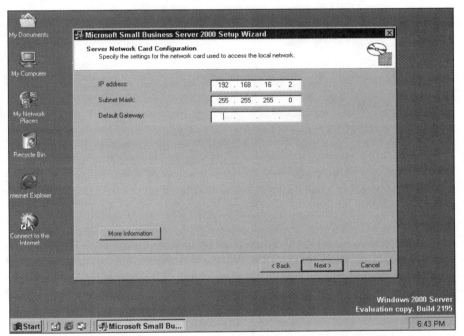

**Figure 24-8:** The Server Network Card Configuration screen allows you to provide basic IP addressing information.

28. Provide your full DNS domain name information, as well as the downstream NT-like domain name (NetBIOS domain name), on the New Domain Information screen, shown in Figure 24-9. By default, the Domain NetBIOS Name field is completed with the first term you supplied in the "Full DNS name for new domain" name field.

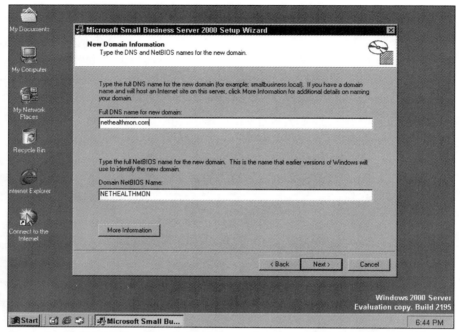

**Figure 24-9:** Critical domain naming information that cannot be changed without reinstalling Small Business Server is entered on the New Domain Information screen.

29. Change or accept the data folder locations on the Data Folders screen and click Next. At this point, additional Windows 2000 installation activity occurs (such as the configuration of Terminal Services), and Active Directory is installed in unattended mode. A component progress screen will keep you informed of the setup status.

30. Windows 2000 will reboot automatically after Active Directory and related components are installed. An automatic logon occurs, and the Small Business Server Setup Wizard starts again, allowing the Windows 2000–related components to continue installation and configuration.

31. The Component Selection screen appears, as shown in Figure 24-10. Select the components to install, the location for the installation, and click Next.

32. You will receive a notice that a Windows 2000 Server service pack will be installed. Click OK.

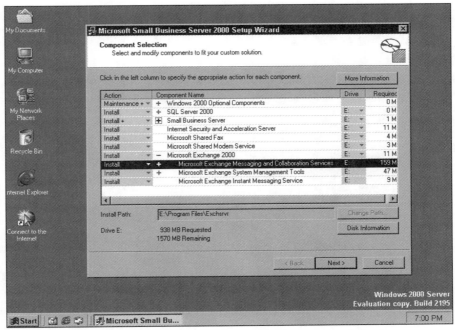

**Figure 24-10:** Making installation decisions on the Component Selection screen

**33.** Complete the ISA Server Cache Drivers screen and click Next. On this screen, you will select whether or not ISA Server caching is enabled and which drive will hold the cache files. Note that only an NTFS drive can be used for ISA caching. The default cache size is 100MB.

**34.** Select your network adapter card on the ISA Server Construct Local Address Table screen so that a Local Address Table (LAT) can automatically be constructed. LAT is used by the Network Address Translation (NAT) function in ISA Server. Click Next.

**35.** The ISA Server Local Address Table Configuration screen allows you to make LAT table entries manually. Click Next.

**36.** The Exchange 2000 Server Installation Type screen appears. Select the option to create a new organization if this is a brand new installation of Small Business Server. If you are upgrading from Small Business Server 4.5, select the Join or Upgrade option. Click Next.

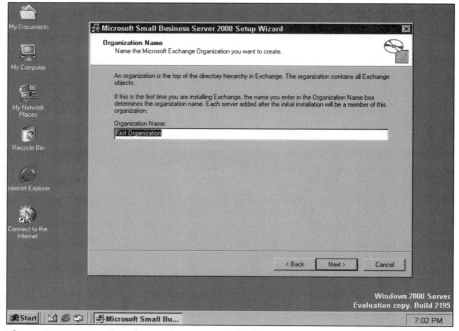

**Figure 24-11:** Naming the Exchange organization

**37.** On the Organization Name screen, shown in Figure 24-11, accept the default First Organization name for Exchange 2000 Server and click Next. If you want, you can change this to the organization name of your choice.

**38.** On the Data Folders screen, you have the opportunity to identify which drive will host the Small Business Server client applications (Outlook 2000 and so on) on the Small Business Server server machine. Make the changes and click Next.

**39.** Confirm the installation choices (applications, drive locations) on the Installation Summary screen and click Next.

**40.** If you get a message indicating that the Windows 2000 Directory Schema must be extended, click OK.

The Small Business Server installation continues. You can monitor the progress of the installation on the Component Progress screen, shown in Figure 24-12. Depending on the speed of your machine, this part of the installation process takes from one to three hours.

**41.** Click Finish on the Completing the Microsoft Small Business Server 2000 Wizard screen. Answer Yes when asked to reboot. The base installation of Small Business Server is now complete.

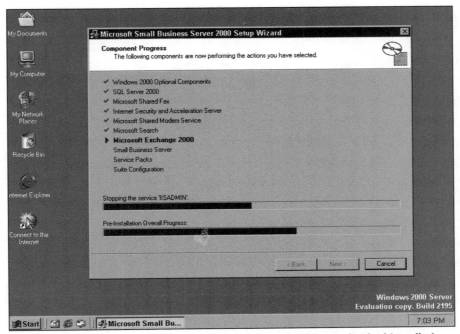

**Figure 24-12:** The Component Progress screen reports both individual installation progress and overall installation progress.

# Workstation Setup

After the Small Business Server machine completes its last reboot, as discussed in the last section, and you log on as the administrator, you're ready to move to the workstation setup stage. In this section, you will create the magic disk and run it on a workstation.

1. Make sure you are logged on to the Small Business Server server machine as an administrator.

2. Launch the Small Business Server Administrator Console by clicking the Start button on the lower-left corner of your display. Select Programs ⇨ Microsoft Small Business Server ⇨ Small Business Server Administrator Console.

3. Launch the To Do List by selecting the BackOffice To Do List found in the left pane.

4. Select Add User. The Add User Wizard launches, as seen in Figure 24-13. Click Next after reading the basic welcome information.

5. Complete the User Account Information screen with the user name, as seen in Figure 24-14.

**Figure 24-13:** Add User Wizard in Small Business Server

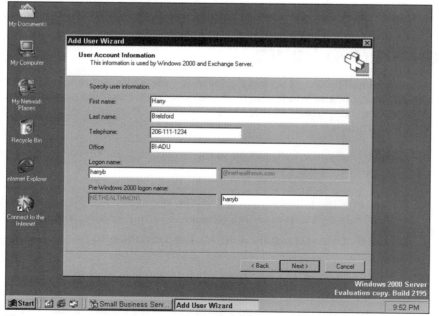

**Figure 24-14:** Providing user naming information

6. Complete the Password Generation screen. Select the "I will specify the user's password" radio button and type the password for the user. Click Next.

7. On the Mailbox Information screen, accept the default information. Click Next.

8. On the User Properties screen, shown in Figure 24-15, select the type of user template that best describes the account (Administrator, Power User, User). For example, you might select Small Business Power User if the individual you are adding to the Small Business Server network will assist in some network management duties. Click Next.

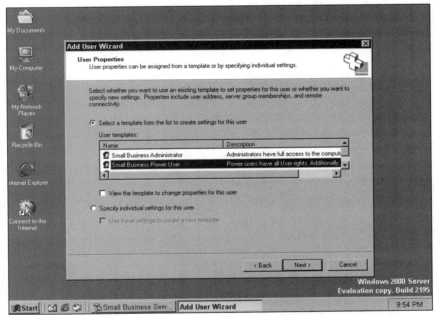

**Figure 24-15:** User templates are new in Small Business Server 2000.

9. Select whether to set up the computer now or later on the Run the Set Up Computer Wizard page. Click Next.

10. Assuming you elected to set up the computer now, provide a computer name. Click Next.

11. Select the Small Business Server client-side applications to install on the Applications screen. Click Next.

**12.** Choose whether or not to create a network setup disk on the Networking Setup Disk screen. Click Next. Insert a disk in Drive A, and the networking setup files are copied to the disk.

**13.** Click Finish on the Completing Add User Wizard screen to complete the creation of the user account and the client computer.

You will now go to the workstation that you want to add to the Small Business Server network and turn it on. After successfully booting into the workstation operating system (for example, Windows 2000 Professional), you start the Small Business Server workstation setup tasks. The setup program installs and configures the workstation-side network components (networking protocol, networking client, domain name, and machine name), sets up the specified user, and reboots the client computer. You then log on to the client computer, and the desktop shortcuts to the shared network folders are created and the applications are installed. Here are the steps:

**1.** Insert the Small Business Server workstation setup disk (magic disk) into the floppy drive of your computer. Run the Setup command from the disk. This is typically **a:\setup.exe** and can be executed from the Run dialog box of Windows 2000 Professional, Windows Me, Windows 9x, or Windows NT Workstation 4.0. The Run command is accessed via the Start button from your desktop.

**2.** The Microsoft Client Network Setup Wizard launches, and the Welcome screen appears. Click Next.

**3.** Select the computer name on the Computer Name screen and click Next.

**4.** Select the user or users you want to associate with this client computer. These people will be installed in the local Administrators group on the client machines (so they have permission to install applications locally). Click Next.

**5.** Provide the domain administrator account name and password on the Network Authentication screen. Click Next. Note that the administrator logon credentials are necessary for the client computer to join the Small Business Server domain during the client computer setup.

**6.** Click Finish on the Complete the Small Business Server Client Networking Setup Wizard screen. You will receive a message in the Windows 2000 Networking Wizard dialog box. After reading the message, click Begin. The Windows Client Setup Status dialog box will inform you of the Windows 2000 networking setup status (installing, configuring, or finishing).

7. After reading the client computer setup message regarding user, machine, and domain name, click Begin to proceed.

8. After the networking is set up, the System Settings Change dialog box appears asking if you want to restart your computer. Click Yes.

9. When prompted via the Network Logon dialog box, log on as the user you have added to this machine.

10. Click Start Now when the Application Launcher dialog box appears. This will start the installation of the Small Business Server client computer applications. The applications are installed in the following order: Microsoft Shared Modem Service client, Microsoft Shared Fax client, MS ISA client, and finally Outlook 2000 and Internet Explorer 5.

    You may track the progress of the Small Business Server client computer application setup process by observing the status information displayed in the Application Launcher dialog box.

11. Click OK when the Application Launcher dialog box reports that you have successfully installed the applications on the client computer.

# Management

The two Small Business Server Consoles are where you will perform the majority of your management tasks. The Small Business Server Personal Console offers limited selections and is typically used by power users at the client site who assist you, the MCSE consultant, in managing the network.

The real fun starts with the Small Business Server Administrator Console, shown in Figure 24-16. This is where all of the Small Business Server components may be managed. Both consoles are based on the MMC in Windows 2000.

 **Note** Both consoles may be customized to meet your needs. You are encouraged to read the Small Business Server 2000 Resource Kit from Microsoft Press for more information on console customization.

Note that Small Business Server automatically installs Terminal Services in remote administration mode, allowing you to manage the Small Business Server machine from a remote location. This is something you will want to take advantage of as an MCSE consultant.

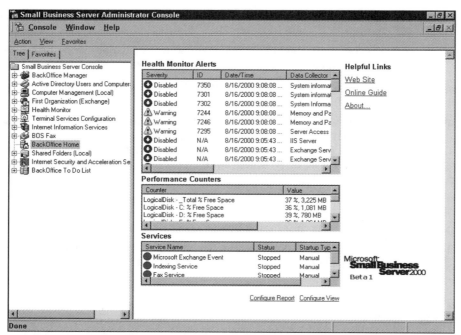

**Figure 24-16:** The Small Business Server Administrator Console

# Configuring Components

Small Business Server uses wizards launched from the consoles to implement and configure its various components. As an example in this chapter, I'll configure the Internet connection.

1. Click Start ➪ Programs ➪ Microsoft Small Business Server ➪ Small Business Server Administrator Console.

2. Select BackOffice To Do List in the tree console.

3. Click Internet Connection Wizard. The Internet Connection Wizard launches and appears.

4. Click Next after reading the Welcome notice.

5. The Configure Hardware screen appears, as seen in Figure 24-17. Select the type of hardware configuration you have and click Next. In this example, I have selected Full-time Broadband Connection.

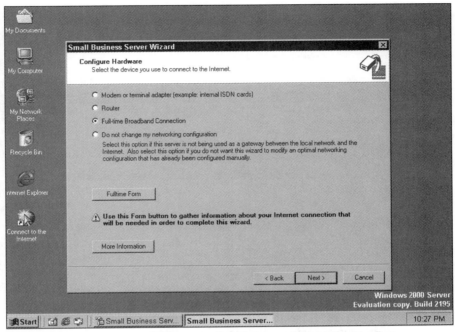

**Figure 24-17:** Selecting Full-time Broadband Connection on the Configure Hardware screen

6. On the Configure Network Adapters screen, select the inside LAN card and the outside WAN card from the listed network adapter cards and click Next. This is shown in Figure 24-18.

7. Complete the "Specify your ISP connection information" screen with default gateway and DNS server address information, as seen in Figure 24-19, and click Next.

8. Complete the Configure Internet Mail Settings screen, shown in Figure 24-20, and click Next.

9. Complete the domain name field on the Configure Internet Domain Name screen and click Next. This is shown in Figure 24-21.

10. Complete the Configure SMTP Server Address screen. Unless advised otherwise by your ISP, you typically use DNS for mail delivery. Click Next.

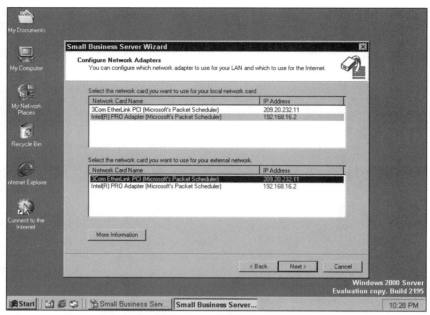

**Figure 24-18:** By selecting the inside and outside network adapter cards, you are helping to configure the firewall capabilities.

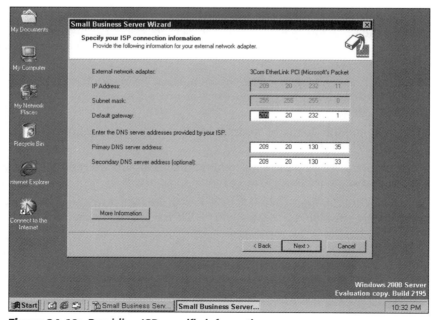

**Figure 24-19:** Providing ISP-specific information

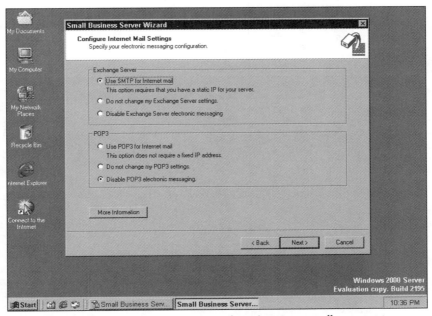

**Figure 24-20:** The Configure Internet Mail Settings screen allows you to configure SMTP and POP3 mail.

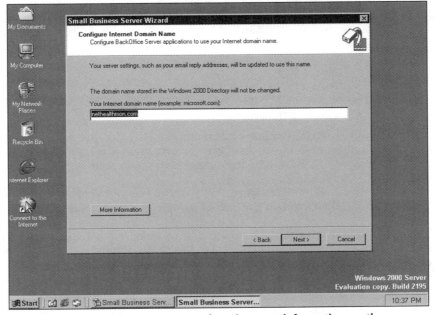

**Figure 24-21:** Provide your Internet domain name information on the Configure Internet Domain Name screen.

**11.** Complete the Configure Firewall Settings screen, as shown in Figure 24-22. This will allow you to set the ISA Server firewall settings for mail, Web Server, VPN, POP3, FTP, and Terminal Server. Click Next.

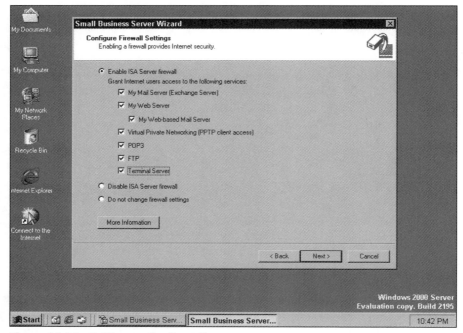

**Figure 24-22:** Setting up the firewall

**12.** Click OK if you receive an ISA warning in a Configure Firewall Settings dialog box. This warning will not appear on all systems (it warns you about overwriting existing settings).

**13.** Carefully read the summary information on the Completing the Small Business Server Internet Connection Wizard screen, shown in Figure 24-23. This is your last chance to back out of any changes, so read carefully. Click Finish.

The Internet Connection Configure Status dialog box will show you the progress of the Internet configuration on the Small Business Server machine.

This example was representative of how you configure Small Business Server. The key to being a successful Small Business Server consultant is to accomplish the configuration tasks from the management consoles.

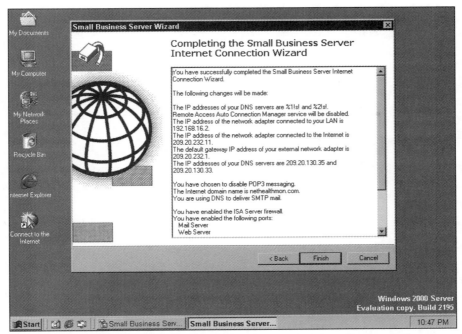

**Figure 24-23:** Important summary information is presented on the completion screen.

## Summary

So there you have a primer on being an MCSE consultant in the Small Business Server consulting space. In this chapter, Small Business Server was defined. Small Business Server–related consulting opportunities were highlighted. A competitive analysis featuring Novell's and IBM's small business product lines was offered, and the error-proof steps for installation and configuration of Small Business Server were presented.

✦      ✦      ✦

# General Technology Advising and Consulting

**N**o book on MCSE consulting would be complete without a chapter on general technology advising and consulting. For a long time, this professional services area wasn't well respected and engaged in by the MCSE technical community. Advising someone rather than implementing technology solutions didn't make much sense to the hands-on world of MCSEs. But two fundamental shifts in thinking have occurred. The first is that the years of work for many MCSEs have passed quickly. Some MCSE certification holders are now entering middle age and don't find downloading a driver at 2:00 A.M. to be fun anymore. Also, the Windows 2000 MCSE designation, with the upper-level designing exams, emphasizes a consulting role. In accordance with these shifts in thinking, I'll explore general technology consulting and advising opportunities in this chapter.

## Benefits of General Technology Consulting

You might feel that as an MCSE consultant you are going against the norm of technical hands-on consulting to stand proud and announce you're providing general technology consulting services. However, there are some compelling reasons to make this your MCSE consulting focus.

## Better money

The free marketplace is a funny thing. It keeps score with money, something that is easily quantifiable. A low-level MCSE acting in a technician role might be able to bill as high as $100 per hour. An accomplished MCSE who is hands-on, has a niche, and can engage in some systems analysis work might peak at $200 per hour. But a well-established technology advisor who reports directly to the executive level at large client sites is akin to a law partner or senior accounting partner. Bill rates here exceed $300 per hour.

Let me, using the analogy of accounting, make my point. A young accountant joins an accounting firm performing repetitive tasks. This individual makes a relatively low salary (for example, in the $30,000 per year range) and bills out at the lower bill rates in the firm. As the accountant gets more seasoned, the tasks performed become less repetitive and more original. This accountant at mid-career makes better pay and bills out at the higher bill rates. The senior accountant who has made partner bills out at the highest bill rates, makes the most money, and per-forms complex tasks that are unique. This ascension in professional services is common and can be observed in the MCSE consulting community as well. This value-added consulting career food chain is shown in Figure 25-1.

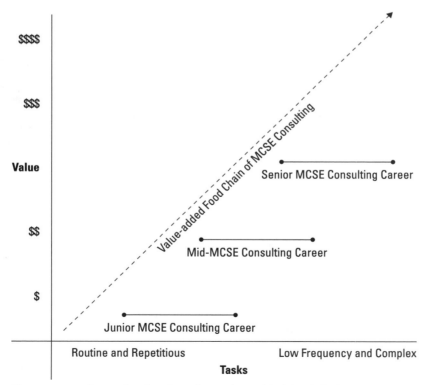

**Figure 25-1:** The professional services value-added food chain

Senior MCSE consultants who want to position themselves as general technology advisors to kings, queens, and CEOs can do quite well financially. The biggest problem that I've observed with MCSE consultants and general technology consulting is that they generally don't want to do it. MCSE consultants, including yours truly, still very much enjoy working with their hands at the keyboard, not talking in front of the whiteboard.

## Corner office company

Another factor that might make you consider a general technology consulting practice is the company you will keep. At the high end of general technology consulting, you'll be golfing with C-level management team members, such as the chief executive officer (CEO), chief information officer (CIO), chief financial officer (CFO), and chief operating officer (COO) of various companies. That's good company to keep at some point in your MCSE career. The social events you'll be invited to are wonderful.

## Goodbye pager

Another consideration skewed to the pragmatic side is that the higher up you ascend in the value-added food chain, the fewer emergency calls you'll take. A technician in a low-level MCSE consulting role may be paged several times a weekend. A high-level MCSE consultant serving the C-level may be paged once or twice a year.

## Up or out

As an MCSE consultant you will at some level feel pressure to raise your bill rates. If you work for a consulting firm, the pressure might be overt. Partners will put pressure on you to find a way to raise your rates or exit the firm because those partners will increase their profits if your rates are higher. If you stagnate, that affects their pocketbooks and may cause them to question whether of not the seat you are occupying could be held by someone who will be more successful in raising their bill rates.

If you work for yourself, you won't feel the same explicit pressure to increase your rates. However, life's events might drive you to this. For example, the kids need dental work, followed by college tuition. In short, your own internal pressures will eventually push you to raise your bill rates.

There are several types of competitors in the general technology consulting and advising space that are also seeking many of the same benefits just described. The competitors that an MCSE consultant in the general technology consulting field will encounter are different from those in other niches, such as SQL Server. Here you are in the domain of large accounting firms, such as the Big Five, and second-tier regional firms. When you bid on work in this consulting space, you'll be up against well-mannered, well-spoken professional service providers. My advice to you is to dress and speak well while staying on your best business behavior, and you'll do fine.

# Aligned with Microsoft

Believe it or not, acting as a general technology consultant in the MCSE community positions you to take advantage of Microsoft's new thinking in the Windows 2000 MCSE track. If you look at the three upper-level designing exams (70-219, 70-220, and 70-221), you will notice the first objectives relate to general business and technology analysis. I bring up this theme several times in this book in the context of positioning Windows 2000 MCSEs as consultants, not just technicians. For example, in Chapter 3, I speak strongly about how the consulting mindset, as evidenced by my list of consulting fundamentals, is the cornerstone to your success as a true consultant who is professional and communicative. Later in this chapter, I list specific upper-level MCSE exam objectives and relate them to the general technology consulting discussion.

# MBA-Side Perspective

If you hold both an MBA and an MCSE, the general technology consulting area is tailor-made for you. A couple of opportunities viewed from the MBA perspective are performing needs analysis and writing technology studies.

## Reflective and contemplative

One day, as I was driving between consulting engagements, I was listening to a popular news show called *All Things Considered* on my local public radio station. A person being interviewed spoke at length about the value of education, including attending humanities courses. The points raised in this interview were that leaders in business and commerce are typically better educated than others who are less successful. So how does this apply to general technology consulting for the MCSE consultant? Very simply, a more educated person is likely to reflect on ambiguous situations before offering advice on specific solutions. And this individual is more likely to contemplate alternative strategies and not just charge ahead. It is this thinking process that is a hallmark of general technology consulting and advising. It is a way of thinking that certainly comes more from the MBA community than it does from the MCSE community.

## Needs analysis

MBAs love needs analysis. I guess it comes from the case study–based curriculum found in so many MBA programs. Needs analysis refers to assessing a current situation and determining what a client's technology needs are. Do they need a new computer system or just an upgrade to an existing system? You will have a chance to analyze a case study later in this chapter.

MCSE consultants that elect the general technology path can do very well to learn more about needs analysis and incorporate that knowledge into their consulting services. A good starting point to learn more is to visit the bookstore of a college in your area and purchase an upper-level or a graduate-level management information systems text. Here you will find significant information on needs analysis.

## Technology studies

There are many people making good livings in this world writing technology studies for large clients. This work falls into the realm of general technology consulting and is often performed by MBAs as much as by MCSEs. It's good work if you can find it. Be advised that on many occasions, just like oft-ignored thick government studies, the well-written recommendations in technology studies that you may write are never implemented.

### Guest Sermon — Where Ideas Come From

This guest sermon is offered by Matthew Gonzalez from the great state of Texas. I met Matthew at a *Microsoft Certified Professional Magazine* TechMentor conference in San Francisco. After speaking with him at length, I knew he was the perfect person to deliver the guest sermon for this chapter.

Matthew began his career working with data warehousing in the insurance industry, where he worked on configuring the second and third tiers of a data-warehousing environment. This entailed setting up a Windows NT Server and IIS environment to host multiple decision support queries between the client and the data-warehousing database. Matthew was also responsible for co-leading the development of an interface to the Web-based decision support system and the development of ad hoc queries. His endeavors meshed well with the I/T architecture function, where he worked on establishing an XML architecture framework, co-developed and managed an architecture compliance process, and served as the communication arm within an I/T architecture environment. Matthew's educational background includes the following: B.B.A. in Information Systems (University of Texas at San Antonio); MCSE (InfoTech); MBA in General Business (St. Mary's University); and P.M.P. — Project Management Professional (Project Management Institute).

Matthew is currently being mentored as an instructor at the University of Phoenix Online, where he has been pre-approved to teach select undergraduate and graduate courses in the MCSE curriculum. He is the founder of his own company, CommuniQué, which still takes much of his attention. He is beginning to develop his business plan writing skills for start-ups that wish to present their idea(s) to potential investors but remains focused through CommuniQué on helping companies with Technology Feasibility and Readiness Assessment Analysis. Matthew can be reached by email at matthew_gonzalez@yahoo.com.

*Continued*

*Continued*

From all that education and experience, Matthew gives the following guidance and words of wisdom:

*The basic evaluation of purchasing or developing a piece of technology is often based on the cost of the product along with a few industry comparisons against competitor's products. The business case and desired features of the chosen hardware, software, or application in question also make quality a strong candidate in the evaluation of technology by analyzing how others have implemented, succeeded, and/or failed. Oftentimes, companies invest in technology without evaluating and thinking about it from a time perspective and how long it will take to achieve a return on investment (ROI). CommuniQué was founded based on the notion that people within companies need to understand a piece of technology with all three project management cornerstones (time, cost, and quality) in mind before adopting or investing in the new piece of technology prematurely.*

*CommuniQué focuses on developing Technology Feasibility Analysis and Technology Readiness Assessments for companies and investors alike who are on the verge of adopting or developing a new piece of hardware, software, network, or application. As an MCSE, I found it beneficial, for myself as well as my clients, to first understand the business needs and constraints of my clients before implementing and recommending a piece of technology that may not fit their needs whatsoever. You would be surprised at the number of companies that invest in technology without analyzing their own business reasons, budgets, expertise level, ROI, and industry adoption rate of the technology. Having made myself aware of this, I used the aforementioned project management cornerstones as my company's primary assessment criterion, over my own technology expertise, in recommending technology solutions. A majority of my research comes from secondary research consortiums that specialize in researching; however, my knowledge of technology plays a strong role in my ability to primarily research, analyze, and comprehend various industries and their use of technology.*

*Here's an interesting example of a company based in England for which I performed some primary research. In the end, the company decided not to accept any of my recommendations. Essentially, the company already had an existing technology infrastructure in place to sell products over the Internet but didn't have the capability to interface a shopping cart solution with a relational database to store customer profile and history of purchasing information. I had an absolute deadline (time) to propose several solutions to address their needs, and I knew the recommended technology had to fit within their existing infrastructure and be available at all times (quality). I didn't have an exact monetary figure to work with other than the shopping cart solution had to be cheap. Upon reviewing my recommendations, the company decided not to implement any of the solutions that I had proposed simply because they were too expensive (cost). Yes, I probably could have recommended freeware/shareware to fit their unannounced budget needs, but would the software really meet the time and especially quality aspects of their needs. Probably not. Although, they didn't adopt any of my recommendations, I felt that CommuniQué and I had done our job because my recommendations forced them to go back and calculate/estimate a solid budget for their anticipated shopping cart solution. This is a perfect example of how important it is to leverage your background in technology while staying focused on the client's business needs and constraints first.*

# MCSE-Side Perspective

To be honest, I don't expect this area of consulting to appeal to most MCSEs, at least not in the early part of their consulting careers. How can I say that? I've observed many less experienced MCSEs to be more interested in the mechanics of hardware and software solutions than in the overall understanding of processes and flows. Less experienced MCSEs tend to make solutions more complicated than necessary, all in the name of being technical. For example, an MCSE I once worked with named Joe was known for telling you how to build a watch when you asked what time it was. The point is that general technology consulting and advising takes a certain level of emotional and professional maturity that isn't necessarily required to make a Registry entry in Windows 2000 Server. But given the passage of time and growing maturity, more MCSE consultants will look at the general technology consulting and advising role as a viable practice area.

## Emphasis is general

This kind of consulting represents a substantial paradigm shift for the average MCSE consultant. Placing an emphasis on general technology consulting instead of specific discrete solution sets, such as a sophisticated logon script, is something new to most MCSE consultants. It's a way of practicing the technology craft that isn't well indoctrinated into the MCSE culture.

## Relating MCSE exam objectives to general consulting

Microsoft is helping promote the delivery of general technology consulting in the MCSE community. How so? The Windows 2000 MCSE exams are implicitly endorsing general technology consulting. To prove this point, in Table 25-1 I list and describe the business-related exam objectives for the 70-219: Designing a Microsoft Windows 2000 Directory Services Infrastructure exam. For example, Microsoft has an exam objective to identify company priorities. The exam objectives listed in Table 25-1 are taken from Microsoft's published list of MCSE exam objectives.

| Table 25-1 70-219 Business Exam Objectives | |
| --- | --- |
| **Objective** | **Description** |
| Analyze Business Requirements. | This is the general discussion about business. |
| Analyze the existing and planned business models. | Business models typically are the underlying strategies that guide the firm. |

*Continued*

| Table 25-1 *(continued)* | |
|---|---|
| **Objective** | **Description** |
| Analyze the company model and the geographical scope. Models include regional, national, international, subsidiary, and branch offices. | This addresses how the company is organized geographically. |
| Analyze company processes. Processes include information flow, communication flow, service and product life cycles, and decision-making. | This addresses operations. |
| Analyze the existing and planned organizational structures. Considerations include management model; company organization; vendor, partner, and customer relationships; and acquisition plans. | This addresses centralized, decentralized, project, and matrix organizational forms. |
| Analyze factors that influence company strategies. | This is the stakeholders analysis. What stakeholders inside and outside the company influence strategy? |
| Identify company priorities. | This addresses the need to be aware of communicated (formal) and grapevine (informal) company priorities. |
| Identify the projected growth and growth strategy. | How will the company grow? Through mergers? Acquisitions? Growth of core businesses? |
| Identify relevant laws and regulations. | This is known as environmental scanning. If applicable, how does the legal and regulatory environment affect the firm? |
| Identify the company's tolerance for risk. | This is risk assessment. Is the firm risk tolerant or risk adverse? |
| Identify the total cost of operations. | This is total cost of operations analysis. The big push in technology consulting is to lower the firm's total cost of operations by using technology. |
| Analyze the structure of IT management. Considerations include type of administration, such as centralized or decentralized; funding model; outsourcing; decision-making process; and change-management process. | This is taking much of the preceding business analysis and applying it to the technology department inside the firm. Basically, this is a business needs analysis of the IT department. |

# General Technology Consulting Service Examples

One example of a general technology consulting practice that you could provide to clients as an MCSE consultant is the formation and management of a technology committee. Often it takes an outside consultant, well versed in both technology specifics and general business topics, to get an organization to takes its technology seriously. As this type of consultant, you can act as an organizational focal point for getting competing factions together. It's often hard for an internal staff member to take the lead in organizing a technology committee.

A technology committee typically meets quarterly to review outstanding technology issues, as well as plan for future technology upgrades and enhancements. The suggested roles on the technology committee are defined in Figure 25-2.

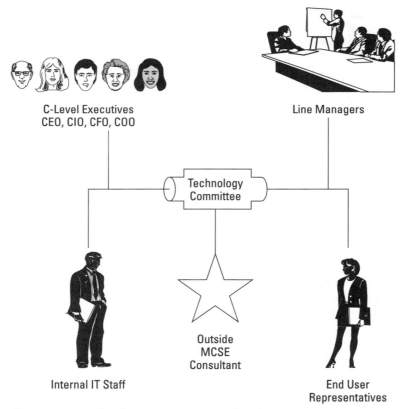

**Figure 25-2:** Technology committee membership

## Case analysis

Another general consulting example is one that I've periodically mentioned: needs analysis. What better way to present that than to share with you a business technology case study with background facts, problem identification, and a solution set. This fictional case study of Warbucks MIC, Inc., is your welcome to the world of MCSE consulting in the general technology advising area.

## Warbucks MIC

In 1998, Warbucks MIC had a Texas-sized computing problem. Twenty-one separate information systems fiefdoms spread across seven business units were attempting, with ever-diminishing success, to maintain control over a tangle of computing systems.

A desktop machine might run UNIX or OS/2 or Windows 95, Windows for Workgroups or Windows 3.1 or DOS. No fewer than eight separate messaging systems, including Microsoft Mail, Lotus Notes, IBM PROFS, DEC All-in-One, and cc:Mail, were operating. The company supported several word processors, multiple spreadsheets, myriad databases, and on the connectivity front, at least four unrelated networking protocols. "We were on a variety of file servers, and they were at different release levels," says Frank Ditt, CIO of the Denver-based company since September 1996. "The infrastructure was very hard to operate on a day-to-day basis, and it didn't support key objectives of the business such as implementing SAP finance."

Warbucks MIC was struggling to make its business practices more competitive, even as it grappled with management structures left over from the 1970s and 1980s. IS management was every bit as decentralized and ineffective as the computing infrastructure it was trying to control. A small, cloistered corporate data center presided in name only over far-flung IS departments. The CIO, who served corporate headquarters only, could recommend desktop and network standards, but had no authority to enforce those guidelines with individual IS managers in the various divisions. "If you asked an IS manager if his department was a mess, he'd say no. The next IS manager felt that his department was under control, too, except that he worked with a completely different set of tools and systems and software," recalls Vinny Benk, director of industry and technology information systems and a 23-year Warbucks MIC veteran who was given the responsibility for managing the changes to come at Warbucks MIC. "As long as you were communicating only in your own space, the world seemed fine."

## Problems to the third power

The multiple platforms, applications, and networks created some productivity-busting difficulties. "We didn't have common back-office tools, so we were speaking different languages," says Ditt. "The chairman couldn't even send a global e-mail message to the troops."

Workers were using such a wide variety of desktop applications that common office tasks such as sharing PC attachments turned into major problems. "If somebody wanted a document, I had to copy it onto a floppy. Now I just download a file to them, and I know they're going to be able to open the document," says Connie Ackman, senior marketing executive in Warbucks MIC's process control division in O'Hare Township, a suburb of Boston. "The network was always crashing. Your machine would just freeze. Now the reliability is an order of magnitude better."

Despite all the process concerns, Ditt and other managers emphasize Warbucks MIC's principal concern was cash. "A lot of [the problem] just hinged frankly on the number of people in IT. It was as high as 1,250," says Ditt. Support costs in particular were troubling; one estimate had 67 percent of the information systems staff (two-thirds) working simply to keep the diverse systems up and running.

The costs remained hidden in multiple departments' bottom lines until a top-management overhaul in 1996 brought in a new chairman and, early in 1997, a new CFO, Frank Raynolds. As part of an overall business audit, Raynolds' staff calculated for the first time IS costs from each individual business unit. That number shocked everyone. "When you totaled up information systems costs at the corporate level, which was very difficult to extract, it looked like a very large number," says Benk. According to Ditt, Warbucks MIC spent $250 million on information technology in 1996.

In the early summer of 1996, Raynolds turned to The MCSE Consulting Group (MCSE-CG), a Plano, Texas, consultancy that specializes in information technology strategy and that also fills in for and recruits senior IS managers. MCSE-CG employees directed IS at Warbucks MIC for just over two months, until Ditt arrived in the fall of 1996; its consultants conducted an initial study that revealed the level of both technical and managerial inefficiencies and, with Warbucks MIC senior management's approval, set to work on this three-pronged strategy to change the situation:

✦ Develop an architecture that will cut costs and meet business requirements for the next five years.

✦ Reorganize the managerial structure of information systems.

✦ Hire a new CIO.

**Tip** The discussion here is focused on the type of general technology consulting and advising discussed in this chapter.

Thus was born SIT, or the Strategic Information Technology initiative, a plan for Warbucks MIC to build a common, centrally managed system of tightly integrated networks, file and print servers running standard interoperable messaging, and desktop applications; on the organizational side, the plan called for an empowered central technology division responsible for making all infrastructure decisions and for creating a centralized help desk for the whole company.

## Solutions, solutions, solutions

From the outset, MCSE-CG focused most intensely on the nuts and bolts of the infrastructure. "We really couldn't get after anything else without fixing the plumbing first," says Bobby-Joe Graham, a consultant with MCSE-CG who served as director of IT services at Warbucks MIC during the two-year span. The MCSE-CG team also concluded that the fastest way to reduce support costs was to cut back the huge number of desktop applications, operating systems, and network protocols as much as possible. Warbucks MIC would then be able to reduce support personnel, take advantage of volume procurements, and boost employee productivity.

Warbucks MIC settled on its vendors with lightning speed: IBM and Microsoft were on board just one month after MCSE-CG presented the broad outline of SIT to the Warbucks MIC chairman's council in early September 1996.

Since volume procurement was one of the leading goals of SIT, says Graham, the team from the outset sought the widest range of products with the highest degree of integration from the fewest number of vendors. Backoffice functionality was deemed more important than applications. Desktop applications weren't a first priority because most office suites offer nearly identical functionality in their business programs, Graham says. Ackman agrees: "Whether it's Microsoft or WordPerfect, I don't have a preference, as long as I have something that works." Before SIT began, in fact, Ackman switched from WordPerfect to Microsoft Word on her own initiative to share files more easily with outside contacts.

Was Warbucks MIC foolhardy to select Microsoft as its top-to-bottom software provider rather than test each component against its individual competitors? Ditt, who came on board a year after the initiative began, says no. "I don't think the decision was a follow-the-leader thing," he says. "You can narrow products down to a few choices fast." On the server, for example, Warbucks had a choice of UNIX, NetWare, or Windows 2000 Server. Windows Server simply beat out the competition. "It took more NetWare servers than it takes Windows 2000 Server–based servers to do what we want to do," Ditt says. And when ease of administration is a key objective, the degree of integration among products is as important as the individual performance of each. Achieving compatibility between elements such as network adapters and device drivers can cost companies "a lot of overhead," Ditt says. Such problems are virtually nonexistent when buying from a single vendor.

Settling on IBM for hardware and Microsoft for software (Windows 2000 Server and BackOffice) eliminated the need to make a lot of subsequent decisions. "When you say, 'I'm going to pick Microsoft BackOffice,' that moves you into a second set of easier decisions," says Benk. In addition, for a company with Warbucks MIC's clout, he says, "selecting IBM as the hardware vendor not just for the desktop but also for the servers meant we would get great pricing and special help from the vendor in putting it all together."

# Managing change

Though MCSE-CG and Warbucks MIC imagined and agreed upon a plan, translating it to reality wasn't without its managerial challenges.

Although SIT called for supporting a single set of standardized desktop applications, workers were allowed to keep certain legacy applications under limited conditions. "People first had to provide proof that they needed a legacy application; plus, management had to assure us that was a valid software need," explains Benk. Once those criteria were met, employees presented the application to the so-called Legion Lab, which had been created specifically to measure existing applications against the new SIT configuration. Connie Ackman, for example, needed to maintain a copy of WordPerfect on her system simply because so many of her old files were in that format. "I checked with the Legion Lab, and they were very flexible," says Ackman. "They weren't being the IT police; they just wanted to make sure it worked okay." Like the vast majority of Warbucks MIC workers, Ackman is happy with the new software and uses her legacy word processor only to retrieve archived files. "They did a good job of communicating the goals of SIT," says Ackman. The promotional information alleviated some of the workers' fears and helped them understand how they could benefit from using standardized desktop software, she says.

Reorganizing the IS staff was more painful. Warbucks MIC established a Customer Support Center (CSC) at company headquarters. "We built a truly centralized help desk for the whole company," says Graham, "where before we had had multiple systems engineers, PC, and desktop support people reporting locally." With CSC, all calls are directed to the help desk and then bounced to a level-two team if they can't be resolved. If the problem still needs attention, an on-site support worker can be dispatched to a worker's desk.

The plans called for some 80 people to work at the data center in Orlando. At the central help desk, Warbucks MIC wanted a ratio of 300 desktops per support worker; on-site, the goal was 200 to 1. Previously, the ratios varied from department to department, says Ditt, but averaged between 50 and 75 workers per support staffer in the field. With the new ratios in hand, managers simply determined how many people worked at a given site, assigned the correct number of support staff, and then reduced the number of employees accordingly. So far, Warbucks has reduced its IS workforce by 250 people.

Warbucks MIC managers struggled to find the best way to determine who would stay and who would go. "We tried to let people know they wouldn't have a long-term job in some cases a year or more in advance," says Graham. "It was the most humane way we could think of." Once new technology positions were established, employees could apply for those jobs. Again, the company tried to let people know as soon as possible if they would in fact be on the team at the new Warbucks MIC.

MCSE-CG consultants, including Mannie Jones, who was acting CIO at Warbucks until Ditt's arrival, and the consultancy's founder, Charlie Brelsford (no relation to the author of this book), recruited candidates to fill the revitalized CIO position that would entail taking direct responsibility for all information systems activities, both at headquarters and in the field. The MCSE-CG team "ran the technical filter" to make sure applicants were capable, says Ditt, and then Warbucks MIC management vetted the list of candidates, seeking someone compatible with the company's new vision and management style. Frank Ditt joined the company in late September of 1996 from Thompson Aerospace Electronics of Seattle.

## As the dust settles

Now, on the eve of a historic split that will separate the company's industrial and power businesses from its media holdings, the newly streamlined and energized Warbucks MIC is working on an end-to-end applications plan that exploits its new infrastructure.

Warbucks MIC, and Ditt in particular, are pleased with the payback of the SIT project thus far (the rollout is expected to be completed in late 1999 or early 2000). The project is self-funding, as annual investment and return both add up to about $25 million. And other benefits are readily apparent, Ditt says: "There are 250 fewer people in support and our acquisition price for assets is significantly lower than before. We're able to acquire tier-one equipment at tier-two prices."

In addition, workers now have a "common language" of uniform messaging and shared applications based on Microsoft BackOffice that allows them to communicate easily across departments and up and down the hierarchy. The central help desk, which fields some 10,000 queries a month, closes half of those calls on the first try, and Warbucks MIC's many networks are now managed centrally, saving IS workers time and effort. "From a delivery perspective, we're able to support and roll out things like client/server application changes with very low overhead," says Ditt. "When we need a new virus scan sent out, it takes almost no effort at all."

Warbucks MIC may have undertaken SIT to clean up its bottom line, but the benefits quickly trickled down to the end users as well. "Our Microsoft Exchange–based e-mail is working very well, and the Windows 2000 network is better," reported one highly placed Warbucks MIC executive.

## The technical solution

Now that you've worked through the business technology side of the case study over the past few pages, here is the technical solution for Warbucks MIC:

✦ **Operating system and suite** — Microsoft Corp.'s Windows 2000 Server, Microsoft BackOffice

✦ **Client computers** — Windows 2000 Professional, 450 MHz Pentiums with 128MB RAM, a 256KB cache, CD-ROM, 10GB hard drive, and 19-inch monitor

✦ **Desktop applications** — Microsoft Office 2000

✦ **Messaging** — Microsoft Exchange Server as part of BackOffice

✦ **Network management** — Microsoft's Systems Management Server as part of BackOffice

✦ **Servers** — Four ("4") dual 600 MHz IBM Pentiums with 512MB RAM and 200GB hard disks (RAID 5), 512 Kbps cache, Ethernet 10/100 connection, and an FDDI network adapter

So you have now had the opportunity in this exercise to read a case study, identify the problems, look at a solution, and observe the technical implementation of that solution.

# Summary

As an MCSE consultant working for yourself or a firm, you'll feel pressure over the years to increase your bill rates. It's a natural progression in the professional services field to start out as an inexperienced consultant with a lower bill rate and ultimately bill at a higher rate when you have more professional experience. Many MCSE consultants both enjoy general technology consulting and advising consulting opportunities and are seeking a way to bill at higher rates. This chapter has defined high yielding general technology consulting opportunities that are available for the MCSE consultant, including needs analysis, technology plan writing, and technology committee membership.

✦     ✦     ✦

# Training While Consulting

I've heard it said time and time again that consultants are natural trainers. This observation certainly applies to the ideal MCSE consultant who is communicative, technically proficient, and enthusiastic. Those three elements, in my mind, define a trainer.

If you ever have the occasion to step back and watch an MCSE consultant toil, you notice that the job isn't just bits and bytes. MCSE consultants are just as likely to show a procedure to a power user as they are to a client representative. For many MCSE consultants, this is the ideal mixture: working with technology and people.

You don't need to be a know-it-all to be a superior trainer. To be successful, your communication skills and the ability to go find the right answer are more important than your BackOffice wisdom.

All MCSE consultants put on a training hat at one time or another, whether they know it or not. Many MCSE consultants are really just frustrated trainers and often add training as another professional service that they can deliver on a billable hour basis. And once they get a taste of training, I've even seen a few who ultimately make the full-time jump to the training community. Hey—the technology industry is big enough for all of us: part-timers, full-timers, and anything in between. However, for the purposes of this chapter, I'll focus primarily on MCSE consultants who are doing both consulting and training.

# If You Really Want To Learn — Teach

You've likely heard the phrase that if you really want to learn a subject, then go teach it. That certainly applies to my MCSE consulting career. It was one thing to poke around with the early Microsoft network solutions such as Windows NT Advanced Server 3.1 and even to pass the early MCSE exams. It was entirely another thing to stand in front of 25 eager MCSE wannabes and pontificate long and loud about the virtues of NT.

I thought I had paid my dues when I put in my hours to pass my MCSE exams and to work with BackOffice and Microsoft server solutions. I was amazed at the preparation I needed to become a bona fide instructor teaching MCSE courses. I truly increased my own knowledge level as part of the course preparation phase. I was exposed at an expert level to things such as the Advanced RISC Computing (ARC) specification naming convention in Windows NT that I really didn't use on a day-to-day basis as an MCSE consultant in the trenches. The point is that teaching rounds out your knowledge base.

# Those Who Can — Train

You've likely heard the saying before about those who wash out of industry and go away to become teachers. It has been my experience as a trainer that this thinking really doesn't apply to MCSEs who also want to be trainers.

Just as in the movie *Top Gun,* starring Tom Cruise, the best fighter pilots in America were invited to conduct elite fighter pilot training, I like to invite top MCSE students to submit their resumes to Seattle Pacific University to become certification instructors. The best and brightest MCSEs today are exactly the types of instructor we need to teach the MCSEs of tomorrow. On more than one occasion, MCSE program alumni have returned to help out as instructors. It's a wonderful and proven trainer-recruiting vehicle.

Top performing MCSE consultants often teach a class here or there if for no other reason than they are true professionals and achievers. I attribute this to the old phrase, "If you want to get something done, assign it to a busy person." Some MCSE consultants are well rounded, very busy and involved, and work long full days. These are the individuals who choose to teach a certification class on the way home from a long day of consulting.

# Those Who Can't — Train

If you're now thinking you don't want the stresses and strains of being an MCSE consultant, being a trainer might just be the calling for you. Education is long known for attracting sharp people who don't want the politics and ungodly long hours of the private sector.

Perhaps you're one of these types who has forsaken private industry, and for whatever reasons you have, you don't want to be an MCSE consultant. Then may I be the first to welcome you to the training community. There is a shortage of dedicated and enthusiastic technology trainers. If your gift isn't MCSE consulting, perhaps being an MCSE trainer is your niche.

# Rule of Ten — Considering Training Services

There are many reasons to consider training as an outlet for your MCSE skill set. I've listed ten that stand out.

## 1 — Seeking enjoyment and fulfillment

Perhaps you feel guilty that success as an MCSE consultant has come easy to you. The lucrative pay scale, late model car, and new home are wonderful, but you've got an empty feeling inside. I've seen MCSE consultants feed that hunger by giving something back as an instructor. These people aren't teaching for the pay. In fact, being a trainer can cost them money (training hours often pay less than consulting hours in the college and technical institute environments). These people simply enjoy training and like to help people be successful. Call them MCSE mentors with a serious work ethic.

## 2 — Doing both

There's nothing wrong with adding another arrow in your MCSE consulting quiver. If economic times turn bad, you may be firing those arrows to pay the mortgage and put food on the table. The Alaskan oil recession of the mid-1980s was one of the key reasons I got into teaching. I never stopped doing the trainer thing, and it became a habit. One day I looked at a calendar and realized I had been both a technology professional and technology trainer for over a dozen years.

## 3 — Moonlighting

So you're in it for the money. At some level many of us are in it for the money, whether that money sends our kids to college or funds a decent retirement. Many adjunct trainers teach a class here and there to earn mad money. They've been some of the best MCSE trainers I've had the pleasure to work with because they are usually happy to be in the classroom. It beats tending bar at night to make a few extra bucks.

More importantly, circling back to an earlier theme, attracting the best and brightest from the MCSE consulting community necessitates using part-timers who are moonlighting after hours. For them, it's a new dimension to the MCSE professional experience.

## 4 – Gaining competitive advantage

The trainer role is an opportunity to give yourself a competitive advantage in the field of MCSE consulting. Instead of paying for $1,800 per week for courses, you're now teaching them. Not only do you get your hands on the thick curriculum books, but also you don't have to pay for them. You effectively get paid to take the courses.

This strategy should also help meet your need to stay current with your MCSE designation (especially in light of the aggressive Windows 2000 recertification requirements).

## 5 – Avoiding pager burnout – no overtime

One advantage in the training community is the respite that's received by not having to carry the pager or to work long after-hours. By and large, certification trainers end class at a fixed time, say goodbye, and go home. No pagers and no unexpected overtime are required. There's the occasional follow-up e-mail from a student seeking an answer, but that's minor league compared to the time demands of MCSE consulting in the private sector.

## 6 – Selling billable hours

Not surprisingly, the act of teaching is also the act of paid marketing at its finest. Where else can you get paid to demonstrate your capabilities before a captive audience for hours on end? On more than one occasion, I've converted my class-room time as a trainer to billable time as an MCSE consultant. For example, I've delivered courses on Networking Essentials to business audiences as part of the Microsoft seminar channel at Microsoft's PacWest office (www.microsoft.com/pacwest). Microsoft has training and conference facilities that it often books with presentations for both general and technical audiences. After teaching a Networking Essentials class to an average audience of 70 attendees, I would often receive a half dozen business cards for consulting work follow-up. This would result in approximately three sales calls and, ultimately, one engagement for my Small Business Server consulting services. Given the four-hour time commitment I made to deliver the Networking Essentials presentation, the one engagement (which typically exceeded $10,000 in billable time) was a wonderful reward. Now step back and appreciate the fact I gave these presentations once per month, and you can see that it was a very good use of time.

## 7 – Finding leads to interesting job opportunities

If you are just starting out as an MCSE consultant, training is a credible professional endeavor, so it's a wonderful way to cover an unemployment gap in your work history. More relevant, vocational technical education institutions, community colleges, and other training organizations frequently advertise for contract trainers.

Depending on the particular organization's needs, such as a "Can you start in one hour?" request, you may find yourself quickly hired and standing before a class of technology students with little or no practical training experience. I got my very first teaching job at an Alaskan vocational technical school as an immediate emergency hire. That base of training experience (deep in the trenches, I might add) has lead to numerous and higher quality training opportunities over the years, including my current home at Seattle Pacific University.

## 8 — Finding leads to other nonjob opportunities

As an MCSE trainer, you'll probably enjoy staying in touch with former students, as I have over the years. Occasionally, you will bump into these students at job sites or out and about. Past students have been an avenue for me to join boards of directors, participate in civic volunteer opportunities, and otherwise engage in commerce and industry activities. I've even gotten a free dinner or two from grateful former students.

## 9 — Working retirement

There's nothing like a working retirement as an instructor. The hours are mellow, the job doesn't kill you, and you get to stay involved with technology, making you employable if you want to go back to industry.

What has stood out about the working retired as trainers is that these individuals have food and shelter covered with retirement pay and that the teaching pay is mad money. More importantly, these individuals typically have more time than harried adjunct instructors to do a great job of class preparation.

## 10 — Writing and selling books

Publishers and executive editors look for certain signals when recruiting writers, including accomplishments in different fields and a broad background. Being a trainer opened the door slightly for me to become a writer. More importantly today, as an instructor, I enjoy the almost unfair benefit of specifying my books as a required or recommended text for the courses I teach. It's a time-honored teacher tradition to sell books, and students enjoy the cachet of learning from the person who wrote the book.

# Training Styles

Part of being a trainer is that you deliver your style of training. This style is in large part what makes you the trainer you are. It exposes your strengths and weaknesses, and it places your personality front and center. In this section, I discuss two common teaching styles.

## Guide by the side

It has been noted that in the delivery of technology content as a trainer, you're more likely to be a guide or coach than a droning know-it-all at the head of the room. MCSE courses lend themselves to performing lab work and to helping students complete exercises. These courses are traditionally light on theory and modeling when compared to liberal arts coursework.

More importantly, you're likely to be no smarter than some of your experienced MCSE certification candidates who are working with the technology every day are. If you play the know-it-all, you'll get burned by the student who happens to know more than you do. It's better to be the guide and draw out those valuable contributions and comments that other students have to share with everyone. Not a course goes by where a student doesn't teach me something I didn't know.

## Sage on the stage

Suppose it turns out that you really do know it all. And not only that, but suppose you've been placed on stage in a huge lecture auditorium. Under these conditions, you really have to be the sage on the stage.

**Tip**    It has been my experience that the larger the audience, the less detail you can convey and the more comedy you need to weave into your lecture. Call it the law of large numbers.

There are those instructors who take the sage on the stage approach in the smaller MCSE lab-based classroom environments and pull it off successfully. While it doesn't work for me personally, it's a style that I recognize and appreciate.

# Rule of Ten — Training Success Factors

I'll use the next couple of pages to discuss factors that when developed help you to teach and train effectively. The Rule of Ten for being a successful trainer includes the following characteristics:

## 1 — Communication skills

The true mark of a great trainer is good communication skills. Whether you speak using examples, metaphors, war stories, analogies, or even fables, the students look to the instructor to be a superior communicator. This is especially important and challenging in the technology environment of Microsoft BackOffice and .NET server-based solutions as well as in the world of the MCSE consultant. I've emphasized the importance of strong communication skills many times in this book, particularly in Chapter 3. The up side to being both a trainer and an MCSE consultant is that you can use the training experience to improve your speaking and presentation skills.

This is a growth opportunity that will favorably impact your role as an MCSE consultant because you'll be a better communicator with your clients. More importantly, you're effectively being paid to learn a new skill. Contrast this with the costs of joining a public speaking organization, such as Toastmasters International. In the training scenario, you are paid; in the Toastmasters International scenario, you pay.

## 2 – Technical know how

Since you're teaching technology courses (I'm assuming MCSE courses), the baseline assumption is that you grasp what you're talking about. You don't have to be the smartest MCSE in the land to teach, but you *have* to be technically competent.

## 3 – Pacing

Nothing is more frustrating to students than poor time management. This takes two forms: too slow and too fast. Too slow usually occurs due to poor time management or too much nonsensical rambling. What tends to happen is that too much time is spent on early topics or topics of little import, leaving only enough time to race through the topics at the end.

Too fast is just as bad. Here your instructor should be called Sir Speedy for the record setting pace in delivering the courseware. The problem here is that these instructors tend to finish way too early, leaving the students with much of their training time free and sensing they haven't received full value. Instructors that are too fast tend to convey a sense of disinterest.

Another scenario is the disappearing instructor. These are trainers that take extremely long breaks and disappear. Students feel abandoned and unappreciated. The trainer in these cases has often forgotten who's paying for their services (the students, of course).

## 4 – Follow through

Keeping your promises to find an answer and report back to the class is critical to maintaining your credibility. As a student, it's always an affront to have an instructor promise to get the answers to questions he or she doesn't know and then drop the ball and offer no answers or solutions.

Another angle to the follow through discussion is the desk work dimension. Do you grade your papers and homework in a timely manner? Do you keep a current grade book so students know where they stand? It has been my experience, painfully learned at times when I'm too busy with my MCSE consulting activity, that students are expressing some level of disappointment in the attention you're giving to them as a trainer if they need to ask for feedback on their work, ask you what their current grade is, and so on. It's a warning sign to receive these inquiries from students, one that can be avoided by simply staying current in your grading process. Students find that commitment from you to stay current to be a strong sign of caring.

## 5 — Self-assessment skills

Success as an instructor correlates to sticking to topics you know well. I once turned down a training opportunity because the educational center wanted me to teach courses in the Microsoft Certified Solution Developer (MCSD) track. This former C programming flunk out wasn't going down that road.

## 6 — Availability

Students have favorable impressions of instructors based on availability. Do you return telephone calls? Do you answer e-mails? Do you maintain regular office hours, or are you available before or after class to answer questions? These qualities all contribute to your success as an MCSE instructor.

## 7 — Organization and preparedness

I once taught a class in Microsoft Systems Management Server (SMS), a topic for which I had little practical hands-on experience. However, I got through the experience by being extremely well versed in the courseware, hands-on labs, materials, handouts, and so on. I borrowed training videos from Microsoft employees on the Redmond, Washington, campus; read magazine articles on SMS; and repeatedly ran through the lab exercises on my test network. My reviews for that course were strong, a total surprise to me. The lesson learned is that a well organized, well prepared, communicative instructor with sufficient technical knowledge can be successful.

## 8 — Facilitation

Part of being a trainer is to draw out the best in people. Perhaps you've seen this in instructors who teach via the case study method, place everyone in a circle, and create a high-participation environment. The skill being displayed here is that of fostering real learning through the interchange between and among participants. Students also enjoy it when you aren't doing all the talking.

## 9 — Tenacity

No matter how long you've taught and how great you think you are, reading student reviews is sobering. Your instructor emotions will run the gamut from elation to utter depression. Students can be so brutal sometimes.

It has been my experience that out of ten students, you will have days where you barely please half of them. Call it my Rule of Ten for student evaluations. If you consistently please less than five students out of ten total, it's time to exit training and return to MCSE consulting. Granted, it's okay to have a bad training day here and there. My comments refer to long-term training trends (over a year of training or longer).

**Note** Student evaluations need to be viewed as long-term trends over an extended period of time. You can't teach a course one time and take the feedback as noting more than a contribution to the trend line. It takes an instructor a couple of rounds to learn the course, at which time the evaluation scores will reflect more accurately how things are going.

## 10 — Humor

You better be armed with humor. In delivering technology topics such as the MCSE curriculum, you're dealing with adult learners, and adult learners can be tough. Some are angry and mean-spirited. Some are big talkers. You've likely attended classes and seen these types and more. What's the bottom line? As the tenth success factor, you need to brush up your socially acceptable humor and keep it handy.

# Competitive Analysis

Here are some factors that may affect the demand for your training services:

✦ **The Web** — The delivery of education over the Internet is still an emerging area, so it's difficult to say whether it will be more or less labor intensive when it comes to the need for trainers. I discuss online training at the end of this chapter.

✦ **Other technology training offerings** — What if a major industry merger, say between IBM and Novell (which hasn't happened as of this writing), causes a major shift in the technology industry? It's not that far-fetched to imagine how other technologies, with their own training communities, could lessen the demand for your MCSE-related training skills.

✦ **Books** — There is always a segment of learners who believe they can study and learn on their own.

✦ **Video courses** — I have been especially impressed with some of the video courses you can purchase or even download for free to learn Microsoft technologies and to get your MCSE at the same time. I can recommend the technical videos offered by KeyStone Learning Systems (www.keystonetraining. com) as being of consistently high quality. You can also benefit from short, free technology training videos from Microsoft's Direct Access site at www. microsoft.com/directaccess.

## Guest Sermon — The Interview

I found a few minutes to get together with Alan Carter recently to discuss the world of MCSE training. Alan is the best-selling author of such IDG Worldwide, Inc., books as *Windows 2000 MCSE Study System, Windows NT Server 4.0 MCSE Study System,* and *Windows NT Workstation 4.0 MCSE Study System.*

Q: How did you get interested in training?

A: *I have always wanted to teach, and when I was in the Air Force, I got a chance to teach and took it. I then spent the last four years I was in the Air Force teaching.*

Q: Do you both train and work as a technology consultant? Why? Why not?

A: *I spend most of my time teaching and writing and very little time consulting. I consider much of my classroom training time as consulting because of the questions I get on a broad range of implementation types and sizes. I tend to avoid long-term consulting gigs because then I end up serving two masters — a server goes down, and at the same time I have 12 paying students. Who do you help then? I avoid this issue by doing only small consulting projects.*

Q: What type of training have you done? CTEC? Private clients?

A: *I have taught at Novell Authorized Education Centers (NAECs) and Microsoft Certified Technical Education Centers (CTECs), and I also do a fair amount of private teaching for large clients.*

Q: What are the success factors for being a superior trainer? Being an all-knowing technical guru? Being a great communicator?

A: *The most important thing for a trainer is enjoying seeing your students get it. If you enjoy that, you will probably be able to develop the necessary skills. You do need to be knowledgeable and be able to communicate clearly without reading directly from the course materials. The second most important thing is to be able to say, "I don't know." Saying "I don't know" actually builds your credibility because students will believe the other information you give out. Giving out false information will destroy your credibility.*

Q: In general terms, can an MCSE who becomes an MCT expect to earn less, the same, or more than they can as a practicing consultant?

A: *Trainer and consultant salaries are fairly similar. In other words, for the same number of years of experience, a trainer that works for a training center is probably making about the same salary as a consultant working for a consulting firm. And a trainer who owns his own business will make about the same as a consultant who owns his own business. There are variations where there are large income disparities; however, those disparities usually involve skill level differences and can involve salary/fee negotiation skill as well.*

Q: How does the Windows 2000 MCSE track differ from the Windows NT 4 MCSE era? Perhaps you could mention the top three differences.

A: *The first difference is in the level of difficulty of the questions; Win2K questions are more difficult.*

*The next difference is the inclusion of a design exam in the core requirements. Microsoft is testing to see if you can design/engineer stuff, instead of just testing implementation skills.*

*The third difference involves the depth of the product. Win2K is significantly more complex both because of Active Directory and because of all of the additional networking and security features that have been added to it.*

# Becoming a Microsoft Certified Trainer

If you are sold on adding the Microsoft Certified Trainer (MCT) designation to your MCSE credentials, here's how you become one.

## What is an MCT?

Microsoft Certified Trainers are qualified instructors who are certified in Microsoft technologies and considered capable of teaching Microsoft Official Curriculum (MOC) courses. These courses are taught at Microsoft Certified Technical Education Centers (CTECs) and Microsoft Authorized Academic Training Program Institutions (AATPs).

### Ask the Guru

Today I share reader mail from someone who read my column in *Microsoft Certified Professional Magazine* in late 1998 and had a question about becoming a trainer. My reply follows:

*Mr. Brelsford,*

*I just read your column in the November MCP Magazine. I noted in your bio that you're doing some teaching on the side at SPU. I've also been interested in taking up teaching, but am uncertain about the market for MCSEs in teaching. I was wondering if you could share your experience on this: Was it hard? What are the opportunities that you've seen; salary and so on, at community and four-year colleges? Private training institutes?*

*-Steve B, MCSE, Senior Systems Engineer*

*Germantown, MD*

*Continued*

*Continued*

Dear Steve,

Thanks for the kind words. The hardest step in becoming a teacher is getting your first teaching assignment. For a number of reasons, educators would prefer to hire someone who has already been in the classroom and has their rookie errors behind them. I can't say I find this thinking to be wrong, but it does present the chicken-and-egg problem facing many professionals in many industries. You have to get experience to get the job, and you have to have the job to get experience.

It has been my own experience that private training institutes in the vocational-technical educational community are more open-minded about helping people launch as trainers. In fact, my first teaching assignment was as an emergency hire for a vocational-technical training institute in Anchorage, Alaska. That teaching experience allowed me to be hired at a true four-year university. Before I knew it, approximately 18 months later, I was teaching a graduate-level course in project management. So the point is that the first teaching job is the hardest job you'll every get, but then the jobs flow in much easier after that.

In answer to your other questions, after you get some basic teaching experience, I'm assuming at the vocational-technical level, the community college level is a logical next choice and one you may enjoy (because the emphasis is more on hands-on instruction and less on theory). The four-year level and above tend to emphasize more theory, so that tends to be an awkward adjustment for many MCSEs to teach. As you know, MCSEs, in general, have a hands-on mentality.

Regarding opportunities and pay, I can say the following: Clearly, the great opportunities are in technology training where there is the greatest shortage of qualified trainers. Adjunct training contracts at the vocation-technical and college levels tend to average between one and a few thousand dollars per semester. It's not especially high pay, but I've always felt it was fair given that it's often moonlighting money and beats being a food delivery driver.

## MCT steps

In this section, I have outlined the procedures for becoming an MCT from the premium designation requirement to the steps for being certified on individual courses. This process is shown graphically in Figure 26-1.

### Holding a premium designation

First, a new requirement for MCTs is that you must hold at least one premium designation in the Microsoft certification program:

✦ Microsoft Certified Systems Engineer (MCSE)

✦ Microsoft Certified Solution Developer (MCSD)

✦ Microsoft Certified Database Administrator (MCDBA)

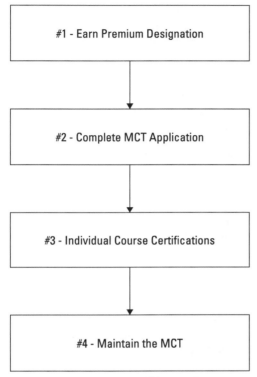

**Figure 26-1:** Steps toward becoming an MCT

 **Note**    Microsoft has institutionalized the MCSE and trainer relationship by requiring MCTs to hold a premium designation such as the MCSE.

## Completing the MCT application process

You must complete the comprehensive MCT application and mail it to Microsoft for processing. There are several steps to this process.

First, you must complete the actual MCT application, which may be downloaded from www.microsoft.com/mct as a standard Microsoft Word document. This application contains several sections that need to be filled in and answered. Once approved, you are temporarily granted the MCT designation for 90 days. This allows you to log on to the private MCT Members only Web site.

   **A. Applicant Information** — This section includes standard name, address, city, state, and zip code information.

   **B. Microsoft Certified Professional ID Number** — This is your MCP ID number that you receive when you are first certified. You will also need to attach your latest MCP transcripts to the MCT application.

**Note**  You should always carefully guard your MCP ID number. This is the primary data identifier for doing business with Microsoft. In a sense, it is similar to your Social Security number. If someone obtains your MCP number, they are certainly one major step closer to impersonating you.

**C. Employer Information** — This part of the MCT application will have you list your CTEC affiliation or declare yourself as an independent or freelance trainer. If you are a freelance trainer, you will need to pay a $200 registration fee to Microsoft.

**Note**  If you are teaching for an AATP and not a CTEC, you enter the AATP name and identification number in this section of the MCT application.

**D. Instructional Skills Requirement** — In this section, you will declare and provide evidence (such as a certificate of attendance) that you have attended an approved "train the trainer" course. Vendors that provide these types of courses are listed at *Microsoft Certified Professional Magazine*'s Web site (www.mcpmag.com). I have attended one of these courses to earn my MCT designation and found the experience to be valuable. The instructor did not know a thing about technology, which was perfect for teaching a bunch of MCSE tech heads how to be trainers. This type of course focuses on instructional methods.

**Note**  If you are a Certified Technical Trainer (CTT), you do not need to attend the Microsoft "train the trainer" course. Note that college teaching experience, even if you're a tenured professor, doesn't count here.

**E. Terms and Agreements** — This is the legal stuff under the title "Microsoft Certified Trainer Preliminary Agreement." One of the terms being communicated is that you are being granted a provisional (temporary) certification that allows you to access the private MCT Web site.

**Note**  To teach a Microsoft course, you must satisfy the requirements for the course. For all courses, this includes passing the certification exam for that class. If you're going to teach the class and help others pass the exam, you should have passed the exam yourself. Other course requirements include attending the class prior to teaching it.

**F. Signature** — Sign the application.

Review the application checklist, which is a preparation checklist for teaching a Microsoft course (and includes tasks such as read the course book, set up the classroom, perform lab exercises, view the trainer video, and so on). You will sign and date the course preparation checklist. You will mail this MCT application to Microsoft for processing. In several weeks, the MCT Welcome Kit will arrive with logo, certificate, and hats and horns for celebrating (I'm just kidding on that last point).

## Qualifying for individual course certifications

Once you've completed the paperwork and obtained the provisional MCT designation, you need to qualify on a course-by-course basis to teach the class. These requirements can vary, but as alluded to in the last section, you must at least pass the exam for the class you plan to teach. The standard process is as follows:

1. Pass any required prerequisite MCP exams to measure your current technical knowledge.

2. Prepare to teach the MOC course. You should obtain and complete the MOC trainer kit (which is separate from the student workbook). Depending on the class, you may be required to attend the class you are seeking to teach. There are two types of MOC courses you can attend. One is the trainer preparation (T-prep) course at a Microsoft CTEC. T-prep courses are designed for trainers and are focused on course materials, delivery styles, labs, and classroom setup and management. The other type of course you might be asked to attend is the public course taught day in and day out at CTECs.

3. Pass any additional exam requirements to measure any additional product knowledge that pertains to the course. This typically involves Microsoft trainer exams. Trainer exams are developed when no public certification exam will be available to take or when Microsoft really wants to raise the bar of competency for instructors that teach the course.

4. Submit your course preparation checklist to Microsoft so that your additional accreditations are reflected on your transcripts.

 **Note**    These are general steps for preparing to teach a Microsoft course. Requirements vary, so you should monitor the private MCT Web site (which I discuss in a moment).

## Maintaining the MCT

Microsoft will periodically communicate new requirements for MCTs. This information is typically communicated via the private MCT Web site. Also, you will want to stay version current with the courses you teach, even if you're not currently teaching a class. For example, if you obtained your MCT in the SQL Server 6.5 era and have taught recently, it's still in your best interest as a trainer to stay current. In this example, you should be proficient in SQL Server 2000 and should have passed the SQL Server 2000 certification exam.

I also recommend you occasionally look at the public certification Web site maintained by Microsoft at `www.microsoft.com/trainingandservices` and shown in Figure 26-2.

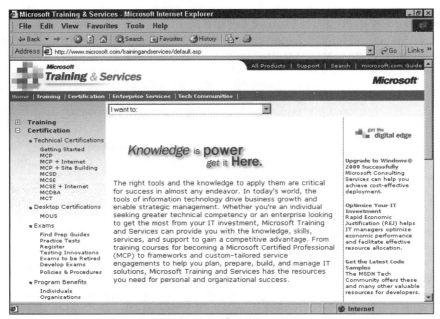

**Figure 26-2:** Microsoft's public certification Web site

## Private MCT Web site

The private MCT Web site at `partnering.one.microsoft.com` is the MCT portal for communicating anything and everything about the MCT designation and is shown in Figure 26-3. Note you must be a bona fide MCT with logon credentials to access this page, hence the term *private*. However, I thought you might enjoy a sneak peek at what's on the other side of this secure site.

One huge benefit is the ability to peruse the courseware library. This is shown in Figure 26-4.

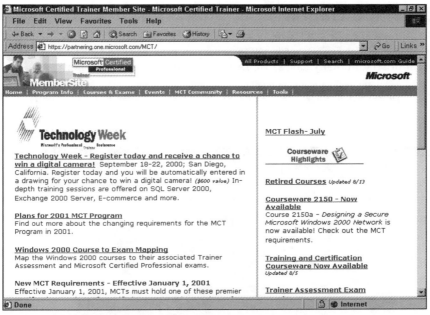

**Figure 26-3:** The private MCT Web site

**Figure 26-4:** Microsoft courseware listing

## MCT compensation

As shown by the *Microsoft Certified Professional Magazine* 2000 Salary Survey in Figure 26-5, compensation for MCTs is very comparable to MCSEs working in private industry. In many cases, MCTs are earning over $100,000 per year.

Cross-Reference    See Appendix E for more details on the *MCP Magazine* 2000 Salary Survey.

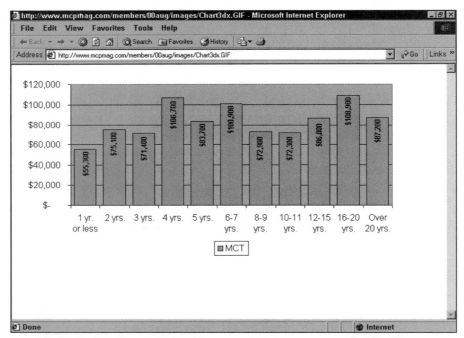

**Figure 26-5:** MCT salaries ranked by years of training experience. The wide variation in salary levels between year classifications reflects a small sample size.

You can benefit in other ways as an MCT, such as by attending the well regarded Technology Week Conference, which is also known as Microsoft's Professional Trainer Conference. Figure 26-6 shows information from a recent Technology Week held in San Diego, California.

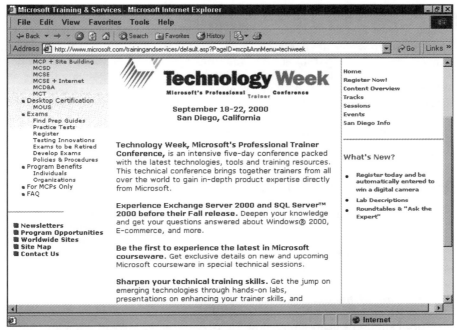

**Figure 26-6:** MCTs should consider attending the Technology Week conference, such as this one recently held in San Diego.

# Custom Training

An interesting training opportunity that is not specific to Microsoft solutions is providing custom training services to clients. I love this work. You are typically paid to develop and deliver training on custom internal applications. This tends to pay well, at or near MCSE consulting rates. You also learn another application or two along the way.

Tip      I've learned a few valuable lessons about custom training along the way. First, you need to bill at least two hours of development time for every hour of in-class training time. I've even seen this ratio approach 10:1. In one of my early custom training gigs, I didn't charge for development time and billed only for the in-class instruction. So it happened that I worked many hours preparing for the class (approximately 40 hours) and billed only for eight of these hours. Needless to say, this billing time management error on my behalf made the engagement unprofitable.

# Third-Party Product Training

The MCSE often works at an infrastructure level to provide support for nonMicrosoft applications. These apparent at-odds solutions are complementary. You can be an MCSE consultant delivering one set of solutions and a trainer teaching third-party applications in the next breath. I've experienced consulting houses that have their MCSEs also work with Great Plains accounting systems, Oracle databases, and so on. It's okay to be an MCSE and train on nonMicrosoft products. There are some great billing opportunities here.

# Being an Adjunct Instructor

As you know after reading the last two sections, not all training opportunities for MCSEs necessarily need to come from the MCT angle. One opportunity that I have participated in and have seen other MCSEs pursue is the adjunct instructor path at colleges. This can include vocational-technical training institutions, community colleges, junior colleges, two-year programs, four-year undergraduate programs, and graduate-level programs. To some extent, I discussed this earlier in the chapter in the *Ask the Guru* feature.

The story I spin now is about a fellow MCT-level trainer at Seattle Pacific University named Michael who found his MCSE course one quarter wasn't going to proceed as scheduled. It was a Windows NT course offered after Windows 2000 had launched, and the enrollment interest had waned. Michael and I discussed his situation and looked around the other schools at the university. It turned out the School of Business had an opening for an adjunct instructor to teach a graduate-level MBA introductory course in computer networking and telephony. Michael accepted the teaching assignment, did a great job according to the students, and filled a gap in his training schedule (allowing him to make money during a down period). Michael had a Masters degree (MBA) that allowed him to teach at the graduate-level, so you should be aware that credentials are essential in the academic environment.

If you are interested in being an adjunct instructor for a college, I have the same words of advice you as I had for my reader in the *Ask the Guru* section earlier in the chapter. Get your start with a vocational-technical college. Then, if you so desire, move over to a community college or four-year college to ply your teaching craft. Most communities have a local college, and you might even consider teaching at local military bases, which have college programs such as Chapman University (www.chapman.edu). Chapman University, shown in Figure 26-7, is based in California and has distance learning satellite branches at many U.S. military facilities. I once had the great pleasure of teaching a finance class for Chapman University at Elmendorf Air Force Base in Anchorage, Alaska. I was impressed with the college's instructor feedback system, where after the course the campus director sat down with you to go over student evaluations. This is the only university I've worked for where an administrator took the time to work so closely with and mentor the instructors.

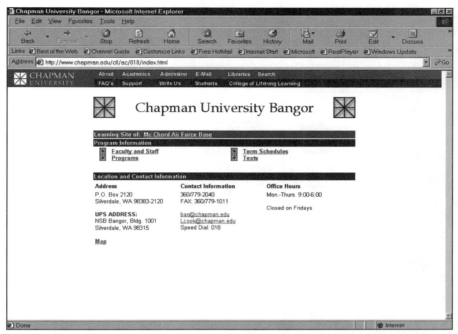

**Figure 26-7:** Chapman University has a distance learning campus at Bangor Submarine Base in Washington State, as well as at many other military facilities.

# Online Training

Many times in this book I have emphasized finding a niche as an MCSE consultant and reaping the rewards that accrue to specialists. This is certainly not the first time you're reading such insights between the covers of this book. I sincerely believe an emerging niche in the MCSE community for trainers is online education.

I feel so strongly about this niche opportunity that several years ago I started teaching online MCSE certification courses in addition to my classroom instruction. In 2000, I stopped teaching in the classroom completely to focus my training efforts strictly online. And as any good nicher does, I attend a professional conference focused on the niche, in this case the OnLine Learning 2000 conference and exposition in Denver, Colorado (www.onlinelearning2000.com, as seen in Figure 26-8). At this conference, I was dumbstruck by how much interest the online education area was generating. Over 7,000 attendees met for several days to explore online education in-depth. The vendor exposition was approximately four football fields in size. This conference is held annually, and the Web link given previously will route you to the current conference home page (which is Los Angles for 2001). The conference has grown so much in popularity that it now includes an Asian and European version. If you think you might like to make online training a niche in your MCSE consulting practice, I highly recommend you consider this industry-leading conference. I look forward to meeting you there.

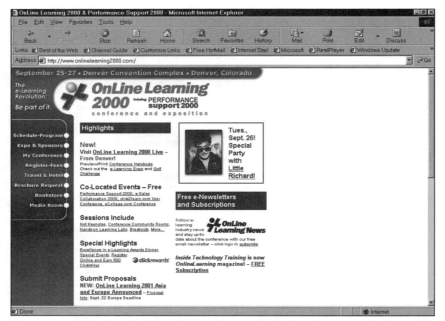

**Figure 26-8:** The OnLine Learning conference is the leading gathering for online educators and trainers.

Let me take a few pages to show you what the Seattle Pacific University online MCSE virtual campus looks like. This virtual campus is hosted on a Windows NT Server–based machine and uses an online campus software application called Blackboard (see Figure 26-9).

The content for the online MCSE courses has been provided both by others and by myself at Seattle Pacific University. The virtual campus, accessible from nearly any modern Web browser, is protected by logon authentication security. After logging on, you see the Announcements page (see Figure 26-10), where daily secrets and general announcements are posted.

A few other pages from the virtual campus give you the flavor of how the course is delivered. A weekly reading assignment, shown in Figure 26-11, is displayed in the Adobe Acrobat file format.

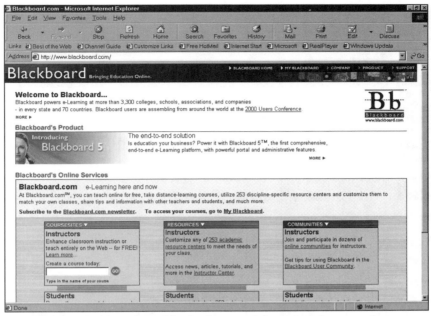

**Figure 26-9:** Blackboard provides both a standalone virtual campus for purchase and a virtual campus hosting service.

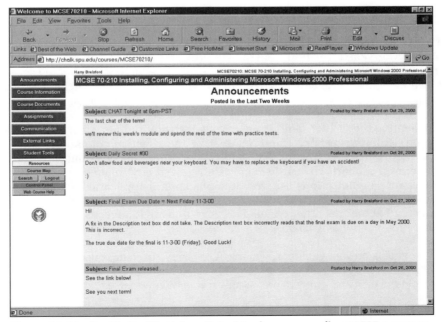

**Figure 26-10:** Seattle Pacific University's virtual campus online MCSE program home page

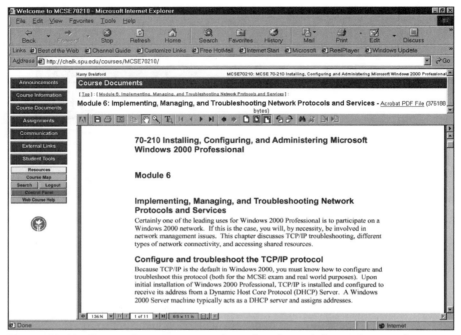

**Figure 26-11:** Course documents are released each week for student reading as part of the online MCSE course.

A multimedia lecture using a program called Authorware allows the students to hear a lecture delivered by the instructor on the weekly topic. Students download the Authorware client the first time the lecture component is run. Afterwards, future lectures launch with a single click. The multimedia lecture opening screen is shown in Figure 26-12. Other capabilities of the virtual campus include a thread discussion board, an online grade book, instant quizzes, and exams.

Supplementing the virtual campus are weekly instructor chats using Microsoft Exchange Conferencing Server and NetMeeting and constant communication between instructor and student via e-mail. Many other online training environments are structured similarly to Seattle Pacific University's environment. In fact, many online training organizations use the same Blackboard application. Other organizations offering online MCSE training include the major CTECs, the University of Phoenix, and numerous other training organizations that advertise in *Microsoft Certified Professional Magazine* (www.mcpmag.com).

**Tip**    Depending on your gumption, you might consider launching your own online training portal. However, take my advice and use an existing tool such as Blackboard to avoid the pain and agony of programming your own Web site.

**Figure 26-12:** A multimedia lecture by the instructor supplements the course readings. Note the multimedia lecture is bandwidth intensive.

## Summary

This chapter highlighted training opportunities that MCSE consultants should consider. Not only does providing training services benefit you intellectually, it can also benefit you financially, as this chapter has demonstrated. At a minimum, offering training services broadens the types of services you can offer as an MCSE consultant and diversifies your income stream. For those of you aspiring to climb the socioeconomic ladder, whether you want to be an executive, a politician, or a statesman, if you look at the backgrounds of leaders, you will often find these people are degreed, are published, and have taught. Keep that thought in mind as you map out the next steps in your career.

✦      ✦      ✦

# Strategies For Staying Current

**E**very MCSE consultant inherently knows the need to stay current. It's how you add value to the consulting services you offer. Knowledge, at least in technology, has declining value over time. You must periodically renew the technical knowledge you have so you can continue to add value to the consulting relationship.

In this chapter, I present several strategies for staying current.

## User Groups

Believe it or not, it's getting harder to find good user groups. At a basic level, user groups can be defined as a regular gathering of like-minded technology enthusiasts. For example, a user group may be organized to discuss a particular product — such as Intuit's QuickBooks — or it may focus on certain segments of the technology community (e.g., "Women in Computing – Northwest Chapter"). Typically, user groups meet each month in the evenings and have a guest speaker and an open forum for questions and answers. This agenda may vary slightly between user groups, but having attended many of these evenings, I know that the format is pretty much the same from user group to user group.

In the past, user groups played a more central and dominant role in the technology community. These gatherings were often used for product releases and major events. In many cases, the central role of user groups has declined in the late 1990s and early 21st century (although I feel strongly enough about them to place this discussion at the top of this chapter). Why? With the advent of the Internet, it's getting harder for people to justify the time commitment to user groups, even if the commitment is just one meeting a month. It's now far easier to access the Internet and surf the newsgroups instead.

There are still good user groups around, including the BackOffice Professionals Association (BOPA) at `www.bopa.org`, shown in Figure 27-1.

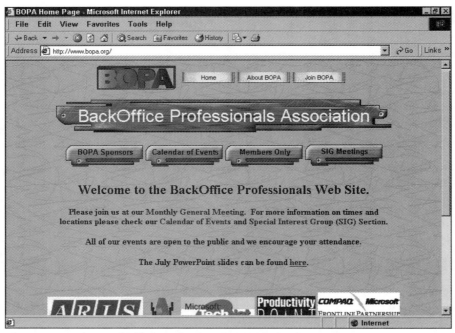

**Figure 27-1:** The BackOffice Professionals Association home page

It's likely your community or region has an active user group that is of interest to you. You should check with local computer resellers for information on how to contact these groups. Attending user group events is a great way to stay current in your technology field.

## Trade Associations

Closely related to user groups are trade associations. Trade associations tend to place a greater emphasis on membership issues and typically aren't as technical as user groups. Trade associations may have political lobbying functions, social events, and group insurance packages. As an example of a trade group, Figure 27-2 displays the Washington Software Alliance (WSA) at `www.wsa1.org`.

**Figure 27-2:** The Washington Software Alliance home page

Participating in a trade association is a great way to expand your contacts. But why would that be important for an MCSE consultant with what appears to be an endless supply of billing opportunities serving business clients? Because just as fast as Dot-Coms became Dot-Gones, the business climate for MCSE consultants could change. Having gone through a couple of business recessions myself, I can attest that my business relationships and social contacts helped in no small part to keep my plate full with work. I've seen this in other industries, where in-house attorneys were downsized after a change at their companies. Those that participated in the local bar association had a wealth of contacts and were quickly re-employed. A few others, without such contacts, often went to a different kind of bar and made contacts of a dubious nature.

# Microsoft TechNet Subscription

One of the best values I can think of is the annual Microsoft TechNet CD-ROM library subscription. Each month, you receive a disc mailer with the current TechNet technical reference library. TechNet, shown in Figure 27-3, is an open window to Microsoft technical support resources.

There is also a Web component to Microsoft TechNet, seen in Figure 27-4 and found at www.microsoft.com/technet.

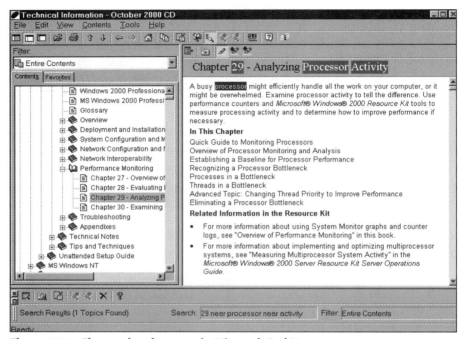

**Figure 27-3:** The results of a query in Microsoft TechNet

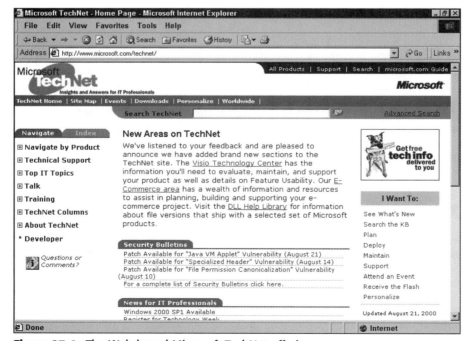

**Figure 27-4:** The Web-based Microsoft TechNet offering

**Note** The CD-ROM disc-based TechNet and the Web-based TechNet are different offerings, as you might have guessed. The CD-ROM TechNet offers greater research resources, including knowledge base articles, product support resolution topics, training courses, white papers, and software utilities. The Web-based TechNet focuses on knowledge base articles and product support resolution topics.

## Guest Sermon — The Finishing Touch

I asked my good friend, George Myers, to speak about the importance of being a life-learner as a professional. Here's George's Guest Sermon:

*For an MCSE, gaining technical experience is one of the most critical requirements for obtaining future success. There's no substitute for getting into an environment where hard-earned knowledge can be developed through practical, daily "real world" experiences. But along with these real-world environments comes those other challenging aspects of the real world — interacting with others and working together on all the various projects we're assigned or must take on.*

*It's no secret that there is a substantial and increasing need for quality technical workers who are also good with people and projects. While the stereotype of the typical "techie" that's great with computers but lousy with real-life forms is inaccurate, there is no question that a technical worker is going to experience much greater success if they have good people and project skills. I've known many a true-blue techie who invested themselves in this area of their professional portfolio and the difference was remarkable, both in improving their ability to create a positive, successful working environment, and in being able to advance their career.*

*Not very many of us want to admit we can benefit from learning how to work better with others, but the truth is there are many important advantages to be gained from developing these skills. Hopefully, your technical studies included role-plays where challenging workplace situations were discussed and worked through, but just like classroom labs, this type of practice only goes so far.*

*Some companies and individuals seem to operate as if people and organizational skills are either something you're born with, or something that you somehow magically learn as you go. While there are personality types that are by nature more people-oriented, or more organizationally inclined, all of us can benefit from learning about our style, temperament, and personality traits and how to effectively incorporate what we know about ourselves into the workplace. The good news is there are a number of programs available at many institutions and organizations that can provide excellent opportunities to acquire this learning, and they don't cost an arm and a leg, or require an extensive time commitment.*

*One investment that is always worthwhile to make is brushing up on people skills. This isn't about learning the right words or postures or techniques because, as you know, people aren't interested in having the right command typed in at their prompt, so to speak.*

*Continued*

*Continued*

*Cosmetic approaches of this type will be sniffed out and usually end up backfiring because people can inherently sense insincerity. (I suspect you can think of someone who's used this approach with you!) Furthermore, working effectively with others isn't something that can be learned at a seminar or workshop or by reading a book. You can certainly gain some good knowledge that way, but to acquire genuine people skills takes some time and effort. It can be done, but you have to be willing to dig in a little and get your hands dirty. However, with some honest self-awareness, a thorough understanding of the various ways people tend to work, and a safe environment to learn how to integrate the two, a lot can be accomplished.*

*If you decide to make this investment and develop your people skills, make sure the format you learn in is interactive, provides an extended learning model with a minimum of ten class sessions over five weeks, and has a well-trained instructor. We can all put on our best self for a few hours, but working under pressure is a more realistic reflection of the workplace, and so a learning environment where honest questions and difficult situations come up and others have a chance to challenge us will create the best opportunity for us to really learn and improve our skills. The goal isn't necessarily to learn how to DO something, but how to BE someone who understands themselves and others enough to work effectively for, and with, all involved. Once you have that foundation, your people skills can flourish.*

*Another worthwhile area of study is coursework in project management. All organizations have some type of business plan, and project management training can help you learn how to break down and analyze aspects of that plan to find its strengths and weaknesses before you spend valuable time or company finances. Learning the analytical tools that experts use to map out the steps involved in working through a proposal will come in handy for both large, formal projects and smaller, more informal tasks. This type of training also helps you identify the most powerful agendas involved in the real world—the unwritten and unspoken ones!*

*There are many other related courses that can be helpful, but these are two areas of development that can help put a finishing touch on any certification. And in today's marketplace, they will add extensive value to what you've already worked hard to earn!*

Byline: George Myers has a personal and professional passion for excellence in the challenging and often neglected art of effective administration. As the Director of the Center for Professional Development in the School of Business and Economics at Seattle Pacific University, George has been responsible for the creation of in-class and online technical education programs in Microsoft 2000, Cisco, CompTIA, and Linux. The Center also offers executive education programs and tailored courses by request to help meet the needs of businesses in the Puget Sound region. In his spare time, George performs extensively as a member of The Nowhere Men, an all-Beatles band, and has recently finished a CD of his original music.

# Professional Development Courses

After you've mastered the depth of your MCSE consulting role, you may want to consider lateral educational improvement. Assuming you find and develop a technology niche and learn how to run a consulting practice, you may be interested in a broader professional development course, such as the type offered by professional development arms of universities. As an example, you can see the Web page for Seattle Pacific University's Center for Professional Development (`www.spu.edu/prolearn`), shown in Figure 27-5.

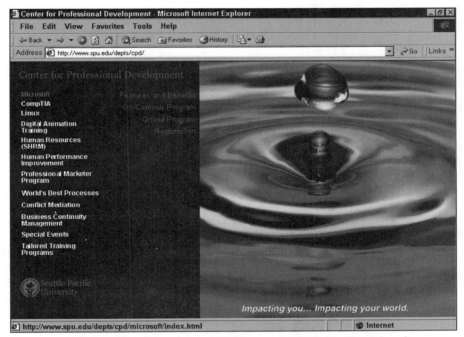

**Figure 27-5:** Professional development offerings at Seattle Pacific University

Professional development courses are offered in a wide range of topics, including conflict mediation and total quality management.

# College Courses

Some MCSE consultants are likely to hunger for more than the occasional professional development course at the local college. You may find it rewarding to pursue a Masters degree or other educational degree. An example of an MBA program with a technology emphasis offered by the University of Denver (`www.du.edu/grad/DCB_degrees.html`) is shown in Figure 27-6.

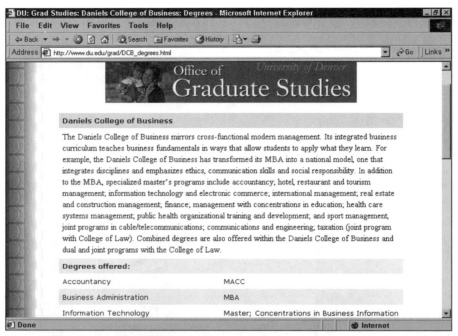

**Figure 27-6:** University of Denver graduate programs

Granted, your situation might be that you really need to pursue an undergraduate degree (perhaps you haven't attended college before). Numerous colleges offer undergraduate degrees with a technology emphasis. Heck, I've even seen MCSEs who return to college to pursue liberal arts degrees in fields far from the nuts and bolts of Microsoft technology solutions. Does this make sense? You bet it does. Degrees in the liberal arts and humanities emphasize writing and communication. And with the end of this *MCSE Consulting Bible* book approaching, it shouldn't be lost on you that being reflective and communicative are success factors for all MCSE consultants.

# Microsoft Direct Access

A Microsoft Web site called Direct Access that is billed as the portal to communicating with technology consultants is shown in Figure 27-7. Direct Access can be found at `www.microsoft.com/directaccess`. DirectAccess offers a wealth of information to support the MCSE consultant, general technology advisor, reseller, and value-added provider (VAP). Basically, it's a site with something for everyone with technical and professional postings meant to educate you and run your service provider business better. This is one of Microsoft's primary ways of supporting the "channel" of its third-party solution providers, such as MCSE consultants. A recent tour of the Direct Access revealed discussion on:

✦ Interviews with noted industry gurus

✦ Interviews with Microsoft management team members

✦ Feature overviews of newly released Microsoft products

✦ An events listing

✦ Details on promotions, including how to earn bonus points for a new color LCD TV if you're a Windows 2000 reseller

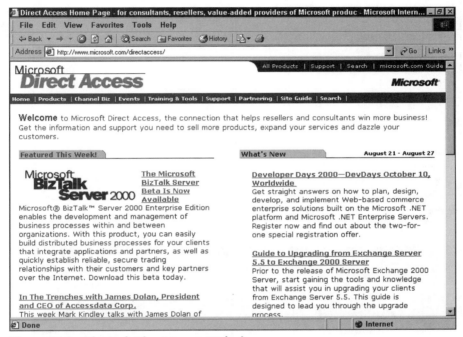

**Figure 27-7:** Microsoft Direct Access Web site

Direct Access is also supplemented by a periodic e-mail newsletter, shown in Figure 27-8.

# Conferences

Finally, as a professional, it is paramount that you try to attend at least one conference per year (with the key point being at least one conference per year). And as an MCSE consultant, the best-positioned conference for you to attend is TechMentor from *Microsoft Certified Professional Magazine* (www.techmentorevents.com). The TechMentor event's Web site is displayed in Figure 27-9.

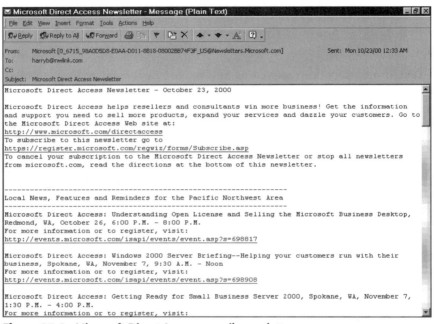

**Figure 27-8:** Microsoft Direct Access e-mail newsletter

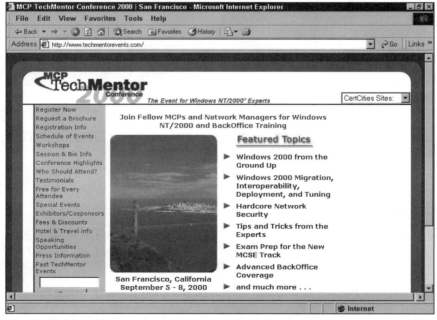

**Figure 27-9:** TechMentor has emerged as the annual gathering spot for MCSEs.

The key point about TechMentor is that it's a conference dedicated to and focused on the MCSE community. It has technical tracks, as you would expect, along with management tracks and certification tracks. Other conferences tend to focus on technical issues. You can even find conferences dedicated to management issues, such as those hosted by the American Management Association. And surprisingly, there are few other conferences focused on certification topics. TechMentor is wonderful in that it brings all three dimensions under one roof (or at least one conference center).

There are other conferences worthy of your attention:

✦ Microsoft's TechEd, hosted annually, was originally focused on trainers and the like as an educational conference. It has since grown to a large conference appealing to technology executives, developers, and salespeople. It's used as a forum for product launches.

✦ Microsoft Fusion is the annual conference for Microsoft partners and solution providers. If you are a Microsoft Certified Solution Provider, this is your annual convention.

✦ IDG, the parent company of IDG Books Worldwide, Inc. (which has published this book), has a large division dedicated to hosting conferences. The conferences include Windows 2000 Conference and Expo (which was the launch event for Windows 2000 Server), LinuxWorld Conference and Expo, COMNET, Internet Commerce Expo, ASPWorld Conference, Internet Entertainment Expo, Macworld Conference and Expo, and countless others discussed at www.idg.com.

# Summary

This chapter has provided you with a range of options for staying current as an MCSE technology consultant. These options included attending user groups, joining a trade association, subscribing to Microsoft TechNet, attending professional development and graduate courses at the college of your choice, monitoring the Microsoft Direct Access site, and attending conferences.

So why is staying current so important? Believe me, there is nothing sadder than seeing an MCSE consultant fall from greatness because of an obsolete technical skill set. Granted, consulting isn't just about having a current technical skills set, it is also about communicating, business development, and managing the business your already have. But you can't deny that a sufficient technical skills set is required as an MCSE consultant. And to maintain your technical skill set in the fast changing world of technology, you clearly need to "stay current."

✦         ✦         ✦

# Strategies For Being a Successful MCSE Consultant

**T**his book is here as a reference for you to visit again and again, but much of your future success depends on your own efforts. Being a successful MCSE consultant is no easy task. The hours, if not long, are intense. The work is challenging, and the clients even more so. The good news is that MCSE consultants are practicing what's preached in this book every day, finding the work fulfilling and making a good living at it.

## Bringing It All Together

Take a moment to savor the MCSE consulting journey on which you've embarked. For many readers, this is nothing less than a major professional life transformation for you. For others, you've already nailed your consulting business model and are heading in the right direction. Perhaps this book has enlightened you to turn the bow of the MCSE consulting ship a few degrees and make a slight course correction.

This book was based on the tried-and-true consulting business model of finder, minder, and grinder. It's difficult to find any one person who can be good at all three dimensions, as you're really talking about radical shifts in personality traits — so go easy on yourself as you mature into a successful MCSE consultant.

# Rule of Ten: MCSE Consulting Success Tips

Good writing is about following procedures. No one writing rule will make or break a book. In that spirit, I am using the next few pages to summarize several points presented throughout this text, that when combined, can help you to become a successful MCSE consultant.

## 1 — Minimize your mistakes

First and foremost, recognize that times are good in the MCSE consulting field. Microsoft is arguably operating at its peak performance as a company. MCSEs are busy. It's relatively easy to be successful. Minimize your mistakes, and you can't help but be successful.

## 2 — Communicate

Yes, one more pitch to be a communicator. The free marketplace greatly rewards technology consultants who are strong communicators. You can communicate your way right into a small fortune.

## 3 — Master a technology niche

Do your own research, and you will find that millionaires often made their money by identifying niches that others ignored. I've listed a few such niches in this book, including Microsoft's Digital Dashboard solution for presenting information.

## 4 — Savor working for yourself

Some of us were born to work for ourselves. I, for one, have truly enjoyed working for myself and find that my productivity is much greater and my creativity is much higher. May such fortunes await you if you decide to go it alone.

## 5 — Grow with the opportunity

Business cycles will wane and wax. Clients will come and go, as will employees if you choose to hire them. Software product releases will increment. But through it all, you'll be a technology consultant, so grow with the opportunity. You might enjoy serving clients today by implementing Windows 2000 solutions. Tomorrow you may be more interested in SQL Server and managing data. But above all, stay current with the technology area in which you consult.

## 6 — Don't overbook yourself

I'd be remiss if I didn't mention again that you've got to manage your time. If you're overbooked, you're selling your clients short.

## 7 — Watch your finances

Keep current with your billings and record keeping. If you read popular business books, such as *The Millionaire Mind* (Stanley), you'll find that more than one successful business person at some point learned to watch their finances the hard way by allowing a company to go broke while making money. How could this be? Simple. The accounts receivable grew too large and choked the cash flow out of the business. It can happen to you, the MCSE consultant, as well. Hey, I've had a sleepless night or two myself wondering how I was going to meet payroll, all while billing many consulting hours to great clients.

## 8 — Don't sweat the small stuff

Call it generic business advice, but pick your battles carefully. It's easy to focus myopically on the small stuff and perhaps miss out on the bigger picture. Keep your problems in perspective and minimize the impact of the insignificant problems.

## Ask the Guru

Here is another e-mail from a loyal reader of my MCSE column. This e-mail, while an interesting story that raises many points presented in this book, also ends with an area of concern, burnout, that I address in the reply.

*December 1998*

*Dear Harry,*

*I have truly enjoyed your articles in* MCP Magazine. *This month's article was exceptionally good, and I would have to agree full force with everything. I usually did not hold a job for longer than 9 months before I left for another. My parents would lean on me and tell me, "You're a family man now. You need to put some roots down." You probably know the rest. Then I would tell them that I am doing the same thing for 20 to 30 percent more money, and they would just nod their heads and leave it at that.*

*I have been in the position where I had to train myself to pass the Microsoft certifications because the employer who hired me promised training and a hefty bonus when I would receive my MCSE. The fine print said that I must complete the certs within 6 months of being hired. Of course, the training was scheduled to start on my seventh month of employment. Having received the MCSE in 4 months, this employer refused to do right by me, so I left. And to think I left for my previous employer, who paid me very well this time!*

*Continued*

*Continued*

*So I made the decision to leave and I went to a few other consultant firms who billed me out at triple my pay, which would not normally bother me if I had great benefits, but I did not. Finally, I found a firm I am somewhat happy with. I have been there for over a year. And yes, I still can go somewhere else for 20% more in earnings, but the reason I am staying is on the first page of your article: . . . Management. I realize that the key players in this field are not only technical, they also have business/board room savvy. With the consulting company I am with now, I was assigned a mentor. This mentor guided me through a difficult discussion of leaving this company or staying (leaving meant 20% more pay for doing the same thing).*

*While at a client site, my mentor walked me into the server room and pointed out the highest paid Novell engineer. Then he explained that the company was going to NT and that he would be out of a job soon, and market value for this individual was not as high as his salary. This individual had few people skills and the mentor eluded to the fact that the Novell guru was only experiencing inflationary raises. In fact, his salary has not changed in 2 years. My mentor explained that this individual opted for more money back in the day when Novell was hot (and what amounted to a short-term strategy), rather than take the opportunity that I was enjoying as an established MCSE consultant.*

*Today, I design infrastructures and mail systems. I provide direction and recommendations, and only once in a while, if I get a chance, I build a server to keep old skills fresh. I am still with the same company as an engineer, but now I wrap business drivers around technology and deal with technical people as well as directors. I am continually trying to develop my management skills, and with the mentor I have, I feel that this is an understatement.*

*Oh! Loved the article on Burnout. I was even looking to move to other states at the time I read your article. Sometimes a different perspective increases one's awareness of the real issues at hand. You have a clear view of the industry and share it objectively.*

*Keep up the great work, and I will be looking forward to your next article.*

*Elias V., MCSE + I, CNA, CWA*

Elias,

Your insightful story is a pocket guide to street smart MCSE consulting. You've learned, sometimes the hard way, how to be a successful MCSE consultant. In particular I like the maturity you displayed in weighing other factors than the paycheck in making some of your career decisions. It also sounds like you developed a keen sense of judgment about what type of firms you are comfortable working for. And you really hit a home run with the description of your mentoring experience. I consider the mentor role (both being a mentor and being mentored) a key MCSE consulting success factor. Thanks for the kind words about my other column on burnout. Too many MCSE consultants run too hard for too long, resulting in burnout in some form. I'm glad you were able to think outside the box after reading my burnout column and enjoy a period of renewal. Best continued wishes to you.

Cheers,

harryb

## 9 – Pay your taxes

Pay your taxes on time to the taxing authority. If you don't do that, it really won't matter how technically proficient you are when you're behind bars in debtors' prison. First claim to your financial resources, even ahead of your lenders, is the tax man. Which is a dramatic way of saying you should stay current with your tax payments. Don't believe me? The next time you see a construction company with a big padlock on the gate to its equipment yard, stop in and ask them if they paid their payroll taxes on time.

## 10 – Mentor other MCSEs

Successful people should help other people. It's just good karma. Take a young person to the monthly user group meeting and introduce him or her to everyone. Good things will come your way.

# Next Steps

So, are you bound for bigger and better things as an MCSE consultant? Or are you content with where you're at right now, making money, going home on time, and so on? The next steps you choose are up to you. But the MCSE consulting framework provides many opportunities for where you want to go. Some of you will join established MCSE consulting firms and enjoy working on a team of fellow MCSE consultants. Other readers of this book will start their own business, seeking the freedom of self-employment over the security of full-time employment for someone else. But in all cases, having completed this book, you're in better shape to make the best decision for you prior to when you started reading this guide.

## Case Study – What Others Say

Don't just take my word for it when it comes to defining technology consulting success factors. One of the best Web sites for articulating consulting success factors is from Keane Consulting Group (www.kcg.keane.com), as seen in the accompanying figure. This group presents a pyramid of success emphasizing the following points:

✦ **Strategic Memorable Recommendations** – This relates to the strong communication skills needed by a consultant.

✦ **Productivity and Profitability** – This relates to being a profitable business.

✦ **Staff Development** – This relates to mentoring and training.

*Continued*

*Continued*

✦ **Leadership** — A successful consultant should be a leader as well.

✦ **Practice Development** — Finally, a successful consultant needs to be successful in developing business.

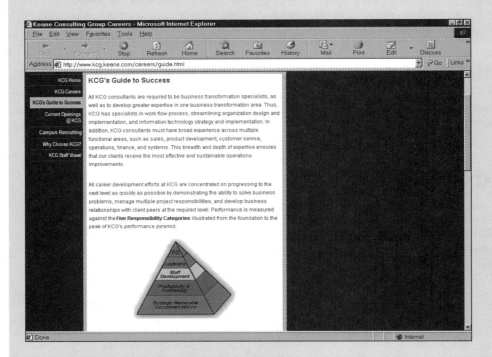

Keane further believe that consultants need to persevere in problem solving and seek help when the problem can't be solved. Inspiring fellow teammates and taking advantage of self-improvement opportunities are also hallmarks of the Keane method. And don't forget high client satisfaction-levels and building business friendships, as other points emphasized by Keane.

So your case study assignment is to use the Web to find, perhaps via one of the popular search engines such as www.google.com, other consulting sites that post technology consulting success factors. Print these Web pages out and save them in your personal development file. And when time allows, and you're in a strategic thinking mindset, revisit these printouts to renew yourself and find a new source of professional motivation. As the famous Nike slogan says, "Just do it!"

# Summary

These pages have presented both the broad strokes of MCSE consultant wisdom and the down-and-dirty details involved in MCSE consulting, such as accounting debit and credit entries. In short, this book has tried, in the course of several hundred pages, to make your professional life as an MCSE consultant better. But in the next breath, let me quickly add that though this book is truly a bible, providing guidance to you, as an MCSE consultant, you're a creature of free will. You will have to fill in the blanks and make hundreds of future decisions on your own as an MCSE consultant. That's a pretty heady responsibility, but the payoff in terms of financial and personal satisfaction is high.

So there you have it — darn near everything you need to be an MCSE consultant. Best wishes.

✦     ✦     ✦

# Windows 2000 MCSE Track

◆ ◆ ◆ ◆

**In This Appendix**

Testing requirements
for becoming an
MCSE

Understanding the
MCSE certification
tracks

Additional MCSE
certification process
insights

◆ ◆ ◆ ◆

**W**hile the Windows 2000 MCSE track appears straight-forward at first glance, a few twists in it need explanation. I will first present the requirements for becoming MCSE certified. I will follow that with analysis of the Windows 2000 MCSE track to unravel any mysteries.

Let me give you a quick word about the exams themselves. The official public relations press release states that "these exams are developed with the input of professionals in the industry and reflect how Microsoft products are used in organizations throughout the world." These exams are more difficult than the Windows NT 4.0 MCSE track exams. The problems tend to be the longer story problems instead of simple multiple-choice, memorization-based questions (such as "What is the definition of TCP/IP?"). More importantly, the exams are much more analytical, requiring you to draw on your knowledge from two or three areas of Microsoft computing to answer a question. For example, a question on the Windows 2000 Server exam (70-215) will have elements of TCP/IP and Windows 2000 Professional embedded in a particular story problem. Finally, the exams have a business needs analysis dimension that was absent in the Windows NT 4.0 MCSE track. It's kind of like you have to be part MBA to successfully pass the upper-level Windows 2000 designing exams. Those of you with significant business experience will do well here.

## Requirements for Windows 2000 MCSE

MCSE candidates in the Windows 2000 track are required to pass seven certification exams. Of these exams, five are core exams and two are elective exams. Microsoft's intent and mission statement for the Windows 2000 MCSE track is to provide a valid and reliable measure of technical proficiency and expertise in Windows 2000 solution design and implementation.

 **Note** An additional accelerated exam (70-240) is offered for a limited time to individuals who have passed the three core exams on the Windows NT 4.0 MCSE track (70-067: Implementing and Supporting Microsoft Windows NT Server 4.0, 70-068: Implementing and Supporting Microsoft Windows NT Server 4.0 in the Enterprise, and 70-073: Microsoft Windows NT Workstation 4.0). This exam may be taken only one time and is considered to have a high degree of difficulty. If you pass it, you avoid taking the four Windows 2000 core exams.

# Windows 2000 MCSE Track

The Windows 2000 MCSE track can be broken into core and elective exams.

## Core exams

For candidates who have not already passed Windows NT 4.0 exams, all four of the following core exams are required:

- ✦ **Exam 70-210:** Installing, Configuring and Administering Microsoft Windows 2000 Professional
- ✦ **Exam 70-215:** Installing, Configuring and Administering Microsoft Windows 2000 Server
- ✦ **Exam 70-216:** Implementing and Administering a Microsoft Windows 2000 Network Infrastructure
- ✦ **Exam 70-217:** Implementing and Administering a Microsoft Windows 2000 Directory Services Infrastructure
- ✦ **Exam 70-240:** Microsoft Windows 2000 Accelerated Exam for MCPs Certified on Microsoft Windows NT 4.0 — This accelerated exam is available June 30, 2000, through December 31, 2001, and covers the core skills tested in exams 70-210, 70-215, 70-216, and 70-217.

## One more core

For all Windows 2000 MCSE candidates one of the following exams is required:

- ✦ **Exam 70-219:** Designing a Microsoft Windows 2000 Directory Services Infrastructure
- ✦ **Exam 70-220:** Designing Security for a Microsoft Windows 2000 Network
- ✦ **Exam 70-221:** Designing a Microsoft Windows 2000 Network Infrastructure

## Electives

In addition, all candidates are required to take two of the following elective exams:

✦ Any current MCSE electives

✦ **Exam 70-219:** Designing a Microsoft Windows 2000 Directory Services Infrastructure

✦ **Exam 70-220:** Designing Security for a Microsoft Windows 2000 Network

✦ **Exam 70-221:** Designing a Microsoft Windows 2000 Network Infrastructure

✦ **Exam 70-222:** Migrating from Microsoft Windows NT 4.0 to Microsoft Windows 2000

**Note**   Core exams that can also be used as elective exams may be counted only once toward a certification. In other words, if a candidate receives credit for an exam as a core in one track, the candidate will not receive credit for that same exam as an elective in the same track.

## Accelerated exam

Candidates who have passed three Windows NT 4.0 exams (Exams 70-067, 70-068, and 70-073) may take Exam 70-240: Microsoft Windows 2000 Accelerated Exam for MCPs Certified on Microsoft Windows NT 4.0 instead of the four core exams. This intensive exam is available June 30, 2000, through December 31, 2001, and covers the core skills addressed in exams 70-210, 70-215, 70-216, and 70-217. You may take this exam only once.

# Substance over Form

If you look closely at how the selection list for what I call the "one more core" exam relates to the elective exams, you will see there is very little difference in the two lists, except for the 70-222 upgrading exam listed in the electives category. So what does this mean? Microsoft is not really giving you as much flexibility as you might have believed.

# Additional Resources

You should visit *Microsoft Certified Professional Magazine's* Web site at www.mcpmag. com for the latest certification news, tips, and tricks, and Microsoft's Web site is certainly your source for the official certification exam policies, procedures, and test objectives: www.microsoft.com/train_cert.

**Tip**    One of the best resources for navigating, preparing for, and passing the demanding Windows 2000 MCSE exams is a wonderful 1,500-page book by my friend Alan Carter: *Windows 2000 MCSE Study System*, published by IDG Books Worldwide, Inc.

✦    ✦    ✦

# Federal, State, and Local Legalities

◆    ◆    ◆    ◆

**In This Appendix**

Federal- or national-level regulations and issues

State- or province-level regulations and issues

Local, including county and city, regulations and issues

◆    ◆    ◆    ◆

**T**his appendix discusses regulatory requirements related to starting and operating a business in the United States, and may not apply to overseas readers. Furthermore, when the discussed regulations are at the state and local levels, the focus is on Washington and the Seattle area specifically. I use Seattle, Washington, for my examples, as I am most familiar with the workings of the government organizations in this region. The situations covered may not apply directly to you, but they may still raise issues you need to consider.

Although everyone's business situation is unique, there are common regulatory matters all MCSE consultants must honor. For example, it's unlikely that you can simply start billing clients and receiving funds no matter who you are and where you live. At some level, you will likely need some type of license to do business.

## General Considerations

Before jumping into a discussion on legalities, there are some general issues to consider. First, you need to decide where to locate your business. You might live in one county, but locate your business in another. This may affect where you will realize your income, and so on.

**Note**   I am not an attorney, nor am I an accountant. The information presented in this appendix is based on my experience and business regulatory information in the public domains. As always, you should consult with a qualified attorney and accountant when starting any business enterprise.

# Insurance

This section discusses the different business insurance needs. Many people ask the following questions about insurance: Why do you need insurance at all? Isn't insurance a financial expense that can be considered a waste of money if nothing ever happens to what is insured? For example, what if you purchase auto theft insurance and your car is never stolen? In this case, aren't the monthly premiums a waste of money? Perhaps all that is true, but I think most people would view insurance as a necessity for minimizing uncertainty and risk in business.

## Errors and omissions liability insurance

A general organizational consideration is the issue of errors and omissions insurance in the United States. In other countries, this might have the title "professional liability insurance." But no matter what you call it, many clients and contractors you do business with (especially Fortune 1000 companies) will insist that you carry a reasonable amount of professional liability insurance — this ensures that if your actions cause damage, there will be enough money to satisfy everyone's claims.

**Note**     Obtaining professional liability insurance can be likened to a construction contractor's getting bonded. A construction contractor's being properly bonded is the equivalent of an MCSE consultant's getting professional liability insurance. Without being bonded, a construction contractor is not allowed to bid on projects, which curtails the development of that contractor's business. In the same way, not having professional liability insurance may affect your ability to grow larger, since you may be ineligible for certain types of MCSE consulting work, may not be awarded jobs, and so on.

## Property insurance

Be sure you have sufficient property insurance to protect that BackOffice network in your consulting office against fire, flood, and theft. When your business is in the early stages of development, a theft can easily put you out of commission if you have no insurance to purchase new computer hardware and software.

## Business interruption insurance

As important as property insurance is business interruption insurance. You may be down and unproductive for a few weeks while the replacement hardware and software is ordered and installed. This type of insurance compensates you for lost revenues so you can pay your utilities, rent, employee salaries, and so on. It typically pays out enough to cover your fixed costs — but not enough for you to go on vacation.

## "Key man" insurance

When you're the "Bill Gates" of your own MCSE consulting operation, you're a "key man." Key man insurance is typically required as part of the bank's lending process.

The lender wants to be repaid if anything should happen to you, causing your MCSE consulting practice to fold. (Surprisingly enough, this condition applies to residential, as well as business, loans.)

### Automobile insurance

It's likely that you drive your car on company business — you may even have a company car. In either case, your car should be insured for a number of reasons, the least being that accidents happen.

### Officer and director insurance

If you've made it to the big time as an MCSE consultant and are suddenly surrounded by a board of directors and corporate officers, you'll need to indemnify your board and officers so they can't be personally liable for decisions made on behalf of the company. Blame the asbestos and tobacco litigation era for this one, but in order to attract top talent, you'll need officer and director insurance.

### Homeowner's policy — home office

If you work at home, like many of us MCSE consultants do, your homeowner's insurance policy should cover the basics, such as theft of your home-based business hardware and software.

## Business organization

Another general consideration is the form your business will take, which may affect how the regulations apply to your MCSE consulting business. In general, there are three types of business organization: sole proprietorship, partnership, and corporation.

**Note**    Within the three broad business organization classes, there are subcategories not detailed here that you should discuss thoroughly with your attorney and accountant. For example, do you live in a community property state in the United States? That can affect you even as a sole proprietorship in the event of death or divorce. There are situations where partnerships have partners that aren't humans but corporate entities. There are many variations of corporate entities including Subchapter S, professional service corporations, and limited liability corporations.

### Sole proprietorship

This is the simplest form of business organization. It's you and you only hanging your shingle out for business. The regulatory paperwork for this type of business organization is the least burdensome of the three types — and you have absolute control over all business decisions.

It has been my experience that many MCSE consultants start here for two reasons. First, it's the easiest way to open up for business. You can always select a more sophisticated organization later as your needs dictate. Second, many MCSE consultants just want to keep things simple, just bill hours, and not run a company entity. A sole proprietorship is best visualized as an individual, as seen in Figure B-1.

**Figure B-1:** The individual view defines the sole proprietorship.

## Partnership

Partnerships, like marriage, take considerable work. My brother, an attorney, raised that point to me when I mentioned that I was planning to team up with an MCSE buddy and start a consulting firm. And he brought up another important point as well—with a partnership, to make it work you either need to really love the work you do or need to have the potential to make significantly more money than you could as a sole proprietor.

As you become a bona fide, successful MCSE consultant, your clients may insist that you select a more sophisticated form of business organization. Large corporations such as Boeing and Microsoft will have language in their vendor applications and contracts that mandate you be organized as a partnership or corporation. Your insurance company or bank may also have the same requirement.

You may seek a partner for the added benefit of companionship, or simply for the expertise to your MCSE consulting firm that such a person provides. It has been my experience that the need for companionship drives many MCSEs to partner in the consulting field. There is also a need for coverage so you can take days off for vacation, illness, or training. You might have a niche and either want a partner with the same niche so your consulting reputation grows or want a partner with a different niche so you can become more of a full-service provider to your clients.

There are two basic types of partnerships: general and limited. Loosely speaking, a general partnership is made up of general partners, each with a say in running the business based on their equity stake. In a general partnership, all partners have unlimited liability

A limited partnership is a slightly different animal. Here, you have one general partner with decision-making capabilities who has exposure to unlimited risk. The other partnership members are limited partners who must remain silent with respect to the day-to-day operations of the entity. Limited partners enjoy limited liability, and can only lose a maximum of their invested capital. That last point is a key reason people become limited partners.

Although the courts have found that a partnership can be formed through verbal agreement (watch that BackOffice and backroom bravado), partnerships are typically evidenced by written agreements covering the following salient points:

- ✦ **Definition of business** — What type of business is this?
- ✦ **Capital contribution** — What is the amount of equity funds invested by each partner?
- ✦ **Distribution of profits or losses** — How will the fruits of the labor be divided?
- ✦ **Payroll issues** — How will the partners be compensated?
- ✦ **Division of assets upon closure** — How will the distribution of assets occur upon the dissolution of the partnership? Dissolutions can occur for a number of reasons, including death, divorce, or simple disagreement.
- ✦ **Duration of the partnership** — Does the agreement spell out a termination date?
- ✦ **Implementation of changes** — Does the partnership agreement spell out how changes or even dissolution of the partnership will occur?
- ✦ **Dispute resolution** — Is there a clause for settling disputes in the partnership? Perhaps mediation should be considered, as it's significantly cheaper than litigation.
- ✦ **Authority definition** — Who has the authority to spend money and incur expenses?
- ✦ **Other clauses** — Numerous other clauses may be inserted into a partnership agreement, so this list merely highlights the broad partnership agreement terms. One such additional item often addresses how one partner can buy out the other.

## Corporation

Several factors drive the need to become a corporation. First and foremost, corporations provide limited liability for the owners, a benefit (to many people's minds) that outweighs the primary disadvantage of incorporation: double taxation of net income. Double taxation means that your earnings are taxed twice, once at the corporate level and once at the dividend distribution level.

Another reason for MCSEs to incorporate is that it provides them the opportunity to learn how to run a corporation (board meetings, etc) and ultimately go public in an initial public offering (IPO). An IPO drives many to incorporate early.

Some specific facts about being a corporation include the following:

+ **Ownership is defined by shares owned** — While this may be obvious to many readers, you should know that stock options (the right to purchase shares) do not constitute ownership.

+ **Control is exercised by ownership of shares** — You only need to own 51 percent of the shares in a company to own the company. In large publicly held companies, you can effectively control the company by holding an even smaller percentage ownership.

+ **Record keeping and administration increase** — Corporations have stricter reporting requirements than other business organizations. You can't "keep it all in your head" anymore — like the business entrepreneur. You must keep minutes, file tax forms on time, and so on.

**Note**    You should avoid using off-the-shelf software solutions to form your business organization. Although numerous packages are available to help you create a partnership or to incorporate, these fill-in-the-blank templates typically don't account for the unique aspects of your situation. You're far better off working with a qualified attorney or accountant on these critical business matters.

Figure B-2 visualizes the corporate form.

## Miscellaneous forms

Two organizational forms are recognized in Washington and many other states: the Limited Liability Company (LLC) and the Limited Liability Partnership (LLP). An LLC or LLP is formed by two or more individuals or entities through a special written agreement. The agreement details the organization of the LLC or LLP, including provisions for management, assignability of interests, and distribution of profits or losses. Limited liability companies and limited liability partnerships are permitted to engage in any lawful, for-profit business endeavor except the banking or insurance industries.

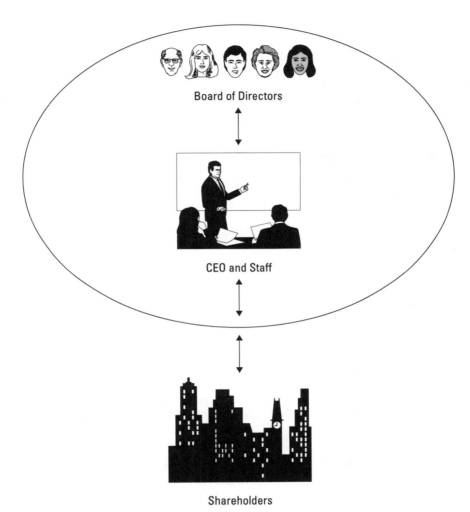

**Board of Directors**

**CEO and Staff**

**Shareholders**

**Figure B-2:** Corporate entity

# Federal-level Considerations

Numerous federal-level considerations demand your attention as you operate as an MCSE consultant in the United States. This section provides information about most of them.

## Fictitious business name

Suppose you have a unique company name, such as "ABC Corporation." In your state, that name isn't registered perhaps. But the broadcast company ABC, with significant operations in New York and California, will certainly object to your using such a name. This is typically a state issue (see "State-level Considerations" below), but implications exist at the national level.

## Trademarks, patents, and copyrights

By definition, trademarks are names or symbols. Trademarks are registered with the Trademark Office in the U.S. Department of Commerce (call 1-800-786-9199). State and federally registered trademarks may conflict with each other, often resulting in litigation.

Patents protect inventors from infringement. They also foster an economy based on innovation because those that create something, based on their unique idea, know that they're protected and will have a fair chance to recoup their investment and make a profit. (For information on registering a patent, see www.uspto.gov.)

Copyrights protect the written ideas of authors and composers. (Contact the U.S. Library of Congress at www.loc.gov for more information.)

# Federal taxation

Of course, the old adage that applies to MCSE consultants is that you can't escape death, taxes, or Microsoft recertification requirements. A discussion on federal taxes follows.

### Federal income tax

Just when you thought nothing could surpass the revision cycle for Microsoft server applications, you were turned on to federal income tax forms, rules, and regulations. Very few of us are exempt from paying federal income taxes. Consult with an accountant to determine your fair share. Also, visit the U.S. Internal Revenue Service (IRS) site at www.irs.gov for more information.

### Federal self-employment Tax

The federal self-employment tax is how the self-employed pay their Social Security taxes, since they don't have an employer to withhold them. In addition to the IRS Web site listed in the section immediately above, you can contact the IRS at 1-800-829-1040 to get the straight facts on this critical tax area.

### Federal Employer's Identification Number

You will need to apply for an Employer Identification Number (EIN) number if you are not using your Social Security Number (SSN) for taxation identification purposes. Contact the IRS for more information.

## Employment Eligibility Verification form

You must verify the employment eligibility of new employees using the Employment Eligibility Verification Form I-9. This is the old "two pieces of ID" routine specified by the Federal Immigration Reform and Control Act of 1986.

## Health and safety: OSHA-style

For businesses with bona fide work places, the Federal Occupational Safety and Health Administration (OSHA) details how employees are to be protected from workplace hazards. This is done by highly detailed health and safety standards. See the OSHA Web site at www.osha.gov for more information.

## Minimum wage

In the MCSE consulting arena, it's highly unlikely you'll have to contend with any minimum wage issues. However, just in case, visit the U.S. Department of Labor, Wage and Hour Division, for the very latest information on federal minimum wages (see www.dol.gov).

## Miscellaneous issues

I've not even touched on issues such as the Uniform Commercial Code (UCC) that discusses the legal framework for conducting business, defining transactions, defining you as a "merchant of the trade," and so on. Those topics are discussed in massive legal tomes, not here.

# State-level Considerations

One of the lessons I hope you learn in this appendix is that you will need to interact with nearly every level of government as you launch and maintain an MCSE consulting practice. This section discusses state-level matters.

## Business license

Many states, including Washington, have you apply for a business license as part of the Master Licensing Application.

# Fictitious business name, trademarks, and service marks

You would register your fictitious business name at the state level. This includes trademarks and service marks as well. A fictitious business name is the name of your business in legal parlance. Business entities are really fictitious organizations with respect to naming while the people who own and run the business are real. You register these business names, trademarks, and service marks so others can't take them from you. Your business identity is an asset that you protect by the types of registration discussed here.

In Washington state, this is accomplished via the Master Licensing Application. Once a trade name (which encompasses the three topics presented here) is registered, the registration typically remains in effect until the business owner cancels it.

# Taxation

State tax law is, in my humble opinion, as complex as federal tax law. There are fifty states with about as many different taxing approaches.

## Sales tax

Washington and many other states assess sales taxes as the primary source of revenue generation. This affects the MCSE consultant in two ways. First, are the services provided by the MCSE consultant taxable to the client? This will vary depending on how the Legislature feels in any given year. Are the goods sold by the MCSE consultant (say software and hardware) taxable? The answer is usually yes.

Second, will the MCSE consultant be exempt from paying sales tax on goods held for resale? The answer, again, is typically yes.

## Unemployment insurance tax

In general, at the state level, businesses are required to pay unemployment insurance tax if the company has one or more employees for 20 weeks in a calendar year, or if it has paid gross wages of $1,500 or more in a calendar year. Typically, these taxes are payable at a rate of 2.7 percent on the first $8,500 in annual wages of an employee. This area is subject to change and you should, as in the case of all taxation discussion, check with the taxing authority for your state.

## Business and occupation tax

Another taxing mechanism used in Washington and other states is the business and occupation (B&O) tax. This applies only to businesses and is typically based on a formula involving the real estate occupied and business assets owned by a business. This hated tax by businesses is often the central theme behind tax reduction initiatives.

### State income tax

Many states have state income taxes assessed at both the business and personal levels. This varies by state, so you are advised to check with the state government where you live.

## Workers' compensation insurance

If a business employs three or more people, workers' compensation insurance must be carried at all times to provide protection to those injured in on-the-job accidents. MCSE consultants operate in environments that contain hazards. For example, those big server rooms are loaded with high voltage connections!

## Unified Business Identifier

In Washington and other states, you will apply for an identification number—a Unified Business Identifier—used to identify your entity for all transactions and business you have with the state government. This is an improvement over the old days, when many state agencies had their own primary data identification number and none of these numbers were cross-referenced.

In some states, the Unified Business Identifier (UBI) is known as the Sales Tax Number.

# Local-level Considerations

My local regulatory discussion includes the county and city level. After consulting a political science textbook, I discovered that the local level is also comprised of untold political entities like boroughs and wards. Political jurisdictional naming issues aside, the following regulatory topics likely apply to you.

Don't underestimate the complexity of local governments regulating small businesses. When large companies look to relocate, treatment by local governments often ranks high on their list of selection criteria.

## Business license

County and city business licenses are common requirements. Other permits and certificates may be required that don't carry the title "business license." My advice is to check the Web site for your local government to get the information you need to make an informed decision about what business licenses you need. As an example, the Web site for King County, Washington, is shown in Figure B-3.

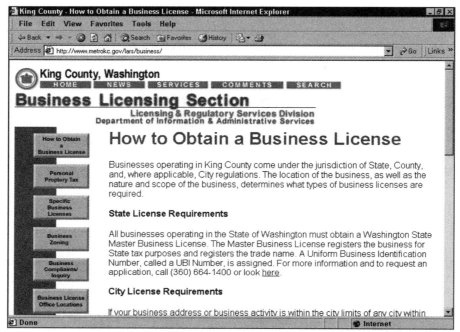

**Figure B-3:** Sample county business licensing information

# Certificate of occupancy

Before you can move into the new office space, you'll need the local governing authority to issue a certificate of occupancy. What weight does this paperwork have? Typically, real property leases, such as the leasing of office space, aren't valid until you have an appropriate certificate of occupancy in hand.

# Zoning

Something that has become an issue in the MCSE consulting community is the topic of zoning. Running a business out of a leased office space is usually devoid of zoning issues. But having an office at home becomes tricky. Some locales don't allow home-based businesses, while others don't allow accessory dwelling units, such as the home office you want to build above the garage. Zoning varies greatly by county and city, so check with a local real estate attorney if you plan to run a business from home.

# Other Resources

By now I'm sure you join me in appreciating the complexities in running any business endeavor, including an MCSE consulting practice. There are days where both you and I will take any help we can get in running our organizations. The good news is that there are many good business resources to help you run your business better. These include Web sites, books, and the good old-fashioned telephone.

## Small Business Administration

The ground zero for finding information about owning and operating a small business, such as an MCSE consulting practice, is the Small Business Administration (SBA) Web site, which can be found at www.sba.gov. Not only can you gather federal regulatory information here, but also links to your state on state-related matters are provided. The SBA Web site is shown in Figure B-4.

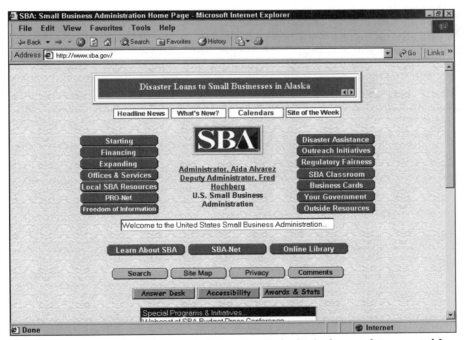

**Figure B-4:** The Small Business Administration Web site is the regulatory portal for MCSE consultants.

**Note**   Just as specific state Web sites are referenced from the SBA site, state Web sites typically link to specific county and city Web sites. This makes it more important that you start your regulatory journey at the SBA Web site and drill down.

## Books

One book to consider reading for more regulatory information is *Small Business For Dummies* by Eric Tyson and Jim Schell, published by IDG Books Worldwide, Inc. Chapters 15 and 16 of this book are especially relevant.

BizBooks, found at www.bizbooks.com, offers numerous books on "How To Do Business in Washington" (insert your state name instead of Washington). This is a helpful series of guides that expands on the regulatory discussion presented in this appendix.

## Summary

No one said all those dollars you're currently earning or will earn as an MCSE consultant were going to come easy. And after the dollars are earned you need to go to great lengths to protect them from taxation, litigation, and other traps that await you. Keeping your affairs straight with the regulatory bodies that affect your MCSE consulting enterprise is one of the all-time important business decisions you'll make. To help, this appendix covered federal or national regulations and issues, state-level regulations and issues, and local regulations and issues (which included the county and city levels).

✦   ✦   ✦

# Sample Technology Proposals

**T**his appendix contains two real-world sample technology proposals that you are welcome to use as the framework for your own proposals. The first proposal is for a Microsoft Small Business Server implementation project. The second proposal defines the scope of work for a public library system.

# Sample Proposal: Microsoft Small Business Server

February 22, 1999

Name
Client Company
Address
Seattle, WA 98*xxx*

BY FAX: (206) 555-*xxxx*

RE:    Small Business Server Computer Proposal

Dear (Insert name),

With great pleasure, we are submitting our proposal for implementing Small Business Server (SBS).

As previously discussed, our SBS methodology consists of five discrete steps that are detailed below. The total proposed costs for the work that we have defined below as SBS Phases A–E is **$9,007.50**. Kindly recall that we bill by the actual hours worked, so it is likely the above figure overstates the amount we will actually charge you. It is also possible to significantly lower our proposed costs by assisting us in the setup of the workstations. You should also be aware that the above costs contain a 30 percent contingency factor to account for unknown problems we might encounter during the implementation of your SBS network; if fewer problems are encountered, the above costs will be lower.

A few comments about M\BA Consulting and our approach to performing our work.

We are a true consulting firm. That means we serve in a couple of roles and not others. We initially act as your technology advisers in the planning/needs analysis/pre-project phases of our engagement. When the actual work is performed, we serve as consulting engineers and administrators with very much of a hands-on orientation. We are not a reseller of hardware or software. That benefits you in two ways. First, we are not necessarily aligned nor contractually committed to any specific hardware or software vendor. Second, we typically endeavor to represent you as you purchase the necessary hardware and software from national resellers/warehouses (such as PCZone or Data Comm Warehouse). It has been our experience that by coordinating your purchase from these national vendors, we are able to demonstrate substantial cost savings over purchases from local vendors.

We believe that, as a professional services firm, we are selling you much more than installation and maintenance services. We are selling you communication, control, and trust.

✦ **Communication** — This detailed proposal attempts to leave no stone unturned. Attached to this letter you will find an SBS project checklist, project schedule, biographies, an SBS advertisement, an SBS article penned by the undersigned, a sample site visit report, and a default engagement letter. Note that each visit to your site will be followed by a detailed site visit report that identifies the work we performed and to which phase this work was billed. We also want to stress that we are a consulting firm and not a reseller of hardware or software. If you need to purchase hardware or software for this conversion project, we will endeavor to help you write the purchase specifications and to obtain the lowest priced competitive bids possible.

✦ **Control** — Your billings from M\BA Consulting will match what we communicated via our site reports. Billing information will also be presented by project phase so that, at a glance, you can determine if the project is over or under budget. Note that our base hourly rates are as follows:

- Server-related work: $125/hour.

- Workstation-related work: $80/hour

- Note that we do bill for travel time. See our engagement letter for full details.

✦ **Trust** — We adhere to the "Ten Commandments of Client Service" as written by the founding partners of the firm. This document, which emphasizes trust-building practices, is available upon request.

Our proposal is organized in the following way:

1. Project phases A–E
2. Additional services
3. Schedule

# Project phases A–E

A breakdown of Phases A–E follows.

## Phase A: preproject planning

Server-related hours = 10 hours at $125/hour

Workstation-related hours = 10 hours at $80/hour

Estimated Phase A costs = **$2,050**

Timeline: These hours are typically billed over 5 to 10 business days.

This work includes meeting with the client to review our engagement letter, making a final assessment of your needs, reviewing our project checklist, confirming the placement of the workstations and server, and discussing infrastructure matters such as wiring, hardware, and software orders, service orders (telco, Internet service), and so on. The key client contact is identified, and issues such as building access are resolved. Our SBS workstation specialist will perform a walk-through of the site with the key client contact. Finally, installation issues such as machine names, domain names, user names, drive mappings, and so on are resolved.

## Phase B: server build

Server-related hours = 22.5 hours (at $125/hour)

Phase B costs = **$2,812.50**

Timeline: These hours are typically billed over several business days commencing at the end of Phase A.

This phase includes setup of the server and installation and optimization of SBS so that, at the end of this phase, the (CLIENT NAME HERE) has a functional file server that performs the following functions/roles: file server, print server, internal e-mail, and tape backups (including the installation of third-party backup applications such as Backup Exec). The network printer(s) is/are installed at this phase, and the user names and machine names are added to the SBS server console. User security is implemented. An emergency repair disk is created.

Phase B does not include the following:

+ Installing external Internet e-mail, remote access, or faxing services at this stage. This is accomplished in Phase D over a period of a few weeks.

+ Migrating data from the existing server. This is considered additional work (see the "Additional Services" section of the proposal).

+ Installing or configuring additional servers (see the "Additional Services" section of the proposal)

+ Converting existing Macintosh data. This is considered additional work (see the "Additional Services" section of the proposal).

We will attempt to install Microsoft Small Business Server and a third-party tape backup application up to two times as part of the work defined in Phase B. Any additional installation attempts beyond two attempts will be billed as "Additional Services" at $125 per hour with your prior approval. Specific tasks for Phase B are defined on the attached SBS Methodology Checklist.

## Phase C: workstation build

Workstation-related hours = 3 hours per workstation (billed at $80/hour)

Phase C costs = **$1,920** (assumes 8 workstations)

Timeline: These hours are typically billed over a 7- to 10-day period commencing at the end of Phase B.

This work includes the physical installation and SBS client setup of each workstation (client operating system, printers, modem sharing client, proxy client, faxing client, Microsoft Outlook, Microsoft Internet Explorer, and so on). Up to one hour per user is dedicated by the SBS workstation specialist to answer user questions, provide basic SBS functionality training on a one-on-one basis, and so forth. Additional time spent beyond this one hour assisting users during Phase C is charged as "Additional Services" at $80 per hour.

Phase C does not include the following:

- ✦ Installation/troubleshooting of user specific applications (for example, TimeSlips)
- ✦ Migration of user data

We will make up to two attempts to install the SBS client components on a workstation. Additional SBS client component installation attempts will be billed as "Additional Services."

After Phase C you will be contacted by Dotti Harris from our office to complete a midpoint client survey. The results from this survey typically allow us to redirect our future efforts if necessary.

## Phase D: weekly follow-ups

Server-based hours = 1 hour per week $125/hour.

Workstation-based hours = 4 hours per week at $80/hour (minimum)

(We assume five weeks of follow-up.)

Phase D cost = **$2,225**

Timeline: One day per week for five weeks following Phase C.

The weekly follow-ups are a mandatory and necessary component of our proposal. Each week, starting with the first week after Phase C is complete, we visit to install a new feature of SBS and to provide ongoing support and user training. This work includes up to one full day per weekly visit. We suggest the following schedule:

- ✦ **Week one** — Internet e-mail via Microsoft Exchange (including modem pool turn up). Basic Outlook functionality. Proxy Server (firewall) will be configured.

- ✦ **Week two** — Remote access. You will note that we strongly recommend PCAnywhere. We no longer support Microsoft's inbound RAS capabilities. If we are asked to implement and support the inbound capabilities of RAS, we will bill this time as "Additional Services" at $80/hour.

- ✦ **Week three** — Faxing, inbound and outbound.

- ✦ **Week four** — Advanced Outlook training for users/implementation of advanced Outlook features such as shared calendars, shared contacts, public folders, and so on.

- ✦ **Week five** — To be determined/WWW page/troubleshooting/Internet development. We typically hand off network administration duties to in-house staff at this point.

Note that these weekly visits typically include the ordinary and necessary resolution/troubleshooting of end user problems, network problems, and so on. We also encourage users to ask questions during each weekly visit so that they may better make use of the new SBS network.

### Phase E: end of project
Phase E cost = $0

This is a milestone wherein we typically recognize the discrete end of the SBS project and answer your final questions. This meeting typically takes the form of a celebration lunch.

After Phase E, we are happy to provide you either ongoing scheduled support on a regular basis or emergency/unplanned support on an as-needed basis. We will discuss these options with you further during Phase E. These services will be billed as "Additional Services."

An employee from our office will contact you again in Phase E with an end-of-project client survey. These results will be used to assist us in assessing our next steps together.

## Additional services

We are unable to include the following work in our standard SBS five-phase project proposal and will perform such work as additional services beyond the scope of the SBS project:

Office 2000 application suite = 1 hour *minimum* per workstation at $80 per hour to install if it is not already installed.

Specific server-based and user-based applications (for example, TimeSlips, marine applications, legal applications, and so on) will be installed at $125 per hour on a time-and-materials basis, as approved by the client. The hours dedicated to this type of work may vary depending on the assignment. We will attempt to provide an hourly estimate on a case-by-case basis.

Technical support and end user support beyond the scope of the five-phase SBS project will be billed at the server and workstation bill rates defined below depending on the work performed.

We offer training classes in SBS administration, Microsoft Outlook basics, and Advanced Microsoft Outlook at our Bellevue training center. These classes range from $150/half day to $300/day and are beyond the scope of this proposal. Please ask us for details if you are interested.

Additional work as requested and approved will be performed subject to these rates:

✦ **Server-related work** — $125 per hour.

✦ **Workstation-related work and end user support** — $80 per hour.

Note that we will charge one hour of travel time for each site visit when we are providing "Additional Services."

## Bottom line — proposed total service costs for the SBS project

The proposed costs, by phase, are listed in Table C-1:

| Table C-1 Proposed Total Service Costs for SBS Project | |
| --- | --- |
| Phase A costs | $2,050.00 |
| Phase B costs | $2,812.50 |
| Phase C costs | $1,920.00 |
| Phase D costs | $2,225.00 |
| Phase E costs | $0 |
| Total project costs for Phases A–E | $9,007.50 |

Note that total hardware and software costs will vary depending on the final purchase configuration. The total costs for our services may vary depending on the amount of planning and follow-up that you authorize.

## Schedule

Note that we can perform the work described above in the month of March 1999. Note that we perform only two SBS installations per month to guarantee that you receive our full attention.

We greatly look forward to working with you on your SBS computer project. We do not consider this proposal complete until we have had the chance to discuss the specific phases above with you and answered your questions.

With best regards.

Very truly yours,

(Insert consultant name)

Attachments

# Sample Proposal: Scope of Work for Public Library System

NT Installation/LAN Conversion Project Scope of Work

Prepared for: Public Library System

DATE

Prepared by: MCSE Consulting Firm, Anytown, State, USA

## Statement of reciprocal confidentiality

MCSE Consulting Firm acknowledges that the information contained in this document is confidential and proprietary to Public Library. MCSE Consulting Firm agrees to use the same degree of care to protect the confidentiality of this information as it uses to protect its own.

The stated implementation techniques used in this document are the intellectual property of MCSE Consulting Firm. It is the responsibility of each recipient of this document to ensure that unauthorized duplication or distribution of this material outside Public Library is not permitted without prior written consent of MCSE Consulting Firm.

 **Tip**    Follow the confidentiality statement with a table of contents clearly outlining what areas the proposal will cover.

## Overview

The request for a Local Area Network Conversion Plan for Public Library will be identified in a series of documents and outlined in two phases — Scope of Work and Installation Guide) Each phase will consist of the specific detailed information needed to complete this transition and will be documented accordingly. The phases are prerequisite to each other and must be implemented in the same manner.

Having collected initial data specific to your current networking environment and your *immediate* and *long-term* objectives, the Scope of Work Document will be generated to address this information. This information along with accompanying documentation of existing equipment, environmental conditions, applications, and procedures will be compiled, bound, and reviewed. This portion outlines "where you are" in terms of your existing configuration.

Upon completion of both the analysis of your *existing* configuration and our recommendations to transition you to your optimal configuration, a section will be created portraying your new configuration. This portion outlines "where you want to be" based on your objectives and our review and will also be bound with all the previous data and this Scope of Work.

Once the Scope of Work and all bound documentation and recommendations, quotes, and so on have been reviewed and approved by Public Library and MCSE Consulting Firm, Phase II begins and an Installation Guide is generated to detail any and all tasks and configuration options necessary to complete the installation. This portion outlines "how you get there" based on all materials previously correlated and is drawn directly from the Scope of Work Document.

It is understood that the Scope of Work Document will be accepted by both parties and that upon acceptance changes, additions, and deletions will constitute a Change in Scope of Work. Such changes will be documented and approved accordingly.

This document details the requirements for Phase I of the *Public Library NT Installation/LAN Conversion Project*.

## Introduction

This Scope of Work is intended to define the Project known as *Public Library NT Installation/LAN Conversion Project* contracted by MCSE Consulting Firm of Framingham, Massachusetts, and the Public Library of Rhode Island.

The Scope of Work is intended to define all requirements necessary for a successful implementation and includes postservice support information.

This Scope of Work is not intended as a contract, but rather it provides a basis for discussion of the required project planning and services to be provided by MCSE Consulting Firm.

## Summary

Public Library has identified the need for the following:

+ Initial analysis, evaluation, and quotations as to the hardware and software platform required to provide a successful conversion from their LanTastic/ DOS and Windows 3.1–based configuration to an NT/DiscPort Executive/Win95 configuration

+ Presentation, analysis, and review of existing and proposed configurations (Scope of Work)

+ Presentation and review of installation procedures with timeline (Installation Guide)

+ Project management and on-site system engineering to install, configure, upgrade, verify, and test server and workstation reconfigurations

+ Basic server and workstation administration training

+ Basic application software installation and administration on NT 4.0 DiskPort Server

### Hardware and software requirements and recommendations

Determine requirements based on each respective workstation:

+ MSD, master workstation inventory, and workstation inventory sheets:
    • Identify/confirm desktop platform — hardware configuration.
    • Identify/confirm desktop operating system, utilities, and applications.
    • Identify/confirm desktop network hardware requirements.
+ Server/workstation application software matrix:
    • Identify/confirm desktop network software requirements.
    • Identify/confirm desktop applications software requirements.
+ Identify/confirm printer configurations and needs.
+ Identify/confirm cable requirements.

## Preinstallation tasks

Arrange for a site survey of the designated Public Library at least 30 days prior to the installation date:

✦ Floor plan document

✦ Network diagram(s) current and proposed

✦ HVAC requirements (power and environment conditioning)

- Router/hub/patch panel location
- Server location
- Workstation locations and redeployment plan

Designate on-site and alternate manager for contact and administration.

Coordinate efforts with Public Library project manager, branch managers, MCSE Consulting Firm technical resources, and outside vendors/contractors to prepare site for installation and acquisition of workstation(s), for memory upgrades, and for support for transitioning to new configuration:

✦ Schedule/confirm site inventory.

✦ Schedule/confirm electrical and HVAC contractor (if required).

✦ Schedule/confirm cable contractor (if required).

✦ Schedule/confirm router configuration and IP addressing scheme.

✦ Schedule/confirm workstation upgrades hardware.

✦ Schedule/confirm workstation upgrades software.

✦ Schedule postinstallation maintenance support (hardware and software).

✦ Schedule postinstallation training of branch administrator.

Address workstation/communication equipment hardware and software requirements:

✦ Present documented hardware and software requirements:

- Hardware network adapter cards
- Hardware network patch cables
- Hardware network patch panel
- Software Win95 upgrades

✦ Obtain acknowledgment of purchase order and estimated delivery dates.

Verify all contracted services have been performed:

- ✦ Obtain necessary connectivity information:
  - IP addressing
  - Naming conventions (if required)
- ✦ Prepare checklist for verification that all services performed are to specification:
  - Verify site inspection and floor plan.
  - Verify workstation/printer inventory.
  - Verify workstation hardware/software upgrades.
  - Verify cable and HVAC installation.

## Site Installation tasks

Schedule on-site installation dates.

Verify contracted services:

- ✦ Verify cable installation including patch panel.
- ✦ Verify new PC installation.
- ✦ Verify memory upgrades on existing PC configurations.

Perform server installation procedures:

- ✦ Acquire Microtest DiscPort Tower.
- ✦ Configure NT.
- ✦ Install/configure DiscPort.
- ✦ Determine and add user profiles.
- ✦ Install software applications.
- ✦ Modify security for user access to applications.

Perform workstation installation procedures:

- ✦ Inventory all hardware and software.
- ✦ Upgrade/configure all existing workstation hardware, memory, and Win95.
- ✦ Configure new workstations (Win95).
- ✦ Test and verify installation of hardware, memory, OS, and software applications.

Document problems and escalation procedures:

- ✦ Prepare installation control log.
- ✦ Document all problems in detail.
- ✦ Follow installation problem escalation procedures.

Prepare documentation of completion (Installation Guide):

- ✦ Obtain branch manager sign off.
- ✦ Obtain project management sign off.

## Description of services

MCSE Consulting Firm will provide project management and technical resources for communication and workstation services for the *Public Library NT Installation/LAN Conversion Project*. The services the MCSE Consulting Firm will provide include the following:

- ✦ A preinstallation site survey
- ✦ Assistance with the preparation of the site environment, including but not limited to the following: HVAC, cabling, existing workstation reconfiguration and deployment, and new workstation configuration and deployment
- ✦ Equipment selection/purchase
- ✦ Equipment configuration/installation
- ✦ Software application configuration/installation
- ✦ Administration training
- ✦ Maintenance and communication of all record keeping associated with these activities

All MCSE Consulting Firm provided installation services are to be performed during normal business hours or on a prearranged basis during nonbusiness hours when so required. MCSE Consulting Firm will work in partnership with Public Library project management to finalize the required timeline of NT Installation/LAN Conversion Project installation.

The implementation of the NT Installation/LAN Conversion Project will be evaluated based on the results of this Scope of Work Document and subsequent Phase I meetings and analysis.

The goals of Phase I are as follows:

+ Determine the approximate time require to perform and document the site survey.

+ Refine the checklist "Site survey."

+ Determine the approximate time required to source outside contractors and perform the necessary installations: HVAC, cabling, and so on.

+ Refine the checklist "Outside contractor scheduling, verification, and testing."

+ Determine the approximate time required to configure and install the NT Server, both hardware and software.

+ Refine the checklist "Server installation."

+ Determine the approximate time required to upgrade the new and existing workstations, both hardware and software.

+ Refine the checklist "Workstation upgrades."

+ Determine the approximate time required to install all applications software on NT Server for workstation access.

+ Refine the checklist "Application software."

+ Determine the approximate time required for in-house administration training.

+ Refine the training procedures for hardware and software.

+ Refine control log documentation.

+ Refine timeline and schedule as needed.

+ Refine status control log procedures for project planning.

+ Refine escalation and problem resolution procedures.

+ Refine sign off procedures.

+ Establish postinstallation support procedures.

+ Refine postinstallation support procedures.

## MCSE Consulting Firm responsibilities

MCSE Consulting Firm will work in partnership with the designated project manager to develop the Installation Guide. A preliminary draft of this guide is included as a separate document titled *Public Library NT Installation/LAN Conversion Installation Guide*.

MCSE Consulting Firm will provide the project management, hardware/software, and technical services for the Public Library installation.

MCSE Consulting Firm will designate a project team for the entire project. This team will have the required skill set for the implementation and postservice support of this project, including hardware support, software installation and configuration, and Windows NT/Windows 95 communication connectivity specific to LAN and WAN platforms.

MCSE Consulting Firm will provide management and technical services at the main branch location. All services provided will follow the procedures set forth in the *Public Library NT Installation/LAN Conversion Installation Guide*.

MCSE Consulting Firm will assist with the contracting of outside resources and equipment purchases; however, MCSE Consulting Firm cannot guarantee the workmanship and schedules as performed and determined by the outside resources.

MCSE Consulting Firm will provide if requested a list of the MCSE Consulting Firm resources assigned to the project. MCSE Consulting Firm has the right to remove and/or assign additional resources if so required.

## Public Library responsibilities

In order to provide successful management and technical services, MCSE Consulting Firm requires the following information to be submitted at least 45 days prior to the scheduled implementation dates:

- ✦ List of branch offices
  - Contacts (primary and alternate)
  - Address
  - Telephone/fax numbers
- ✦ Floor plan (blueprint), if available
- ✦ Complete listing of all applications software to be installed
- ✦ Complete set of all applications software to be installed (for bench preinstallation)
- ✦ Workstation and printer inventory, including make, model, and configuration

Public Library will be responsible for workstation hardware compatibility if provided by outside vendor.

Public Library will be responsible to purchase the equipment recommended by MCSE Consulting Firm. In the event the equipment recommended is not available and/or substitution is required, MCSE Consulting Firm will be notified immediately.

## Considerations

MCSE Consulting Firm will install and implement the Public Library NT Installation/ LAN Conversion according to the specifications listed in the *Public Library NT Installation/LAN Conversion Installation Guide*.

# Transition plan

MCSE Consulting Firm believes that a five-tiered transition process will be required to successfully implement the required NT Installation/LAN Conversion. The five tiers of this transition process include the following:

1. Scope of Work completion and approval

2. Installation Guide generation and approval with time lines

3. Benchmarking installation procedures (benching preinstall)

4. Installation/training

5. Postinstallation review and approval

# Completion statement

MCSE Consulting Firm will consider the Public Library NT Installation/LAN Conversion Project complete when the following items are deemed operational:

✦ NT 4.0 Server is configured and installed with DiskPort Executive software, and all applications software is made available to the specific workstations in the LAN based on the server/workstation applications software matrix.

✦ All existing and new workstations are upgraded, verified, and tested in the designated Public Library locations within the branch.

✦ Public Library project management team representative sign-offs at completion of job.

✦ All control log and tracking information is completed and included in the final report on project status (Labor Reports).

✦ The MCSE Consulting Firm Project Manager completes all postinstallation procedures.

MCSE Consulting Firm acknowledges that Public Library has ultimate responsibility for the implementation and operational use of the Public Library NT Installation/LAN Conversion. Certain factors are out of MCSE Consulting Firm control; therefore when MCSE Consulting Firm satisfies the above requirements, Public Library takes responsibility for maintaining and using the NT 4.0 Server/DiskPort Executive properly.

# Scope of Project acceptance

The preceding Public Library NT Installation/LAN Conversion Scope of Work Documentation is satisfactory and hereby accepted. You are authorized to perform the services described in this document and do the work as specified. (This section of the proposal will leave space to allow the client to sign and date their acceptance of the Scope of Work proposal. Further space for notes or comments may also be left after the acceptance section of the proposal.)

✦　　✦　　✦

# MCSE Consulting Working Papers

✦ ✦ ✦ ✦

**In This Appendix**

Needs analysis listings

Systems analysis questions to ask

Sample project checklist

Relevant business forms

✦ ✦ ✦ ✦

This appendix includes a potpourri of checklists, working papers, Web site listings, and other useful information to help the MCSE consultant to set up shop quickly. The resources offered in this appendix are based on my years of experience as an MCSE consultant. The goal for this appendix is to save you time. If I save you one hour of time with these papers, then you've just paid for the price of the book, if not more. If I save you hundreds of hours, then I've met my personal goal of being a good MCSE consulting citizen and mentoring those that follow in my footsteps. Also, just like characters in the fall 2000 hit movie *Pay It Forward* helped others after they had been helped, I ask that you in turn mentor some MCSE consultant that follows behind you.

## Windows 2000 MCSE Needs Analysis

The following needs analysis lists are designed to assist you in performing needs analysis as an MCSE consultant. I present four lists: business needs, infrastructure, directory services, and security. You can use these lists to structure your planning engagement with the client. More importantly, you can append, delete, and otherwise modify these lists to meet your general needs as an MCSE consultant and the specific needs of your client. These lists are living documents, not static forms that lock you into one structure.

Table D-1 presents the list of areas you should analyze in the business needs department.

| Table D-1 Business Needs Analysis | |
| --- | --- |
| *Analysis Area* | *Findings* |
| Analyze the existing and planned business models. | |
| Analyze the company model and the geographical scope: Regional, national, international, subsidiary, and branch offices. | |
| Analyze company processes: Information flow; communication flow; service and product life cycles; and decision-making process. | |
| Analyze the existing and planned organizational structures: Management model; company organization; vendor; partner; customer relationships; and acquisitions plans. | |
| Analyze factors that influence company strategies. | |
| Identify company priorities. | |
| Identify the projected growth and growth strategy. | |
| Identify relevant laws and regulations. | |
| Identify the company's tolerance for risk. | |
| Identify the total cost of operations. | |
| Analyze the structure of IT management: Type of administration (centralized or decentralized); funding model; outsourcing; decision-making process; and change-management process. | |

Table D-2 presents analysis elements for infrastructure needs.

| Table D-2 Infrastructure Needs Analysis | |
| --- | --- |
| *Analysis Area* | *Findings* |
| **Technical Requirements Analysis** | |
| Evaluate the company's existing and planned technical environment and goals. | |
| Analyze company size and user and resource distribution. | |
| Assess the available connectivity between the geographic location of work sites and remote sites. | |
| Assess net available bandwidth and latency issues. | |
| Analyze performance, availability, and scalability requirements of services. | |

| Analysis Area | Findings |
|---|---|
| **Technical Requirements Analysis** | |
| Analyze data and system access patterns. | |
| Analyze network roles and responsibilities. | |
| Analyze security considerations. | |
| Analyze the impact of infrastructure design on the existing and planned technical environment. | |
| Assess current applications. | |
| Analyze network infrastructure, protocols, and hosts. | |
| Evaluate network services. | |
| Analyze TCP/IP infrastructure. | |
| Assess current hardware. | |
| Identify existing and planned upgrades and rollouts. | |
| Analyze technical support structure. | |
| Analyze existing and planned network and systems management. | |
| Analyze the network requirements for client computer access. | |
| Analyze end user work needs. | |
| Analyze end user usage patterns. | |
| Analyze the existing disaster recovery strategy for client computers, servers, and the network. | |
| **Network Infrastructure Analysis** | |
| Modify and design a network topology. | |
| Design a TCP/IP networking strategy. | |
| Analyze IP subnet requirements. | |
| Design a TCP/IP addressing and implementation plan. | |
| Measure and optimize a TCP/IP infrastructure design. | |
| Integrate software routing into existing networks. | |
| Integrate TCP/IP with existing WAN requirements. | |
| Design a DHCP strategy. | |
| Integrate DHCP into a routed environment. | |
| Integrate DHCP with Windows 2000. | |

*Continued*

## Table D-2 *(continued)*

| Analysis Area | Findings |
|---|---|
| **Network Infrastructure Analysis** | |
| Design a DHCP service for remote locations. | |
| Measure and optimize a DHCP infrastructure design. | |
| Design name resolution services. | |
| Create an integrated DNS design. | |
| Create a secure DNS design. | |
| Create a highly available DNS design. | |
| Measure and optimize a DNS infrastructure design. | |
| Design a DNS deployment strategy. | |
| Create a WINS design. | |
| Create a secure WINS design. | |
| Measure and optimize a WINS infrastructure design. | |
| Design a WINS deployment strategy. | |
| Design a multiprotocol strategy. Protocols include IPX/SPX and SNA. | |
| Design a Distributed File System (Dfs) strategy. | |
| Design the placement of a Dfs root. | |
| Design a Dfs root replica strategy. | |
| Designing for Internet Connectivity | |
| Design an Internet and extranet access solution using any or all of these solution components: Firewall (with caching); routing and remote access; Network Address Translation (NAT); connection sharing; Web server; and Mail server. | |
| Design a load-balancing strategy. | |
| Designing a Wide Area Network Infrastructure | |
| Design an implementation strategy for dial-up remote access. | |
| Design a remote access solution that uses Routing and Remote Access. | |
| Integrate authentication with Remote Authentication Dial-In User Service (RADIUS). | |
| Design a virtual private network (VPN) strategy. | |
| Design a Routing and Remote Access routing solution to connect locations. | |

| Analysis Area | Findings |
|---|---|
| **Network Infrastructure Analysis** | |
| Design a demand-dial routing strategy. | |
| Designing a Management and Implementation Strategy for Windows 2000 Networking | |
| Design a strategy for monitoring and managing Windows 2000 network services: Global catalog; Lightweight Directory Access Protocol (LDAP) services; certificate services; DNS; DHCP; WINS; routing and remote access; ISA Server/Proxy Server; and Dfs. | |
| Design network services that support application architecture. | |
| Design a plan for the interaction of Windows 2000 network services such as WINS, DHCP, and DNS. | |
| Design a resource strategy. | |
| Plan for the placement and management of resources. | |
| Plan for growth. | |
| Plan for decentralized resources or centralized resources. | |

Table D-3 focuses on directory services needs analysis.

## Table D-3
## Active Directory – Directory Services Needs Analysis

| Analysis Area | Findings |
|---|---|
| Analyzing Directory Services Technical Requirements | |
| Evaluate the company's existing and planned technical environment. | |
| Analyze company size and user and resource distribution. | |
| Assess the available connectivity between the geographic location of work sites and remote sites. | |
| Assess the net available bandwidth. | |
| Analyze performance requirements. | |
| Analyze data and system access patterns. | |
| Analyze network roles and responsibilities. | |
| Analyze security considerations. | |

*Continued*

| Table D-3 (continued) | |
|---|---|
| **Analysis Area** | **Findings** |
| Analyze the impact of Active Directory on the existing and planned technical environment. | |
| Assess existing systems and applications. | |
| Identify existing and planned upgrades and rollouts. | |
| Analyze technical support structure. | |
| Analyze existing and planned network and systems management. | |
| Analyze the business requirements for client computer desktop management. | |
| Analyze end user work needs. | |
| Identify technical support needs for end users. | |
| Establish the required client computer environment. | |
| Designing a Directory Service Architecture | |
| Design an Active Directory forest and domain structure. | |
| Design a forest and schema structure. | |
| Design a domain structure. | |
| Analyze and optimize trust relationships. | |
| Design an Active Directory naming strategy. | |
| Establish the scope of the Active Directory. | |
| Design the namespace. | |
| Plan DNS strategy. | |
| Design and plan the structure of organizational units (OUs). Considerations you should include are: Administration control; existing resource domains; administrative policy; geographic locations; and company structure. | |
| Develop an OU delegation plan. | |
| Plan Group Policy object management. | |
| Plan policy management for client computers. | |
| Plan for the coexistence of Active Directory and other directory services. | |
| Design an Active Directory site topology. | |
| Design a replication strategy. | |

| Analysis Area | Findings |
|---|---|
| Define site boundaries. | |
| Design a schema modification policy. | |
| Design an Active Directory implementation plan. | |
| Designing Service Locations | |
| Design the placement of operations masters. (Considerations include performance, fault tolerance, functionality, and manageability.) | |
| Design the placement of global catalog servers. (Considerations include performance, fault tolerance, functionality, and manageability.) | |
| Design the placement of domain controllers. (Considerations include performance, fault tolerance, functionality, and manageability.) | |
| Design the placement of DNS servers. (Considerations include performance, fault tolerance, functionality, and manageability.) | |
| Plan for interoperability with the existing DNS. | |

Table D-4 addresses areas of analysis for security needs.

| Table D-4 Security Needs Analysis | |
|---|---|
| Analysis Area | Findings |
| Business security needs | |
| Analyze the current physical model and information security model. | |
| Analyze internal and external security risks. | |
| Analyzing Security Technical Requirements | |
| Evaluate the company's existing and planned technical environment. | |
| Analyze company size and user and resource distribution. | |
| Assess the available connectivity between the geographic location of work sites and remote sites. | |

*Continued*

| Table D-4 *(continued)* | |
| --- | --- |
| *Analysis Area* | *Findings* |
| Assess the net available bandwidth. | |
| Analyze performance requirements. | |
| Analyze the method of accessing data and systems. | |
| Analyze network roles and responsibilities. Roles include administrative, user, service, resource ownership, and application. | |
| Analyze the impact of the security design on the existing and planned technical environment. | |
| Assess existing systems and applications. | |
| Identify existing and planned upgrades and rollouts. | |
| Analyze technical support structure. | |
| Analyze existing and planned network and systems management. | |
| Analyzing Security Requirements | |
| Design a security baseline for a Windows 2000 network. The analysis should include: Domain controllers; operations masters; application servers; file and print servers; RAS servers and desktop computers; and portable computers. | |
| Identify the required level of security for each these resources: printers, files, shares, Internet access, and dial-in access. | |
| Designing a Windows 2000 Security Solution | |
| Design an audit policy. | |
| Design a delegation of authority strategy. | |
| Design the placement and inheritance of security policies for sites, domains, and organizational units. | |
| Design an Encrypting File System strategy. | |
| Design an authentication strategy. | |
| Select authentication methods: Certificate-based authentication; Kerberos authentication; clear-text passwords; digest authentication; smart cards; NTLM; RADIUS; and SSL. | |
| Design an authentication strategy for integration with other systems. | |
| Design a security group strategy. | |
| Design a Public Key Infrastructure. | |
| Design Certificate Authority (CA) hierarchies. | |

| Analysis Area | Findings |
|---|---|
| Identify certificate server roles. | |
| Manage certificates. | |
| Integrate with third-party CAs. | |
| Map certificates. | |
| Design Windows 2000 network services security. | |
| Design Windows 2000 DNS security. | |
| Design Windows 2000 Remote Installation Services (RIS) security. | |
| Design Windows 2000 SNMP security. | |
| Design Windows 2000 Terminal Services security. | |
| Designing a Security Solution for Access Between Networks | |
| Provide secure access to public networks from a private network. | |
| Provide external users with secure access to private network resources. | |
| Provide secure access between private networks. | |
| Provide secure access within a LAN. | |
| Provide secure access within a WAN. | |
| Provide secure access across a public network. | |
| Design Windows 2000 security for remote access users. | |
| Designing Security for Communication Channels | |
| Design an SMB-signing solution. | |
| Design an IPSec solution. | |
| Design an IPSec encryption scheme. | |
| Design an IPSec management strategy. | |
| Design negotiation policies. | |
| Design security policies. | |
| Design IP filters. | |
| Define security levels. | |

The next section lists system analysis questions taken from some of my earlier consulting work (before Windows 2000 arrived). This is relevant as it provides more general technology questions you may use to fortify your MCSE consulting checklists for use in the field.

## Systems analysis — networking

These questions pertain to choosing the type of network.

+ Approximately how many users does the network at your site serve?

+ Is there data and resources on your network that need to be restricted or regulated?

+ Can the users on your network take care of their own network administration and management needs?

+ Does your network need extensive data security?

+ Are you allowed to share your own network resources and set other network policies for your computer?

+ Does your network use centralized security?

+ Does your network have one central administrator who sets network policies?

+ Does your network have more than one server?

+ Approximately how many servers does your network have?

+ Will your network's servers be centrally located or spread out in different locations?

+ Will some of your network's servers be in a secure location?

+ Are some of the servers designated for special tasks?

+ Circle the tasks below that will apply to your servers:

  • Communication

  • Backup/redundancy

  • Application

  • Database

  • E-mail

  • Fax

  • Print

  • User directories

  • General data storage

+ Approximately how many users does the network at your site serve?

+ Is cost a consideration in choosing your network topology?

+ Does your building have drop ceilings?

+ Is these easy access to crawl spaces or wiring conduits?

✦ Is ease of troubleshooting important?

✦ Does the physical layout of the computers and office space naturally lend itself to a particular topology?

✦ Is ease of reconfiguration important?

✦ Is there existing wiring in the building that could be used for your new network?

# Cabling

The following questions relate to cabling types that are used.

## Unshielded twisted pair

✦ Are most of your computers within 100 meters of your wiring closet?

✦ Is ease of reconfiguration important?

✦ Does any of your staff have experience with UTP cable?

## Shielded twisted pair

✦ Does your network have any existing STP cabling?

✦ Does the topology or network card you want require the use of STP cable?

✦ Do you have a need for cable that is more resistant to EMI (interference) than UTP?

## Coaxial

✦ Do you have existing coaxial cabling in your network?

✦ Is your network going to be installed in an open area using cubicles to separate work areas?

## Fiber optic

✦ Do you have a need for network cabling that is immune to EMI (interference)?

✦ Do you have a need for network cabling that is relatively secure from most eavesdropping or corporate intelligence gathering equipment?

✦ Do you have a need for network transmission speeds that are higher than those supported by copper media?

✦ Do you have a need for longer cabling distances than those supported by copper media?

✦ Do you have the budget to absorb the costs of implementing fiber?

### Wireless network communications

✦ Do users on your network need to physically move their computers in the course of their work day?

✦ Are there limitations that make it very difficult or impossible to cable computers to the network?

# Network adapter cards, drivers, protocols

This section has questions relating to the network adapter cards, drivers, and protocols that are used.

### Network adapter card

✦ What type of network adapter card are you using/will you be using?

✦ Are there drivers/updated drivers available for the card that will work with the existing/future operating system(s)?

✦ Is the card compatible with the cable type and topology you have chosen?

✦ Is the card compatible with the type of computer into which it will be installed?

### Drivers

✦ Does the hardware you are planning to buy come with drivers for the type of computer and OS you plan to use?

✦ Has the vendor of the OS you want to use tested the card and driver you plan to purchase in the type of computer you intend to install it in?

✦ Is the network adapter card on the HCL?

### Protocol — IPX/NWLink IPX

✦ Is IPX the default protocol for the NOS you are installing?

✦ Does the network software you are installing support IPX?

✦ Does the network need to support routing?

✦ Do you have to support network servers or clients running NetWare server or client software?

### Protocol — TCP/IP

✦ Is TCP/IP the default protocol for the network operating system you are installing?

✦ Does the network software you are installing support TCP/IP?

✦ Does the network need to support routing?

✦ Do the computers on the network need access to the Internet?

✦ Do you have to support network clients from multiple vendors?

### AppleTalk

✦ Is AppleTalk the default protocol for the network operating system you are installing?

✦ Do any of the computers you are installing require support for AppleTalk?

✦ Does the network need to support routing?

✦ Does the network software you are installing support AppleTalk?

## Network operations

✦ Is your server hardware on the HCL?

✦ Do you have correct (current) drivers for all of the hardware in your server?

✦ Do you have the minimum amount of memory in your server to support your current network operating system?

✦ Does your server have the minimum amount of hard disk space recommended to support all of your storage needs?

✦ Does your server have the minimum processing power needed to support your network?

✦ Do you have all of your network bindings implemented correctly, and are the most used bindings listed first?

✦ Do your client computers have the correct client software loaded (redirector)?

## Printers

✦ Are there particular users or groups of users who will produce an exceptional amount of printed output?

✦ Are there printers for each group that have been identified as producing a lot of printer output?

✦ Are print jobs at certain printers spending too much time in print queues?

✦ Based on the preceding discussion, how many printers will your organization need?

## Faxing

✦ Will you need to support network faxing?

✦ How will this be accomplished?

## E-mail

✦ What type of e-mail do you use?

✦ Will it meet your growth needs?

✦ Do you need to share e-mail with other users outside of your company?

✦ What type of e-mail gateway will you use?

## Network Operating Systems (NOSs)

✦ Is there a need for more than one NOS in your environment? Discuss.

✦ Does each client computer have the redirectors required to communicate with the appropriate servers?

## Client/server environment

✦ Are you currently running the following applications in a non-client/server environment? (If more than 10 people use either of the following, consider implementing client/server versions.)

- Database
- Groupware

## Security

✦ Do you want to put most shared resources on dedicated servers, but leave some to be shared in a peer-to-peer fashion?

✦ Do you want to give permissions to resources by group memberships?

✦ Will everyone in your organization leave the server alone if it is left out in an open space?

✦ Are there employees or visitors who should not have access to any network resources?

✦ Could passwords get passed around, borrowed, or stolen in your environment?

✦ Are there users working with sensitive data?

✦ Is there the possibility that some users at your site would attempt to use someone else's computer without permission or log on to the network under someone else's name?

✦ Is it possible that some users at your site might not know how to implement passwords?

✦ Does your company use temporary, contract, or other non-permanent employees?

✦ Is there a need to monitor or restrict access to any particular sensitive network resources or peripherals, or a need to identify which users have accessed which resources over a given period of time?

✦ Is there a concern that temps, contractors, etc., might intentionally copy data to disks, download data, or take it off-premises?

✦ How sensitive is your data? Could it be used against you?

✦ Is your network currently protected from viruses?

## Managing network performance

✦ Do any users in your organization ever experience erratic or inconsistent network performance?

✦ Will you be using any network management tools like SMS?

✦ Does your network have a written history? Is it easily accessible?

✦ Are you currently keeping a record of your network's behavior?

✦ Have you established and recorded a baseline based on monitoring information?

## Data loss

✦ How do you currently protect your data from data loss?

✦ Who is responsible for the backup?

✦ What is the backup schedule and rotation?

## Modems

✦ Do you need to communicate with BBSs like CompuServe, MSN, or AOL?

✦ Do you need individual connectivity to the Internet?

✦ Do you need to periodically transfer files with another user at a different location?

✦ Do several users at once ever need to communicate with an online server or remote resource?

✦ Do you have users that need to access the network from home or while on the road?

The next sections relate to creating larger networks, such as wide area networks.

## Switches

✦ Does your network run slower than you would like?

✦ Do certain departments only transmit data within their department?

## Routers

✦ Do you need to join several LAN segments into a single network?

✦ Do you need to connect different types of network architectures (Ethernet, Token Ring)?

✦ Do you need to isolate or filter traffic between multiple segments?

✦ Are network performance and data important enough to maintain redundant paths between multiple segments simultaneously?

✦ If you have multiple paths, do you want packets routed on a "best path" algorithm?

## Gateways

✦ Do you need to allow communications between unlike systems (PC to Mainframe, etc.)? Discuss.

## Advanced WAN technologies

✦ Do you have only two sites to link? (If yes, consider point-to-point service.)

✦ Does your system need to link multiple sites to a central location? (If yes, consider a point-to-multipoint service.)

✦ Does your system need to link many points simultaneously? (If yes, consider multipoint-to-multipoint.)

✦ Is the data you transmit critical enough that you require multiple links between sites to provide redundancy in case of link failure?

✦ What kind of network traffic will be on the link?

- Voice
- E-mail
- Light file transfer
- Heavy file transfer
- Client/server database activity
- Client computer database activity with files stored on remote server

✦ Based on the amount of network traffic you have, what type of network bandwidth do you need: 56 Kbps? more than 1 Mbps?

# Project Checklist

Table D-5 shows a detailed, multiphase checklist for hands-on work tasks. I use this list in my Small Business Server (SBS) consulting engagements. Here again, it can easily be modified for your use on other projects.

| Table D-5 Detailed Project Checklist | | |
| --- | --- | --- |
| **Work Phase** | **Task** | **Completed (Y/N)** |
| Phase A: Preproject planning | First Meeting | |
| | Review meeting agenda. | |
| | Review order of events — rough timeline. | |
| | Mention possible delays (HW/SW failures, third-party relations, and so on). | |
| | Stress the importance of training and continuous learning. | |
| | Check infrastructure — existing equipment and cabling. | |
| | *Hub* | |
| | *Cabling* | |
| | *Wall jacks* | |
| | Proposal written, delivered, and discussed. | |
| | Network layout discussed and described. | |

*Continued*

## Table D-5 *(continued)*

| Work Phase | Task | Completed (Y/N) |
|---|---|---|
| Phase A: Preproject planning | SBS checklist/methodology discussed and revised as needed. | |
| | Write and deliver confirmation letters recounting meeting and telephone conversations. | |
| | Review engagement letter. | |
| | Discrete outcomes | |
| | *Written agenda* | |
| | *Written proposal* | |
| | *Written confirmation letters detailing meeting content and telephone conversations* | |
| | *Written SBS checklist* | |
| | *Written project schedule and calendar* | |
| | Next steps | |
| | *Acceptance of proposal* | |
| | *Receipt of signed engagement letter* | |
| | Second Meeting: Plan for Deployment | |
| | Specifically identify a point of contact for the project. | |
| | Review estimated timeline. | |
| | Make yourself available by pager, voice mail, and e-mail. | |
| | Offer written and/or verbal updates periodically. | |
| | Have the client order all services and equipment. | |
| | Order data service. | |
| | Make sure domain name move is underway if necessary. | |
| | Order all hardware. | |
| | Order router from ISP if necessary. | |
| | Order all software. | |

| Work Phase | Task | Completed (Y/N) |
|---|---|---|
| | Confirm the correct number of SBS licenses are available. | |
| | Order infrastructure (Ethernet jacks). | |
| | Discrete outcomes | |
| | *Written confirmation letters detailing meeting content and telephone conversations* | |
| | *Revised project schedule* | |
| | Pre-Implementation Walkthrough | |
| | Building access | |
| | All computer access (people off their machines for client installation) | |
| | Assess training needs. | |
| | *Outlook* | |
| | *Operating system (Win2K, WinMe/Win9x)* | |
| | Installation plan — location map, and so on. | |
| | Server | |
| | *Where will it sit?* | |
| | *Who should be in the administrator's group?* | |
| | Workstation issues | |
| | Get a list of names of users with correct spelling. | |
| | Printers | |
| | Routers and hubs | |
| | Special circumstances | |
| | Discrete outcomes | |
| | *List of user names with correct spelling* | |
| | *Location map — installation map* | |
| | Next steps | |
| | *Phase B: Server Installation* | |

*Continued*

| | Table D-5 *(continued)* | |
|---|---|---|
| **Work Phase** | **Task** | **Completed (Y/N)** |
| Phase B: Server Installation | Physically unpack and construct server. | |
| | Install SBS—floppy, CD-ROM installation. | |
| | Complete server installation information sheet (partitions, drive mappings, Dynamics modifications, passwords, and so on). | |
| | Add SBS licenses. | |
| | Add any server-based printers to the network. | |
| | Add users to network via SBS console. | |
| | Add workstations to network via SBS console. | |
| | Implement and verify Microsoft Exchange is working internally. | |
| | Begin a system log on the server. | |
| | Take note of any unusual circumstances. | |
| | Provide training on password security. | |
| | Test tape backup/restore. | |
| | Implement tape backup policy. | |
| | Verify virus protection is working. | |
| | Make ERD. | |
| | Discrete outcomes | |
| | *Phase B summary report* | |
| | Next Steps | |
| | *Phase C: Workstation Installation* | |
| Phase C: Workstation Installation | Physically unpack and construct workstations. | |
| | Complete installation of client operating system (Win2K, WinMe/9x). | |
| | Create installation disk for each workstation. | |
| | Install SBS client components on each workstation. | |
| | Perform basic SBS client component tests, answer limited user questions, and so on. | |
| | Enable and demonstrate Network file sharing from client PCs | |

| Work Phase | Task | Completed (Y/N) |
|---|---|---|
| | Enable and demonstrate Network printing from client PCs | |
| | Enable and demonstrate basic internal e-mail via Outlook. | |
| | Set a date to return to fully configure Outlook (calendar, contact list, and so on). | |
| | Propose a date for Outlook training. | |
| | Discrete outcomes | |
| | *Phase C summary report* | |
| | *Client completes midpoint quality survey* | |
| | Next Steps | |
| | *Phase D: Weekly Visits* | |
| Phase D: Weekly Visits | | |
| Week One — Outlook and Microsoft Exchange external Internet connection | Minimum criteria for proceeding with this phase: | |
| | *Server installed and configured.* | |
| | *Clients installed and configured.* | |
| | Data transport service available from phone company (dial-up, ISDN, T-1, and so on) | |
| | ISP service available and ready to go with domain name in place | |
| | Implement externally connectivity. | |
| | Configure Proxy and Exchange to use Outlook externally. | |
| | Configure and use Outlook externally and with Public Folders (contact lists, calendars). | |
| | Verify external e-mail and Web browsing. | |
| Week Two — Remote Users | Implement PCAnywhere or RAS-based solution. | |
| | Test remote user solution. | |
| | Configure user machines for remote connectivity. | |
| | Train users on remote connectivity. | |

*Continued*

## Table D-5 *(continued)*

| Work Phase | Task | Completed (Y/N) |
|---|---|---|
| Week Three — Faxing | Implement inbound/outbound faxing services at server per client specifications. | |
| | Implement inbound/outbound faxing client configuration at user workstations. | |
| Week Four — Internet development | Install IIS 4.0. | |
| | .asp pages | |
| | Internal Web applications | |
| | Encrypted e-mail | |
| Week Five — Network administration wrap-up/punch list | Test backups. | |
| | Check security. | |
| | Apply OS fixes and upgrades. | |
| | Resolve configuration issues: printers, modems, SBS clients, and so on. | |
| Week Six and forward — other work as agreed | Discrete outcomes | |
| | *Weekly activity/summary report* | |
| | *Daily site visit reports* | |
| | Next Steps | |
| | *Phase E: Project Completion* | |
| Phase E: Project completion | Client/consultant lunch and so forth to celebrate and review project. | |
| | Discrete outcomes | |
| | *Client completes final quality survey* | |
| | Next Steps | |
| | *Additional work performed on an as-needed and by-request basis.* | |

# Business Forms

This section includes several business forms for your consideration, including a project versus actual variance reporting worksheet.

## Variance reporting

In Table D-6, I present a variance reporting form.

| Table D-6 **Variance Reporting** | | | | | | | | |
|---|---|---|---|---|---|---|---|---|
| **Project Budget vs. Actual Variance Reporting** | **MCSE Consultant** | **PHASE A – Hours** | | | **PHASE A – Costs** | | | |
| | | **Orig. Budget** | **Current Budget** | **Actual** | **Orig. Budget** | **Current Budget** | **Actual** | |
| | Harry ($125/hour) | 2 | 2 | 2 | 250 | 250 | 250 | |
| | Steve ($80/hour) | 5 | 5 | 7.5 | 400 | 400 | 600 | |
| | Total | 7 | 7 | 9.5 | 650 | 650 | 850 | |

## Sample engagement letter

Here is a sample engagement letter for MCSE consulting.

*March 31, 2001*

*SBS Customer*

*RE: SBS Implementation Engagement Letter*

*Dear NAME,*

*Thank you for selecting MCSE Consulting, Inc., to provide CLIENT with consulting services. This letter is to confirm our responsibilities and our rates relating to your engagement of our firm. We look forward to the opportunity to serve you, and we welcome CLIENT as a client of MCSE Consulting, Inc.*

*It is our desire to provide you with the highest quality consulting and computer services that are delivered in the most efficient manner. Our goal is your satisfaction with the services that we provide. The key to a successful professional relationship is clear and candid communication. Please contact me immediately if you have questions regarding any matter that MCSE Consulting, Inc., is handling for you.*

*The consulting service you have asked us to perform is Small Business Server implementation and training services. These services are fully described in our proposal letter of DATE. You have selected the hardware and software for the implementation of this system. Furthermore, we have not been contracted to perform a needs analysis to determine if this system satisfies the requirements of your company. Therefore, we are not responsible for any shortcomings of the new system. You are responsible for maintaining all equipment and for the safeguarding and updating of all hardware, software, and data stored.*

*Our rate for these services currently is as follows:*

*Harry Brelsford — $125.00 per hour (portal to portal)*

*There is a two (2) hour minimum for on-site support. Telephone/modem support is billed on a time-spent basis with the minimum charge of one-quarter hour. Services requested and performed outside of normal business hours (Monday–Friday 8:00 a.m.– 5:00 p.m.) will be billed at time and one half. Out-of-pocket expenses incurred on your behalf will be billed directly to you. Payment for software and hardware ordered by CLIENT is due 50 percent on order and the remaining balance upon delivery.*

*In order to effect the prompt delivery of services, the employees of CLIENT are authorized to place orders or requests for the services of MCSE Consulting, Inc. An authorized member of your staff must approve requests of services that are estimated to be in excess of $750.00.*

*Invoices will be mailed on a monthly basis for the services performed and cost incurred during the previous month. Payment is due 15 days after the date of our invoice. Invoices unpaid within 15 days will be subject to a late charge of 1.5 percent per month (18 percent per year) on the unpaid balance commencing from the date of the invoice and continuing until paid. If any of our invoices remain unpaid or if you exceed your credit limit of $10,000.00, we may cease to perform services until satisfactory arrangements are made for the payment of invoices due and prospective future fees.*

*CLIENT understands that while performing services MCSE Consulting, Inc., does not make any warranties with respect to the computer systems or software, particularly to warranties of merchantability, of fitness for a particular purpose, or against infringement.*

*It is agreed that MCSE Consulting, Inc., will not be liable for special, consequential, exemplary, indirect, or incidental damages. CLIENT's recourse on software warranties is dictated by the terms and conditions of the specific software warranty agreement that is provided by the software manufacturer. CLIENT is responsible for reviewing and understanding the software manufacturer's warranty terms.*

*Given the nature and complexity of the services we will be providing you, should any misunderstandings arise relating to the services described in this letter, we will do our best to resolve such issues as soon as possible to the mutual satisfaction of all parties involved. If we are not able to accomplish that result, any disputes arising under this agreement (including the scope, nature, and quality of services, fees, or other terms of the engagement) shall be submitted to mediation. A competent and impartial third party, acceptable to both parties, shall be appointed to mediate, and each disputing party shall pay an equal percentage of the mediator's fees and expenses. No suit or arbitration proceedings shall be commenced under this agreement until at least 60 days after the mediator's first meeting with the involved parties. If the dispute requires litigation, the court shall be authorized to impose all defense costs against any nonprevailing party found not to have participated in the mediation process in good faith.*

*If you find the terms of our engagement letter as set forth above to be satisfactory, please acknowledge your acceptance by signing this letter and returning it to MCSE Consulting, Inc.*

*If you have any questions regarding any aspect of our engagement, feel free to contact me. It is important that we begin our arrangement on an open and mutually satisfactory basis.*

*Yours very truly,*                                      *Executed By:*

*MCSE CONSULTING, INC.*                                  *CLIENT*

*Harry Brelsford, MCSE, MCT*

*President*

*Title: _____*

*Date: _____*

# Early Small Business Server interview questions

A list of SBS interview questions is presented in Table D-7.

| Table D-7 Small Business Server Interview Questions – Early Stage | |
|---|---|
| **Question** | **Answer** |
| List the three reasons that you intend to use SBS. | |
| What is the time frame for implementing SBS? | |
| What roadblocks or problems can you identify today that may make the SBS project more difficult to complete? | |
| How have you arranged for training for the new SBS network? | |
| ADD | |
| ADD | |

# Third-party/ISV software assessment form

Table D-8 provides a list of questions to assess the fitness of a third-party software product for your client.

| Table D-8 Third-party Software Questionnaire | |
|---|---|
| **Questions** | **Response** |
| How long has product been on market? | |
| How many versions? | |
| How many releases per version? | |
| How long after new Dynamics version is third-party software new version released? | |
| How many installations? | |
| Three to five references. | |
| Any VAR licensing arrangements? | |
| Does ISV have a formal training program for partners? customers? | |
| Web site address? | |
| Marketing materials? | |
| Any printed manuals and/or installation guides? | |

| Questions | Response |
|---|---|
| Any online manuals? | |
| Demo data? | |
| How many employees does ISV have? | |
| How many help desk people, consultants, developers, and trainers? | |
| Future plans for revisions, direction of product? | |
| Interfaces with other third-party products? | |
| What platforms/databases does software perform on (LAN, SQL), (Btrieve, Ctree SQL), and are there significant installation considerations? | |
| Does ISV have plans to maintain product on above platforms? | |
| Is third-party software Great Plains Logo compliant? | |
| Any awards received for product? | |
| Other products ISV has or is developing? | |
| Does product interface only with Dynamics? Is it also stand-alone? | |
| Can users modify forms and reports through Dynamics report writer and VBA modifier? | |
| What programming language is product written in? | |
| System requirements? | |

# Sample site visit report

This is a sample site report for a visit to a client site.

*August 14, 2001*

*CLIENT*

*RE: Work Performed August 10, 2001*

*Dear Jon,*

*This letter will serve as our site visit report for the work performed by the undersigned on your behalf.*

*On August 10, we performed the following:*

1. *Updated our checklists and project schedule and discussed the project internally with Steve B. and Vernon L.*

2. *Accepted a support telephone call from you wherein we provided extensive guidance with respect to the Paradox database. At our request, you modified the properties for the Paradox application shortcut icon so that the shortcut icon pointed to the proper application and working directory.*

3. *Directed your efforts to add everyone to the Administrators group so that we could efficiently resolve a Great Plains Dynamics security authentication issue.*

4. *Fixed the WSP-related conflict on the workstation running CompuServe.*

5. *Resolved a logon problem at a user's workstation by having that workstation authenticate on the network via the IPX/SPX protocol.*

6. *Fixed the Raiser's Edge client application installation on Lynette's PC and mapped Drive R to DS01.*

7. *Modified the Paradox network configuration files as per instructions from Borland support. This modification work included changing the network identity from NetWare to Other (which apparently supports Windows NT Server, the underlying network operating system for SBS).*

8. *Assisted in the resolution of Mike's Great Plains Dynamics data reporting problem by first verifying the status of the data copy from the old NetWare server to the new SBS server. Next we paged and instructed Vernon Loveless to proceed to your site. Once Vernon arrived, we advised Vernon of our progress and assisted him in performing several Dynamics-related tests. We also assisted Vernon in retransferring the Dynamics-related data from the old NetWare server to the new SBS server.*

*For this work we billed the following:*

✦ *For item #1 we billed one ("1") hour at $125/hour to Phase B of the project.*

✦ *For item #2 we billed 0.5 hours at $125 per hour to "Additional Services" for the project.*

✦ *For items #3 to #8 we billed three hours ("3") to "Additional Services" and one hour ("1") to Phase B of the project.*

*If your understanding of the above work differs from ours, please contact our office so we may discuss this matter. Thank you for your continued use of MCSE Consulting, Inc.*

*With best regards.*

*Very truly yours,*

*Your Loyal MCSE Consultant!*

# Web-based Resources

Obviously the Web is a tremendous repository of resources for the MCSE consultant seeking to run a more effective and efficient consulting practice. Here is a list of Web sites to get you started on seeking out the many useful consulting resources that have been posted. You can also use the major search engines and search on keywords such as consulting if you like.

✦ Small Business Administration: www.sba.gov

✦ Service Corps Of Retired Executives (SCORE): www.score.org

✦ CNN's financial/business Web page: cnnfn.cnn.com

✦ CNET: www.cnet.com

✦ Onvia: www.onvia.com

✦ Workz: www.workz.com

**Tip**

I encourage you to monitor my company Web site at www.nethealthmon.com for additional MCSE consulting working papers. At this site, you'll find a sample business plan I've written that you can download and modify for your own use among other things. See you online.

# Summary

This appendix was included in this book to save you time. I've provided forms for your modification and use. I've provided some Web page links to further your development as the owner and operator of and worker in an MCSE consulting firm. Good luck!

✦     ✦     ✦

# MCP Magazine Salary Survey

**O**ne of the reasons you likely purchased this book and
are looking forward to a career as an MCSE consultant
is that you want to make money. This appendix provides a
glimpse of a recent annual salary survey from *Microsoft
Certified Professional (MCP) Magazine* (www.mcpmag.com),
portions of which are reprinted here by permission. This
salary survey is published annually, so be sure to check the
Web site for the most recent work.

## MCSE Consulting Compensation

What is interesting to note from observing the long-term trend
of the *MCP Magazine* Salary Surveys is that the average annual
MCSE salary has remained in the mid- to upper-$60,000 range
despite significant growth in the sheer numbers of MCSE titleholders. You would expect some dilution of earnings to occur
as the base grows larger, but such hasn't been the case as of
the early twenty-first century.

**Note**

Here is an example of dilution of earnings to better understand the concept I'm trying to convey. This comes from
the world of corporate finance and makes my point that a
large base (be it MCSE title holders or shares of stock outstanding) will effectively dilute per unit earnings. If a firm
has 100 shares of stock from which it made $100 in profit,
the earnings per share are one dollar per share. However, if
the firm proceeds to issue another 100 shares with the
same earnings ($100 in profit), the earnings per share
drops to $0.50 per share. This is typical with financial
instruments such as stocks, and the math is relatively easy
to compute.

It is a positive sign that MCSE compensation has held steady or slightly increased in the *MCP Magazine* Salary Survey because the base of MCSE titleholders has more than increased fivefold during that time. If you do the math, this means the aggregate economic sector that supports MCSEs (that is, firms who have a demand for the services of MCSEs) has kept pace and is growing at a similar or slightly faster rate. Otherwise, as the number of MCSEs went from roughly 50,000 to over 250,000 during the first five years of the *MCP Magazine* Salary Survey, you would have seen a significant decline in per MCSE annual salary. Again, it's a linear mathematical formula, but the bottom line is that this area of the economy is very robust.

**Note**
Another interesting angle to this economic data and the strength in the demand for MCSEs is that the *MCP Magazine* Salary Surveys have chronicled how with the huge growth in the number of MCSE titleholders the average years of work experience per MCSE has decreased slightly. Technology professionals with less work experience are earning their MCSE titles. Such a decrease is expected. Why? For two reasons. First, work experience is a linear function of time (one year worked is one year of work experience). Second, as the number of MCSEs (for example) grew over fivefold during the first five years of the *MCP Magazine* Salary Survey, less experienced titleholders have no doubt entered the field. The fact that the *MCP Magazine* Salary Survey can report increasing compensation while the MCSE base is growing and while the average years of experience is declining is a true testament to the economic viability of holding the MCSE certification title.

You will also note with interest in the reprinted article below that the $60,000 annual compensation figure is an aggregate amount for all MCSEs. Those MCSEs employed in an in-house position on salary are slightly below this average annual compensation figure and MCSE consultants are 20 percent higher (at $73,000) than their in-house counterparts. The differential between in-house and external MCSE knowledge workers is significant and favorable for the self-employed MCSE consultant.

I will now share part of the fifth annual *MCP Magazine* Salary Survey (*Smart Money* by Linda Briggs, Copyright 2000). Visit the magazine's Web site at www.mcpmag.com for the most recent salary survey (remember that business decisions you make such as becoming an MCSE consultant should be based on the most current data available). Note this article has been edited and condensed.

# Smart Money

"Not surprisingly in today's job market, salaries are up, up, up for just about everyone. You can move ever higher in the compensation pile with these tickets: job experience, developer talent, or Windows 2000 skills.

In MCP Magazine's U.S. Salary Survey, everyone's a winner this year — except perhaps the hiring managers who must deal with a rising tide of IT salaries. Despite a doubling in the number of MCSEs in the past year and a huge increase in the numbers of MCPs overall, our fifth annual salary survey shows compensation holding strong for all Microsoft Certified Professionals. In line with general increases in the IT industry driven by strong demand, salaries for MCSEs, for example, are up four percent, from a base salary last year of $65,100, to this year's $67,800. The compensation picture is considerably different, though, for someone just entering the IT field. Those with a year or less of experience, as 23 percent of our respondents reported, and who have passed a single Microsoft exam and thus hold the entry-level Microsoft Certified Professional title, reported an average base salary of $45,800. Experience, as always, is the key differentiator in salary, followed by area of the country and job function. Other factors, including age and gender, also play into the salary equation.

## The value of experience

As always, our survey emphasizes the tight relationship between pay and time on the job. It also highlights how quickly the certification program has grown. Respondents, who represent a statistical sampling of all MCPs in the U.S., have an average of 5.5 years of experience — down from 6.6 years in 1999. In particular, average experience among those holding the MCSE title has dropped almost a full year, from 6.8 to 5.9. Last year, notably, we saw a surprising rise in average experience among MCSEs and speculated that the program might be attracting more experienced IT workers expanding on Novell and UNIX-centered skill sets. This year it appears that the huge influx of newcomers into the certification program is pulling down the average. For example, MCSEs have grown from around 140,000 worldwide when we conducted our survey last spring, to over 260,000 today. Microsoft's program overall includes at least 800,000 certified individuals worldwide, up from about 500,000 a year ago.

## Footing the bill

We observed a drop again this year in the number of companies paying for certification. In 1998, 58 percent of respondents said their companies paid for certification entirely; in 1999, that had dropped to 50 percent; this year, just 39 percent of companies pick up the certification bill completely.

Given the increasing prevalence of certification in IT, we find this surprising. Apparently, in a red-hot job market, employers are reluctant to pay for skills that they think may increase an employee's worth or attractiveness elsewhere. Interestingly, salaries for those whose companies paid for certification were much higher (averaging $71,400) than those who paid for certification themselves ($58,500). Perhaps the more valued and highly compensated the employee, the more negotiating power that individual has in convincing an employer to pick up the tab.

## Internal versus external

We consistently found a big difference in salary between those who work in corporate IT/IS supplying internal services to other employees and those who primarily supply external services (working for solution providers, value-added retailers, and systems integration companies). IT professionals supplying external services averaged $73,000 in base salary, 20 percent above the $60,600 of those who supply services primarily to corporate IT departments. Part of the reason may be that companies tend to use more experienced people for outside assignments. Also, working with outside clients may demand more skills and expertise than working with internal employees. Also, our survey showed that companies supplying external services tend to have a higher percentage of IT workers with expensive talents, including security, UNIX, and programming skills.

*Bonuses were also higher for those at external service firms, averaging $5,700 a year versus $4,500 for those supplying internal services.*

## Outside income and hours worked

Despite high salaries, performing outside work for extra income remains lucrative to many in IT. Among our respondents, two-thirds reported receiving some income from "other job-related sources." The amount earned was relatively low for those with little experience, peaking among those with 5–6 years of experience at $6,400 this year. Outside income then dropped as experience increased, perhaps as respondents with more responsibility — and higher salaries — felt less inclination to moonlight. In an industry with a reputation for long hours and sudden weekend emergencies, number of hours worked was surprisingly reasonable.

## Self-employed

We asked the 10 percent of respondents who are self-employed to complete information on hourly rates and how work is contracted. Half of those responding contract directly with clients (receive IRS form 1099s and are responsible for their own taxes). We defined self-employed as "You assume risk of profit or loss and are responsible for all business overhead." Another 14 percent work through brokers, placement firms, or IT staffing companies. The remaining third combine contract and direct assignments. The average hourly rate reported by those who contract directly with clients is $67. This breaks down to averages of $57 an hour for an MCP, $71 an hour for an MCSE, $84 an hour for an MCSE+I, and $87 an hour for an MCSD. Those holding premium titles probably have more experience and a broader skill set than the average respondent, and hence command more per hour for that reason, not solely because of a certification title.

## Gender bias

As it does each year, our survey shows that women in information technology make significantly less than men across all titles and job descriptions. Women are also poorly represented in the industry as MCPs. Just 11 percent of all Microsoft Certified Professionals in the U.S. are women; the MCSD title reflects the lowest percent of females (9 percent), while the entry-level MCP title has the highest, at 14 percent. On average across all titles and years of experience, women reported earning just under

$10,000 less than men. Note, however, that that's partly because they tend to have less experience, are less likely to be IT managers, and because fewer of them hold premier titles. In every certification, job title, or years-of-experience comparison we ran, though, women fell short of men. Male MCSEs with an NT 4.0 focus, for example, average $67,800 in base pay; females, $57,700. Men with two to three years of experience average $60,600; women, $51,500. This follows the pattern of past years and, in fact, shows a slightly greater salary gap than in 1999.

## Does education pay off?

Education affects compensation, but as is typical in IT, it isn't the most important factor. For example, our survey found that high school graduates reported earning slightly more, on average, than those who had attended some college or graduated from a two-year college program. Perhaps high school graduates have dived into an IT profession and are moving up quickly, while those attending some college or holding a two-year degree either tend to be career-changers or are spending part of their time and efforts on school rather than work. Most common among respondents (31 percent) was a four-year college degree; the average salary for a college graduate was $67,800. Earning a master's degree added $5,300; adding a doctorate, assuming all else remains equal, added just another $1,400 on top of that.

## Add up the numbers

Hot salaries abound, but remember that if yours doesn't match one of the averages we show, there are many factors determining compensation. As you compare your pay to our figures, consider: How much actual, hands-on experience do you have? That's the single biggest influencer on salary, and there's really no way to move quickly from having less than a year's experience to having three or four years in IT. Also weigh in where you live and work. If you're in a major metropolitan area, where the cost of living is higher and where many high-tech firms tend to compete for workers, expect more dollars. If you've chosen a more rural lifestyle, compensation will correspond. Finally, managers and team leads, because of their greater responsibility, also earn more, so you may want to consider that as you plot your career. We can't discount certifications and job skills. The two go hand-in-hand. MCSEs consistently make more than MCPs, but they also typically have more experience and a bigger set of skills. Part of that comes from the certification process; part certainly comes from time on the job developing a broader and deeper skill set.

Finally, our survey shows that those working with Windows 2000 now, and planning to certify this year, are making more than those who aren't. For now, we conclude that it's because the most experienced people are getting assigned to Win2K rollouts. But some analysts have predicted that Win2K skills will be in huge demand if companies deploy the new OS at the predicted rates. Add to that Microsoft's attempts to raise the MCSE bar for Win2K and you can be assured that Windows 2000 skills will be a valuable rarity, at least for a while."

## Additional Information

"Since salaries are affected by many variables, we encourage you to check out other surveys and compare their numbers with ours. Although *MCP Magazine* conducts the only survey that focuses on the effect of Microsoft certification on pay, you can find a growing number of high-tech salary surveys available these days. When viewing other surveys, check the number of respondents polled (some are too small to be worthwhile) and consider the method by which respondents are selected. Many surveys simply invite any IT professional to visit a Web site and enter salary numbers. In those cases, remember that it's unlikely that the numbers represent a statistical sampling of the IT workforce.

Like many industry publications, *Computerworld* keeps a constant eye on IT salaries. To view numbers and articles on pay ranging from CTOs to help desk support, go to www.computerworld.com and click on "IT Resources"; then under the Surveys & Reports header, click on "Annual Salary Survey."

SANS is a research and educational institute focusing on systems and security at www.sans.org. You can sign up to receive an almost-instant e-mail of its 1999 survey, with data for 7,151 respondents with titles like network administrator, security admin, or system admin.

www.computerjobs.com is a technical-job-focused site that sponsors a nationwide survey, in which you can participate. While it's not a statistically accurate way to conduct a salary survey, you may find the results interesting. The site also includes a handy list of other IT salary surveys.

The survey at www.asponline.com covers titles like Support Technician or Analyst/Project Manager. If you're a member of the Association of Support Professionals, the latest survey is free. Otherwise, you have to pay—or access 1999 data for free.

If you're a federal government employee, pay rates for any classification and scale, not just in IT, are available at www.seemyad.com/gov/salary.htm.

www.Realrates.com solicits salary information from the computer consultants who visit its site. For $25 you can download a copy of its salary database, which provides such details as skills, location by city and state, length of contract, rate paid by client, and the like.

If you're interested in pursuing one of the technical certifications offered by Lotus, check out that company's own salary survey of Certified Lotus Professionals at www.lotus.com/home.nsf/welcome/clpsurvey."

# Summary

So what lessons can be gleamed by looking at the fifth annual salary survey from *Microsoft Certified Professional Magazine*? First, regardless of the year the salary survey was conducted, there are several significant trends worth noting that have held steady from year to year in this survey: experience is important; premium titles are meaningful, as are other educational achievements; and external MCSE consultants make significantly more money than salaried in-house employees. The specific compensation figures, while very interesting, represent values obtained during a limited survey. These figures can and do change from year to year, so you will want to check the *Microsoft Certified Professional Magazine* Web site at `www.mcpmag.com` periodically to see if new, specific compensation figures have been published.

✦    ✦    ✦

# MCSE Consulting Toolkit

The MCSE toolkit is much more than just a bunch of tools you should have handy when performing surgery on a fallen NT server. It strikes at the core of what you are and aren't as an MCSE. Are you a professional or skilled tradesperson? Your role and duties determine the type of toolkit you should have. A professional may carry a leather briefcase with monogrammed initials, and a tradesperson may have a toolkit akin to those carried by electricians. Use your judgement and carry an appropriate toolkit for the work you perform, the image you want to convey as an MCSE, and the expectations of your clients and supervisors.

The good news is that the MCSE community is big enough to accommodate people from different walks of life. Perhaps you've worn only the white collar-and-tie combo in your MCSE consulting career. In that case, your toolkit may consist of information that allows you to communicate with your clients, solve problems, and provide solutions, such as a small CD-ROM library containing TechNet. On the other hand, maybe you're part of a break-fix hardware organization. In that case, your toolkit is more likely to contain tools such as a cable tester, solder gun, and Phillips screwdriver. Both types are needed in the MCSE consulting community for clients to be able to use their BackOffice technologies effectively. Don't forget that even cardiologists and oncologists have such tools as saws and drills in their toolkits. No one is above carrying at least a few tools.

What type of toolkit should you possess? This discussion will focus primarily on MCSEs, but I'll also provide some detail on what MCTs and MCSDs may need.

# The Prepared MCSE

I'm an MCSE, first and foremost. What's in my toolkit? I carry a limited set of real tools, including two Phillips screwdrivers, two flat-head screwdrivers, a Compaq screwdriver that has a star pattern on the end to open older Compaq servers, a chip extractor, and a static energy discharger wristband. You can purchase these types of kits from national resellers such as PCZone and Data Comm Warehouse for under $50. It's safe to say this type of toolkit is a necessary and required fixture for any MCSE. You must be able to connect a cable or open a workstation if you want to earn the lofty salaries paid to MCSEs.

Because the leather pouch that contains my real toolkit has extra room, I carry other invaluable items. These include a modern network adapter such as the 3Com 3C9xx series and an old-fashioned, true NE2000 network adapter. The modern network adapter helps me fix the common point of failure on workstations and servers: layer one of the OSI model (better known as the network adapter). Anyone with the MCSE title should at least be able to replace this component. The NE2000 network adapter shows my age. In the old days when knights were bold and kings owned all the gold, the NE2000 network adapter was fashionable. Today, I carry my remaining NE2000 because it always works. I've had some late nights at client sites when I've been up to my neck with Plug-and-Play (PNP) and needed to be saved by my trusty ISA-based NE2000 card. It's a trick worth remembering and an item worth adding to your MCSE toolkit.

Two extra items that I've added to my toolkit based on my own errors and omissions are a small dental mirror that extends several inches and a pen-sized flashlight. With these tools working in tandem, I can easily see the backside of components and motherboards during "surgery." Such visibility makes a difference when you're trying to insert RAM chips into tight slots.

# Important CDs

Other MCSE toolkit items you may carry in your vehicle, but not necessarily on your person, include CDs that you'll need to access. Here's what I currently carry in my soft-sided CD-ROM carrier:

+ **Microsoft TechNet** — I carry the full edition of six CDs including the Technical Information Network, Client Utilities, Microsoft BackOffice Products Evaluation, Service Packs, Server Utilities, and Supplemental Drivers and Patches CDs. This collection of CDs is invaluable.

**Note**

Using the term *near* when performing Boolean-type searches in TechNet typically works best. *Near* finds matches within 15 words. It seems like fuzzy logic, but it's a search that works well for us humanoids.

+ **Compaq SmartStart** — This resource is, of course, invaluable when you're working with Compaq servers and workstations.

✦ **Hewlett Packard JetAdmin software for JetDirect print servers**—You'd be surprised how often you need to implement a new JetDirect card and don't have the correct software. The CD version I carry has drivers for every network known to humankind (from AppleTalk to Unix).

✦ **Business Resources Kit and Sales Training Interactive CD**—These CDs are provided by Microsoft as part of the Microsoft Certified Solution Provider program. I use these CDs to fortify my sales efforts.

✦ *Windows 2000 Server Secrets* **CD-ROM**—This is one of those CD-ROMs that ships with almost all retail books today. In this case, the book is *Windows 2000 Server Secrets*, a book of mine that was published by Hungry Minds, Inc., formerly IDG Books Worldwide, Inc. These book-based CDs are typically best for finding something like WinZip so that you can "zip" a client's data file and send it quickly over the Internet. Don't forget that many of the CDs found at the back of books have sample MCSE exams. That's an invaluable freebie for MCSE candidates.

✦ **Windows support source CD**—This is a CD-ROM subscription service from Cobb, the well-known newsletter publisher. It contains an archive of articles that may interest the practicing MCSE.

✦ **Internet service provider (ISP) CD**—I carry the CD that my ISP issues, which contains ISP-specific sign-up information, drivers, and FAQs. This CD is extremely helpful in the field, especially if you implement Internet service for your clients.

✦ **Microsoft Project 2000 CD Disc 1**—This CD contains blank project templates for creating your BackOffice migration project schedule. It saves lots of time during the management of your project.

✦ **Novell Support Connection CD**—The life of an MCSE consultant is one of working in multi-vendor environments. Rare is the network that only has Microsoft solutions. Rather, you're likely to see NetWare on many of the networks you help manage. Thus, you need to consider the monthly subscription to the Novell Support Connection CD library.

✦ **Microsoft BackOffice CDs**—How many times are you asked to insert a specific CD to complete the installation of a driver? How many times do you need the BackOffice CD library to install SQL Server books online after the fact? How many times have you tried to install client management tools for SMS, only to discover that you didn't have your BackOffice CD library handy? Enough said.

✦ **Windows 2000 Professional, Windows NT Workstation, Windows Me, and Windows 9x**—Here again, how many times are you asked to insert a CD so that a driver will finishing installing?

**Note**

You'll need to carry at least two versions of these CDs: the original retail version and the upgrade version. Windows 9x has a nasty way of knowing whether an operating system was previously installed on the machine, so it'll ask for one type of CD over the other.

✦ **Windows 2000 Server and Workstation Resource Kit CDs** — You need both CDs. The Server edition contains several more utilities than the Workstation version does. However, these CDs are no substitute for having the hard copy resource kits, as I'll discuss in a moment.

✦ **Windows 2000 Service Pack CDs** — How many times have you gone to a site only to discover that the Windows 2000 machines didn't have the latest service packs installed? Just try getting help from Microsoft's official technical support without the latest service pack applied.

✦ **Microsoft Office 2000 CD** — Have you ever been caught needing the Microsoft Exchange Server resource driver for Outlook 2000? I'll bet you discovered that it wasn't on your operating system CD. One of the places it's magically kept is on the Office 2000 CD. Just try setting up an Exchange-based mailbox — not personal folders — without this resource.

✦ **NPA West technical CD** — This goodie contains cross-platform utilities, product demos, and an article archive. I've found this CD valuable when I'm working in heterogeneous networking environments. Information regarding this CD can be found at www.npa.com.

✦ **Virus Detector CDs** — It's always a good idea to carry virus detection tools to your sites. My preference is McAfee VirusScan, but there are other good products, such as Norton and Trend Micro. One note about software licensing here: Be careful to honor the licensing agreement requiring that McAfee VirusScan be installed on only one machine at a time. I typically install, run, and uninstall McAfee VirusScan prior to performing surgery on a machine. The reasons are obvious. You can carry the virus protection program media of your choice (McAfee, Trend Micro, Norton, and so on).

# Other Convenient Tools

Besides CDs, you may carry a variety of other useful items in your vehicle, including the following:

✦ **3.5-inch disks** — Still very much alive, floppies offer valuable help in an MCSE toolkit. I carry an old-fashioned, bootable MS-DOS 6.22 disk with EDIT, XCOPY, and a few other invaluable tools on it. How many times, for reasons you can't quite explain, have you needed to boot from **A:>** into a "real" DOS environment to get something done? Applications like the INSTALL.EXE contained on 3Com's EtherDisk disk (another mandatory floppy to carry) still run only in a true MS-DOS environment. In many cases, this is the only way you'll be able to test your 3Com network adapter accurately for failure, configuration settings, and so on. Making and carrying a copy of the emergency repair disk for your favorite Windows NT Servers are also not bad ideas. You never know when you'll need those emergency repair disks.

✦ **Resource kits and other books** — Having a resource kit or two, along with your favorite books, spread out in front of you when performing server surgery can be an invaluable aid.

✦ **Catalogs** — The monthly catalog mailings from the national hardware/software resellers come in handy when discussing technology solutions with clients, particularly when you need to draw a few prices out of thin air.

✦ **Monthly newspapers for computer users** — In Seattle, the January issue of the Puget Sound Computer User (www.pscu.com) lists a potpourri of local reseller, consulting, labor, and publishing resources for the technology community. It's called the Business Directory issue, and this type of publication is also available in many other North American areas. The January issue helps me refer my clients to competent professionals in technical areas that I don't serve (such as Unix).

✦ **Handheld tape recorder** — Having a recorded journal of the steps you took to troubleshoot a problem or build a server allows you to access your own previous work as one of the sources on which you draw for help.

✦ **Laptop computer** — You'll need a computer with the ability to access the Internet, download drivers, and search Microsoft's knowledge base (www.microsoft.com). If you live in Seattle, the San Francisco Bay area, or Washington, D.C., you can use the Ricochet modem (www.ricochet.net) to establish a high-speed connection to the Internet without tying up a fax or voice line.

✦ **External modem with modem cable (serial 9 to 25 pinout)** — Sometimes the client's modem just won't function correctly and work needs to get done. Because of my experience with Small Business Server, I now carry an external U.S. Robotics 33.6 K Sportster modem just in case, and it always works.

✦ **A long telephone line and an analog telephone** — The long telephone line is for reaching the telco wall jack that's always across the room. The analog telephone is to plug into that wall jack to test the telephone service thoroughly.

✦ **Telephone numbers of peers to call for advice** — Calling a BackOffice buddy to help you out of a jam is a strategy that you shouldn't overlook.

✦ **A portable file cabinet** — This file cabinet can help you maintain working client files with office layout drawings, field notes, and billable-hour charge sheets.

✦ **Kneepads** — I carry them to protect my old skier's knees when I'm fishing cable around a crowded server room.

✦ **Working clothes** — As MCSEs, we must face today's formal versus casual clothing challenge. One moment you're selling your MCSE services in a glass tower. The next minute you're implementing SBS in a dusty warehouse. It's best to carry a change of clothes.

✦ ✦ ✦

# Index

*Continued*

*Continued*

# O

*Continued*

*Continued*

*Continued*

# my2cents.idgbooks.com

## Register This Book — And Win!

Visit **http://my2cents.idgbooks.com** to register this book and we'll automatically enter you in our fantastic monthly prize giveaway. It's also your opportunity to give us feedback: let us know what you thought of this book and how you would like to see other topics covered.

## Discover IDG Books Online!

The IDG Books Online Web site is your online resource for tackling technology — at home and at the office. Frequently updated, the IDG Books Online Web site features exclusive software, insider information, online books, and live events!

### 10 Productive & Career-Enhancing Things You Can Do at www.idgbooks.com

- Nab source code for your own programming projects.

- Download software.

- Read Web exclusives: special articles and book excerpts by IDG Books Worldwide authors.

- Take advantage of resources to help you advance your career as a Novell or Microsoft professional.

- Buy IDG Books Worldwide titles or find a convenient bookstore that carries them.

- Register your book and win a prize.

- Chat live online with authors.

- Sign up for regular e-mail updates about our latest books.

- Suggest a book you'd like to read or write.

- Give us your 2¢ about our books and about our Web site.

You say you're not on the Web yet? It's easy to get started with IDG Books' *Discover the Internet,* available at local retailers everywhere.